William Shakspere

AFTER WARD'S BRONZE STATUE IN THE CENTRAL PARK, NEW YORK

ENGRAVED BY H.B. HALL & SONS.

J. B. FORD & Co. N.Y.

EDITED BY

WILLIAM CULLEN BRYANT

Illustrated

WITH STEEL PORTRAITS, WOOD ENGRAVINGS BY ENGLISH AND AMERICAN ARTISTS, SILHOUETTE TITLES, MANUSCRIPT FAC-SIMILES, ETC., ETC.

New York
J. B. FORD AND COMPANY

PUBLISHERS' PREFACE.

THE marked success of "A Library of Poetry and Song," as issued in the year 1870, showed that the work supplied a real popular need. Since the date of its publication, between seventy and eighty thousand copies of the book have been taken by the public, whose confidence in the name of Mr. Bryant, as its editor, has been borne out by the work itself.

Although its popular acceptability seems no whit diminished, in its original octavo form, the publishers have thought it worthy of a thorough revision, enlargement, and improvement. Accordingly, with Mr. Bryant's active co-operation, the work has undergone an entire reconstruction, both as to matter and form. About one fifth of the material of the former volume has been eliminated, and twice as much new matter added; great pains having been taken to insure the correctness of the text with a view to making it a standard for reference, as well as to give an ample provision for general or special reading.

The book has been prepared with the aim of gathering into a single volume the largest practicable compilation of the best Poems of the English language, making it as nearly as possible the choicest and most complete general collection of Poetry yet published.

The name "Library," which has been given it, indicates the principle upon which the book has been made, namely: that it might serve as a book of reference; as a comprehensive exhibit of the history, growth, and condition of poetical literature; and, more especially, as a companion, at the will of its possessor, for the varying moods of the mind.

Necessarily limited in extent, it yet contains one quarter more matter than any similar publication, presenting nearly two thousand selections, from more than five hundred authors. It is believed that of the poetical writers acknowledged by the intelligent and cultivated to be great, none, whether English, Scotch, Irish, or American, will be found unrepresented in the volume; while many verses, of merit though not of fame, found in old books or caught out of the passing current of literature, have been here presented side by side with those more notable. And the chief object of the collection — to present an array of good poetry so widely representative and so varied in its tone as to offer an answering chord to every mood and phase of human feeling — has been carefully kept in view, both in the selection and the arrangement of its contents. So that, in all senses, the realization of its significant title has been an objective point.

In pursuance of this plan, the highest standard of literary criticism has not been made the only test of worth for selection, since many poems have been included, which, though less perfect than others in form, have, by some power of touching the heart, gained and maintained a sure place in the popular esteem.

The enlargement and reconstruction of this work has entailed upon Mr. Bryant much labor, in conscientious and thorough revision of all the material, — cancelling, inserting, suggesting, even copying out with his own hand many poems not readily attainable except from his private library, — in short, giving the work not only the sanction of his widely honored name, but also the genuine influence of his fine poetic sense, his unquestioned taste, his broad and scholarly acquaintance with literature. To assist him, especially in the principal gathering and classification of the material, the Publishers, with his concurrence, obtained the services of Mr. Edward H. Knight, of Washington, D. C., of whose good judgment, singular industry, and peculiar talent for systematization they had availed themselves in the first preparation of the original work. The work has also had the advantage of the nice critical discrimination of Professor Robert R. Raymond, of Brooklyn, N. Y., who has made it his care to revise all the copy before sending it to the printers, to correct erroneous readings perpetuated from careless editions of various authors, to perfect the progressive shading of the arrangement of the poems within their several classifications, and to add the numberless and nameless final touches of the literary artist.

The Publishers desire to return their cordial thanks for the courtesy freely extended to them, by which many copyrighted American poems have been allowed to appear in this collection. In regard to a large number of them, permission has been accorded by the authors themselves; other poems, having been gathered as waifs and strays, have been necessarily used without especial authority, and where due credit is not given, or where the authorship may have been erroneously ascribed, future editions will afford opportunity for the correction, which will be gladly made. Particular acknowledgments are offered to Messrs. D. Appleton & Co. for extracts from the works of Fitz-Greene Halleck, and from the poems of William Cullen Bryant; to Messrs. Harper and Brothers for poems of Charles G. Halpine and Will Carleton; to Messrs. J. B. Lippincott & Co. for quotations from the writings of T. Buchanan Read; to Messrs. Charles Scribner & Co. for extracts from Dr. J. G. Holland's poems; and more especially to the house of Messrs. James R. Osgood & Co., — whose good taste, liberality, and intelligent enterprise have given them an unequalled list of American poetical writers, comprising many of the most eminent poets of the land, — for their courtesy in the liberal extracts granted from the writings of Thomas Bailey Aldrich, Ralph Waldo Emerson, Oliver Wendell Holmes, Henry Wadsworth Longfellow, James Russell Lowell, Florence Percy, John Godfrey Saxe, Harriet Beecher Stowe, Edmund Clarence Stedman, Bayard Taylor, Bret Harte, John Townsend Trowbridge, Mrs. Celia Thaxter, John Greenleaf Whittier, and others.

In addition to the above special acknowledgments, readers will see in the "Index of Authors" references enabling them to find the publishers of the entire works of any American writer to whom their attention has been called by any fragment or poem printed in this volume. This "Library" contains specimens of many styles, and it is believed that, so far from preventing the purchase of special authors, it serves to draw attention to their merits; and the courtesy of their publishers in granting the use of some of their poems here will find ample and *practical* recognition.

Contents.

TABLE OF CONTENTS.

INDEX OF AUTHORS.

Names of American Publishers of the poetical works of American writers may be found in connection with the Authors' names.

Illustrations.

LIST OF ILLUSTRATIONS.

I.

STEEL PORTRAITS.

II.

ENGRAVINGS ON WOOD.

III.

ORNAMENTAL TITLES IN SILHOUETTE.

IV.

MANUSCRIPT AND AUTOGRAPH FAC-SIMILES.

MEMOIR OF

William Cullen Bryant

By James Grant Wilson

MEMOIR

OF

WILLIAM CULLEN BRYANT.

BY JAMES GRANT WILSON.

CHAPTER I.

"THE gravity and stillness of your youth
The world hath noted, and your name is great
In mouths of wisest censure."

SHAKESPEARE.

"HE had the wisdom of age in his youth, and the fire of youth in his age."

MARK HOPKINS.

ANCESTORS — BIRTH — CHILDHOOD — SCHOOL AND COLLEGE DAYS — LEGAL STUDIES — MARRIAGE — PUBLICATION OF POEMS.

SIR WALTER SCOTT relates that, when some one was mentioned as a "fine old man" to Dean Swift, he exclaimed with violence that there was no such thing. "If the man you speak of had either a mind or a body worth a farthing, they would have worn him out long ago." Béranger and Brougham, Goethe and Guizot, Humboldt and Sir Henry Holland, Lyndhurst and Palmerston, Earl Russell and Field-Marshal Moltke, and among Americans, J. Q. Adams and Taney, Professors Henry and Hodge, Horace Binney and Richard Henry Dana, now ninety-one—the age at which Titian said that genius never grows old—may be cited among the men of the nineteenth century in refutation of this theory, which it may be presumed has nothing to do with thews or stature. But if we wanted a bright and shining example of faculties, and faculties of a high order, remaining unimpaired in mind and body till long past the grand climacteric, we might name William Cullen Bryant, the beloved patriarch of American poetry, and "the most accomplished, the most distinguished, and the most universally honored citizen of the United States," who, having lived under every President of our country, completed his fourscore years and three, cheerful and full of conversation, and continued until the last week of May, 1878, to heartily enjoy what Dr. Johnson happily calls "the sunshine of life."

No name in our contemporaneous literature, either in England or America, is crowned with more successful honors than that of William Cullen Bryant. Born among the granite hills of Massachusetts, at a period when our colonial literature, like our people, was but recently under the dominion of Great Britain, he lived to see that literature expand from its infancy and take a proud place in the republic of letters, and he survived to see the Republic itself, starting from its revolutionary birth, spring up to a giant power, after passing most triumphantly through a giant rebellion. Surrounded by such historic and heroic associations, men like Bryant, who survive, embody in their lives the annals of a people, and represent in their individuality the history of a nation.

Pursuing beyond the age of fourscore an energetic literary career, the poet was also an active co-laborer in all worthy movements to promote the advancement of the arts and literature. A liberal patron of art himself, he was always the judicious and eloquent advocate of the claims of artists. On the completion of the beautiful Venetian temple to art erected by the New York Academy of Design, Mr. Bryant delivered the address inaugurating the building and consecrating it to its uses. Foremost in the literary circles of his adopted city, he was for many years the president of that time-honored institution of New York, the Century Club, which has always embraced among its members men of letters, prominent artists, and leading gentlemen of the liberal professions: the poet's predecessors in that office were Gulian C. Verplanck and George Bancroft. Philanthropic in his nature, Bryant was ever the consistent promoter of all subjects having for their tendency the elevation of the race and the furtherance of the interests of humanity. Connected with the leading evening metropolitan journal, and one of the oldest in the United States, he was enabled to bring the powerful influence of the press to bear with his own great literary renown and personal weight upon whatever measure he supported in the cause of philanthropy, letters, and the promotion of art.

William Cullen Bryant was born in a log-house at Cummington, Hampshire County, Massachusetts, November 3d, 1794.* He was a descendant of the English and Scotch families of Alden, Ames, Harris, Hayward, Howard, Keith, Mitchell, Packard, Snell, and Washburn, and through them from several of the Pilgrims who landed from the Mayflower at Plymouth, on the 22d of December, 1620—not a bad genealogy for an American citizen, nor unlike that of his brother-poet Halleck, who was descended from the Pilgrim Fathers, including John Eliot, the apostle to the Indians. Bryant also had a worthy clerical ancestor in the person of James Keith, the first minister of Bridgewater, Massachusetts, who, after having preached from the same pulpit fifty-six years, died in that town in 1719.

Stephen Bryant, the first of the poet's American ancestors of his own name, who is known to have been at Plymouth, Massachusetts, as early as 1632, and who some time before 1650 married Abigail Shaw, had several children, one of whom was also named Stephen. He was the father of Ichabod Bryant, who moved from Raynham

* A general misapprehension exists as to Mr. Bryant's birthplace. He was born, as he told the writer, not in what is now known as the "Bryant Homestead," but in a small house constructed of square logs and long since removed. This fact is further confirmed by the following note from the poet to a friend, dated December 5th, 1876: "Your uncle Eliphalet Packard was quite right in designating my birthplace. As the tradition of my family goes, I was born in a house which then stood at the north-west corner of a road leading north of the burying-ground on the hill, and directly opposite to the burying-ground. The house was afterwards removed and placed near that occupied then by Daniel Dawes. I suppose there is nothing left of it now."

to West Bridgewater in 1745, bringing with him a certificate of dismission from the church at Raynham, and a recommendation to that of his new place of residence. Philip, the eldest of his five sons, studied medicine, and settled in North Bridgewater, now Brockton, where his house is still standing. Dr. Philip Bryant married Silence Howard, daughter of Dr. Abiel Howard, with whom he studied medicine. One of their nine children, a son called Peter, born in the year 1767, studied his father's profession, and succeeded to his practice. At that time there lived in the same town a revolutionary veteran, "stern and severe," named Ebenezer Snell, of whom a small boy of the period, still living, informs the writer that "all the boys of Bridgewater were dreadfully afraid," so austere and authoritative were his manners. The old soldier had a pretty daughter who won the susceptible young doctor's affections, so that when Squire Snell removed with his family to Cummington, and built what is now known as the "Bryant Homestead," Peter Bryant followed, establishing himself there as a physician and surgeon, and in 1792 was married to "sweet Sarah Snell," as she is called in one of the youthful doctor's poetic effusions. Five sons and two daughters were the fruit of this happy marriage, their second son being the subject of this sketch. Of these seven children but two sons survive, Arthur and John Howard Bryant of Illinois, who were present at the poet's funeral.

Dr. Peter Bryant's bearing, I am told by an aged man who remembers him, was the very reverse of that of his gruff father-in-law. Although reserved, he was gentle in manner, with a low soft voice, and always attired with scrupulous neatness. While not above the height of his gifted son, he was broad-shouldered, and would sometimes exhibit his great strength by lifting a barrel of cider from the ground over the wheel into a wagon. According to the account of another who knew him, he was "possessed of extensive literary and scientific acquirements, an unusually vigorous and well-disciplined mind, and an elegant and refined taste." He was for his son William an able and skilful instructor, who chastened, improved, and encouraged the first rude efforts of his boyish genius. A personal friend of the poet wrote of him in 1840, "his father, his guide in the first attempts at versification, taught him the value of correctness and compression, and enabled him to distinguish between true poetic enthusiasm and fustian."

The son in after-life commemorated the teachings and trainings of the father in a poem entitled "Hymn to Death," published in 1825, which has often been quoted for its beauty and pathos :

"For he is in his grave who taught my youth
The art of verse, and in the end of life
Offered me the Muses. Oh, cut off
Untimely ! when the reason in its strength,
Ripened by years of toil and studious search,
And watch of nature's silent lessons, taught
Thy hand to practise best the lenient art
To which thou gavest thy laborious days
And lost thy life."

The poet's great-grandfather, Dr. Abiel Howard, a graduate of Harvard College of the class of 1729, had an extensive library for those times, and in his youth wrote verses. Some of these were in Mr. Bryant's possession, and, to quote his own words, " show no small power of poetic expression." The inclination to express themselves in poetic form reappeared in Dr. Howard's grandchildren. Dr. Bryant wrote many songs and love stanzas in his younger days, and some satirical political poems in middle age. His sister Ruth Bryant, who died young, left behind several meritorious poems which her nephew had read in manuscript. When Mr. Bryant was studying law, the late Judge Daniel Howard asked him from whom he inherited his poetic gift; he promptly replied, from his great-grandfather Dr. Howard. One of the poet's surviving brothers recently said to the writer, " We were all addicted, more or less, to the unprofitable business of rhyming."

It was the dream of Dr. Bryant's life to educate a child for his own and his father's loved profession, and so it came to pass that his second son was named after one of the great Scottish medical lights of that era, William Cullen, an eminent Edinburgh physician. The child was frail, and his head was deemed too large for his body, which fact so disturbed the worthy doctor that, unable to find in the books any remedy for excessive cerebral development, he decided upon a remedy of his own, and directed that the child should be daily ducked in an adjoining spring of clear cold water. Two of Dr. Bryant's students were deputed to carry the child from his bed each morning and to immerse him and his immense head. The tradition is that the embryo-poet fought stoutly against this singular proceeding, of which the young mother did not approve, but which notwithstanding was continued till the discrepancy of proportion between the head and the body disappeared and the father no longer deemed its continuance necessary.

As a child Bryant exhibited extraordinary precocity. He received instruction at home from his mother, whose school education, like that of most American women of her day, was limited to the ordinary English branches. He also was instructed by his father and an uncle, who taught him

" A little Latine and less Greeke."

Bryant has happily told the story of his boyhood* in better and more entertaining style than it can by any possibility be narrated by another. It forms a charming chapter in an autobiography to which the venerable poet devoted an occasional hour during the closing years of his long career. Says Mr. Bryant:

"The boys of the generation to which I belonged—that is to say, who were born in the last years of the last century or the earliest of this—were brought up under a system of discipline which put a far greater distance between parents and their children than now exists. The parents seemed to think this necessary in order to secure obedience. They were believers in the old maxim that familiarity breeds contempt. My own parents lived in the house with my grandfather and grandmother on the mother's side. My grandfather was a disciplinarian of the stricter sort, and I can hardly find words to express the awe in which I stood of him—an awe so great as almost to prevent anything like affection on my part, although he was in

* " The Boys of my Boyhood." *St. Nicholas Magazine*, December, 1876.

the main kind, and certainly never thought of being severe beyond what was necessary to maintain a proper degree of order in the family.

"The other boys in that part of the country, my schoolmates and playfellows, were educated on the same system. Yet there were at that time some indications that this very severe discipline was beginning to relax. With my father and mother I was on much easier terms than with my grandfather. If a favor was to be asked of my grandfather, it was asked with fear and trembling; the request was postponed to the last moment, and then made with hesitation and blushes and a confused utterance.

"One of the means of keeping the boys of that generation in order was a little bundle of birchen rods, bound together by a small cord, and generally suspended on a nail against the wall in the kitchen. This was esteemed as much a part of the necessary furniture as the crane that hung in the kitchen fireplace, or the shovel and tongs. It sometimes happened that the boy suffered a fate similar to that of the eagle in the fable, wounded by an arrow fledged with a feather from his own wing; in other words, the boy was made to gather the twigs intended for his own castigation.

. . . .

"The awe in which the boys of that time held their parents extended to all elderly persons, toward whom our behavior was more than merely respectful, for we all observed a hushed and subdued demeanor in their presence. Toward the ministers of the Gospel this behavior was particularly marked. At that time every township in Massachusetts, the State in which I lived, had its minister, who was settled there for life, and when he once came among his people was understood to have entered into a connection with them scarcely less lasting than the marriage-tie. The community in which he lived regarded him with great veneration, and the visits which from time to time he made to the district schools seemed to the boys important occasions, for which special preparation was made. When he came to visit the school which I attended, we all had on our Sunday clothes, and were ready for him with a few answers to the questions in the 'Westminster Catechism.' He heard us recite our lessons, examined us in the catechism, and then began a little address, which I remember was the same on every occasion. He told us how much greater were the advantages of education which we enjoyed than those which had fallen to the lot of our parents, and exhorted us to make the best possible use of them, both for our own sakes and that of our parents, who were ready to make any sacrifice for us, even so far as to take the bread out of their own mouths to give us. I remember being disgusted with this illustration of parental kindness, which I was obliged to listen to twice at least in every year.

"The good man had, perhaps, less reason than he supposed to magnify the advantages of education enjoyed in the common schools at that time. Reading, spelling, writing, and arithmetic, with a little grammar and a little geography, were all that was taught, and these by persons much less qualified, for the most part, than those who now give instruction. Those, however, who wished to proceed further took lessons from graduates of the colleges, who were then much more numerous in proportion to the population than they now are.

. . . .

"One of the entertainments of the boys of my time was what were called the 'raisings,' meaning the erection of the timber-frames of houses or barns, to which the boards were to be afterward nailed. Here the minister made a point of being present, and hither the able-bodied men of the neighborhood, the young men especially, were summoned, and took part in the work with great alacrity. It was a spectacle for us next to that of a performer on the tight-rope to see the young men walk steadily on the narrow footing of the beams at a great height from the ground, or as they stood to catch in their hands the wooden pins and the braces flung to them from below. They vied with each other in the dexterity and daring with which they went through with the work, and when the skeleton of the building was put together, some one among them generally capped the climax of fearless activity by standing on the ridge-pole with his head downward and his heels in the air. At that time even the presence of the minister was no restraint upon the flow of milk-punch and grog, which, in some cases, was taken to excess. The practice of calling the neighbors to these 'raisings' is now discontinued in the rural neighborhoods; the carpenters provide their own workmen for the business of adjusting the timbers of the new building to each other, and there is no consumption of grog.

"Another of the entertainments of rustic life in the region of which I am speaking was the making of maple sugar. This was a favorite frolic of the boys.

. . . .

"In autumn, the task of stripping the husks from the ears of Indian corn was made the occasion of social meetings, in which the boys took a special part. A farmer would appoint what was called 'a husking,' to which he invited his neighbors. The ears of maize in the husk, sometimes along with part of the stalk, were heaped on the barn floor. In the evening lanterns were brought, and, seated on piles of dry husks, the men and boys stripped the ears of their covering, and, breaking them from the stem with a sudden jerk, threw them into baskets placed for the purpose. It was often a merry time: the gossip of the neighborhood was talked over, stories were told, jests went round, and at the proper hour the assembly adjourned to the dwelling-house, and were treated to pumpkin-pie and cider, which in that season had not been so long from the press as to have parted with its sweetness.

"Quite as cheerful were the 'apple-parings,' which on autumn evenings brought together the young people of both sexes in little circles. The fruit of the orchards was pared and quartered and the core extracted, and a supply of apples in this state provided for making what was called 'apple-sauce,' a kind of preserve of which every family laid in a large quantity every year.

"The cider-making season in autumn was, at the time of which I am speaking, somewhat correspondent to the vintage in the wine countries of Europe. Large tracts of land in New England were overshadowed by rows of apple-trees, and in the month of May a journey through that region was a journey through a wilderness of bloom. In the month of October the whole population was busy gathering apples under the trees, from which they fell in heavy showers as the branches were shaken by the strong arms of the farmers. The creak of the cider-mill, turned by a horse moving in a circle, was heard in every neighborhood as one of the most common of rural sounds. The freshly-pressed juice of the apples was most agreeable to boyish tastes, and the whole process of gathering the fruit and making the cider came in among the more laborious rural occupations in a way which diversified them pleasantly, and which made it seem a pastime. The time that was given to making cider, and the number of barrels made and stored in the cellars of the farm-houses, would now seem incredible. A hundred barrels to a single farm was no uncommon proportion, and the quantity swallowed by the men of that day led to the habits of intemperance which at length alarmed the more thoughtful part of the community, and gave occasion to the formation of temperance societies and the introduction of better habits.

. . . .

"The streams which bickered through the narrow glens of the region in which I lived were much better stocked with trout in those days than now, for the country had been newly opened to settlement. The boys all were anglers. I confess to having felt a strong interest in that 'sport,' as I no longer call it. I have long since been weaned from the propensity of which I speak; but I have no doubt that the instinct which inclines so many to it, and some of them our grave divines, is a remnant of the original wild nature of man.

. . . .

"I have not mentioned other sports and games of the boys of that day; that is to say, of seventy or eighty years since—such as wrestling, running, leaping, base-ball, and the like, for in these there was nothing to distinguish them from the same pastimes at the present day. There were no public lectures at that time on subjects of general interest; the profession of public lecturer was then unknown, and eminent men were not solicited, as they now are, to appear before audiences in distant parts of the country, and gratify the curiosity of strangers by letting them hear the sound of their voices. But the men of those days were far more given to attendance on public worship than those who now occupy their place, and of course they took their boys with them.

. . . .

"Every parish had its tything-men, two in number generally, whose business it was to maintain order in the church during divine service, and who sat with a stern countenance through the sermon, keeping a vigilant eye on the boys in the distant pews and in the galleries. Sometimes, when he detected two of them communicating with each other, he went to one of them, took him by the button, and, leading him away, seated him beside himself. His power extended to other delinquencies. He was directed by law to see that the Sabbath was not profaned by people wandering in the fields and angling in the brooks. At that time a law, no longer in force, directed that any person who absented himself unnecessarily from public worship for a certain length of time should pay a fine into the treasury of the county. I remember several persons of whom it was said that they had been compelled to pay this fine, but I do not remember any of them who went to church afterward."

Bryant's education was continued under his uncle the Rev. Thomas Snell,* of Brookfield, in whose family he lived and studied for one year; and by the Rev. Moses Hallock, of Plainfield, he was prepared for college. One of his surviving brothers remembers that when the young poet came home on visits from his uncle Snell's or "Parson Hallock's," he was in the habit of playing at games with them, and of amusing them in various ways; that he excelled as a runner and had many successful running contests with his college classmates; also that he was accustomed on his home visits to declaim, for the entertainment of the family circle, some of his own compositions, both in prose and verse. He was when studying with the pastor, a small, delicate, and handsome youth, very shy and reserved, and a great reader, devouring every volume that he could meet with, and resembling the hero of Waverley in "driving through a sea of books like a vessel without pilot or rudder." He was, I am also told by one who studied with him at that time,—now nearly seventy years ago,—a natural scholar like his father, and although but fifteen, he had already accumulated a vast stock of information. In a letter to the Rev. H. Seymour, of Northampton, Massachusetts, published since Mr. Bryant's death, he speaks as follows of his early studies of Greek. "I began with the Greek alphabet, passed to the declensions and conjugations, which I committed to memory, and was put into the Gospel of St. John. In two calendar months from the time of beginning with the powers of the Greek alphabet I had read every book in the New Testament. I supposed, at the time, that I had made pretty good progress, but do not even now know whether that was very extraordinary." He found more pleasure in books, and in silent rambles among the hills and valleys, than in the usual sports and pastimes of youth of that age.

In October, 1810, when in his sixteenth year, he entered the sophomore class of Williams College. He continued his studies there during one winter with the same

* Dr. Snell was pastor of the North Parish of Brookfield for sixty-four years.

ardor as before, but not with the same enthusiasm or pleasure. He did not like his college life, some features of which were distasteful to his shy and sensitive nature, and so with his father's permission he obtained an honorable dismissal in May, 1811, and in due time he received the degree as a member of the class of 1813, of which there are now (July, 1878) but two survivors, the Rev. Elisha D. Barrett, of Missouri, and the Hon. Charles F. Sedgwick, of Connecticut. Dr. Calvin Durfee, the historian of Williams College, writes to me that Mr. Bryant "did not graduate in a regular course with his class; still years ago, by vote of the trustees of the college, he was restored to his place in the class, and has been enrolled among the alumni."

Judge Sedgwick, under date Sharon, July 3d, writes:

"I have your favor asking me to give you some of my recollections of the college life of my classmate W. C. Bryant. It gives me great pleasure to comply with your request, so far as I am able; but the short time during which he remained a member of the college could not be productive of many events of very great interest. Since his decease, many incorrect statements in relation to this portion of his history have gone forth, most of them intimating that he was a member of the college for two years. The truth is that, having entered the sophomore class in October, 1810, and then having continued his membership for two terms, he took a dismission in May, 1811, intending to complete his collegiate education at Yale College. As stated above, he entered our class at the commencement of the sophomore year. His room-mate was John Avery, of Conway, Mass., who was some eight years his senior in age. Bryant had not then attained to the physical dimensions which he afterwards reached, but his bodily structure was remarkably regular and systematic. He had a prolific growth of dark brown hair, and I do not remember ever to have known a person in whom the progress of years made so great a difference in personal appearance as it did in the case of Mr. Bryant. I met him twice near the close of his life at Williams College Commencements, and if I had not seen pictures of him as he appeared in old age, I would hardly have been persuaded of his identity with the Bryant I knew in early life.

"When he entered college, it was known that he was the reputed author of two or three short poems which had recently been published, and which indicated decidedly promising talent on the part of their author. When spoken to in relation to these poetical effusions, he was reticent and modest, and in fact his modesty in everything was a peculiar trait of his character. It was very difficult to obtain from him any specimens of his talent as a poet. One exercise demanded of the students was the occasional writing of a composition, to be read to the tutor in presence of the class, and once Bryant, in fulfilling this requirement, read a short poem which received the decided approval of the tutor, and once he translated one of the Odes of Horace which he showed to a few personal friends. Those were the only examples of his poetry that I now remember of his furnishing during his college life. It may be stated here that the tutor who instructed Mr. Bryant in college was the Rev. Orange Lyman, who was afterwards the Presbyterian clergyman at Vernon, Oneida County, N. Y.

. . . .

"Bryant, during all his college experience, was remarkably quiet, pleasant, and unobtrusive in his manners, and studious in the literary course. His lessons were all well mastered, and not a single event occurred during his residence which received the least disapproval of the faculty.

. . . .

"Your letter reminds me of the fact that there are but very few persons left who knew Mr. Bryant in college. 'The Flood of Years' has swept them all away except the Rev.

Herman Halsey, of the class of 1811, who yet survives in Western New York, and my classmate the Rev. E. D. Barrett, of Missouri, and myself. If I live to see the first day of September, I shall have completed eighty-three years of life."

The Rev. E. D. Barrett, under date Sedalia, Missouri, July 9th, writes :

"I well remember Bryant's first appearance at college in my sophomore year. Many of the class were assembled in one of our rooms when he presented himself. A friendly greeting passed round the circle, and all seemed to enjoy the arrival of the young stranger and poet. News of Mr. Bryant's precocious intellect, his poetical genius, and his literary taste had preceded his arrival. He was looked up to with great respect, and regarded as an honor to the class of which he had become a member, and to the college which had now received him as his *alma mater*. I was the poet's senior by more than four years, having been born in January, 1790, and am, with the single exception of Charles F. Sedgwick, the sole survivor of the Williams College class of 1813."

No American poet has equalled Bryant in early poetic development. In that particular he surpassed Pope and Cowley and Byron.* At the age of nine we find him composing tolerably clever verses, and four years later writing "The Embargo," a political as well as a poetical satire upon the Jeffersonian party of that day. The poem is also remarkable as having manifested at that early age a political order of mind which continued to develop in an equal ratio with his poetical nature through life. That mind, indeed, taking higher range, was not active in the turmoils and schemes of politicians ; but it investigated the great questions of political economy, and grappled with principles of the gravest moment to society and humanity.

"The Embargo ; or, Sketch of the Times, a Satire," we could easily imagine had been written in 1878, instead of seventy-one years ago, when, our fathers tell us, demagogism was unknown :

"E'en while I sing, see Faction urge her claim,
Mislead with falsehood, and with zeal inflame ;
Lift her black banner, spread her empire wide,
And stalk triumphant with a Fury's stride !
She blows her brazen trump, and at the sound
A motley throng obedient flock around :
A mist of changing hue around she flings,
And darkness perches on her dragon wings."

This poem, printed in Boston, attracted the public attention, and the edition was soon sold. To the second edition, containing "The Spanish Revolution" and several other juvenile pieces,† was prefixed this curious advertisement, dated February, 1809 :

---

* The *Saturday Review* of June 22d says, "The death of Bryant does not indeed deprive America of her oldest poet—for the memorable Dana still survives—but even Mr. Dana can hardly have published verses earlier than the 'Infantalia' of Mr. Bryant. He lisped in numbers which were duly printed when he was but ten years of age, and in his early lines, published in 1804, shows a precocity as great as that of the late Bishop of St. David's"—Dr. Connop Thirlwall.

† Mr. Bryant, in a note to the writer, says, "the first edition of my poem called 'The Embargo' did not contain any other poems. They were added in the second edition."

"A doubt having been intimated in the *Monthly Anthology* of June last whether a youth of thirteen years could have been the author of this poem, in justice to his merits, the friends of the writer feel obliged to certify the fact from their personal knowledge of himself and his family, as well as his literary improvement and extraordinary talents. They would premise that they do not come uncalled before the public to bear this testimony: they would prefer that he should be judged by his works without favor or affection. As the doubt has been suggested, they deem it merely an act of justice to remove it; after which they leave him a candidate for favor in common with other literary adventurers. They therefore assure the public that Mr. Bryant, the author, is a native of Cummington, in the county of Hampshire, and in the month of November last arrived at the age of fourteen years. The facts can be authenticated by many of the inhabitants of that place, as well as by several of his friends who give this notice. And if it be deemed worthy of further inquiry, the printer is enabled to disclose their names and places of residence."

In September, 1817, appeared in the *North American Review* the poem entitled "Thanatopsis," which Professor Wilson said "was alone sufficient to establish the author's claims to the honors of genius." It was written in a few weeks, in his eighteenth year,* and but slightly retouched during the time that elapsed between its composition and its first appearance in print. The poem created a marked sensation at the time of its appearance, not unlike that caused by the publication of Halleck's "Marco Bozzaris," a few years later. Richard H. Dana was then a member of the committee which conducted the *Review*, and received the manuscript poems "Thanatopsis" and the "Inscription on the Entrance to a Wood." The former was understood to have been written by Dr. Bryant, and the latter by his son. When Dana learned the name, and heard that the author of "Thanatopsis" was a member of the State legislature, he proceeded to the senate chamber to observe the new poet. He saw there a man of dark complexion, with iron-gray hair, thick eyebrows, well-developed forehead, with an intellectual expression in which, however, he failed to find

"The vision and the faculty divine."

He went away puzzled and mortified at his lack of discernment. When Bryant in 1821 delivered at Harvard University his didactic poem entitled "The Ages"—a comprehensive poetical essay reviewing the world's progress in a panoramic view of the ages, and glowing with a prophetic vision of the future of America—Dana

---

* In a letter to the writer, dated March 15th, 1869, Mr. Bryant says, "I return your article, the great fault of which is too kind an appreciation of its subject. . . . I am not certain that the poem entitled 'Thanatopsis' was not written a year earlier than you have made it; indeed I am much inclined to think it was in my eighteenth year. I was not a college student at the time, though I was pursuing college studies with a view of entering Yale College, having taken a dismission from Williams College for the purpose, which, however, was never accomplished."

The poem may be found on p. 308.

alluded in complimentary terms to Dr. Bryant's "Thanatopsis," and then learned for the first time that the son was the author of both poems.

It is related that when the father showed a copy of "Thanatopsis" in manuscript, before its publication, to a lady well qualified to judge of its merits, simply saying, "Here are some lines that our Willie has been writing," she read the poem, raised her eyes to the father's face, and burst into tears, in which Dr. Bryant, a somewhat reserved and silent man, was not ashamed to join. "And no wonder," continues the writer; "it must have seemed a mystery that in the bosom of eighteen had grown up thoughts that even in boyhood shaped themselves into solemn harmonies, majestic as the diapason of ocean, fit for a temple-service beneath the vault of heaven."

Mr. Bryant continued his classical and mathematical studies at home with a view to entering Yale College; but, abandoning this purpose, he became a law student in the office of Judge Howe, of Worthington, afterwards completing his course of legal study with William Baylies, of West Bridgewater. He was admitted to the bar at Plymouth in 1815, and began practice at Plainfield, where he remained one year and then removed to Great Barrington (all these towns being in the State of Massachusetts). At Great Barrington he made the acquaintance of the author Catherine M. Sedgwick, who afterwards dedicated to him her novel, "Redwood," and of Miss Frances Fairchild. The lovely qualities of this latter lady the young lawyer celebrated in verses which, for simple purity and delicate imagery, are most characteristic of our poet's genius. As they are not elsewhere given in the "Library," it will be of interest to read them here, in connection with the incidents of their origin:

"Oh, fairest of the rural maids!
Thy birth was in the forest shades;
Green boughs, and glimpses of the sky,
Were all that met thine infant eye.

"Thy sports, thy wanderings, when a child,
Were ever in the sylvan wild,
And all the beauty of the place
Is in thy heart and on thy face.

"The twilight of the trees and rocks
Is in the light shade of thy locks;
Thy step is as the wind, that weaves
Its playful way among the leaves.

"Thine eyes are springs, in whose serene
And silent waters heaven is seen;
Their lashes are the herbs that look
On their young figures in the brook.

"The forest depths, by foot unpressed,
Are not more sinless than thy breast;
The holy peace, that fills the air
Of those calm solitudes, is there."

Miss Fairchild became Mr. Bryant's wife in 1821, and for more than twoscore years was the "good angel of his life." She is mentioned in many of the poet's stanzas. "The Future Life" * is addressed to her. "It was written," says Mr. Bryant in a note to me, "during the lifetime of my wife and some twenty years after our marriage—that is to say, about 1840, or possibly two or three years after." "The Life that Is" was also inspired by Mrs. Bryant, the poet having written it on the occasion of her recovery from a serious illness in Italy in 1858. It is of so personal a character that the author hesitated about publishing it.

"Twice wert thou given me; once in thy fair prime,
Fresh from the fields of youth, when first we met,
And all the blossoms of that hopeful time
Clustered and glowed where'er thy steps were set.

"And now, in thy ripe autumn, once again
Given back to fervent prayers and yearnings strong,
From the drear realm of sickness and of pain
When we had watched, and feared, and trembled long."

A few months after the young poet's marriage a small volume of forty-four dingy pages was published by Hilliard & Metcalf, of Cambridge, Mass., entitled "Poems by William Cullen Bryant." A copy is now lying before me. It contains "The Ages," "To a Waterfowl," "Translation of a Fragment of Simonides," "Inscription for the Entrance to a Wood," "The Yellow Violet," "Song," "Green River," and "Thanatopsis." In this rare little volume the first and last paragraphs of the latter poem appear as they now stand, the version originally published in the *North American Review* having commenced with the lines,

"Yet a few days, and thee
The all-beholding sun shall see no more
In all his course;"

and ended with the words,

"And make their bed with thee."

Last winter I met Mr. Bryant in a Broadway bookstore and showed him a copy of this early edition of his poetical writings, which the dealer in literary wares had just sold for ten dollars. He laughingly remarked, "Well, that's more than I received for its contents."

---

* To be found on page 263.

CHAPTER II.

"THIS little life-boat of an earth, with its noisy crew of a mankind, and their troubled history, will one day have vanished; faded like a cloud-speck from the azure of the all! What, then, is man? He endures but for an hour, and is crushed before the moth. Yet, in the being and in the working of a faithful man is there already (as all faith, from the beginning, gives assurance) a something that pertains not to this wild death-element of time; that triumphs over time, and is, will be, when time shall be no more."—THOMAS CARLYLE.

LITERARY CAREER — AUTHOR, EDITOR, AND POET—FOREIGN TRAVELS — SEVENTIETH BIRTHDAY FESTIVAL—COUNTRY HOUSES—EIGHTIETH BIRTHDAY—POETICAL AND PROSE WRITINGS—PUBLIC ADDRESSES.

IN the year 1824 Mr. Bryant's picturesque poem, "A Forest Hymn," * "The Old Man's Funeral," "The Murdered Traveler," and other poetical compositions appeared in the *United States Literary Gazette*, a weekly journal issued in Boston. The same year, at the suggestion of the Sedgwick family, he made his first visit to New York City, where, through their influence, he was introduced to many of the leading literary men of the metropolis. From the first, Bryant was averse to the dull and distasteful routine of his profession—

"Forced to drudge for the dregs of men
And scrawl strange words with a barbarous pen."

He could not like it, and his aversion for it daily increased. With *Slender* he could say, "if there be no great love in the beginning, yet heaven may decrease it upon better acquaintance." His visit to New York decided his destiny. Abandoning the law, in which he had met with a fair measure of success, having enjoyed for nine years a reasonable share of the local practice of Great Barrington, he determined upon pursuing the career of a man of letters, so well described by Carlyle, the "Censor of the Age," as "an anarchic, nomadic, and entirely aërial and ill-conditioned profession," and he accordingly, in 1825, removed to New York, which continued to be his place of residence for more than half a century. Here he lived from earnest youth to venerable age—from eighteen to eighty-four—in one unbroken path of honor and success.

Establishing himself as a literary man in New York, the poet entered upon the editorship of a monthly magazine, to which he contributed "The Death of the Flowers" and many other popular poems, as well as numerous articles on art and kindred subjects. This position soon introduced Bryant into a very charming circle, composed of Chancellor Kent; Cooper, just achieving popularity by his American

---

* See page 414.

novels; the young poets Halleck, Hillhouse, and Percival; the painters Dunlap, Durand, Inman, and Morse; the scholars Charles King and Verplanck, and many other choice spirits, all long since passed away.

A few days after the poet's arrival in New York he met Cooper, to whom he had been previously introduced, who said:

"Come and dine with me to-morrow; I live at No. 345 Greenwich Street."

"Please put that down for me," said Bryant, "or I shall forget the place."

"Can't you remember three-four-five?" replied Cooper, bluntly.

Bryant did "remember three-four-five" not only for the day, but ever afterward. He dined with the novelist according to appointment, the additional guest, besides Cooper's immediate family, being Fitz-Greene Halleck. The warm friendship of these three gifted men was severed only by death.

It was chiefly through the influence of the brothers Robert and Henry D. Sedgwick that Mr. Bryant was induced to abandon the uncongenial pursuit of the law; and it was through the influence of the same gentlemen that, during the year 1826, he became connected with the *Evening Post.* Mr. H. D. Sedgwick, who was among the first to appreciate the genius of young Bryant, was a brother of Miss Sedgwick, the author, and at the time of his death, in 1831, he was among the most prominent lawyers and political writers of that day. To the *Evening Post* Mr. Bryant brought a varied experience of literary taste and learning, and even at that time a literary reputation. Halleck at that period rendered in *The Recorder* a richly-deserved compliment to his brother bard, when he wrote:

"Bryant, whose songs are thoughts that bless
The heart—its teachers and its joy—
As mothers blend with their caress
Lessons of truth and gentleness
And virtue for the listening boy.
Spring's lovelier flowers for many a day
Have blossomed on his wandering way;
Beings of beauty and decay,
They slumber in their autumn tomb;
But those that graced his own Green River
And wreathed the lattice of his home,
Charmed by his song from mortal doom,
Bloom on, and will bloom on forever."

The Evening Post was founded by William Coleman, a lawyer of Massachusetts, its first number being issued on the 16th of November, 1801. Mr. Coleman dying in [illegible], the well remembered William Leggett became its assistant editor, in which capacity he continued for ten years. Mr. Bryant soon after his return from Europe in 1836, upon the retirement of Mr. Leggett, assumed the sole editorial charge of the paper, performing those duties, with intervals of absence, till the 29th day of May, 1878, when he sat at his desk for the last time. To the *Post,* originally a Federal journal, Mr. Bryant early gave a strongly Democratic tone, taking decided ground against all class legislation, and strongly advocating freedom of trade. When his party at a later day passed under the yoke of slavery, the poet followed his principles out of the party, becoming before the war a strong Republican. In its management he was for a long time assisted by his son-in-law, Parke Godwin, and John Bigelow, late United States minister to France. Besides these able coadjutors, the *Post* has had the benefit of many eminent writers of prose and verse. To its columns Drake and Halleck contributed those sprightly and sparkling *jeux d'esprit*, "The Croakers," which, after nearly sixty years, are still read with pleasure. At the expiration of the *Post's* first half century, Mr. Bryant prepared a history of the veteran journal, in which his versatile pen and well-stored mind had ample range and material, in men and incidents, to do justice to the very interesting and eventful period through which the paper had passed.

The following terse and just characterization of Mr. Bryant as a political journalist, taken from an article which appeared in the editorial column of the *Post* since his death, gives an admirable summary of the man's life and work :

"Mr. Bryant's political life was so closely associated with his journalistic life that they must necessarily be considered together. He never sought public office ; he repeatedly refused to hold it. He made no effort either to secure or to use influence in politics except through his newspaper and by his silent, individual vote at the polls. The same methods marked his political and his journalistic life. He could be a stout party man upon occasion, but only when the party promoted what he believed to be right principles. When the party with which he was accustomed to act did what according to his judgment was wrong, he would denounce and oppose it as readily and as heartily as he would the other party. . . .

"He used the newspaper conscientiously to advocate views of political and social subjects which he believed to be correct. He set before himself principles whose prevalence he regarded as beneficial to the country or to the world, and his constant purpose was to promote their prevalence. He looked upon the journal which he conducted as a conscientious statesman looks upon the official trust which has been committed to him, or the work which he has undertaken—not with a view to do what is to be done to-day in the easiest or most brilliant way, but so to do it that it may tell upon what is to be done to-morrow, and all other days, until the worthiest object of ambition is achieved. This is the most useful journalism ; and, first and last, it is the most effective and influential."

The lines with which Dr. Johnson concluded a memoir of James Thomson may with equal truth be applied to the writings of William Cullen Bryant : "The highest praise which he has received ought not to be suppressed : it is said by Lord Lyttleton, in the Prologue to his posthumous play, that his works contained

"No line which, dying, he could wish to blot."

Though actively and constantly connected with a daily paper, the poet found ample time to devote to verse and other literary pursuits.

In 1827 and the two following years Mr. Bryant was associated with Verplanck and Robert C. Sands in an annual publication called "The Talisman," consisting of miscellanies in prose and verse written almost exclusively by the trio of literary partners, in Sands's library at Hoboken. Verplanck had a curious habit of balancing himself on two legs of a chair with his feet placed on two others, and while occupying this novel position he dictated his portion of the three volumes to Bryant and

Sands, who alternately acted as his amanuensis. In 1832 Bryant was again associated with Sands in a brace of volumes entitled "Tales of the Glauber Spa," to which Paulding, Leggett, and Miss Sedgwick were also contributors. In 1839 Mr. Bryant made a most admirable selection from the American poets, which was published by the Harpers in two volumes during the following year. At the same time they brought out a similar collection from the British poets, edited by Halleck.

So far back as 1827, Washington Irving writes from Spain to his friend Henry Brevoort of the growing fame of Bryant and Halleck. He says, "I have been charmed with what I have seen of the writings of Bryant and Halleck. Are you acquainted with them? I should like to know something of them personally. Their vein of thinking is quite above that of ordinary men and ordinary poets, and they are masters of the magic of poetical language." Four years later, Mr. Bryant, in a letter to Irving, informs him of the publication, in New York, of a volume comprising all his poems which he thought worth printing, and expresses a desire for their republication by a respectable English house. In order to anticipate their reproduction by any other, he requested Mr. Irving's kind aid in securing their publication. They appeared, with an introduction by Irving, in London in 1832. Professor Wilson said, in a periodical distinguished for its contempt of mediocrity: "Bryant's poetry overflows with natural religion—with what Wordsworth calls 'the religion of the gods.' The reverential awe of the irresistible pervades the verses entitled 'Thanatopsis' and 'Forest Hymn,' imparting to them a sweet solemnity, which must affect all thinking hearts." Another British periodical, very chary of its praise of anything American, remarked: "The verses of Mr. Bryant come as assuredly from the 'well of English undefiled' as the finer compositions of Wordsworth; indeed the resemblance between the two living authors might justify a much more invidious comparison."

Irving left behind him the following picture of the poetry of this distinguished American whom his own country delighted to honor: "Bryant's writings transport us into the depths of the solemn primeval forest, to the shore of the lovely lake, the banks of the wild nameless stream, or the brow of the rocky upland, rising like a promontory from amidst a wide ocean of foliage, while they shed around us the glories of a climate fierce in its extremes but splendid in all its vicissitudes." Dana has expressed his opinion of Bryant's poetry in equally admiring terms, and Halleck said to the writer, after repeating the whole of one of Bryant's later poems, "The Planting of the Apple Tree," * "His genius is almost the only instance of a high order of thought becoming popular; not that the people do not prize literary worth, but because they are unable to comprehend obscure poetry. Bryant's

* "I was most agreeably surprised, as well as flattered, the other day to receive from General Wilson, who has collected the poetical writings of Halleck, and is engaged in preparing his Life and Letters for the press, a copy in the poet's handwriting of some verses of mine entitled "The Planting of the Apple Tree," which he had taken the pains to transcribe, and which General Wilson had heard him repeat from memory in his own fine manner."—*Bryant's address on Halleck*, 1869.

The poem may be found on p. 419.

pieces seem to be fragments of one and the same poem, and require only a common plot to constitute a unique epic."

Since the appearance of the first English edition of Bryant's poems, many others, mostly unauthorized, have been published in Great Britain, with but slight, if any, pecuniary advantage to their author. With one of these, which I bought at an English railway-stand for a shilling of their currency, and brought back with me to present to the poet in October, 1855, he appeared much amused, as it contained a villainous portrait of himself which looked, he said, "more like Jack Ketch than a respectable poet." Many American editions of his poetical writings have appeared, from which Mr. Bryant derived a considerable amount of copyright, notwithstanding the remark he once made to the writer: "I should have starved if I had been obliged to depend upon my poetry for a living." Of one of these editions, known as the Red-line, there were five thousand copies sold in 1870, the year in which it appeared; and of another beautiful illustrated edition issued in 1877, the entire edition was exhausted in the course of a few months.

Intensely American in his feelings, the love of home and of his native land being among his most cherished sentiments, Mr. Bryant, like all truly cultivated and liberal minds, possessed an enlarged appreciation of the poetical associations of other lands. The inspirations of the East, the glowing imagery and romantic history of Spain, the balmy breezes and sunshine of the island of Cuba—all had an enchantment and charm for his most appreciative genius. The range of his poetic gift embraced with comprehensive sympathy the progress and struggles of humanity, seeking its vindication in a universal and enlightened liberty, in the beauties and harmonies of nature in her many forms, and the inspirations of art in its truthfulness to nature; and all these find their legitimate expression in productions of his muse.

Between the years 1834 and 1867, inclusive, Mr. Bryant made six visits to the Old World.* In 1872 still another long journey was undertaken by him—a second voyage to Cuba, his tour being extended to the city of Mexico. Bryant was fond of travel, and seemed as unwilling as that ancient worthy, Ulysses, whose wanderings he not long ago put in such pleasing English verse, to let his faculties rest in idleness. His letters to the *Evening Post*, embracing his observations and opinions of Cuba and the Old World, were collected and published after his third visit to Europe in 1849, and were entitled "The Letters of a Traveler." A few years later, after recrossing the Atlantic for the fifth time, he put forth in book form his letters from Spain and the East. These charming volumes, "born from his traveling thigh," as Ben Jonson quaintly expressed it, are written in a style of English prose distinguished for its purity and directness. The genial love of nature and the lurking tendency to humor which they everywhere betray prevent their severe simplicity from running into hardness, and give them a freshness and occasional glow in spite

* In a letter to the writer Mr. Bryant says, "I went six times to Europe. In 1834 with my wife and family, returning in 1836. In 1845; but I did not visit the Shetland Islands till four years later, in 1849. My fourth visit was in 1852, when I went to the Holy Land. In 1857 I made a fifth voyage to Europe with my wife and younger daughter. In 1867 I went over the sixth time. In both these last voyages I visited Spain."

of their prevailing propriety and reserve. The reception which Mr. Bryant always met among literary men of distinction, especially in Great Britain, was a direct testimony to his own fine qualities. The poets Wordsworth and Rogers particularly extended to him most cordial and intimately friendly attention.

Bryant's sympathy for the kindred arts was reciprocated by its votaries—though happily not in a posthumous form—in a novel and most beautiful manner, by a tribute paid to the poet on the anniversary of his seventieth birthday. I allude to the offering of paintings and poems made to Mr. Bryant on the evening of November 5th, 1864—which was selected for the festival—by the painters and poets of America, who cherished a love and veneration for one standing as a high-priest at the altar of nature, singing its praises in most harmonious numbers, and encouraging art in all its glowing beauties. An appropriate place for the offering was the Century Club of New York, of which but five of the one hundred founders are now living. On the occasion of the festival—a memorable one not only in the annals of the society itself, but in the history of American art and letters, Bancroft delivered the congratulatory address in most touching and eloquent words, and was followed by Ralph Waldo Emerson, Richard H. Dana, Jr., and William M. Evarts, in equally felicitous addresses. Miss Sedgwick, Mrs. Sherwood, the elder Dana, Edward Everett, Halleck, Longfellow, Lowell, Whittier, Willis, and others who were unable to be present, sent poems and epistles of affectionate greeting. Mr. Everett wrote : "I congratulate the Century Club on the opportunity of paying this richly-earned tribute of respect and admiration to their veteran, and him on the well-deserved honor. Happy the community that has the discernment to appreciate its gifted sons ; happy the poet, the artist, the scholar, who is permitted to enjoy, in this way, a foretaste of posthumous commemoration and fame !" Halleck, from a sick-chamber, sent these words : "Though far off in body, I shall be near him in spirit, repeating the homage which with heart, voice, and pen I have, during more than forty years of his threescore and ten, delighted to pay him." Longfellow in his letter said : "I assure you, nothing would give me greater pleasure than to do honor to Bryant at all times and in all ways, both as a poet and a man. He has written noble verse and led a noble life, and we are all proud of him." Whittier in felicitous stanzas, written, be it remembered, in the third year of the war, exclaims :

"I praise not here the poet's art,
  The rounded fitness of his song :
Who weighs him from his life apart
  Must do his nobler nature wrong.

. . . .

"When Freedom hath her own again,
  Let happy lips his songs rehearse ;
His life is now his noblest strain,
  His manhood better than his verse.

. . . .

"Thank God ! his hand on nature's keys
  Its cunning keeps at life's full span ;
But dimmed and dwarfed, in times like these,
  The poet seems beside the Man."

Other poetical tributes were addressed to Mr. Bryant by Boker, Buchanan Read, Mrs. Howe, Mrs. Sigourney, Holmes, Street, Tuckerman, and Bayard Taylor ; but the feature of the festival was the presentation to the venerable poet, in an eloquent address by the President of the National Academy, of upward of twoscore oil-paintings—gifts of the artist-members of the Century Club, including Church, Darley, Durand, Gifford, Huntington, Eastman Johnson, and others.

Shelley, in his "Defence of Poetry," asserts that "No living poet ever arrived at the fullness of his fame : the jury which sits in judgment upon a poet, belonging, as he does, to all time, must be composed of his peers, it must be impaneled by Time from the selectest of the wise of many generations." Does not the continual sale of the beloved Bryant's poems, on which criticism and panegyric are alike unneeded, and on which the American world has pronounced a judgment of unanimous admiration, prove him to be an exception to the rule laid down by the *dictum* of the gifted Shelley ?

As promised in his "Inscription for the Entrance of a Wood," to him who should enter and "view the haunts of Nature" "the calm shade shall bring a kindred calm," so did he truly seem to have received a quietude of spirit, a purity and elevation of thought, a "various language" of expression, which held him at once in subtle sympathy with nature and in ready communion with the minds of men. George William Curtis writes in his editorial Easy Chair of *Harper's Magazine* for August, 1878, "What Nature said to him was plainly spoken and clearly heard and perfectly repeated. His art was exquisite. It was absolutely unsuspected ; but it served its truest purpose, for it removed every obstruction to full and complete delivery of his message."

In December, 1867, Mr. Bryant responded in a beautiful letter to an invitation of the alumni of Williams College to read a poem at their next meeting. The brief letter of declination is poetical in its sympathy, and expresses, with pathos, not the decline of the powers of a mind yet vigorous, but a conscientious distrust of reaching that degree of excellence which his admirers might expect from his previous poems :

"You ask me for a few lines of verse to be read at your annual festival of the alumni of Williams College. I am ever ill at occasional verses. Such as it is, my vein is not of that sort. I find it difficult to satisfy myself. Besides, it is the December of life with me, I try to keep a few flowers in pots—mere remembrances of a more genial season which is now with the things of the past. If I have a carnation or two for Christmas, I think myself fortunate. You write as if I had nothing to do, in fulfilling your request, but to go out and gather under the hedges and by the brooks a bouquet of flowers that spring spontaneously, and throw upon your table. If I am to try, what would you say if it proved to be only a little bundle of devil-stalks and withered leaves, which my dim sight had mistaken for fresh, green sprays and blossoms ? So I must excuse myself as well as I can, and content myself with wishing a very pleasant evening to the foster-children of old "Williams" who meet on New Year's Day, and all manner of prosperity and honor to the excellent institution of learning in which they were nurtured."

On the evening of the 17th of May, 1870, Mr. Bryant delivered an address before the New York Historical Society, his subject being the "Life and

Writings of Gulian C. Verplanck." The venerable poet spoke of his friend, as in previous years he had spoken of their contemporaries, Thomas Cole, the painter, and the authors Fenimore Cooper, Washington Irving, and Fitz-Greene Halleck. These charming orations, together with various addresses, including those made at the unveiling of the Shakespeare, Scott, and Morse statues in the Central Park, were published in 1872 in a volume worthy of being possessed by all Bryant's admirers.

The literary life which began more than sixty years ago was crowned by his translations of Homer. He was more than threescore and ten, when he set himself to the formidable task of adding another to the many translations of the "Iliad" and "Odyssey." The former occupied most of his leisure hours for three years, and the latter about two ; being completed when Mr. Bryant was well advanced in his seventy-seventh year. The opinion has been pronounced by competent critics that these will hold their own with the translations of Pope, Chapman, Newman, or the late Earl Derby, of which latter Halleck said to the writer that "it was an admirable translation of the 'Iliad' with the poetry omitted !" *

To the breakfast-table at Roslyn I remember that Mr. Bryant one day brought some pages in manuscript, being his morning's work on Homer ; for, like Scott, he was always an early riser, and by that excellent habit he gained some hours each day. That Bryant, Bayard Taylor, and Longfellow should have, during the past decade, simultaneously appeared as translators of Homer, Goethe, and Dante, and that their work should compare favorably with any previous renderings into English of "Faust," the "Divina Commedia," and of the "Iliad" and "Odyssey," is certainly a striking illustration of advancing literary culture in the New World.

In 1873 Mr. Bryant's name appeared as the editor of "Picturesque America," a handsome illustrated quarto published by the Appletons ; and the latest prose work with which he was associated is a "History of the United States," now in course of publication by the Scribners, the second volume having been completed shortly before Mr. Bryant's death, the residue of the work remaining in the hands of its associate author, Sidney Howard Gay.

To the readers of this memoir a topic of especial interest will be Mr. Bryant's connection with the volume which incloses it—"The Library of Poetry and Song." This began in 1870, with the origination of the book in its octavo form, and continued with constant interest, through the reconstruction and enlargement of the work in its more elaborate quarto form until its completion in 1878. His own words best show how it happened that Mr. Bryant became the sponsor of this book, which in its various editions has already taken his name into nearly a hundred thousand American homes. "At the request of the publishers," he says, "I undertook to

* Of Mr. Bryant's translations of the "Iliad" and the "Odyssey" the *Athenæum* remarks: "These translations are with Mr. Bryant, as with Lord Derby, the work of the ripened scholarship and honorable leisure of age, and the impulse is natural to compare the products of the two minds. Mr. Bryant's translations seem less laboriously rounded and ornate, but perhaps even more forceful and vigorous, than Lord Derby's ;" while the London *Times* expresses the judgment that "his performance fell flat on the ears of an educated audience, after the efforts of Lord Derby and others in the same direction."

write an Introduction to the present work, and in pursuance of this design I find that I have come into a somewhat closer personal relation with the book. In its progress it has passed entirely under my revision. . . . I have, as requested, exercised a free hand both in excluding and in adding matter according to my judgment of what was best adapted to the purposes of the enterprise." Every poem took its place after passing under his clear eye. Many were dropped out by him; more were suggested, found, often copied out by him for addition. In the little notes accompanying his frequent forwarding of matter to the publishers, he casually included many interesting points and hints of criticism or opinion: "I send also some extracts from an American poet who is one of our best—Richard H. Dana." "I would request that more of the poems of Jones Very be inserted. I think them quite remarkable." "Do not, I pray you, forget Thomson's 'Castle of Indolence,' the first canto of which is one of the most magnificent things in the language, and altogether free from the faults of style which deform his blank verse." "The lines are pretty enough, though there is a bad rhyme—*toes* and *clothes;* but I have seen a similar one in Dryden—*clothes* pronounced as *cloes*—and I think I have seen the same thing in Whittier."

He was not a man given to humorous turns, yet he was not deficient in the sense of the comical. In forwarding some correction for an indexed name, he writes: "It is difficult always to get the names of authors right. Please read the inclosed, and see that Mrs. —— be not put into a pair of breeches."

In specifying some additional poems of Stedman's for insertion, he says: "I think 'Alectryon' a very beautiful poem. It is rather long. . . . 'The Old Admiral' should go in—under the head of 'Patriotism' I think; or, better, under that of 'Personal.' 'The Door Step' is a poem of 'Love;' but it is pretty enough for anywhere," etc. "I do not exactly like the poem 'To a Girl in her Thirteenth Year,' on account of the bad rhymes; nor am I quite pleased with Praed's 'I remember, I remember,' printed just after Hood's—it seems to me a little flippant, which is Praed's fault." The scrupulous care which Mr. Bryant exercised in keeping the compilation clean and pure was exemplified in his habitual name for it in correspondence and conversation—"The Family Book;" "The Family Library." He writes: "I have made more suggestions for the omission of poems in the humorous department than in any other; several of them being deficient in the requisite literary merit. As to the convivial poems, the more I think of it the more I am inclined to advise their total omission."

When the book appeared in 1870, it met with an instant and remarkable popular welcome, selling more than twenty thousand copies during the first six months, which, for a book costing five dollars in its least expensive style, was certainly unusual. In 1876 it was determined to give the work a thorough revision, although it had been from time to time benefiting by the amendments sent by Mr. Bryant or suggested by use. Mr. Bryant took a keen interest in this enlargement and reconstruction, and, as stated in the Publisher's Preface to the quarto edition, it "entailed upon him much labor, in conscientious and thorough revision of all the material—canceling, inserting, suggesting, even copying out with his own hand many poems not attainable save from his private library; in short, giving the work not only the sanction of his widely honored name, but also the genuine influence of his fine poetic sense, his unquestioned taste, his broad and scholarly acquaintance with literature." Both the octavo and the quarto editions now contain his much-admired Introduction, in the form of an essay on "The Poets and Poetry of the English Language." Of this, Edmund Clarence Stedman, in an admirable paper on Bryant as "The Man of Letters," contributed to *The Evening Post* since the poet's death, says: "This is a model of expressive English prose, as simple as that of the *Spectator* essayists and far more to the purpose. Like all his productions, it ends when the writer's proper work is done. The essay, it may be added, contains in succinct language the poet's own views of the scope and method of song, a reflection of the instinct governing his entire poetical career."

Bryant's prose has always received high commendation. A little collection of extracts from his writings has been compiled for use in schools, as a model of style. The secret of it, so far as genius can communicate its secrets, may be found in a letter addressed by Mr. Bryant to one of the editors of the *Christian Intelligencer*, in reply to some questions, and published in the issue of that journal, July 11th, 1878:

"ROSLYN, LONG ISLAND, July 6, 1864.

. . . .

"It seems to me that in style we ought first, and above all things, to aim at clearness of expression. An obscure style is, of course, a bad style. In writing we should always consider not only whether we have expressed the thought in a manner which meets our own comprehension, but whether it will be understood by readers in general.

"The quality of style next in importance is attractiveness. It should invite and agreeably detain the reader. To acquire such a style, I know of no other way than to contemplate good models and consider the observations of able critics. The Latin and Greek classics of which you speak are certainly important helps in forming a taste in respect to style, but to attain a good English style something more is necessary—the diligent study of good English authors. I would recur for this purpose to the elder worthies of our literature—to such writers as Jeremy Taylor and Barrow and Thomas Fuller—whose works are perfect treasures of the riches of our language. Many modern writers have great excellences of style, but few are without some deficiency. . . . . . .

"I have but one more counsel to give in regard to the formation of a style in composition, and that is to read the poets—the nobler and grander ones of our language. In this way warmth and energy is communicated to the diction and a musical flow to the sentences.

"I have here treated the subject very briefly and meagrely, but I have given you my own method and the rules by which I have been guided through many years mostly passed in literary labors and studies."

Quite recently the writer has seen a document which, in these days of international copyright agitation, is of some interest. It runs thus: "*The British and American Copyright League* is an association having for its object the passage of an International Copyright Law in America and in England, and in favor of such other countries as are willing to reciprocate, which shall secure to *authors* the same control over their own productions as is accorded to inventors, who, if they so elect, can patent their inventions in all the countries of Europe. This is the first organized attempt that has been made to bring about this very desirable result. As a preliminary step, it is proposed to get the approval of those immediately interested, and your signature to the inclosed circular is therefore respectfully requested." This is signed "Wm. C. Bryant, Secretary of the British and American Copyright League." The "inclosed circular" is a brief declaration of approval of the efforts of the League to secure the passage of an international copyright law, and bears the signatures of Bryant, Longfellow, Emerson, Whittier, Garrison, Beecher, Holmes, Mrs. Stowe, Miss Alcott, Prof. Dana, Howells, Aldrich, and other well-known authors. This excellent beginning was made in 1873, but for some reason was not pushed to any practical outcome. It was, however, one of the signs of the change now becoming manifest.

On Mr. Bryant's eightieth birthday he received a congratulatory letter with its thousands of signatures, sent from every State and Territory of his native land, followed soon after by the presentation, in Chickering Hall, New York, in the presence of a large and appreciative audience, of a superb silver vase, the gift of many hundred admirers in various portions of the country. This exquisite and valuable specimen of American silver work is now in the possession of the Metropolitan Museum of Art. Standing before it, the spectator may fitly recall those noble lines of Keats upon a Grecian urn:

"When old age shall this generation waste
Thou shalt remain, in midst of other woe
Than ours, a friend to men: to whom thou sayest,
'Beauty is truth, truth beauty; that is all
Ye know on earth, and all ye need to know.'"

A few months later, the venerable poet presented to the citizens of Roslyn a new hall and public reading-room, having previously given one to his native town. It was the wish of his fellow-citizens that the handsome hall should be named in honor of Mr. Bryant; but as he proposed that it should be known simply as "The Hall," that title was bestowed upon it by popular acclamation.

The "Centennial Ode," written by Bryant for the opening of the International Exposition at Philadelphia, is worthy of the great fame of its author. Another of his recent compositions, and one of his noblest, elicited from a prominent foreign journal the following mention: "The venerable American poet, who was born before Keats, and who has seen so many tides of influence sweep over the literature of his own country and of England, presents us here with a short but very noble and characteristic poem, which carries a singular weight with it as embodying the reflection of a very old man of genius on the mutability of all things, and the hurrying tide of years that cover the past as with a flood of waters. In a vein that reminds us of 'Thanatopsis,' the grand symphonic blank verse of which was published no less than sixty-one years ago, Mr. Bryant reviews the mortal life of man as the ridge of a wave ever hurrying to oblivion the forms that appear on its surface for a moment." In this worthy companion to "Thanatopsis," written in his eighty-second year, the poet strikes the old familiar key-note that he took so successfully in his greatest poem in 1812, in "The Ages" in 1821, and again in "Among the Trees" in 1874. It originally appeared in *Scribner's Magazine*, and was subsequently published by the Putnams as a holiday gift-book in beautiful form, artistically illustrated by Linton, the famous engraver, from his own designs. It is entitled "The Flood of Years."

"A MIGHTY HAND, from an exhaustless urn,
Pours forth the never ending Flood of Years
Among the nations. How the rushing waves
Bear all before them! On their foremost edge,
And there alone, is Life; the Present there
Tosses and foams and fills the air with roar
Of mingled noises. There are they who toil,
And they who strive, and they who feast, and they
Who hurry to and fro. The sturdy hind—
Woodman and delver with the spade—are there,
And busy artisan beside his bench,
And pallid student with his written roll.
A moment on the mounting billow seen—
The flood sweeps over them and they are gone.
There groups of revelers, whose brows are twined
With roses, ride the topmost swell awhile,
And as they raise their flowing cups to touch
The clinking brim to brim, are whirled beneath
The waves and disappear. I hear the jar
Of beaten drums, and thunders that break forth
From cannon, where the advancing billow sends
Up to the sight long files of armed men,
That hurry to the charge through flame and smoke.
The torrent bears them under, whelmed and hid,
Slayer and slain, in heaps of bloody foam.
Down go the steed and rider; the plumed chief
Sinks with his followers; the head that wears
The imperial diadem goes down beside
The felon's with cropped ear and branded cheek.
A funeral train—the torrent sweeps away
Bearers and bier and mourners. By the bed
Of one who dies men gather sorrowing,
And women weep aloud; the flood rolls on;
The wail is stifled, and the sobbing group
Borne under. Hark to that shrill sudden shout—
The cry of an applauding multitude
Swayed by some loud-tongued orator who wields
The living mass, as if he were its soul.
The waters choke the shout and all is still.
Lo, next, a kneeling crowd and one who spreads
The hands in prayer; the engulfing wave o'ertakes
And swallows them and him. A sculptor wields
The chisel, and the stricken marble grows
To beauty; at his easel, eager-eyed,
A painter stands, and sunshine, at his touch,
Gathers upon the canvas, and life glows;
A poet, as he paces to and fro,
Murmurs his sounding line. Awhile they ride

The advancing billow, till its tossing crest
Strikes them and flings them under while their tasks
Are yet unfinished. See a mother smile
On her young babe that smiles to her again—
The torrent wrests it from her arms ; she shrieks,
And weeps, and midst her tears is carried down.
A beam like that of moonlight turns the spray
To glistening pearls ; two lovers, hand in hand,
Rise on the billowy swell and fondly look
Into each other's eyes. The rushing flood
Flings them apart ; the youth goes down ; the maid,
With hands outstretched in vain and streaming eyes,
Waits for the next high wave to follow him.
An aged man succeeds ; his bending form
Sinks slowly ; mingling with the sullen stream
Gleam the white locks and then are seen no more.
  Lo, wider grows the stream ; a sea-like flood
Saps earth's walled cities ; massive palaces
Crumble before it ; fortresses and towers
Dissolve in the swift waters ; populous realms,
Swept by the torrent, see their ancient tribes
Engulfed and lost, their very languages
Stifled and never to be uttered more.
  I pause and turn my eyes, and, looking back,
Where that tumultuous flood has passed, I see
The silent Ocean of the Past, a waste
Of waters weltering over graves, its shores
Strewn with the wreck of fleets, where mast and hull
Drop away piecemeal ; battlemented walls
Frown idly, green with moss, and temples stand
Unroofed, forsaken by the worshipers.
There lie memorial stones, whence time has gnawed
The graven legends, thrones of kings o'erturned,
The broken altars of forgotten gods,
Foundations of old cities and long streets
Where never fall of human foot is heard
Upon the desolate pavement. I behold
Dim glimmerings of lost jewels far within
The sleeping waters, diamond, sardonyx,
Ruby and topaz, pearl and chrysolite,
Once glittering at the banquet on fair brows
That long ago were dust ; and all around,
Strewn on the waters of that silent sea,
Are withering bridal wreaths, and glossy locks
Shorn from fair brows by loving hands, and scrolls
O'erwritten—haply with fond words of love
And vows of friendship—and fair pages flung
Fresh from the printer's engine. There they lie
A moment and then sink away from sight.
  I look, and the quick tears are in my eyes,
For I behold, in every one of these,
A blighted hope, a separate history

Of human sorrow, telling of dear ties
Suddenly broken, dreams of happiness
Dissolved in air, and happy days, too brief,
That sorrowfully ended, and I think
How painfully must the poor heart have beat
In bosoms without number, as the blow
Was struck that slew their hope or broke their peace.
  Sadly I turn, and look before, where yet
The Flood must pass, and I behold a mist
Where swarm dissolving forms, the brood of Hope,
Divinely fair, that rest on banks of flowers
Or wander among rainbows, fading soon
And reappearing, haply giving place
To shapes of grisly aspect, such as Fear
Moulds from the idle air; where serpents lift
The head to strike, and skeletons stretch forth
The bony arm in menace. Further on
A belt of darkness seems to bar the way,
Long, low and distant, where the Life that Is
Touches the Life to come. The Flood of Years
Rolls toward it, nearer and nearer. It must pass
That dismal barrier. What is there beyond?
Hear what the wise and good have said Beyond
That belt of darkness still the years roll on
More gently, but with not less mighty sweep.
They gather up again and softly bear
All the sweet lives that late were overwhelmed
And lost to sight—all that in them was good,
Noble, and truly great and worthy of love—
The lives of infants and ingenuous youths,
Sages and saintly women who have made
Their households happy—all are raised and borne
By that great current on its onward sweep,
Wandering and rippling with caressing waves
Around green islands, fragrant with the breath
Of flowers that never wither. So they pass,
From stage to stage, along the shining course
Of that fair river broadening like a sea.
As its smooth eddies curl along their way,
They bring old friends together; hands are clasped
In joy unspeakable; the mother's arms
Again are folded round the child she loved
And lost. Old sorrows are forgotten now,
Or but remembered to make sweet the hour
That overpays them; wounded hearts that bled
Or broke are healed forever. In the room
Of this grief-shadowed Present there shall be
A Present in whose reign no grief shall gnaw
The heart, and never shall a tender tie
Be broken—in whose reign the eternal Change
That waits on growth and action shall proceed
With everlasting Concord hand in hand."

A gentleman who had been recently bereaved was so struck by the unquestioning faith in immortality expressed in the concluding lines of this poem that he wrote to the poet, asking if they represented his own belief. Mr. Bryant answered him in the following note, dated Cummington, August 10th, 1876 : "Certainly I believe all that is said in the lines you have quoted. If I had not, I could not have written them. I believe in the everlasting life of the soul ; and it seems to me that immortality would be but an imperfect gift without the recognition in the life to come of those who are dear to us here."

If the harmony of the poet's career was sustained in his writings and his love of art, it was further manifested in the taste and affection which governed him in the selection of his homes. Like the historian Prescott, Bryant had three residences—a town-house and two country homes. One of these is near the picturesque village of Roslyn, Long Island, and commands a view which in its varied aspect takes in a mingled scene of outspreading land and water. The mansion, embosomed in trees and vines, an ample dwelling-place situated at the top of the hills, was built by Richard Kirk in 1781. Mr. Bryant, who was ever mindful of the injunction given by the dying Scotch laird to his son, "Be aye sticking in a tree, Jock : it will be growing while ye are sleeping," alternated recreations of tree planting and pruning and other rural occupations with his literary labor. Not extensive, but excellent in wide and judicious selections, was his library of several thousand volumes. The poet's knowledge of ancient and living languages enabled him to add with advantage to his collection of books the works of the best French, German, Italian, and Spanish authors. Among his poems may be found admirable translations from these various languages as well as from the Greek and Latin.

The poet's country-seat at Roslyn, called "Cedarmere," has been the resort of many distinguished men of art and literature, of travelers and statesmen, gone thither to pay their respects to the sage, philosopher, and author. They were always welcomed, and enjoyed the purity of taste and simplicity of manner which presided over the mansion. Here the venerable host continued to the last to enjoy the society of his friends ; and here much of his best literary work has been done since his purchase of the place in 1845. He was accustomed to spend most of the time there from May to the end of November of each year, excepting the months of August and September, which were given to the old Homestead at Cummington, Mass.

Cedarmere is an extensive estate, and rich in a great variety of trees. As I was walking on a sunny October afternoon with the poet through his loved domain, he pointed out a Spanish chestnut-tree laden with fruit, and, springing lithely on a fence despite his seventy-six summers, caught an open burr hanging from one of the lower branches, opened it, and, jumping down with the agility of a youth, handed to his city guest the contents, consisting of two as large chestnuts as I ever saw in Spain. The Madeira and Pecan nuts were also successfully cultivated by him at Cedarmere. During another walk, Mr. Bryant gave a jump and caught the branch of a tree with his hands, and, after swinging backward and forward several times with his feet raised, he swung himself over a fence without touching it.

About a quarter of a mile from the mansion, he pointed out a black-walnut tree, which was planted by Adam Smith, and first made its appearance above ground in 1713. It had attained a girth of twenty-five feet and an immense breadth of branches. It was the comfortable home of a small army of squirrels, and every year strewed the ground around its gigantic stem with an abundance of "heavy fruit." The tree is alluded to in one of Mr. Bryant's poems :

"On my cornice linger the ripe black grapes ungathered ;
Children fill the groves with the echoes of their glee,
Gathering tawny chestnuts, and shouting when beside them
Drops the heavy fruit of the tall black-walnut tree."

The taste displayed by the poet in the selection and adornment of his residence at Roslyn was more than equaled by the affection and veneration which fourteen years ago prompted him to purchase the old Bryant Homestead and estate at Cummington, which had some thirty years previous passed out of the family into other hands. The mansion is situated among the Hampshire hills, and is a spot that nature has surrounded with scenes calculated to awaken the early dreams of the poet, and to fill his soul with purest inspiration. In the midst of such scenes the young singer received his earliest impressions, and descriptive of them he has embodied some of his most cherished and home-endearing poetry. To a friend who requested information about the home of his boyhood, Mr. Bryant in 1872 wrote as follows :

"I am afraid that I can not say much that will interest you or any body else. A hundred years since this broad highland region lying between the Housatonic and the Connecticut was principally forest, and bore the name of Pontoosuc. In a few places settlers had cleared away woodlands and cultivated the cleared spots. Bears, catamounts, and deer were not uncommon here. Wolves were sometimes seen, and the woods were dense and dark, without any natural openings or meadows. My grandfather on the mother's side came up from Plymouth County, in Massachusetts, when a young man, in the year 1773, and chose a farm on a commanding site overlooking an extensive prospect, cut down the trees on a part of it, and built a house of square logs with a chimney as large as some kitchens, within which I remember to have sat on a bench in my childhood. About ten years afterward he purchased, of an original settler, the contiguous farm, now called the Bryant Homestead, and having built beside a little brook, not very far from a spring from which water was to be drawn in pipes, the house which is now mine, he removed to it with his family. The soil of this region was then exceedingly fertile, all the settlers prospered, and my grandfather among the rest. My father, a physician and surgeon, married his daughter, and after a while came to live with him on the homestead. He made some enlargements of the house, in one part of which he had his office, and in this, during my boyhood, were generally two or three students of medicine, who sometimes accompanied my father in his visits to his patients, always on horseback, which was the mode of traveling at that time. To this place my father brought me in my early childhood, and I have scarce an early recollection which does not relate to it.

"On the farm beside the little brook, and at a short distance from the house, stood the district school-house, of which nothing now remains but a little hollow where was once a cellar. Here I received my earliest lessons in learning, except such as were given me by my mother, and here, when ten years old, I declaimed a copy of verses composed by me as a description of a district school. The little brook which runs by the house, on the site of the old district school-house, was in after-years made the subject of a little poem, entitled 'The Rivulet.' To the south of the house is a wood of tall trees clothing a declivity, and touching with its outermost boughs the grass of a moist meadow at the foot of the hill, which suggested the poem entitled 'An Inscription for the Entrance to a Wood.'

"In the year 1835 the place passed out of the family; and at the end of thirty years I repurchased it, and made various repairs of the house and additions to its size. A part of the building which my father had added, and which contained his office, had, in the mean time, been detached from it, and moved off down a steep hill to the side of the Westfield River. I supplied its place by a new wing with the same external form, though of less size, in which is now my library.

"The site of the house is uncommonly beautiful. Before it, to the east, the ground descends, first gradually, and then rapidly, to the Westfield River, flowing in a deep and narrow valley, from which is heard, after a copious rain, the roar of its swollen current, itself unseen. In the spring-time, when the frost-bound waters are loosened by a warm rain, the roar and crash are remarkably loud as the icy crust of the stream is broken, and the masses of ice are swept along by the flood over the stones with which the bed of the river is paved. Beyond the narrow valley of the Westfield the surface of the country rises again gradually, carrying the eye over a region of vast extent, interspersed with farm-houses, pasture-grounds, and wooded heights, where on a showery day you sometimes see two or three different showers, each watering its own separate district; and in winter-time two or three different snow-storms dimly moving from place to place."

"The soil of the whole of this highland region is disintegrated mica slate, for the most part. It has its peculiar growth of trees, shrubs, and wild flowers, differing considerably from those of the eastern part of the State. In autumn, the woods are peculiarly beautiful with their brightness and variety of hues. The higher farms of this region lie nearly two thousand feet above tide-water. The air is pure and healthful; the summer temperature is most agreeable; but the spring is coy in her approaches, and winter often comes before he is bidden. No venomous reptile inhabits any part of this region, as I think there is no tradition of a rattlesnake or copperhead having been seen here."

The serenity and dignity so manifest in Bryant's writings were notable also in his person. The poet was often depicted with pencil and pen. The phrenologists exhausted their skill upon his noble head, and the painters and engravers their art upon his face. The former believed him to approach the ideal of Spurzheim in his phrenological developments, and the latter deemed him to possess the fine artistic features of Titian and the Greek poet whom he translated. It is a consolation to age, when protected by a wise and orderly regulated life, that its inherent dignity supplies the want, if not the place, of youth, and that the veneration and serenity which surround it more than compensate for the passions which turbulence renders dangerous. To such an honored age as this Bryant attained; calm, circumspect, and sedate, he passed the perilous portals of Parnassus with his crown of laurel untarnished and unwithered by the baser breath that sometimes lurks like a poison within its leaves. To my conception, he more resembled Dante in the calm dignity of his nature, though happily not in the violent and oppressive affliction of his life, than any other poet in history.

Having passed, by more than three winters, what the Psalmist calls "the days of our years," and escaped the "labor and sorrow" that are foreboded to the strength that attains fourscore, Bryant continued to perform his daily editorial duties, to pursue his studies, and to give the world his much prized utterances, without exhibiting any evidences of physical or mental decay, although for a good part of half a century he was under whip and spur, with the daily press forever, as Scott expressed it, "clattering and thundering at his heels." On the evening of January 31st, 1878, he walked out on the wildest night of the winter, when a blinding snow-storm kept many younger men at home, to address a meeting of the American Geographical Society, and to take part in the cordial welcome extended to the Earl of Dufferin, the accomplished Governor-General of Canada. When the president of the society sent for a carriage and urged the aged poet, at the close of the meeting, to make use of it, he sturdily refused, saying that he preferred to walk home.

Among Mr. Bryant's latest utterances was the following noble ode, written for Washington's last birthday, February 22d, 1878, for *The Sunday School Times:*

"Pale is the February sky,
And brief the mid-day's sunny hours;
The wind-swept forest seems to sigh
For the sweet time of leaves and flowers.

"Yet has no month a prouder day,
Not even when the Summer broods
O'er meadows in their fresh array,
Or Autumn tints the glowing woods.

"For this chill season now again
Brings, in its annual round, the morn
When, greatest of the sons of men,
Our glorious Washington was born.

"Lo, where, beneath an icy shield,
Calmly the mighty Hudson flows!
By snow-clad fell and frozen field
Broadening the lordly river goes.

"The wildest storm that sweeps through space,
And rends the oak with sudden force,
Can raise no ripple on his face
Or slacken his majestic course.

"Thus, 'mid the wreck of thrones, shall live
Unmarred, undimmed, our hero's fame,
And years succeeding years shall give
Increase of honors to his name."

Still later (May 15th, 1878) Mr. Bryant wrote at Roslyn the following characteristic sentiment contributed to a Decoration Day number of *The Recorder.*

"In expressing my regard for the memory of those who fell in the late civil war, I can not omit to say that, for one result of what they did and endured—namely, the extinction of slavery in this great republic—they deserve the imperishable gratitude of mankind. Their memory will survive many thousands of the generations of spring flowers which men will gather to-day on their graves. Nay, they will not be forgotten while the world has a written history."

CHAPTER III.

"Of no distemper, of no blast he died,
But fell like autumn fruit that mellow'd long:
Even wonder'd at, because he dropt no sooner.
Fate seem'd to wind him up for fourscore years;
Yet freshly ran he on three winters more;
Till, like a clock worn out with eating time,
The wheels of weary life at last stood still."

John Dryden.

Mazzini Address—Last Words—Accident—Sickness—Death—Burial at Roslyn—Tributes to his Memory.

In accordance with the expressed wishes of many personal friends of the patriarch of American poetry, who was so recently laid in his grave with many tears, and also remembering that posterity likes details in regard to the latest actions and utterances of eminent men, I have recorded, to the best of my recollection, some particulars of his conversation during the afternoon of Wednesday, May 29th, his last hours of consciousness. He was appointed to deliver an oration on the occasion of unveiling a bronze bust of Mazzini, the Italian revolutionist and statesman, in the Central Park. I met Mr. Bryant in the Park about half an hour before the commencement of the ceremonies, conversing with him during that time, and again for a similar period after those ceremonials were concluded. While I was walking with Mr. Bryant for the last time, he quoted an aphorism from his friend Sainte-Beuve, that "To know another man well, especially if he be a noted and illustrious character, is a great thing not to be despised." It was my good fortune to have enjoyed for nearly or quite a quarter of a century the privilege and pleasure of Mr. Bryant's acquaintance, and in all that time I never met him in a more cheerful and conversational mood than on the above-mentioned afternoon, and never saw him exhibit an equal depth and tenderness of feeling, either in his public utterances or in his private talk.

At the proper time Mr. Bryant took his seat on the platform—for he had been standing or seated under the welcome shade of adjoining elms—and presently he proceeded with the delivery of the last of a long series of scholarly addresses delivered in New York during the past thirty years. As I gazed on the majestic man, with his snow-white hair and flowing beard, his small, keen, but gentle blue eye, his light but firm lithe figure, standing so erect and apparently with undiminished vigor, enunciating with such distinctness, I thought of what Napoleon said of another great singer who, like our American poet, reached an advanced age to which but few attain, and which was equally true of Bryant: "Behold a man!"

The delivery of the oration, which affords most interesting evidence of the enthusiasm and mental energy of its aged author, it is to be feared drew too heavily on the poet's failing powers. It was uttered with an unusual depth of feeling, and for the first time in his public addresses, so far as I am aware, he hesitated and showed some difficulty in finding his place in the printed slip which was spread before him, and in proceeding with his remarks. During the delivery of his speech he was but slightly exposed to the hot sun, an umbrella being held over his

"Good gray head, which all men knew,"

till he reached his peroration, when he stepped from under its shelter, and, looking up at the bust, delivered with power and great emphasis, while exposed to the sun, the concluding paragraph of his address:

"Image of the illustrious champion of civil and religious liberty, cast in enduring bronze to typify the imperishable renown of thy original! Remain for ages yet to come where we place thee, in this resort of millions; remain till the day shall dawn—far distant though it may be—when the rights and duties of human brotherhood shall be acknowledged by all the races of mankind!"

At the conclusion, Mr. Bryant was loudly applauded, and resuming his seat again on the platform, he remained an interested listener to the address in Italian which followed his. At the close of the ceremonies, and when the poet was left almost alone on the platform, he took my offered arm to accompany me to my home, saying that he was perfectly able to walk there, or indeed to his own house in Sixteenth Street. Before proceeding, I again proposed that we should take a carriage, when the poet said, in a determined manner, "I am not tired, and prefer to walk." As we set off, I raised my umbrella to protect him from the sun, when he said, in a most decided tone, "Don't hold that umbrella up on my account; I like the warmth of the sunshine." He was much interested in the fine flock of sheep, together with the shepherd and his intelligent Scotch collie, that he observed as we passed across the green.

Mr. Bryant alluded to the death of Lord John Russell the day before, and asked if I had ever met him or heard him speak in public, adding: "For a statesman, he devoted a good deal of time to literature, and he appears to have been a man of respectable talents. How old was he?" "Eighty-six." "Why, he was older than I am; but I expect to beat that and to live as long as my friend Dana, who is ninety-one." "Have you any theory as to the cause of your good health?" "Oh, yes," he answered; "it is all summed up in one word—moderation. As you know, I am a moderate eater and drinker, moderate in my work, as well as in my pleasures, and I believe the best way to preserve the mental and physical faculties is to keep them employed. Don't allow them to rust." "But surely," I added, "there is no moderation in a man of eighty-three, after walking more than two miles, mounting eight or nine pairs of stairs to his office." "Oh," he merrily replied, "I confess to the two or three miles down-town, but I do not often mount the stairs; and if I do sometimes, when the elevator is not there, I do not see that it does me any harm. I can walk and work as well as ever, and have been at the office to-day, as usual."

Some mention having been made of Lord Houghton's and Tupper's recent travels in this country, the poet asked: "Did I ever tell you of Lord Houghton's visit to Roslyn a few years ago? He was accompanied by his valet, who announced in my kitchen that his 'master was the greatest poet in England,' when one of my servants, not to be outdone, thereupon said, 'Our man is the greatest poet in America.'" The use of the words "master" and "man," I may remark, are worthy of notice, and appeared to amuse the poet when relating the incident.

Passing the Halleck statue, Mr. Bryant paused to speak of it, of other statues in similar sitting posture, and of Halleck himself and his genius, for several minutes.

Still continuing to lean on my arm, he asked my little daughter, whose hand he had held and continued to hold during our walk, if she knew the names of the robbins and sparrows that attracted his attention, and also the names of some flowering shrubs that we passed. Her correct answers pleased him, and he then inquired if she had ever heard some little verses about the bobolink. She answered yes, and that she also knew the poet who wrote them. This caused him much amusement, and he said, "I think I shall have to write them out for you. "Mary, do you know the name of that tree with the pretty blue flowers?" he asked, and as she did not know, he told her that it was "called the *Paulownia imperialis*—a hard name for a little girl to remember; it was named in honor of a princess, and was brought from Japan."

Arriving at the Morse statue at the Seventy-second Street gate, we stopped, and he said: "This recalls to my mind a curious circumstance. You remember Launt Thompson's bust which the Commissioners refused to admit in the Park, on the ground that I was living? Well, soon after, this statue of Morse was placed here, although he was alive, and [laughingly] I was asked to deliver the address on the occasion of its unveiling, which I did." "Do you like your bust?" "Yes, I think it is a good work of art, and the likeness is pleasing and satisfactory, I believe, to my friends." "Which do you think your best portrait?" "Unlike Irving, I prefer the portraits made of me in old age. Of the earlier pictures, I presume the best are Inman's and my friend Durand's,* which you perhaps remember hangs in the parlor at Roslyn."

As we approached my house, about four o'clock, Mr. Bryant was recalling the scenes of the previous year on the occasion of President Hayes's first visit to New York, and he was still, I think, cheerfully conversing on that subject as we walked up arm in arm, and all entered the vestibule. Disengaging my arm, I took a step in advance to open the inner door, and during those few

* The most important portraits of the poet, mentioned as nearly as possible in the order in which they were painted, are by Henry Inman (1835); Prof. S. F. B. Morse (1836); Henry Peters Gray, S. W. Cheney, Charles Martin (1851); Charles L. Elliott, A. B. Durand (1854); Samuel Lawrence (1856); Paul Duggan, C. G. Thompson, A. H. Wenzler (1861); Thomas Hicks (1863); and Charles Fisher (1875). Of these I have engravings on steel now before me from Inman's, Martin's, Elliott's, Durand's, and Lawrence's portraits, as well as several taken from recent photographs. The portrait of Mr. Bryant which appears in this work is engraved from an admirable photograph taken by Sarony.

seconds, without the slightest warning of any kind, the venerable poet, while my back was turned, dropped my daughter's hand and fell suddenly backward through the open outer door, striking his head on the steps. I turned just in time to see the silvered head striking the stone, and, springing to his side, hastily raised him up. He was unconscious, and I supposed that he was dead. Ice-water was immediately applied to his head, and, with the assistance of a neighbor's son and the servants, he was carried into the parlor and laid unconscious at full length on the sofa. He soon moved, became restless, and in a few minutes sat up and drank the contents of a goblet filled with iced sherry, which partially restored him, and he asked, with a bewildered look, "Where am I? I do not feel at all well. Oh, my head! my poor head!" accompanying the words by raising his right hand to his forehead. After a little, at his earnest request, I accompanied him to his own house, and, leaving him in charge of his niece, went for his family physician, Dr. John F. Gray. The following is a portion of the statement made by Dr. Gray after the poet's death:

"I sent for Dr. Carnochan, the surgeon. He could find no injury to the skull, and therefore thought there was a chance of recovery. Mr. Bryant, during the first few days, would get up and walk about the library or sit in his favorite chair. He would occasionally say something about diet and air. When his daughter arrived from Atlantic City, where she had been for her health, she thought her father recognized her. It is uncertain how far he recognized her or any of his friends. The family were hopeful and made the most out of every sign of consciousness or recognition.

"On the eighth day after the fall, hemorrhage took place in the brain, resulting in paralysis, technically called hemiplegia, and extending down the right side of the body. After this he was most of the time comatose. He ceased to recognize his friends in any way, and lay much of the time asleep. He was unable to speak, and when he attempted to swallow his food lodged in his larynx and choked him. He was greatly troubled with phlegm, and could not clear his throat. There was only that one attack of hemorrhage of the brain, and that was due to what is called traumatic inflammation. After the fourteenth day he died.

"He was a man who made little demonstration of affection or emotion, but he had a profoundly sympathetic feeling for the life and mission of Mazzini, and on the day when he delivered the address he exhibited considerable emotion. That and the walk afterwards certainly exhausted him, and led to the swoon. He overtaxed his strength during the winter, in attending evening entertainments and in public speaking. He had few intimate acquaintances, and was so extremely modest in expressing approbation or liking that one could scarcely tell the extent of his friendly feeling. Though I had attended him for many years, and often visited him at Roslyn, and also at his old homestead in Massachusetts, I never noticed an expression of more than ordinary friendship till I was prostrated by sickness. He made an impression ordinarily of coldness, but his poems show that he had plenty of feeling, and great sympathy for mankind.

"Once when at Roslyn we visited the grave of his wife in the village cemetery, and we saw the place by her side reserved for him. He frequently requested that his funeral should be simple and without ostentation. He has had fulfilled his wish to die in June.

"Mr. Bryant owed his long life to an exceedingly tenacious and tough constitution and very prudent living. I always found him an early riser. Although he was slight of body and limb, he seemed to me unconscious of fatigue, and he would walk many a stronger man off his legs. He did not walk rapidly, but seemed as wiry as an Indian."

In April, 1867, Mr. Bryant expressed to the writer a wish that he might not survive the loss of his mental faculties like Southey, Scott, Wilson, Lockhart, and the Ettrick Shepherd, who all suffered from softening of the brain, and mentioned his hope that he should be permitted to complete his translation of Homer before death or mental imbecility, with a failure of physical strength, should overtake him. On another occasion he said, "If I am worthy, I would wish for sudden death, with no interregnum between *I cease to exercise reason* and *I cease to exist.*" In these wishes he was happily gratified, as well as in the time of his being laid away to his final rest, as expressed in the following beautiful and characteristic lines to JUNE:

"I gazed upon the glorious sky,
 And the green mountains round,
And thought that when I came to lie
 At rest within the ground,
'Twere pleasant that in flowery June,
When brooks send up a cheerful tune,
 And groves a cheerful sound,
The sexton's hand, my grave to make,
The rich, green mountain turf should break.

"A cell within the frozen mould,
 A coffin borne through sleet,
And icy clods above it rolled,
 While fierce the tempests beat—
Away! I will not think of these—
Blue be the sky and soft the breeze,
 Earth green beneath the feet,
And be the damp mould gently pressed
Into my narrow place of rest.

"There, through the long, long, summer hours,
 The golden light should lie,
And thick young herbs and groups of flowers
 Stand in their beauty by.
The oriole should build and tell
His love-tale close beside my cell;
 The idle butterfly
Should rest him there, and there be heard
The housewife bee and humming-bird.

"And what if cheerful shouts at noon
 Come, from the village sent,
Or song of maids beneath the moon
 With fairy laughter blent?
And what if, in the evening light,
Betrothed lovers walk in sight
 Of my low monument?
I would the lovely scene around
Might know no sadder sight nor sound.

"I know that I no more should see
The season's glorious show,
Nor would its brightness shine for me,
Nor its wild music flow;
But if, around my place of sleep,
The friends I love should come to weep,
They might not haste to go.
Soft airs, and song, and light and bloom
Should keep them lingering by my tomb.

These to their softened hearts should bear
The thought of what has been,
And speak of one who can not share
The gladness of the scene;
Whose part, in all the pomp that fills
The circuit of the summer hills,
Is that his grave is green;
And deeply would their hearts rejoice
To hear again his living voice."

It was indeed a glorious day, and the daisies were dancing and glimmering over the fields as the poet's family, a few old friends, and the villagers saw him laid in his last resting-place at Roslyn, after a few words fitly spoken by his pastor, and beheld his coffin covered with roses and other summer flowers by a little band of country children, who gently dropped them as they circled round the poet's grave. This act completed, we left the aged minstrel amid the melody dearest of all to him in life—the music of the gentle June breezes murmuring through the tree-tops, from whence also came the songs of summer birds.

The following, from the pen of Paul H. Hayne, of South Carolina, is one of the many tributes to Mr. Bryant's character and genius, that have appeared since the poet's death, from the pens of Curtis, Holland, Osgood, Powers, Stedman, Stoddard, Street, Symington (a Scottish singer), and many others:

"Lo! there he lies, our Patriarch Poet, dead!
The solemn angel of eternal peace
Has waved a wand of mystery o'er his head,
Touched his strong heart, and bade his pulses cease.

"Behold, in marble quietude he lies!
Pallid and cold, divorced from earthly breath,
With tranquil brow, lax hands, and dreamless eyes;—
Yet the closed lips would seem to smile at death.

"Well may they smile; for death, to such as he,
Brings purer freedom, loftier thought and aim;
And, in grand truce with immortality,
Lifts to song's fadeless heaven his star-like fame!"

I can not forbear adding to this expression of appreciative affection a few words from the funeral address uttered by his pastor, the Rev. Dr. Bellows, at the commemorative ceremony held in New York, on the 14th of June, at All Souls' Church, of which Mr. Bryant was for the last fifteen years of his life an active and honored member. Dr. Bellows said :

"Never, perhaps, was there an instance of such precocity in point of wisdom and maturity as that which marked 'Thanatopsis,' written at eighteen, or of such persistency in judgment, force, and melody as that exhibited in his last public ode, written at eighty-three, on occasion of Washington's last birthday. Between these two bounds lies one even path, high, finished, faultless, in which comes a succession of poems, always meditative, always steeped in the love and knowledge of nature, always pure and melodious, always stamped with his sign manual of faultless taste and gem-like purity. . . .

"A devoted lover of religious liberty, he was an equal lover of religion itself—not in any precise dogmatic form, but in its righteousness, reverence, and charity. . . .

"It is the glory of this man that his character outshone even his great talent and his large fame. Distinguished equally for his native gifts and his consummate culture, his poetic inspiration and his exquisite art, he is honored and loved to-day even more for his stainless purity of life, his unswerving rectitude of will, his devotion to the higher interests of his race, his unfeigned patriotism, and his broad humanity. . . .

"The increasing sweetness and beneficence of his character, meanwhile, must have struck his familiar friends. His last years were his devoutest and most humane years. He became beneficent as he grew able to be so, and his hand was open to all just needs and to many unreasonable claimants."

No more appropriate concluding paragraph can be added to this memorial paper, which I could wish worthier of the good and gifted Bryant—*Integer vitæ scelerisque purus*—than his own beautiful words, applied to his contemporary Washington Irving. "If it were becoming," said the poet, "to address our departed friend as if in his immediate presence, I would say, 'Farewell, thou who hast entered into the rest prepared from the foundation of the world for serene and gentle spirits like thine. Farewell, happy in thy life, happy in thy death, happier in the reward to which that death is the assured passage ; fortunate in attracting the admiration of the world to thy beautiful writings ; still more fortunate in having written nothing which did not tend to promote the reign of magnanimous forbearance and generous sympathies among thy fellow-men. The brightness of that enduring fame which thou hast won on earth is but a shadowy symbol of the glory to which thou art admitted in the world beyond the grave. Thy errand on earth was an errand of peace and good-will to men, and thou art now in a region where hatred and strife never enter, and where the harmonious activity of those who inhabit it acknowledges no impulse less noble or less pure than love."

JAMES GRANT WILSON.

NEW YORK, July, 1878.

Eng.d by H.B.Hall & Sons, New York.

Yours very truly,
W. C. Bryant.

J. B. FORD & Co. NEW YORK.

THE EDITOR TO THE READER.

THE present enlarged edition of the "Library of Poetry and Song" has been projected with a view of making the collection more perfect, both in the choice of poems and the variety of sources from which they are derived. Within a very few years past several names of eminence have been added to the list of poets in our language, and every reader would expect to find samples of their verse in an anthology like this, to say nothing of the air of freshness which these would give.

That the demand for compilations of this character is genuine and very general is sufficiently demonstrated by the appearance, since the first edition of this was published, of Emerson's "Parnassus" and Whittier's "Songs of Three Centuries." These, however, do not seem to have supplanted Dana's "Household Book of Poetry," which still retains its popularity. It often happens that the same household contains several of these publications. The present volume, moreover, in addition to the fullness of its material, has been got up with much expense in the way of engraved illustrations, so that it will occupy a place by itself. Regarded from a literary point of view, it owes much to the expert hands of Mr. Knight and Mr. Raymond, who have assisted in its compilation and the perfecting of its details. The first edition has proved, commercially speaking, one of the most successful publications of the day; and if the compilation in its present shape should meet with the same favor, the Publishers, it seems to me, can ask no more.

When I saw that Mr. Emerson had omitted to include any of his own poems in the collection entitled "Parnassus," I doubted, for a while, whether

I ought not to have practiced the same reserve. Yet when I considered that the omission on his part was so far a defect, and that there is not a reader of his volume who would not have been better pleased to possess several of his poems along with the others, I became better satisfied with what I had done, and allowed such of my poems as I had included to remain. In one respect, at least, the present compilation will have the advantage over Mr. Emerson's, namely, that it contains several of the poems with which he has enriched our literature.

WILLIAM CULLEN BRYANT.

July, 1876.

The Poet.

Thou who wouldst wear the name
Of Poet midst thy brethren of mankind,
And clothe, in words of flame,
Thoughts that shall live within the general mind,
Deem not the framing of a deathless lay
The pastime of a drowsy summer day.

But gather all thy powers,
And wreak them on the verse that thou dost weave;
And, in thy lonely hours,
At silent morning or at wakeful eve,
While the warm current tingles through thy veins,
Set forth the burning words in fluent strains.

No smooth array of phrase,
Artfully sought and ordered though it be,
Which the cold rhymer lays
Upon the page with languid industry,
Can wake the listless pulse to livelier speed,
Or fill, with sudden tears, the eyes that read,

The secret wouldst thou know
To touch the heart or fire the blood at will,
Let thine eyes o'erflow;
Let thy lips quiver with the passionate thrill;
Seize the great thought ere yet its power be past,
And bind, in words, the fleet emotion fast.

Then, should thy verse appear
Halting and harsh and all unaptly wrought,
Touch the crude line with fear,
Save in the moment of impassioned thought;
Then summon back the orginal glow and mend
The strain with rapture that with fire was penned.

Yet let no empty gust
Of passion find an utterance in thy lay;
A blast that whirls the dust
Along the howling street and dies away;
But feelings of calm power and mighty sweep,
Like currents journeying through the windless deep.

Seek'st thou in living lays
To limn the beauty of the earth and sky?
Before thine inner gaze
Let all that beauty in clear vision lie;
Look on it with exceeding love and write
The words inspired by wonder and delight.

Of tempests wouldst thou sing,
Or tell of battles; make thyself a part
Of the great tumult; cling
To the tossed wreck with terror in thy heart;
Scale, with the assaulting host, the ramparts' height,
And strike and struggle in the thickest fight.

So shalt thou frame a lay
Which haply may endure from age to age;
And they who read shall say:
"What witchery hangs upon this poet's page!
"What art is his the written spells to find
"That sway, from mood to mood, the willing mind!"

William Cullen Bryant.

Copied, Dec. 1875.

INTRODUCTION:

POETS AND POETRY OF THE ENGLISH LANGUAGE.

I SUPPOSE it is not necessary to give a reason for adding another to the collections of this nature, already in print. They abound in every language, for the simple reason that there is a demand for them. German literature, prolific as it is in verse, has many of them, and some of them compiled by distinguished authors. The parlor table and the winter fireside require a book which, when one is in the humor for reading poetry and knows not what author to take up, will supply exactly what he wants.

I have known persons who frankly said that they took no pleasure in reading poetry, and perhaps the number of those who make this admission would be greater were it not for the fear of appearing singular. But to the great mass of mankind poetry is really a delight and a refreshment. To many, perhaps to most, it is not requisite that it should be of the highest degree of merit. Nor, although it be true that the poems which are most famous and most highly prized are works of considerable length, can it be said that the pleasure they give is in any degree proportionate to the extent of their plan. It seems to me that it is only poems of a moderate length, or else portions of the greater works to which I refer, that produce the effect upon the mind and heart which make the charm of this kind of writing. The proper office of poetry, in filling the mind with delightful images and awakening the gentler emotions, is not accomplished on a first and rapid perusal, but requires that the words should be dwelt upon until they become in a certain sense our own, and are adopted as the utterance of our own minds. A collection such as this is intended to be furnishes for this purpose portions of the best English verse suited to any of the varying moods of its readers.

Such a work also, if sufficiently extensive, gives the reader an opportunity of comparing the poetic literature of one period with that of another; of noting the fluctuations of taste, and how the poetic forms which are in fashion during one age are laid aside in the next; of observing the changes which take place in our language, and the sentiments which at different periods challenge the public approbation. Specimens of the poetry of different centuries presented in this way show how the great stream of human thought in its poetic form eddies now to the right and now to the left, wearing away its banks first on one side and then on the other. Some author of more than common faculties and more than common boldness catches the public attention, and immediately he has a crowd of followers who form their taste on his and seek to divide with him the praise. Thus Cowley, with his undeniable genius, was the head of a numerous class who made poetry consist in far-fetched conceits, ideas oddly brought together, and quaint turns of thought. Pope, following close upon Dryden, and learning much from him, was the founder of a school of longer duration, which found its models in Boileau and other poets of the reign of Louis the Fourteenth, — a school in which the wit predominated over the poetry, — a school marked by striking oppositions of thought, frequent happinesses of expression, and a carefully balanced modulation, — numbers pleasing at first, but in the end fatiguing. As this school degenerated the wit almost disappeared, but there was no new infusion of poetry in its place. When Scott gave the public the *Lay of the Last Minstrel*, and other poems, which certainly, considered as mere narratives, are the best we have, carrying the reader forward without weariness and with an interest which the author never allows to subside, a crowd of imitators pressed after him, the greater part of whom are no longer read. Wordsworth had, and still has, his school; the stamp of his example is visible on the writings of all the poets of the present day. Even Byron showed himself, in the third canto of *Childe Harold*, to be one of his disciples, though he fiercely resented being called so. The same poet did not disdain to learn of Scott in composing his narrative poems, such as the *Bride of Abydos* and the *Giaour*, though he could never tell a story in verse without occasional tediousness. In our day the style of writing adopted by eminent living poets is often seen reflected in the verses of their younger contemporaries, — sometimes with an effect like that of a face beheld in a tarnished mirror. Thus it is that poets are formed by their influence on one another; the greatest of them are more or less indebted for what they are to their predecessors and their contemporaries.

While speaking of these changes in the public taste, I am tempted to caution the reader against the mistake often made of estimating the merit of one poet by the too easy process of comparing him with another. The varieties of poetic excellence are as great as the varieties of beauty in flowers or in the female face. There is no poet, indeed no author in any department of literature, who can be taken as a standard in judging of others; the true standard is an ideal one, and even this is not the same in all men's minds. One delights in grace, another in strength; one in a fiery vehemence and enthusiasm on the surface, another in majestic repose and the expression of feeling too deep to be noisy; one loves simple and obvious images strikingly employed, or familiar thoughts placed in a new light, another is satisfied only with novelties of thought and expression, with uncommon illustrations and images far sought. It is certain that each of these modes of treating a subject may have its peculiar merit, and that it is absurd to require of those whose genius inclines them to one that they should adopt its opposite, or to set one down as inferior to another because he is not of the same class. As well, in looking through an astronomer's telescope at that beautiful phenomenon, a double star, in which the twin flames are one of a roseate and the other of a golden tint, might we quarrel with either of them because it is not colored like its fellow. Some of the comparisons made by critics between one poet and another are scarcely less preposterous than would be a comparison between a river and a mountain.

The compiler of this collection has gone as far back as to the author who may

Etch.d by H. B. Hall N.Y. 1875

Geoffroy Chaucer.

J. B. FORD & Co NEW YORK.

properly be called the father of English poetry, and who wrote while our language was like the lion in Milton's account of the creation, when rising from the earth at the Divine command and

"... . pawing to get free
His hinder parts,"—

for it was still clogged by the unassimilated portions of the French tongue, to which in part is owed its origin. These were to be thrown aside in after years. The versification had also one characteristic of French verse which was soon after Chaucer's time laid aside, — the mute or final *e* had in his lines the value of a syllable by itself, especially when the next word began with a consonant. But though these peculiarities somewhat embarrass the reader, he still finds in the writings of the old poet a fund of the good old English of the Saxon fireside, which makes them worthy to be studied were it only to strengthen our hold on our language. He delighted in describing natural objects which still retained their Saxon names, and this he did with great beauty and sweetness. In the sentiments also the critics ascribe to him a degree of delicacy which one could scarcely have looked for in the age in which he wrote, though at other times he avails himself of the license then allowed. There is no majesty, no stately march of numbers, in his poetry, still less is there of fire, rapidity, or conciseness; the French and Italian narrative poets from whom he learned his art wrote as if the people of their time had nothing to do but to attend to long stories, and Chaucer, who translated from the French the *Romaunt of the Rose*, though a greater poet than any of those whom he took for his models, made small improvement upon them in this respect. His *Troylus and Cryseyde*, with but little action and incident, is as long as either of the epics of Homer. The *Canterbury Tales*, Chaucer's best things, have less of this defect; but even there the narrative is overminute, and the personages, as Taine, the French critic, remarks, although they talk well, talk too much. The taste for this prolixity in narratives and conversations had a long duration in English poetry, since we find the same tediousness, to call it by its true name, in Shakespeare's *Venus and Adonis* and his *Lucrece*, written more than two hundred years later. Yet in the mean time the old popular ballads of England and Scotland had been composed, in which the incidents follow each other in quick succession, and the briefest possible speeches are uttered by the personages. The scholars and court poets doubtless disdained to learn anything of these poets of the people, and the *Davideis* of Cowley, who lived three hundred years after Chaucer, is as remarkable for the sluggish progress of the story and the tediousness of the harangues as for any other characteristics.

Between the time of Chaucer and that of Sidney and Spenser we find little in the poetic literature of our language to detain our attention. That age produced many obscure versifiers, and metrical romances continued to be written after the fashion of the French and Italian poets, whom Chaucer acknowledged as his masters. During this period appeared Skelton, the poet and jester, whose special talent was facility in rhyming, who rhymed as if he could not help it, — as if he had only to put pen to paper, and the words leaped of their own accord into regular measure with an inevitable jingle at the endings. Meantime our language was undergoing a process which gradually separated the nobler parts from the dross, rejecting the French additions for which there was no occasion, or which could not easily be made to take upon themselves the familiar forms of our tongue. The prosody of English became also fixed in that period; the final *e* which so perplexes the modern reader in Chaucer's verse was no longer permitted to figure as a distinct syllable. The poets, however, still allowed themselves the liberty of sometimes making, after the French manner, two syllables of the terminations *tion* and *ion*, so that *nation* became a word of three syllables and *opinion* a word of four. The Sonnets of Sidney, written on the Italian model, have all the grace and ingenuity of those of Petrarch. In the *Faerie Queene* of Spenser it seems to me that we find the English language, so far as the purposes of poetry require, in a degree of perfection beyond which it has not been since carried, and, I suppose, never will be. A vast assemblage of poetic endowments contributed to the composition of this poem, yet I think it would not be easy to name one of the same length, and the work of a genius equally great, in any language, which more fatigues the reader in a steady perusal from beginning to end. In it we have an invention ever awake, active, and apparently inexhaustible; an affluence of imagery grand, beautiful, or magnificent, as the subject may require; wise observations on human life steeped in a poetic coloring, and not without touches of pathos; a wonderful mastery of versification, and the aptest forms of expression. We read at first with admiration, yet to this erelong succeeds a sense of satiety, and we lay down the book, not unwilling, however, after an interval, to take it up with renewed admiration. I once heard an eminent poet say that he thought the second part of the *Faerie Queene* inferior to the first; yet I am inclined to ascribe the remark rather to a falling off in the attention of the reader than in the merit of the work. A poet, however, would be more likely to persevere to the end than any other reader, since in every stanza he would meet with some lesson in his art.

In that fortunate age of English literature arose a greater than Spenser. Let me only say of Shakespeare, that in his dramas, amid certain faults imputable to the taste of the English public, there is to be found every conceivable kind of poetic excellence. At the same time and immediately after him flourished a group of dramatic poets who drew their inspiration from nature and wrote with manly vigor. One would naturally suppose that their example, along with the more illustrious ones of Spenser and Shakespeare, would influence and form the taste of the succeeding age; but almost before they had ceased to claim the attention of the public, and while the eminent divines, Barrow, Jeremy Taylor, and others, wrote nobly in prose with a genuine eloquence and a fervor scarcely less than poetic, appeared the school of writers in verse whom Johnson, by a phrase the propriety of which has been disputed, calls the metaphysical poets, — a class of wits whose whole aim was to extort admiration by ingenious conceits, thoughts of such unexpectedness and singularity that one wondered how they could ever come into the mind of the author. For what they regarded as poetic effect they depended, not upon the sense of beauty or grandeur, not upon depth or earnestness of feeling, but simply upon surprise at quaint and strange resemblances, contrasts, and combinations of ideas. These were delivered for the most part in rugged diction, and in numbers so harsh as to be almost unmanageable by the reader. Cowley, a man of real genius, and of a more musical versification than his fellows, was the most distinguished example of this school. Milton, born a little before Cowley, and like him an eminent poet in his teens, is almost the only instance of escape from the infection of this vicious style; his genius was of too robust a mold for such petty employments, and he would have made, if he had condescended to them, as ill a figure as his own Samson on the stage of a mountebank. Dryden himself, in some of his earlier poems, appears as a pupil of this school; but he soon outgrew — in great part, at least — the false taste of the time, and set an example of a nobler treatment of poetic subjects.

Yet though the genius of Dryden reacted against this perversion of the art of verse, it had not the power to raise the poetry of our language to the height which it occupied in the Elizabethan age. Within a limited range he was a true poet; his imagination was far from fertile, nor had he much skill in awakening emotion, but he could treat certain subjects magnificently in verse, and often where his imagination fails him he is sustained by the vigor of his understanding and the largeness of his knowledge. He gave an example of versification in the heroic couplet, which has commanded the admiration of succeeding poets down to our time, — a versification manly, majestic, and of varied modulation, of which Pope took only a certain part as the model of his own, and, contracting its range and reducing it to more regular pauses, made it at first appear more musical to the reader, but in the end fatigued him by its monotony. Dryden drew scarcely a single image from his own observation of external nature; and Pope, though less insensible than he to natural beauty, was still merely the poet of the drawing-room. Yet he is the author of more happy lines, which have passed into the common speech and are quoted as proverbial sayings, than any author we have save Shakespeare; and, whatever may be said in his dispraise, he is likely to be quoted as long as the English is a living language. The footprints of Pope are not those of a giant, but he has left them scattered all over the field of our literature, although the fashion of writing like him has wholly passed away.

Certain faculties of the poetic mind seem to have slumbered from the time of Milton to that of Thomson, who showed the literary world of Great Britain, to its astonishment, what a profusion of materials for poetry Nature offers to him who directly consults her instead of taking his images at second-hand. Thomson's blank verse, however, is often swollen and bladdery to a painful degree. He seems to have imagined, like many other writers of his time, that blank verse could not support itself without the aid of a stilted phraseology; for that fine poem of his, in the Spenserian stanza, the *Castle of Indolence*, shows that when he wrote in rhyme he did not think it necessary to depart from a natural style.

Wordsworth is generally spoken of as one who gave to our literature that impulse which brought the poets back from the capricious forms of expression in vogue before his time to a certain fearless simplicity; for it must be acknowledged that until he arose there was scarce any English poet who did not seem in some degree to labor under the apprehension of becoming too simple and natural, — to imagine that a certain pomp of words is necessary to elevate the style and make that grand and noble which in its direct expression would be homely and trivial. Yet the poetry of Wordsworth was but the consummation of a tendency already existing and active. Cowper had already felt it in writing his *Task*, and in his longer rhymed poems had not only attempted a freer versification than that of Pope, but had clothed his thoughts in the manly English of the better age of our poetry. Percy's *Reliques* had accustomed English readers to perceive the extreme beauty of the old ballads in their absolute simplicity, and shown how much superior these were to such productions as Percy's own *Hermit of Warkworth* and Goldsmith's *Edwin and Angelina*, in their feeble elegance. Burns's inimitable Scottish poems — his English verses are tumid and wordy — had taught the same lesson. We may infer that the genius of Wordsworth was in a great degree influenced by these, just as he in his turn contributed to form the taste of those who wrote after him. It was long, however, before he reached the eminence which he now holds in the estimation of the literary world. His *Lyrical Ballads*, published about the close of the last century, were at first little read, and of those who liked them there were few who were not afraid to express their admiration. Yet his fame has slowly climbed from stage to stage until now his influence is perceived in all the English poetry of the day. If this were the place to criticise his poetry, I should say, of his more stately poems in blank verse, that they often lack compression, — that the thought suffers by too great expansion. Wordsworth was unnecessarily afraid of being epigrammatic. He abhorred what is called a point as much as Dennis is said to have abhorred a pun. Yet I must own that even his most diffuse amplifications have in them a certain grandeur that fills the mind.

At a somewhat later period arose the poet Keats, who wrote in a manner which carried the reader back to the time when those charming passages of lyrical enthusiasm were produced which we occasionally find in the plays of Shakespeare, in those of Beaumont and Fletcher, and in Milton's *Comus*. The verses of Keats are occasionally disfigured, especially in his *Endymion*, by a flatness almost childish, but in the finer passages they clothe the thought in the richest imagery and in words each of which is a poem. Lowell has justly called Keats "over-languaged," but there is scarce a word that we should be willing to part with in his *Ode to the Nightingale*, and that on a *Grecian Urn*, and the same thing may be said of the greater part of his *Hyperion*. His poems were ridiculed in the Edinburgh Review, but they survived the ridicule, and now, fifty years after their first publication, the poetry of the present day, by certain resemblances of manner, testifies to the admiration with which he is still read.

The genius of Byron was of a more vigorous mold than that of Keats; but notwithstanding his great popularity and the number of his imitators at one time, he made a less permanent impression on the character of English poetry. His misanthropy and gloom, his scoffing vein, and the fierceness of his animosities, after the first glow of admiration was over, had a repellent effect upon readers, and made them turn to more cheerful strains. Moore had in his time many imitators, but all his gayety, his brilliant fancy, his somewhat feminine graces, and the elaborate music of his numbers, have not saved him from the fate of being imitated no more. Coleridge and Southey were of the same school with Wordsworth, and only added to the effect of his example upon our literature. Coleridge is the author of the two most perfect poetical translations which our language in his day could boast, those of Schiller's *Piccolomini* and *Death of Wallenstein*, in which the English verse falls in no respect short of the original German. Southey divides with Scott the honor of writing the first long narrative poems in our language which can be read without occasional weariness.

Of the later poets, educated in part by the generation of authors which produced Wordsworth and Byron and in part by each other, yet possessing their individual peculiarities, I should perhaps speak with more reserve. The number of those who are attempting to win a name in this walk of literature is great, and several of them have already gained, and through many years held, the public favor. To some of them will be assigned an enduring station among the eminent of their class.

There are two tendencies by which the seekers after poetic fame in our day are apt to be misled, through both the example of others and the applause of critics. One of these is the desire to extort admiration by striking novelties of expression; and the other, the ambition to distinguish themselves by subtilties of thought, remote from the common apprehension.

With regard to the first of these I have only to say what has been often said before, that, however favorable may be the idea which this luxuriance of poetic imagery and of epithet at first gives us of the author's talent, our admiration soon exhausts itself. We feel that the thought moves heavily under its load of garments, some of which perhaps strike us as tawdry and others as ill-fitting, and we lay down the book to take it up no more.

The other mistake, if I may so call it, deserves more attention, since we find able critics speaking with high praise of passages in the poetry of the day to which the general reader is puzzled to attach a meaning. This is often the case when the words themselves seem simple enough, and keep within the range of the Saxon or household element of our language. The obscurity lies sometimes in the phrase itself, and sometimes in the recondite or remote allusion. I will not say that certain minds are not affected by this, as others are by verses in plainer English. To the few it may be genuine poetry, although it may be a riddle to the mass of readers. I remember reading somewhere of a mathematician who was affected with a sense of sublimity by the happy solution of an algebraical or geometrical problem, and I have been assured by one who devoted himself to the science of mathematics that the phenomenon is no uncommon one. Let us beware, therefore, of assigning too narrow limits to the causes which produce the poetic exaltation of mind. The genius of those who write in this manner may be freely acknowledged, but they do not write for mankind at large.

To me it seems that one of the most important requisites for a great poet is a luminous style. The elements of poetry lie in natural objects, in the vicissitudes of human life, in the emotions of the human heart, and the relations of man to man. He who can present them in combinations and lights which at once affect the mind with a deep sense of their truth and beauty is the poet for his own age and the ages that succeed it. It is no disparagement either to his skill or his power that he finds them near at hand; the nearer they lie to the common track of the human intelligence, the more certain is he of the sympathy of his own generation, and of those which shall come after him. The metaphysician, the subtile thinker, the dealer in abstruse speculations, whatever his skill in versification, misapplies it when he abandons the more convenient form of prose and perplexes himself with the attempt to express his ideas in poetic numbers.

Let me say for the poets of the present day, that in one important respect they have profited by the example of their immediate predecessors; they have learned to go directly to nature for their imagery, instead of taking it from what had once been regarded as the common stock of the guild of poets. I have often had occasion to verify this remark with no less delight than surprise on meeting in recent verse new images in their untarnished luster, like coins fresh from the mint, unworn and unsoiled by passing from pocket to pocket. It is curious, also, to observe how a certain set of hackneyed phrases, which Leigh Hunt, I believe, was the first to ridicule, and which were once used for the convenience of rounding out a line or supplying a rhyme, have disappeared from our poetry, and how our blank verse in the hands of the most popular writers has dropped its stiff Latinisms and all the awkward distortions resorted to by those who thought that by putting a sentence out of its proper shape they were writing like Milton.

I have now brought this brief survey of the progress of our poetry down to the present time, and refer the reader, for samples of it in the different stages of its existence, to those which are set before him in this volume.

Such is the wide range of English verse, and such the abundance of the materials, that a compilation of this kind must be like a bouquet gathered from the fields in June, when hundreds of flowers will be left in unvisited spots, as beautiful as those which have been taken. It may happen, therefore, that many who have learned to delight in some particular poem will turn these pages, as they might those of other collections, without finding their favorite. Nor should it be matter of surprise, considering the multitude of authors from whom the compilation is made, if it be found that some are overlooked, especially the more recent, of equal merit with many whose poems appear in these pages. It may happen, also, that the compiler, in consequence of some particular association, has been sensible of a beauty and a power of awakening emotions and recalling images in certain poems which other readers will fail to perceive. It should be considered, moreover, that in poetry, as in painting, different artists have different modes of presenting their conceptions, each of which may possess its peculiar merit, yet those whose taste is formed by contemplating the productions of one class take little pleasure in any other. Crabb Robinson relates that Wordsworth once admitted to him that he did not much admire contemporary poetry, not because of its want of poetic merit, but because he had been accustomed to poetry of a different sort, and added that but for this he might have read it with pleasure. I quote from memory. It is to be hoped that every reader of this collection, however he may have been trained, will find in the great variety of its contents something conformable to his taste.

WILLIAM CULLEN BRYANT.

POEMS OF
INFANCY AND YOUTH

The angel wrote, and vanish'd. The next night
It came again, with a great wakening light,
And shew'd the names whom love of God had bless'd,
And lo! Ben Adhem's name led all the rest.

Leigh Hunt

"Here on this blest Thanksgiving Night,
We raise to Thee our grateful voice;
For what thou doest, Lord, is right
And thus believing, we rejoice."

A. G. Spalding

J. G. Holland

J. B. FORD & Co NEW YORK

POEMS OF INFANCY AND YOUTH.

INFANCY.

PHILIP, MY KING.

"Who bears upon his baby brow the round
And top of sovereignty."

LOOK at me with thy large brown eyes,
Philip, my king!
For round thee the purple shadow lies
Of babyhood's royal dignities.
Lay on my neck thy tiny hand
With Love's invisible sceptre laden;
I am thine Esther, to command
Till thou shalt find thy queen-handmaiden,
Philip, my king!

O, the day when thou goest a-wooing,
Philip, my king!
When those beautiful lips 'gin suing,
And, some gentle heart's bars undoing,
Thou dost enter, love-crowned, and there
Sittest love-glorified! — Rule kindly,
Tenderly over thy kingdom fair;
For we that love, ah! we love so blindly,
Philip, my king!

I gaze from thy sweet mouth up to thy brow,
Philip, my king!
The spirit that there lies sleeping now
May rise like a giant, and make men bow
As to one Heaven-chosen amongst his peers.
My Saul, than thy brethren higher and fairer,
Let me behold thee in future years!
Yet thy head needeth a circlet rarer,
Philip, my king; —

A wreath, not of gold, but palm. One day,
Philip, my king!
Thou too must tread, as we trod, a way
Thorny, and cruel, and cold, and gray;
Rebels within thee and foes without
Will snatch at thy crown. But march on, glorious,
Martyr, yet monarch! till angels shout,
As thou sitt'st at the feet of God victorious,
"Philip, the king!"

DINAH MULOCK CRAIK.

CRADLE SONG.

FROM "BITTER-SWEET."

WHAT is the little one thinking about?
Very wonderful things, no doubt;
Unwritten history!
Unfathomed mystery!
Yet he chuckles, and crows, and nods, and winks,
As if his head were as full of kinks
And curious riddles as any sphinx!
Warped by colic, and wet by tears,
Punctured by pins, and tortured by fears,
Our little nephew will lose two years;
And he'll never know
Where the summers go;
He need not laugh, for he'll find it so.

Who can tell what a baby thinks?
Who can follow the gossamer links
By which the manikin feels his way
Out from the shore of the great unknown,
Blind, and wailing, and alone,
Into the light of day?
Out from the shore of the unknown sea,
Tossing in pitiful agony;
Of the unknown sea that reels and rolls,
Specked with the barks of little souls, —
Barks that were launched on the other side,
And slipped from heaven on an ebbing tide!
What does he think of his mother's eyes?
What does he think of his mother's hair?
What of the cradle-roof, that flies
Forward and backward through the air?
What does he think of his mother's breast,
Bare and beautiful, smooth and white,
Seeking it ever with fresh delight,
Cup of his life, and couch of his rest?
What does he think when her quick embrace
Presses his hand and buries his face
Deep where the heart-throbs sink and swell,
With a tenderness she can never tell,
Though she murmur the words
Of all the birds, —
Words she has learned to murmur well?
Now he thinks he'll go to sleep!
I can see the shadow creep

Over his eyes in soft eclipse,
Over his brow and over his lips,
Out to his little finger-tips!
Softly sinking, down he goes!
Down he goes! down he goes!
See! he 's hushed in sweet repose.

JOSIAH GILBERT HOLLAND.

THE BABY.

NAKED on parents' knees, a new-born child,
Weeping thou sat'st when all around thee smiled:
So live, that, sinking to thy last long sleep,
Thou then mayst smile while all around thee weep.

From the Portuguese of CALIDASA,
by SIR WILLIAM JONES.

BABY MAY.

CHEEKS as soft as July peaches;
Lips whose dewy scarlet teaches
Poppies paleness; round large eyes
Ever great with new surprise;
Minutes filled with shadeless gladness;
Minutes just as brimmed with sadness;
Happy smiles and wailing cries;
Crows, and laughs, and tearful eyes;
Lights and shadows, swifter born
Than on wind-swept autumn corn;
Ever some new tiny notion,
Making every limb all motion;
Catchings up of legs and arms;
Throwings back and small alarms;
Clutching fingers; straightening jerks;
Twining feet whose each toe works;
Kickings up and straining risings;
Mother's ever new surprisings;
Hands all wants and looks all wonder
At all things the heavens under;
Tiny scorns of smiled reprovings
That have more of love than lovings;
Mischiefs done with such a winning
Archness that we prize such sinning;
Breakings dire of plates and glasses;
Graspings small at all that passes;
Pullings off of all that 's able
To be caught from tray or table;
Silences, — small meditations
Deep as thoughts of cares for nations;
Breaking into wisest speeches
In a tongue that nothing teaches;
All the thoughts of whose possessing
Must be wooed to light by guessing;
Slumbers, — such sweet angel-seemings
That we 'd ever have such dreamings;
Till from sleep we see thee breaking,
And we 'd always have thee waking;
Wealth for which we know no measure;
Pleasure high above all pleasure;
Gladness brimming over gladness;
Joy in care; delight in sadness;
Loveliness beyond completeness;
Sweetness distancing all sweetness;
Beauty all that beauty may be; —
That 's May Bennett; that 's my baby.

WILLIAM C. BENNETT.

CHOOSING A NAME.

I HAVE got a new-born sister;
I was nigh the first that kissed her.
When the nursing-woman brought her
To papa, his infant daughter,
How papa's dear eyes did glisten! —
She will shortly be to christen;
And papa has made the offer,
I shall have the naming of her.

Now I wonder what would please her, —
Charlotte, Julia, or Louisa?
Ann and Mary, they 're too common;
Joan 's too formal for a woman;
Jane 's a prettier name beside;
But we had a Jane that died.
They would say, if 't was Rebecca,
That she was a little Quaker.
Edith 's pretty, but that looks
Better in old English books;
Ellen 's left off long ago;
Blanche is out of fashion now.
None that I have named as yet
Are so good as Margaret.
Emily is neat and fine;
What do you think of Caroline?
How I 'm puzzled and perplexed
What to choose or think of next!
I am in a little fever
Lest the name that I should give her
Should disgrace her or defame her; —
I will leave papa to name her.

MARY LAMB.

THE BABY.

WHERE did you come from, baby dear?
Out of the everywhere into here.

Where did you get your eyes so blue?
Out of the sky as I came through.

Where did you get that little tear?
I found it waiting when I got here.

What makes your forehead so smooth and high?
A soft hand stroked it as I went by.

What makes your cheek like a warm white rose?
I saw something better than any one knows.

Whence that three-cornered smile of bliss?
Three angels gave me at once a kiss.

Where did you get this pearly ear?
God spoke, and it came out to hear.

Where did you get those arms and hands?
Love made itself into hooks and bands.

Feet, whence did you come, you darling things?
From the same box as the cherubs' wings.

How did they all come to be you?
God thought about me, and so I grew.

But how did you come to us, you dear?
God thought about you, and so I am here.

GEORGE MACDONALD.

LITTLE FEET.

Two little feet, so small that both may nestle
In one caressing hand, —
Two tender feet upon the untried border
Of life's mysterious land.

Dimpled, and soft, and pink as peach-tree blossoms,
In April's fragrant days,
How can they walk among the briery tangles,
Edging the world's rough ways?

These rose-white feet, along the doubtful future,
Must bear a mother's load;
Alas! since Woman has the heaviest burden,
And walks the harder road.

Love, for a while, will make the path before them
All dainty, smooth, and fair, —
Will cull away the brambles, letting only
The roses blossom there.

But when the mother's watchful eyes are shrouded
Away from sight of men,
And these dear feet are left without her guiding,
Who shall direct them then?

How will they be allured, betrayed, deluded,
Poor little untaught feet!
Into what dreary mazes will they wander,
What dangers will they meet?

Will they go stumbling blindly in the darkness
Of Sorrow's tearful shades?
Or find the upland slopes of Peace and Beauty,
Whose sunlight never fades?

Will they go toiling up Ambition's summit,
The common world above?
Or in some nameless vale, securely sheltered,
Walk side by side with Love?

Some feet there be which walk Life's track unwounded,
Which find but pleasant ways:
Some hearts there be to which this life is only
A round of happy days.

But these are few. Far more there are who wander
Without a hope or friend, —
Who find their journey full of pains and losses,
And long to reach the end.

How shall it be with her, the tender stranger,
Fair-faced and gentle-eyed,
Before whose unstained feet the world's rude highway
Stretches so fair and wide?

Ah! who may read the future? For our darling
We crave all blessings sweet,
And pray that He who feeds the crying ravens
Will guide the baby's feet.

ANONYMOUS.

CRADLE SONG.

SLEEP, little baby of mine,
Night and the darkness are near,
But Jesus looks down
Through the shadows that frown,
And baby has nothing to fear.

Shut, little sleepy blue eyes;
Dear little head, be at rest;
Jesus, like you,
Was a baby once, too,
And slept on his own mother's breast.

Sleep, little baby of mine,
Soft on your pillow so white;
Jesus is here
To watch over you, dear,
And nothing can harm you to-night.

O, little darling of mine,
What can you know of the bliss,
The comfort I keep,
Awake and asleep,
Because I am certain of this?

ANONYMOUS.

MY BIRD.

Ere last year's moon had left the sky
 A birdling sought my Indian nest,
And folded, oh! so lovingly,
 Her tiny wings upon my breast.

From morn till evening's purple tinge,
 In winsome helplessness she lies;
Two rose-leaves, with a silken fringe,
 Shut softly o'er her starry eyes.

There 's not in Ind a lovelier bird;
 Broad earth owns not a happier nest;
O God! thou hast a fountain stirred,
 Whose waters nevermore shall rest.

This beautiful, mysterious thing,
 This seeming visitant from heaven,
This bird with the immortal wing,
 To me, to me Thy hand has given.

The pulse first caught its tiny stroke,
 The blood its crimson hue, from mine:
This life which I have dared invoke,
 Henceforth is parallel with Thine!

A silent awe is in my room,
 I tremble with delicious fear;
The future with its light and gloom,
 Time and eternity are here.

Doubts, hopes, in eager tumult rise;
 Hear, O my God! one earnest prayer;
Room for my bird in Paradise,
 And give her angel-plumage there!

Emily C. Judson.

NURSE'S WATCH.

[From the "Boy's Horn of Wonders," a German Book of Nursery Rhymes.]

 The moon it shines,
 My darling whines;
The clock strikes twelve: — God cheer
The sick, both far and near.

 God knoweth all;
 Mousy nibbles in the wall;
The clock strikes one: — like day,
Dreams o'er thy pillow play.

 The matin-bell
 Wakes the nun in convent cell;
The clock strikes two: — they go
To choir in a row.

 The wind it blows,
 The cock he crows;
The clock strikes three: — the wagoner
In his straw bed begins to stir.

 The steed he paws the floor,
 Creaks the stable door;
The clock strikes four: — 't is plain,
The coachman sifts his grain.

 The swallow's laugh the still air shakes,
 The sun awakes;
The clock strikes five: — the traveller must be gone,
He puts his stockings on.

 The hen is clacking,
 The ducks are quacking;
The clock strikes six: — awake, arise,
Thou lazy hag; come, ope thy eyes.

 Quick to the baker's run;
 The rolls are done;
The clock strikes seven: —
'T is time the milk were in the oven.

 Put in some butter, do,
 And some fine sugar too;
The clock strikes eight: —
Now bring my baby's porridge straight.

Translation of Charles T. Brooks.

OLD GAELIC LULLABY.

Hush! the waves are rolling in,
 White with foam, white with foam;
Father toils amid the din,
 But baby sleeps at home.

Hush! the winds roar hoarse and deep, —
 On they come, on they come!
Brother seeks the wandering sheep,
 But baby sleeps at home.

Hush! the rain sweeps o'er the knowes
 Where they roam, where they roam;
Sister goes to seek the cows,
 But baby sleeps at home.

THE HOUSEHOLD SOVEREIGN.

FROM THE "HANGING OF THE CRANE."

The picture fades; as at a village fair
A showman's views dissolve into the air,
 To reappear transfigured on the screen,
So in my fancy this; and now once more

In part transfigured through the open door
Appears the selfsame scene.

Seated I see the two again,
But not alone; they entertain
A little angel unaware,
With face as round as is the moon;
A royal guest with flaxen hair,
Who, throned upon his lofty chair,
Drums on the table with his spoon,
Then drops it careless on the floor,
To grasp at things unseen before.
Are these celestial manners? these
The ways that win, the arts that please?
Ah, yes; consider well the guest,
And whatsoe'er he does seems best;
He ruleth by the right divine
Of helplessness, so lately born
In purple chambers of the morn,
As sovereign over thee and thine.
He speaketh not, and yet there lies
A conversation in his eyes;
The golden silence of the Greek,
The gravest wisdom of the wise,
Not spoken in language, but in looks
More legible than printed books,
As if he could but would not speak.

And now, O monarch absolute,
Thy power is put to proof; for lo!
Resistless, fathomless, and slow,
The nurse comes rustling like the sea,
And pushes back thy chair and thee,
And so good night to King Canute.

As one who walking in the forest sees
A lovely landscape through the parted trees,
Then sees it not for boughs that intervene,
Or as we see the moon sometimes revealed
Through drifting clouds, and then again concealed,
So I beheld the scene.

There are two guests at table now;
The king, deposed, and older grown,
No longer occupies the throne, —
The crown is on his sister's brow;
A princess from the Fairy Tales;
The very pattern girl of girls,
All covered and embowered in curls,
Rose tinted from the Isle of Flowers,
And sailing with soft silken sails
From far-off Dreamland into ours.
Above their bowls with rims of blue
Four azure eyes of deeper hue
Are looking, dreamy with delight;
Limpid as planets that emerge
Above the ocean's rounded verge,
Soft shining through the summer night,
Steadfast they gaze, yet nothing see
Beyond the horizon of their bowls;
Nor care they for the world that rolls
With all its freight of troubled souls
Into the days that are to be.

HENRY WADSWORTH LONGFELLOW.

BABY LOUISE.

I 'M in love with you, Baby Louise!
With your silken hair, and your soft blue eyes,
And the dreamy wisdom that in them lies,
And the faint, sweet smile you brought from the skies, —
God's sunshine, Baby Louise.

When you fold your hands, Baby Louise,
Your hands, like a fairy's, so tiny and fair,
With a pretty, innocent, saint-like air,
Are you trying to think of some angel-taught prayer
You learned above, Baby Louise?

I 'm in love with you, Baby Louise!
Why! you never raise your beautiful head!
Some day, little one, your cheek will grow red
With a flush of delight, to hear the words said,
"I love you," Baby Louise.

Do you hear me, Baby Louise?
I have sung your praises for nearly an hour,
And your lashes keep drooping lower and lower,
And — you 've gone to sleep, like a weary flower,
Ungrateful Baby Louise!

MARGARET EYTINGE.

THE ANGEL'S WHISPER.

[In Ireland they have a pretty fancy, that, when a child smiles in its sleep, it is "talking with angels."]

A BABY was sleeping;
Its mother was weeping,
For her husband was far on the wild raging sea;
And the tempest was swelling
Round the fisherman's dwelling;
And she cried, "Dermot, darling, O come back to me!"

Her beads while she numbered,
The baby still slumbered,
And smiled in her face as she bended her knee:
"O, blest be that warning,
My child, thy sleep adorning,
For I know that the angels are whispering with thee.

"And while they are keeping
Bright watch o'er thy sleeping,
O, pray to them softly, my baby, with me!
And say thou wouldst rather
They 'd watch o'er thy father!
For I know that the angels are whispering to thee."

The dawn of the morning
Saw Dermot returning,
And the wife wept with joy her babe's father to see;
And closely caressing
Her child with a blessing,
Said, "I knew that the angels were whispering with thee."

SAMUEL LOVER.

SMILING IN HIS SLEEP.

The baby sleeps and smiles.
What fairy thought beguiles
His little brain?
He sleeps and smiles again,
Flings his white arms about,
Half opes his sweet blue eye
As if he thought to spy,
By coyly peeping out,
The funny elf that brought
That tiny fairy thought
Unto his infant mind.
Would I some way could find
To know just how they seem,
Those dreams that infants dream.
I wonder what they are, —
Those thoughts that seem to wear
So sweet a guise?
What picture, tiny, fair,
What vision, lovely, rare,
Delights *his* eyes?
See! now he smiles once more;
Perhaps there is before
His mental sight portrayed
Some vision blest
Of that dear land of rest,
That far-off heaven,
From whence his new-created soul
Has lately strayed;
Or to his ear, perchance, are given
Those echoes sweet that roll
From angel harps we may not hear,
We, who have added year to year,
And sin to sin.
As yet his soul is spotless. Why
Should not angelic harmony
Reach his unsullied ear?
Why not within
His infant fancy transient gleams
Of heaven find their way in dreams?
And still the baby sleeps,
And as he sleeps he smiles. Ah, now
He starts, he wakes, he weeps;
Earth-shadows cloud his baby-brow.
His smiles how fleeting; how
Profuse his tears!
Dreams he of coming years,
Checkered by shadow and by light,
Unlike that vision holy, bright, —
That fairy gleam,
That infant dream
That made him sweetly smile?
Do coming sin and sorrow,
Phantoms of dark to-morrow,
Their shadows cast before,
Clouding all o'er
His baby-dreams, erewhile
So beautiful?

HARRIET W. STILLMAN.

BABY BYE.

Baby Bye,
Here 's a fly;
Let us watch him, you and I.
How he crawls
Up the walls,
Yet he never falls!
I believe with six such legs
You and I could walk on eggs.
There he goes
On his toes,
Tickling Baby's nose.

Spots of red
Dot his head;
Rainbows on his back are spread;
That small speck
Is his neck;
See him nod and beck.
I can show you, if you choose,
Where to look to find his shoes, —
Three small pairs,
Made of hairs;
These he always wears.

Black and brown
Is his gown;
He can wear it upside down;
It is laced
Round his waist;
I admire his taste.
Yet though tight his clothes are made,
He will lose them, I 'm afraid,
If to-night
He gets sight
Of the candle-light.

In the sun
Webs are spun;
What if he gets into one?
When it rains
He complains
On the window-panes.
Tongue to talk have you and I;
God has given the little fly
No such things,
So he sings
With his buzzing wings.

He can eat
Bread and meat;
There 's his mouth between his feet.
On his back
Is a pack
Like a pedler's sack.
Does the baby understand?
Then the fly shall kiss her hand;
Put a crumb
On her thumb,
Maybe he will come.

Catch him? No,
Let him go;
Never hurt an insect so;
But no doubt
He flies out
Just to gad about.
Now you see his wings of silk
Drabbled in the baby's milk;
Fie, O fie,
Foolish fly!
How will he get dry?

All wet flies
Twist their thighs;
Thus they wipe their heads and eyes;
Cats, you know,
Wash just so,
Then their whiskers grow.
Flies have hairs too short to comb,
So they fly bareheaded home;
But the gnat
Wears a hat.
Do you believe that?

Flies can see
More than we,
So how bright their eyes must be!
Little fly,
Ope your eye;
Spiders are near by.
For a secret I can tell, —
Spiders never use flies well.
Then away!
Do not stay.
Little fly, good day.

THEODORE TILTON.

NO BABY IN THE HOUSE.

No baby in the house, I know,
'T is far too nice and clean.
No toys, by careless fingers strewn,
Upon the floors are seen.
No finger-marks are on the panes,
No scratches on the chairs;
No wooden men set up in rows,
Or marshaled off in pairs;
No little stockings to be darned,
All ragged at the toes;
No pile of mending to be done,
Made up of baby-clothes;
No little troubles to be soothed;
No little hands to fold;
No grimy fingers to be washed;
No stories to be told;
No tender kisses to be given;
No nicknames, "Dove" and "Mouse";
No merry frolics after tea, —
No baby in the house!

CLARA G. DOLLIVER.

BABY'S SHOES.

O, THOSE little, those little blue shoes!
Those shoes that no little feet use!
O, the price were high
That those shoes would buy,
Those little blue unused shoes!

For they hold the small shape of feet
That no more their mother's eyes meet,
That, by God's good-will,
Years since, grew still,
And ceased from their totter so sweet.

And O, since that baby slept,
So hushed, how the mother has kept,
With a tearful pleasure,
That little dear treasure,
And over them thought and wept!

For they mind her forevermore
Of a patter along the floor;
And blue eyes she sees
Look up from her knees
With the look that in life they wore.

As they lie before her there,
There babbles from chair to chair
A little sweet face
That 's a gleam in the place,
With its little gold curls of hair.

Then O, wonder not that her heart
From all else would rather part
Than those tiny blue shoes
That no little feet use,
And whose sight makes such fond tears start!

WILLIAM C. BENNETT.

A CRADLE SONG.

HUSH, my dear! lie still and slumber!
Holy angels guard thy bed;
Heavenly blessings without number
Gently falling on thy head.

Sleep, my babe! thy food and raiment,
House and home, thy friends provide;
All without thy care or payment,
All thy wants are well supplied.

How much better thou 'rt attended
Than the Son of God could be,
When from heaven he descended,
And became a child like thee.

Soft and easy is thy cradle:
Coarse and hard thy Saviour lay:
When his birthplace was a stable,
And his softest bed was hay.

See the kindly shepherds round him,
Telling wonders from the sky!
Where they sought him, there they found him,
With his Virgin-Mother by.

See the lovely babe a-dressing:
Lovely infant, how he smiled!
When he wept, the mother's blessing
Soothed and hushed the holy child.

Lo, he slumbers in his manger,
Where the hornèd oxen fed;
— Peace, my darling! here 's no danger!
Here 's no ox anear thy bed!

— May'st thou live to know and fear him,
Trust and love him all thy days.
Then go dwell forever near him;
See his face, and sing his praise.

I could give thee thousand kisses,
Hoping what I most desire:
Not a mother's fondest wishes
Can to greater joys aspire.

ISAAC WATTS.

THE MOTHER'S STRATAGEM.

AN INFANT PLAYING NEAR A PRECIPICE.

WHILE on the cliff with calm delight she kneels,
And the blue vales a thousand joys recall,
See, to the last, last verge her infant steals!
O, fly — yet stir not, speak not, lest it fall. —
Far better taught, she lays her bosom bare,
And the fond boy springs back to nestle there.

From the Greek of LEONIDAS of Alexandria,
by SAMUEL ROGERS.

WILLIE WINKIE.

WEE Willie Winkie rins through the town,
Up stairs and doon stairs, in his nicht-gown,
Tirlin' at the window, cryin' at the lock,
"Are the weans in their bed? — for it 's now ten o'clock."

Hey, Willie Winkie! are ye comin' ben?
The cat 's singin' gay thrums to the sleepin' hen,
The doug 's speldered on the floor, and disna gie a cheep;
But here 's a waukrife laddie, that winna fa' asleep.

Ony thing but sleep, ye rogue: — glow'rin' like the moon,
Rattlin' in an airn jug wi' an airn spoon,
Rumblin', tumblin' roun' about, crawin' like a cock,
Skirlin' like a kenna-what — wauknin' sleepin' folk!

Hey, Willie Winkie! the wean 's in a creel!
Waumblin' aff a bodie's knee like a vera eel,
Ruggin' at the cat's lug, and ravellin' a' her thrums:
Hey, Willie Winkie! — See, there he comes!

Wearie is the mither that has a storie wean,
A wee stumpie stoussie, that canna rin his lane,
That has a battle aye wi' sleep, before he 'll close an ee;
But a kiss frae aff his rosy lips gies strength anew to me.

WILLIAM MILLER.

LITTLE PUSS.

SLEEK coat, eyes of fire,
Four paws that never tire,
That 's puss.

Ways playful, tail on high,
Twisting often toward the sky,
That 's puss.

LITTLE PUSS.

"Sleek coat, eyes of fire,
Four paws that never tire.
That's puss.

"Ways playful, tail on high,
Twisting often towards the sky,
That's puss."

In the larder, stealing meat,
Patter, patter, little feet,
That 's puss.

After ball, reel, or string,
Wild as any living thing,
That 's puss.

Round and round, after tail,
Fast as any postal mail,
That 's puss.

Curled up, like a ball,
On the door-mat in the hall,
That 's puss.

Purring loud on missis' lap,
Having toast, then a nap,
That 's puss.

Black as night, with talons long,
Scratching, which is very wrong,
That 's puss.

From a saucer lapping milk,
Soft, as soft as washing silk,
That 's puss.

Rolling on the dewy grass,
Getting wet, all in a mass,
That 's puss.

Climbing tree, and catching bird,
Little twitter nevermore heard,
That 's puss.

Killing fly, rat, or mouse,
As it runs about the house,
That 's puss.

Pet of missis, "Itte mite,"
Never must be out of sight,
That 's puss.

ANONYMOUS.

THE KITTEN AND FALLING LEAVES.

THAT way look, my Infant, lo!
What a pretty baby-show!
See the Kitten on the wall,
Sporting with the leaves that fall,
Withered leaves — one — two — and three —
From the lofty elder-tree!
Through the calm and frosty air
Of this morning bright and fair,
Eddying round and round they sink
Softly, slowly: one might think,
From the motions that are made,
Every little leaf conveyed
Sylph or faery hither tending, —
To this lower world descending,
Each invisible and mute,
In his wavering parachute.
— But the Kitten, how she starts,
Crouches, stretches, paws, and darts!
First at one, and then its fellow
Just as light and just as yellow;
There are many now — now one —
Now they stop, and there are none:
What intenseness of desire
In her upward eye of fire!
With a tiger-leap half-way
Now she meets the coming prey,
Lets it go as fast, and then
Has it in her power again:
Now she works with three or four,
Like an Indian conjurer;
Quick as he in feats of art,
Far beyond in joy of heart.
Were her antics played in th' eye
Of a thousand standers-by,
Clapping hands with shout and stare,
What would little Tabby care
For the plaudits of the crowd?
Over happy to be proud,
Over wealthy in the treasure
Of her own exceeding pleasure!
'Tis a pretty baby-treat;
Nor, I deem, for me unmeet;
Here, for neither Babe nor me,
Other playmate can I see.
Of the countless living things,
That with stir of feet and wings
(In the sun or under shade,
Upon bough or grassy blade)
And with busy revelings,
Chirp and song, and murmurings,
Made this orchard's narrow space
And this vale so blithe a place, —
Multitudes are swept away
Nevermore to breathe the day:
Some are sleeping; some in bands
Traveled into distant lands;
Others slunk to moor and wood,
Far from human neighborhood;
And, among the kinds that keep
With us closer fellowship,
With us openly abide,
All have laid their mirth aside.
Where is he, that giddy sprite,
Blue-cap, with his colors bright,
Who was blest as bird could be,
Feeding in the apple-tree;

Made such wanton spoil and rout,
Turning blossoms inside out;
Hung — head pointing towards the ground —
Fluttered, perched, into a round
Bound himself, and then unbound;
Lithest, gaudiest Harlequin;
Prettiest Tumbler ever seen;
Light of heart and light of limb;
What is now become of him?
Lambs, that through the mountains went
Frisking, bleating merriment,
When the year was in its prime,
They are sobered by this time.
If you look to vale or hill,
If you listen, all is still,
Save a little neighboring rill,
That from out the rocky ground
Strikes a solitary sound.
Vainly glitter hill and plain,
And the air is calm in vain;
Vainly Morning spreads the lure
Of a sky serene and pure;
Creature none can she decoy
Into open sign of joy:
Is it that they have a fear
Of the dreary season near?
Or that other pleasures be
Sweeter e'en than gayety?
 Yet, whate'er enjoyments dwell
In the impenetrable cell
Of the silent heart which Nature
Furnishes to every creature;
Whatsoe'er we feel and know
Too sedate for outward show, —
Such a light of gladness breaks,
Pretty Kitten! from thy freaks, —
Spreads with such a living grace
O'er my little Dora's face;
Yes, the sight so stirs and charms
Thee, Baby, laughing in my arms,
That almost I could repine
That your transports are not mine,
That I do not wholly fare
Even as ye do, thoughtless pair!
And I will have my careless season,
Spite of melancholy reason;
Will walk through life in such a way
That, when time brings on decay,
Now and then I may possess
Hours of perfect gladsomeness.
— Pleased by any random toy;
By a kitten's busy joy,
Or an infant's laughing eye
Sharing in the ecstasy;
I would fare like that or this,
Find my wisdom in my bliss;
Keep the sprightly soul awake;
And have faculties to take,
Even from things by sorrow wrought,
Matter for a jocund thought;
Spite of care, and spite of grief,
To gambol with Life's falling Leaf.

WILLIAM WORDSWORTH.

"COMPLIMENTS OF THE SEASON."

LITTLE Four Years, little Two Years,
Merry Christmas! Happy New-Year's!
That is what I wish for you;
Shall I tell you what to do
That will make my wish come true?

Cheerful looks and words are very
Sure to make the Christmas merry:
Tongues that speak the truth sincere,
Hearts that hold each other dear,
These will make a happy year.

Four Years is of Two the double, —
Should be twice as brave in trouble,
Twice as gentle, twice as kind,
Always twice as much inclined
Mother's words to keep in mind;

So that Two Years, when she 's older,
May remember what is told her,
Just as Four Years did before, —
Only think! in two years more
Little Two Years will be Four!

ROSSITER W. RAYMOND.

NOW I LAY ME DOWN TO SLEEP.

GOLDEN head so lowly bending,
 Little feet so white and bare,
Dewy eyes, half shut, half opened,
 Lisping out her evening prayer.

"Now I lay," — repeat it, darling —
 "Lay me," lisped the tiny lips
Of my daughter, kneeling, bending
 O'er the folded finger-tips.

"Down to sleep," — "To sleep," she murmured,
 And the curly head bent low;
"I pray the Lord," I gently added,
 "You can say it all, I know."

"Pray the Lord," — the sound came faintly,
 Fainter still, — "my soul to keep";
Then the tired head fairly nodded,
 And the child was fast asleep.

But the dewy eyes half opened
 When I clasped her to my breast,

And the dear voice softly whispered,
"Mamma, God knows all the rest."

O, the trusting, sweet confiding
Of the child-heart! Would that I
Thus might trust my Heavenly Father,
He who hears my feeblest cry.

O, the rapture, sweet, unbroken,
Of the soul who wrote that prayer!
Children's myriad voices, floating
Up to Heaven, record it there.

If, of all that has been written,
I could choose what might be mine,
It should be that child's petition,
Rising to the throne divine.

ANONYMOUS.

LITTLE PUSS.

A LITTLE golden head close to my knee,
Sweet eyes of tender, gentianella blue
Fixed upon mine, a little coaxing voice, —
Only we two.

"Tell it again!" Insatiate demand!
And like a toiling spider where I sat,
I wove and spun the many-colored webs
Of this and that.

Of Dotty Pringle sweeping out her hall;
Of Greedy Bear; of Santa Claus the good;
And how the little children met the Months
Within the wood.

"Tell it again!" and though the sand-man came,
Dropping his drowsy grains in each blue eye,
"Tell it again! O, just once more!" was still
The sleepy cry.

My spring-time violet! early snatched away
To fairer gardens all unknown to me, —
Gardens of whose invisible, guarded gates
I have no key, —

I weave my fancies now for other ears, —
Thy sister-blossom's, who beside me sits,
Rosy, imperative, and quick to mark
My lagging wits.

But still the stories bear thy name, are thine,
Part of the sunshine of thy brief, sweet day,
Though in *her* little warm and living hands
This book I lay.

SUSAN COOLIDGE.

LITTLE GOLDENHAIR.

GOLDENHAIR climbed up on grandpapa's knee;
Dear little Goldenhair, tired was she,
All the day busy as busy could be.

Up in the morning as soon as 't was light,
Out with the birds and butterflies bright,
Skipping about till the coming of night.

Grandpapa toyed with the curls on her head.
"What has my darling been doing," he said,
"Since she rose with the sun from her bed?"

"Pitty much," answered the sweet little one.
"I cannot tell so much things I have done,
Played with my dolly and feeded my bun.

"And then I jumped with my little jump-rope,
And I made out of some water and soap
Bootiful worlds, mamma's castles of hope.

"Then I have readed in my picture-book,
And Bella and I, we went to look
For the smooth little stones by the side of the brook.

"And then I comed home and eated my tea,
And I climbed up on grandpapa's knee,
And I jes as tired as tired can be."

Lower and lower the little head pressed,
Until it had dropped upon grandpapa's breast;
Dear little Goldenhair, sweet be thy rest!

We are but children; things that we do
Are as sports of a babe to the Infinite view
That marks all our weakness, and pities it too.

God grant that when night overshadows our way,
And we shall be called to account for our day,
He shall find us as guileless as Goldenhair's lay!

And O, when aweary, may we be so blest,
And sink like the innocent child to our rest,
And feel ourselves clasped to the Infinite breast!

ANONYMOUS.

BENNY.

I HAD told him, Christmas morning,
As he sat upon my knee,
Holding fast his little stockings,
Stuffed as full as full could be,
And attentive, listening to me,
With a face demure and mild,
That old Santa Claus, who filled them,
Did not love a naughty child.

"But we 'll be good, won't we, moder?"
  And from off my lap he slid,
Digging deep among the goodies
  In his crimson stockings hid,
While I turned me to my table,
  Where a tempting goblet stood,
With a dainty drink brimmed over,
  Sent me by a neighbor good.

But the kitten, there before me,
  With his white paw, nothing loth,
Sat, by way of entertainment,
  Slapping off the shining froth;
And in not the gentlest humor
  At the loss of such a treat,
I confess, I rather rudely,
  Thrust him out into the street.

Then how Benny's blue eyes kindled!
  Gathering up the precious store
He had busily been pouring
  In his tiny pinafore,
With a generous look that shamed me,
  Sprang he from the carpet bright,
Showing, by his mien indignant,
  All a baby's sense of right.

"Come back, Harney," called he loudly,
  As he held his apron white,
"You shall have my candy wabbit";
  But the door was fastened tight.
So he stood, abashed and silent,
  In the center of the floor,
With defeated look alternate
  Bent on me and on the door.

Then, as by some sudden impulse,
  Quickly ran he to the fire,
And while eagerly his bright eyes
  Watched the flames go high and higher,
In a brave, clear key, he shouted,
  Like some lordly little elf,
"Santa Caus, come down de chimney,
  Make my moder 'have herself."

"I will be a good girl, Benny,"
  Said I, feeling the reproof;
And straightway recalled poor Harney,
  Mewing on the gallery roof.
Soon the anger was forgotten,
  Laughter chased away the frown,
And they gamboled 'neath the live-oaks
  Till the dusky night came down.

In my dim, fire-lighted chamber
  Harney purred beneath my chair,
And my play-worn boy beside me
  Knelt to say his evening prayer:

"God bess fader, God bess moder,
  God bess sister," — then a pause,
And the sweet young lips devoutly
  Murmured, "God bess Santa Kaus."

He is sleeping; brown and silken
  Lie the lashes, long and meek,
Like caressing, clinging shadows
  On his plump and peachy cheek;
And I bend above him, weeping
  Thankful tears, O Undefiled!
For a woman's crown of glory,
  For the blessing of a child.

ANNIE C. KETCHUM.

TO MY INFANT SON.

THOU happy, happy elf!
(But stop, first let me kiss away that tear,)
  Thou tiny image of myself!
(My love, he 's poking peas into his ear!)
Thou merry, laughing sprite,
With spirits feather light,
Untouched by sorrow, and unsoiled by sin;
(My dear, the child is swallowing a pin!)

Thou little tricksy Puck!
With antic toys so funnily bestuck,
Light as the singing bird that wings the air,—
(The door! the door! he 'll tumble down the stair!)
Thou darling of thy sire!
(Why, Jane, he 'll set his pinafore afire!)
  Thou imp of mirth and joy!
In love's dear chain so bright a link,
  Thou idol of thy parents; — (Drat the boy!
There goes my ink.)

  Thou cherub, but of earth;
Fit playfellow for fays, by moonlight pale,
  In harmless sport and mirth,
(That dog will bite him, if he pulls his tail!)
  Thou human humming-bee, extracting honey
From every blossom in the world that blows,
  Singing in youth's Elysium ever sunny, —
(Another tumble! That 's his precious nose!)
Thy father's pride and hope!
(He 'll break the mirror with that skipping-rope!)
With pure heart newly stamped from nature's mint,
(Where *did* he learn that squint?)

Thou young domestic dove!
(He 'll have that ring off with another shove,)
Dear nursling of the hymeneal nest!
(Are these torn clothes his best?)

Little epitome of man!
(He 'll climb upon the table, that 's his plan!)
Touched with the beauteous tints of dawning life,
(He 's got a knife!)
Thou enviable being!
No storms, no clouds, in thy blue sky foreseeing,
Play on, play on,
My elfin John!
Toss the light ball, bestride the stick, —
(I knew so many cakes would make him sick!)
With fancies buoyant as the thistle-down,
Prompting the face grotesque, and antic brisk,
With many a lamb-like frisk!
(He 's got the scissors, snipping at your gown!)
Thou pretty opening rose!
(Go to your mother, child, and wipe your nose!)
Balmy and breathing music like the south,
(He really brings my heart into my mouth!)
Bold as the hawk, yet gentle as the dove;
(I 'll tell you what, my love,
I cannot write unless he 's sent above.)

THOMAS HOOD.

THE LOST HEIR.

"O where, and O where,
Is my bonnie laddie gone?" — OLD SONG.

ONE day, as I was going by
That part of Holborn christened High,
I heard a loud and sudden cry
That chilled my very blood;
And lo! from out a dirty alley,
Where pigs and Irish wont to rally,
I saw a crazy woman sally,
Bedaubed with grease and mud.
She turned her East, she turned her West,
Staring like Pythoness possest,
With streaming hair and heaving breast,
As one stark mad with grief.

"O Lord! O dear, my heart will break, I shall go stick stark staring wild!
Has ever a one seen anything about the streets like a crying lost-looking child?
Lawk help me, I don't know where to look, or to run, if I only knew which way —
A Child as is lost about London streets, and especially Seven Dials, is a needle in a bottle of hay.
I am all in a quiver — get out of my sight, do, you wretch, you little Kitty M'Nab!
You promised to have half an eye to him, you know you did, you dirty deceitful young drab!
The last time as ever I see him, poor thing, was with my own blessed Motherly eyes,
Sitting as good as gold in the gutter, a playing at making little dirt-pies.
I wonder he left the court, where he was better off than all the other young boys,
With two bricks, an old shoe, nine oyster-shells, and a dead kitten, by way of toys.
When his Father comes home, and he always comes home as sure as ever the clock strikes one,
He 'll be rampant, he will, at his child being lost; and the beef and the inguns not done!
La bless you, good folks, mind your own consarns, and don't be making a mob in the street;
O Sergeant M'Farlane! you have not come across my poor little boy, have you, in your beat?
Do, good people, move on! don't stand staring at me like a parcel of stupid stuck pigs;
Saints forbid! but he 's p'r'aps been inviggled away up a court for the sake of his clothes by the prigs;
He 'd a very good jacket, for certain, for I bought it myself for a shilling one day in Rag Fair;
And his trousers considering not very much patched, and red plush, they was once his Father's best pair.
His shirt, it 's very lucky I 'd got washing in the tub, or that might have gone with the rest;
But he 'd got on a very good pinafore with only two slits and a burn on the breast.
He 'd a goodish sort of hat, if the crown was sewed in, and not quite so much jagged at the brim;
With one shoe on, and the other shoe is a boot, and not a fit, and you 'll know by that if it 's him.
And then he has got such dear winning ways — but O, I never, never shall see him no more!
O dear! to think of losing him just after nussing him back from death's door!
Only the very last month when the windfalls, hang 'em, was at twenty a penny;
And the threepence he 'd got by grottoing was spent in plums, and sixty for a child is too many.
And the Cholera man came and whitewashed us all, and, drat him! made a seize of our hog. —
It 's no use to send the Crier to cry him about, he 's such a blunderin' drunken old dog;
The last time he was fetched to find a lost child he was guzzling with his bell at the Crown,
And went and cried a boy instead of a girl, for a distracted Mother and Father about Town.
Billy — where are you, Billy, I say? come, Billy, come home, to your best of Mothers!
I 'm scared when I think of them Cabroleys, they drive so, they 'd run over their own Sisters and Brothers.

Or maybe he 's stole by some chimbly-sweeping wretch, to stick fast in narrow flues and what not,
And be poked up behind with a picked pointed pole, when the soot has ketched, and the chimbly 's red-hot.
O, I 'd give the whole wide world, if the world was mine, to clap my two longin' eyes on his face;
For he 's my darlin' of darlin's, and if he don't soon come back, you 'll see me drop stone dead on the place.
I only wish I 'd got him safe in these two Motherly arms, and would n't I hug him and kiss him!
Lawk! I never knew what a precious he was — but a child don't not feel like a child till you miss him.
Why, there he is! Punch and Judy hunting, the young wretch, it 's that Billy as sartin as sin!
But let me get him home, with a good grip of his hair, and I 'm blest if he shall have a whole bone in his skin!

THOMAS HOOD.

THE THREE SONS.

I HAVE a son, a little son, a boy just five years old,
With eyes of thoughtful earnestness, and mind of gentle mould.
They tell me that unusual grace in all his ways appears,
That my child is grave and wise of heart beyond his childish years.
I cannot say how this may be; I know his face is fair, —
And yet his chiefest comeliness is his sweet and serious air;
I know his heart is kind and fond; I know he loveth me;
But loveth yet his mother more with grateful fervency.
But that which others most admire, is the thought which fills his mind,
The food for grave inquiring speech he everywhere doth find.
Strange questions doth he ask of me, when we together walk;
He scarcely thinks as children think, or talks as children talk.
Nor cares he much for childish sports, dotes not on bat or ball,
But looks on manhood's ways and works, and aptly mimics all.
His little heart is busy still, and oftentimes perplext
With thoughts about this world of ours, and thoughts about the next.
He kneels at his dear mother's knee; she teacheth him to pray;
And strange, and sweet, and solemn then are the words which he will say.
O, should my gentle child be spared to manhood's years like me,
A holier and a wiser man I trust that he will be;
And when I look into his eyes, and stroke his thoughtful brow,
I dare not think what I should feel, were I to lose him now.

I have a son, a second son, a simple child of three;
I 'll not declare how bright and fair his little features be,
How silver sweet those tones of his when he prattles on my knee;
I do not think his light-blue eye is, like his brother's, keen,
Nor his brow so full of childish thought as his hath ever been;
But his little heart 's a fountain pure of kind and tender feeling;
And his every look 's a gleam of light, rich depths of love revealing.
When he walks with me, the country folk, who pass us in the street,
Will shout for joy, and bless my boy, he looks so mild and sweet.
A playfellow is he to all; and yet, with cheerful tone,
Will sing his little song of love, when left to sport alone.
His presence is like sunshine sent to gladden home and hearth,
To comfort us in all our griefs, and sweeten all our mirth.
Should he grow up to riper years, God grant his heart may prove
As sweet a home for heavenly grace as now for earthly love;
And if, beside his grave, the tears our aching eyes must dim,
God comfort us for all the love which we shall lose in him.

I have a son, a third sweet son; his age I cannot tell,
For they reckon not by years and months where he has gone to dwell.
To us, for fourteen anxious months, his infant smiles were given;

And then he bade farewell to earth, and went to live in heaven.
I cannot tell what form is his, what looks he weareth now,
Nor guess how bright a glory crowns his shining seraph brow.
The thoughts that fill his sinless soul, the bliss which he doth feel,
Are numbered with the secret things which God will not reveal.
But I know (for God hath told me this) that he is now at rest,
Where other blessed infants be, on their Saviour's loving breast.
I know his spirit feels no more this weary load of flesh,
But his sleep is blessed with endless dreams of joy forever fresh.
I know the angels fold him close beneath their glittering wings,
And soothe him with a song that breathes of Heaven's divinest things.
I know that we shall meet our babe (his mother dear and I)
Where God for aye shall wipe away all tears from every eye.
Whate'er befalls his brethren twain, his bliss can never cease;
Their lot may here be grief and fear, but his is certain peace.
It may be that the tempter's wiles their souls from bliss may sever;
But, if our own poor faith fail not, he must be ours forever.
When we think of what our darling is, and what we still must be, —
When we muse on that world's perfect bliss, and this world's misery, —
When we groan beneath this load of sin, and feel this grief and pain, —
Oh! we 'd rather lose our other two, than have him here again.

JOHN MOULTRIE.

GOOD NIGHT AND GOOD MORNING.

A FAIR little girl sat under a tree
Sewing as long as her eyes could see;
Then smoothed her work and folded it right,
And said, "Dear work, good night, good night!"

Such a number of rooks came over her head,
Crying "Caw, caw!" on their way to bed,
She said, as she watched their curious flight,
"Little black things, good night, good night!"

The horses neighed, and the oxen lowed,
The sheep's "Bleat! bleat!" came over the road;
All seeming to say, with a quiet delight,
"Good little girl, good night, good night!"

She did not say to the sun, "Good night!"
Though she saw him there like a ball of light;
For she knew he had God's time to keep
All over the world and never could sleep.

The tall pink foxglove bowed his head;
The violets courtesied, and went to bed;
And good little Lucy tied up her hair,
And said, on her knees, her favorite prayer.

And, while on her pillow she softly lay,
She knew nothing more till again it was day;
And all things said to the beautiful sun,
"Good morning, good morning! our work is begun."

RICHARD MONCKTON MILNES.
(LORD HOUGHTON.)

THE GAMBOLS OF CHILDREN.

DOWN the dimpled greensward dancing
Bursts a flaxen-headed bevy, —
Bud-lipt boys and girls advancing,
Love's irregular little levy.

Rows of liquid eyes in laughter,
How they glimmer, how they quiver!
Sparkling one another after,
Like bright ripples on a river.

Tipsy band of rubious faces,
Flushed with Joy's ethereal spirit,
Make your mocks and sly grimaces
At Love's self, and do not fear it.

GEORGE DARLEY.

UNDER MY WINDOW.

UNDER my window, under my window,
All in the Midsummer weather,
Three little girls with fluttering curls
Flit to and fro together: —
There 's Bell with her bonnet of satin sheen,
And Maud with her mantle of silver-green,
And Kate with her scarlet feather.

Under my window, under my window,
Leaning stealthily over,
Merry and clear, the voice I hear,
Of each glad-hearted rover.
Ah! sly little Kate, she steals my roses;
And Maud and Bell twine wreaths and posies,
As merry as bees in clover.

Under my window, under my window,
  In the blue midsummer weather,
Stealing slow, on a hushed tiptoe,
  I catch them all together: —
Bell with her bonnet of satin sheen,
And Maud with her mantle of silver-green,
  And Kate with the scarlet feather.

Under my window, under my window,
  And off through the orchard closes;
While Maud she flouts, and Bell she pouts,
  They scamper and drop their posies;
But dear little Kate takes naught amiss,
And leaps in my arms with a loving kiss,
  And I give her all my roses.

THOMAS WESTWOOD.

THE MOTHER'S HEART.

WHEN first thou camest, gentle, shy, and fond,
  My eldest born, first hope, and dearest treasure,
My heart received thee with a joy beyond
  All that it yet had felt of earthly pleasure;
Nor thought that any love again might be
So deep and strong as that I felt for thee.

Faithful and true, with sense beyond thy years,
  And natural piety that leaned to heaven;
Wrung by a harsh word suddenly to tears,
  Yet patient to rebuke when justly given;
Obedient, easy to be reconciled,
And meekly cheerful; such wert thou, my child!

Not willing to be left — still by my side,
  Haunting my walks, while summer-day was dying;
Nor leaving in thy turn, but pleased to glide
  Through the dark room where I was sadly lying;
Or by the couch of pain, a sitter meek,
Watch the dim eye, and kiss the fevered cheek.

O boy! of such as thou are oftenest made
  Earth's fragile idols; like a tender flower,
No strength in all thy freshness, prone to fade,
  And bending weakly to the thunder-shower;
Still, round the loved, thy heart found force to bind,
And clung, like woodbine shaken in the wind!

Then THOU, my merry love, — bold in thy glee,
  Under the bough, or by the firelight dancing,
With thy sweet temper, and thy spirit free, —
  Didst come, as restless as a bird's wing glancing,
Full of a wild and irrepressible mirth,
Like a young sunbeam to the gladdened earth!

Thine was the shout, the song, the burst of joy,
  Which sweet from childhood's rosy lip resoundeth;
Thine was the eager spirit naught could cloy,
  And the glad heart from which all grief reboundeth;
And many a mirthful jest and mock reply
Lurked in the laughter of thy dark-blue eye.

And thine was many an art to win and bless,
  The cold and stern to joy and fondness warming;
The coaxing smile, the frequent soft caress,
  The earnest, tearful prayer all wrath disarming!
Again my heart a new affection found,
But thought that love with thee had reached its bound.

At length THOU camest, — thou, the last and least,
  Nicknamed "the Emperor" by thy laughing brothers,
Because a haughty spirit swelled thy breast,
  And thou didst seek to rule and sway the others,
Mingling with every playful infant wile
A mimic majesty that made us smile.

And O, most like a regal child wert thou!
  An eye of resolute and successful scheming!
Fair shoulders, curling lips, and dauntless brow,
  Fit for the world's strife, not for poet's dreaming;
And proud the lifting of thy stately head,
And the firm bearing of thy conscious tread.

Different from both! yet each succeeding claim
  I, that all other love had been forswearing,
Forthwith admitted, equal and the same;
  Nor injured either by this love's comparing,
Nor stole a fraction for the newer call, —
But in the mother's heart found room for all!

CAROLINE E. NORTON.

THE MOTHER'S HOPE.

Is there, when the winds are singing
  In the happy summer time, —
When the raptured air is ringing
With Earth's music heavenward springing,
  Forest chirp, and village chime, —
Is there, of the sounds that float
Sighingly, a single note
Half so sweet, and clear, and wild,
As the laughter of a child?

Listen! and be now delighted:
  Morn hath touched her golden strings;
Earth and Sky their vows have plighted;
Life and Light are reunited
  Amid countless carolings;
Yet, delicious as they are,
There 's a sound that 's sweeter far, —
One that makes the heart rejoice
More than all, — the human voice!

Organ finer, deeper, clearer,
  Though it be a stranger's tone, —
Than the winds or waters dearer,
More enchanting to the hearer,
  For it answereth to his own.
But, of all its witching words,
All its myriad magic chords,
Those are sweetest, bubbling wild
Through the laughter of a child.

Harmonies from time-touched towers,
  Haunted strains from rivulets,
Hum of bees among the flowers,
Rustling leaves, and silver showers, —
  These, ere long, the ear forgets;
But in mine there is a sound
Ringing on the whole year round, —
Heart-deep laughter that I heard
Ere my child could speak a word.

Ah! 't was heard by ear far purer,
  Fondlier formed to catch the strain, —
Ear of one whose love is surer, —
Hers, the mother, the endurer
  Of the deepest share of pain;
Hers the deepest bliss to treasure
Memories of that cry of pleasure;
Hers to hoard, a lifetime after,
Echoes of that infant laughter.

'T is a mother's large affection
  Hears with a mysterious sense, —
Breathings that evade detection,
Whisper faint, and fine inflection,
  Thrill in her with power intense.
Childhood's honeyed words untaught
Hiveth she in loving thought,
Tones that never thence depart;
For she listens — with her heart.

LAMAN BLANCHARD.

SEVEN TIMES ONE.

THERE 's no dew left on the daisies and clover,
  There 's no rain left in heaven.
I 've said my "seven times" over and over, —
  Seven times one are seven.

I am old, — so old I can write a letter;
  My birthday lessons are done.
The lambs play always, — they know no better;
  They are only one times one.

O Moon! in the night I have seen you sailing
  And shining so round and low.
You were bright — ah, bright — but your light is failing;
  You are nothing now but a bow.

You Moon! have you done something wrong in heaven,
  That God has hidden your face?
I hope, if you have, you will soon be forgiven,
  And shine again in your place.

O velvet Bee! you 're a dusty fellow, —
  You 've powdered your legs with gold.
O brave marsh Mary-buds, rich and yellow,
  Give me your money to hold!

O Columbine! open your folded wrapper,
  Where two twin turtle-doves dwell!
O Cuckoopint! toll me the purple clapper
  That hangs in your clear green bell!

And show me your nest, with the young ones in it —
  I will not steal them away:
I am old! you may trust me, linnet, linnet!
  I am seven times one to-day.

JEAN INGELOW.

SEVEN TIMES FOUR.

HEIGH-HO! daisies and buttercups,
  Fair yellow daffodils, stately and tall!
When the wind wakes how they rock in the grasses,
  And dance with the cuckoo-buds slender and small!
Here 's two bonny boys, and here 's mother's own lasses,
  Eager to gather them all.

Heigh-ho! daisies and buttercups!
  Mother shall thread them a daisy chain;
Sing them a song of the pretty hedge-sparrow,
  That loved her brown little ones, loved them full fain;
Sing, "Heart, thou art wide though the house be but narrow," —
  Sing once, and sing it again.

Heigh-ho! daisies and buttercups,
Sweet wagging cowslips, they bend and they bow;
A ship sails afar over warm ocean waters,
And haply one musing doth stand at her prow.
O bonny brown sons, and O sweet little daughters,
Maybe he thinks on you now!

Heigh-ho! daisies and buttercups,
Fair yellow daffodils, stately and tall —
A sunshiny world full of laughter and leisure,
And fresh hearts unconscious of sorrow and thrall!
Send down on their pleasure smiles passing its measure,
God that is over us all!

JEAN INGELOW.

WE ARE SEVEN.

A SIMPLE child,
That lightly draws its breath,
And feels its life in every limb,
What should it know of death?

I met a little cottage girl:
She was eight years old, she said;
Her hair was thick with many a curl
That clustered round her head.

She had a rustic, woodland air,
And she was wildly clad;
Her eyes were fair, and very fair; —
Her beauty made me glad.

"Sisters and brothers, little maid,
How many may you be?"
"How many? Seven in all," she said,
And wondering looked at me.

"And where are they? I pray you tell."
She answered, "Seven are we;
And two of us at Conway dwell,
And two are gone to sea;

"Two of us in the churchyard lie,
My sister and my brother;
And, in the churchyard cottage, I
Dwell near them with my mother."

"You say that two at Conway dwell,
And two are gone to sea,
Yet ye are seven! I pray you tell,
Sweet maid, how this may be."

Then did the little maid reply,
"Seven boys and girls are we;
Two of us in the churchyard lie
Beneath the churchyard tree."

"You run about, my little maid;
Your limbs they are alive;
If two are in the churchyard laid,
Then ye are only five."

"Their graves are green, they may be seen,"
The little maid replied:
"Twelve steps or more from my mother's door,
And they are side by side.

"My stockings there I often knit;
My kerchief there I hem;
And there upon the ground I sit,
And sing a song to them.

"And often after sunset, sir,
When it is light and fair,
I take my little porringer,
And eat my supper there.

"The first that died was Sister Jane;
In bed she moaning lay,
Till God released her of her pain;
And then she went away.

"So in the churchyard she was laid;
And, when the grass was dry,
Together round her grave we played,
My brother John and I.

"And when the ground was white with snow,
And I could run and slide,
My brother John was forced to go,
And he lies by her side."

"How many are you, then," said I,
"If they two are in heaven?"
Quick was the little maid's reply:
"O Master! we are seven."

"But they are dead; those two are dead!
Their spirits are in heaven!" —
'T was throwing words away; for still
The little maid would have her will,
And said, "Nay, we are seven!"

WILLIAM WORDSWORTH.

TO A CHILD, DURING SICKNESS.

SLEEP breathes at last from out thee,
My little patient boy;
And balmy rest about thee
Smooths off the day's annoy.

I sit me down, and think
Of all thy winning ways ;
Yet almost wish, with sudden shrink,
That I had less to praise.

Thy sidelong pillowed meekness ;
Thy thanks to all that aid ;
Thy heart, in pain and weakness,
Of fancied faults afraid ;
The little trembling hand
That wipes thy quiet tears, —
These, these are things that may demand
Dread memories for years.

Sorrows I 've had, severe ones,
I will not think of now ;
And calmly, midst my dear ones,
Have wasted with dry brow ;
But when thy fingers press
And pat my stooping head,
I cannot bear the gentleness, —
The tears are in their bed.

Ah, first-born of thy mother,
When life and hope were new ;
Kind playmate of thy brother,
Thy sister, father too ;
My light, where'er I go ;
My bird, when prison-bound ;
My hand-in-hand companion — No,
My prayers shall hold thee round.

To say, "He has departed" —
"His voice"—"his face"— "is gone,"
To feel impatient-hearted,
Yet feel we must bear on, —
Ah, I could not endure
To whisper of such woe,
Unless I felt this sleep insure
That it will not be so.

Yes, still he 's fixed, and sleeping !
This silence too the while, —
Its very hush and creeping
Seem whispering us a smile ;
Something divine and dim
Seems going by one's ear,
Like parting wings of cherubim,
Who say, "We 've finished here."

LEIGH HUNT.

THE PET NAME.

"The name
Which from *their* lips seemed a caress."
MISS MITFORD'S *Dramatic Scenes.*

I HAVE a name, a little name,
Uncadenced for the ear,
Unhonored by ancestral claim,
Unsanctified by prayer and psalm
The solemn font anear.

It never did, to pages wove
For gay romance, belong.
It never dedicate did move
As "Sacharissa," unto love, —
"Orinda," unto song.

Though I write books, it will be read
Upon the leaves of none,
And afterward, when I am dead,
Will ne'er be graved for sight or tread,
Across my funeral-stone.

This name, whoever chance to call,
Perhaps your smile may win.
Nay, do not smile ! mine eyelids fall
Over mine eyes, and feel withal
The sudden tears within.

Is there a leaf that greenly grows
Where summer meadows bloom,
But gathereth the winter snows,
And changeth to the hue of those,
If lasting till they come ?

Is there a word, or jest, or game,
But time encrusteth round
With sad associate thoughts the same ?
And so to me my very name
Assumes a mournful sound.

My brother gave that name to me
When we were children twain, —
When names acquired baptismally
Were hard to utter, as to see
That life had any pain.

No shade was on us then, save one
Of chestnuts from the hill, —
And through the word our laugh did run
As part thereof. The mirth being done,
He calls me by it still.

Nay, do not smile ! I hear in it
What none of you can hear, —
The talk upon the willow seat,
The bird and wind that did repeat
Around, our human cheer.

I hear the birthday's noisy bliss,
My sisters' woodland glee, —
My father's praise I did not miss,
When, stooping down, he cared to kiss
The poet at his knee, —

And voices which, to name me, aye
Their tenderest tones were keeping, —
To some I nevermore can say
An answer, till God wipes away
In heaven these drops of weeping.

My name to me a sadness wears;
No murmurs cross my mind.
Now God be thanked for these thick tears,
Which show, of those departed years,
Sweet memories left behind.

Now God be thanked for years enwrought
With love which softens yet.
Now God be thanked for every thought
Which is so tender it has caught
Earth's guerdon of regret.

Earth saddens, never shall remove,
Affections purely given;
And e'en that mortal grief shall prove
The immortality of love,
And heighten it with Heaven.

ELIZABETH BARRETT BROWNING.

OLD-SCHOOL PUNISHMENT.

OLD Master Brown brought his ferule down,
And his face looked angry and red.
"Go, seat you there, now, Anthony Blair,
Along with the girls," he said.
Then Anthony Blair, with a mortified air,
With his head down on his breast,
Took his penitent seat by the maiden sweet
That he loved, of all, the best.
And Anthony Blair seemed whimpering there,
But the rogue only made believe;
For he peeped at the girls with the beautiful curls,
And oggled them over his sleeve.

ANONYMOUS.

THE SMACK IN SCHOOL.

A DISTRICT school, not far away,
Mid Berkshire hills, one winter's day,
Was humming with its wonted noise
Of threescore mingled girls and boys;
Some few upon their tasks intent,
But more on furtive mischief bent.
The while the master's downward look
Was fastened on a copy-book;
When suddenly, behind his back,
Rose sharp and clear a rousing smack!
As 't were a battery of bliss
Let off in one tremendous kiss!
"What 's that?" the startled master cries;
"That, thir," a little imp replies,
"Wath William Willith, if you pleathe, —
I thaw him kith Thuthanna Peathe!"
With frown to make a statue thrill,
The master thundered, "Hither, Will!"
Like wretch o'ertaken in his track,
With stolen chattels on his back,
Will hung his head in fear and shame,
And to the awful presence came, —
A great, green, bashful simpleton,
The butt of all good-natured fun.
With smile suppressed, and birch upraised,
The threatener faltered, — "I 'm amazed
That you, my biggest pupil, should
Be guilty of an act so rude!
Before the whole set school to boot, —
What evil genius put you to 't?"
"'T was she herself, sir," sobbed the lad,
"I did not mean to be so bad;
But when Susannah shook her curls,
And whispered, I was 'fraid of girls,
And dursn't kiss a baby's doll,
I could n't stand it, sir, at all,
But up and kissed her on the spot!
I know — boo-hoo — I ought to not,
But, somehow, from her looks — boo-hoo —
I thought she kind o' wished me to!"

J. W. PALMER.

THE BAREFOOT BOY.

BLESSINGS on thee, little man,
Barefoot boy, with cheek of tan!
With thy turned-up pantaloons,
And thy merry whistled tunes;
With thy red lip, redder still
Kissed by strawberries on the hill;
With the sunshine on thy face,
Through thy torn brim's jaunty grace;
From my heart I give thee joy, —
I was once a barefoot boy!
Prince thou art, — the grown-up man
Only is republican.
Let the million-dollared ride!
Barefoot, trudging at his side,
Thou hast more than he can buy
In the reach of ear and eye, —
Outward sunshine, inward joy:
Blessings on thee, barefoot boy!

O for boyhood's painless play,
Sleep that wakes in laughing day,
Health that mocks the doctor's rules,
Knowledge never learned of schools,
Of the wild bee's morning chase,
Of the wild-flower's time and place,
Flight of fowl and habitude
Of the tenants of the wood;
How the tortoise bears his shell,
How the woodchuck digs his cell,
And the ground-mole sinks his well;
How the robin feeds her young,
How the oriole's nest is hung;

Where the whitest lilies blow,
Where the freshest berries grow,
Where the groundnut trails its vine,
Where the wood-grape's clusters shine;
Of the black wasp's cunning way,
Mason of his walls of clay,
And the architectural plans
Of gray hornet artisans! —
For, eschewing books and tasks,
Nature answers all he asks;
Hand in hand with her he walks,
Face to face with her he talks,
Part and parcel of her joy, —
Blessings on the barefoot boy!

O for boyhood's time of June,
Crowding years in one brief moon,
When all things I heard or saw,
Me, their master, waited for.
I was rich in flowers and trees,
Humming-birds and honey-bees;
For my sport the squirrel played,
Plied the snouted mole his spade;
For my taste the blackberry cone
Purpled over hedge and stone;
Laughed the brook for my delight
Through the day and through the night,
Whispering at the garden wall,
Talked with me from fall to fall;
Mine the sand-rimmed pickerel pond,
Mine the walnut slopes beyond,
Mine, on bending orchard trees,
Apples of Hesperides!
Still, as my horizon grew,
Larger grew my riches too;
All the world I saw or knew
Seemed a complex Chinese toy,
Fashioned for a barefoot boy!

O for festal dainties spread,
Like my bowl of milk and bread, —
Pewter spoon and bowl of wood,
On the door-stone, gray and rude!
O'er me, like a regal tent,
Cloudy-ribbed, the sunset bent,
Purple-curtained, fringed with gold,
Looped in many a wind-swung fold;
While for music came the play
Of the pied frogs' orchestra;
And, to light the noisy choir,
Lit the fly his lamp of fire.
I was monarch: pomp and joy
Waited on the barefoot boy!

Cheerly, then, my little man,
Live and laugh, as boyhood can!
Though the flinty slopes be hard,
Stubble-speared the new-mown sward,
Every morn shall lead thee through
Fresh baptisms of the dew;
Every evening from thy feet
Shall the cool wind kiss the heat:
All too soon these feet must hide
In the prison cells of pride,
Lose the freedom of the sod,
Like a colt's for work be shod,
Made to tread the mills of toil,
Up and down in ceaseless moil:
Happy if their track be found
Never on forbidden ground;
Happy if they sink not in
Quick and treacherous sands of sin.
Ah! that thou couldst know thy joy,
Ere it passes, barefoot boy!

JOHN GREENLEAF WHITTIER.

BOYHOOD.

Ah, then how sweetly closed those crowded days!
The minutes parting one by one like rays
  That fade upon a summer's eve.
But O, what charm or magic numbers
Can give me back the gentle slumbers
  Those weary, happy days did leave?
When by my bed I saw my mother kneel,
  And with her blessing took her nightly kiss;
  Whatever Time destroys, he cannot this; —
E'en now that nameless kiss I feel.

WASHINGTON ALLSTON.

OUR WEE WHITE ROSE.

All in our marriage garden
  Grew, smiling up to God,
A bonnier flower than ever
  Suckt the green warmth of the sod;
O beautiful unfathomably
  Its little life unfurled;
And crown of all things was our wee
  White Rose of all the world.

From out a balmy bosom
  Our bud of beauty grew;
It fed on smiles for sunshine,
  On tears for daintier dew:
Aye nestling warm and tenderly,
  Our leaves of love were curled
So close and close about our wee
  White Rose of all the world.

With mystical faint fragrance
  Our house of life she filled;
Revealed each hour some fairy tower
  Where wingèd hopes might build!

We saw — though none like us might see —
  Such precious promise pearled
Upon the petals of our wee
  White Rose of all the world.

But evermore the halo
  Of angel-light increased,
Like the mystery of moonlight
  That folds some fairy feast.
Snow-white, snow-soft, snow-silently
  Our darling bud up-curled,
And dropt i' the grave — God's lap — our wee
  White Rose of all the world.

Our Rose was but in blossom,
  Our life was but in spring,
When down the solemn midnight
  We heard the spirits sing,
"Another bud of infancy
  With holy dews impearled!"
And in their hands they bore our wee
  White Rose of all the world.

You scarce could think so small a thing
  Could leave a loss so large;
Her little light such shadow fling
  From dawn to sunset's marge.
In other springs our life may be
  In bannered bloom unfurled,
But never, never match our wee
  White Rose of all the world.

GERALD MASSEY.

PICTURES OF MEMORY.

AMONG the beautiful pictures
  That hang on Memory's wall
Is one of a dim old forest,
  That seemeth best of all;
Not for its gnarled oaks olden,
  Dark with the mistletoe;
Not for the violets golden
  That sprinkle the vale below;
Not for the milk-white lilies
  That lean from the fragrant ledge,
Coquetting all day with the sunbeams,
  And stealing their golden edge;
Not for the vines on the upland,
  Where the bright red berries rest,
Nor the pinks, nor the pale sweet cowslip,
  It seemeth to me the best.

I once had a little brother,
  With eyes that were dark and deep;
In the lap of that old dim forest
  He lieth in peace asleep:
Light as the down of the thistle,
  Free as the winds that blow,
We roved there the beautiful summers,
  The summers of long ago;
But his feet on the hills grew weary,
  And, one of the autumn eves,
I made for my little brother
  A bed of the yellow leaves.
Sweetly his pale arms folded
  My neck in a meek embrace,
As the light of immortal beauty
  Silently covered his face;
And when the arrows of sunset
  Lodged in the tree-tops bright,
He fell, in his saint-like beauty,
  Asleep by the gates of light.
Therefore, of all the pictures
  That hang on Memory's wall,
The one of the dim old forest
  Seemeth the best of all.

ALICE CARY.

HARRY ASHLAND, ONE OF MY LOVERS.

I HAVE a lover, a little lover, he rolls on the grass and plays in the clover;
He builds block-houses and digs clay wells, and makes sand-pies in his hat.
On Sundays he swings in the little porch, or has a clean collar and goes to church,
And asks me to marry him, when he grows up, and live in a house "like that."
He wears a great apron like a sack, — it 's hard they don't put him in trousers and jackets;
But his soul is far above buttons, and his hopes for the future o'ershoot them,
For Harry, like larger lovers, will court, without any visible means of support,
And ask you to give him your heart and hand, when he does n't know where to put them.

All day he 's tumbling, and leaping, and jumping, — running and calling, hammering and thumping,
Playing "bo-peep" with the blue-eyed babe, or chasing the cows in the lane;
But at twilight around my chair he lingers, clasping my hand in his dimpled fingers,
And I wonder if love so pure and fresh I shall ever inspire again!
The men that kneel and declaim their passion, — the men that "annex" you in stately fashion, —
There is not so much of truth and warmth in all the hearts of a score, —
And I look in the honest eyes of this baby, and wonder what would have happened, maybe,
If Heaven had not made me be twenty now, while Harry is only four.

I have a little rival named Ada, she clings to a promise that Harry made her,
"To build her a house all full of doors," and live with her there some day;
But Ada is growing lank and thin, — they say she will have a peaked chin,
And I think had nearly outgrown her "first love" before I came in the way.
She wears short skirts, and a pink-trimmed Shaker, the nicest aprons her mother can make her,
And a Sunday hat with feathers; but it does n't matter how she is dressed,
For Harry — sweetest of earthly lispers — has said in my ear, in loudest whispers,
With his dear short arms around my neck, that he "likes the *grown-up* bonnets best."

He says he shall learn to be a lawyer, but his private preference is a sawyer,
And counselors, not less than carpenters, live by "sawdust" and by *bores*.
It 's easier to saw a plank in two than to bore a judicial blockhead through,
And if panels of jurors fail to yield, he can always panel doors.
It 's a question of enterprise *versus* wood, and if his hammer and will be good,
If his energetic little brown hand be as steady and busy then,
Though chisel or pen be the weapon he 's needing, whether his business is planing or pleading,
Harry will cut his way through the ranks, and stand at the head of you men!

I say to him sometimes, "My dearest Harry, we have n't money enough to marry";
He has sixty cents in his little tin "bank," and a keepsake in his drawer;
But he always promises, "I 'll get plenty — I 'll find where they make it, when I 'm twenty;
I 'll go down town where the other men do, and bring it out of the store."
And then he describes such wonderful dresses, and gives me such gallant hugs and caresses,
With items of courtship from Mother Goose, silk cushions and rings of gold,
And I think what a fond true breast to dream on, what a dear, brave heart for a woman to lean on,
What a king and kingdom are saving up for some baby a twelvemonth old!

Twenty years hence, when I am forty, and Harry a young man, gay and naughty,
Flirting and dancing, and shooting guns, driving fast horses and cracking whips,
The handsomest fellow! — Heaven bless him! — setting the girls all wild to possess him, —
With his dark mustache and hazel eyes, and cigars in those pretty lips!
O, do you think he will *quite* forget me, — do you believe he will ever regret me?
Will he wish the twenty years back again, or deem this an idle myth,
While I shall sometimes push up my glasses, and sigh as my baby-lover passes,
And wonder if Heaven sets this world right, as I look at Mr. Smith!

ANONYMOUS.

THE MITHERLESS BAIRN.

[Thom gives the following narrative as to the origin of "The Mitherless Bairn": "When I was livin' in Aberdeen, I was limping roun' the house to my garret, when I heard the greetin' o' a wean. A lassie was thumpin' a bairn, when out cam a big dame, bellowin', 'Ye hussie, will ye lick a mitherless bairn!' I hobbled up the stair and wrote the sang afore sleepin'."]

WHEN a' ither bairnies are hushed to their hame
By aunty, or cousin, or frecky grand-dame,
Wha stands last and lanely, an' naebody carin'?
'T is the puir doited loonie, — the mitherless bairn!

The mitherless bairn gangs to his lane bed;
Nane covers his cauld back, or haps his bare head;
His wee hackit heelies are hard as the airn,
An' litheless the lair o' the mitherless bairn.

Aneath his cauld brow siccan dreams hover there,
O' hands that wont kindly to kame his dark hair;
But mornin' brings clutches, a' reckless an' stern,
That lo'e nae the locks o' the mitherless bairn!

Yon sister that sang o'er his saftly rocked bed
Now rests in the mools where her mammie is laid;
The father toils sair their wee bannock to earn,
An' kens na the wrangs o' his mitherless bairn.

Her spirit, that passed in yon hour o' his birth,
Still watches his wearisome wanderings on earth;
Recording in heaven the blessings they earn
Wha couthilie deal wi' the mitherless bairn!

O, speak him na harshly, — he trembles the while,
He bends to your bidding, and blesses your smile;
In their dark hour o' anguish the heartless shall learn
That God deals the blow for the mitherless bairn!

WILLIAM THOM.

THE OLD ARM-CHAIR.

I LOVE it, I love it! and who shall dare
To chide me for loving that old arm-chair?
I 've treasured it long as a sainted prize,
I 've bedewed it with tears, I 've embalmed it with sighs.
'T is bound by a thousand bands to my heart;
Not a tie will break, not a link will start;
Would you know the spell?—a mother sat there!
And a sacred thing is that old arm-chair.

In childhood's hour I lingered near
The hallowed seat with listening ear;
And gentle words that mother would give
To fit me to die, and teach me to live.
She told me that shame would never betide,
With Truth for my creed, and God for my guide;
She taught me to lisp my earliest prayer,
As I knelt beside that old arm-chair.

I sat, and watched her many a day,
When her eye grew dim, and her locks were gray;
And I almost worshiped her when she smiled,
And turned from her Bible to bless her child.
Years rolled on, but the last one sped, —
My idol was shattered, my earth-star fled!
And I learned how much the heart can bear,
When I saw her die in her old arm-chair.

'T is past, 't is past! but I gaze on it now,
With quivering breath and throbbing brow:
'T was there she nursed me, 't was there she died,
And memory flows with lava tide.
Say it is folly, and deem me weak,
Whilst scalding drops start down my cheek;
But I love it, I love it, and cannot tear
My soul from a mother's old arm-chair.

ELIZA COOK.

THE OLD OAKEN BUCKET.

How dear to this heart are the scenes of my childhood,
When fond recollection presents them to view!
The orchard, the meadow, the deep-tangled wild-wood,
And every loved spot which my infancy knew;—
The wide-spreading pond, and the mill which stood by it,
The bridge, and the rock where the cataract fell;
The cot of my father, the dairy-house nigh it,
And e'en the rude bucket which hung in the well.
The old oaken bucket, the iron-bound bucket,
The moss-covered bucket which hung in the well.

That moss-covered vessel I hail as a treasure;
For often, at noon, when returned from the field,
I found it the source of an exquisite pleasure,
The purest and sweetest that nature can yield.
How ardent I seized it, with hands that were glowing!
And quick to the white-pebbled bottom it fell;
Then soon, with the emblem of truth overflowing,
And dripping with coolness, it rose from the well;
The old oaken bucket, the iron-bound bucket,
The moss-covered bucket, arose from the well.

How sweet from the green mossy brim to receive it,
As, poised on the curb, it inclined to my lips!
Not a full blushing goblet could tempt me to leave it,
Though filled with the nectar that Jupiter sips.
And now, far removed from the loved situation,
The tear of regret will intrusively swell,
As fancy reverts to my father's plantation,
And sighs for the bucket which hangs in the well;
The old oaken bucket, the iron-bound bucket,
The moss-covered bucket which hangs in the well.

SAMUEL WOODWORTH.

I REMEMBER, I REMEMBER.

I REMEMBER, I remember
The house where I was born,
The little window where the sun
Came peeping in at morn.
He never came a wink too soon,
Nor brought too long a day;
But now I often wish the night
Had borne my breath away!

I remember, I remember
The roses, red and white,
The violets, and the lily-cups, —
Those flowers made of light!
The lilacs where the robin built,
And where my brother set
The laburnum on his birthday, —
The tree is living yet!

I remember, I remember
Where I was used to swing,
And thought the air must rush as fresh
To swallows on the wing;
My spirit flew in feathers then,
That is so heavy now,
And summer pools could hardly cool
The fever on my brow!

MY MOTHER AND HER BIBLE.

"*I sat and watched her many a day,*
When her eye grew dim, and her locks were gray;
And I almost worshiped her when she smiled,
And turned from her Bible to bless her child."

I remember, I remember
  The fir-trees dark and high;
I used to think their slender tops
  Were close against the sky.
It was a childish ignorance,
  But now 't is little joy
To know I 'm farther off from heaven
  Than when I was a boy.

THOMAS HOOD.

WOODMAN, SPARE THAT TREE.

WOODMAN, spare that tree!
  Touch not a single bough!
In youth it sheltered me,
  And I 'll protect it now.
'T was my forefather's hand
  That placed it near his cot;
There, woodman, let it stand,
  Thy ax shall harm it not!

That old familiar tree,
  Whose glory and renown
Are spread o'er land and sea,
  And wouldst thou hew it down?
Woodman, forbear thy stroke!
  Cut not its earth-bound ties;
O, spare that aged oak,
  Now towering to the skies!

When but an idle boy
  I sought its grateful shade;
In all their gushing joy
  Here too my sisters played.
My mother kissed me here;
  My father pressed my hand —
Forgive this foolish tear,
  But let that old oak stand!

My heart-strings round thee ling,
  Close as thy bark, old friend!
Here shall the wild-bird sing,
  And still thy branches bend.
Old tree! the storm still brave!
  And, woodman, leave the spot;
While I 've a hand to save,
  Thy ax shall harm it not.

GEORGE P. MORRIS.

YOUTH.

THE ROMANCE OF THE SWAN'S NEST.

Little Ellie sits alone
Mid the beeches of a meadow,
By a stream-side, on the grass,
And the trees are showering down
Doubles of their leaves in shadow
On her shining hair and face.

She has thrown her bonnet by,
And her feet she has been dipping
In the shallow water's flow.
Now she holds them nakedly
In her hands all sleek and dripping,
While she rocketh to and fro.

Little Ellie sits alone,
And the smile she softly uses
Fills the silence like a speech,
While she thinks what shall be done, —
And the sweetest pleasure chooses
For her future within reach.

Little Ellie in her smile
Chooses . . . . "I will have a lover,
Riding on a steed of steeds!
He shall love me without guile,
And to *him* I will discover
The swan's nest among the reeds.

"And the steed shall be red-roan,
And the lover shall be noble,
With an eye that takes the breath.
And the lute he plays upon
Shall strike ladies into trouble,
As his sword strikes men to death.

"And the steed it shall be shod
All in silver, housed in azure,
And the mane shall swim the wind;
And the hoofs along the sod
Shall flash onward and keep measure,
Till the shepherds look behind.

"But my lover will not prize
All the glory that he rides in,
When he gazes in my face.
He will say, 'O Love, thine eyes
Build the shrine my soul abides in,
And I kneel here for thy grace.'

"Then, ay, then — he shall kneel low,
With the red-roan steed anear him,
Which shall seem to understand —
Till I answer, 'Rise and go!
For the world must love and fear him
Whom I gift with heart and hand.'

"Then he will arise so pale,
I shall feel my own lips tremble
With a *yes* I must not say;
Nathless maiden-brave, 'Farewell,'
I will utter, and dissemble; —
'Light to-morrow with to-day.'

"Then he'll ride among the hills
To the wide world past the river,
There to put away all wrong;
To make straight distorted wills,
And to empty the broad quiver
Which the wicked bear along.

"Three times shall a young foot-page
Swim the stream and climb the mountain
And kneel down beside my feet; —
'Lo, my master sends this gage,
Lady, for thy pity's counting!
What wilt thou exchange for it?'

"And the first time, I will send
A white rosebud for a guerdon, —
And the second time, a glove;
But the third time, I may bend
From my pride, and answer, 'Pardon,
If he comes to take my love.'

"Then the young foot-page will run, —
Then my lover will ride faster,
Till he kneeleth at my knee:
'I am a Duke's eldest son!
Thousand serfs do call me master, —
But, O Love, I love but *thee!*'

"He will kiss me on the mouth
Then, and lead me as a lover
Through the crowds that praise his deeds;
And, when soul-tied by one troth,
Unto *him* I will discover
That swan's nest among the reeds."

Little Ellie, with her smile
Not yet ended, rose up gayly,
Tied the bonnet, donned the shoe,
And went homeward, round a mile,
Just to see, as she did daily,
What more eggs were with the two.

Pushing through the elm-tree copse,
Winding up the stream, light-hearted,
Where the osier pathway leads, —
Past the boughs she stoops — and stops.
Lo, the wild swan had deserted,
And a rat had gnawed the reeds.

Ellie went home sad and slow.
If she found the lover ever,
With his red-roan steed of steeds,
Sooth I know not! but I know
She could never show him — never,
That swan's nest among the reeds!

ELIZABETH BARRETT BROWNING.

LITTLE BELL.

PIPED the blackbird on the beechwood spray,
"Pretty maid, slow wandering this way,
What 's your name?" quoth he, —
"What's your name? O, stop and straight unfold,
Pretty maid with showery curls of gold." —
"Little Bell," said she.

Little Bell sat down beneath the rocks,
Tossed aside her gleaming golden locks, —
"Bonny bird," quoth she,
"Sing me your best song before I go."
"Here 's the very finest song I know,
Little Bell," said he.

And the blackbird piped; you never heard
Half so gay a song from any bird, —
Full of quips and wiles,
Now so round and rich, now soft and slow,
All for love of that sweet face below,
Dimpled o'er with smiles.

And the while the bonny bird did pour
His full heart freely o'er and o'er
'Neath the morning skies,
In the little childish heart below
All the sweetness seemed to grow and grow,
And shine forth in happy overflow
From the blue, bright eyes.

Down the dell she tripped and through the glade,
Peeped the squirrel from the hazel shade,
And from out the tree
Swung, and leaped, and frolicked, void of fear;
While bold blackbird piped that all might hear, —
"Little Bell," piped he.

Little Bell sat down amid the fern, —
"Squirrel, squirrel, to your task return;
Bring me nuts," quoth she.
Up away the frisky squirrel hies, —
Golden wood-lights glancing in his eyes, —
And adown the tree
Great ripe nuts, kissed brown by July sun,
In the little lap dropped one by one.
Hark, how blackbird pipes to see the fun!
"Happy Bell," pipes he.

Little Bell looked up and down the glade, —
"Squirrel, squirrel, if you 're not afraid,
Come and share with me!"
Down came squirrel eager for his fare,
Down came bonny blackbird, I declare;
Little Bell gave each his honest share, —
Ah the merry three!
And the while these frolic playmates twain
Piped and frisked from bough to bough again,
'Neath the morning skies,
In the little childish heart below
All the sweetness seems to grow and grow,
And shine out in happy overflow
From her blue, bright eyes.

By her snow-white cot at close of day,
Knelt sweet Bell, with folded palms, to pray;
Very calm and clear
Rose the praying voice to where, unseen,
In blue heaven, an angel shape serene
Paused awhile to hear.
"What good child is this," the angel said,
"That with happy heart beside her bed
Prays so lovingly?"
Low and soft, O, very low and soft,
Crooned the blackbird in the orchard croft,
"Bell, dear Bell!" crooned he.

"Whom God's creatures love," the angel fair
Murmured, "God doth bless with angels' care;
Child, thy bed shall be
Folded safe from harm. Love, deep and kind,
Shall watch around and leave good gifts behind,
Little Bell, for thee!"

THOMAS WESTWOOD.

A VISIT FROM ST. NICHOLAS.

'T WAS the night before Christmas, when all through the house
Not a creature was stirring, not even a mouse;
The stockings were hung by the chimney with care,
In hopes that St. Nicholas soon would be there:
The children were nestled all snug in their beds,
While visions of sugar-plums danced in their heads;
And mamma in her kerchief, and I in my cap,
Had just settled our brains for a long winter's nap, —

When out on the lawn there arose such a clatter,
I sprang from my bed to see what was the matter.
Away to the window I flew like a flash,
Tore open the shutters and threw up the sash.
The moon on the breast of the new-fallen snow
Gave a lustre of midday to objects below;
When, what to my wondering eyes should appear,
But a miniature sleigh and eight tiny reindeer,
With a little old driver, so lively and quick
I knew in a moment it must be St. Nick.
More rapid than eagles his coursers they came,
And he whistled and shouted, and called them by name:
"Now, Dasher! now, Dancer! now, Prancer and Vixen!
On, Comet! on, Cupid! on, Donder and Blitzen!
To the top of the porch, to the top of the wall!
Now dash away, dash away, dash away all!"
As dry leaves that before the wild hurricane fly,
When they meet with an obstacle, mount to the sky,
So up to the house-top the coursers they flew,
With the sleigh full of toys, — and St. Nicholas too.
And then in a twinkling I heard on the roof
The prancing and pawing of each little hoof.
As I drew in my head, and was turning around,
Down the chimney St. Nicholas came with a bound.
He was dressed all in fur from his head to his foot,
And his clothes were all tarnished with ashes and soot;
A bundle of toys he had flung on his back,
And he looked like a pedler just opening his pack.
His eyes how they twinkled! his dimples how merry!
His cheeks were like roses, his nose like a cherry;
His droll little mouth was drawn up like a bow,
And the beard on his chin was as white as the snow.
The stump of a pipe he held tight in his teeth,
And the smoke it encircled his head like a wreath.
He had a broad face and a little round belly
That shook, when he laughed, like a bowl full of jelly.
He was chubby and plump, — a right jolly old elf;
And I laughed, when I saw him, in spite of myself.
A wink of his eye and a twist of his head
Soon gave me to know I had nothing to dread.
He spoke not a word, but went straight to his work,
And filled all the stockings; then turned with a jerk,
And laying his finger aside of his nose,
And giving a nod, up the chimney he rose.
He sprang to his sleigh, to his team gave a whistle,
And away they all flew like the down of a thistle;
But I heard him exclaim, ere he drove out of sight,
"Happy Christmas to all, and to all a good-night!"

CLEMENT C. MOORE.

THE FROST.

THE Frost looked forth, one still, clear night,
And he said, "Now I shall be out of sight;
So through the valley and over the height
In silence I'll take my way.
I will not go like that blustering train,
The wind and the snow, the hail and the rain,
Who make so much bustle and noise in vain,
But I'll be as busy as they!"

Then he went to the mountain, and powdered its crest,
He climbed up the trees, and their boughs he dressed
With diamonds and pearls, and over the breast
Of the quivering lake he spread
A coat of mail, that it need not fear
The downward point of many a spear
That he hung on its margin, far and near,
Where a rock could rear its head.

He went to the windows of those who slept,
And over each pane like a fairy crept:
Wherever he breathed, wherever he stepped,
By the light of the moon was seen
Most beautiful things. There were flowers and trees,
There were bevies of birds and swarms of bees,
There were cities, thrones, temples, and towers, and these
All pictured in silver sheen!

But he did one thing that was hardly fair, —
He peeped in the cupboard, and, finding there
That all had forgotten for him to prepare, —
"Now, just to set them a thinking,
I'll bite this basket of fruit," said he;
"This costly pitcher I'll burst in three,
And the glass of water they've left for me
Shall '*tchick!*' to tell them I'm drinking."

HANNAH F. GOULD.

A PORTRAIT.

"One name is Elizabeth." — BEN JONSON.

I WILL paint her as I see her,
Ten times have the lilies blown
Since she looked upon the sun.

And her face is lily-clear,
Lily-shaped, and dropped in duty
To the law of its own beauty.

Oval cheeks encolored faintly,
Which a trail of golden hair
Keeps from fading off to air;

And a forehead fair and saintly,
  Which two blue eyes undershine,
  Like meek prayers before a shrine.

Face and figure of a child, —
  Though too calm, you think, and tender,
  For the childhood you would lend her.

Yet child-simple, undefiled,
  Frank, obedient, — waiting still
  On the turnings of your will.

Moving light, as all your things,
  As young birds, or early wheat,
  When the wind blows over it.

Only, free from flutterings
  Of loud mirth that scorneth measure, —
  Taking love for her chief pleasure.

Choosing pleasures, for the rest,
  Which come softly, — just as she,
  When she nestles at your knee.

Quiet talk she liketh best,
  In a bower of gentle looks, —
  Watering flowers, or reading books.

And her voice, it murmurs lowly,
  As a silver stream may run,
  Which yet feels, you feel, the sun.

And her smile it seems half holy,
  As if drawn from thoughts more far
  Than our common jestings are.

And if any poet knew her,
  He would sing of her with falls
  Used in lovely madrigals.

And if any painter drew her,
  He would paint her unaware
  With a halo round the hair.

And if reader read the poem,
  He would whisper, "You have done a
  Consecrated little Una."

And a dreamer (did you show him
  That same picture) would exclaim,
  "'T is my angel, with a name!"

And a stranger, when he sees her
  In the street even, smileth stilly,
  Just as you would at a lily.

And all voices that address her
  Soften, sleeken every word,
  As if speaking to a bird.

And all fancies yearn to cover
  The hard earth whereon she passes,
  With the thymy-scented grasses.

And all hearts do pray, "God love her!"—
  Ay, and certes, in good sooth,
  We may all be sure he doth.

ELIZABETH BARRETT BROWNING.

THE CHILDREN'S HOUR.

BETWEEN the dark and the daylight,
  When night is beginning to lower,
Comes a pause in the day's occupations,
  That is known as the children's hour.

I hear in the chamber above me
  The patter of little feet,
The sound of a door that is opened,
  And voices soft and sweet.

From my study I see in the lamplight,
  Descending the broad hall stair,
Grave Alice and laughing Allegra,
  And Edith with golden hair.

A whisper and then a silence;
  Yet I know by their merry eyes
They are plotting and planning together
  To take me by surprise.

A sudden rush from the stairway,
  A sudden raid from the hall, —
By three doors left unguarded,
  They enter my castle wall.

They climb up into my turret,
  O'er the arms and back of my chair;
If I try to escape, they surround me:
  They seem to be everywhere.

They almost devour me with kisses,
  Their arms about me entwine,
Till I think of the Bishop of Bingen
  In his Mouse-Tower on the Rhine.

Do you think, O blue-eyed banditti,
  Because you have scaled the wall,
Such an old mustache as I am
  Is not a match for you all?

I have you fast in my fortress,
  And will not let you depart,
But put you into the dungeon
  In the round-tower of my heart.

And there will I keep you forever,
Yes, forever and a day,
Till the walls shall crumble to ruin,
And moulder in dust away.

H. W. LONGFELLOW.

THREAD AND SONG.

SWEETER and sweeter,
Soft and low,
Neat little nymph,
Thy numbers flow,
Urging thy thimble,
Thrift's tidy symbol,
Busy and nimble,
To and fro;
Prettily plying
Thread and song,
Keeping them flying
Late and long,
Though the stitch linger,
Kissing thy finger
Quick, — as it skips along.

Many an echo,
Soft and low,
Follows thy flying
Fancy so, —
Melodies thrilling,
Tenderly filling
Thee with their trilling,
Come and go;
Memory's finger,
Quick as thine,
Loving to linger
On the line,
Writes of another,
Dearer than brother:
Would that the name were mine!

JOHN WILKINSON PALMER.

SEVEN TIMES TWO.

ROMANCE.

YOU bells in the steeple, ring, ring out your changes,
How many soever they be,
And let the brown meadow-lark's note as he ranges
Come over, come over to me.

Yet birds' clearest carol by fall or by swelling
No magical sense conveys,
And bells have forgotten their old art of telling
The fortune of future days.

"Turn again, turn again," once they rang cheerily
While a boy listened alone:
Made his heart yearn again, musing so wearily
All by himself on a stone.

Poor bells! I forgive you; your good days are over,
And mine, they are yet to be;
No listening, no longing, shall aught, aught discover:
You leave the story to me.

The foxglove shoots out of the green matted heather,
Preparing her hoods of snow;
She was idle, and slept till the sunshiny weather:
O, children take long to grow.

I wish, and I wish that the spring would go faster,
Nor long summer bide so late;
And I could grow on like the foxglove and aster,
For some things are ill to wait.

I wait for the day when dear hearts shall discover,
While dear hands are laid on my head;
"The child is a woman, the book may close over,
For all the lessons are said."

I wait for my story — the birds cannot sing it,
Not one, as he sits on the tree;
The bells cannot ring it, but long years, O bring it!
Such as I wish it to be.

JEAN INGELOW.

RAIN ON THE ROOF.

WHEN the showery vapors gather over all the starry spheres,
And the melancholy darkness gently weeps in rainy tears,
'T is a joy to press the pillow of a cottage chamber bed,
And listen to the patter of the soft rain overhead.

Every tinkle on the shingles has an echo in the heart,
And a thousand dreary fancies into busy being start;
And a thousand recollections weave their bright hues into woof,
As I listen to the patter of the soft rain on the roof.

There in fancy comes my mother, as she used to years agone,
To survey the infant sleepers ere she left them till the dawn.

I can see her bending o'er me, as I listen to the strain
Which is played upon the shingles by the patter of the rain.

Then my little seraph sister, with her wings and waving hair,
And her bright-eyed cherub brother, — a serene, angelic pair, —
Glide around my wakeful pillow with their praise or mild reproof,
As I listen to the murmur of the soft rain on the roof.

And another comes to thrill me with her eyes' delicious blue.
I forget, as gazing on her, that her heart was all untrue;
I remember that I loved her as I ne'er may love again,
And my heart's quick pulses vibrate to the patter of the rain.

There is naught in art's bravuras that can work with such a spell,
In the spirit's pure, deep fountains, whence the holy passions swell,
As that melody of nature, — that subdued, subduing strain,
Which is played upon the shingles by the patter of the rain.

COATES KINNEY.

THE EDUCATION OF NATURE.

THREE years she grew in sun and shower;
Then Nature said, "A lovelier flower
On earth was never sown:
This child I to myself will take;
She shall be mine, and I will make
A lady of my own.

"Myself will to my darling be
Both law and impulse; and with me
The girl, in rock and plain,
In earth and heaven, in glade and bower,
Shall feel an overseeing power
To kindle or restrain.

"She shall be sportive as the fawn
That wild with glee across the lawn
Or up the mountain springs;
And hers shall be the breathing balm,
And hers the silence and the calm,
Of mute insensate things.

"The floating clouds their state shall lend
To her; for her the willow bend;
Nor shall she fail to see
E'en in the motions of the storm
Grace that shall mould the maiden's form
By silent sympathy.

"The stars of midnight shall be dear
To her; and she shall lean her ear
In many a secret place
Where rivulets dance their wayward round,
And beauty born of murmuring sound
Shall pass into her face.

"And vital feelings of delight
Shall rear her form to stately height,
Her virgin bosom swell;
Such thoughts to Lucy I will give
While she and I together live
Here in this happy dell."

Thus Nature spake. The work was done, —
How soon my Lucy's race was run!
She died, and left to me
This heath, this calm and quiet scene;
The memory of what has been,
And nevermore will be.

WILLIAM WORDSWORTH.

MAIDENHOOD.

MAIDEN! with the meek brown eyes,
In whose orbs a shadow lies
Like the dusk in evening skies!

Thou whose locks outshine the sun, —
Golden tresses wreathed in one,
As the braided streamlets run!

Standing, with reluctant feet,
Where the brook and river meet,
Womanhood and childhood fleet!

Gazing, with a timid glance,
On the brooklet's swift advance,
On the river's broad expanse!

Deep and still, that gliding stream
Beautiful to thee must seem
As the river of a dream.

Then why pause with indecision,
When bright angels in thy vision
Beckon thee to fields Elysian?

Seest thou shadows sailing by,
As the dove, with startled eye,
Sees the falcon's shadow fly?

Hearest thou voices on the shore,
That our ears perceive no more,
Deafened by the cataract's roar?

O thou child of many prayers !
Life hath quicksands, Life hath snares !
Care and age come unawares !

Like the swell of some sweet tune,
Morning rises into noon,
May glides onward into June.

Childhood is the bough where slumbered
Birds and blossoms many-numbered ;—
Age, that bough with snows encumbered.

Gather, then, each flower that grows,
When the young heart overflows,
To embalm that tent of snows.

Bear a lily in thy hand ;
Gates of brass cannot withstand
One touch of that magic wand.

Bear through sorrow, wrong, and ruth,
In thy heart the dew of youth,
On thy lips the smile of truth.

O, that dew, like balm, shall steal
Into wounds that cannot heal,
Even as sleep our eyes doth seal ;

And that smile, like sunshine, dart
Into many a sunless heart,
For a smile of God thou art.

H. W. LONGFELLOW.

CASTARA.

LIKE the violet, which alone
Prospers in some happy shade,
My Castara lives unknown,
To no ruder eye betrayed ;
For she 's to herself untrue
Who delights i' the public view.

Such is her beauty as no arts
Have enriched with borrowed grace.
Her high birth no pride imparts,
For she blushes in her place.
Folly boasts a glorious blood, —
She is noblest being good.

Cautious, she knew never yet
What a wanton courtship meant ;
Nor speaks loud to boast her wit,
In her silence eloquent.
Of herself survey she takes,
But 'tween men no difference makes.

She obeys with speedy will
Her grave parents' wise commands ;
And so innocent, that ill
She nor acts nor understands.
Women's feet run still astray
If to ill they know the way.

She sails by that rock, the court,
Where oft virtue splits her mast ;
And retiredness thinks the port,
Where her fame may anchor cast.
Virtue safely cannot sit
Where vice is enthroned for wit.

She holds that day's pleasure best
Where sin waits not on delight ;
Without mask, or ball, or feast,
Sweetly spends a winter's night.
O'er that darkness whence is thrust
Prayer and sleep, oft governs lust.

She her throne makes reason climb,
While wild passions captive lie ;
And each article of time,
Her pure thoughts to heaven fly ;
All her vows religious be,
And she vows her love to me.

WILLIAM HABINGTON.

THE PRETTY GIRL OF LOCH DAN.

THE shades of eve had crossed the glen
That frowns o'er infant Avonmore,
When, nigh Loch Dan, two weary men,
We stopped before a cottage door.

"God save all here," my comrade cries,
And rattles on the raised latch-pin ;
"God save you kindly," quick replies
A clear sweet voice, and asks us in.

We enter ; from the wheel she starts,
A rosy girl with soft black eyes ;
Her fluttering court'sy takes our hearts,
Her blushing grace and pleased surprise.

Poor Mary, she was quite alone,
For, all the way to Glenmalure,
Her mother had that morning gone,
And left the house in charge with her.

But neither household cares, nor yet
The shame that startled virgins feel,
Could make the generous girl forget
Her wonted hospitable zeal.

She brought us in a beechen bowl
Sweet milk that smacked of mountain thyme,
Oat cake, and such a yellow roll
Of butter, — it gilds all my rhyme !

And, while we ate the grateful food
(With weary limbs on bench reclined),
Considerate and discreet, she stood
Apart, and listened to the wind.

Kind wishes both our souls engaged,
From breast to breast spontaneous ran
The mutual thought, — we stood and pledged
THE MODEST ROSE ABOVE LOCH DAN.

"The milk we drink is not more pure,
Sweet Mary, — bless those budding charms! —
Than your own generous heart, I 'm sure,
Nor whiter than the breast it warms!"

She turned and gazed, unused to hear
Such language in that homely glen;
But, Mary, you have naught to fear,
Though smiled on by two stranger-men.

Not for a crown would I alarm
Your virgin pride by word or sign,
Nor need a painful blush disarm
My friend of thoughts as pure as mine.

Her simple heart could not but feel
The words we spoke were free from guile;
She stooped, she blushed, she fixed her wheel, —
'T is all in vain, — she can't but smile!

Just like sweet April's dawn appears
Her modest face, — I see it yet, —
And though I lived a hundred years
Methinks I never could forget

The pleasure that, despite her heart,
Fills all her downcast eyes with light,
The lips reluctantly apart,
The white teeth struggling into sight,

The dimples eddying o'er her cheek, —
The rosy cheek that won't be still; —
O, who could blame what flatterers speak,
Did smiles like this reward their skill?

For such another smile, I vow,
Though loudly beats the midnight rain,
I 'd take the mountain-side e'en now,
And walk to Luggelaw again!

SAMUEL FERGUSON.

RUTH.

SHE stood breast high amid the corn,
Clasped by the golden light of morn,
Like the sweetheart of the sun,
Who many a glowing kiss had won.

On her cheek an autumn flush
Deeply ripened; — such a blush
In the midst of brown was born,
Like red poppies grown with corn.

Round her eyes her tresses fell, —
Which were blackest none could tell;
But long lashes veiled a light
That had else been all too bright.

And her hat, with shady brim,
Made her tressy forehead dim; —
Thus she stood amid the stooks,
Praising God with sweetest looks.

Sure, I said, Heaven did not mean
Where I reap thou shouldst but glean;
Lay thy sheaf adown and come,
Share my harvest and my home.

THOMAS HOOD.

LUCY.

SHE dwelt among the untrodden ways
Beside the springs of Dove;
A maid whom there were none to praise,
And very few to love.

A violet by a mossy stone
Half hidden from the eye!
— Fair as a star, when only one
Is shining in the sky.

She lived unknown, and few could know
When Lucy ceased to be;
But she is in her grave, and O,
The difference to me!

WILLIAM WORDSWORTH.

TO THE HIGHLAND GIRL OF INVERSNAID.

SWEET Highland Girl, a very shower
Of beauty is thy earthly dower!
Twice seven consenting years have shed
Their utmost bounty on thy head;
And these gray rocks, this household lawn,
These trees, — a veil just half withdrawn, —
This fall of water that doth make
A murmur near the silent lake,
This little bay, a quiet road
That holds in shelter thy abode;
In truth together ye do seem
Like something fashioned in a dream;
Such forms as from their covert peep
When earthly cares are laid asleep!

But O fair Creature! in the light
Of common day so heavenly bright,
I bless thee, Vision as thou art,
I bless thee with a human heart:
God shield thee to thy latest years!
I neither know thee nor thy peers;
And yet my eyes are filled with tears.

With earnest feeling I shall pray
For thee when I am far away;
For never saw I mien or face
In which more plainly I could trace
Benignity and home-bred sense
Ripening in perfect innocence.
Here scattered like a random seed,
Remote from men, thou dost not need
The embarrassed look of shy distress,
And maidenly shamefacedness:
Thou wear'st upon thy forehead clear
The freedom of a mountaineer;
A face with gladness overspread,
Soft smiles, by human kindness bred;
And seemliness complete, that sways
Thy courtesies, about thee plays;
With no restraint, but such as springs
From quick and eager visitings
Of thoughts that lie beyond the reach
Of thy few words of English speech, —
A bondage sweetly brooked, a strife
That gives thy gestures grace and life!
So have I, not unmoved in mind,
Seen birds of tempest-loving kind,
Thus beating up against the wind.

What hand but would a garland cull
For thee who art so beautiful?
O happy pleasure! here to dwell
Beside thee in some heathy dell;
Adopt your homely ways and dress,
A shepherd, thou a shepherdess!
But I could frame a wish for thee
More like a grave reality:
Thou art to me but as a wave
Of the wild sea; and I would have
Some claim upon thee, if I could,
Though but of common neighborhood.
What joy to hear thee, and to see!
Thy elder brother I would be,
Thy father, — anything to thee.

Now thanks to Heaven! that of its grace
Hath led me to this lonely place;
Joy have I had; and going hence
I bear away my recompense.
In spots like these it is we prize
Our Memory, feel that she hath eyes:
Then why should I be loath to stir?
I feel this place was made for her;
To give new pleasure like the past,
Continued long as life shall last.
Nor am I loath, though pleased at heart,
Sweet Highland Girl! from thee to part;
For I, methinks, till I grow old
As fair before me shall behold
As I do now, the cabin small,
The lake, the bay, the waterfall;
And thee, the spirit of them all!

WILLIAM WORDSWORTH.

JENNY KISSED ME.

JENNY kissed me when we met,
  Jumping from the chair she sat in.
Time, you thief! who love to get
  Sweets into your list, put that in.
Say I 'm weary, say I 'm sad;
  Say that health and wealth have missed me;
Say I 'm growing old, but add —
  Jenny kissed me!

LEIGH HUNT.

NARCISSA.

"YOUNG, gay, and fortunate!" Each yields a theme.
And, first, thy youth: what says it to gray hairs?
Narcissa, I 'm become thy pupil now;
Early, bright, transient, chaste as morning dew,
She sparkled, was exhaled, and went to heaven.

EDWARD YOUNG.

SWEET STREAM, THAT WINDS.

SWEET stream, that winds through yonder glade,
Apt emblem of a virtuous maid, —
Silent and chaste, she steals along,
Far from the world's gay, busy throng;
With gentle yet prevailing force,
Intent upon her destined course;
Graceful and useful all she does,
Blessing and blest where'er she goes;
Pure-bosomed as that watery glass,
And Heaven reflected in her face.

WILLIAM COWPER.

AFTER THE BALL.

THEY sat and combed their beautiful hair,
  Their long, bright tresses, one by one,
As they laughed and talked in the chamber there,
  After the revel was done.

Idly they talked of waltz and quadrille,
  Idly they laughed, like other girls,

Who over the fire, when all is still,
  Comb out their braids and curls.

Robe of satin and Brussels lace,
  Knots of flowers and ribbons, too,
Scattered about in every place,
  For the revel is through.

And Maud and Madge in robes of white,
  The prettiest nightgowns under the sun,
Stockingless, slipperless, sit in the night,
  For the revel is done, —

Sit and comb their beautiful hair,
  Those wonderful waves of brown and gold,
Till the fire is out in the chamber there,
  And the little bare feet are cold.

Then out of the gathering winter chill,
  All out of the bitter St. Agnes weather,
While the fire is out and the house is still,
  Maud and Madge together, —

Maud and Madge in robes of white,
  The prettiest nightgowns under the sun,
Curtained away from the chilly night,
  After the revel is done, —

Float along in a splendid dream,
  To a golden gittern's tinkling tune,
While a thousand lusters shimmering stream
  In a palace's grand saloon.

Flashing of jewels and flutter of laces,
  Tropical odors sweeter than musk,
Men and women with beautiful faces,
  And eyes of tropical dusk, —

And one face shining out like a star,
  One face haunting the dreams of each,
And one voice, sweeter than others are,
  Breaking into silvery speech, —

Telling, through lips of bearded bloom,
  An old, old story over again,
As down the royal bannered room,
  To the golden gittern's strain,

Two and two, they dreamily walk,
  While an unseen spirit walks beside,
And all unheard in the lovers' talk.
  He claimeth one for a bride.

O Maud and Madge, dream on together,
  With never a pang of jealous fear!
For, ere the bitter St. Agnes weather
  Shall whiten another year,

Robed for the bridal, and robed for the tomb,
  Braided brown hair and golden tress,
There 'll be only one of you left for the bloom
  Of the bearded lips to press, —

Only one for the bridal pearls,
  The robe of satin and Brussels lace, —
Only one to blush through her curls
  At the sight of a lover's face.

O beautiful Madge, in your bridal white,
  For you the revel has just begun;
But for her who sleeps in your arms to-night
  The revel of Life is done!

But, robed and crowned with your saintly bliss,
  Queen of heaven and bride of the sun,
O beautiful Maud, you 'll never miss
  The kisses another hath won!

NORA PERRY.

NEIGHBOR NELLY.

I 'M in love with neighbor Nelly,
  Though I know she 's only ten,
While, alas! I 'm eight-and-forty
  And the *marriedest* of men!
I 've a wife who weighs me double,
  I 've three daughters all with *beaux*:
I 've a son with noble whiskers,
  Who at me turns up his nose.

Though a square-toes, and a fogey,
  Still I 've sunshine in my heart;
Still I 'm fond of cakes and marbles,
  Can appreciate a tart.
I can love my neighbor Nelly
  Just as though I were a boy:
I could hand her nuts and apples
  From my depths of corduroy.

She is tall, and growing taller,
  She is vigorous of limb;
(You should see her play at cricket,
  With her little brother Jim.)
She has eyes as blue as damsons,
  She has pounds of auburn curls,
She regrets the game of leap-frog
  Is prohibited to girls.

I adore my neighbor Nelly,
  I invite her in to tea;
And I let her nurse the baby, —
  All her pretty ways to see.
Such a darling bud of woman,
  Yet remote from any teens, —
I have learnt from neighbor Nelly
  What the girl's doll-instinct means.

O, to see her with the baby!
He adores her more than I, —
How she choruses his crowing, —
How she hushes every cry!
How she loves to pit his dimples
With her light forefinger deep!
How she boasts to me in triumph
When she 's got him off to sleep!

We must part, my neighbor Nelly,
For the summers quickly flee;
And your middle-aged admirer
Must supplanted quickly be.
Yet as jealous as a mother, —
A distempered, cankered churl,
I look vainly for the setting
To be worthy such a pearl.

ROBERT B. BROUGH.

SATURDAY AFTERNOON.

I LOVE to look on a scene like this,
Of wild and careless play,
And persuade myself that I am not old
And my locks are not yet gray;
For it stirs the blood in an old man's heart,
And it makes his pulses fly,
To catch the thrill of a happy voice,
And the light of a pleasant eye.

I have walked the world for fourscore years;
And they say that I am old,
And my heart is ripe for the reaper Death,
And my years are wellnigh told:
It is very true; it is very true;
I am old, and I bide my time;
But my heart will leap at a scene like this,
And I half renew my prime.

Play on, play on; I am with you there,
In the midst of your merry ring;
I can feel the thrill of the daring jump,
And the rush of the breathless swing.
I hide with you in the fragrant hay,
And I whoop the smothered call;
And my feet slip up on the seedy floor,
And I care not for the fall.

I am willing to die when my time shall come,
And I shall be glad to go;
For the world at best is a weary place
And my pulse is getting low:
But the grave is dark, and the heart will fail
In treading its gloomy way;
But it wiles my heart from its dreariness,
To see the young so gay.

NATHANIEL PARKER WILLIS.

IT NEVER COMES AGAIN.

THERE are gains for all our losses,
There are balms for all our pain;
But when youth, the dream, departs,
It takes something from our hearts,
And it never comes again.

We are stronger, and are better,
Under manhood's sterner reign;
Still we feel that something sweet
Followed youth, with flying feet,
And will never come again.

Something beautiful is vanished,
And we sigh for it in vain;
We behold it everywhere,
On the earth, and in the air,
But it never comes again.

RICHARD HENRY STODDARD.

POEMS of FRIENDSHIP

An angel face: – its sunny wealth of hair
In radiant ripples bathed the graceful throat
And dimpled shoulders; round the rosy curve
Of the sweet mouth a smile seemed wandering ever;
While in the depths of azure fire that gleamed
Beneath the drooping lashes, slept a world
Of eloquent meaning, passionate yet pure –
Dreamy – subdued – but oh, how beautiful!

Edgar A Poe.

Epitaph.

Here rests his Head upon the Lap of Earth
A Youth, to Fortune & to Fame unknown:
Fair Science frown'd not on his humble Birth,
And Melancholy mark'd him for her own.
Large was his Bounty, & his Soul sincere;
Heav'n did a Recompense as largely send:
He gave to Mis'ry all he had, a Tear,
He gain'd from Heav'n ('twas all he wish'd) a Friend
No farther seek his Merits to disclose,
Or draw his Frailties from their dread Abode,
(There they alike in trembling Hope repose)
The Bosom of his Father, & his God.

T Gray.

POEMS OF FRIENDSHIP.

BENEDICITE.

God's love and peace be with thee, where
Soe'er this soft autumnal air
Lifts the dark tresses of thy hair!

Whether through city casements comes
Its kiss to thee, in crowded rooms,
Or, out among the woodland blooms,

It freshens o'er thy thoughtful face,
Imparting, in its glad embrace,
Beauty to beauty, grace to grace!

Fair Nature's book together read,
The old wood-paths that knew our tread,
The maple shadows overhead, —

The hills we climbed, the river seen
By gleams along its deep ravine, —
All keep thy memory fresh and green.

Where'er I look, where'er I stray,
Thy thought goes with me on my way,
And hence the prayer I breathe to-day:

O'er lapse of time and change of scene,
The weary waste which lies between
Thyself and me, my heart I lean.

Thou lack'st not Friendship's spellword, nor
The half-unconscious power to draw
All hearts to thine by Love's sweet law.

With these good gifts of God is cast
Thy lot, and many a charm thou hast
To hold the blessèd angels fast.

If, then, a fervent wish for thee
The gracious heavens will heed from me,
What should, dear heart, its burden be?

The sighing of a shaken reed, —
What can I more than meekly plead
The greatness of our common need?

God's love, — unchanging, pure, and true, —
The Paraclete white-shining through
His peace, — the fall of Hermon's dew!

With such a prayer, on this sweet day,
As thou mayst hear and I may say,
I greet thee, dearest, far away!

John Greenleaf Whittier.

AN INVITATION.

Nine years have slipt like hour-glass sand
   From life's still-emptying globe away
Since last, dear friend, I clasped your hand,
And stood upon the impoverished land,
   Watching the steamer down the bay.

I held the token which you gave,
   While slowly the smoke-pennon curled
O'er the vague rim 'tween sky and wave,
And shut the distance like a grave,
   Leaving me in the colder world.

The old worn world of hurry and heat,
   The young, fresh world of thought and scope,
While you, where beckoning billows fleet
Climb far sky-beaches still and sweet,
   Sank wavering down the ocean slope.

You sought the new world in the old,
   I found the old world in the new,
All that our human hearts can hold,
The inward world of deathless mold,
   The same that Father Adam knew.

He needs no ship to cross the tide,
   Who, in the lives about him, sees
Fair window-prospects opening wide
O'er history's fields on every side,
   To Ind and Egypt, Rome and Greece.

Whatever molds of various brain
   E'er shaped the world to weal or woe,
Whatever empires wax and wane,

To him that hath not eyes in vain,
  Our village-microcosm can show.

Come back our ancient walks to tread,
  Dear haunts of lost or scattered friends,
Old Harvard's scholar-factories red,
Where song and smoke and laughter sped
  The nights to proctor-haunted ends.

Constant are all our former loves,
  Unchanged the icehouse-girdled pond,
Its hemlock glooms, its shadowy coves,
Where floats the coot and never moves,
  Its slope of long-tamed green beyond.

Our old familiars are not laid,
  Though snapt our wands and sunk our books;
They beckon, not to be gainsaid,
Where, round broad meads that mowers wade,
  The Charles his steel-blue sickle crooks.

Where, as the cloudbergs eastward blow,
  From glow to gloom the hillsides shift
Their plumps of orchard trees arow,
Their lakes of rye that wave and flow,
  Their snowy whiteweed's summer drift.

There have we watched the West unfurl
  A cloud Byzantium newly born,
With flickering spires and domes of pearl,
And vapory surfs that crowd and curl
  Into the sunset's Golden Horn.

There, as the flaming occident
  Burned slowly down to ashes gray,
Night pitched o'erhead her silent tent,
And glimmering gold from Hesper sprent
  Upon the darkened river lay,

Where a twin sky but just before
  Deepened, and double swallows skimmed,
And, from a visionary shore,
Hung visioned trees, that, more and more,
  Grew dusk as those above were dimmed.

Then eastward saw we slowly grow
  Clear-edged the lines of roof and spire,
While great elm-masses blacken slow,
And linden-ricks their round heads show
  Against a flush of widening fire.

Doubtful at first and far away,
  The moon-flood creeps more wide and wide;
Up a ridged beach of cloudy gray,
Curved round the east as round a bay,
  It slips and spreads its gradual tide.

Then suddenly, in lurid mood,
  The moon looms large o'er town and field,
As upon Adam, red like blood,
'Tween him and Eden's happy wood,
  Glared the commissioned angel's shield.

Or let us seek the seaside, there
  To wander idly as we list,
Whether, on rocky headlands bare,
Sharp cedar-horns, like breakers, tear
  The trailing fringes of gray mist,

Or whether, under skies full flown,
  The brightening surfs, with foamy din,
Their breeze-caught forelocks backward blown,
Against the beach's yellow zone,
  Curl slow, and plunge forever in.

And as we watch those canvas towers
  That lean along the horizon's rim,
"Sail on," I'll say; "may sunniest hours
Convoy you from this land of ours,
  Since from my side you bear not him!"

For years thrice three, wise Horace said,
  A poem rare let silence bind;
And love may ripen in the shade,
Like ours, for nine long seasons laid
  In deepest arches of the mind.

Come back! Not ours the Old World's good,
  The Old World's ill, thank God, not ours;
But here, far better understood,
The days enforce our native mood,
  And challenge all our manlier powers.

Kindlier to me the place of birth
  That first my tottering footsteps trod;
There may be fairer spots of earth,
But all their glories are not worth
  The virtue of the native sod.

Thence climbs an influence more benign
  Through pulse and nerve, through heart and brain;
Sacred to me those fibers fine
That first clasped earth. O, ne'er be mine
  The alien sun and alien rain!

These nourish not like homelier glows
  Or waterings of familiar skies,
And nature fairer blooms bestows
On the heaped hush of wintry snows,
  In pastures dear to childhood's eyes,

Than where Italian earth receives
  The partial sunshine's ampler boons,
Where vines carve friezes 'neath the eaves,
And, in dark firmaments of leaves,
  The orange lifts its golden moons.

JAMES RUSSELL LOWELL.

DREAMS AND REALITIES.

O Rosamond, thou fair and good
And perfect flower of womanhood!
Thou royal rose of June!
Why didst thou droop before thy time?
Why wither in the first sweet prime?
Why didst thou die so soon?

For, looking backward through my tears
On thee, and on my wasted years,
I cannot choose but say,
If thou hadst lived to be my guide,
Or thou hadst lived and I had died,
'T were better far to-day.

O child of light, O golden head! —
Bright sunbeam for one moment shed
Upon life's lonely way, —
Why didst thou vanish from our sight?
Could they not spare my little light
From heaven's unclouded day?

O friend so true, O friend so good! —
Thou one dream of my maidenhood,
That gave youth all its charms, —
What had I done, or what hadst thou,
That, through this lonesome world till now,
We walk with empty arms?

And yet this poor soul had been fed
With all it loved and coveted;
Had life been always fair,
Would these dear dreams that ne'er depart,
That thrill with bliss my inmost heart,
Forever tremble there?

If still they kept their earthly place,
The friends I held in my embrace,
And gave to death, alas!
Could I have learned that clear, calm faith
That looks beyond the bonds of death,
And almost longs to pass?

Sometimes, I think, the things we see
Are shadows of the things to be;
That what we plan we build;
That every hope that hath been crossed,
And every dream we thought was lost,
In heaven shall be fulfilled;

That even the children of the brain
Have not been born and died in vain,
Though here unclothed and dumb;
But on some brighter, better shore
They live, embodied evermore,
And wait for us to come.

And when on that last day we rise,
Caught up between the earth and skies,
Then shall we hear our Lord
Say, Thou hast done with doubt and death,
Henceforth, according to thy faith,
Shall be thy faith's reward.

Phœbe Cary.

THE OLD SCHOOL-HOUSE.

I sat an hour to-day, John,
Beside the old brook-stream, —
Where we were school-boys in old time,
When manhood was a dream;
The brook is choked with fallen leaves,
The pond is dried away,
I scarce believe that you would know
The dear old place to-day.

The school-house is no more, John, —
Beneath our locust-trees,
The wild rose by the window's side
No more waves in the breeze;
The scattered stones look desolate;
The sod they rested on
Has been plowed up by stranger hands,
Since you and I were gone.

The chestnut-tree is dead, John, —
And what is sadder now,
The grapevine of that same old swing
Hangs on the withered bough.
I read our names upon the bark,
And found the pebbles rare
Laid up beneath the hollow side,
As we had piled them there.

Beneath the grass-grown bank, John, —
I looked for our old spring,
That bubbled down the alder-path
Three paces from the swing;
The rushes grow upon the brink,
The pool is black and bare,
And not a foot for many a day,
It seems, has trodden there.

I took the old blind road, John,
That wandered up the hill, —
'T is darker than it used to be,
And seems so lone and still;
The birds yet sing upon the boughs
Where once the sweet grapes hung,
But not a voice of human kind
Where all our voices rung.

I sat me on the fence, John,
That lies as in old time,

The same half-panel in the path
  We used so oft to climb, —
And thought how, o'er the bars of life,
  Our playmates had passed on,
And left me counting on the spot
  The faces that were gone.

ANONYMOUS.

BILL AND JOE.

Come, dear old comrade, you and I
Will steal an hour from days gone by, —
The shining days when life was new,
And all was bright as morning dew, —
The lusty days of long ago,
When you were Bill and I was Joe.

Your name may flaunt a titled trail,
Proud as a cockerel's rainbow tail;
And mine as brief appendix wear
As Tam O'Shanter's luckless mare;
To-day, old friend, remember still
That I am Joe and you are Bill.

You 've won the great world's envied prize,
And grand you look in people's eyes,
With H O N. and L L. D.
In big brave letters, fair to see, —
Your fist, old fellow! off they go!
How are you, Bill? How are you, Joe?

You 've worn the judge's ermined robe;
You 've taught your name to half the globe;
You 've sung mankind a deathless strain;
You 've made the dead past live again:
The world may call you what it will,
But you and I are Joe and Bill.

The chaffing young folks stare and say,
"See those old buffers, bent and gray;
They talk like fellows in their teens!
Mad, poor old boys! That 's what it means," —
And shake their heads; they little know
The throbbing hearts of Bill and Joe!

How Bill forgets his hour of pride,
While Joe sits smiling at his side;
How Joe, in spite of time's disguise,
Finds the old schoolmate in his eyes, —
Those calm, stern eyes that melt and fill
As Joe looks fondly up at Bill.

Ah, pensive scholar, what is fame?
A fitful tongue of leaping flame;
A giddy whirlwind's fickle gust,
That lifts a pinch of mortal dust:
A few swift years, and who can show
Which dust was Bill, and which was Joe?

The weary idol takes his stand,
Holds out his bruised and aching hand,
While gaping thousands come and go, —
How vain it seems, this empty show!
Till all at once his pulses thrill,
'T is poor old Joe's "God bless you, Bill!"

And shall we breathe in happier spheres
The names that pleased our mortal ears, —
In some sweet lull of harp and song,
For earth-born spirits none too long, —
Just whispering of the world below,
Where this was Bill, and that was Joe?

No matter; while our home is here
No sounding name is half so dear;
When fades at length our lingering day,
Who cares what pompous tombstones say?
Read on the hearts that love us still,
Hic jacet Joe. *Hic jacet* Bill.

OLIVER WENDELL HOLMES.

THE DEAD FRIEND.

FROM "IN MEMORIAM."

The path by which we twain did go,
  Which led by tracts that pleased us well,
  Through four sweet years arose and fell,
From flower to flower, from snow to snow.

. . . . . .

But where the path we walked began
  To slant the fifth autumnal slope,
  As we descended following Hope,
There sat the Shadow feared of man;

Who broke our fair companionship,
  And spread his mantle dark and cold,
  And wrapped thee formless in the fold,
And dulled the murmur on thy lip.

. . . . . .

When each by turns was guide to each,
  And Fancy light from Fancy caught,
  And Thought leapt out to wed with Thought
Ere Thought could wed itself with Speech;

And all we met was fair and good,
  And all was good that Time could bring,
  And all the secret of the Spring
Moved in the chambers of the blood;

. . . . . .

I know that this was Life, — the track
  Whereon with equal feet we fared;
  And then, as now, the day prepared
The daily burden for the back.

But this it was that made me move
  As light as carrier-birds in air;
  I loved the weight I had to bear
Because it needed help of Love:

Nor could I weary, heart or limb,
  When mighty Love would cleave in twain
  The lading of a single pain,
And part it, giving half to him.

. . . . .

But I remained, whose hopes were dim,
  Whose life, whose thoughts were little worth,
  To wander on a darkened earth,
Where all things round me breathed of him.

O friendship, equal-poised control,
  O heart, with kindliest motion warm,
  O sacred essence, other form,
O solemn ghost, O crownèd soul!

Yet none could better know than I,
  How much of act at human hands
  The sense of human will demands
By which we dare to live or die.

Whatever way my days decline,
  I felt and feel, though left alone,
  His being working in mine own,
The footsteps of his life in mine.

. . . . . .

My pulses therefore beat again
  For other friends that once I met:
  Nor can it suit me to forget
The mighty hopes that make us men.

I woo your love: I count it crime
  To mourn for any overmuch;
  I, the divided half of such
A friendship as had mastered Time;

Which masters Time, indeed, and is
  Eternal, separate from fears:
  The all-assuming months and years
Can take no part away from this.

. . . . . .

O days and hours, your work is this,
  To hold me from my proper place,
  A little while from his embrace,
For fuller gain of after bliss:

That out of distance might ensue
  Desire of nearness doubly sweet;
  And unto meeting when we meet,
Delight a hundred-fold accrue.

. . . . . .

The hills are shadows, and they flow
  From form to form, and nothing stands;
  They melt like mist, the solid lands,
Like clouds they shape themselves and go.

But in my spirit will I dwell,
  And dream my dream, and hold it true;
  For though my lips may breathe adieu,
I cannot think the thing farewell.

ALFRED TENNYSON.

THE MEETING OF THE SHIPS.

"We take each other by the hand, and we exchange a few words and looks of kindness, and we rejoice together for a few short moments; and then days, months, years intervene, and we see and know nothing of each other." — WASHINGTON IRVING.

Two barks met on the deep mid-sea,
  When calms had stilled the tide;
A few bright days of summer glee
  There found them side by side.

And voices of the fair and brave
  Rose mingling thence in mirth;
And sweetly floated o'er the wave
  The melodies of earth.

Moonlight on that lone Indian main
  Cloudless and lovely slept;
While dancing step and festive strain
  Each deck in triumph swept.

And hands were linked, and answering eyes
  With kindly meaning shone;
O, brief and passing sympathies,
  Like leaves together blown!

A little while such joy was cast
  Over the deep's repose,
Till the loud singing winds at last
  Like trumpet music rose.

And proudly, freely on their way
  The parting vessels bore;
In calm or storm, by rock or bay,
  To meet — O nevermore!

Never to blend in victory's cheer,
  To aid in hours of woe;
And thus bright spirits mingle here,
  Such ties are formed below.

FELICIA HEMANS.

JAFFAR.

JAFFAR, the Barmecide, the good vizier,
The poor man's hope, the friend without a peer, —
Jaffar was dead, slain by a doom unjust;
And guilty Haroun, sullen with mistrust
Of what the good, and e'en the bad, might say,
Ordained that no man living, from that day,
Should dare to speak his name on pain of death.
All Araby and Persia held their breath:

All but the brave Mondeer ; he, proud to show
How far for love a grateful soul could go,
And facing death for very scorn and grief
(For his great heart wanted a great relief),
Stood forth in Bagdad, daily, in the square
Where once had stood a happy house, and there
Harangued the tremblers at the scimitar
On all they owed to the divine Jaffar.

"Bring me this man," the caliph cried ; the man
Was brought, was gazed upon. The mutes began
To bind his arms. "Welcome, brave cords," cried he,
"From bonds far worse Jaffar delivered me ;
From wants, from shames, from loveless household fears ;
Made a man's eyes friends with delicious tears ;
Restored me, loved me, put me on a par
With his great self. How can I pay Jaffar ?"

Haroun, who felt that on a soul like this
The mightiest vengeance could but fall amiss,
Now deigned to smile, as one great lord of fate
Might smile upon another half as great.
He said, "Let worth grow frenzied if it will ;
The caliph's judgment shall be master still;
Go, and since gifts so move thee, take this gem,
The richest in the Tartar's diadem,
And hold the giver as thou deemest fit !"
"Gifts !" cried the friend ; he took and holding it,
High toward the heavens, as though to meet his star,
Exclaimed, "This, too, I owe to thee, Jaffar !"

LEIGH HUNT.

WE HAVE BEEN FRIENDS TOGETHER.

WE have been friends together
In sunshine and in shade,
Since first beneath the chestnut-tree
In infancy we played.
But coldness dwells within thy heart,
A cloud is on thy brow ;
We have been friends together,
Shall a light word part us now ?

We have been gay together ;
We have laughed at little jests ;
For the fount of hope was gushing
Warm and joyous in our breasts.
But laughter now hath fled thy lip,
And sullen glooms thy brow ;
We have been gay together,
Shall a light word part us now ?

We have been sad together ;
We have wept with bitter tears
O'er the grass-grown graves where slumbered
The hopes of early years.
The voices which were silent then
Would bid thee clear thy brow ;
We have been sad together,
Shall a light word part us now ?

CAROLINE E. NORTON.

KINDRED HEARTS.

O, ASK not, hope thou not, too much
Of sympathy below ;
Beware the hearts whence one same touch
Bids the sweet fountains flow :
Few — and by still conflicting powers
Forbidden here to meet —
Such ties would make this life of ours
Too fair for aught so fleet.

It may be that thy brother's eye
Sees not as thine, which turns
In such deep reverence to the sky
Where the rich sunset burns ;
It may be that the breath of spring,
Born amidst violets lone,
A rapture o'er thy soul can bring, —
A dream, to his unknown.

The tune that speaks of other times, —
A sorrowful delight ! —
The melody of distant chimes,
The sound of waves by night ;
The wind that, with so many a tone,
Some chord within can thrill, —
These may have language all thine own,
To *him* a mystery still.

Yet scorn thou not for this the true
And steadfast love of years ;
The kindly, that from childhood grew,
The faithful to thy tears !
If there be one that o'er the dead
Hath in thy grief borne part,
And watched through sickness by thy bed,
Call *his* a kindred heart !

But for those bonds all perfect made,
Wherein bright spirits blend,
Like sister flowers of one sweet shade
With the same breeze that bend,
For that full bliss of thought allied,
Never to mortals given,
O, lay thy lovely dreams aside,
Or lift them unto heaven !

FELICIA HEMANS.

G. Richmond Pinx^t

Eng^d by H. B. Hall & Sons N.Y.

Thomas Moore

FORDS, HOWARD & HULBERT, N.Y.

THE VALE OF AVOCA.

There is not in this wide world a valley so sweet
As that vale in whose bosom the bright waters meet;
O, the last ray of feeling and life must depart
Ere the bloom of that valley shall fade from my heart!

Yet it was not that Nature had shed o'er the scene
Her purest of crystal and brightest of green;
'T was not the soft magic of streamlet or hill, —
O, no! it was something more exquisite still.

'T was that friends, the beloved of my bosom, were near,
Who made every dear scene of enchantment more dear,
And who felt how the best charms of nature improve,
When we see them reflected from looks that we love.

Sweet Vale of Avoca! how calm could I rest
In thy bosom of shade, with the friends I love best;
Where the storms that we feel in this cold world should cease,
And our hearts, like thy waters, be mingled in peace.

THOMAS MOORE.

THE ROYAL GUEST.

They tell me I am shrewd with other men;
With thee I 'm slow, and difficult of speech.
With others I may guide the car of talk;
Thou wing'st it oft to realms beyond my reach.

If other guests should come, I 'd deck my hair,
And choose my newest garment from the shelf;
When thou art bidden, I would clothe my heart
With holiest purpose, as for God himself.

For them I while the hours with tale or song,
Or web of fancy, fringed with careless rhyme;
But how to find a fitting lay for thee,
Who hast the harmonies of every time?

O friend beloved! I sit apart and dumb, —
Sometimes in sorrow, oft in joy divine;
My lip will falter, but my prisoned heart
Springs forth to measure its faint pulse with thine.

Thou art to me most like a royal guest,
Whose travels bring him to some lowly roof,
Where simple rustics spread their festal fare
And, blushing, own it is not good enough.

Bethink thee, then, whene'er thou com'st to me,
From high emprise and noble toil to rest,
My thoughts are weak and trivial, matched with thine;
But the poor mansion offers thee its best.

JULIA WARD HOWE.

THE QUARREL OF FRIENDS.

FROM "CHRISTABEL."

Alas! they had been friends in youth:
But whispering tongues can poison truth;
And constancy lives in realms above;
And life is thorny; and youth is vain;
And to be wroth with one we love
Doth work like madness in the brain.
And thus it chanced, as I divine,
With Roland and Sir Leoline!
Each spoke words of high disdain
And insult to his heart's best brother;
They parted, — ne'er to meet again!
But never either found another
To free the hollow heart from paining.
They stood aloof, the scars remaining,
Like cliffs which had been rent asunder;
A dreary sea now flows between,
But neither heat, nor frost, nor thunder
Shall wholly do away, I ween,
The marks of that which once hath been.

S. T. COLERIDGE.

FRIENDSHIP.

A ruddy drop of manly blood
The surging sea outweighs;
The world uncertain comes and goes,
The lover rooted stays.
I fancied he was fled, —
And, after many a year,
Glowed unexhausted kindliness,
Like daily sunrise there.
My careful heart was free again;
O friend, my bosom said,
Through thee alone the sky is arched,
Through thee the rose is red;
All things through thee take nobler form,
And look beyond the earth;
The mill-round of our fate appears
A sun-path in thy worth.
Me too thy nobleness has taught
To master my despair;
The fountains of my hidden life
Are through thy friendship fair.

RALPH WALDO EMERSON.

FRIENDSHIP.

HAM. Horatio, thou art e'en as just a man
As e'er my conversation coped withal.
HOR. O, my dear lord —
HAM. Nay, do not think I flatter:
For what advancement may I hope from thee
That no revénue hast but thy good spirits,
To feed and clothe thee? Why should the poor be flattered?
No, let the candied tongue lick absurd pomp,
And crook the pregnant hinges of the knee,
Where thrift may follow fawning. Dost thou hear?
Since my dear soul was mistress of her choice,
And could of men distinguish, her election
Hath sealed thee for herself; for thou hast been
As one, in suffering all, that suffers nothing, —
A man that Fortune's buffets and rewards
Hast ta'en with equal thanks; and blessed are those
Whose blood and judgment are so well co-mingled,
That they are not a pipe for Fortune's finger
To sound what stop she please: Give me that man
That is not passion's slave, and I will wear him
In my heart's core, ay, in my heart of heart,
As I do thee.

SHAKESPEARE.

MARTIAL FRIENDSHIP.

FROM "CORIOLANUS."

[Aufidius the Volscian to Caius Marcius Coriolanus.]

AUF. O Marcius, Marcius!
Each word thou hast spoke hath weeded from my heart
A root of ancient envy. If Jupiter
Should from yond' cloud speak divine things, and say,
"'T is true," I 'd not believe them more than thee,
All-noble Marcius. — Let me twine
Mine arms about that body, where-against
My grainèd ash an hundred times hath broke,
And scared the moon with splinters! Here I clip
The anvil of my sword; and do contest
As hotly and as nobly with thy love,
As ever in ambitious strength I did
Contend against thy valor. Know thou first,
I loved the maid I married; never man
Sighed truer breath; but that I see thee here,
Thou noble thing! more dances my rapt heart
Than when I first my wedded mistress saw
Bestride my threshold. Why, thou Mars! I tell thee,
We have a power on foot; and I had purpose
Once more to hew thy target from thy brawn,
Or lose mine arm for 't. Thou hast beat me out
Twelve several times, and I have nightly since
Dreamt of encounters 'twixt thyself and me,
We have been down together in my sleep,
Unbuckling helms, fisting each other's throat,
And waked half dead with nothing. Worthy Marcius,
Had we no other quarrel else to Rome, but that
Thou art thence banished, we would muster all
From twelve to seventy; and, pouring war
Into the bowels of ungrateful Rome,
Like a bold flood o'erbear. O, come! go in,
And take our friendly senators by the hands,
Who now are here, taking their leaves of me,
Who am prepared against your territories,
Though not for Rome itself.
A thousand welcomes!
And more a friend than e'er an enemy;
Yet, Marcius, that was much.

SHAKESPEARE.

THE MEMORY OF THE HEART.

IF stores of dry and learnèd lore we gain,
We keep them in the memory of the brain;
Names, things, and facts, — whate'er we knowledge call, —
There is the common ledger for them all;
And images on this cold surface traced
Make slight impression, and are soon effaced.
But we 've a page, more glowing and more bright,
On which our friendship and our love to write;
That these may never from the soul depart,
We trust them to the memory of the heart.
There is no dimming, no effacement there;
Each new pulsation keeps the record clear;
Warm, golden letters all the tablet fill,
Nor lose their luster till the heart stands still.

DANIEL WEBSTER.

WHEN TO THE SESSIONS OF SWEET SILENT THOUGHT.

SONNET.

WHEN to the sessions of sweet silent thought
I summon up remembrance of things past,
I sigh the lack of many a thing I sought,
And with old woes new wail my dear time's waste.
Then can I drown an eye, unused to flow,
For precious friends hid in death's dateless night,
And weep afresh love's long since cancelled woe,
And moan th' expense of many a vanished sight.
Then can I grieve at grievances foregone,
And heavily from woe to woe tell o'er
The sad account of fore-bemoanèd moan,
Which I new pay, as if not paid before;
But if the while I think on thee, dear friend,
All losses are restored, and sorrows end.

SHAKESPEARE.

EARLY FRIENDSHIP.

The half-seen memories of childish days,
When pains and pleasures lightly came and went;
The sympathies of boyhood rashly spent
In fearful wanderings through forbidden ways;
The vague, but manly wish to tread the maze
Of life to noble ends, — whereon intent,
Asking to know for what man here is sent,
The bravest heart must often pause, and gaze,—
The firm resolve to seek the chosen end
Of manhood's judgment, cautious and mature, —
Each of these viewless bonds binds friend to friend
With strength no selfish purpose can secure:
My happy lot is this, that all attend
That friendship which first came, and which shall
last endure.

AUBREY DE VERE.

A TEMPLE TO FRIENDSHIP.

"A temple to Friendship," cried Laura, enchanted,
"I 'll build in this garden; the thought is divine."
So the temple was built, and she now only wanted
An image of Friendship, to place on the shrine.

So she flew to the sculptor, who sat down before her
An image, the fairest his art could invent;
But so cold, and so dull, that the youthful adorer
Saw plainly this was not the Friendship she meant.

"O, never," said she, "could I think of enshrining
An image whose looks are so joyless and dim;
But yon little god upon roses reclining,
We 'll make, if you please, sir, a Friendship of him."

So the bargain was struck; with the little god laden,
She joyfully flew to her home in the grove.
"Farewell," said the sculptor, "you 're not the first maiden
Who came but for Friendship, and took away Love!"

THOMAS MOORE.

PLATONIC.

I had sworn to be a bachelor, she had sworn to be a maid,
For we quite agreed in doubting whether matrimony paid;
Besides, we had our higher loves, — fair science ruled my heart,
And she said her young affections were all wound up in art.

So we laughed at those wise men who say that friendship cannot live
'Twixt man and woman, unless each has something more to give:
We would be friends, and friends as true as e'er were man and man;
I 'd be a second David, and she Miss Jonathan.

We scorned all sentimental trash, — vows, kisses, tears, and sighs;
High friendship, such as ours, might well such childish arts despise;
We *liked* each other, that was all, quite all there was to say,
So we just shook hands upon it, in a business sort of way.

We shared our secrets and our joys, together hoped and feared,
With common purpose sought the goal that young Ambition reared;
We dreamed together of the days, the dream-bright days to come,
We were strictly confidential, and we called each other "chum."

And many a day we wandered together o'er the hills,
I seeking bugs and butterflies, and she, the ruined mills
And rustic bridges, and the like, that picture-makers prize
To run in with their waterfalls, and groves, and summer skies.

And many a quiet evening, in hours of silent ease,
We floated down the river, or strolled beneath the trees,
And talked, in long gradation from the poets to the weather,
While the western skies and my cigar burned slowly out together.

Yet through it all no whispered word, no tell-tale glance or sigh,
Told aught of warmer sentiment than friendly sympathy.
We talked of love as coolly as we talked of nebulæ,
And thought no more of being *one* than we did of being *three*.

. . . . . .

"Well, good by, chum!" I took her hand, for the time had come to go.
My going meant our parting, when to meet, we did not know.
I had lingered long, and said farewell with a very heavy heart;
For although we were but *friends*, 't is hard for honest friends to part.

"Good by, old fellow! don't forget your friends beyond the sea,
And some day, when you 've lots of time, drop a line or two to me."
The words came lightly, gayly, but a great sob, just behind,
Welled upward with a story of quite a different kind.

And then she raised her eyes to mine, — great liquid eyes of blue,
Filled to the brim, and running o'er, like violet cups of dew;
One long, long glance, and then I did, what I never did before —
Perhaps the *tears* meant friendship, but I 'm sure the *kiss* meant more.

WILLIAM B. TERRETT.

POEMS OF LOVE.

COMPLIMENT AND ADMIRATION.

WHEN IN THE CHRONICLE OF WASTED TIME.

SONNET.

WHEN in the chronicle of wasted time
I see descriptions of the fairest wights,
And beauty making beautiful old rhyme,
In praise of ladies dead, and lovely knights;
Then, in the blazon of sweet beauty's best
Of hand, of foot, of lip, of eye, of brow,
I see their antique pen would have expressed
Even such a beauty as you master now.
So all their praises are but prophecies
Of this our time, all you prefiguring;
And, for they looked but with divining eyes,
They had not skill enough your worth to sing;
For we, which now behold these present days,
Have eyes to wonder, but lack tongues to praise.

SHAKESPEARE.

O MISTRESS MINE.

O MISTRESS mine, where are you roaming?
O, stay and hear! your true-love's coming
That can sing both high and low;
Trip no further, pretty sweeting!
Journeys end in lovers' meeting, —
Every wise man's son doth know.

What is love? 't is not hereafter;
Present mirth hath present laughter;
What's to come is still unsure:
In delay there lies no plenty, —
Then come kiss me, Sweet-and-twenty,
Youth's a stuff will not endure.

SHAKESPEARE.

OLIVIA.

FROM "TWELFTH NIGHT."

VIOLA. 'T is beauty truly blent, whose red and white
Nature's own sweet and cunning hand laid on:
Lady, you are the cruel'st she alive,
If you will lead these graces to the grave,
And leave the world no copy.

SHAKESPEARE.

PORTIA'S PICTURE.

FROM "THE MERCHANT OF VENICE."

FAIR Portia's counterfeit? What demigod
Hath come so near creation? Move these eyes?
Or whether, riding on the balls of mine,
Seem they in motion? Here are severed lips,
Parted with sugar breath; so sweet a bar
Should sunder such sweet friends: Here in her hairs
The painter plays the spider; and hath woven
A golden mesh to entrap the hearts of men,
Faster than gnats in cobwebs: But her eyes, —
How could he see to do them? having made one,
Methinks it should have power to steal both his,
And leave itself unfurnished.

SHAKESPEARE.

THE NIGHT PIECE.

TO JULIA.

HER eyes the glow-worme lend thee,
The shooting-starres attend thee;
And the elves also,
Whose little eyes glow
Like the sparks of fire, befriend thee.

No Will-o'-th'-wispe mislight thee,
Nor snake nor slow-worm bite thee;
But on thy way,
Not making stay,
Since ghost there's none t' affright thee!

Let not the darke thee cumber;
What though the moon does slumber?
The stars of the night
Will lend thee their light,
Like tapers cleare, without number.

Then, Julia, let me woo thee,
Thus, thus to come unto me;
And when I shall meet
Thy silvery feet,
My soule I'll pour into thee!

ROBERT HERRICK.

THE FORWARD VIOLET THUS DID I CHIDE.

SONNET.

The forward violet thus did I chide:—
Sweet thief, whence didst thou steal thy sweet that smells,
If not from my love's breath? the purple pride
Which on thy soft cheek for complexion dwells,
In my love's veins thou hast too grossly dyed.
The lily I condemnèd for thy hand,
And buds of marjoram had stolen thy hair:
The roses fearfully on thorns did stand,
One blushing shame, another white despair;
A third, nor red nor white, had stolen of both,
And to this robbery had annexed thy breath;
But, for his theft, in pride of all his growth
A vengeful canker eat him up to death.
More flowers I noted, yet I none could see,
But sweet or color it had stolen from thee.

SHAKESPEARE.

GOOD AND FAIR.

How near to good is what is fair!
Which we no sooner see,
But with the lines and outward air
Our senses taken be.
We wish to see it still, and prove
What ways we may deserve;
We court, we praise, we more than love,
We are not grieved to serve.

BEN JONSON.

SAMELA.

Like to Diana in her summer weed,
Girt with a crimson robe of brightest dye,
Goes fair Samela;
Whiter than be the flocks that straggling feed,
When washed by Arethusa faint they lie,
Is fair Samela;
As fair Aurora in her morning gray,
Decked with the ruddy glister of her love,
Is fair Samela;
Like lovely Thetis on a calmed day,
Whenas her brightness Neptune's fancy move,
Shines fair Samela;
Her tresses gold, her eyes like glassy streams,
Her teeth are pearl, the breasts are ivory
Of fair Samela;
Her cheeks, like rose and lily yield forth gleams,
Her brows' bright arches framed of ebony;
Thus fair Samela
Passeth fair Venus in her bravest hue,
And Juno in the show of majesty,
For she 's Samela:
Pallas in wit, all three, if you will view,
For beauty, wit, and matchless dignity,
Yield to Samela.

ROBERT GREENE.

THERE IS A GARDEN IN HER FACE.

FROM "AN HOURE'S RECREATION IN MUSICKE." 1606.

There is a garden in her face,
Where roses and white lilies blow;
A heavenly paradise is that place,
Wherein all pleasant fruits do grow;
There cherries grow that none may buy,
Till cherry-ripe themselves do cry.

Those cherries fairly do enclose
Of orient pearl a double row,
Which when her lovely laughter shows,
They look like rosebuds filled with snow;
Yet them no peer nor prince may buy,
Till cherry-ripe themselves do cry.

Her eyes like angels watch them still,
Her brows like bended bows do stand,
Threatening with piercing frowns to kill
All that approach with eye or hand
These sacred cherries to come nigh,
Till cherry-ripe themselves do cry.

RICHARD ALLISON.

THE WHITE ROSE.

SENT BY A YORKISH LOVER TO HIS LANCASTRIAN MISTRESS.

If this fair rose offend thy sight,
Placed in thy bosom bare,
'T will blush to find itself less white,
And turn Lancastrian there.

But if thy ruby lip it spy,
As kiss it thou mayest deign,
With envy pale 't will lose its dye,
And Yorkish turn again.

ANONYMOUS.

MY SWEET SWEETING.

FROM A MANUSCRIPT OF THE TIME OF HENRY VIII.

Ah, my sweet sweeting;
My little pretty sweeting,
My sweeting will I love wherever I go;
She is so proper and pure,
Full, steadfast, stable, and demure,
There is none such, you may be sure,
As my sweet sweeting.

In all this world, as thinketh me,
Is none so pleasant to my e'e,
That I am glad so oft to see,
As my sweet sweeting.
When I behold my sweeting sweet,
Her face, her hands, her minion feet,
They seem to me there is none so mete
As my sweet sweeting.

Above all other praise must I,
And love my pretty pygsnye,
For none I find so womanly
As my sweet sweeting.

ANONYMOUS.

A VISION OF BEAUTY.

It was a beauty that I saw, —
So pure, so perfect, as the frame
Of all the universe were lame
To that one figure, could I draw,
Or give least line of it a law:
A skein of silk without a knot!
A fair march made without a halt!
A curious form without a fault!
A printed book without a blot!
All beauty! — and without a spot.

BEN JONSON.

GIVE PLACE, YE LOVERS.

Give place, ye lovers, here before
That spent your boasts and brags in vain;
My lady's beauty passeth more
The best of yours, I dare well sayen,
Than doth the sun the candle-light,
Or brightest day the darkest night.

And thereto hath a troth as just
As had Penelope the fair;
For what she saith, ye may it trust,
As it by writing sealèd were:
And virtues hath she many mo'
Than I with pen have skill to show.

I could rehearse, if that I would,
The whole effect of Nature's plaint,
When she had lost the perfect mold,
The like to whom she could not paint:
With wringing hands, how she did cry,
And what she said, I know it aye.

I know she swore with raging mind,
Her kingdom only set apart,
There was no loss by law of kind
That could have gone so near her heart;
And this was chiefly all her pain;
"She could not make the like again."

Sith Nature thus gave her the praise,
To be the chiefest work she wrought,
In faith, methink, some better ways
On your behalf might well be sought,
Than to compare, as ye have done,
To match the candle with the sun.

LORD SURREY.

PHILLIS IS MY ONLY JOY.

Phillis is my only joy;
Faithless as the wind or seas;
Sometimes coming, sometimes coy,
Yet she never fails to please.
If with a frown
I am cast down,
Phillis, smiling
And beguiling,
Makes me happier than before.

Though, alas! too late I find
Nothing can her fancy fix;
Yet the moment she is kind
I forgive her all her tricks;
Which though I see,
I can't get free;
She deceiving,
I believing,
What need lovers wish for more?

SIR CHARLES SEDLEY.

YOU MEANER BEAUTIES.

You meaner beauties of the night,
That poorly satisfy our eyes
More by your number than your light, —
You common people of the skies,
What are you when the moon shall rise?

You curious chanters of the wood,
That warble forth Dame Nature's lays,
Thinking your passions understood
By your weak accents, — what 's your praise
When Philomel her voice shall raise?

You violets that first appear,
By your pure purple mantles known,
Like the proud virgins of the year,
As if the spring were all your own, —
What are you when the rose is blown?

So when my mistress shall be seen
In form and beauty of her mind:
By virtue first, then choice, a queen, —
Tell me, if she were not designed
Th' eclipse and glory of her kind?

SIR HENRY WOTTON.

GO, LOVELY ROSE.

Go, lovely rose !
Tell her that wastes her time and me,
That now she knows,
When I resemble her to thee,
How sweet and fair she seems to be.

Tell her that 's young,
And shuns to have her graces spied,
That hadst thou sprung
In deserts, where no men abide,
Thou must have uncommended died.

Small is the worth
Of beauty from the light retired ;
Bid her come forth,
Suffer herself to be desired,
And not blush so to be admired.

Then die, that she
The common fate of all things rare
May read in thee ;
How small a part of time they share,
That are so wondrous, sweet, and fair.

EDMUND WALLER.

STANZA ADDED BY HENRY KIRKE WHITE.

Yet, though thou fade,
From thy dead leaves let fragrance rise ;
And teach the maid,
That goodness Time's rude hand defies,
That virtue lives when beauty dies.

MY LOVE IN HER ATTIRE.

My Love in her attire doth show her wit,
It doth so well become her :
For every season she hath dressings fit,
For Winter, Spring, and Summer.
No beauty she doth miss
When all her robes are on :
But beauty's self she is
When all her robes are gone.

ANONYMOUS.

BELINDA.

FROM THE "RAPE OF THE LOCK."

On her white breast a sparkling cross she wore,
Which Jews might kiss, and Infidels adore.
Her lively looks a sprightly mind disclose,
Quick as her eyes, and as unfixed as those :
Favors to none, to all she smiles extends :
Oft she rejects, but never once offends.
Bright as the sun, her eyes the gazers strike,
And, like the sun, they shine on all alike.
Yet, graceful ease, and sweetness void of pride,
Might hide her faults, if belles had faults to hide ;
If to her share some female errors fall,
Look on her face, and you 'll forget them all.

ALEXANDER POPE.

MOODS.

Out upon it. I have loved
Three whole days together ;
And am like to love three more,
If it prove fair weather.

Time shall moult away his wings,
Ere he shall discover
In the whole wide world again
Such a constant lover.

But the spite on 't is, no praise
Is due at all to me :
Love with me had made no stays,
Had it any been but she.

Had it any been but she,
And that very face,
There had been at least ere this
A dozen dozen in her place.

SIR JOHN SUCKLING.

"MY LOVE IS ALWAYS NEAR."

My only love is always near, —
In country or in town
I see her twinkling feet, I hear
The whisper of her gown.

She foots it ever fair and young,
Her locks are tied in haste,
And one is o'er her shoulder flung,
And hangs below her waist.

She ran before me in the meads ;
And down this world-worn track
She leads me on ; but while she leads
She never gazes back.

And yet her voice is in my dreams,
To witch me more and more ;
That wooing voice ! Ah me, it seems
Less near me than of yore.

Lightly I sped when hope was high,
And youth beguiled the chase, —
I follow, follow still ; but I
Shall never see her face.

FREDERICK LOCKER.

AT THE CHURCH GATE.

Although I enter not,
Yet round about the spot
 Ofttimes I hover;
And near the sacred gate,
With longing eyes I wait,
 Expectant of her.

The minster bell tolls out
Above the city's rout
 And noise and humming;
They 've hushed the minster bell;
The organ 'gins to swell;
 She 's coming, coming!

My lady comes at last,
Timid and stepping fast,
 And hastening hither,
With modest eyes downcast;
She comes, — she 's here, — she 's past!
 May Heaven go with her!

Kneel undisturbed, fair saint!
Pour out your praise or plaint
 Meekly and duly:
I will not enter there,
To sully your pure prayer
 With thoughts unruly.

But suffer me to pace
Round the forbidden place,
 Lingering a minute,
Like outcast spirits, who wait,
And see, through heaven's gate,
 Angels within it.

William Makepeace Thackeray.

SHE WAS A PHANTOM OF DELIGHT.

She was a phantom of delight
When first she gleamed upon my sight;
A lovely apparition, sent
To be a moment's ornament;
Her eyes as stars of twilight fair;
Like Twilight's, too, her dusky hair;
But all things else about her drawn
From May-time and the cheerful dawn;
A dancing shape, an image gay,
To haunt, to startle, and waylay.

I saw her upon nearer view,
A spirit, yet a woman too!
Her household motions light and free,
And steps of virgin-liberty;
A countenance in which did meet
Sweet records, promises as sweet;
A creature not too bright or good
For human nature's daily food,
For transient sorrows, simple wiles,
Praise, blame, love, kisses, tears, and smiles.

And now I see with eye serene
The very pulse of the machine;
A being breathing thoughtful breath,
A traveller between life and death:
The reason firm, the temperate will,
Endurance, foresight, strength, and skill;
A perfect woman, nobly planned
To warn, to comfort, and command;
And yet a spirit still, and bright
With something of an angel-light.

William Wordsworth.

SHE WALKS IN BEAUTY.

She walks in beauty, like the night
 Of cloudless climes and starry skies,
And all that 's best of dark and bright
 Meets in her aspect and her eyes,
Thus mellowed to that tender light
 Which heaven to gaudy day denies.

One shade the more, one ray the less,
 Had half impaired the nameless grace
Which waves in every raven tress
 Or softly lightens o'er her face,
Where thoughts serenely sweet express
 How pure, how dear their dwelling-place.

And on that cheek and o'er that brow
 So soft, so calm, yet eloquent,
The smiles that win, the tints that glow,
 But tell of days in goodness spent, —
A mind at peace with all below,
 A heart whose love is innocent.

Lord Byron.

THE MILKING-MAID.

The year stood at its equinox,
 And bluff the North was blowing;
A bleat of lambs came from the flocks,
 Green hardy things were growing;
I met a maid with shining locks
 Where milky kine were lowing.

She wore a kerchief on her neck,
 Her bare arm showed its dimple,
Her apron spread without a speck,
 Her air was frank and simple.

She milked into a wooden pail,
 And sang a country ditty, —

An innocent fond lovers' tale,
  That was nor wise nor witty,
Pathetically rustical,
  Too pointless for the city.

She kept in time without a beat,
  As true as church-bell ringers,
Unless she tapped time with her feet,
  Or squeezed it with her fingers ;
Her clear, unstudied notes were sweet
  As many a practiced singer's.

I stood a minute out of sight,
  Stood silent for a minute,
To eye the pail, and creamy white
  The frothing milk within it, —

To eye the comely milking-maid,
  Herself so fresh and creamy.
"Good day to you !" at last I said ;
  She turned her head to see me.
"Good day !" she said, with lifted head ;
  Her eyes looked soft and dreamy.

And all the while she milked and milked
  The grave cow heavy-laden :
I 've seen grand ladies, plumed and silked,
  But not a sweeter maiden ;

But not a sweeter, fresher maid
  Than this in homely cotton,
Whose pleasant face and silky braid
  I have not yet forgotten.

Seven springs have passed since then, as I
  Count with a sober sorrow ;
Seven springs have come and passed me by,
  And spring sets in to-morrow.

I 've half a mind to shake myself
  Free, just for once, from London,
To set my work upon the shelf,
  And leave it done or undone ;

To run down by the early train,
  Whirl down with shriek and whistle,
And feel the bluff North blow again,
  And mark the sprouting thistle
Set up on waste patch of the lane
  Its green and tender bristle ;

And spy the scarce-blown violet banks,
  Crisp primrose-leaves and others,
And watch the lambs leap at their pranks,
  And butt their patient mothers.

Alas ! one point in all my plan
  My serious thoughts demur to :
Seven years have passed for maid and man,
  Seven years have passed for her too.

Perhaps my rose is over-blown,
  Not rosy or too rosy ;
Perhaps in farm-house of her own
  Some husband keeps her cosy,
Where I should show a face unknown, —
  Good by, my wayside posy !

CHRISTINA GEORGINA ROSSETTI.

A VIOLET IN HER HAIR.

A VIOLET in her lovely hair,
A rose upon her bosom fair !
    But O, her eyes
A lovelier violet disclose,
And her ripe lips the sweetest rose
    That 's 'neath the skies.

A lute beneath her graceful hand
Breathes music forth at her command ;
    But still her tongue
Far richer music calls to birth
Than all the minstrel power on earth
    Can give to song.

And thus she moves in tender light,
The purest ray, where all is bright,
    Serene, and sweet ;
And sheds a graceful influence round,
That hallows e'en the very ground
    Beneath her feet !

CHARLES SWAIN.

THE ROSE OF THE WORLD.

LO, when the Lord made north and south,
  And sun and moon ordainèd, he,
Forth bringing each by word of mouth
  In order of its dignity,
Did man from the crude clay express
  By sequence, and, all else decreed,
He formed the woman ; nor might less
  Than Sabbath such a work succeed.

And still with favor singled out,
  Marred less than man by mortal fall,
Her disposition is devout,
  Her countenance angelical.
No faithless thought her instinct shrouds,
  But fancy checkers settled sense,
Like alteration of the clouds
  On noonday's azure permanence.
Pure courtesy, composure, ease,
  Declare affections nobly fixed,

Eng^d by H B Hall & Sons, N.Y.

Paul Hamilton Hayne

J. B. FORD & Co NEW YORK

And impulse sprung from due degrees
  Of sense and spirit sweetly mixed.
Her modesty, her chiefest grace,
  The cestus clasping Venus' side,
Is potent to deject the face
  Of him who would affront its pride.
Wrong dares not in her presence speak,
  Nor spotted thought its taint disclose
Under the protest of a cheek
  Outbragging Nature's boast, the rose.
In mind and manners how discreet!
  How artless in her very art!
How candid in discourse! how sweet
  The concord of her lips and heart!
How (not to call true instinct's bent
  And woman's very nature harm),
How amiable and innocent
  Her pleasure in her power to charm!
How humbly careful to attract,
  Though crowned with all the soul desires,
Connubial aptitude exact,
  Diversity that never tires!

COVENTRY PATMORE.

SWEET, BE NOT PROUD.

Sweet, be not proud of those two eyes,
Which starlike sparkle in their skies;
Nor be you proud that you can see
All hearts your captives, yours yet free.
Be you not proud of that rich hair,
Which wantons with the love-sick air;
Whenas that ruby which you wear,
Sunk from the tip of your soft ear,
Will last to be a precious stone
When all your world of beauty 's gone.

ROBERT HERRICK.

LOVE.

IF IT BE TRUE THAT ANY BEAUTEOUS THING.

If it be true that any beauteous thing
Raises the pure and just desire of man
From earth to God, the eternal fount of all,
Such I believe my love; for as in her
So fair, in whom I all besides forget,
I view the gentle work of her Creator,
I have no care for any other thing,
Whilst thus I love. Nor is it marvelous,
Since the effect is not of my own power,
If the soul doth, by nature tempted forth,
Enamored through the eyes,
Repose upon the eyes which it resembleth,
And through them riseth to the Primal Love,
As to its end, and honors in admiring;
For who adores the Maker needs must love his work.

From the Italian of MICHAEL ANGELO,
by J. E. TAYLOR.

THE MIGHT OF ONE FAIR FACE.

The might of one fair face sublimes my love,
For it hath weaned my heart from low desires;
Nor death I heed, nor purgatorial fires.
Thy beauty, antepast of joys above,
Instructs me in the bliss that saints approve;
For O, how good, how beautiful, must be
The God that made so good a thing as thee,
So fair an image of the heavenly Dove!
Forgive me if I cannot turn away
From those sweet eyes that are my earthly heaven,
For they are guiding stars, benignly given
To tempt my footsteps to the upward way;
And if I dwell too fondly in thy sight,
I live and love in God's peculiar light.

From the Italian of MICHAEL ANGELO,
by J. E. TAYLOR.

LOVE SCORNS DEGREES.

FROM "THE MOUNTAIN OF THE LOVERS."

Love scorns degrees; the low he lifteth high,
The high he draweth down to that fair plain
Whereon, in his divine equality,
Two loving hearts may meet, nor meet in vain;
'Gainst such sweet leveling Custom cries amain,
But o'er its harshest utterance one bland sigh,
Breathed passion-wise, doth mount victorious still,
For Love, earth's lord, must have his lordly will.

PAUL H. HAYNE.

PHILLIS THE FAIR.

On a hill there grows a flower,
  Fair befall the dainty sweet!
By that flower there is a bower
  Where the heavenly muses meet.

In that bower there is a chair,
Fringèd all about with gold,
Where doth sit the fairest fair
That ever eye did yet behold.

It is Phillis, fair and bright,
She that is the shepherd's joy,
She that Venus did despite,
And did blind her little boy.

Who would not that face admire?
Who would not this saint adore?
Who would not this sight desire,
Though he thought to see no more?

Thou that art the shepherd's queen,
Look upon thy love-sick swain!
By thy comfort have been seen
Dead men brought to life again.

NICHOLAS BRETON.

LOVE IS A SICKNESS.

LOVE is a sickness full of woes,
All remedies refusing;
A plant that most with cutting grows,
Most barren with best using.
Why so?
More we enjoy it, more it dies;
If not enjoyed, it sighing cries
Heigh-ho!

Love is a torment of the mind,
A tempest everlasting;
And Jove hath made it of a kind,
Not well, nor full, nor fasting.
Why so?
More we enjoy it, more it dies;
If not enjoyed, it sighing cries
Heigh-ho!

SAMUEL DANIEL.

AH! WHAT IS LOVE?

AH! what is love? It is a pretty thing,
As sweet unto a shepherd as a king,
And sweeter too;
For kings have cares that wait upon a crown,
And cares can make the sweetest face to frown:
Ah then, ah then,
If country loves such sweet desires gain,
What lady would not love a shepherd swain?

His flocks are folded; he comes home at night
As merry as a king in his delight,
And merrier too;
For kings bethink them what the state require,
Where shepherds, careless, carol by the fire:
Ah then, ah then,
If country love such sweet desires gain,
What lady would not love a shepherd swain?

He kisseth first, then sits as blithe to eat
His cream and curd as doth the king his meat,
And blither too;
For kings have often fears when they sup,
Where shepherds dread no poison in their cup:
Ah then, ah then,
If country loves such sweet desires gain,
What lady would not love a shepherd swain?

Upon his couch of straw he sleeps as sound
As doth the king upon his beds of down,
More sounder too;
For cares cause kings full oft their sleep to spill,
Where weary shepherds lie and snort their fill:
Ah then, ah then,
If country loves such sweet desires gain,
What lady would not love a shepherd swain?

Thus with his wife he spends the year as blithe
As doth the king at every tide or syth,
And blither too;
For kings have wars and broil, to take in hand,
When shepherds laugh, and love upon the land:
Ah then, ah then,
If country loves such sweet desires gain,
What lady would not love a shepherd swain?

ROBERT GREENE.

TELL ME, MY HEART, IF THIS BE LOVE.

WHEN Delia on the plain appears,
Awed by a thousand tender fears,
I would approach, but dare not move;—
Tell me, my heart, if this be love.

Whene'er she speaks, my ravished ear
No other voice than hers can hear;
No other wit but hers approve;—
Tell me, my heart, if this be love.

If she some other swain commend,
Though I was once his fondest friend,
His instant enemy I prove;—
Tell me, my heart, if this be love.

When she is absent, I no more
Delight in all that pleased before,
The clearest spring, the shadiest grove;—
Tell me, my heart, if this be love.

When fond of power, of beauty vain,
Her nets she spread for every swain,
I strove to hate, but vainly strove;—
Tell me, my heart, if this be love.

GEORGE, LORD LYTTELTON.

GO, HAPPY ROSE!

Go, happy Rose! and, interwove
With other flowers, bind my love!
Tell her, too, she must not be
Longer flowing, longer free,
That so oft hath fettered me.

Say, if she 's fretful, I have bands
Of pearl and gold to bind her hands;
Tell her, if she struggle still,
I have myrtle rods at will,
For to tame, though not to kill.

Take then my blessing thus, and go,
And tell her this, — but do not so!
Lest a handsome anger fly,
Like a lightning from her eye,
And burn thee up, as well as I.

ROBERT HERRICK.

LOVE.

FROM "THE MERCHANT OF VENICE."

Tell me where is Fancy bred,
Or in the heart, or in the head?
How begot, how nourishèd?
Reply, reply.

It is engendered in the eyes,
With gazing fed; and Fancy dies
In the cradle where it lies.
Let us all ring Fancy's knell;
I 'll begin it, — Ding, dong, bell.
Ding, dong, bell.

SHAKESPEARE.

THE DECEIVED LOVER SUETH ONLY FOR LIBERTY.

If chance assigned
Were to my mind,
By every kind
Of destiny;
Yet would I crave
Naught else to have
But dearest life and liberty.

Then were I sure
I might endure
The displeasure
Of cruelty;
Where now I plain
Alas! in vain,
Lacking my life for liberty.

For without th' one,
Th' other is gone,
And there can none
It remedy;
If th' one be past,
Th' other doth waste,
And all for lack of liberty.

And so I drive,
As yet alive,
Although I strive
With misery;
Drawing my breath,
Looking for death,
And loss of life for liberty.

But thou that still
Mayst at thy will
Turn all this ill
Adversity;
For the repair
Of my welfare,
Grant me but life and liberty.

And if not so,
Then let all go
To wretched woe,
And let me die;
For th' one or th' other,
There is none other;
My death, or life with liberty.

SIR THOMAS WYATT.

HOPE.

My banks they are furnished with bees,
Whose murmur invites one to sleep;
My grottos are shaded with trees,
And my hills are white over with sheep;
I seldom have met with a loss,
Such health do my fountains bestow;
My fountains all bordered with moss,
Where the harebells and violets grow.

Not a pine in my grove is there seen
But with tendrils of woodbine is bound;
Not a beach 's more beautiful green,
But a sweetbrier entwines it around.
Not my fields, in the prime of the year,
More charms than my cattle unfold;
Not a brook that is limpid and clear,
But it glitters with fishes of gold.

One would think she might like to retire
To the bower I have labored to rear;
Not a shrub that I heard her admire
But I hasted and planted it there.

O how sudden the jessamine strove
With the lilac, to render it gay!
Already it calls for my love
To prune the wild branches away.

From the plains, from the woodlands, and groves,
What strains of wild melody flow:
How the nightingales warble their loves,
From thickets of roses that blow!
And when her bright form shall appear,
Each bird shall harmoniously join
For a concert so soft and so clear,
As she may not be fond to resign.

I have found out a gift for my fair;
I have found where the wood-pigeons breed:
But let me that plunder forbear, —
She will say 't was a barbarous deed.
For he ne'er could be true, she averred,
Who could rob a poor bird of his young;
And I loved her the more when I heard
Such tenderness fall from her tongue.

I have heard her with sweetness unfold
How that pity was due to a dove;
That it ever attended the bold,
And she called it the sister of Love.
But her words such a pleasure convey,
So much I her accents adore,
Let her speak, and, whatever she say,
Methinks I should love her the more.

Can a bosom so gentle remain
Unmoved when her Carydon sighs?
Will a nymph that is fond of the plain
These plains and this valley despise?
Dear regions of silence and shade!
Soft scenes of contentment and ease!
Where I could have pleasingly strayed,
If aught in her absence could please.

But where does my Phyllida stray?
And where are her grots and her bowers?
Are the groves and the valleys as gay,
And the shepherds as gentle as ours?
The groves may perhaps be as fair,
And the face of the valleys as fine;
The swains may in manners compare,
But their love is not equal to mine.

WILLIAM SHENSTONE.

MY TRUE-LOVE HATH MY HEART.

MY true-love hath my heart, and I have his,
By just exchange one to the other given:
I hold his dear, and mine he cannot miss,
There never was a better bargain driven:
My true-love hath my heart, and I have his.

His heart in me keeps him and me in one;
My heart in him his thoughts and senses guides:
He loves my heart, for once it was his own;
I cherish his because in me it bides:
My true-love hath my heart, and I have his.

SIR PHILIP SIDNEY.

I SAW TWO CLOUDS AT MORNING.

I SAW two clouds at morning,
Tinged by the rising sun,
And in the dawn they floated on,
And mingled into one;
I thought that morning cloud was blessed,
It moved so sweetly to the west.

I saw two summer currents
Flow smoothly to their meeting,
And join their course, with silent force,
In peace each other greeting;
Calm was their course through banks of green,
While dimpling eddies played between.

Such be your gentle motion,
Till life's last pulse shall beat;
Like summer's beam, and summer's stream,
Float on, in joy, to meet
A calmer sea, where storms shall cease,
A purer sky, where all is peace.

JOHN G. C. BRAINARD.

THE FRIAR OF ORDERS GRAY.

IT was a friar of orders gray
Walked forth to tell his beads;
And he met with a lady fair
Clad in a pilgrim's weeds.

"Now Christ thee save, thou reverend friar;
I pray thee tell to me,
If ever at yon holy shrine
My true-love thou didst see."

"And how should I know your true-love
From many another one?"
"O, by his cockle hat, and staff,
And by his sandal shoon.

"But chiefly by his face and mien,
That were so fair to view;
His flaxen locks that sweetly curled,
And eyes of lovely blue."

"O lady, he is dead and gone!
Lady, he 's dead and gone!
And at his head a green grass turf,
And at his heels a stone.

"Within these holy cloisters long
He languished, and he died,
Lamenting of a lady's love,
And 'plaining of her pride.

"Here bore him barefaced on his bier
Six proper youths and tall,
And many a tear bedewed his grave
Within yon kirk-yard wall."

"And art thou dead, thou gentle youth?
And art thou dead and gone?
And didst thou die for love of me?
Break, cruel heart of stone!"

"O weep not, lady, weep not so;
Some ghostly comfort seek;
Let not vain sorrow rive thy heart,
Nor tears bedew thy cheek."

"O do not, do not, holy friar,
My sorrow now reprove;
For I have lost the sweetest youth
That e'er won lady's love.

"And now, alas! for thy sad loss
I 'll evermore weep and sigh:
For thee I only wished to live,
For thee I wish to die."

"Weep no more, lady, weep no more,
Thy sorrow is in vain;
For violets plucked, the sweetest showers
Will ne'er make grow again.

"Our joys as wingèd dreams do fly;
Why then should sorrow last?
Since grief but aggravates thy loss,
Grieve not for what is past."

"O say not so, thou holy friar;
I pray thee, say not so;
For since my true-love died for me,
'T is meet my tears should flow.

"And will he never come again?
Will he ne'er come again?
Ah! no, he is dead and laid in his grave,
Forever to remain.

"His cheek was redder than the rose;
The comeliest youth was he!
But he is dead and laid in his grave:
Alas, and woe is me!"

"Sigh no more, lady, sigh no more,
Men were deceivers ever:
One foot on sea and one on land,
To one thing constant never.

"Hadst thou been fond, he had been false,
And left thee sad and heavy;
For young men ever were fickle found,
Since summer trees were leafy."

"Now say not so, thou holy friar,
I pray thee say not so;
My love he had the truest heart, —
O, he was ever true!

"And art thou dead, thou much-loved youth,
And didst thou die for me?
Then farewell home; forevermore
A pilgrim I will be.

"But first upon my true-love's grave
My weary limbs I 'll lay,
And thrice I 'll kiss the green-grass turf
That wraps his breathless clay."

"Yet stay, fair lady: rest awhile
Beneath this cloister wall;
See through the hawthorn blows the cold wind,
And drizzly rain doth fall."

"O stay me not, thou holy friar,
O stay me not, I pray;
No drizzly rain that falls on me
Can wash my fault away."

"Yet stay, fair lady, turn again,
And dry those pearly tears;
For see, beneath this gown of gray
Thy own true-love appears.

"Here forced by grief and hopeless love,
These holy weeds I sought;
And here, amid these lonely walls,
To end my days I thought.

"But haply, for my year of grace
Is not yet passed away,
Might I still hope to win thy love,
No longer would I stay."

"Now farewell grief, and welcome joy
Once more unto my heart;
For since I have found thee, lovely youth,
We nevermore will part."

Adapted by THOMAS PERCY.

ON LOVE.

THERE is no worldly pleasure here below,
Which by experience doth not folly prove;
But among all the follies that I know,
The sweetest folly in the world is love:

But not that passion which, with fools' consent,
  Above the reason bears imperious sway,
Making their lifetime a perpetual Lent,
  As if a man were born to fast and pray.
No, that is not the humor I approve,
  As either yielding pleasure or promotion ;
I like a mild and lukewarm zeal in love,
  Although I do not like it in devotion ;
For it has no coherence with my creed,
  To think that lovers die as they pretend;
If all that say they dy had dy'd indeed,
  Sure long ere now the world had had an end.
Besides, we need not love but if we please,
  No destiny can force men's disposition ;
And how can any die of that disease
  Whereof himself may be his own physician?
But some seem so distracted of their wits,
  That I would think it but a venial sin
To take some of those innocents that sits
  In Bedlam out, and put some lovers in.
Yet some men, rather than incur the slander
  Of true apostates, will false martyrs prove,
But I am neither Iphis nor Leander,
  I 'll neither drown nor hang myself for love.
Methinks a wise man's actions should be such
  As always yield to reason's best advice ;
Now for to love too little or too much
  Are both extreams, and all extreams are vice.
Yet have I been a lover by report,
  Yea I have dy'd for love, as others do;
But, praised be God, it was in such a sort,
  That I revived within an hour or two.
Thus have I lived, thus have I lov'd till now,
  And find no reason to repent me yet ;
And whosoever otherways will do,
  His courage is as little as his wit.

SIR ROBERT AYTON.

THE LADY'S LOOKING-GLASS.

Celia and I, the other day,
Walked o'er the sand-hills to the sea :
The setting sun adorned the coast,
His beams entire his fierceness lost :
And on the surface of the deep
The winds lay only not asleep :
The nymphs did, like the scene, appear
Serenely pleasant, calmly fair ;
Soft felt her words as flew the air.
With secret joy I heard her say
That she would never miss one day
A walk so fine, a sight so gay ;
But O, the change ! The winds grow high,
Impending tempests charge the sky,
The lightning flies, the thunder roars,
The big waves lash the frightened shores.
Struck with the horror of the sight,
She turns her head and wings her flight ;
And, trembling, vows she 'll ne'er again
Approach the shore or view the main.

"Once more at least look back," said I,
"Thyself in that large glass descry :
When thou art in good-humor drest,
When gentle reason rules thy breast,
The sun upon the calmest sea
Appears not half so bright as thee :
'T is then that with delight I rove
Upon the boundless depth of love :
I bless my chain, I hand my oar,
Nor think on all I left on shore.

"But when vain doubt and groundless fear
Do that dear foolish bosom tear ;
When the big lip and watery eye
Tell me the rising storm is nigh ;
'T is then thou art yon angry main
Deformed by winds and dashed by rain ;
And the poor sailor that must try
Its fury labors less than I.
Shipwrecked, in vain to land I make,
While love and fate still drive me back :
Forced to dote on thee thy own way,
I chide thee first, and then obey :
Wretched when from thee, vexed when nigh,
I with thee, or without thee, die."

MATTHEW PRIOR.

"SHALL I TELL YOU WHOM I LOVE?"

FROM "BRITANNIA'S PASTORALS."

Shall I tell you whom I love ?
  Hearken then awhile to me ;
And if such a woman move,
  As I now shall versifie,
Be assured, 't is she or none
That I love, and love alone.

Nature did her so much right
  As she scorns the helpe of art,
In as many vertues dight
  As e'er yet imbraced a heart.
So much good so truly tride,
Some for lesse were deifide.

Wit she hath without desire
  To make knowne how much she hath ;
And her anger flames no higher
  Than may fitly sweeten wrath.
Full of pitty as may be,
Though perhaps not so to me.

Reason masters every sense,
  And her vertues grace her birth :

Lovely as all excellence,
  Modest in her most of mirth :
Likelihood enough to prove,
Onely worth could kindle love.

Such she is : and if you know
  Such a one as I have sung ;
Be she brown or faire, or so
  That she be but somewhile young,
Be assured 't is she or none
That I love, and love alone.

WILLIAM BROWNE.

LOVE NOT ME FOR COMELY GRACE.

LOVE not me for comely grace,
For my pleasing eye or face,
Nor for any outward part,
No, nor for my constant heart ;
  For those may fail or turn to ill,
    So thou and I shall sever ;
Keep therefore a true woman's eye,
And love me still, but know not why.
  So hast thou the same reason still
    To dote upon me ever.

ANONYMOUS.

HE THAT LOVES A ROSY CHEEK.

HE that loves a rosy cheek,
  Or a coral lip admires,
Or from starlike eyes doth seek
  Fuel to maintain his fires ;
As old Time makes these decay,
So his flames must waste away.

But a smooth and steadfast mind,
  Gentle thoughts, and calm desires,
Hearts with equal love combined,
  Kindle never-dying fires : —
Where these are not, I despise
Lovely cheeks or lips or eyes.

THOMAS CAREW.

LOVE ME LITTLE, LOVE ME LONG.

ORIGINALLY PRINTED IN 1569.

LOVE me little, love me long !
Is the burden of my song :
Love that is too hot and strong
    Burneth soon to waste.
Still I would not have thee cold, —
Not too backward, nor too bold ;
Love that lasteth till 't is old
    Fadeth not in haste.
Love me little, love me long !
Is the burden of my song.

If thou lovest me too much,
'T will not prove as true a touch ;
Love me little more than such, —
    For I fear the end.
I 'm with little well content,
And a little from thee sent
Is enough, with true intent
    To be steadfast, friend.

Say thou lovest me, while thou live
I to thee my love will give,
Never dreaming to deceive
    While that life endures ;
Nay, and after death, in sooth,
I to thee will keep my truth,
As now when in my May of youth :
    This my love assures.

Constant love is moderate ever,
And it will through life perséver ;
Give me that with true endeavor, —
    I will it restore.
A suit of durance let it be,
For all weathers, — that for me, —
For the land or for the sea :
    Lasting evermore.

Winter's cold or summer's heat,
Autumn's tempests on it beat ;
It can never know defeat,
    Never can rebel :
Such the love that I would gain,
Such the love, I tell thee plain,
Thou must give, or woo in vain :
    So to thee — farewell !

ANONYMOUS.

I DO NOT LOVE THEE FOR THAT FAIR.

I DO not love thee for that fair
Rich fan of thy most curious hair,
Though the wires thereof be drawn
Finer than the threads of lawn,
And are softer than the leaves
On which the subtle spider weaves.

I do not love thee for those flowers
Growing on thy cheeks — love's bowers -
Though such cunning them hath spread,
None can paint them white and red.
Love's golden arrows thence are shot,
Yet for them I love thee not.

I do not love thee for those soft
Red coral lips I 've kissed so oft ;
Nor teeth of pearl, the double guard
To speech whence music still is heard,

Though from those lips a kiss being taken
Might tyrants melt, and death awaken.

I do not love thee, O my fairest,
For that richest, for that rarest
Silver pillar, which stands under
Thy sound head, that globe of wonder;
Though that neck be whiter far
Than towers of polished ivory are.

THOMAS CAREW.

A HEALTH.

I FILL this cup to one made up
  Of loveliness alone;
A woman, of her gentle sex
  The seeming paragon;
To whom the better elements
  And kindly stars have given
A form so fair that, like the air,
  'T is less of earth than heaven.

Her every tone is music's own,
  Like those of morning birds,
And something more than melody
  Dwells ever in her words;
The coinage of her heart are they,
  And from her lips each flows
As one may see the burdened bee
  Forth issue from the rose.

Affections are as thoughts to her,
  The measures of her hours;
Her feelings have the fragrancy,
  The freshness of young flowers;
And lovely passions, changing oft,
  So fill her, she appears
The image of themselves by turns, —
  The idol of past years!

Of her bright face one glance will trace
  A picture on the brain,
And of her voice in echoing hearts
  A sound must long remain;
But memory, such as mine of her,
  So very much endears,
When death is nigh my latest sigh
  Will not be life's, but hers.

I fill this cup to one made up
  Of loveliness alone,
A woman, of her gentle sex
  The seeming paragon.
Her health! and would on earth there stood
  Some more of such a frame,
That life might be all poetry,
  And weariness a name.

EDWARD COATE PINCKNEY.

FAIRER THAN THEE.

FAIRER than thee, beloved,
  Fairer than thee! —
There is one thing, beloved,
  Fairer than thee.

Not the glad sun, beloved,
  Bright though it beams;
Not the green earth, beloved,
  Silver with streams;

Not the gay birds, beloved,
  Happy and free:
Yet there 's one thing, beloved,
  Fairer than thee.

Not the clear day, beloved,
  Glowing with light;
Not (fairer still, beloved)
  Star-crownèd night.

Truth in her might, beloved,
  Grand in her sway;
Truth with her eyes, beloved,
  Clearer than day;

Holy and pure, beloved,
  Spotless and free,
Is the one thing, beloved,
  Fairer than thee.

Guard well thy soul, beloved;
  Truth, dwelling there,
Shall shadow forth, beloved,
  Her image rare.

Then shall I deem, beloved,
  That thou art she;
And there 'll be naught, beloved,
  Fairer than thee.

ANONYMOUS.

THE MAIDEN'S CHOICE.

GENTEEL in personage,
Conduct, and equipage;
Noble by heritage;
  Generous and free;

Brave, not romantic;
Learned, not pedantic;
Frolic, not frantic, —
  This must he be.

Honor maintaining,
Meanness disdaining,
Still entertaining,
  Engaging and new;

Neat, but not finical;
Sage, but not cynical;
Never tyrannical,
But ever true.

HENRY FIELDING.

THE LOVELINESS OF LOVE.

It is not Beauty I demand,
A crystal brow, the moon's despair,
Nor the snow's daughter, a white hand,
Nor mermaid's yellow pride of hair:

Tell me not of your starry eyes,
Your lips that seem on roses fed,
Your breasts, where Cupid tumbling lies,
Nor sleeps for kissing of his bed, —

A bloomy pair of vermeil cheeks,
Like Hebe's in her ruddiest hours,
A breath that softer music speaks
Than summer winds a-wooing flowers; —

These are but gauds: nay, what are lips?
Coral beneath the ocean-stream,
Whose brink when your adventurer slips
Full oft he perisheth on them.

And what are cheeks, but ensigns oft
That wave hot youth to fields of blood?
Did Helen's breast, though ne'er so soft,
Do Greece or Ilium any good?

Eyes can with baleful ardor burn;
Breath can poison that erst perfumed;
There 's many a white hand holds an urn,
With lovers' hearts to dust consumed.

For crystal brows, there 's naught within;
They are but empty cells for pride;
He who the Siren's hair would win
Is mostly strangled in the tide.

Give me, instead of Beauty's bust,
A tender heart, a loyal mind,
Which with temptation I would trust,
Yet never linked with error find, —

One in whose gentle bosom I
Could pour my secret heart of woes,
Like the care-burdened honey-fly
That hides his murmurs in the rose, —

My earthly Comforter! whose love
So indefeasible might be
That, when my spirit wonned above,
Hers could not stay, for sympathy.

ANONYMOUS.

THE LANDLADY'S DAUGHTER.

Three students were traveling over the Rhine;
They stopped when they came to the landlady's sign;
"Good landlady, have you good beer and wine?
And where is that dear little daughter of thine?"

"My beer and wine are fresh and clear;
My daughter she lies on the cold death-bier!"
And when to the chamber they made their way,
There, dead, in a coal-black shrine, she lay.

The first he drew near, and the veil gently raised,
And on her pale face he mournfully gazed.
"Ah! wert thou but living yet," he said,
"I 'd love thee from this time forth, fair maid!"

The second he slowly put back the shroud,
And turned him away and wept aloud:
"Ah! that thou liest in the cold death-bier!
Alas! I have loved thee for many a year!"

The third he once more uplifted the veil,
And kissed her upon her mouth so pale:
"Thee loved I always; I love still but thee;
And thee will I love through eternity!"

From the German of UHLAND,
by J. S. DWIGHT.

"THREE LOVES."

There were three maidens who loved a king;
They sat together beside the sea;
One cried, "I love him, and I would die,
If but for one day he might love me!"

The second whispered, "And I would die
To gladden his life, or make him great."
The third one spoke not, but gazed afar
With dreamy eyes that were sad as Fate.

The king he loved the first for a day,
The second his life with fond love blest;
And yet the woman who never spoke
Was the one of the three who loved him best.

LUCY H. HOOPER.

TO A GENTILWOMAN

THAT SAYD: ALL MEN BE FALSE, THEY THINK NOT WHAT THEY SAY.

Some women fayne that Paris was
The falsest louer that could bee:
Who for his [life] did nothing passe,
As all the world might playnly see:
But ventred life and limmes and all,
To keepe his freend from Greekish thrall:
With many a broyle hee dearely bought,
His [Hellen] whom hee long had sought.

For first [Dame Venus] granted him,
A gallant gifte of Beauties fleece :
Which boldely for to seeke to win,
By surging Seas hee sayld to Greece :
And when he was arrived theare,
By earnest sute to win his Deare
No greater paynes might man endure,
Than Paris did for Hellen sure.
Besides all this when they were well,
Both hee and shee arryu'd at Troy :
Kinge Menelaüs wrath did swell,
And swore, by sword, to rid their ioye :
And so hee did for ten yeres' space,
Hee lay before the Troyan face ;
With all the hoste that he could make,
To bee reveng'd for Hellens sake.
Loe ? thus much did poore Paris bide,
Who is accounted most untrue :
All men bee false it hath bin sayd,
They think not what they speake, (say you)
Yes Paris spoke, and sped with speede,
As all the heavenly Gods decreed
And prooud himselfe a louer iust
Till stately Troy was turned to dust.
I doo not reade of any man,
That so much was unfaythfull found.
You did us wrong, t' accuse us than,
And say our freendship is not sound :
If any fault bee found at all,
To womens lot it needes must fall :
If Hellen had not bin so light
Sir Paris had not died in fight.
The falsest men I can excuse
That euer you in stories reade :
Therefore all men for to accuse,
Methinkes it was not well decreede :
It is a signe you have not tride
What stedfastnesse in men doth bide :
But when your time shal try them true,
This judgment then you must renue.
I know not every mans devise
But commonly they stedfast are :
Though you doo make them of no price,
They breake their vowes but very rare :
They will performe theyr promis well,
And specially where loue doth dwell :
Where freendship doth not iustly frame,
Then men (forsooth) must beare the blame.

O. R.

From "A gorgious Gallery of Gallant Inuentions"
Imprinted at London, 1578.

NOT OURS THE VOWS—

Not ours the vows of such as plight
Their troth in sunny weather,
While leaves are green, and skies are bright,
To walk on flowers together.

But we have loved as those who tread
The thorny path of sorrow,
With clouds above, and cause to dread
Yet deeper gloom to-morrow.

That thorny path, those stormy skies,
Have drawn our spirits nearer ;
And rendered us, by sorrow's ties,
Each to the other dearer.

Love, born in hours of joy and mirth,
With mirth and joy may perish ;
That to which darker hours gave birth
Still more and more we cherish.

It looks beyond the clouds of time,
And through death's shadowy portal ;
Made by adversity sublime,
By faith and hope immortal.

BERNARD BARTON.

A "MERCENARY" MARRIAGE.

She moves as light across the grass
As moves my shadow large and tall ;
And like my shadow, close yet free,
The thought of her aye follows me,
My little maid of Moreton Hall.

No matter how or where we loved,
Or when we 'll wed, or what befall ;
I only feel she 's mine at last,
I only know I 'll hold her fast,
Though to dust crumbles Moreton Hall.

Her pedigree — good sooth, 't is long !
Her grim sires stare from every wall ;
And centuries of ancestral grace
Revive in her sweet girlish face,
As meek she glides through Moreton Hall.

Whilst I have — nothing ; save, perhaps,
Some worthless heaps of idle gold
And a true heart, — the which her eye
Through glittering dross spied, womanly ;
Therefore they say *her* heart was sold !

I laugh ; she laughs ; the hills and vales
Laugh as we ride 'neath chestnuts tall,
Or start the deer that silent graze,
And look up, large-eyed, with soft gaze,
At the fair maid of Moreton Hall ;

We let the neighbors talk their fill,
For life is sweet, and love is strong,
And two, close knit in marriage ties,
The whole world's shams may well despise, —
Its folly, madness, shame, and wrong.

OVER THE WATER.

" With wary step across the stream
My darling on my heart I bore.
She clasped my neck, and did not dream,
Herself a child, that I was more.

" O Death, too soon thy shadowy tide
She passed alone, who was so dear!
Tell her upon the farther side
What I would fain have told her here!"

We are not proud, with a fool's pride,
Nor cowards, — to be held in thrall
By pelf or lineage, rank or lands:
One honest heart, two honest hands,
Are worth far more than Moreton Hall.

Therefore we laugh to scorn — we two —
The bars that weaker souls appall:
I take her hand, and hold it fast,
Knowing she 'll love me to the last,
My dearest maid of Moreton Hall.

DINAH MULOCK CRAIK.

SONG.

SHALL I love you like the wind, love,
That is so fierce and strong,
That sweeps all barriers from its path
And recks not right or wrong?
The passion of the wind, love,
Can never last for long.

Shall I love you like the fire, love,
With furious heat and noise,
To waken in you all love's fears
And little of love's joys?
The passion of the fire, love,
Whate'er it finds, destroys.

I will love you like the stars, love,
Set in the heavenly blue,
That only shine the brighter
After weeping tears of dew;
Above the wind and fire, love,
They love the ages through.

And when this life is o'er, love,
With all its joys and jars,
We 'll leave behind the wind and fire
To wage their boisterous wars, —
Then we shall only be, love,
The nearer to the stars!

R. W. RAYMOND.

A WOMAN'S QUESTION.

BEFORE I trust my fate to thee,
Or place my hand in thine,
Before I let thy future give
Color and form to mine,
Before I peril all for thee,
Question thy soul to-night for me.

I break all slighter bonds, nor feel
A shadow of regret:
Is there one link within the past
That holds thy spirit yet?
Or is thy faith as clear and free
As that which I can pledge to thee?

Does there within thy dimmest dreams
A possible future shine,
Wherein thy life could henceforth breathe,
Untouched, unshared by mine?
If so, at any pain or cost,
O, tell me before all is lost!

Look deeper still: if thou canst feel,
Within thy inmost soul,
That thou hast kept a portion back,
While I have staked the whole,
Let no false pity spare the blow,
But in true mercy tell me so.

Is there within thy heart a need
That mine cannot fulfill?
One chord that any other hand
Could better wake or still?
Speak now, lest at some future day
My whole life wither and decay.

Lives there within thy nature hid
The demon-spirit, change,
Shedding a passing glory still
On all things new and strange?
It may not be thy fault alone, —
But shield my heart against thine own.

Couldst thou withdraw thy hand one day
And answer to my claim,
That fate, and that to-day's mistake, —
Not thou, — had been to blame?
Some soothe their conscience thus; but thou
Wilt surely warn and save me now.

Nay, answer *not*, — I dare not hear,
The words would come too late;
Yet I would spare thee all remorse,
So comfort thee, my fate:
Whatever on my heart may fall,
Remember, I *would* risk it all!

ADELAIDE ANNE PROCTER.

THE LADY'S "YES."

"YES," I answered you last night;
"No," this morning, sir, I say.
Colors seen by candlelight
Will not look the same by day.

When the viols played their best,
Lamps above, and laughs below,
Love me sounded like a jest,
Fit for *yes* or fit for *no*.

Call me false or call me free,
  Vow, whatever light may shine,
No man on your face shall see
  Any grief for change on mine.

Yet the sin is on us both ;
  Time to dance is not to woo ;
Wooing light makes fickle troth ;
  Scorn of *me* recoils on *you*.

Learn to win a lady's faith
  Nobly, as the thing is high,
Bravely, as for life and death,
  With a loyal gravity.

Lead her from the festive boards,
  Point her to the starry skies,
Guard her, by your truthful words,
  Pure from courtship's flatteries.

By your truth she shall be true,
  Ever true, as wives of yore ;
And her *yes*, once said to you,
  SHALL be Yes forevermore.

ELIZABETH BARRETT BROWNING.

LOVE'S SILENCE.

BECAUSE I breathe not love to everie one,
  Nor do not use set colors for to weare,
  Nor nourish special locks of vowèd haire,
Nor give each speech a full point of a groane, —
The courtlie nymphs, acquainted with the moane
  Of them who on their lips Love's standard beare,
  "What, he?" say they of me ; "now I dare sweare
He cannot love : No, no ! let him alone."
  And think so still, — if Stella know my minde.

Profess, indeed, I do not Cupid's art ;
  But you, faire maids, at length this true shall finde, —
That his right badge is but worne in the hearte.
  Dumb swans, not chattering pies, do lovers prove :
  They love indeed who quake to say they love.

SIR PHILIP SIDNEY.

THE MAID'S REMONSTRANCE.

NEVER wedding, ever wooing,
Still a love-lorn heart pursuing,
Read you not the wrong you 're doing
  In my cheek's pale hue ?
All my life with sorrow strewing,
  Wed, or cease to woo.

Rivals banished, bosoms plighted,
Still our days are disunited ;
Now the lamp of hope is lighted,
  Now half quenched appears,
Damped and wavering and benighted
  Midst my sighs and tears.

Charms you call your dearest blessing,
Lips that thrill at your caressing,
Eyes a mutual soul confessing,
  Soon you 'll make them grow
Dim, and worthless your possessing,
  Not with age, but woe !

THOMAS CAMPBELL.

GIVE ME MORE LOVE OR MORE DISDAIN.

GIVE me more love or more disdain ;
  The torrid or the frozen zone
Brings equal ease unto my pain ;
  The temperate affords me none ;
Either extreme, of love or hate,
Is sweeter than a calm estate.

Give me a storm ; if it be love,
  Like Danaë in a golden shower,
I swim in pleasure ; if it prove
  Disdain, that torrent will devour
My vulture hopes ; and he 's possessed
Of heaven that 's but from hell released ;
Then crown my joys, or cure my pain ;
Give me more love or more disdain.

THOMAS CAREW.

LOVE DISSEMBLED.

FROM "AS YOU LIKE IT."

THINK not I love him, though I ask for him ;
'T is but a peevish boy : — yet he talks well ; —
But what care I for words ? — yet words do well,
When he that speaks them pleases those that hear.
But, sure, he 's proud ; and yet his pride becomes him :
He 'll make a proper man : The best thing in him
Is his complexion ; and faster than his tongue
Did make offense, his eye did heal it up.
He is not very tall ; yet for his years he 's tall ;
His leg is but so so ; and yet 't is well :
There was a pretty redness in his lip,
A little riper and more lusty red
Than that mixed in his cheek ; 't was just the difference
Betwixt the constant red, and mingled damask.
There be some women, Silvius, had they marked him
In parcels, as I did, would have gone near
To fall in love with him : but, for my part,
I love him not, nor hate him not ; and yet

I have more cause to hate him than to love him:
For what had he to do to chide at me?
He said mine eyes were black, and my hair black;
And, now I am remembered, scorned at me:
I marvel, why I answered not again:
But that's all one; omittance is no quittance.

SHAKESPEARE.

MILLAIS'S "HUGUENOTS."

TO H., PLAYING ONE OF MENDELSSOHN'S "SONGS WITHOUT WORDS."

YOUR fav'rite picture rises up before me,
Whene'er you play that tune;
I see two figures standing in a garden,
In the still August noon.

One is a girl's, with pleading face turned upwards,
Wild with great alarm;
Trembling with haste she binds her broidered kerchief
About the other's arm,

Whose gaze is bent on her in tender pity,
Whose eyes look into hers
With a deep meaning, though she cannot read it,
Hers are so dim with tears.

What are they saying in the sunny garden,
With summer flowers ablow?
What gives the woman's voice its passionate pleading?
What makes the man's so low?

"See, love!" she murmurs; "you shall wear my kerchief,
It is the badge, I know;
And it will bear you safely through the conflict,
If — if, indeed, you go!

"You will not wear it? Will not wear my kerchief?
Nay! Do not tell me why,
I will not listen! If you go without it,
You will go hence to die.

"Hush! Do not answer! It is death, I tell you!
Indeed, I speak the truth.
You, standing there, so warm with life and vigor,
So bright with health and youth;

"You would go hence, out of the glowing sunshine,
Out of the garden's bloom,
Out of the living, thinking, feeling present,
Into the unknown gloom!"

Then he makes answer, "Hush! O, hush, my darling!
Life is so sweet to me,
So full of hope, you need not bid me guard it,
If such a thing might be!

"If such a thing might be! — but not through falsehood,
I could not come to you;
I dare not stand here in your pure, sweet presence,
Knowing myself untrue."

"It is no sin!" the wild voice interrupts him,
"This is no open strife.
Have you not often dreamt a nobler warfare,
In which to spend your life?

"Oh! for my sake — though but for my sake, wear it!
Think what my life would be
If you, who gave it first true worth and meaning,
Were taken now from me.

"Think of the long, long days, so slowly passing!
Think of the endless years!
I am so young! Must I live out my lifetime
With neither hopes nor fears?"

He speaks again, in mournful tones and tender,
But with unswerving faith:
"Should not love make us braver, ay, and stronger,
Either for life or death?

"And life is hardest! O my love! my treasure!
If I could bear your part
Of this great sorrow, I would go to meet it
With an unshrinking heart.

"Child! child! I little dreamt in that bright summer,
When first your love I sought,
Of all the future store of woe and anguish
Which I, unknowing, wrought.

"But you'll forgive me? Yes, you will forgive me,
I know, when I am dead!
I would have loved you, — but words have scant meaning;
God loved you more instead!"

Then there is silence in the sunny garden,
Until, with faltering tone,
She sobs, the while still clinging closer to him,
"Forgive me — go — my own!"

So human love, and death by faith unshaken,
Mingle their glorious psalm,
Albeit low, until the passionate pleading
Is hushed in deepest calm.

ANONYMOUS.

WILL YOU LOVE ME WHEN I'M OLD?

Will affection still infold me
When the day of life declines,
When old age with ruthless rigor
Plows my face in furrowed lines;
When the eye forgets its seeing,
And the hand forgets its skill,
And the very words prove rebel
To the mind's once kingly will;

When the deaf ear, strained to listen,
Scarcely hears the opening word,
And the unfathomed depths of feeling
Are by no swift current stirred;
When fond memory, like a limner,
Many a line perspective casts,
Spreading out our bygone pleasures
On the canvas of the Past;

When the leaping blood grows sluggish,
And the fire of youth has fled;
When the friends who now surround us
Half are numbered with the dead;
When the years appear to shorten,
Scarcely leaving us a trace;
When old Time with bold approaches
Marks his dial on my face;

When our present hopes, all gathered,
Lie like dead flowers on our track;
When the whole of our existence
Is one fearful looking back;
When each wasted hour of talent,
Hardly measured now at all,
Sends its witness back to haunt us,
Like the writing on the wall;

When the ready tongue is palsied,
And the form is bowed with care;
When our only hope is Heaven,
And our only help is prayer;
When our idols, broken round us,
Fall amid the ranks of men;
Until Death uplifts the curtain, —
Will thy love endure till then?

ANONYMOUS.

A PASTORAL.

I sat with Doris, the shepherd maiden;
Her crook was laden with wreathèd flowers;
I sat and wooed her through sunlight wheeling,
And shadows stealing, for hours and hours.

And she, my Doris, whose lap incloses
Wild summer roses of faint perfume,
The while I sued her, kept hushed, and hearkened
Till shades had darkened from gloss to gloom.

She touched my shoulder with fearful finger;
She said, "We linger, we must not stay;
My flock 's in danger, my sheep will wander;
Behold them yonder, how far they stray!"

I answered, bolder, "Nay, let me hear you,
And still be near you, and still adore!
No wolf nor stranger will touch one yearling, —
Ah! stay, my darling, a moment more!"

She whispered, sighing, "There will be sorrow
Beyond to-morrow, if I lose to-day;
My fold unguarded, my flock unfolded, —
I shall be scolded and sent away!"

Said I, replying, "If they do miss you,
They ought to kiss you when you get home;
And well rewarded by friend and neighbor
Should be the labor from which you come."

"They might remember," she answered, meekly,
"That lambs are weakly and sheep are wild;
But if they love me, it 's none so fervent —
I am a servant, and not a child."

Then each hot ember glowed quick within me,
And love did win me to swift reply:
"Ah! do but prove me, and none shall bind you,
Nor fray, nor find you, until I die!"

She blushed and started, and stood awaiting,
As if debating in dreams divine;
But I did brave them, — I told her plainly,
She doubted vainly, she must be mine.

So we, twin-hearted, from all the valley
Did rouse and rally her nibbling ewes;
And homeward drove them, we two together,
Through blooming heather and gleaming dews.

That simple duty such grace did lend her,
My Doris tender, my Doris true,
That I, her warder, did always bless her,
And often press her to take her due.

And now in beauty she fills my dwelling
With love excelling and undefiled;
And love doth guard her, both fast and fervent,
No more a servant, nor yet a child.

ARTHUR J. MUNDY.

FETCHING WATER FROM THE WELL.

Early on a sunny morning, while the lark was singing sweet,
Came, beyond the ancient farm-house, sounds of lightly tripping feet.

'T was a lowly cottage maiden going — why, let young hearts tell —
With her homely pitcher laden, fetching water from the well.
Shadows lay athwart the pathway, all along the quiet lane,
And the breezes of the morning moved them to and fro again.
O'er the sunshine, o'er the shadow, passed the maiden of the farm,
With a charmèd heart within her, thinking of no ill nor harm.
Pleasant, surely, were her musings, for the nodding leaves in vain
Sought to press their bright'ning image on her ever-busy brain.
Leaves and joyous birds went by her, like a dim, half-waking dream ;
And her soul was only conscious of life's gladdest summer gleam.
At the old lane's shady turning lay a well of water bright,
Singing, soft, its hallelujah to the gracious morning light.
Fern-leaves, broad and green, bent o'er it where its silvery droplets fell,
And the fairies dwelt beside it, in the spotted foxglove bell.
Back she bent the shading fern-leaves, dipt the pitcher in the tide, —
Drew it, with the dripping waters flowing o'er its glazèd side ;
But before her arm could place it on her shiny, wavy hair,
By her side a youth was standing ! — Love rejoiced to see the pair !
Tones of tremulous emotion trailed upon the morning breeze,
Gentle words of heart-devotion whispered 'neath the ancient trees ;
But the holy, blessed secrets it becomes me not to tell :
Life had met another meaning, fetching water from the well !
Down the rural lane they sauntered. He the burden-pitcher bore ;
She, with dewy eyes down-looking, grew more beauteous than before !
When they neared the silent homestead, up he raised the pitcher light ;
Like a fitting crown he placed it on her hair of wavelets bright :
Emblems of the coming burdens that for love of him she 'd bear,
Calling every burden blessed, if his love but lighted there.
Then, still waving benedictions, farther, farther off he drew,
While his shadow seemed a glory that across the pathway grew.
Now about her household duties silently the maiden went,
And an ever-radiant halo o'er her daily life was blent.
Little knew the aged matron as her feet like music fell,
What abundant treasure found she, fetching water from the well !

ANONYMOUS.

OTHELLO'S DEFENSE.

OTHELLO. I 'll present
How I did thrive in this fair lady's love,
And she in mine.
Her father loved me ; oft invited me ;
Still questioned me the story of my life,
From year to year ; — the battles, sieges, fortunes,
That I have passed.
I ran it through, even from my boyish days,
To the very moment that he bade me tell it :
Wherein I spake of most disastrous chances,
Of moving accidents by flood and field ;
Of hair-breadth 'scapes i' the imminent deadly breach ;
Of being taken by the insolent foe,
And sold to slavery ; of my redemption thence,
And portance in my travel's history :
Wherein of antres vast, and deserts idle,
Rough quarries, rocks, and hills whose heads touch heaven,
It was my hint to speak, — such was the process ;
And of the Cannibals that each other eat,
The Anthropophagi, and men whose heads
Do grow beneath their shoulders. This to hear,
Would Desdemona seriously incline :
But still the house affairs would draw her thence ;
Which ever as she could with haste dispatch,
She 'd come again, and with a greedy ear
Devour up my discourse. Which I observing,
Took once a pliant hour ; and found good means
To draw from her a prayer of earnest heart,
That I would all my pilgrimage dilate,
Whereof by parcels she had something heard,
But not intentively : I did consent ;
And often did beguile her of her tears,
When I did speak of some distressful stroke
That my youth suffered. My story being done,
She gave me for my pains a world of sighs :
She swore, — in faith 't was strange, 't was passing strange ;
'T was pitiful, 't was wondrous pitiful :
She wished she had not heard it, yet she wished
That Heaven had made her such a man : she thanked me ;

And bade me, if I had a friend that loved her,
I should teach him how to tell my story,
And that would woo her. Upon this hint, I spake:
She loved me for the dangers I had passed;
And I loved her that she did pity them.
This only is the witchcraft I have used:
Here comes the lady, let her witness it.

SHAKESPEARE.

FOLLOW A SHADOW, IT STILL FLIES YOU.

Follow a shadow, it still flies you;
Seem to fly it, it will pursue:
So court a mistress, she denies you;
Let her alone, she will court you.
Say, are not women truly, then,
Styled but the shadows of us men?

At morn and even, shades are longest;
At noon they are or short or none:
So men at weakest they are strongest,
But grant us perfect, they 're not known.
Say, are not women truly, then,
Styled but the shadows of us men?

BEN JONSON.

THE PURITAN LOVERS.

Drawn out, like lingering bees, to share
The last, sweet summer weather,
Beneath the reddening maples walked
Two Puritans together, —

A youth and maiden, heeding not
The woods which round them brightened,
Just conscious of each other's thoughts,
Half happy and half frightened.

Grave were their brows, and few their words,
And coarse their garb and simple;
The maiden's very cheek seemed shy
To own its worldly dimple.

For stern the time; they dwelt with Care,
And Fear was oft a comer;
A sober April ushered in
The Pilgrim's toilful summer.

And stern their creed; they tarried here
Mere desert-land sojourners:
They must not dream of mirth or rest,
God's humble lesson-learners.

The temple's sacred perfume round
Their week-day robes was clinging;
Their mirth was but the golden bells
On priestly garments ringing.

But as to-day they softly talked,
That serious youth and maiden,
Their plainest words strange beauty wore,
Like weeds with dewdrops laden.

The saddest theme had something sweet,
The gravest, something tender,
While with slow steps they wandered on,
Mid summer's fading splendor.

He said, "Next week the church will hold
A day of prayer and fasting";
And then he stopped, and bent to pick
A white life-everlasting, —

A silvery bloom, with fadeless leaves;
He gave it to her, sighing;
A mute confession was his glance,
Her blush, a mute replying.

"Mehetabel!" (at last he spoke,)
"My fairest one and dearest!
One thought is ever to my heart
The sweetest and the nearest.

"You read my soul; you know my wish;
O, grant me its fulfilling!"
She answered low, "If Heaven smiles,
And if my father 's willing!"

No idle passion swayed her heart,
This quaint New England beauty!
Faith was the guardian of her life, —
Obedience was a duty.

Too truthful for reserve, she stood,
Her brown eyes earthward casting,
And held with trembling hand the while
Her white life-everlasting.

Her sober answer pleased the youth, —
Frank, clear, and gravely cheerful;
He left her at her father's door,
Too happy to be fearful.

She looked on high, with earnest plea,
And Heaven seemed bright above her;
And when she shyly spoke his name,
Her father praised her lover.

And when, that night, she sought her couch,
With head-board high and olden,
Her prayer was praise, her pillow down,
And all her dreams were golden.

And still upon her throbbing heart,
In bloom and breath undying,
A few life-everlasting flowers,
Her lover's gift, were lying.

O Venus' myrtles, fresh and green!
  O Cupid's blushing roses!
Not on your classic flowers alone
  The sacred light reposes;

Though gentler care may shield your buds
  From north-winds rude and blasting,
As dear to Love, those few, pale flowers
  Of white life-everlasting.

ANNIE D. GREEN (MARIAN DOUGLAS).

WERE I AS BASE AS IS THE LOWLY PLAIN.

WERE I as base as is the lowly plain,
And you, my love, as high as heaven above,
Yet should the thoughts of me your humble swain
Ascend to heaven, in honor of my love.

Were I as high as heaven above the plain,
And you, my love, as humble and as low
As are the deepest bottoms of the main,
Whereso'er you were, with you my love should
  go.

Were you the earth, dear love, and I the skies,
My love should shine on you like to the sun,
And look upon you with ten thousand eyes
Till heaven waxed blind, and till the world were
  done.

Whereso'er I am, below, or else above you,
Whereso'er you are, my heart shall truly love you.

JOSHUA SYLVESTER.

AH, HOW SWEET!

AH, how sweet it is to love!
  Ah, how gay is young desire!
And what pleasing pains we prove
  When we first approach love's fire!
Pains of love are sweeter far
Than all other pleasures are.

Sighs which are from lovers blown
  Do but gently heave the heart:
E'en the tears they shed alone
  Cure, like trickling balm, their smart.
Lovers, when they lose their breath,
Bleed away in easy death.

Love and Time with reverence use,
  Treat them like a parting friend;
Nor the golden gifts refuse
  Which in youth sincere they send;
For each year their price is more,
And they less simple than before.

Love, like spring-tides full and high,
  Swells in every youthful vein;
But each tide does less supply,
  Till they quite shrink in again.
If a flow in age appear,
'T is but rain, and runs not clear.

JOHN DRYDEN.

THE FIRE OF LOVE.

FROM THE "EXAMEN MISCELLANEUM," 1708.

THE fire of love in youthful blood,
Like what is kindled in brushwood,
    But for a moment burns;
Yet in that moment makes a mighty noise;
It crackles, and to vapor turns,
    And soon itself destroys.

But when crept into aged veins,
It slowly burns, then long remains,
    And with a silent heat,
Like fire in logs, it glows and warms 'em long;
And though the flame be not so great,
    Yet is the heat as strong.

EARL OF DORSET.

CHILD AND MAIDEN.

AH, Chloris! could I now but sit
  As unconcerned as when
Your infant beauty could beget
  No happiness or pain!
When I the dawn used to admire,
  And praised the coming day,
I little thought the rising fire
  Would take my rest away.

Your charms in harmless childhood lay
  Like metals in a mine;
Age from no face takes more away
  Than youth concealed in thine.
But as your charms insensibly
  To their perfection prest,
So love as unperceived did fly,
  And centered in my breast.

My passion with your beauty grew,
  While Cupid at my heart
Still, as his mother favored you,
  Threw a new flaming dart.
Each gloried in their wanton part:
  To make a lover, he
Employed the utmost of his art;
  To make a beauty, she.

SIR CHARLES SEDLEY.

ON A GIRDLE.

THAT which her slender waist confined
Shall now my joyful temples bind;
No monarch but would give his crown,
His arms might do what this hath done.

It was my heaven's extremest sphere,
The pale which held that lovely deer:
My joy, my grief, my hope, my love,
Did all within this circle move.

A narrow compass! and yet there
Dwelt all that 's good, and all that 's fair.
Give me but what this ribbon bound,
Take all the rest the sun goes round!

EDMUND WALLER.

WHY, LOVELY CHARMER?

FROM "THE HIVE."

WHY, lovely charmer, tell me why
So very kind, and yet so shy?
Why does that cold, forbidding air
Give damps of sorrow and despair?
Or why that smile my soul subdue,
And kindle up my flames anew?

In vain you strive with all your art,
By turns to fire and freeze my heart;
When I behold a face so fair,
So sweet a look, so soft an air,
My ravished soul is charmed all o'er,
I cannot love thee less or more.

ANONYMOUS.

I PRITHEE SEND ME BACK MY HEART.

I PRITHEE send me back my heart,
Since I cannot have thine;
For if from yours you will not part,
Why then shouldst thou have mine?

Yet, now I think on 't, let it lie;
To find it were in vain;
For thou 'st a thief in either eye
Would steal it back again.

Why should two hearts in one breast lie,
And yet not lodge together?
O Love! where is thy sympathy
If thus our breasts thou sever?

But love is such a mystery,
I cannot find it out;
For when I think I 'm best resolved
Then I am most in doubt.

Then farewell care, and farewell woe;
I will no longer pine;
For I 'll believe I have her heart
As much as she has mine.

SIR JOHN SUCKLING.

IF DOUGHTY DEEDS MY LADY PLEASE.

IF doughty deeds my lady please,
Right soon I 'll mount my steed,
And strong his arm and fast his seat
That bears frae me the meed.
I 'll wear thy colors in my cap,
Thy picture at my heart,
And he that bends not to thine eye
Shall rue it to his smart!
Then tell me how to woo thee, Love;
O, tell me how to woo thee!
For thy dear sake nae care I 'll take,
Though ne'er another trow me.

If gay attire delight thine eye,
I 'll dight me in array;
I 'll tend thy chamber door all night,
And squire thee all the day.
If sweetest sounds can win thine ear,
These sounds I 'll strive to catch;
Thy voice I 'll steal to woo thysell,
That voice that nane can match.

But if fond love thy heart can gain,
I never broke a vow;
Nae maiden lays her skaith to me;
I never loved but you.
For you alone I ride the ring,
For you I wear the blue;
For you alone I strive to sing,
O, tell me how to woo!
Then tell me how to woo thee, Love;
O, tell me how to woo thee!
For thy dear sake nae care I 'll take,
Though ne'er another trow me.

GRAHAM OF GARTMORE.

TO ALTHEA FROM PRISON.

WHEN Love with unconfinèd wings
Hovers within my gates,
And my divine Althea brings
To whisper at the grates;
When I lie tangled in her hair
And fettered to her eye,
The birds that wanton in the air
Know no such liberty.

When flowing cups run swiftly round
With no allaying Thames,

Our careless heads with roses crowned,
Our hearts with loyal flames ;
When thirsty grief in wine we steep,
When healths and draughts go free,
Fishes that tipple in the deep
Know no such liberty.

When, linnet-like confinèd, I
With shriller throat shall sing
The sweetness, mercy, majesty
And glories of my King ;
When I shall voice aloud how good
He is, how great should be,
Enlargèd winds, that curl the flood,
Know no such liberty.

Stone walls do not a prison make,
Nor iron bars a cage ;
Minds innocent and quiet take
That for an hermitage :
If I have freedom in my love,
And in my soul am free,
Angels alone, that soar above,
Enjoy such liberty.

RICHARD LOVELACE.

WELCOME, WELCOME DO I SING.

Welcome, welcome, do I sing,
Far more welcome than the spring;
He that parteth from you never
Shall enjoy a spring forever.

Love, that to the voice is near,
Breaking from your ivory pale,
Need not walk abroad to hear
The delightful nightingale.
Welcome, welcome, then I sing, etc.

Love, that still looks on your eyes,
Though the winter have begun
To benumb our arteries,
Shall not want the summer's sun.
Welcome, welcome, then I sing, etc.

Love, that still may see your cheeks,
Where all rareness still reposes,
Is a fool if e'er he seeks
Other lilies, other roses.
Welcome, welcome, then I sing, etc.

Love, to whom your soft lip yields,
And perceives your breath in kissing,
All the odors of the fields
Never, never shall be missing.

WILLIAM BROWNE.

RIVALRY IN LOVE.

Of all the torments, all the cares,
With which our lives are curst ;
Of all the plagues a lover bears,
Sure rivals are the worst !
By partners in each other kind,
Afflictions easier grow ;
In love alone we hate to find
Companions of our woe.

Sylvia, for all the pangs you see
Are lab'ring in my breast,
I beg not you would favor me,
Would you but slight the rest !
How great soe'er your rigors are,
With them alone I 'll cope ;
I can endure my own despair,
But not another's hope.

WILLIAM WALSH.

VERSES WRITTEN IN AN ALBUM.

Here is one leaf reserved for me,
From all thy sweet memorials free ;
And here my simple song might tell
The feelings thou must guess so well.
But could I thus, within thy mind,
One little vacant corner find,
Where no impression yet is seen,
Where no memorial yet has been,
O, it should be my sweetest care
To write my name forever there !

THOMAS MOORE.

HER LIKENESS.

A girl who has so many willful ways
She would have caused Job's patience to forsake him,
Yet is so rich in all that 's girlhood's praise,
Did Job himself upon her goodness gaze,
A little better she would surely make him.

Yet is this girl I sing in naught uncommon,
And very far from angel yet, I trow.
Her faults, her sweetnesses, are purely human ;
Yet she 's more lovable as simple woman
Than any one diviner that I know.

Therefore I wish that she may safely keep
This womanhede, and change not, only grow ;
From maid to matron, youth to age, may creep,
And in perennial blessedness still reap,
On every hand, of that which she doth sow.

DINAH MULOCK CRAIK.

A SLEEPING BEAUTY.

Sleep on! and dream of Heaven awhile!
Though shut so close thy laughing eyes,
Thy rosy lips still wear a smile,
And move, and breathe delicious sighs.

Ah! now soft blushes tinge her cheeks
And mantle o'er her neck of snow;
Ah! now she murmurs, now she speaks,
What most I wish, and fear, to know.

She starts, she trembles, and she weeps!
Her fair hands folded on her breast; —
And now, how like a saint she sleeps!
A seraph in the realms of rest!

Sleep on secure! Above control,
Thy thoughts belong to Heaven and thee;
And may the secret of thy soul
Remain within its sanctuary!

SAMUEL ROGERS.

SHE IS NOT FAIR TO OUTWARD VIEW.

She is not fair to outward view,
As many maidens be;
Her loveliness I never knew
Until she smiled on me:
O, then I saw her eye was bright, —
A well of love, a spring of light.

But now her looks are coy and cold;
To mine they ne'er reply;
And yet I cease not to behold
The love-light in her eye:
Her very frowns are better far
Than smiles of other maidens are!

HARTLEY COLERIDGE.

THE FLOWER'S NAME.

Here 's the garden she walked across,
Arm in my arm, such a short while since:
Hark! now I push its wicket, the moss
Hinders the hinges, and makes them wince.
She must have reached this shrub ere she turned,
As back with that murmur the wicket swung;
For she laid the poor snail my chance foot spurned,
To feed and forget it the leaves among.

Down this side of the gravel-walk
She went while her robe's edge brushed the box;
And here she paused in her gracious talk
To point me a moth on the milk-white phlox.
Roses, ranged in valiant row,
I will never think that she passed you by!
She loves you, noble roses, I know;
But yonder see where the rock-plants lie!

This flower she stopped at, finger on lip, —
Stooped over, in doubt, as settling its claim;
Till she gave me, with pride to make no slip,
Its soft meandering Spanish name.
What a name! was it love or praise?
Speech half asleep, or song half awake?
I must learn Spanish one of these days,
Only for that slow sweet name's sake.

Roses, if I live and do well,
I may bring her one of these days,
To fix you fast with as fine a spell, —
Fit you each with his Spanish phrase.
But do not detain me now, for she lingers
There, like sunshine over the ground;
And ever I see her soft white fingers
Searching after the bud she found.

Flower, you Spaniard! look that you grow not, —
Stay as you are, and be loved forever!
Bud, if I kiss you, 't is that you blow not, —
Mind! the shut pink mouth opens never!
For while thus it pouts, her fingers wrestle,
Twinkling the audacious leaves between,
Till round they turn, and down they nestle:
Is not the dear mark still to be seen?

Where I find her not, beauties vanish;
Whither I follow her, beauties flee.
Is there no method to tell her in Spanish
June 's twice June since she breathed it with me?
Come, bud! show me the least of her traces.
Treasure my lady's lightest footfall:
Ah! you may flout and turn up your faces, —
Roses, you are not so fair after all!

ROBERT BROWNING.

WHY?

Why came the rose? Because the sun in shining,
Found in the mould some atoms rare and fine:
And stooping, drew and warmed them into growing, —
Dust, with the spirit's mystic countersign.

What made the perfume? All his wondrous kisses
Fell on the sweet red mouth, till, lost to sight,
The love became too exquisite, and vanished
Into a viewless rapture of the night.

Why did the rose die? Ah, why ask the question?
There is a time to love, — a time to give;
She perished gladly, folding close the secret
Wherein is garnered what it is to live.

MARY LOUISE RITTER.

CORINNA'S GOING A-MAYING.

Get up, get up! for shame! the blooming morn
Upon her wings presents the god unshorn.
See how Aurora throws her fair
Fresh-quilted colors through the air;
Get up, sweet slugabed, and see
The dew bespangling herb and tree.
Each flower has wept, and bowed toward the east,
Above an hour since, yet you are not drest, —
Nay, not so much as out of bed,
When all the birds have matins said,
And sung their thankful hymns: 't is sin,
Nay, profanation, to keep in,
Whenas a thousand virgins on this day
Spring, sooner than the lark, to fetch in May.

Rise, and put on your foliage, and be seen
To come forth, like the spring-time, fresh and green,
And sweet as Flora. Take no care
For jewels for your gown or hair;
Fear not, the leaves will strew
Gems in abundance upon you;
Besides, the childhood of the day has kept,
Against you come, some Orient pearls unwept.
Come, and receive them while the light
Hangs on the dew-locks of the night;
And Titan on the eastern hill
Retires himself, or else stands still
Till you come forth. Wash, dress, be brief in praying:
Few beads are best, when once we go a-Maying.

Come, my Corinna, come! and, coming, mark
How each field turns a street, each street a park,
Made green and trimmed with trees; see how
Devotion gives each house a bough
Or branch; each porch, each door, ere this
An ark, a tabernacle is,
Made up of white thorn neatly interwove,
As if here were those cooler shades of love.
Can such delights be in the street
And open fields, and we not see 't?
Come, we 'll abroad, and let 's obey
The proclamation made for May,
And sin no more, as we have done, by staying;
But, my Corinna, come, let 's go a-Maying.

There 's not a budding boy or girl this day
But is got up and gone to bring in May.
A deal of youth, ere this, is come
Back, and with white thorn laden, home;
Some have dispatched their cakes and cream
Before that we have left to dream;
And some have wept, and wooed, and plighted troth,
And chose their priest, ere we can cast off sloth;
Many a green gown has been given;
Many a kiss, both odd and even;
Many a glance, too, has been sent
From out the eye, love's firmament;
Many a jest told of the keys' betraying
This night, and locks picked, yet we 're not a-Maying.

Come, let us go, while we are in our prime,
And take the harmless folly of the time.
We shall grow old apace, and die,
Before we know our liberty.
Our life is short, and our days run
As fast away as does the sun;
And as a vapor, or a drop of rain,
Once lost, can ne'er be found again,
So when or you or I are made
A fable, song, or fleeting shade,
All love, all liking, all delight,
Lies drowned with us in endless night.
Then, while time serves, and we are but decaying,
Come, my Corinna, come, let 's go a-Maying.

Robert Herrick.

A MATCH.

If love were what the rose is,
And I were like the leaf,
Our lives would grow together
In sad or singing weather,
Blown fields or flowerful closes,
Green pleasure or gray grief;
If love were what the rose is,
And I were like the leaf.

If I were what the words are,
And love were like the tune,
With double sound and single
Delight our lips would mingle,
With kisses glad as birds are
That get sweet rain at noon;
If I were what the words are,
And love were like the tune.

If you were life, my darling,
And I, your love, were death,
We 'd shine and snow together
Ere March made sweet the weather
With daffodil and starling
And hours of fruitful breath;
If you were life, my darling,
And I, your love, were death.

If you were thrall to sorrow,
And I were page to joy,
We 'd play for lives and seasons,
With loving looks and treasons,

And tears of night and morrow,
  And laughs of maid and boy;
If you were thrall to sorrow,
  And I were page to joy.

If you were April's lady,
  And I were lord in May,
We 'd throw with leaves for hours,
And draw for days with flowers,
Till day like night were shady,
  And night were bright like day;
If you were April's lady,
  And I were lord in May.

If you were queen of pleasure,
  And I were king of pain,
We 'd hunt down love together,
Pluck out his flying-feather,
And teach his feet a measure,
  And find his mouth a rein;
If you were queen of pleasure,
  And I were king of pain.

ALGERNON CHARLES SWINBURNE.

THE FLOWER O' DUMBLANE.

THE sun has gane down o'er the lofty Ben Lomond,
  And left the red clouds to preside o'er the scene,
While lanely I stray in the calm summer gloamin',
  To muse on sweet Jessie, the Flower o' Dumblane.

How sweet is the brier, wi' its saft fauldin' blossom,
  And sweet is the birk, wi' its mantle o' green;
Yet sweeter and fairer, and dear to this bosom,
  Is lovely young Jessie, the Flower o' Dumblane.

She 's modest as ony, and blithe as she 's bonnie,—
  For guileless simplicity marks her its ain;
And far be the villain, divested of feeling,
  Wha 'd blight in its bloom the sweet Flower o' Dumblane.

Sing on, thou sweet mavis, thy hymn to the e'ening!—
  Thou 'rt dear to the echoes of Calderwood glen:
Sae dear to this bosom, sae artless and winning,
  Is charming young Jessie, the Flower o' Dumblane.

How lost were my days till I met wi' my Jessie!
  The sports o' the city seemed foolish and vain;
I ne'er saw a nymph I would ca' my dear lassie
  Till charmed wi' sweet Jessie, the Flower o' Dumblane.

Though mine were the station o' loftiest grandeur,
  Amidst its profusion I 'd languish in pain,
And reckon as naething the height o' its splendor,
  If wanting sweet Jessie, the Flower o' Dumblane.

ROBERT TANNAHILL.

THE LASS OF RICHMOND HILL.

ON Richmond Hill there lives a lass
    More bright than May-day morn,
Whose charms all other maids surpass,—
    A rose without a thorn.

This lass so neat, with smiles so sweet,
    Has won my right good-will;
I 'd crowns resign to call her mine,
    Sweet lass of Richmond Hill.

Ye zephyrs gay that fan the air,
    And wanton through the grove,
O, whisper to my charming fair,
    I die for her I love.

How happy will the shepherd be
    Who calls this nymph his own!
O, may her choice be fixed on me!
    Mine 's fixed on her alone.

JAMES UPTON.

MARY MORISON.

O MARY, at thy window be!
  It is the wished, the trysted hour!
Those smiles and glances let me see
  That make the miser's treasure poor:
How blithely wad I bide the stoure,
  A weary slave frae sun to sun,
Could I the rich reward secure,
  The lovely Mary Morison.

Yestreen, when to the trembling string
  The dance gaed through the lighted ha',
To thee my fancy took its wing,—
  I sat, but neither heard nor saw:
Though this was fair, and that was braw,
  And yon the toast of a' the town,
I sighed, and said amang them a',
  "Ye are na Mary Morison."

O Mary, canst thou wreck his peace
  Wha for thy sake wad gladly dee?
Or canst thou break that heart of his,
  Whase only faut is loving thee?
If love for love thou wilt na gie,
  At least be pity to me shown;
A thought ungentle canna be
  The thought o' Mary Morison.

ROBERT BURNS.

THE POSIE.

O, LUVE will venture in where it daurna weel be
seen,
O, luve will venture in where wisdom ance has been!
But I will down yon river rove amang the woods
sae green:
And a' to pu' a posie to my ain dear May.

The primrose I will pu', the firstling o' the year,
And I will pu' the pink, the emblem o' my dear,
For she 's the pink o' womankind, and blooms
without a peer:
And a' to be a posie to my ain dear May.

I 'll pu' the budding rose, when Phœbus peeps
in view,
For it's like a balmy kiss o' her sweet bonnie mou';
The hyacinth 's for constancy, wi' its unchanging
blue:
And a' to be a posie to my ain dear May.

The lily it is pure, and the lily it is fair,
And in her lovely bosom I 'll place the lily there;
The daisy 's for simplicity and unaffected air:
And a' to be a posie to my ain dear May.

The hawthorn I will pu', wi' its locks o' siller gray,
Where, like an aged man, it stands at break o' day;
But the songster's nest within the bush I winna
take away:
And a' to be a posie to my ain dear May.

The woodbine I will pu', when the e'ening star
is near,
And the diamond draps o' dew shall be her een
sae clear;
The violet 's for modesty, which weel she fa's to
wear:
And a' to be a posie to my ain dear May.

I 'll tie the posie round wi' the silken band o' luve,
And I 'll place it in her breast, and I 'll swear by
a' above
That to my latest draught o' life the band shall
ne'er remove:
And this will be a posie to my ain dear May.

ROBERT BURNS.

MARY LEE.

I HAVE traced the valleys fair
In May morning's dewy air,
My bonny Mary Lee!
Wilt thou deign the wreath to wear,
Gathered all for thee?

They are not flowers of Pride,
For they graced the dingle-side;
Yet they grew in Heaven's smile,
My gentle Mary Lee!
Can they fear thy frowns the while
Though offerèd by me?

Here 's the lily of the vale,
That perfumed the morning gale,
My fairy Mary Lee!
All so spotless and so pale,
Like thine own purity.
And might I make it known,
'T is an emblem of my own
Love, — if I dare so name
My esteem for thee.
Surely flowers can bear no blame,
My bonny Mary Lee.

Here 's the violet's modest blue,
That 'neath hawthorns hides from view,
My gentle Mary Lee,
Would show whose heart is true,
While it thinks of thee.
While they choose each lowly spot,
The sun disdains them not;
I 'm as lowly too, indeed,
My charming Mary Lee;
So I 've brought the flowers to plead,
And win a smile from thee.

Here 's a wild rose just in bud;
Spring's beauty in its hood,
My bonny Mary Lee!
'T is the first in all the wood
I could find for thee.
Though a blush is scarcely seen,
Yet it hides its worth within,
Like my love; for I 've no power,
My angel Mary Lee,
To speak unless the flower
Can make excuse for me.

Though they deck no princely halls,
In bouquets for glittering balls,
My gentle Mary Lee,
Richer hues than painted walls
Will make them dear to thee;
For the blue and laughing sky
Spreads a grander canopy
Than all wealth's golden skill,
My charming Mary Lee!
Love would make them dearer still,
That offers them to thee.

My wreathèd flowers are few,
Yet no fairer drink the dew,
My bonny Mary Lee!

They may seem as trifles too, —
Not, I hope, to thee;
Some may boast a richer prize
Under pride and wealth's disguise;
None a fonder offering bore
Than this of mine to thee;
And can true love wish for more?
Surely not, Mary Lee!

JOHN CLARE.

THE BROOKSIDE.

I WANDERED by the brookside,
I wandered by the mill;
I could not hear the brook flow, —
The noisy wheel was still;
There was no burr of grasshopper,
No chirp of any bird,
But the beating of my own heart
Was all the sound I heard.

I sat beneath the elm-tree;
I watched the long, long shade,
And, as it grew still longer,
I did not feel afraid;
For I listened for a footfall,
I listened for a word, —
But the beating of my own heart
Was all the sound I heard.

He came not, — no, he came not, —
The night came on alone, —
The little stars sat one by one,
Each on his golden throne;
The evening wind passed by my cheek,
The leaves above were stirred, —
But the beating of my own heart
Was all the sound I heard.

Fast silent tears were flowing,
When something stood behind;
A hand was on my shoulder, —
I knew its touch was kind:
It drew me nearer, — nearer, —
We did not speak one word,
For the beating of our own hearts
Was all the sound we heard.

RICHARD MONCKTON MILNES.
(LORD HOUGHTON.)

ECHOES.

How sweet the answer Echo makes
To Music at night
When, roused by lute or horn, she wakes,
And far away o'er lawns and lakes
Goes answering light!

Yet Love hath echoes truer far
And far more sweet
Than e'er, beneath the moonlight's star,
Of horn or lute or soft guitar
The songs repeat.

'T is when the sigh — in youth sincere
And only then,
The sigh that 's breathed for one to hear —
Is by that one, that only Dear
Breathed back again.

THOMAS MOORE.

MY DEAR AND ONLY LOVE.

(AN EXCELLENT NEW BALLAD TO THE TUNE OF "I 'LL NEVER LOVE THEE MORE.")

THE FIRST PART.

MY dear and only love, I pray,
That little world, — of THEE, —
Be governed by no other sway
Than purest Monarchie.
For if confusion have a part,
Which virtuous souls abhore,
And have a Synod in thine heart,
I 'll never love thee more.

As Alexander I will reign,
And I will reign alone;
My thoughts shall evermore disdain
A rival on my throne:
He either fears his fate too much,
Or his deserts are small
That puts it not unto the touch,
To win or lose it all.

But I will reign, and govern still,
And always give the law,
And have *each subject at my will*,
And all to stand in awe;
But 'gainst my batteries if I find
Thou kick or vex me sore,
As that thou set me up a blind,
I 'll never love thee more.

And in the Empire of thine heart,
Where I should solely be,
If others do pretend a part,
Or dare to vie with me,
Or if *Committees* thou erect,
And go on such a score,
I 'll laugh and sing at thy neglect,
And never love thee more.

But if thou wilt prove faithful then,
And constant of thy word,
I 'll make thee glorious by my pen
And famous by my sword;

I 'll serve thee in such noble ways
  Was never heard before,
I 'll crown and deck thee all with bays,
  And love thee more and more.

THE SECOND PART.

My dear and only love, take heed
  How thou thyself dispose;
Let not all longing lovers feed
  Upon such looks as those;
I 'll marble wall thee round about,
  Myself shall be the door,
And if thy heart chance to slide out,
  I 'll never love thee more.

Let not their oaths, like volleys shot,
  Make any breach at all,
Nor smoothness of their language plot
  Which way to scale the wall;
Nor balls of wildfire love consume
  The shrine which I adore,
For if such smoke about thee fume,
  I 'll never love thee more.

I know thy virtues be too strong
  To suffer by surprise;
If that thou slight their love too long,
  Their siege at last will rise,
And leave thee conqueror, in that health
  And state thou wast before;
But if thou turn a Commonwealth,
  I 'll never love thee more.

And if by fraud, or by consent,
  Thy heart to ruin come,
I 'll sound no trumpet as I wont,
  Nor march by tuck of drum,
But hold my arms, like Achaüs, up,
  Thy falsehood to deplore,
And bitterly will sigh and weep,
  And never love thee more.

I 'll do with thee as Nero did
  When he set Rome on fire;
Not only all relief forbid,
  But to a hill retire,
And scorn to shed a tear to save
  Thy spirit grown so poor,
But laugh and smile thee to thy grave,
  And never love thee more.

Then shall thy heart be set by mine,
  But in far different case,
For mine was true; so was not thine,
  But looked like Janus' face;

For as the waves with every wind,
  So sails thou every shore
And leaves my constant heart behind, —
  How can I love thee more?

My heart shall with the sun be fix'd,
  For constancy most strange;
And there shall with the moon be mix'd,
  Delighting aye in change;
Thy beauty shined at first so bright!
  And woe is me therefore,
That ever I found thy love so light
  That I could love no more.

Yet for the love I bare thee once,
  Lest that thy name should die,
A monument of marble stone
  The truth shall testify;
That every pilgrim passing by,
  May pity and deplore,
And, sighing, read the reason why
  I cannot love thee more.

The golden laws of love shall be
  Upon these pillars hung;
A single heart; a simple eye;
  A true and constant tongue;
Let no man for more love pretend
  Than he has hearts in store;
True love begun will never end;
  Love one and love no more.

And when all gallants ride about
  These monuments to view,
Whereon is written, in and out,
  Thou traitorous and untrue;
Then, in a passion, they shall pause,
  And thus say, sighing sore,
Alas! he had too just a cause
  Never to love thee more.

And when that tracing goddess Fame
  From east to west shall flee,
She shall record it to thy shame
  How thou hast lovèd me;
And how in odds our love was such
  As few have been before;
Thou lovedst too many, and I too much;
  So I can love no more.

The misty mount, the smoking lake,
  The rock's resounding echo,
The whistling winds, the woods that shake,
  Shall all, with me, sing hey ho!
The tossing seas, the tumbling boats,
  Tears dropping from each oar,
Shall *tune* with me their *turtle notes*, —
  I 'll never love thee more.

As doth the turtle, chaste and true,
  Her fellow's death regret,
And daily mourns for her adieu,
  And ne'er renews her mate;
So, though my faith was ever fast,
  Which grieves me wondrous sore,
Yet I shall live in love so chaste
  That I shall love no more.

JAMES GRAHAM, MARQUIS OF MONTROSE.

ROSALINE.

LIKE to the clear in highest sphere,
Where all imperial glory shines,
Of selfsame color is her hair,
Whether unfolded, or in twines:
  Heigh-ho, fair Rosaline!
Her eyes are sapphires set in snow,
Resembling heaven by every wink;
The gods do fear whenas they glow,
And I do tremble when I think
  Heigh-ho, would she were mine!

Her cheeks are like the blushing cloud
That beautifies Aurora's face,
Or like the silver crimson shroud
That Phœbus' smiling looks doth grace:
  Heigh-ho, fair Rosaline!
Her lips are like two budded roses
Whom ranks of lilies neighbor nigh,
Within which bounds she balm encloses
Apt to entice a deity:
  Heigh-ho, would she were mine!

Her neck is like a stately tower
Where Love himself imprisoned lies,
To watch for glances every hour
From her divine and sacred eyes;
  Heigh-ho, fair Rosaline!
Her paps are centres of delight,
Her breasts are orbs of heavenly frame,
Where Nature moulds the dew of light
To feed perfection with the same:
  Heigh-ho, would she were mine!

With orient pearl, with ruby red,
With marble white, with sapphire blue,
Her body every way is fed,
Yet soft in touch and sweet in view:
  Heigh-ho, fair Rosaline!
Nature herself her shape admires;
The gods are wounded in her sight;
And Love forsakes his heavenly fires
And at her eyes his brand doth light:
  Heigh-ho, would she were mine!

Then muse not, Nymphs, though I bemoan
The absence of fair Rosaline,
Since for a fair there 's fairer none,
Nor for her virtues so divine:
  Heigh-ho, fair Rosaline!
Heigh-ho, my heart! would God that she were mine!

THOMAS LODGE.

FOR LOVE'S SWEET SAKE.

AWAKE! — the starry midnight hour
  Hangs charmed, and pauseth in its flight;
In its own sweetness sleeps the flower,
  And the doves lie hushed in deep delight.
    Awake! awake!
    Look forth, my love, for Love's sweet sake!

Awake! — soft dews will soon arise
  From daisy mead and thorny brake:
Then, sweet, uncloud those eastern eyes,
  And like the tender morning break!
    Awake! awake!
    Dawn forth, my love, for Love's sweet sake!

Awake! — within the musk-rose bower
  I watch, pale flower of love, for thee.
Ah, come! and show the starry hour
  What wealth of love thou hid'st from me!
    Awake! awake!
    Show all thy love, for Love's sweet sake!

Awake! — ne'er heed though listening night
  Steal music from thy silver voice;
Uncloud thy beauty, rare and bright,
  And bid the world and me rejoice!
    Awake! awake! —
    She comes at last, for Love's sweet sake.

BARRY CORNWALL.

LOVE AND TIME.

Two pilgrims from the distant plain
  Come quickly o'er the mossy ground.
One is a boy, with locks of gold
  Thick curling round his face so fair;
The other pilgrim, stern and old,
  Has snowy beard and silver hair.

The youth with many a merry trick
  Goes singing on his careless way;
His old companion walks as quick,
  But speaks no word by night or day.
Where'er the old man treads, the grass
  Fast fadeth with a certain doom;
But where the beauteous boy doth pass
  Unnumbered flowers are seen to bloom.

And thus before the sage, the boy
  Trips lightly o'er the blooming lands,

GUINEVERE.

"I am a queen, but Love of queens is lord;

. . . . .

I am a queen; be merciful to me,
My servant Lancelot. Thee alone I see;
All else is fading from my swimming eyes."

And proudly bears a pretty toy, —
A crystal glass with diamond sands.
A smile o'er any brow would pass
To see him frolic in the sun, —
To see him shake the crystal glass,
And make the sands more quickly run.

And now they leap the streamlet o'er,
A silver thread so white and thin,
And now they reach the open door,
And now they lightly enter in :
"God save all here," — that kind wish flies
Still sweeter from his lips so sweet ;
"God save you kindly," Norah cries,
"Sit down, my child, and rest and eat."

"Thanks, gentle Norah, fair and good,
We 'll rest awhile our weary feet ;
But though this old man needeth food,
There 's nothing here that he can eat.
His taste is strange, he eats alone,
Beneath some ruined cloister's cope,
Or on some tottering turret's stone,
While I can only live on — Hope !

"A week ago, ere you were wed, —
It was the very night before, —
Upon so many sweets I fed
While passing by your mother's door, —
It was that dear, delicious hour
When Owen here the nosegay brought,
And found you in the woodbine bower, —
Since then, indeed, I 've needed naught."

A blush steals over Norah's face,
A smile comes over Owen's brow,
A tranquil joy illumes the place,
As if the moon were shining now ;
The boy beholds the pleasing pain,
The sweet confusion he has done,
And shakes the crystal glass again,
And makes the sands more quickly run.

"Dear Norah, we are pilgrims, bound
Upon an endless path sublime ;
We pace the green earth round and round,
And mortals call us Love and Time ;
He seeks the many, I the few ;
I dwell with peasants, he with kings.
We seldom meet ; but when we do,
I take his glass, and he my wings.

"And thus together on we go,
Where'er I chance or wish to lead ;
And Time, whose lonely steps are slow,
Now sweeps along with lightning speed.
Now on our bright predestined way
We must to other regions pass ;
But take this gift, and night and day
Look well upon its truthful glass.

"How quick or slow the bright sands' fall
Is hid from lovers' eyes alone:
If you can see them move at all,
Be sure your heart has colder grown.
'T is coldness makes the glass grow dry,
The icy hand, the freezing brow ;
But warm the heart and breathe the sigh,
And then they 'll pass, you know not how."

She took the glass where Love's warm hands
A bright impervious vapor cast ;
She looks, but cannot see the sands,
Although she feels they 're falling fast.
But cold hours came, and then, alas !
She saw them falling frozen through,
Till Love's warm light suffused the glass,
And hid the loosening sands from view !

DENIS FLORENCE MACCARTHY.

INVOCATION TO THE ANGEL.

FROM "HEAVEN AND EARTH."

Samiasa !
I call thee, I await thee, and I love thee ;
Many may worship thee, that will I not ;
If that thy spirit down to mine may move thee,
Descend and share my lot !
Though I be formed of clay,
And thou of beams
More bright than those of day
On Eden's streams,
Thine immortality cannot repay
With love more warm than mine
My love. There is a ray
In me, which, though forbidden yet to shine,
I feel was lighted at thy God's and thine.
It may be hidden long : death and decay
Our mother Eve bequeathed us, but my heart
Defies it ; though this life must pass away,
Is *that* a cause for thee and me to part ?
Thou art immortal ; so am I : I feel —
I feel my immortality o'ersweep
All pains, all tears, all time, all fears, and peal,
Like the eternal thunders of the deep,
Into my ears this truth,—"Thou liv'st forever !"

LORD BYRON.

FLY TO THE DESERT, FLY WITH ME.

SONG OF NOURMAHAL IN "THE LIGHT OF THE HAREM."

"Fly to the desert, fly with me,
Our Arab tents are rude for thee ;
But oh ! the choice what heart can doubt
Of tents with love or thrones without ?

"Our rocks are rough, but smiling there
Th' acacia waves her yellow hair,
Lonely and sweet, nor loved the less
For flowering in a wilderness.

"Our sands are bare, but down their slope
The silvery-footed antelope
As gracefully and gayly springs
As o'er the marble courts of kings.

"Then come, — thy Arab maid will be
The loved and lone acacia-tree,
The antelope, whose feet shall bless
With their light sound thy loneliness.

"O, there are looks and tones that dart
An instant sunshine through the heart,
As if the soul that minute caught
Some treasure it through life had sought;

"As if the very lips and eyes
Predestined to have all our sighs,
And never be forgot again,
Sparkled and spoke before as then!

"So came thy every glance and tone,
When first on me they breathed and shone;
New, as if brought from other spheres,
Yet welcome as if loved for years!

"Then fly with me, if thou hast known
No other flame, nor falsely thrown
A gem away, that thou hadst sworn
Should ever in thy heart be worn.

"Come, if the love thou hast for me
Is pure and fresh as mine for thee, —
Fresh as the fountain underground,
When first 't is by the lapwing found.

"But if for me thou dost forsake
Some other maid, and rudely break
Her worshiped image from its base,
To give to me the ruined place,

"Then, fare thee well! — I 'd rather make
My bower upon some icy lake
When thawing suns begin to shine
Than trust to love so false as thine!"

There was a pathos in this lay,
That even without enchantment's art
Would instantly have found its way
Deep into Selim's burning heart;
But breathing, as it did, a tone
To earthly lutes and lips unknown;
With every chord fresh from the touch
Of music's spirit, 't was too much!

Starting, he dashed away the cup, —
Which, all the time of this sweet air,
His hand had held, untasted, up,
As if 't were fixed by magic there, —
And naming her, so long unnamed,
So long unseen, wildly exclaimed,
"O Nourmahal! O Nourmahal!
Hadst thou but sung this witching strain,
I could forget — forgive thee all,
And never leave those eyes again."

The mask is off, — the charm is wrought, —
And Selim to his heart has caught,
In blushes more than ever bright,
His Nourmahal, his Harem's Light!
And well do vanished frowns enhance
The charm of every brightened glance;
And dearer seems each dawning smile
For having lost its light awhile;
And, happier now for all her sighs,
As on his arm her head reposes,
She whispers him, with laughing eyes,
"Remember, love, the Feast of Roses!"

THOMAS MOORE.

COME INTO THE GARDEN, MAUD.

COME into the garden, Maud,
For the black bat, night, has flown!
Come into the garden, Maud,
I am here at the gate alone;
And the woodbine spices are wafted abroad,
And the musk of the roses blown.

For a breeze of morning moves,
And the planet of Love is on high,
Beginning to faint in the light that she loves,
On a bed of daffodil sky, —
To faint in the light of the sun that she loves,
To faint in its light, and to die.

All night have the roses heard
The flute, violin, bassoon;
All night has the casement jessamine stirred
To the dancers dancing in tune, —
Till a silence fell with the waking bird,
And a hush with the setting moon.

I said to the lily, "There is but one
With whom she has heart to be gay.
When will the dancers leave her alone?
She is weary of dance and play."
Now half to the setting moon are gone,
And half to the rising day;
Low on the sand and loud on the stone
The last wheel echoes away.

I said to the rose, "The brief night goes
  In babble and revel and wine.
O young lord-lover, what sighs are those
  For one that will never be thine?
But mine, but mine," so I sware to the rose,
  "For ever and ever mine!"

And the soul of the rose went into my blood,
  As the music clashed in the hall;
And long by the garden lake I stood,
  For I heard your rivulet fall
From the lake to the meadow and on to the wood,
  Our wood, that is dearer than all;

From the meadow your walks have left so sweet
  That, whenever a March-wind sighs,
He sets the jewel-print of your feet
  In violets blue as your eyes,
To the woody hollows in which we meet,
  And the valleys of Paradise.

The slender acacia would not shake
  One long milk-bloom on the tree;
The white lake-blossom fell into the lake,
  As the pimpernel dozed on the lea;
But the rose was awake all night for your sake,
  Knowing your promise to me;
The lilies and roses were all awake,
  They sighed for the dawn and thee.

Queen rose of the rosebud garden of girls,
  Come hither! the dances are done;
In gloss of satin and glimmer of pearls,
  Queen lily and rose in one;
Shine out, little head, sunning over with curls,
  To the flowers, and be their sun.

There has fallen a splendid tear
  From the passion-flower at the gate.
She is coming, my dove, my dear;
  She is coming, my life, my fate!
The red rose cries, "She is near, she is near";
  And the white rose weeps, "She is late";
The larkspur listens, "I hear, I hear";
  And the lily whispers, "I wait."

She is coming, my own, my sweet!
  Were it ever so airy a tread,
My heart would hear her and beat,
  Were it earth in an earthy bed;
My dust would hear her and beat,
  Had I lain for a century dead;
Would start and tremble under her feet,
  And blossom in purple and red.

ALFRED TENNYSON.

KATIE.

It may be through some foreign grace,
And unfamiliar charm of face;
It may be that across the foam
Which bore her from her childhood's home,
By some strange spell, my Katie brought,
Along with English creeds and thought, —
Entangled in her golden hair, —
Some English sunshine, warmth, and air!
I cannot tell — but here to-day,
A thousand billowy leagues away
From that green isle whose twilight skies
No darker are than Katie's eyes,
She seems to me, go where she will,
An English girl in England still.

I meet her on the dusty street,
And daisies spring about her feet;
Or, touched to life beneath her tread,
An English cowslip lifts its head;
And, as to do her grace, rise up
The primrose and the buttercup.
I roam with her through fields of cane,
And seem to stroll an English lane,
Which, white with blossoms of the May,
Spreads its green carpet in her way.
As fancy wills, the path beneath
Is golden gorse, or purple heath;
And now we hear in woodlands dim
Their unarticulated hymn,
Now walk through rippling waves of wheat,
Now sink in mats of clover sweet,
Or see before us from the lawn
The lark go up to greet the dawn.
All birds that love the English sky
Throng round my path when she is by:
The blackbird from a neighboring thorn
With music brims the cup of morn,
And in a thick, melodious rain
The mavis pours her mellow strain.
But only when my Katie's voice
Makes all the listening woods rejoice
I hear — with cheeks that flush and pale —
The passion of the nightingale.
Anon the pictures round her change,
And through an ancient town we range
Whereto the shadowy memory clings
Of one of England's Saxon kings,
And which, to shrine his fading fame,
Still keeps his ashes and his name.
Quaint houses rise on either hand;
But still the airs are fresh and bland,
As if their gentle wings caressed
Some new-born village of the West.
A moment by the Norman tower
We pause; it is the Sabbath hour!
And o'er the city sinks and swells

The chime of old St. Mary's bells,
Which still resound in Katie's ears
As sweet as when in distant years
She heard them peal with jocund din
A merry English Christmas in.
We pass the Abbey's ruined arch,
And statelier grows my Katie's march,
As round her, wearied with the taint
Of Transatlantic pine and paint,
She sees a thousand tokens cast
Of England's venerable past.
Our reverent footsteps lastly claims
The younger chapel of St. James,
Which, though, as English records run,
Not old, had seen full many a sun,
Ere to the cold December gale
The thoughtful Pilgrim spread his sail.
There Katie in her childish days
Spelt out her prayers and lisped her praise,
And doubtless, as her beauty grew,
Did much as other maidens do, —
Across the pews and down the aisle
Sent many a beau-bewildering smile,
And to subserve her spirit's need
Learned other things beside the creed.
There, too, to-day her knee she bows,
And by her one whose darker brows
Betray the Southern heart that burns
Beside her, and which only turns
Its thoughts to Heaven in one request,
Not all unworthy to be blest,
But rising from an earthlier pain
Than might beseem a Christian fane.
Ah ! can the guileless maiden share
The wish that lifts that passionate prayer ?
Is all at peace that breast within ?
Good angels ! warn her of the sin !
Alas ! what boots it ? who can save
A willing victim of the wave ?
Who cleanse a soul that loves its guilt ?
Or gather wine when wine is spilt ?

We quit the holy house and gain
The open air ; then, happy twain,
Adown familiar streets we go,
And now and then she turns to show,
With fears that all is changing fast,
Some spot that 's sacred to her past.
Here, by this way, through shadows cool,
A little maid, she tripped to school ;
And there, each morning used to stop
Before a wonder of a shop
Where, built of apples and of pears,
Rose pyramids of golden spheres ;
While dangling in her dazzled sight,
Ripe cherries cast a crimson light
And made her think of elfin lamps,
And feast and sport in fairy camps,
Whereat upon her royal throne
(Most richly carved in cherry-stone)
Titania ruled, in queenly state,
The boisterous revels of the fête !
'T was yonder, with their "horrid" noise,
Dismissed from books, she met the boys,
Who, with a barbarous scorn of girls,
Glanced lightly at her sunny curls,
And laughed and leaped as reckless by
As though no pretty face were nigh.
But here the maiden grows demure, —
Indeed, she 's not so very sure
That in a year, or haply twain,
Who looked e'er failed to look again ;
And, sooth to say, I little doubt
(Some azure day the truth will out !)
That certain baits in certain eyes
Caught many an unsuspecting prize ;
And somewhere underneath these eaves
A budding flirt put forth its leaves !

Has not the sky a deeper blue,
Have not the trees a greener hue,
And bend they not with lordlier grace
And noble shapes above the place
Whereon, one cloudless winter morn,
My Katie to this life was born ?
Ah, folly ! long hath fled the hour
When love to sight gave keener power,
And lovers looked for special boons
In brighter flowers and larger moons.
But wave the foliage as it may,
And let the sky be ashen gray,
Thus much at least a manly youth
May hold — and yet not blush — as truth :
If near that blessed spot of earth
Which saw the cherished maiden's birth
No softer dews than usual rise,
And life there keeps its wonted guise,
Yet not the less that spot may seem
As lovely as a poet's dream ;
And should a fervid faith incline
To make thereof a sainted shrine,
Who may deny that round us throng
A hundred earthly creeds as wrong,
But meaner far, which yet unblamed
Stalk by us and are not ashamed ?
So, therefore, Katie, as our stroll
Ends at this portal, while you roll
Those lustrous eyes to catch each ray
That may recall some vanished day,
I — let them jeer and laugh who will —
Stoop down and kiss the sacred sill !
So strongly sometimes on the sense
These fancies hold their influence,
That in long well-known streets I stray
Like one who fears to lose his way.
The stranger I, the native she,

Myself, not Kate, had crossed the sea;
And changing place, and mixing times,
I walk in unfamiliar climes.
These houses, free to every breeze
That blows from warm Floridian seas,
Assume a massive English air,
And close around an English square;
While, if I issue from the town,
An English hill looks greenly down,
Or round me rolls an English park,
And in the Broad I hear the lark.
Thus when, where woodland violets hide,
I rove with Katie at my side,
It scarce would seem amiss to say:
"Katie! my home lies far away,
Beyond the pathless waste of brine,
In a young land of palm and pine.
There by the tropic heats the soul
Is touched as if with living coal,
And glows with such a fire as none
Can feel beneath a Northern sun,
Unless — my Katie's heart attest! —
'T is kindled in an English breast.
Such is the land in which I live,
And, Katie! such the soul I give.
Come, ere another morning beam,
We 'll cleave the sea with wings of steam;
And soon, despite of storm or calm,
Beneath my native groves of palm,
Kind friends shall greet, with joy and pride,
The Southron and his English bride!

HENRY TIMROD.

KATIE LEE AND WILLIE GREY.

Two brown heads with tossing curls,
Red lips shutting over pearls,
Bare feet, white and wet with dew,
Two eyes black, and two eyes blue;
Little girl and boy were they,
Katie Lee and Willie Grey.

They were standing where a brook,
Bending like a shepherd's crook,
Flashed its silver, and thick ranks
Of willow fringed its mossy banks;
Half in thought, and half in play,
Katie Lee and Willie Grey.

They had cheeks like cherries red;
He was taller, — near a head;
She, with arms like wreaths of snow,
Swung a basket to and fro
As she loitered, half in play,
Chattering to Willie Grey.

"Pretty Katie," Willie said, —
And there came a dash of red
Through the brownness of his cheek, —
"Boys are strong and girls are weak,
And I 'll carry, so I will,
Katie's basket up the hill."

Katie answered with a laugh,
"You shall carry only half";
And then, tossing back her curls,
"Boys are weak as well as girls."
Do you think that Katie guessed
Half the wisdom she expressed?

Men are only boys grown tall;
Hearts don't change much, after all;
And when, long years from that day,
Katie Lee and Willie Grey
Stood again beside the brook,
Bending like a shepherd's crook, —

Is it strange that Willie said,
While again a dash of red
Crossed the brownness of his cheek,
"I am strong and you are weak;
Life is but a slippery steep,
Hung with shadows cold and deep:

"Will you trust me, Katie dear, —
Walk beside me without fear?
May I carry, if I will,
All your burdens up the hill?"
And she answered, with a laugh,
"No, but you may carry half."

Close beside the little brook,
Bending like a shepherd's crook,
Washing with its silver hands
Late and early at the sands,
Is a cottage, where to-day
Katie lives with Willie Grey.

In a porch she sits, and lo!
Swings a basket to and fro —
Vastly different from the one
That she swung in years agone:
This is long and deep and wide,
And has — *rockers at the side.*

ANONYMOUS.

ENCHANTMENTS.

ALL in the May-time's merriest weather
  Rode two travelers, bride and groom;
Breast and breast went their mules together,
  Fetlock deep through the daisy bloom.
Roses peeped at them out of the hedges,
  White flowers leaned to them down from the thorn,
And up from the furrows with sunlit edges
  Crowded with children that sowed in the corn.

Cheek o'er cheek, and with red so tender
  Rippling bright through the gypsy brown,
Just to see how a lady's splendor
  Shone the heads of the daffodils down.
Ah, but the wonder grows and lingers,
  Ah, but their fields look low and lorn,
Just to think how her jeweled fingers
  Shamed the seeds of their yellow corn !

O, it was sweet, so sweet to be idle !
  Each little sower with fate fell wroth ;
O, but to ride with a spangled bridle !
  O for a saddle with scarlet cloth !
Waving corn — each stalk in tassel ;
  Home, with its thatch and its turf-lit room —
What was this by the side of a castle ?
  What was that to a tossing plume ?

Winds through the violets' misty covering
  Now kissed the white ones and now the blue,
Sang the redbreast over them hovering
  All as the world were but just made new.
And on and on through the golden weather,
  Fear at the faintest and hope at the best,
Went the true lovers riding together,
  Out of the East-land and into the West.

Father and mother in tears abiding,
  Bridemaids all with their favors dressed,
Back and backward the daisies sliding,
  Dove-throat, Black-foot, breast and breast.
Yet hath the bridemaid joy of her pining,
  And grief sits light on the mother's brow ;
Under her cloud is a silver lining, —
  The lowly child is a lady now.

But for the sowers, the eyes held shady
  Either the sun-brown arm or hand ;
Darkly they follow the lord and lady
  With jealous hatred of house and land.
Fine — it was all so fine to be idle ;
  Dull and weary the work-day doom ;
O, but to ride with a spangled bridle !
  O for a cap with a tossing plume !

Nearer the castle, the bells fell ringing,
  And strong men and maidens to work and wait,
Cried, "God's grace on the bride's home-bringing,"
  And master, mistress, rode through the gate.
Five select ladies — maids of the chamber —
  One sewed her silken seams, one kept her rings,
One for the pearl combs, one for the amber,
  And one for her green fan of peacock wings.

And sweetly and long they abode in their castle,
  And daughters and sons to their love were born;
But doves at the dew-fall homeward nestle,
  To lodge in the rafters they left at morn ;
And memory, holding true and tender,
  As pleasures faded and years increased,
Oft bore the lady from all her splendor
  Out of the West-land into the East ;

And far from the couch where sleep so slowly
  Came to her eyes through the purples grand,
Left her to lodge in the bed so lowly,
  Smoothed by the mother's dear, dear hand.
But after all the ado to assemble
  The sunrise pictures to brighten the set,
One there was thrilled her heart to a tremble,
  Half made of envy and half of regret.

Ah, was it this that in playful sporting,
  And not as lamenting her maiden years,
Often she brought from the time of the courting,
  When hopes are the sweeter for little fears,
That one day of the days so pleasant,
  When, while she mused of her lord, as it fell,
Rode from the castle the groom with his present,
  Dear little Dove-throat, beloved so well ?

Or altar, in splendor of lilies and laces,
  Long-tressed bridemaids, or priest close shorn?
Or ride through the daisies, or green field spaces,
  Gay with children that sowed in the corn ?
Ye who have left the noontide behind you,
  And whom dull shadows begin to oppress,
Say, ere the night-time falleth to blind you,
  Which was the picture — pray, do you guess ?

All in the castle was sweet with contentment,
  For Fortune, in granting all favors but one,
Threw over the distance a cruel enchantment
  That darkened the love-light and darkened the sun.
Of alms and of pleasures the life-long bestowers,
  The lord and the lady had just one lament :
O for the lives of the brown little sowers !
  And O for their artless and homely content !

ALICE CARY.

THE WELCOME.

COME in the evening, or come in the morning ;
Come when you 're looked for, or come without warning ;
Kisses and welcome you 'll find here before you,
And the oftener you come here the more I 'll adore you !
  Light is my heart since the day we were plighted ;
  Red is my cheek that they told me was blighted ;
  The green of the trees looks far greener than ever,
  And the linnets are singing, "True lovers don't sever !"

I 'll pull you sweet flowers, to wear if you choose them,
Or, after you 've kissed them, they 'll lie on my bosom;
I 'll fetch from the mountain its breeze to inspire you;
I 'll fetch from my fancy a tale that won't tire you.
Oh! your step 's like the rain to the summer-vexed farmer,
Or sabre and shield to a knight without armor;
I 'll sing you sweet songs till the stars rise above me,
Then, wandering, I 'll wish you in silence to love me.

We 'll look through the trees at the cliff and the eyrie;
We 'll tread round the rath on the track of the fairy;
We 'll look on the stars, and we 'll list to the river,
Till you ask of your darling what gift you can give her.
Oh! she 'll whisper you, — "Love, as unchangeably beaming,
And trust, when in secret, most tunefully streaming;
Till the starlight of heaven above us shall quiver,
As our souls flow in one down eternity's river."

So come in the evening, or come in the morning;
Come when you 're looked for, or come without warning;
Kisses and welcome you 'll find here before you,
And the oftener you come here the more I 'll adore you!
Light is my heart since the day we were plighted;
Red is my cheek that they told me was blighted;
The green of the trees looks far greener than ever,
And the linnets are singing, "True lovers don't sever!"

THOMAS DAVIS.

CA' THE YOWES TO THE KNOWES.

CHORUS.

Ca' the yowes to the knowes,
Ca' them where the heather grows,
Ca' them where the burnie rowes,
My bonnie dearie.

Hark the mavis' evening sang
Sounding Cluden's woods amang;
Then a-faulding let us gang,
My bonnie dearie.
Ca' the, etc.

We 'll gae down by Cluden side,
Thro' the hazels spreading wide,
O'er the waves that sweetly glide
To the moon sae clearly.
Ca' the, etc.

Yonder Cluden's silent towers,
Where at moonshine midnight hours,
O'er the dewy bending flowers,
Fairies dance sae cheerie.
Ca' the, etc.

Ghaist nor bogle shalt thou fear:
Thou 'rt to Love and Heaven sae dear,
Nocht of ill may come thee near,
My bonnie dearie.
Ca' the, etc.

Fair and lovely as thou art,
Thou hast stown my very heart;
I can die — but canna part,
My bonnie dearie.
Ca' the, etc.

While waters wimple to the sea;
While day blinks in the lift sae hie;
Till clay-cauld death shall blin' my e'e,
Ye shall be my dearie.
Ca' the, etc.

ROBERT BURNS.

CHARLIE MACHREE.

A BALLAD.

COME over, come over
The river to me,
If ye are my laddie,
Bold Charlie machree.

Here 's Mary McPherson
And Susy O'Linn,
Who say ye 're faint-hearted,
And darena plunge in.

But the dark rolling water,
Though deep as the sea,
I know willna scare ye,
Nor keep ye frae me;

For stout is yer back,
And strong is yer arm,
And the heart in yer bosom
Is faithful and warm.

Come over, come over
The river to me,
If ye are my laddie,
Bold Charlie machree!

I see him, I see him!
He 's plunged in the tide,
His strong arms are dashing
The big waves aside.

O, the dark rolling water
Shoots swift as the sea,
But blithe is the glance
Of his bonny blue e'e;

And his cheeks are like roses,
Twa buds on a bough;
Who says ye 're faint-hearted,
My brave Charlie, now?

Ho, ho, foaming river,
Ye may roar as ye go,
But ye canna bear Charlie
To the dark loch below!

Come over, come over
The river to me,
My true-hearted laddie,
My Charlie machree!

He 's sinking, he 's sinking,
O, what shall I do!
Strike out, Charlie, boldly,
Ten strokes and ye 're thro'.

He 's sinking, O Heaven!
Ne'er fear, man, ne'er fear;
I 've a kiss for ye, Charlie,
As soon as ye 're here!

He rises, I see him, —
Five strokes, Charlie, mair, —
He 's shaking the wet
From his bonny brown hair;

He conquers the current,
He gains on the sea, —
Ho, where is the swimmer
Like Charlie machree?

Come over the river,
But once come to me,
And I 'll love ye forever,
Dear Charlie machree!

He 's sinking, he 's gone, —
O God! it is I,
It is I, who have killed him —
Help, help! — he must die!

Help, help! — ah, he rises, —
Strike out and ye 're free!
Ho, bravely done, Charlie,
Once more now, for me!

Now cling to the rock,
Now gie us yer hand, —
Ye 're safe, dearest Charlie,
Ye 're safe on the land!

Come rest in my bosom,
If *there* ye can sleep;
I canna speak to ye,
I only can weep.

Ye 've crossed the wild river,
Ye 've risked all for me,
And I 'll part frae ye never,
Dear Charlie machree!

WILLIAM J. HOPPIN.

ROBIN ADAIR.

WHAT 's this dull town to me?
Robin 's not near, —
He whom I wished to see,
Wished for to hear;
Where 's all the joy and mirth
Made life a heaven on earth,
O, they 're all fled with thee,
Robin Adair!

What made the assembly shine?
Robin Adair:
What made the ball so fine?
Robin was there:
What, when the play was o'er,
What made my heart so sore?
O, it was parting with
Robin Adair!

But now thou art far from me,
Robin Adair;
But now I never see
Robin Adair;
Yet him I loved so well
Still in my heart shall dwell;
O, I can ne'er forget
Robin Adair!

Welcome on shore again,
Robin Adair!
Welcome once more again,
Robin Adair!
I feel thy trembling hand;
Tears in thy eyelids stand,
To greet thy native land,
Robin Adair.

Long I ne'er saw thee, love,
Robin Adair;
Still I prayed for thee, love,
Robin Adair;

When thou wert far at sea,
Many made love to me,
But still I thought on thee,
Robin Adair.

Come to my heart again,
Robin Adair;
Never to part again,
Robin Adair;
And if thou still art true,
I will be constant too,
And will wed none but you,
Robin Adair!

LADY CAROLINE KEPPEL.

THE BIRTH OF PORTRAITURE.

As once a Grecian maiden wove
Her garland mid the summer bowers,
There stood a youth, with eyes of love,
To watch her while she wreathed the flowers.
The youth was skilled in painting's art,
But ne'er had studied woman's brow,
Nor knew what magic hues the heart
Can shed o'er Nature's charm, till now.

CHORUS.

Blest be Love, to whom we owe
All that 's fair and bright below.

His hand had pictured many a rose,
And sketched the rays that lit the brook;
But what were these, or what were those,
To woman's blush, to woman's look?
"O, if such magic power there be,
This, this," he cried, "is all my prayer.
To paint that living light I see,
And fix the soul that sparkles there!"

His prayer as soon as breathed was heard;
His pallet touched by Love grew warm,
And painting saw her thus transferred
From lifeless flowers to woman's form.
Still, as from tint to tint he stole,
The fair design shone out the more,
And there was now a life, a soul,
Where only colors glowed before.

Then first carnation learned to speak,
And lilies into life were brought;
While, mantling on the maiden's cheek,
Young roses kindled into thought:
Then hyacinths their darkest dyes
Upon the locks of beauty threw;
And violets transformed to eyes,
Inshrined a soul within their blue.

CHORUS.

Blest be Love, to whom we owe
All that 's bright and fair below;
Song was cold and painting dim,
Till song and painting learned from him.

THOMAS MOORE.

O NANCY, WILT THOU GO WITH ME?

O NANCY, wilt thou go with me,
Nor sigh to leave the flaunting town?
Can silent glens have charms for thee,
The lonely cot and russet gown?
No longer drest in silken sheen,
No longer decked with jewels rare,
Say, canst thou quit each courtly scene
Where thou wert fairest of the fair?

O Nancy! when thou 'rt far away,
Wilt thou not cast a wish behind?
Say, canst thou face the parching ray,
Nor shrink before the wintry wind?
O, can that soft and gentle mien
Extremes of hardship learn to bear,
Nor sad regret each courtly scene
Where thou wert fairest of the fair?

O Nancy! canst thou love so true,
Through perils keen with me to go,
Or when thy swain mishap shall rue,
To share with him the pang of woe?
Say, should disease or pain befall,
Wilt thou assume the nurse's care,
Nor wistful those gay scenes recall
Where thou wert fairest of the fair?

And when at last thy love shall die,
Wilt thou receive his parting breath?
Wilt thou repress each struggling sigh,
And cheer with smiles the bed of death?
And wilt thou o'er his breathless clay,
Strew flowers, and drop the tender tear,
Nor then regret those scenes so gay,
Where thou wert fairest of the fair?

THOMAS PERCY.

WHISTLE, AND I 'LL COME TO YOU, MY LAD.

O WHISTLE and I 'll come to you, my lad,
O whistle, and I 'll come to you, my lad;
Tho' father and mither and a' should gae mad,
O whistle, and I 'll come to you, my lad.

But warily tent, when ye come to court me,
And come na unless the back-yett be a-jee;

Syne up the back stile, and let naebody see,
And come as ye were na' comin' to me.
And come, etc.
O whistle, etc.

At kirk, or at market, whene'er ye meet me,
Gang by me as tho' that ye cared nae a flie ;
But steal me a blink o' your bonnie black e'e,
Yet look as ye were na lookin' at me.
Yet look, etc.
O whistle, etc.

Aye vow and protest that ye care na for me,
And whiles ye may lightly my beauty a wee ;
But court nae anither, tho' jokin' ye be,
For fear that she wile your fancy frae me.
For fear, etc.
O whistle, etc.

ROBERT BURNS.

THE SHEPHERD TO HIS LOVE.

COME, live with me, and be my love,
And we will all the pleasures prove
That valleys, groves, and hills, and fields,
Woods or steepy mountains, yields.

And we will sit upon the rocks,
Seeing the shepherds feed their flocks
By shallow rivers, to whose falls
Melodious birds sing madrigals.

There will I make thee beds of roses
With a thousand fragrant posies ;
A cap of flowers, and a kirtle,
Embroidered all with leaves of myrtle ;

A gown made of the finest wool,
Which from our pretty lambs we pull ;
Fair-linèd slippers for the cold,
With buckles of the purest gold ;

A belt of straw, and ivy buds,
With coral clasps and amber studs :
And if these pleasures may thee move,
Come, live with me, and be my love.

The shepherd swains shall dance and sing
For thy delight each May morning :
If these delights thy mind may move,
Then live with me, and be my love.

CHRISTOPHER MARLOWE.

THE NYMPH'S REPLY.

IF that the world and love were young,
And truth in every shepherd's tongue,
These pretty pleasures might me move
To live with thee and be thy love.

But time drives flocks from field to fold,
When rivers rage, and rocks grow cold ;
And Philomel becometh dumb,
And all complain of cares to come.

The flowers do fade, and wanton fields
To wayward winter reckoning yields ;
A honey tongue, a heart of gall,
Is fancy's spring, but sorrow's fall.

Thy gowns, thy shoes, thy beds of roses,
Thy cap, thy kirtle, and thy posies
Soon break, soon wither, soon forgotten, —
In folly ripe, in reason rotten.

Thy belt of straw and ivy buds,
Thy coral clasps and amber studs, —
All these in me no means can move
To come to thee, and be thy love.

But could youth last, and love still breed,
Had joys no date, nor age no need,
Then these delights my mind might move
To live with thee, and be thy love.

SIR WALTER RALEIGH.

MAUD MULLER.

MAUD MULLER, on a summer's day,
Raked the meadow sweet with hay.

Beneath her torn hat glowed the wealth
Of simple beauty and rustic health.

Singing, she wrought, and her merry glee
The mock-bird echoed from his tree.

But, when she glanced to the far-off town,
White from its hill-slope looking down,

The sweet song died, and a vague unrest
And a nameless longing filled her breast, —

A wish, that she hardly dared to own,
For something better than she had known.

The Judge rode slowly down the lane,
Smoothing his horse's chestnut mane.

He drew his bridle in the shade
Of the apple trees, to greet the maid,

And ask a draught from the spring that flowed
Through the meadow, across the road.

She stooped where the cool spring bubbled up,
And filled for him her small tin cup,

John G. Whittier

J. B. FORD & Co. NEW YORK.

And blushed as she gave it, looking down
On her feet so bare, and her tattered gown.

"Thanks!" said the Judge, "a sweeter draught
From a fairer hand was never quaffed."

He spoke of the grass and flowers and trees,
Of the singing birds and the humming bees;

Then talked of the haying, and wondered whether
The cloud in the west would bring foul weather.

And Maud forgot her brier-torn gown,
And her graceful ankles, bare and brown,

And listened, while a pleased surprise
Looked from her long-lashed hazel eyes.

At last, like one who for delay
Seeks a vain excuse, he rode away.

Maud Muller looked and sighed: "Ah me!
That I the Judge's bride might be!

"He would dress me up in silks so fine,
And praise and toast me at his wine.

"My father should wear a broadcloth coat,
My brother should sail a painted boat.

"I 'd dress my mother so grand and gay,
And the baby should have a new toy each day.

"And I 'd feed the hungry and clothe the poor,
And all should bless me who left our door."

The Judge looked back as he climbed the hill,
And saw Maud Muller standing still:

"A form more fair, a face more sweet,
Ne'er hath it been my lot to meet.

"And her modest answer and graceful air
Show her wise and good as she is fair.

"Would she were mine, and I to-day,
Like her, a harvester of hay.

"No doubtful balance of rights and wrongs,
Nor weary lawyers with endless tongues,

"But low of cattle, and song of birds,
And health, and quiet, and loving words."

But he thought of his sister proud and cold,
And his mother, vain of her rank and gold.

So, closing his heart, the Judge rode on,
And Maud was left in the field alone.

But the lawyers smiled that afternoon,
When he hummed in court an old love tune;

And the young girl mused beside the well,
Till the rain on the unraked clover fell.

He wedded a wife of richest dower,
Who lived for fashion, as he for power.

Yet oft, in his marble hearth's bright glow,
He watched a picture come and go;

And sweet Maud Muller's hazel eyes
Looked out in their innocent surprise.

Oft, when the wine in his glass was red,
He longed for the wayside well instead,

And closed his eyes on his garnished rooms,
To dream of meadows and clover blooms;

And the proud man sighed with a secret pain,
"Ah, that I were free again!

"Free as when I rode that day
Where the barefoot maiden raked the hay."

She wedded a man unlearned and poor,
And many children played round her door.

But care and sorrow, and child-birth pain,
Left their traces on heart and brain.

And oft, when the summer sun shone hot
On the new-mown hay in the meadow lot,

And she heard the little spring brook fall
Over the roadside, through the wall,

In the shade of the apple-tree again
She saw a rider draw his rein,

And, gazing down with a timid grace,
She felt his pleased eyes read her face.

Sometimes her narrow kitchen walls
Stretched away into stately halls;

The weary wheel to a spinnet turned,
The tallow candle an astral burned;

And for him who sat by the chimney lug,
Dozing and grumbling o'er pipe and mug,

A manly form at her side she saw,
And joy was duty and love was law.

Then she took up her burden of life again,
Saying only, "It might have been."

Alas for maiden, alas for judge,
For rich repiner and household drudge!

God pity them both! and pity us all,
Who vainly the dreams of youth recall;

For of all sad words of tongue or pen,
The saddest are these: "It might have been!"

Ah, well! for us all some sweet hope lies
Deeply buried from human eyes;

And, in the hereafter, angels may
Roll the stone from its grave away!

JOHN GREENLEAF WHITTIER.

QUAKERDOM.

THE FORMAL CALL.

THROUGH her forced, abnormal quiet
Flashed the soul of frolic riot,
And a most malicious laughter lighted up her downcast eyes;
All in vain I tried each topic,
Ranged from polar climes to tropic, —
Every commonplace I started met with yes-or-no replies.

For her mother — stiff and stately,
As if starched and ironed lately —
Sat erect, with rigid elbows bedded thus in curving palms;
There she sat on guard before us,
And in words precise, decorous,
And most calm, reviewed the weather, and recited several psalms.

How without abruptly ending
This my visit, and offending
Wealthy neighbors, was the problem which employed my mental care;
When the butler, bowing lowly,
Uttered clearly, stiffly, slowly,
"Madam, please, the gardener wants you," —
Heaven, I thought, has heard my prayer.

"Pardon me!" she grandly uttered;
Bowing low, I gladly muttered,
"Surely, madam!" and, relieved, I turned to scan the daughter's face:
Ha! what pent-up mirth outflashes
From beneath those penciled lashes!
How the drill of Quaker custom yields to Nature's brilliant grace!

Brightly springs the prisoned fountain
From the side of Delphi's mountain,
When the stone that weighed upon its buoyant life is thrust aside;
So the long-enforced stagnation
Of the maiden's conversation
Now imparted fivefold brilliance to its ever-varying tide.

Widely ranging, quickly changing,
Witty, winning, from beginning
Unto end I listened, merely flinging in a casual word;
Eloquent, and yet how simple!
Hand and eye, and eddying dimple,
Tongue and lip together made a music seen as well as heard.

When the noonday woods are ringing,
All the birds of summer singing,
Suddenly there falls a silence, and we know a serpent nigh:
So upon the door a rattle
Stopped our animated tattle,
And the stately mother found us prim enough to suit her eye.

CHARLES G. HALPINE.

THE CHESS-BOARD.

MY little love, do you remember,
Ere we were grown so sadly wise,
Those evenings in the bleak December,
Curtained warm from the snowy weather,
When you and I played chess together,
Checkmated by each other's eyes?

Ah! still I see your soft white hand
Hovering warm o'er Queen and Knight;
Brave Pawns in valiant battle stand;
The double Castles guard the wings;
The Bishop, bent on distant things,
Moves, sidling, through the fight.

Our fingers touch; our glances meet,
And falter; falls your golden hair
Against my cheek; your bosom sweet
Is heaving. Down the field, your Queen
Rides slow, her soldiery all between,
And checks me unaware.

Ah me! the little battle 's done:
Disperst is all its chivalry.
Full many a move since then have we
Mid life's perplexing checkers made,
And many a game with fortune played;
What is it we have won?
This, this at least, — if this alone:

That never, never, nevermore,
As in those old still nights of yore,
(Ere we were grown so sadly wise,)
Can you and I shut out the skies,
Shut out the world and wintry weather,
And, eyes exchanging warmth with eyes,
Play chess, as then we played together.

ROBERT BULWER LYTTON.

DINNA ASK ME.

O, DINNA ask me gin I lo'e ye:
Troth, I daurna tell!
Dinna ask me gin I lo'e ye, —
Ask it o' yoursel'.

O, dinna look sae sair at me,
For weel ye ken me true;
O, gin ye look sae sair at me,
I daurna look at you.

When ye gang to yon braw braw town,
And bonnier lassies see,
O, dinna, Jamie, look at them,
Lest ye should mind na me.

For I could never bide the lass
That ye 'd lo'e mair than me;
And O, I 'm sure my heart wad brak,
Gin ye 'd prove fause to me!

DUNLOP.

SUMMER DAYS.

IN summer, when the days were long,
We walked together in the wood:
Our heart was light, our step was strong;
Sweet flutterings were there in our blood,
In summer, when the days were long.

We strayed from morn till evening came;
We gathered flowers, and wove us crowns;
We walked mid poppies red as flame,
Or sat upon the yellow downs;
And always wished our life the same.

In summer, when the days were long,
We leaped the hedgerow, crossed the brook;
And still her voice flowed forth in song,
Or else she read some graceful book,
In summer, when the days were long.

And then we sat beneath the trees,
With shadows lessening in the noon;
And in the sunlight and the breeze,
We feasted, many a gorgeous June,
While larks were singing o'er the leas.

In summer, when the days were long,
On dainty chicken, snow-white bread,
We feasted, with no grace but song;
We plucked wild strawberries, ripe and red,
In summer, when the days were long.

We loved, and yet we knew it not, —
For loving seemed like breathing then;
We found a heaven in every spot;
Saw angels, too, in all good men;
And dreamed of God in grove and grot.

In summer, when the days are long,
Alone I wander, muse alone.
I see her not; but that old song
Under the fragrant wind is blown,
In summer, when the days are long.

Alone I wander in the wood:
But one fair spirit hears my sighs;
And half I see, so glad and good,
The honest daylight of her eyes,
That charmed me under earlier skies.

In summer, when the days are long,
I love her as we loved of old.
My heart is light, my step is strong;
For love brings back those hours of gold,
In summer, when the days are long.

ANONYMOUS.

GENEVIEVE.

ALL thoughts, all passions, all delights,
Whatever stirs this mortal frame,
All are but ministers of Love,
And feed his sacred flame.

Oft in my waking dreams do I
Live o'er again that happy hour,
When midway on the mount I lay
Beside the ruined tower.

The moonshine stealing o'er the scene
Had blended with the lights of eve;
And she was there, my hope, my joy,
My own dear Genevieve!

She leaned against the armèd man,
The statue of the armèd knight;
She stood and listened to my lay,
Amid the lingering light.

Few sorrows hath she of her own,
My hope! my joy! my Genevieve!
She loves me best, whene'er I sing
The songs that make her grieve.

I played a soft and doleful air,
I sang an old and moving story, —
An old rude song, that suited well
That ruin wild and hoary.

She listened with a flitting blush,
With downcast eyes and modest grace;
For well she knew, I could not choose
But gaze upon her face.

I told her of the Knight that wore
Upon his shield a burning brand;
And that for ten long years he wooed
The Lady of the Land.

I told her how he pined: and ah!
The deep, the low, the pleading tone
With which I sang another's love
Interpreted my own.

She listened with a flitting blush,
With downcast eyes, and modest grace;
And she forgave me, that I gazed
Too fondly on her face.

But when I told the cruel scorn
That crazed that bold and lovely Knight,
And that he crossed the mountain-woods,
Nor rested day nor night;

That sometimes from the savage den,
And sometimes from the darksome shade,
And sometimes starting up at once
In green and sunny glade,

There came and looked him in the face
An angel beautiful and bright;
And that he knew it was a Fiend,
This miserable Knight!

And that, unknowing what he did,
He leaped amid a murderous band,
And saved from outrage worse than death
The Lady of the Land;

And how she wept, and clasped his knees;
And how she tended him in vain;
And ever strove to expiate
The scorn that crazed his brain;

And that she nursed him in a cave,
And how his madness went away,
When on the yellow forest-leaves
A dying man he lay;

— His dying words — but when I reached
That tenderest strain of all the ditty,
My faltering voice and pausing harp
Disturbed her soul with pity.

All impulses of soul and sense
Had thrilled my guileless Genevieve;
The music and the doleful tale,
The rich and balmy eve;

And hopes, and fears that kindle hope,
An undistinguishable throng,
And gentle wishes long subdued,
Subdued and cherished long.

She wept with pity and delight,
She blushed with love, and virgin shame;
And like the murmur of a dream,
I heard her breathe my name.

Her bosom heaved, — she stepped aside,
As conscious of my look she stept, —
Then suddenly, with timorous eye
She fled to me and wept.

She half enclosed me with her arms,
She pressed me with a meek embrace;
And bending back her head, looked up,
And gazed upon my face.

'T was partly love, and partly fear,
And partly 't was a bashful art
That I might rather feel than see
The swelling of her heart.

I calmed her fears, and she was calm,
And told her love with virgin pride;
And so I won my Genevieve,
My bright and beauteous Bride.

SAMUEL TAYLOR COLERIDGE.

WHEN THE KYE COME HAME.

COME, all ye jolly shepherds,
That whistle through the glen!
I 'll tell ye o' a secret
That courtiers dinna ken:
What is the greatest bliss
That the tongue o' man can name?
'T is to woo a bonnie lassie
When the kye come hame.
When the kye come hame,
When the kye come hame, —
'Tween the gloamin' an' the mirk,
When the kye come hame.

'T is not beneath the burgonet,
Nor yet beneath the crown;
'T is not on couch o' velvet,
Nor yet in bed o' down:
'T is beneath the spreading birk,
In the glen without the name,

Wi' a bonnie bonnie lassie,
When the kye come hame.

There the blackbird bigs his nest,
For the mate he lo'es to see,
And on the tapmost bough
O, a happy bird is he!
There he pours his melting ditty,
And love is a' the theme;
And he 'll woo his bonnie lassie,
When the kye come hame.

When the blewart bears a pearl,
And the daisy turns a pea,
And the bonnie lucken gowan
Has fauldit up his ee,
Then the lavrock, frae the blue lift,
Draps down and thinks nae shame
To woo his bonnie lassie,
When the kye come hame.

See yonder pawky shepherd,
That lingers on the hill:
His yowes are in the fauld,
And his lambs are lying still;
Yet he downa gang to bed,
For his heart is in a flame,
To meet his bonnie lassie
When the kye come hame.

When the little wee bit heart
Rises high in the breast,
And the little wee bit starn
Rises red in the east,
O, there 's a joy sae dear
That the heart can hardly frame!
Wi' a bonnie bonnie lassie,
When the kye come hame.

Then since all Nature joins
In this love without alloy,
O, wha wad prove a traitor
To Nature's dearest joy?
Or wha wad choose a crown,
Wi' its perils an' its fame,
And miss his bonnie lassie,
When the kye come hame?

JAMES HOGG.

THE NIGHT BEFORE THE WEDDING OR, TEN YEARS AFTER.

THE country ways are full of mire,
The boughs toss in the fading light,
The winds blow out the sunset's fire,
And sudden droppeth down the night.
I sit in this familiar room,
Where mud-splashed hunting squires resort;
My sole companion in the gloom
This slowly dying pint of port.

'Mong all the joys my soul hath known,
'Mong errors over which it grieves,
I sit at this dark hour alone,
Like Autumn mid his withered leaves.
This is a night of wild farewells
To all the past; the good, the fair;
To-morrow, and my wedding bells
Will make a music in the air.

Like a wet fisher, tempest-tost,
Who sees throughout the weltering night,
Afar on some low-lying coast,
The streaming of a rainy light,
I saw this hour, — and now 't is come;
The rooms are lit, the feast is set;
Within the twilight I am dumb,
My heart filled with a vain regret.

I cannot say, in Eastern style,
Where'er she treads the pansy blows;
Nor call her eyes twin stars, her smile
A sunbeam, and her mouth a rose.
Nor can I, as your bridegrooms do,
Talk of my raptures. O, how sore
The fond romance of twenty-two
Is parodied ere thirty-four.

To-night I shake hands with the past, —
Familiar years, adieu, adieu!
An unknown door is open cast,
An empty future wide and new
Stands waiting. O ye naked rooms,
Void, desolate, without a charm,
Will Love's smile chase your lonely glooms,
And drape your walls, and make them warm?

The man who knew, while he was young,
Some soft and soul-subduing air,
Melts when again he hears it sung,
Although 't is only half so fair.
So I love thee, and love is sweet
(My Florence, 't is the cruel truth)
Because it can to age repeat
That long-lost passion of my youth.

O, often did my spirit melt,
Blurred letters, o'er your artless rhymes!
Fair trees, in which the sunshine dwelt,
I 've kissed you many a million times!
And now 't is done, — my passionate tears,
Mad pleadings with an iron fate,
And all the sweetness of my years,
Are blackened ashes in the grate.

Then ring in the wind, my wedding chimes;
Smile, villagers, at every door;

Old churchyard, stuffed with buried crimes,
  Be clad in sunshine o'er and o'er;
And youthful maidens, white and sweet,
  Scatter your blossoms far and wide;
And with a bridal chorus greet
  This happy bridegroom and his bride.

"This happy bridegroom!" there is sin
  At bottom of my thankless mood:
What if desert alone could win
  For me life's chiefest grace and good?
Love gives itself; and if not given,
  No genius, beauty, state or wit,
No gold of earth, no gem of heaven,
  Is rich enough to purchase it.

It may be, Florence, loving thee,
  My heart will its old memories keep;
Like some worn sea-shell from the sea,
  Filled with the music of the deep.
And you may watch, on nights of rain,
  A shadow on my brow encroach;
Be startled by my sudden pain,
  And tenderness of self-reproach.

It may be that your loving wiles
  Will call a sigh from far-off years;
It may be that your happiest smiles
  Will brim my eyes with hopeless tears;
It may be that my sleeping breath
  Will shake, with painful visions wrung;
And, in the awful trance of death,
  A stranger's name be on my tongue.

Ye phantoms, born of bitter blood,
  Ye ghosts of passion, lean and worn,
Ye terrors of a lonely mood,
  What do ye here on a wedding-morn?
For, as the dawning sweet and fast
  Through all the heaven spreads and flows,
Within life's discord, rude and vast,
  Love's subtle music grows and grows.

And lightened is the weary curse,
  And clearer is the weary road;
The very worm the sea-weeds nurse
  Is cared for by the Eternal God.
My love, pale blossom of the snow,
  Has pierced earth wet with wintry showers, —
O may it drink the sun, and blow,
  Followed by all the year of flowers!

Black Bayard from the stable bring;
  The rain is o'er, the wind is down,
Round stirring farms the birds will sing,
  The dawn stand in the sleeping town,
Within an hour. This is her gate,
  Her sodden roses droop in night,
And, emblem of my happy fate,
  In one dear window there is light.

The dawn is oozing pale and cold
  Through the damp east for many a mile;
When half my tale of life is told,
  Grim-featured Time begins to smile.
Last star of night that lingerest yet
  In that long rift of rainy gray,
Gather thy wasted splendors, set,
  And die unto my wedding day.

ALEXANDER SMITH.

ATALANTA VICTORIOUS.

FROM "ATALANTA'S RACE," IN "THE EARTHLY PARADISE."

AND there two runners did the sign abide
Foot set to foot, — a young man slim and fair,
Crisp-haired, well knit, with firm limbs often tried
In places where no man his strength may spare;
Dainty his thin coat was, and on his hair
A golden circlet of renown he wore,
And in his hand an olive garland bore.

But on this day with whom shall he contend?
A maid stood by him like Diana clad
When in the woods she lists her bow to bend,
Too fair for one to look on and be glad,
Who scarcely yet has thirty summers had,
If he must still behold her from afar;
Too fair to let the world live free from war.

She seemed all earthly matters to forget;
Of all tormenting lines her face was clear;
Her wide gray eyes upon the goal were set
Calm and unmoved as though no soul were near;
But her foe trembled as a man in fear,
Nor from her loveliness one moment turned
His anxious face with fierce desire that burned.

Now through the hush there broke the trumpet's clang,
Just as the setting sun made eventide.
Then from light feet a spurt of dust there sprang,
And swiftly were they running side by side;
But silent did the thronging folk abide
Until the turning-post was reached at last,
And round about it still abreast they passed.

But when the people saw how close they ran,
When half-way to the starting-point they were,
A cry of joy broke forth, whereat the man
Headed the white-foot runner, and drew near
Unto the very end of all his fear;
And scarce his straining feet the ground could feel,
And bliss unhoped for o'er his heart 'gan steal.

But midst the loud victorious shouts he heard
Her footsteps drawing nearer, and the sound
Of fluttering raiment, and thereat afeared
His flushed and eager face he turned around,
And even then he felt her past him bound
Fleet as the wind, but scarcely saw her there
Till on the goal she laid her fingers fair.

There stood she, breathing like a little child
Amid some warlike clamor laid asleep,
For no victorious joy her red lips smiled,
Her cheek its wonted freshness did but keep;
No glance lit up her clear gray eyes and deep,
Though some divine thought softened all her face
As once more rang the trumpet through the place.

But her late foe stopped short amidst his course,
One moment gazed upon her piteously,
Then with a groan his lingering feet did force
To leave the spot whence he her eyes could see;
And, changed like one who knows his time must be
But short and bitter, without any word
He knelt before the bearer of the sword;

Then high rose up the gleaming deadly blade,
Bared of its flowers, and through the crowded place
Was silence now, and midst of it the maid
Went by the poor wretch at a gentle pace,
And he to hers upturned his sad white face;
Nor did his eyes behold another sight
Ere on his soul there fell eternal night.

William Morris.

ATALANTA CONQUERED.

FROM "ATALANTA'S RACE," IN "THE EARTHLY PARADISE."

Now has the lingering month at last gone by,
Again are all folk round the running place,
Nor other seems the dismal pageantry
Than heretofore, but that another face
Looks o'er the smooth course ready for the race,
For now, beheld of all, Milanion
Stands on the spot he twice has looked upon.

But yet — what change is this that holds the maid?
Does she indeed see in his glittering eye
More than disdain of the sharp shearing blade,
Some happy hope of help and victory?
The others seemed to say, "We come to die,
Look down upon us for a little while,
That dead, we may bethink us of thy smile."

But he — what look of mastery was this
He cast on her? why were his lips so red?
Why was his face so flushed with happiness?
So looks not one who deems himself but dead,
E'en if to death he bows a willing head;
So rather looks a god well pleased to find
Some earthly damsel fashioned to his mind.

Why must she drop her lids before his gaze,
And even as she casts adown her eyes
Redden to note his eager glance of praise,
And wish that she were clad in other guise?
Why must the memory to her heart arise
Of things unnoticed when they first were heard,
Some lover's song, some answering maiden's word?

What makes these longings, vague, without a name,
And this vain pity never felt before,
This sudden languor, this contempt of fame,
This tender sorrow for the time past o'er,
These doubts that grow each minute more and more?
Why does she tremble as the time grows near,
And weak defeat and woful victory fear?

But while she seemed to hear her beating heart,
Above their heads the trumpet blast rang out,
And forth they sprang; and she must play her part;
Then flew her white feet, knowing not a doubt,
Though slackening once, she turned her head about,
But then she cried aloud and faster fled
Than e'er before, and all men deemed him dead.

But with no sound he raised aloft his hand,
And thence what seemed a ray of light there flew
And past the maid rolled on along the sand;
Then trembling she her feet together drew,
And in her heart a strong desire there grew
To have the toy; some god she thought had given
That gift to her, to make of earth a heaven.

Then from the course with eager steps she ran,
And in her odorous bosom laid the gold.
But when she turned again, the great-limbed man
Now well ahead she failed not to behold,
And mindful of her glory waxing cold,
Sprang up and followed him in hot pursuit,
Though with one hand she touched the golden fruit.

Note, too, the bow that she was wont to bear
She laid aside to grasp the glittering prize,
And o'er her shoulder from the quiver fair
Three arrows fell and lay before her eyes
Unnoticed, as amidst the people's cries
She sprang to head the strong Milanion,
Who now the turning-post had wellnigh won.

But as he set his mighty hand on it,
White fingers underneath his own were laid,

And white limbs from his dazzled eyes did flit,
Then he the second fruit cast by the maid,
But she ran on awhile, then as afraid
Wavered and stopped, and turned and made no stay
Until the globe with its bright fellow lay.

Then, as a troubled glance she cast around,
Now far ahead the Argive could she see,
And in her garment's hem one hand she wound
To keep the double prize, and strenuously
Sped o'er the course, and little doubt had she
To win the day, though now but scanty space
Was left betwixt him and the winning place.

Short was the way unto such wingèd feet,
Quickly she gained upon him, till at last
He turned about her eager eyes to meet,
And from his hand the third fair apple cast.
She wavered not, but turned and ran so fast
After the prize that should her bliss fulfill,
That in her hand it lay ere it was still.

Nor did she rest, but turned about to win
Once more, an unblest woful victory —
And yet — and yet — why does her breath begin
To fail her, and her feet drag heavily?
Why fails she now to see if far or nigh
The goal is? why do her gray eyes grow dim?
Why do these tremors run through every limb?

She spreads her arms abroad some stay to find
Else must she fall, indeed, and findeth this,
A strong man's arms about her body twined.
Nor may she shudder now to feel his kiss,
So wrapped she is in new, unbroken bliss:
Made happy that the foe the prize hath won,
She weeps glad tears for all her glory done.

WILLIAM MORRIS.

THE SIESTA.

FROM THE SPANISH.

"Vientecico murmurador
Que lo gozas y andas todo," etc.

AIRS, that wander and murmur round,
Bearing delight where'er ye blow!
Make in the elms a lulling sound,
While my lady sleeps in the shade below.

Lighten and lengthen her noonday rest,
Till the heat of the noonday sun is o'er.
Sweet be her slumbers! though in my breast
The pain she has waked may slumber no more.
Breathing soft from the blue profound,
Bearing delight where'er ye blow,
Make in the elms a lulling sound,
While my lady sleeps in the shade below.

Airs! that over the bending boughs,
And under the shade of pendent leaves,
Murmur soft, like my timid vows
Or the secret sighs my bosom heaves, —
Gently sweeping the grassy ground,
Bearing delight where'er ye blow,
Make in the elms a lulling sound,
While my lady sleeps in the shade below.

WILLIAM CULLEN BRYANT.

ACBAR AND NOURMAHAL.

FROM "THE LIGHT OF THE HAREM."

O, BEST of delights, as it everywhere is,
To be near the loved *one*,— what a rapture is his
Who in moonlight and music thus sweetly may glide
O'er the Lake of Cashmere with that *one* by his side!
If woman can make the worst wilderness dear,
Think, think what a heaven she must make of Cashmere!

So felt the magnificent Son of Acbar,
When from power and pomp and the trophies of war
He flew to that valley, forgetting them all
With the Light of the Harem, his young Nourmahal.
When free and uncrowned as the conqueror roved
By the banks of that lake, with his only beloved,
He saw, in the wreaths she would playfully snatch
From the hedges, a glory his crown could not match,
And preferred in his heart the least ringlet that curled
Down her exquisite neck to the throne of the world!

There's a beauty forever unchangingly bright,
Like the long sunny lapse of a summer day's light,
Shining on, shining on, by no shadow made tender,
Till love falls asleep in its sameness of splendor.
This *was* not the beauty — O, nothing like this,
That to young Nourmahal gave such magic of bliss,
But that loveliness, ever in motion, which plays
Like the light upon autumn's soft shadowy days,
Now here and now there, giving warmth as it flies
From the lips to the cheek, from the cheek to the eyes;
Now melting in mist and now breaking in gleams,
Like the glimpses a saint has of heaven in his dreams!
When pensive, it seemed as if that very grace,
That charm of all others, was born with her face;
And when angry, — for even in the tranquilest climes
Light breezes will ruffle the flowers sometimes, —
The short, passing anger but seemed to awaken
New beauty, like flowers that are sweetest when shaken.

If tenderness touched her, the dark of her eye
At once took a darker, a heavenlier dye,
From the depth of whose shadow, like holy revealings
From innermost shrines, came the light of her feelings!
Then her mirth — O, 't was sportive as ever took wing
From the heart with a burst like the wild-bird in spring, —
Illumed by a wit that would fascinate sages,
Yet playful as Peris just loosed from their cages.
While her laugh, full of life, without any control
But the sweet one of gracefulness, rung from her soul;
And where it most sparkled no glance could discover,
In lip, cheek, or eyes, for she brightened all over, —
Like any fair lake that the breeze is upon,
When it breaks into dimples, and laughs in the sun.
Such, such were the peerless enchantments that gave
Nourmahal the proud Lord of the East for her slave;
And though bright was his Harem, — a living parterre
Of the flowers of this planet, — though treasures were there,
For which Solomon's self might have given all the store
That the navy from Ophir e'er winged to his shore,
Yet dim before *her* were the smiles of them all,
And the Light of his Harem was young Nourmahal!

THOMAS MOORE.

PYGMALION AND THE IMAGE.

FROM "THE EARTHLY PARADISE."

A Man of Cyprus, a Sculptor named Pygmalion, made an Image of a Woman, fairer than any that had yet been seen, and in the end came to love his own handiwork as though it had been alive; wherefore, praying to Venus for help, he obtained his end, for she made the image alive indeed, and a Woman, and Pygmalion wedded her.

AT Amathus, that from the southern side
Of Cyprus looks across the Syrian sea,
There did in ancient time a man abide
Known to the island-dwellers, for that he
Had wrought most godlike works in imagery,
And day by day still greater honor won, —
Which man our old books call Pygmalion.

. . . . .

The lessening marble that he worked upon
A woman's form now imaged doubtfully;
And in such guise the work had he begun,
Because when he the untouched block did see
In wandering veins that form there seemed to be,
Whereon he cried out in a careless mood,
"O lady Venus, make this presage good!

"And then this block of stone shall be thy maid,
And, not without rich golden ornament,
Shall bide within thy quivering myrtle-shade."
So spoke he, but the goddess, well content,
Unto his hand such godlike mastery sent,
That like the first artificer he wrought,
Who made the gift that woe to all men brought.

And yet, but such as he was wont to do,
At first indeed that work divine he deemed,
And as the white chips from the chisel flew
Of other matters languidly he dreamed,
For easy to his hand that labor seemed.
And he was stirred with many a troubling thought,
And many a doubt perplexed him as he wrought.

And yet, again, at last there came a day
When smoother and more shapely grew the stone,
And he, grown eager, put all thought away
But that which touched his craftsmanship alone,
And he would gaze at what his hands had done,
Until his heart with boundless joy would swell
That all was wrought so wonderfully well.

Yet long it was ere he was satisfied,
And with his pride that by his mastery
This thing was done, whose equal far and wide
In no town of the world a man could see,
Came burning longing that the work should be
E'en better still, and to his heart there came
A strange and strong desire he could not name.

. . . . .

The night seemed long, and long the twilight seemed,
A vain thing seemed his flowery garden fair;
Though through the night still of his work he dreamed,
And though his smooth-stemmed trees so nigh it were,
That thence he could behold the marble hair,
Naught was enough, until with steel in hand
He came before the wondrous stone to stand.

. . . . .

Blinded with tears, his chisel up he caught,
And, drawing near, and sighing, tenderly
Upon the marvel of the face he wrought,
E'en as he used to pass the long days by;
But his sighs changed to sobbing presently,
And on the floor the useless steel he flung,
And, weeping loud, about the image clung.

"Alas!" he cried, "why have I made thee then,
That thus thou mockest me? I know indeed
That many such as thou are loved of men,
Whose passionate eyes poor wretches still will lead
Into their net, and smile to see them bleed;

But these the Gods made, and this hand made thee
Who wilt not speak one little word to me."

Then from the image did he draw aback
To gaze on it through tears : and you had said,
Regarding it, that little did it lack
To be a living and most lovely maid ;
Naked it was, its unbound locks were laid
Over the lovely shoulders; with one hand
Reached out, as to a lover, did it stand.

The other held a fair rose over-blown ;
No smile was on the parted lips, the eyes
Seemed as if even now great love had shown
Unto them something of its sweet surprise,
Yet saddened them with half-seen mysteries,
And still midst passion maiden-like she seemed,
As though of love unchanged for aye she dreamed.

Reproachfully beholding all her grace,
Pygmalion stood, until he grew dry-eyed,
And then at last he turned away his face
As if from her cold eyes his grief to hide ;
And thus a weary while did he abide.
With nothing in his heart but vain desire,
The ever-burning, unconsuming fire.

. . . . . .

No word indeed the moveless image said,
But with the sweet grave eyes his hands had wrought
Still gazed down on his bowed imploring head ;
Yet his own words some solace to him brought,
Gilding the net wherein his soul was caught
With something like to hope, and all that day
Some tender words he ever found to say ;

And still he felt as something heard him speak;
Sometimes he praised her beauty, and sometimes
Reproached her in a feeble voice and weak,
And at the last drew forth a book of rhymes,
Wherein were writ the tales of many climes,
And read aloud the sweetness hid therein
Of lovers' sorrows and their tangled sin.

And when the sun went down, the frankincense
Again upon the altar-flame he cast
That through the open window floating thence
O'er the fresh odors of the garden passed ;
And so another day was gone at last,
And he no more his lovelorn watch could keep,
But now for utter weariness must sleep.

. . . . . .

But the next morn, e'en while the incense-smoke
At sunrising curled round about her head,
Sweet sound of songs the wonted quiet broke
Down in the street, and he, by something led,
He knew not what, must leave his prayer unsaid,
And through the freshness of the morn must see
The folk who went with that sweet minstrelsy ;

Damsels and youths in wonderful attire,
And in their midst upon a car of gold
An image of the Mother of Desire,
Wrought by his hands in days that seemed grown old,
Though those sweet limbs a garment did enfold,
Colored like flame, enwrought with precious things,
Most fit to be the prize of striving kings.

Then he remembered that the manner was
That fair-clad priests the lovely Queen should take
Thrice in the year, and through the city pass,
And with sweet songs the dreaming folk awake ;
And through the clouds a light there seemed to break
When he remembered all the tales well told
About her glorious kindly deeds of old.

So his unfinished prayer he finished not,
But, kneeling, once more kissed the marble feet,
And, while his heart with many thoughts waxed hot,
He clad himself with fresh attire and meet
For that bright service, and with blossoms sweet
Entwined with tender leaves he crowned his head,
And followed after as the goddess led.

. . . . . .

So there he stood, that help from her to gain,
Bewildered by that twilight midst of day ;
Downcast with listening to the joyous strain
He had no part in, hopeless with delay
Of all the fair things he had meant to say :
Yet, as the incense on the flame he cast,
From stammering lips and pale these words there passed, —

"O thou forgotten help, dost thou yet know
What thing it is I need, when even I,
Bent down before thee in this shame and woe,
Can frame no set of words to tell thee why
I needs must pray, O help me or I die !
Or slay me, and in slaying take from me
Even a dead man's feeble memory.

. . . . . .

Yet soon, indeed, before his door he stood,
And, as a man awaking from a dream,
Seemed waked from his old folly ; naught seemed good
In all the things that he before had deemed
At least worth life, and on his heart there streamed
Cold light of day, — he found himself alone,
Reft of desire, all love and madness gone.

. . . . . .

Thus to his chamber at the last he came,
And, pushing through the still half-opened door,
He stood within ; but there, for very shame
Of all the things that he had done before,
Still kept his eyes bent down upon the floor,

Thinking of all that he had done and said
Since he had wrought that luckless marble maid.

Yet soft his thoughts were, and the very place
Seemed perfumed with some nameless heavenly air.
So gaining courage, did he raise his face
Unto the work his hands had made so fair,
And cried aloud to see the niche all bare
Of that sweet form, while through his heart again
There shot a pang of his old yearning pain.

Yet while he stood, and knew not what to do
With yearning, a strange thrill of hope there came,
A shaft of new desire now pierced him through,
And therewithal a soft voice called his name,
And when he turned, with eager eyes aflame,
He saw betwixt him and the setting sun
The lively image of his lovèd one.

He trembled at the sight, for though her eyes,
Her very lips, were such as he had made,
And though her tresses fell but in such guise
As he had wrought them, now was she arrayed
In that fair garment that the priests had laid
Upon the goddess on that very morn,
Dyed like the setting sun upon the corn.

Speechless he stood, but she now drew anear,
Simple and sweet as she was wont to be,
And once again her silver voice rang clear,
Filling his soul with great felicity,
And thus she spoke, "Wilt thou not come to me,
O dear companion of my new-found life,
For I am called thy lover and thy wife?"

. . . . .

She reached her hand to him, and with kind eyes
Gazed into his; but he the fingers caught
And drew her to him, and midst ecstasies
Passing all words, yea, wellnigh passing thought,
Felt that sweet breath that he so long had sought,
Felt the warm life within her heaving breast
As in his arms his living love he pressed.

But as his cheek touched hers he heard her say,
"Wilt thou not speak, O love? why dost thou weep?
Art thou then sorry for this long-wished day,
Or dost thou think perchance thou wilt not keep
This that thou holdest, but in dreamy sleep?
Nay, let us do the bidding of the Queen,
And hand in hand walk through thy garden green;

"Then shalt thou tell me, still beholding me,
Full many things whereof I wish to know,
And as we walk from whispering tree to tree
Still more familiar to thee shall I grow,
And such things shalt thou say unto me now
As when thou deemedst thou wast quite alone,
A madman kneeling to a thing of stone."

But at that word a smile lit up his eyes
And therewithal he spake some loving word,
And she at first looked up in grave surprise
When his deep voice and musical she heard,
And clung to him as somewhat grown afeard;
Then cried aloud and said, "O mighty one!
What joy with thee to look upon the sun!"

Then into that fair garden did they pass,
And all the story of his love he told,
And as the twain went o'er the dewy grass,
Beneath the risen moon could he behold
The bright tears trickling down, then, waxen bold,
He stopped and said, "Ah, love, what meaneth this?
Seest thou how tears still follow earthly bliss?"

Then both her white arms round his neck she threw,
And sobbing said, "O love, what hurteth me?
When first the sweetness of my life I knew,
Not this I felt, but when I first saw thee
A little pain and great felicity
Rose up within me, and thy talk e'en now
Made pain and pleasure ever greater grow."

"O sweet," he said, "this thing is even love,
Whereof I told thee; that all wise men fear,
But yet escape not; nay, to gods above,
Unless the old tales lie, it draweth near.
But let my happy ears, I pray thee, hear
Thy story too, and how thy blessed birth
Has made a heaven of this once lonely earth."

"My sweet," she said, "as yet I am not wise,
Or stored with words, aright the tale to tell,
But listen: when I opened first mine eyes
I stood within the niche thou knowest well,
And from mine hand a heavy thing there fell
Carved like these flowers, nor could I see things clear,
And but a strange confusèd noise could hear.

"At last mine eyes could see a woman fair,
But awful as this round white moon o'erhead,
So that I trembled when I saw her there,
For with my life was born some touch of dread,
And therewithal I heard her voice that said,
'Come down, and learn to love and be alive,
For thee, a well-prized gift, to-day I give.'

"Then on the floor I stepped, rejoicing much,
Not knowing why, not knowing aught at all,
Till she reached out her hand my breast to touch,
And when her fingers thereupon did fall,

Thought came unto my life, and therewithal
I knew her for a goddess, and began
To murmur in some tongue unknown to man.

"And then indeed not in this guise was I.
No sandals had I, and no saffron gown,
But naked as thou knowest utterly,
E'en as my limbs beneath thine hand had grown,
And this fair perfumed robe then fell adown
Over the goddess' feet and swept the ground,
And round her loins a glittering belt was bound.

"But when the stammering of my tongue she heard
Upon my trembling lips her hand she laid,
And spoke again, 'Nay, say not any word,
All that thine heart would say I know unsaid,
Who even now thine heart and voice have made;
But listen rather, for thou knowest now
What these words mean, and still wilt wiser grow.

"'Thy body, lifeless till I gave it life,
A certain man, my servant, well hath wrought,
I give thee to him as his love and wife,
With all thy dowry of desire and thought,
Since this his yearning heart hath ever sought;
Now from my temple is he on the way,
Deeming to find thee e'en as yesterday;

"'Bide thou his coming by the bed-head there,
And when thou seest him set his eyes upon
Thine empty niche, and hear'st him cry for care,
Then call him by his name, Pygmalion,
And certainly thy lover hast thou won;
But when he stands before thee silently,
Say all these words that I shall teach to thee.'

"With that she said what first I told thee, love,
And then went on, 'Moreover thou shalt say
That I, the daughter of almighty Jove,
Have wrought for him this long-desired day;
In sign whereof, these things that pass away,
Wherein mine image men have well arrayed,
I give thee for thy wedding gear, O maid.'

"Therewith her raiment she put off from her,
And laid bare all her perfect loveliness,
And, smiling on me, came yet more anear,
And on my mortal lips her lips did press,
And said, 'Now herewith shalt thou love no less
Than Psyche loved my son in days of old;
Farewell, of thee shall many a tale be told.'

"And even with that last word was she gone,
How, I know not, and I my limbs arrayed
In her fair gifts, and waited thee alone —
Ah, love, indeed the word is true she said,
For now I love thee so, I grow afraid
Of what the gods upon our heads may send —
I love thee so, I think upon the end."

What words he said? How can I tell again
What words they said beneath the glimmering light,
Some tongue they used unknown to loveless men
As each to each they told their great delight,
Until for stillness of the growing night
Their soft sweet murmuring words seemed growing loud,
And dim the moon grew, hid by fleecy cloud.

WILLIAM MORRIS.

MEETING.

The gray sea, and the long black land;
And the yellow half-moon large and low;
And the startled little waves, that leap
In fiery ringlets from their sleep,
As I gain the cove with pushing prow,
And quench its speed in the slushy sand.

Then a mile of warm, sea-scented beach;
Three fields to cross, till a farm appears:
A tap at the pane, the quick sharp scratch
And blue spurt of a lighted match,
And a voice less loud, through its joys and fears,
Than the two hearts, beating each to each.

ROBERT BROWNING.

A MAIDEN WITH A MILKING-PAIL.

I.

What change has made the pastures sweet,
And reached the daisies at my feet,
And cloud that wears a golden hem?
This lovely world, the hills, the sward, —
They all look fresh, as if our Lord
But yesterday had finished them.

And here's the field with light aglow:
How fresh its boundary lime-trees show!
And how its wet leaves trembling shine!
Between their trunks come through to me
The morning sparkles of the sea,
Below the level browzing line.

I see the pool, more clear by half
Than pools where other waters laugh
Up at the breasts of coot and rail.
There, as she passed it on her way,
I saw reflected yesterday
A maiden with a milking-pail.

There neither slowly nor in haste, —
One hand upon her slender waist,
The other lifted to her pail, —
She, rosy in the morning light,
Among the water-daisies white,
Like some fair sloop appeared to sail.

Against her ankles as she trod
The lucky buttercups did nod:
I leaned upon the gate to see.
The sweet thing looked, but did not speak;
A dimple came in either cheek,
And all my heart was gone from me.

Then, as I lingered on the gate,
And she came up like coming fate,
I saw my picture in her eyes, —
Clear dancing eyes, more black than sloes!
Cheeks like the mountain pink, that grows
Among white-headed majesties!

I said, "A tale was made of old
That I would fain to thee unfold:
Ah! let me, — let me tell the tale."
But high she held her comely head:
"I cannot heed it now," she said,
"For carrying of the milking-pail."

She laughed. What good to make ado?
I held the gate, and she came through,
And took her homeward path anon.
From the clear pool her face had fled;
It rested on my heart instead,
Reflected when the maid was gone.

With happy youth, and work content,
So sweet and stately, on she went,
Right careless of the untold tale.
Each step she took I loved her more,
And followed to her dairy door
The maiden with the milking-pail.

II.

For hearts where wakened love doth lurk,
How fine, how blest a thing is work!
For work does good when reasons fail, —
Good; yet the ax at every stroke
The echo of a name awoke, —
Her name is Mary Martindale.

I'm glad that echo was not heard
Aright by other men. A bird
Knows doubtless what his own notes tell;
And I know not, — but I can say
I felt as shamefaced all that day
As if folks heard her name right well.

And when the west began to glow
I went — I could not choose but go —
To that same dairy on the hill;
And while sweet Mary moved about
Within, I came to her without,
And leaned upon the window-sill.

The garden border where I stood
Was sweet with pinks and southernwood.
I spoke, — her answer seemed to fail.
I smelt the pinks, — I could not see;
The dusk came down and sheltered me;
And in the dusk she heard my tale.

And what is left that I should tell?
I begged a kiss, — I pleaded well:
The rosebud lips did long decline;
But yet, I think — I think 't is true —
That, leaned at last into the dew,
One little instant they were mine!

O life! how dear thou hast become!
She laughed at dawn, and I was dumb!
But evening counsels best prevail.
Fair shine the blue that o'er her spreads,
Green be the pastures where she treads,
The maiden with the milking-pail!

JEAN INGELOW.

THE MILKMAID'S SONG.

TURN, turn, for my cheeks they burn,
Turn by the dale, my Harry!
Fill pail, fill pail,
He has turned by the dale,
And there by the stile waits Harry.
Fill, fill,
Fill pail, fill,
For there by the stile waits Harry!
The world may go round, the world may stand still,
But I can milk and marry,
Fillpail,
I can milk and marry.

Wheugh, wheugh!
O, if we two
Stood down there now by the water,
I know who 'd carry me over the ford
As brave as a soldier, as proud as a lord,
Though I don't live over the water.
Wheugh, wheugh! he 's whistling through,
He 's whistling "The Farmer's Daughter."
Give down, give down,
My crumpled brown!
He shall not take the road to the town,
For I 'll meet him beyond the water.
Give down, give down,
My crumpled brown!

And send me to my Harry.
The folk o' towns
May have silken gowns,
But I can milk and marry,
Fillpail,
I can milk and marry.

Wheugh, wheugh! he has whistled through,
He has whistled through the water.
Fill, fill, with a will, a will,
For he's whistled through the water,
And he's whistling down
The way to the town,
And it's not "The Farmer's Daughter!"
Churr, churr! goes the cockchafer,
The sun sets over the water,
Churr, churr! goes the cockchafer,
I'm too late for my Harry!
And, O, if he goes a-soldiering,
The cows they may low, the bells they may ring,
But I'll neither milk nor marry,
Fillpail,
Neither milk nor marry.

My brow beats on thy flank, Fillpail,
Give down, good wench, give down!
I know the primrose bank, Fillpail,
Between him and the town.
Give down, good wench, give down, Fillpail,
And he shall not reach the town!
Strain, strain! he's whistling again,
He's nearer by half a mile.
More, more! O, never before
Were you such a weary while!
Fill, fill! he's crossed the hill,
I can see him down by the stile,
He's passed the hay, he's coming this way,
He's coming to me, my Harry!
Give silken gowns to the folks o' towns,
He's coming to me, my Harry!
There's not so grand a dame in the land,
That she walks to-night with Harry!
Come late, come soon, come sun, come moon,
O, I can milk and marry,
Fillpail,
I can milk and marry.

Wheugh, wheugh! he has whistled through,
My Harry! my lad! my lover!
Set the sun and fall the dew,
Heigh-ho, merry world, what's to do
That you're smiling over and over?
Up on the hill and down in the dale,
And along the tree-tops over the vale
Shining over and over,
Low in the grass and high on the bough,
Shining over and over,
O world, have you ever a lover?
You were so dull and cold just now,
O world, have you ever a lover?
I could not see a leaf on the tree,
And now I could count them, one, two, three,
Count them over and over,
Leaf from leaf like lips apart,
Like lips apart for a lover.
And the hillside beats with my beating heart,
And the apple-tree blushes all over,
And the May bough touched me and made me start,
And the wind breathes warm like a lover.

Pull, pull! and the pail is full,
And milking's done and over.
Who would not sit here under the tree?
What a fair fair thing's a green field to see!
Brim, brim, to the rim, ah me!
I have set my pail on the daisies!
It seems so light, — can the sun be set?
The dews must be heavy, my cheeks are wet.
I could cry to have hurt the daisies!
Harry is near, Harry is near,
My heart's as sick as if he were here,
My lips are burning, my cheeks are wet,
He has n't uttered a word as yet,
But the air's astir with his praises.
My Harry!
The air's astir with your praises.

He has scaled the rock by the pixy's stone,
He's among the kingcups — he picks me one,
I love the grass that I tread upon
When I go to my Harry!
He has jumped the brook, he has climbed the knowe,
There's never a faster foot I trow,
But still he seems to tarry.
O Harry! O Harry! my love, my pride,
My heart is leaping, my arms are wide!
Roll up, roll up, you dull hillside,
Roll up, and bring my Harry!
They may talk of glory over the sea,
But Harry's alive, and Harry's for me,
My love, my lad, my Harry!
Come spring, come winter, come sun, come snow,
What cares Dolly, whether or no,
While I can milk and marry?
Right or wrong, and wrong or right,
Quarrel who quarrel, and fight who fight,
But I'll bring my pail home every night
To love, and home, and Harry!
We'll drink our can, we'll eat our cake,
There's beer in the barrel, there's bread in the bake,
The world may sleep, the world may wake,
But I shall milk and marry,
And marry,
I shall milk and marry.

SYDNEY DOBELL.

AUF WIEDERSEHEN.*

SUMMER.

THE little gate was reached at last,
Half hid in lilacs down the lane;
She pushed it wide, and, as she past,
A wistful look she backward cast,
And said, "*Auf wiedersehen!*"

With hand on latch, a vision white
Lingered reluctant, and again,
Half doubting if she did aright,
Soft as the dews that fell that night,
She said, "*Auf wiedersehen!*"

The lamp's clear gleam flits up the stair;
I linger in delicious pain;
Ah, in that chamber, whose rich air
To breathe in thought I scarcely dare,
Thinks she, "*Auf wiedersehen!*"

'T is thirteen years: once more I press
The turf that silences the lane;
I hear the rustle of her dress,
I smell the lilacs, and — ah yes,
I hear "*Auf wiedersehen!*"

Sweet piece of bashful maiden art!
The English words had seemed too fain,
But these — they drew us heart to heart,
Yet held us tenderly apart;
She said, "*Auf wiedersehen!*"

JAMES RUSSELL LOWELL.

* Till we meet again; like *au revoir* in French.

SWEET MEETING OF DESIRES.

I GREW assured, before I asked,
That she 'd be mine without reserve,
And in her unclaimed graces basked
At leisure, till the time should serve, —
With just enough of dread to thrill
The hope, and make it trebly dear:
Thus loath to speak the word, to kill
Either the hope or happy fear.

Till once, through lanes returning late,
Her laughing sisters lagged behind;
And ere we reached her father's gate,
We paused with one presentient mind:
And, in the dim and perfumed mist
Their coming stayed, who, blithe and free,
And very women, loved to assist
A lover's opportunity.

Twice rose, twice died, my trembling word;
To faint and frail cathedral chimes
Spake time in music, and we heard
The chafers rustling in the limes.
Her dress, that touched me where I stood;
The warmth of her confided arm;
Her bosom's gentle neighborhood;
Her pleasure in her power to charm;

Her look, her love, her form, her touch!
The least seemed most by blissful turn, —
Blissful but that it pleased too much,
And taught the wayward soul to yearn.
It was as if a harp with wires
Was traversed by the breath I drew;
And O, sweet meeting of desires!
She, answering, owned that she loved too.

COVENTRY PATMORE.

ZARA'S EAR-RINGS.

FROM THE SPANISH.

"MY ear-rings! my ear-rings! they 've dropt into the well,
And what to say to Muça, I cannot, cannot tell."
'T was thus, Granada's fountain by, spoke Albuharez' daughter, —
"The well is deep, far down they lie, beneath the cold blue water.
To me did Muça give them, when he spake his sad farewell,
And what to say when he comes back, alas! I cannot tell.

"My ear-rings! my ear-rings! they were pearls in silver set,
That when my Moor was far away, I ne'er should him forget,
That I ne'er to other tongue should list, nor smile on other's tale,
But remember he my lips had kissed, pure as those ear-rings pale.
When he comes back, and hears that I have dropped them in the well,
O, what will Muça think of me, I cannot, cannot tell.

"My ear-rings! my ear-rings! he 'll say they should have been,
Not of pearl and silver, but of gold and glittering sheen,
Of jasper and of onyx, and of diamond shining clear,
Changing to the changing light, with radiance insincere;
That changeful mind unchanging gems are not befitting well, —
Thus will he think, — and what to say, alas! I cannot tell.

"He 'll think when I to market went I loitered by the way;
He 'll think a willing ear I lent to all the lads might say;

He 'll think some other lover's hand, among my tresses noosed,
From the ears where he had placed them my rings of pearl unloosed;
He 'll think when I was sporting so beside this marble well,
My pearls fell in, — and what to say, alas! I cannot tell.

"He 'll say I am a woman, and we are all the same;
He 'll say I loved when he was here to whisper of his flame, —
But when he went to Tunis my virgin troth had broken,
And thought no more of Muça, and cared not for his token.
My ear-rings! my ear-rings! O, luckless, luckless well!
For what to say to Muça, alas! I cannot tell.

"I 'll tell the truth to Muça, and I hope he will believe
That I 've thought of him at morning, and thought of him at eve;
That musing on my lover, when down the sun was gone,
His ear-rings in my hand I held, by the fountain all alone;
And that my mind was o'er the sea, when from my hand they fell,
And that deep his love lies in my heart, as they lie in the well."

JOHN GIBSON LOCKHART.

"O SWALLOW, SWALLOW, FLYING SOUTH."

FROM "THE PRINCESS."

"O SWALLOW, Swallow, flying, flying South,
Fly to her, and fall upon her gilded eaves,
And tell her, tell her what I tell to thee.

"O tell her, Swallow, thou that knowest each,
That bright and fierce and fickle is the South,
And dark and true and tender is the North.

"O Swallow, Swallow, if I could follow and light
Upon her lattice, I would pipe and trill,
And cheep and twitter twenty million loves.

"O were I thou that she might take me in,
And lay me on her bosom, and her heart
Would rock the snowy cradle till I died!

"Why lingereth she to clothe her heart with love,
Delaying as the tender ash delays
To clothe herself, when all the woods are green?

"O tell her, Swallow, that thy brood is flown:
Say to her, I do but wanton in the South,
But in the North long since my nest is made.

"O tell her, brief is life, but love is long,
And brief the sun of summer in the North,
And brief the moon of beauty in the South.

"O Swallow, flying from the golden woods,
Fly to her, and pipe and woo her, and make her mine,
And tell her, tell her, that I follow thee."

ALFRED TENNYSON.

"ASK ME NO MORE."

FROM "THE PRINCESS."

ASK me no more: the moon may draw the sea;
The cloud may stoop from heaven and take the shape,
With fold to fold, of mountain or of cape;
But, O too fond! when have I answered thee?
Ask me no more.

Ask me no more: what answer should I give?
I love not hollow cheek or faded eye:
Yet, O my friend, I will not have thee die!
Ask me no more, lest I should bid thee live;
Ask me no more.

Ask me no more: thy fate and mine are sealed:
I strove against the stream, and all in vain:
Let the great river take me to the main:
No more, dear love, for at a touch I yield;
Ask me no more.

ALFRED TENNYSON.

ATHULF AND ETHILDA.

ATHULF. . . . Appeared
The princess with that merry child Prince Guy:
He loves me well, and made her stop and sit,
And sat upon her knee, and it so chanced
That in his various chatter he denied
That I could hold his hand within my own
So closely as to hide it: this being tried
Was proved against him; he insisted then
I could not by his royal sister's hand
Do likewise. Starting at the random word,
And dumb with trepidation, there I stood
Some seconds as bewitched; then I looked up,
And in her face beheld an orient flush
Of half-bewildered pleasure: from which trance
She with an instant ease resumed herself,
And frankly, with a pleasant laugh, held out
Her arrowy hand.
I thought it trembled as it lay in mine,
But yet her looks were clear, direct, and free,

And said that she felt nothing.
SIDROC. And what felt'st thou?
ATHULF. A sort of swarming, curling, tremulous tumbling,
As though there were an ant-hill in my bosom.
I said I was ashamed. — Sidroc, you smile,
If at my folly, well! But if you smile,
Suspicious of a taint upon my heart,
Wide is your error, and you never loved.

HENRY TAYLOR.

SEVEN TIMES THREE.

LOVE.

I LEANED out of window, I smelt the white clover,
Dark, dark was the garden, I saw not the gate;
"Now, if there be footsteps, he comes, my one lover —
Hush, nightingale, hush! O sweet nightingale, wait
Till I listen and hear
If a step draweth near,
For my love he is late!

"The skies in the darkness stoop nearer and nearer,
A cluster of stars hangs like fruit in the tree,
The fall of the water comes sweeter, comes clearer:
To what art thou listening, and what dost thou see?
Let the star-clusters glow,
Let the sweet waters flow,
And cross quickly to me.

"You night-moths that hover where honey brims over
From sycamore blossoms, or settle or sleep;
You glow-worms, shine out, and the pathway discover
To him that comes darkling along the rough steep.
Ah, my sailor, make haste,
For the time runs to waste,
And my love lieth deep, —

"Too deep for swift telling; and yet, my one lover,
I've conned thee an answer, it waits thee to-night."
By the sycamore passed he, and through the white clover;
Then all the sweet speech I had fashioned took flight;
But I'll love him more, more
Than e'er wife loved before,
Be the days dark or bright.

JEAN INGELOW.

FATIMA AND RADUAN.

FROM THE SPANISH.

"Diamante falso y fingido,
Engastado en pedernal," etc.

"FALSE diamond set in flint! hard heart in haughty breast!
By a softer, warmer bosom the tiger's couch is prest.
Thou art fickle as the sea, thou art wandering as the wind,
And the restless ever-mounting flame is not more hard to bind.
If the tears I shed were tongues, yet all too few would be
To tell of all the treachery that thou hast shown to me.
Oh! I could chide thee sharply, — but every maiden knows
That she who chides her lover forgives him ere he goes.

"Thou hast called me oft the flower of all Granada's maids,
Thou hast said that by the side of me the first and fairest fades;
And they thought thy heart was mine, and it seemed to every one
That what thou didst to win my love, for love of me was done.
Alas! if they but knew thee, as mine it is to know,
They well might see another mark to which thine arrows go;
But thou giv'st little heed, — for I speak to one who knows
That she who chides her lover forgives him ere he goes.

"It wearies me, mine enemy, that I must weep and bear
What fills thy heart with triumph, and fills my own with care.
Thou art leagued with those that hate me, and ah! thou know'st I feel
That cruel words as surely kill as sharpest blades of steel.
'T was the doubt that thou wert false that wrung my heart with pain;
But, now I know thy perfidy, I shall be well again.
I would proclaim thee as thou art — but every maiden knows
That she who chides her lover forgives him ere he goes."

Thus Fatima complained to the valiant Raduan,
Where underneath the myrtles Alhambra's fountains ran:
The Moor was inly moved, and blameless as he was,
He took her white hand in his own, and pleaded thus his cause:

"O lady, dry those star-like eyes, — their dimness does me wrong;
If my heart be made of flint, at least 't will keep thy image long;
Thou hast uttered cruel words, — but I grieve the less for those,
Since she who chides her lover forgives him ere he goes."

WILLIAM CULLEN BRYANT.

THE SPINNING-WHEEL SONG.

Mellow the moonlight to shine is beginning;
Close by the window young Eileen is spinning;
Bent o'er the fire, her blind grandmother, sitting,
Is croaning, and moaning, and drowsily knitting, —
"Eileen, achora, I hear some one tapping."
"'T is the ivy, dear mother, against the glass flapping."
"Eileen, I surely hear somebody sighing."
"'T is the sound, mother dear, of the summer wind dying."
Merrily, cheerily, noisily whirring,
Swings the wheel, spins the reel, while the foot 's stirring;
Sprightly, and lightly, and airily ringing,
Thrills the sweet voice of the young maiden singing.

"What 's that noise that I hear at the window, I wonder!"
"'T is the little birds chirping the holly-bush under."
"What makes you be shoving and moving your stool on,
And singing all wrong that old song of 'The Coolun'?"
There 's a form at the casement, — the form of her true-love, —
And he whispers, with face bent, "I 'm waiting for you, love;
Get up on the stool, through the lattice step lightly,
We 'll rove in the grove while the moon 's shining brightly."
Merrily, cheerily, noisily whirring,
Swings the wheel, spins the reel, while the foot 's stirring;
Sprightly, and lightly, and airily ringing,
Thrills the sweet voice of the young maiden singing.

The maid shakes her head, on her lip lays her fingers,
Steals up from her seat, — longs to go, and yet lingers;
A frightened glance turns to her drowsy grandmother,
Puts one foot on the stool, spins the wheel with the other.
Lazily, easily, swings now the wheel round;
Slowly and lowly is heard now the reel's sound;
Noiseless and light to the lattice above her
The maid steps, — then leaps to the arms of her lover.
Slower — and slower — and slower the wheel swings;
Lower — and lower — and lower the reel rings;
Ere the reel and the wheel stop their ringing and moving,
Through the grove the young lovers by moonlight are roving.

JOHN FRANCIS WALLER.

A SPINSTER'S STINT.

Six skeins and three, six skeins and three!
Good mother, so you stinted me,
And here they be, — ay, six and three!

Stop, busy wheel! stop, noisy wheel!
Long shadows down my chamber steal,
And warn me to make haste and reel.

'T is done, — the spinning work complete;
O heart of mine, what makes you beat
So fast and sweet, so fast and sweet?

I must have wheat and pinks, to stick
My hat from brim to ribbon, thick, —
Slow hands of mine, be quick, be quick!

One, two, three stars along the skies
Begin to wink their golden eyes, —
I 'll leave my thread all knots and ties.

O moon, so red! O moon, so red!
Sweetheart of night, go straight to bed;
Love's light will answer in your stead.

A-tiptoe, beckoning me, he stands, —
Stop trembling, little foolish hands,
And stop the bands, and stop the bands!

ALICE CARY.

SOMEBODY.

Somebody 's courting somebody
  Somewhere or other to-night;
Somebody 's whispering to somebody,
Somebody 's listening to somebody,
  Under this clear moonlight.

Near the bright river's flow,
Running so still and slow,
Talking so soft and low,
  She sits with somebody.

Pacing the ocean's shore,
Edged by the foaming roar,
Words never used before
  Sound sweet to somebody.

Under the maple-tree
Deep though the shadow be,
Plain enough they can see,
  Bright eyes has somebody.

No one sits up to wait,
Though she is out so late,
All know she 's at the gate,
  Talking with somebody.

Tiptoe to parlor door,
Two shadows on the floor,
Moonlight, reveal no more,
  Susy and somebody.

Two, sitting side by side,
Float with the ebbing tide,
"Thus, dearest, may we glide
  Through life," says somebody.

Somewhere, somebody
Makes love to somebody
  To-night.

ANONYMOUS.

THE MISTRESS.

If he 's capricious, she 'll be so;
  But, if his duties constant are,
She lets her loving favor glow
  As steady as a tropic star.
Appears there naught for which to weep,
  She 'll weep for naught for his dear sake;
She clasps her sister in her sleep;
  Her love in dreams is most awake.
Her soul, that once with pleasure shook
  Did any eyes her beauty own,
Now wonders how they dare to look
  On what belongs to him alone.
The indignity of taking gifts
  Exhilarates her loving breast;
A rapture of submission lifts
  Her life into celestial rest.
There 's nothing left of what she was, —
  Back to the babe the woman dies;
And all the wisdom that she has
  Is to love him for being wise.
She 's confident because she fears;
  And, though discreet when he 's away,
If none but her dear despot hears,
  She 'll prattle like a child at play.
Perchance, when all her praise is said,
  He tells the news, — a battle won —
On either side ten thousand dead, —
  Describing how the whole was done:
She thinks, "He 's looking on my face!
  I am his joy; whate'er I do,
He sees such time-contenting grace
  In that, he 'd have me always so!"
And, evermore, for either's sake,
  To the sweet folly of the dove
She joins the cunning of the snake,
  To rivet and exalt his love.
Her mode of candor is deceit;
  And what she thinks from what she 'll say
(Although I 'll never call her cheat)
  Lies far as Scotland from Cathay.
Without his knowledge he was won,
  Against his nature kept devout;
She 'll never tell him how 't was done,
  And he will never find it out.
If, sudden, he suspects her wiles,
  And hears her forging chain and trap,
And looks, — she sits in simple smiles,
  Her two hands lying in her lap!
Her secret (privilege of the Bard,
  Whose fancy is of either sex)
Is mine; but let the darkness guard
  Mysteries that light would more perplex.

COVENTRY PATMORE.

BONNIE WEE THING.

Bonnie wee thing! cannie wee thing!
  Lovely wee thing! wert thou mine,
I wad wear thee in my bosom,
  Lest my jewel I should tine.
Wishfully I look, and languish,
  In that bonnie face o' thine;
And my heart it stounds wi' anguish,
  Lest my wee thing be na mine.

Wit and grace, and love and beauty,
  In ae constellation shine;
To adore thee is my duty,
  Goddess o' this soul o' mine!
Bonnie wee thing, cannie wee thing,
  Lovely wee thing, wert thou mine,
I wad wear thee in my bosom,
  Lest my jewel I should tine.

ROBERT BURNS.

BELIEVE ME, IF ALL THOSE ENDEARING YOUNG CHARMS.

Believe me, if all those endearing young charms,
  Which I gaze on so fondly to-day,
Were to change by to-morrow, and fleet in my arms,
  Like fairy-gifts fading away,

Thou wouldst still be adored, as this moment thou art,
Let thy loveliness fade as it will,
And around the dear ruin each wish of my heart
Would entwine itself verdantly still.

It is not while beauty and youth are thine own,
And thy cheeks unprofaned by a tear,
That the fervor and faith of a soul may be known,
To which time will but make thee more dear!
O, the heart that has truly loved never forgets,
But as truly loves on to the close,
As the sunflower turns to her god when he sets
The same look which she turned when he rose!

THOMAS MOORE.

THE SLEEPING BEAUTY.

FROM "THE DAY DREAM."

Year after year unto her feet,
She lying on her couch alone,
Across the purple coverlet,
The maiden's jet-black hair has grown;
On either side her trancèd form
Forth streaming from a braid of pearl;
The slumb'rous light is rich and warm,
And moves not on the rounded curl.

The silk star-broidered coverlid
Unto her limbs itself doth mould,
Languidly ever; and amid
Her full black ringlets, downward rolled,
Glows forth each softly shadowed arm,
With bracelets of the diamond bright.
Her constant beauty doth inform
Stillness with love, and day with light.

She sleeps; her breathings are not heard
In palace chambers far apart.
The fragrant tresses are not stirred
That lie upon her charmèd heart.
She sleeps; on either hand upswells
The gold-fringed pillow lightly prest;
She sleeps, nor dreams, but ever dwells
A perfect form in perfect rest.

ALFRED TENNYSON.

THE REVIVAL OF THE "SLEEPING BEAUTY."

FROM "THE DAY DREAM."

A touch, a kiss! the charm was snapt.
There rose a noise of striking clocks;
And feet that ran, and doors that clapt,
And barking dogs, and crowing cocks;
A fuller light illumined all;
A breeze through all the garden swept;
A sudden hubbub shook the hall;
And sixty feet the fountain leapt.

The hedge broke in, the banner blew,
The butler drank, the steward scrawled,
The fire shot up, the martin flew,
The parrot screamed, the peacock squalled;
The maid and page renewed their strife;
The palace banged, and buzzed, and clackt;
And all the long-pent stream of life
Dashed downward in a cataract.

And last of all the king awoke,
And in his chair himself upreared,
And yawned, and rubbed his face, and spoke:
"By holy rood, a royal beard!
How say you? we have slept, my lords;
My beard has grown into my lap."
The barons swore, with many words,
'T was but an after-dinner's nap.

"Pardy!" returned the king, "but still
My joints are something stiff or so.
My lord, and shall we pass the bill
I mentioned half an hour ago?"
The chancellor, sedate and vain,
In courteous words returned reply;
But dallied with his golden chain,
And, smiling, put the question by.

ALFRED TENNYSON.

THE "SLEEPING BEAUTY" DEPARTS WITH HER LOVER.

FROM "THE DAY DREAM."

And on her lover's arm she leant,
And round her waist she felt it fold;
And far across the hills they went
In that new world which is the old.
Across the hills, and far away
Beyond their utmost purple rim,
And deep into the dying day,
The happy princess followed him.

"I 'd sleep another hundred years,
O love, for such another kiss!"
"O, wake forever, love," she hears,
"O love, 't was such as this and this."
And o'er them many a sliding star,
And many a merry wind was borne,
And, streamed through many a golden bar,
The twilight melted into morn.

"O eyes long laid in happy sleep!"
"O happy sleep, that lightly fled!"
"O happy kiss, that woke thy sleep!"
"O love, thy kiss would wake the dead!"
And o'er them many a flowing range
Of vapor buoyed the crescent bark;
And, rapt through many a rosy change,
The twilight died into the dark.

"A hundred summers! can it be?
 And whither goest thou, tell me where!"
"O, seek my father's court with me,
 For there are greater wonders there."
And o'er the hills, and far away
 Beyond their utmost purple rim,
Beyond the night, across the day,
 Through all the world she followed him.

ALFRED TENNYSON.

THE EVE OF ST. AGNES.

I.

St. Agnes' Eve, — ah, bitter chill it was!
The owl, for all his feathers, was a-cold;
The hare limped trembling through the frozen grass,
And silent was the flock in woolly fold:
Numb were the beadsman's fingers while he told
His rosary, and while his frosted breath,
Like pious incense from a censer old,
Seemed taking flight for heaven without a death,
Past the sweet virgin's picture, while his prayer he saith.

II.

His prayer he saith, this patient, holy man;
Then takes his lamp, and riseth from his knees,
And back returneth, meagre, barefoot, wan,
Along the chapel aisle by slow degrees;
The sculptured dead, on each side seemed to freeze,
Imprisoned in black, purgatorial rails;
Knights, ladies, praying in dumb orat'ries,
He passeth by; and his weak spirit fails
To think how they may ache in icy hoods and mails.

III.

Northward he turneth through a little door,
And scarce three steps, ere music's golden tongue
Flattered to tears this aged man and poor;
But no, — already had his death-bell rung;
The joys of all his life were said and sung;
His was harsh penance on St. Agnes' Eve;
Another way he went, and soon among
Rough ashes sat he for his soul's reprieve,
And all night kept awake, for sinners' sake to grieve.

IV.

That ancient beadsman heard the prelude soft:
And so it chanced, for many a door was wide,
From hurry to and fro. Soon, up aloft,
The silver, snarling trumpets 'gan to chide;
The level chambers, ready with their pride,
Were glowing to receive a thousand guests;
The carvèd angels, ever eager-eyed,
Stared, where upon their heads the cornice rests,
With hair blown back, and wings put crosswise on their breasts.

V.

At length burst in the argent revelry,
With plume, tiara, and all rich array,
Numerous as shadows haunting fairily
The brain, new-stuffed, in youth, with triumphs gay
Of old romance. These let us wish away;
And turn, sole-thoughted, to one lady there,
Whose heart had brooded, all that wintry day,
On love, and winged St. Agnes' saintly care,
As she had heard old dames full many times declare.

VI.

They told her how, upon St. Agnes' Eve,
Young virgins might have visions of delight,
And soft adorings from their loves receive
Upon the honeyed middle of the night,
If ceremonies due they did aright;
As, supperless to bed they must retire,
And couch supine their beauties, lily white;
Nor look behind, nor sideways, but require
Of heaven with upward eyes for all that they desire.

VII.

Full of this whim was thoughtful Madeline;
The music, yearning like a god in pain,
She scarcely heard; her maiden eyes divine,
Fixed on the floor, saw many a sweeping train
Pass by, — she heeded not at all; in vain
Came many a tiptoe, amorous cavalier,
And back retired, not cooled by high disdain,
But she saw not; her heart was otherwhere;
She sighed for Agnes' dreams, the sweetest of the year.

VIII.

She danced along with vague, regardless eyes,
Anxious her lips, her breathing quick and short;
The hallowed hour was near at hand; she sighs
Amid the timbrels, and the thronged resort
Of whisperers in anger, or in sport;
Mid looks of love, defiance, hate, and scorn,
Hoodwinked with fairy fancy; all amort
Save to St. Agnes and her lambs unshorn,
And all the bliss to be before to-morrow morn.

IX.

So, purposing each moment to retire,
She lingered still. Meantime, across the moors,
Had come young Porphyro, with heart on fire
For Madeline. Beside the portal doors,
Buttressed from moonlight, stands he, and implores
All saints to give him sight of Madeline;
But for one moment in the tedious hours,
That he might gaze and worship all unseen;
Perchance speak, kneel, touch, kiss, — in sooth such things have been.

X.

He ventures in ; let no buzzed whisper tell ;
All eyes be muffled, or a hundred swords
Will storm his heart, love's feverous citadel ;
For him, those chambers held barbarian hordes,
Hyena foemen, and hot-blooded lords,
Whose very dogs would execrations howl
Against his lineage ; not one breast affords
Him any mercy, in that mansion foul,
Save one old beldame, weak in body and in soul.

XI.

Ah, happy chance ! the aged creature came,
Shuffling along with ivory-headed wand,
To where he stood, hid from the torch's flame,
Behind a broad hall-pillar, far beyond
The sound of merriment and chorus bland.
He startled her ; but soon she knew his face,
And grasped his fingers in her palsied hand,
Saying, "Mercy, Porphyro ! hie thee from this place ;
They are all here to-night, the whole bloodthirsty race !

XII.

"Get hence ! get hence ! there 's dwarfish Hildebrand ;
He had a fever late, and in the fit
He cursèd thee and thine, both house and land ;
Then there 's that old Lord Maurice, not a whit
More tame for his gray hairs — alas me ! flit !
Flit like a ghost away !" — "Ah, gossip dear,
We 're safe enough ; here in this arm-chair sit,
And tell me how" — "Good saints, not here, not here ;
Follow me, child, or else these stones will be thy bier."

XIII.

He followed through a lowly archèd way,
Brushing the cobwebs with his lofty plume :
And as she muttered "Well-a — well-a-day !"
He found him in a little moonlight room,
Pale, latticed, chill, and silent as a tomb.
"Now tell me where is Madeline," said he ;
"O, tell me, Angela, by the holy loom
Which none but secret sisterhood may see,
When they St. Agnes' wool are weaving piously."

XIV.

"St. Agnes ! Ah ! it is St. Agnes' Eve, —
Yet men will murder upon holy days ;
Thou must hold water in a witch's sieve,
And be liege-lord of all the elves and fays,
To venture so. It fills me with amaze
To see thee, Porphyro ! — St. Agnes' Eve !
God's help ! my lady fair the conjurer plays
This very night ; good angels her deceive !
But let me laugh awhile, I 've mickle time to grieve."

XV.

Feebly she laugheth in the languid moon,
While Porphyro upon her face doth look,
Like puzzled urchin on an aged crone
Who keepeth closed a wondrous riddle-book,
As spectacled she sits in chimney nook.
But soon his eyes grew brilliant, when she told
His lady's purpose ; and he scarce could brook
Tears, at the thought of those enchantments cold,
And Madeline asleep in lap of legends old.

XVI.

Sudden a thought came like a full-blown rose,
Flushing his brow, and in his painèd heart
Made purple riot ; then doth he propose
A stratagem that makes the beldame start :
"A cruel man and impious thou art !
Sweet lady, let her pray, and sleep and dream
Alone with her good angels, far apart
From wicked men like thee. Go, go ! I deem
Thou canst not surely be the same that thou didst seem."

XVII.

"I will not harm her, by all saints I swear !"
Quoth Porphyro ; "O, may I ne'er find grace
When my weak voice shall whisper its last prayer,
If one of her soft ringlets I displace,
Or look with ruffian passion in her face :
Good Angela, believe me by these tears ;
Or I will, even in a moment's space,
Awake, with horrid shout, my foemen's ears,
And beard them, though they be more fanged than wolves and bears."

XVIII.

"Ah ! why wilt thou affright a feeble soul ?
A poor, weak, palsy-stricken, churchyard thing,
Whose passing-bell may ere the midnight toll ;
Whose prayers for thee, each morn and evening,
Were never missed." Thus plaining, doth she bring
A gentler speech from burning Porphyro ;
So woful, and of such deep sorrowing,
That Angela gives promise she will do
Whatever he shall wish, betide her weal or woe.

XIX.

Which was, to lead him, in close secrecy,
Even to Madeline's chamber, and there hide
Him in a closet, of such privacy
That he might see her beauty unespied,
And win perhaps that night a peerless bride ;
While legioned fairies paced the coverlet,
And pale enchantment held her sleepy-eyed.
Never on such a night have lovers met,
Since Merlin paid his demon all the monstrous debt.

XX.

"It shall be as thou wishest," said the dame;
"All cates and dainties shall be storèd there
Quickly on this feast-night; by the tambour frame
Her own lute thou wilt see; no time to spare,
For I am slow and feeble, and scarce dare
On such a catering trust my dizzy head.
Wait here, my child, with patience kneel in prayer
The while. Ah! thou must needs the lady wed,
Or may I never leave my grave among the dead."

XXI.

So saying, she hobbled off with busy fear.
The lover's endless minutes slowly passed:
The dame returned, and whispered in his ear
To follow her; with aged eyes aghast
From fright of dim espial. Safe at last,
Through many a dusky gallery, they gain
The maiden's chamber, silken, hushed and chaste;
Where Porphyro took covert, pleased amain.
His poor guide hurried back with agues in her brain.

XXII.

Her faltering hand upon the balustrade,
Old Angela was feeling for the stair,
When Madeline, St. Agnes' charmèd maid,
Rose, like a missioned spirit, unaware;
With silver taper's light, and pious care,
She turned, and down the aged gossip led
To a safe level matting. Now prepare,
Young Porphyro, for gazing on that bed!
She comes, she comes again, like a ring-dove frayed and fled.

XXIII.

Out went the taper as she hurried in;
Its little smoke, in pallid moonshine, died;
She closed the door, she panted, all akin
To spirits of the air, and visions wide;
No uttered syllable, or, woe betide!
But to her heart, her heart was voluble,
Paining with eloquence her balmy side;
As though a tongueless nightingale should swell
Her throat in vain, and die, heart-stifled in her dell.

XXIV.

A casement high and triple-arched there was,
All garlanded with carven imageries
Of fruits, and flowers, and bunches of knot-grass,
And diamonded with panes of quaint device,
Innumerable of stains and splendid dyes,
As are the tiger-moth's deep-damasked wings;
And in the midst, 'mong thousand heraldries,
And twilight saints, and dim emblazonings,
A shielded scutcheon blushed with blood of queens and kings.

XXV.

Full on this casement shone the wintry moon,
And threw warm gules on Madeline's fair breast,
As down she knelt for heaven's grace and boon;
Rose-bloom fell on her hands, together prest,
And on her silver cross soft amethyst,
And on her hair a glory, like a saint;
She seemed a splendid angel, newly drest,
Save wings, for heaven. Porphyro grew faint:
She knelt, so pure a thing, so free from mortal taint.

XXVI.

Anon his heart revives; her vespers done,
Of all its wreathèd pearls her hair she frees;
Unclasps her warmèd jewels one by one;
Loosens her fragrant bodice; by degrees
Her rich attire creeps rustling to her knees;
Half hidden, like a mermaid in sea-weed,
Pensive awhile she dreams awake, and sees,
In fancy, fair St. Agnes in her bed,
But dares not look behind, or all the charm is fled.

XXVII.

Soon, trembling in her soft and chilly nest,
In sort of wakeful swoon, perplexed she lay,
Until the poppied warmth of sleep oppressed
Her soothèd limbs, and soul fatigued away;
Flown like a thought, until the morrow-day;
Blissfully havened both from joy and pain;
Clasped like a missal where swart Paynims pray;
Blinded alike from sunshine and from rain,
As though a rose should shut, and be a bud again.

XXVIII.

Stolen to this paradise, and so entranced,
Porphyro gazed upon her empty dress,
And listened to her breathing, if it chanced
To wake into a slumberous tenderness;
Which when he heard, that minute did he bless,
And breathed himself; then from the closet crept,
Noiseless as fear in a wide wilderness,
And over the hushed carpet, silent, stept,
And 'tween the curtains peeped, where, lo!—how fast she slept.

XXIX.

Then by the bedside, where the faded moon
Made a dim, silver twilight, soft he set
A table, and, half anguished, threw thereon
A cloth of woven crimson, gold, and jet:—
O for some drowsy Morphean amulet!
The boisterous, midnight, festive clarion,
The kettle-drum, and far-heard clarionet,

Affray his ears, though but in dying tone : —
The hall-door shuts again, and all the noise is gone.

XXX.

And still she slept an azure-lidded sleep,
In blanchèd linen, smooth, and lavendered ;
While he from forth the closet brought a heap
Of candied apple, quince, and plum, and gourd;
With jellies soother than the creamy curd,
And lucent syrops, tinct with cinnamon ;
Manna and dates, in argosy transferred
From Fez ; and spicèd dainties, every one,
From silken Samarcand to cedared Lebanon.

XXXI.

These delicates he heaped with glowing hand
On golden dishes and in baskets bright
Of wreathèd silver. Sumptuous they stand
In the retired quiet of the night,
Filling the chilly room with perfume light. —
"And now, my love, my seraph fair, awake!
Thou art my heaven, and I thine eremite ;
Open thine eyes, for meek St. Agnes' sake,
Or I shall drowse beside thee, so my soul doth ache."

XXXII.

Thus whispering, his warm, unnervèd arm
Sank in her pillow. Shaded was her dream
By the dusk curtains ; —'t was a midnight charm
Impossible to melt as icèd stream :
The lustrous salvers in the moonlight gleam
Broad golden fringe upon the carpet lies ;
It seemed he never, never could redeem
From such a steadfast spell his lady's eyes ;
So mused awhile, entoiled in woofèd fantasies.

XXXIII.

Awakening up, he took her hollow lute, —
Tumultuous, — and, in chords that tenderest be,
He played an ancient ditty, long since mute,
In Provence called "La belle dame sans mercy";
Close to her ear touching the melody ;—
Wherewith disturbed, she uttered a soft moan ;
He ceased — she panted quick — and suddenly
Her blue affrayèd eyes wide open shone ;
Upon his knees he sank, pale as smooth-sculptured
stone.

XXXIV.

Her eyes were open, but she still beheld,
Now wide awake, the vision of her sleep.
There was a painful change, that nigh expelled
The blisses of her dream so pure and deep ;
At which fair Madeline began to weep,
And moan forth witless words with many a sigh;
While still her gaze on Porphyro would keep.
Who knelt, with joinèd hands and piteous eye,
Fearing to move or speak, she looked so dreamingly.

XXXV.

"Ah, Porphyro!" said she, "but even now
Thy voice was at sweet tremble in mine ear,
Made tunable with every sweetest vow ;
And those sad eyes were spiritual and clear ;
How changed thou art ! how pallid, chill, and
drear !
Give me that voice again, my Porphyro,
Those looks immortal, those complainings dear !
O, leave me not in this eternal woe,
For if thou diest, my love, I know not where to go."

XXXVI.

Beyond a mortal man impassioned far
At these voluptuous accents, he arose,
Ethereal, flushed, and like a throbbing star
Seen mid the sapphire heaven's deep repose ;
Into her dream he melted, as the rose
Blendeth its odor with the violet, —
Solution sweet ; meantime the frost-wind blows
Like love's alarum pattering the sharp sleet
Against the window-panes; St. Agnes' moon hath
set.

XXXVII.

'T is dark ; quick pattereth the flaw-blown sleet ;
"This is no dream, my bride, my Madeline !"
'T is dark ; the icèd gusts still rave and beat :
"No dream, alas ! alas ! and woe is mine !
Porphyro will leave me here to fade and pine. —
Cruel ! what traitor could thee hither bring ?
I curse not, for my heart is lost in thine,
Though thou forsakest a deceivèd thing ; —
A dove forlorn and lost, with sick, unprunèd wing."

XXXVIII.

"My Madeline ! sweet dreamer ! lovely bride !
Say, may I be for aye thy vassal blest ?
Thy beauty's shield, heart-shaped and vermeil
dyed ?
Ah, silver shrine, here will I take my rest
After so many hours of toil and quest,
A famished pilgrim, — saved by miracle.
Though I have found, I will not rob thy nest,
Saving of thy sweet self ; if thou think'st well
To trust, fair Madeline, to no rude infidel.

. . . . . .

XLI.

They glide, like phantoms, into the wide hall !
Like phantoms to the iron porch they glide,
Where lay the porter, in uneasy sprawl,
With a huge empty flagon by his side ;
The wakeful bloodhound rose, and shook his hide,
But his sagacious eye an inmate owns ;
By one, and one, the bolts full easy slide ;
The chains lie silent on the footworn stones ;
The key turns, and the door upon its hinges groans.

XLII.

And they are gone! ay, ages long ago
These lovers fled away into the storm.
That night the baron dreamt of many a woe,
And all his warrior-guests, with shade and form
Of witch, and demon, and large coffin-worm,
Were long be-nightmared. Angela the old
Died palsy-twitched, with meagre face deform;
The beadsman, after thousand aves told,
For aye unsought-for slept among his ashes cold.

JOHN KEATS.

THE LITTLE MILLINER.

MY girl hath violet eyes and yellow hair,
A soft hand, like a lady's, small and fair,
A sweet face pouting in a white straw bonnet,
A tiny foot, and little boot upon it;
And all her finery to charm beholders
Is the gray shawl drawn tight around her shoulders,
The plain stuff-gown and collar white as snow,
And sweet red petticoat that peeps below.
But gladly in the busy town goes she,
Summer and winter, fearing nobodie;
She pats the pavement with her fairy feet,
With fearless eyes she charms the crowded street;
And in her pocket lie, in lieu of gold,
A lucky sixpence and a thimble old.

We lodged in the same house a year ago
She on the topmost floor, I just below, —
She, a poor milliner, content and wise,
I, a poor city clerk, with hopes to rise;
And, long ere we were friends, I learnt to love
The little angel on the floor above.
For, every morn, ere from my bed I stirred,
Her chamber door would open, and I heard, —
And listened, blushing, to her coming down,
And palpitated with her rustling gown,
And tingled while her foot went downward slow,
Creaked like a cricket, passed, and died below;
Then, peeping from the window, pleased and sly,
I saw the pretty shining face go by,
Healthy and rosy, fresh from slumber sweet, —
A sunbeam in the quiet morning street.

And every night, when in from work she tript,
Red to the ears, I from my chamber slipt,
That I might hear upon the narrow stair
Her low "Good evening," as she passed me there.
And when her door was closed, below sat I,
And hearkened stilly as she stirred on high, —
Watched the red firelight shadows in the room,
Fashioned her face before me in the gloom,
And heard her close the window, lock the door,
Moving about more lightly than before,
And thought, "She is undressing now!" and O,
My cheeks were hot, my heart was in a glow!
And I made pictures of her, — standing bright
Before the looking-glass in bed-gown white,
Unbinding in a knot her yellow hair,
Then kneeling timidly to say a prayer;
Till, last, the floor creaked softly overhead,
'Neath bare feet tripping to the little bed, —
And all was hushed. Yet still I hearkened on,
Till the faint sounds about the streets were gone;
And saw her slumbering with lips apart,
One little hand upon her little heart,
The other pillowing a face that smiled
In slumber like the slumber of a child,
The bright hair shining round the small white ear,
The soft breath stealing visible and clear,
And mixing with the moon's, whose frosty gleam
Made round her rest a vaporous light of dream.

How free she wandered in the wicked place,
Protected only by her gentle face!
She saw bad things, — how could she choose but see? —
She heard of wantonness and misery;
The city closed around her night and day,
But lightly, happily, she went her way.
Nothing of evil that she saw or heard
Could touch a heart so innocently stirred
By simple hopes that cheered it through the storm,
And little flutterings that kept it warm.
No power had she to reason out her needs,
To give the whence and wherefore of her deeds;
But she was good and pure amid the strife,
By virtue of the joy that was her life.
Here, where a thousand spirits daily fall,
Where heart and soul and senses turn to gall,
She floated, pure as innocent could be,
Like a small sea-bird on a stormy sea,
Which breasts the billows, wafted to and fro,
Fearless, uninjured, while the strong winds blow,
While the clouds gather, and the waters roar,
And mighty ships are broken on the shore.

. . . . .

'T was when the spring was coming, when the snow
Had melted, and fresh winds began to blow,
And girls were selling violets in the town,
That suddenly a fever struck me down.
The world was changed, the sense of life was pained,
And nothing but a shadow-land remained;
Death came in a dark mist and looked at me,
I felt his breathing, though I could not see,
But heavily I lay and did not stir,
And had strange images and dreams of her.
Then came a vacancy: with feeble breath,
I shivered under the cold touch of Death,
And swooned among strange visions of the dead,
When a voice called from heaven, and he fled;

And suddenly I wakened, as it seemed,
From a deep sleep wherein I had not dreamed.

And it was night, and I could see and hear,
And I was in the room I held so dear,
And unaware, stretched out upon my bed,
I hearkened for a footstep overhead.

But all was hushed. I looked around the room,
And slowly made out shapes amid the gloom.
The wall was reddened by a rosy light,
A faint fire flickered, and I knew 't was night,
Because below there was a sound of feet
Dying away along the quiet street, —
When, turning my pale face and sighing low,
I saw a vision in the quiet glow:
A little figure, in a cotton gown,
Looking upon the fire and stooping down,
Her side to me, her face illumed, she eyed
Two chestnuts burning slowly, side by side, —
Her lips apart, her clear eyes strained to see,
Her little hands clasped tight around her knee,
The firelight gleaming on her golden head,
And tinting her white neck to rosy red,
Her features bright, and beautiful, and pure,
With childish fear and yearning half demure.
O sweet, sweet dream! I thought, and strained mine eyes,
Fearing to break the spell with words and sighs.

Softly she stooped, her dear face sweetly fair,
And sweeter since a light like love was there,
Brightening, watching, more and more elate,
As the nuts glowed together in the grate,
Crackling with little jets of fiery light,
Till side by side they turned to ashes white, —
Then up she leapt, her face cast off its fear
For rapture that itself was radiance clear,
And would have clapped her little hands in glee,
But, pausing, bit her lips and peeped at me,
And met the face that yearned on her so whitely,
And gave a cry and trembled, blushing brightly,
While, raised on elbow, as she turned to flee,
"*Polly!*" I cried, — and grew as red as she!

It was no dream! for soon my thoughts were clear,
And she could tell me all, and I could hear:
How in my sickness friendless I had lain;
How the hard people pitied not my pain;
How, in despite of what bad people said,
She left her labors, stopped beside my bed,
And nursed me, thinking sadly I would die;
How, in the end, the danger passed me by;
How she had sought to steal away before
The sickness passed, and I was strong once more.
By fits she told the story in mine ear,
And troubled all the telling with a fear
Lest by my cold man's heart she should be chid,
Lest I should think her bold in what she did;
But, lying on my bed, I dared to say,
How I had watched and loved her many a day;
How dear she was to me, and dearer still
For that strange kindness done while I was ill;
And how I could but think that Heaven above
Had done it all to bind our lives in love.
And Polly cried, turning her face away,
And seemed afraid, and answered "yea" nor "nay";
Then stealing close, with little pants and sighs,
Looked on my pale thin face and earnest eyes,
And seemed in act to fling her arms about
My neck, then, blushing, paused, in fluttering doubt.
Last, sprang upon my heart, sighing and sobbing, —
That I might feel how gladly hers was throbbing!

Ah! ne'er shall I forget until I die
How happily the dreamy days went by,
While I grew well, and lay with soft heart-beats,
Heark'ning the pleasant murmur from the streets,
And Polly by me like a sunny beam,
And life all changed, and love a drowsy dream!
'T was happiness enough to lie and see
The little golden head bent droopingly
Over its sewing, while the still time flew,
And my fond eyes were dim with happy dew!
And then, when I was nearly well and strong,
And she went back to labor all day long,
How sweet to lie alone with half-shut eyes,
And hear the distant murmurs and the cries,
And think how pure she was from pain and sin, —
And how the summer days were coming in!
Then, as the sunset faded from the room,
To listen for her footstep in the gloom,
To pant as it came stealing up the stair,
To feel my whole life brighten unaware
When the soft tap came to the door, and when
The door was opened for her smile again!
Best, the long evenings! — when, till late at night,
She sat beside me in the quiet light,
And happy things were said and kisses won,
And serious gladness found its vent in fun.
Sometimes I would draw close her shining head,
And pour her bright hair out upon the bed,
And she would laugh, and blush, and try to scold,
While "Here," I cried, "I count my wealth in gold!"

Once, like a little sinner for transgression,
She blushed upon my breast, and made confession:
How, when that night I woke and looked around,
I found her busy with a charm profound, —
One chestnut was herself, my girl confessed,
The other was the person she loved best,

And if they burned together side by side,
He loved her, and she would become his bride;
And burn indeed they did, to her delight, —
And had the pretty charm not proven right?
Thus much, and more, with timorous joy, she said,
While her confessor, too, grew rosy red, —
And close together pressed two blissful faces,
As I absolved the sinner, with embraces.

And here is winter come again, winds blow,
The houses and the streets are white with snow;
And in the long and pleasant eventide,
Why, what is Polly making at my side?
What but a silk gown, beautiful and grand,
We bought together lately in the Strand!
What but a dress to go to church in soon,
And wear right queenly 'neath a honey-moon!
And who shall match her with her new straw bonnet,
Her tiny foot and little boot upon it,
Embroidered petticoat and silk gown new,
And shawl she wears as few fine ladies do?
And she will keep, to charm away all ill,
The lucky sixpence in her pocket still;
And we will turn, come fair or cloudy weather,
To ashes, like the chestnuts, close together!

ROBERT BUCHANAN.

THE PASSIONATE PILGRIM'S SONG.

FROM "THE BRIDEGROOM OF BEAUTY."

LIKE a tree beside the river
Of her life that runs from me,
Do I lean me, murmuring ever
In my love's idolatry.
Lo, I reach out hands of blessing;
Lo, I stretch out hands of prayer;
And, with passionate caressing,
Pour my life upon the air,
In my ears the siren river
Sings, and smiles up in my face;
But forever, and forever,
Runs from my embrace.

Spring by spring, the branches duly
Clothe themselves in tender flower;
And for her sweet sake as truly
All their fruit and fragrance shower.
But the stream, with careless laughter,
Runs in merry beauty by,
And it leaves me yearning after,
Lorn to droop and lone to die.
In my ears the siren river
Sings, and smiles up in my face;
But forever, and forever,
Runs from my embrace.

I stand mazèd in the moonlight,
O'er its happy face to dream;
I am parchèd in the moonlight
By that cool and brimming stream;
I am dying by the river
Of her life that runs from me,
And it sparkles by me ever,
With its cool felicity.
In my ears the siren river
Sings, and smiles up in my face;
But forever, and forever,
Runs from my embrace.

GERALD MASSEY.

ONCE.

THE June roses covered the hedges with blushes,
And wooed with their perfume the murmuring bee;
And white were the cups of the odorous lilies,
When fate stole the joy of existence from me.

With hands closely clasped, and with lips pressed together,
One instant we stood, while the heart in my breast
Leapt eager and wild, as the callow birds flutter
When the wing of the mother sweeps over the nest.

One star is the type of the glory of heaven;
A shell from the beach whispers still of the sea;
To a rose all the sweetness of summer is given;
A kiss tells what living and loving might be.

MARY LOUISE RITTER.

THE MILLER'S DAUGHTER.

IT is the miller's daughter,
And she is grown so dear, so dear,
That I would be the jewel
That trembles at her ear;
For, hid in ringlets day and night,
I 'd touch her neck so warm and white.

And I would be the girdle
About her dainty, dainty waist,
And her heart would beat against me
In sorrow and in rest;
And I should know if it beat right,
I 'd clasp it round so close and tight.

And I would be the necklace,
And all day long to fall and rise
Upon her balmy bosom
With her laughter or her sighs;
And I would lie so light, so light,
I scarce should be unclasped at night.

ALFRED TENNYSON.

BLEST AS THE IMMORTAL GODS.

BLEST as the immortal gods is he,
The youth who fondly sits by thee,
And hears and sees thee all the while
Softly speak, and sweetly smile.

'T was this deprived my soul of rest,
And raised such tumults in my breast:
For while I gazed, in transport tost,
My breath was gone, my voice was lost.

My bosom glowed; the subtle flame
Ran quick through all my vital frame:
O'er my dim eyes a darkness hung;
My ears with hollow murmurs rung.

In dewy damps my limbs were chilled;
My blood with gentle horrors thrilled:
My feeble pulse forgot to play —
I fainted, sunk, and died away.

From the Greek of SAPPHO,
by AMBROSE PHILLIPS.

THOSE EYES.

AH! do not wanton with those eyes,
  Lest I be sick with seeing;
Nor cast them down, but let them rise,
  Lest shame destroy their being.

Ah! be not angry with those fires,
  For then their threats will kill me;
Nor look too kind on my desires,
  For then my hopes will spill me.

Ah! do not steep them in thy tears,
  For so will sorrow slay me;
Nor spread them as distraught with fears, —
  Mine own enough betray me.

BEN JONSON.

JANE.

SHE came along the little lane,
Where all the bushes dripped with rain,
And robins sung and sung again,

As if with sudden, sheer delight,
For such a world so fresh and bright,
To swing and sing in day and night.

But, coming down the little lane,
She did not heed the robin's strain,
Nor feel the sunshine after rain.

A little face with two brown eyes,
A little form of slender size,
A little head not very wise;

A little heart to match the head,
A foolish little heart, that bled
At every foolish word was said.

So, coming down the little lane, —
I see her now, my little Jane, —
Her foolish heart with foolish pain

Was aching, aching in her breast,
And all her pretty golden crest
Was drooping as if sore opprest.

And something, too, of anger's trace
Was on the flushed and frowning face,
And in the footsteps' quickened pace.

So swift she stept, so low she leant,
Her pretty head on thought intent,
She scarcely saw the way she went,

Nor saw the long, slim shadow fall
Across the little, low stone-wall,
As some one rose up slim and tall, —

Rose up, and came to meet her there;
A youth, with something in his air
That, at a glance, revealed his share

In all this foolish, girlish pain,
This grief and anger and disdain,
That rent the heart of little Jane.

With hastier steps than hers he came,
And in a moment called her name;
And in a moment, red as flame

She blushed, and blushed, and in her eyes
A sudden, soft, and shy surprise
Did suddenly and softly rise.

"What, you?" she cried: "I thought — they said —"
Then stopped, and blushed a deeper red,
And lifted up her drooping head,

Shook back her lovely falling hair,
And arched her neck, and strove to wear
A nonchalant and scornful air.

A moment thus they held apart,
With lovers' love and lovers' art;
Then swift he caught her to his heart.

What pleasure then was born of pain,
What sunshine after cloud and rain,
As they forgave and kissed again!

'T was April then; he talked of May,
And planned therein a wedding-day:
She blushed, but scarcely said him nay.

What pleasure now is mixed with pain,
As, looking down the little lane,
A graybeard grown, I see again,

Through twenty Aprils' rain and mist,
The little sweetheart that I kissed,
The little bride my folly missed!

NORA PERRY.

PAN IN LOVE.

NAY! if you will not sit upon my knee,
Lie on that bank, and listen while I play
A sylvan song upon these reedy pipes.
In the full moonrise as I lay last night
Under the alders on Peneus' banks,
Dabbling my hoofs in the cool stream that welled
Wine-dark with gleamy ripples round their roots,
I made the song the while I shaped the pipes.
'T is all of you and love, as you shall hear.
The drooping lilies, as I sang it, heaved
Upon their broad green leaves, and underneath,
Swift silvery fishes, poised on quivering fins,
Hung motionless to listen; in the grass
The crickets ceased to shrill their tiny bells;
And even the nightingale, that all the eve,
Hid in the grove's deep green, had throbbed and thrilled,
Paused in his strain of love to list to mine.
Bacchus is handsome, but such songs as this
He cannot shape, and better loves the clash
Of brazen cymbals than my reedy pipes.
Fair as he is without, he's coarse within, —
Gross in his nature, loving noise and wine,
And, tipsy, half the time goes reeling round
Leaning on old Silenus' shoulders fat.
But I have scores of songs that no one knows,
Not even Apollo, no, nor Mercury, —
Their strings can never sing like my sweet pipes, —
Some, that will make fierce tigers rub their fur
Against the oak trunks for delight, or stretch
Their plump sides for my pillow on the sward.
Some, that will make the satyrs' clattering hoofs
Leap when they hear, and from their noonday dreams
Start up to stamp a wild and frolic dance
In the green shadows. Ay! and better songs,
Made for the delicate nice ears of nymphs,
Which while I sing my pipes shall imitate
The droning bass of honey-seeking bees,
The tinkling tenor of clear pebbly streams,
The breezy alto of the alder's sighs,
And all the airy sounds that lull the grove
When noon falls fast asleep among the hills.
Nor only these, — for I can pipe to you
Songs that will make the slippery vipers pause,
And stay the stags to gaze with their great eyes;
Such songs — and you shall hear them if you will —
That Bacchus' self would give his hide to hear.
If you 'll but love me every day, I 'll bring
The coyest flowers, such as you never saw,
To deck you with. I know their secret nooks, —
They cannot hide themselves away from Pan.
And you shall have rare garlands; and your bed
Of fragrant mosses shall be sprinkled o'er
With violets like your eyes, — just for a kiss.
Love me, and you shall do whate'er you like,
And shall be tended wheresoe'er you go,
And not a beast shall hurt you, — not a toad
But at your bidding give his jewel up.
The speckled shining snakes shall never sting,
But twist like bracelets round your rosy arms,
And keep your bosom cool in the hot noon.
You shall have berries ripe of every kind,
And luscious peaches, and wild nectarines,
And sun-flecked apricots, and honeyed dates,
And wine from bee-stung grapes, drunk with the sun
(Such wine as Bacchus never tasted yet).
And not a poisonous plant shall have the power
To tetter your white flesh, if you 'll love Pan.
And then I 'll tell you tales that no one knows;
Of what the pines talk in the summer nights,
When far above you hear them murmuring,
As they sway whispering to the lifting breeze;
And what the storm shrieks to the struggling oaks
As it flies through them hurrying to the sea
From mountain crags and cliffs. Or, when you 're sad,
I 'll tell you tales that solemn cypresses
Have whispered to me. There 's not anything
Hid in the woods and dales and dark ravines,
Shadowed in dripping caves, or by the shore,
Slipping from sight, but I can tell to you.
Plump, dull-eared Bacchus, thinking of himself,
Never can catch a syllable of this;
But with my shaggy ear against the grass
I hear the secrets hidden underground,
And know how in the inner forge of Earth,
The pulse-like hammers of creation beat.
Old Pan is ugly, rough, and rude to see,
But no one knows such secrets as old Pan.

WILLIAM W. STORY.

COME, REST IN THIS BOSOM.

FROM "IRISH MELODIES."

COME, rest in this bosom, my own stricken deer,
Though the herd have fled from thee, thy home is still here;
Here still is the smile, that no cloud can o'ercast,
And a heart and a hand all thy own to the last.

Oh! what was love made for, if 't is not the same
Through joy and through torment, through glory and shame?
I know not, I ask not, if guilt 's in that heart,
I but know that I love thee, whatever thou art.

Thou hast called me thy Angel in moments of bliss,
And thy Angel I 'll be, mid the horrors of this,
Through the furnace, unshrinking, thy steps to pursue,
And shield thee, and save thee, — or perish there too!

THOMAS MOORE.

BEDOUIN LOVE-SONG.

FROM the Desert I come to thee,
On a stallion shod with fire;
And the winds are left behind
In the speed of my desire.
Under thy window I stand,
And the midnight hears my cry:
I love thee, I love but thee!
With a love that shall not die
Till the sun grows cold,
And the stars are old,
And the leaves of the Judgment
Book unfold!

Look from thy window, and see
My passion and my pain!
I lie on the sands below,
And I faint in thy disdain.
Let the night-winds touch thy brow
With the heat of my burning sigh,
And melt thee to hear the vow
Of a love that shall not die
Till the sun grows cold,
And the stars are old,
And the leaves of the Judgment
Book unfold!

My steps are nightly driven,
By the fever in my breast,
To hear from thy lattice breathed
The word that shall give me rest.
Open the door of thy heart,
And open thy chamber door,
And my kisses shall teach thy lips
The love that shall fade no more
Till the sun grows cold,
And the stars are old,
And the leaves of the Judgment
Book unfold!

BAYARD TAYLOR.

WHEN YOUR BEAUTY APPEARS.

"WHEN your beauty appears,
In its graces and airs,
All bright as an angel new dropt from the skies,
At distance I gaze, and am awed by my fears,
So strangely you dazzle my eyes!

"But when without art
Your kind thoughts you impart,
When your love runs in blushes through every vein,
When it darts from your eyes, when it pants at your heart,
Then I know that you 're woman again."

"There 's a passion and pride
In our sex," she replied;
"And thus (might I gratify both) I would do, —
Still an angel appear to each lover beside,
But still be a woman for you."

THOMAS PARNELL.

KISS ME SOFTLY.

Da mihi basia. — CATULLUS.

KISS me softly and speak to me low, —
Malice has ever a vigilant ear:
What if Malice were lurking near?
Kiss me, dear!
Kiss me softly and speak to me low.

Kiss me softly and speak to me low, —
Envy too has a watchful ear:
What if Envy should chance to hear?
Kiss me, dear!
Kiss me softly and speak to me low.

Kiss me softly and speak to me low:
Trust me, darling, the time is near
When lovers may love with never a fear, —
Kiss me, dear!
Kiss me softly and speak to me low.

JOHN GODFREY SAXE.

THE FIRST KISS.

How delicious is the winning
Of a kiss at love's beginning,
When two mutual hearts are sighing
For the knot there 's no untying.

Yet remember, midst your wooing,
Love has bliss, but love has ruing;
Other smiles may make you fickle,
Tears for other charms may trickle.

Love he comes, and Love he tarries,
Just as fate or fancy carries, —
Longest stays when sorest chidden,
Laughs and flies when pressed and bidden.

Bind the sea to slumber stilly,
Bind its odor to the lily,
Bind the aspen ne'er to quiver, —
Then bind Love to last forever!

Love 's a fire that needs renewal
Of fresh beauty for its fuel;
Love's wing moults when caged and captured, —
Only free he soars enraptured.

Can you keep the bee from ranging,
Or the ring-dove's neck from changing?
No! nor fettered Love from dying
In the knot there 's no untying.

THOMAS CAMPBELL.

SLY THOUGHTS.

"I SAW him kiss your cheek!" — "'T is true."
"O Modesty!" — "'T was strictly kept:
He thought me asleep; at least, I knew
He thought I thought he thought I slept."

COVENTRY PATMORE.

THE KISS.

1. AMONG thy fancies tell me this:
What is the thing we call a kiss? —
2. I shall resolve ye what it is:

It is a creature born and bred
Between the lips all cherry red,
By love and warm desires fed;
Chor. And makes more soft the bridal bed.

It is an active flame, that flies
First to the babies of the eyes,
And charms them there with lullabies;
Chor. And stills the bride too when she cries.

Then to the chin, the cheek, the ear,
It frisks and flies, — now here, now there;
'T is now far off, and then 't is near;
Chor. And here, and there, and everywhere.

1. Has it a speaking virtue? — 2. Yes.
1. How speaks it, say? — 2. Do you but this:
Part your joined lips, — then speaks your kiss;
Chor. And this love's sweetest language is.

1. Has it a body? — 2. Ay, and wings,
With a thousand rare encolorings;
And as it flies it gently sings;
Chor. Love honey yields, but never stings.

ROBERT HERRICK.

THE DIFFERENCE.

So you call that a kiss, when, in token of parting,
Your lips touched my own with such tremulous fear;
When haste took for wages the most of the honey
And whispered that danger and peril were near.

So you call that a kiss! Let me paint for a minute,
The home of my fancy, my castle of rest,
Where — all the bright dreams of my life stored within it —
I linger for hours with the friends I love best.

The lamps shed a light like the soft glow of moonbeams,
The air breathes warm odors of spice and of balm,
Not a sound breaks the hush, and the spirit, in rapture,
Folds round it the mantle of heavenly calm.

You are there in the stillness and some one beside you,
We 'll say, for the dream's sake, the one you love best,
She is kneeling beside you, your arms are around her,
Her head on your shoulder is pillowed in rest.

You smooth the soft tresses away from her forehead,
Her breath, sweet as summer, floats over your cheek.
You tighten your clasp as you murmur, "My darling,
I am weary and faint for the kisses I seek."

She turns her face toward you, her large eyes uplifted,
Dilated, and dark, with a passionate fire;
And her rich, dewy lips, in their innocent fondness,
Fill up in full measure your cup of desire.

O moment ecstatic — renewed and repeated!
Alas! weary world, with your burden of care,
Your raptures are coldness, your kisses are failures,
When matched with the ones of my castle in air.

MARY LOUISE RITTER.

THE PLAIDIE.

Upon ane stormy Sunday,
Coming adoon the lane,
Were a score of bonnie lassies —
And the sweetest I maintain
Was Caddie,
That I took unneath my plaidie,
To shield her from the rain.

She said that the daisies blushed
For the kiss that I had ta'en;
I wad na hae thought the lassie
Wad sae of a kiss complain:
"Now, laddie!
I winna stay under your plaidie,
If I gang hame in the rain!"

But, on an after Sunday,
When cloud there was not ane,
This selfsame winsome lassie
(We chanced to meet in the lane)
Said, "Laddie,
Why dinna ye wear your plaidie?
Wha kens but it may rain?"

CHARLES SIBLEY.

KISSING 'S NO SIN.

Some say that kissing 's a sin;
But I think it 's nane ava,
For kissing has wonn'd in this warld
Since ever that there was twa.

O, if it wasna lawfu'
Lawyers wadna allow it;
If it wasna holy,
Ministers wadna do it.

If it wasna modest,
Maidens wadna tak' it;
If it wasna plenty,
Puir folk wadna get it.

ANONYMOUS.

LOVE'S PHILOSOPHY.

The fountains mingle with the river,
And the rivers with the ocean;
The winds of heaven mix forever,
With a sweet emotion;
Nothing in the world is single;
All things by a law divine
In one another's being mingle: —
Why not I with thine?

See! the mountains kiss high heaven,
And the waves clasp one another;
No sister flower would be forgiven
If it disdained its brother;
And the sunlight clasps the earth,
And the moonbeams kiss the sea: —
What are all these kissings worth,
If thou kiss not me?

PERCY BYSSHE SHELLEY.

COMIN' THROUGH THE RYE.

Gin a body meet a body
Comin' through the rye,
Gin a body kiss a body,
Need a body cry?
Every lassie has her laddie, —
Ne'er a ane hae I;
Yet a' the lads they smile at me
When comin' through the rye.
Amang the train there is a swain
I dearly lo'e mysel';
But whaur his hame, or what his name,
I dinna care to tell.

Gin a body meet a body
Comin' frae the town,
Gin a body greet a body,
Need a body frown?
Every lassie has her laddie, —
Ne'er a ane hae I;
Yet a' the lads they smile at me
When comin' through the rye.
Amang the train there is a swain
I dearly lo'e mysel';
But whaur his hame, or what his name,
I dinna care to tell.

Adapted by BURNS.

KITTY OF COLERAINE.

As beautiful Kitty one morning was tripping
With a pitcher of milk, from the fair of Coleraine,
When she saw me she stumbled, the pitcher it tumbled,
And all the sweet buttermilk watered the plain.

"O, what shall I do now?— 't was looking at you now!
Sure, sure, such a pitcher I 'll ne'er meet again!
'T was the pride of my dairy: O Barney M'Cleary!
You 're sent as a plague to the girls of Coleraine."

I sat down beside her, and gently did chide her,
That such a misfortune should give her such pain.
A kiss then I gave her; and ere I did leave her,
She vowed for such pleasure she'd break it again.

'T was hay-making season — I can't tell the reason —
Misfortunes will never come single, 't is plain;
For very soon after poor Kitty's disaster
The devil a pitcher was whole in Coleraine.

ANONYMOUS.

THE MOTH'S KISS, FIRST.

FROM "IN A GONDOLA."

THE Moth's kiss, first!
Kiss me as if you made believe
You were not sure, this eve,
How my face, your flower, had pursed
Its petals up; so, here and there
You brush it, till I grow aware
Who wants me, and wide open burst.

The Bee's kiss, now!
Kiss me as if you entered gay
My heart at some noonday,
A bud that dared not disallow
The claim, so all is rendered up,
And passively its shattered cup
Over your head to sleep I bow.

ROBERT BROWNING.

THE LUTE-PLAYER.

FROM "HASSAN BEN KHALED."

"'MUSIC!' they shouted, echoing my demand,
And answered with a beckon of his hand
The gracious host, whereat a maiden, fair
As the last star that leaves the morning air,
Came down the leafy paths. Her veil revealed
The beauty of her face, which, half concealed
Behind its thin blue folds, showed like the moon
Behind a cloud that will forsake it soon.
Her hair was braided darkness, but the glance
Of lightning eyes shot from her countenance,
And showed her neck, that like an ivory tower
Rose o'er the twin domes of her marble breast.
Were all the beauty of this age compressed
Into one form, she would transcend its power.
Her step was lighter than the young gazelle's
And as she walked, her anklet's golden bells
Tinkled with pleasure, but were quickly mute
With jealousy, as from a case she drew
With snowy hands the pieces of her lute,
And took her seat before me. As it grew
To perfect shape, her lovely arms she bent
Around the neck of the sweet instrument,
Till from her soft caresses it awoke
To consciousness, and thus its rapture spoke:
'I was a tree within an Indian vale,
When first I heard the love-sick nightingale
Declare his passion; every leaf was stirred
With the melodious sorrow of the bird,
And when he ceased, the song remained with me.
Men came anon, and felled the harmless tree,
But from the memory of the songs I heard,
The spoiler saved me from the destiny
Whereby my brethren perished. O'er the sea
I came, and from its loud, tumultuous moan
I caught a soft and solemn undertone;
And when I grew beneath the maker's hand
To what thou seest, he sang (the while he planned)
The mirthful measures of a careless heart,
And of my soul his songs became a part.
Now they have laid my head upon a breast
Whiter than marble, I am wholly blest.
The fair hands smite me, and my strings complain
With such melodious cries, they smite again,
Until, with passion and with sorrow swayed,
My torment moves the bosom of the maid,
Who hears it speak her own. I am the voice
Whereby the lovers languish or rejoice;
And they caress me, knowing that my strain
Alone can speak the language of their pain.'

"Here ceased the fingers of the maid to stray
Over the strings; the sweet song died away
In mellow, drowsy murmurs, and the lute
Leaned on her fairest bosom, and was mute.
Better than wine that music was to me;
Not the lute only felt her hands, but she
Played on my heart-strings, till the sounds became
Incarnate in the pulses of my frame.
Speech left my tongue, and in my tears alone
Found utterance. With stretched arms I implored
Continuance, whereat her fingers poured
A tenderer music, answering the tone
Her parted lips released, the while her throat
Throbbed, as a heavenly bird were fluttering there,
And gave her voice the wonder of his note.
'His brow,' she sang, 'is white beneath his hair;
The fertile beard is soft upon his chin,
Shading the mouth that nestles warm within,
As a rose nestles in its leaves; I see
His eyes, but cannot tell what hue they be,
For the sharp eyelash, like a saber, speaks
The martial law of Passion; in his cheeks
The quick blood mounts, and then as quickly goes,
Leaving a tint like marble when a rose
Is held beside it; — bid him veil his eyes,
Lest all my soul should unto mine arise,
And he behold it!' As she sang, her glance
Dwelt on my face; her beauty, like a lance,
Transfixed my heart. I melted into sighs,

Slain by the arrows of her beauteous eyes.
'Why is her bosom made,' I cried, 'a snare?
Why does a single ringlet of her hair
Hold my heart captive?' 'Would you know?' she said;
'It is that you are mad with love, and chains
Were made for madmen.' Then she raised her head
With answering love, that led to other strains,
Until the lute, which shared with her the smart,
Rocked as in storm upon her beating heart.
Thus to its wires she made impassioned cries:
'I swear it by the brightness of his eyes;
I swear it by the darkness of his hair;
By the warm bloom his limbs and bosom wear;
By the fresh pearls his rosy lips enclose;
By the calm majesty of his repose;
By smiles I coveted, and frowns I feared,
And by the shooting myrtles of his beard, —
I swear it, that from him the morning drew
Its freshness, and the moon her silvery hue,
The sun his brightness, and the stars their fire,
And musk and camphor all their odorous breath:
And if he answer not my love's desire,
Day will be night to me, and Life be Death!'"

BAYARD TAYLOR.

SUB SILENTIO.

Hush! the night is calm and quiet
And the crescent moon hangs low;
Silence deep and wide hath power,
And the south wind wanders slow —
Through a casement where the curtain
Faintly rustles to and fro.

Like a spirit softly sighing
Flits it all the chamber round,
Where the dim lamp fading, dying,
Just dispels the gloom profound;
Hangs above two happy dreamers,
By love's perfect promise crowned.

Even through the gates of slumber
To the shadowy land of rest
He still clasps his long-sought treasure
Closely, closely to his breast,
With the ardor of a passion
Long denied and long repressed.

With his lips still warm with kisses
Close and clinging as his own,
Sighing still in happy dreaming
For the joy his heart hath known —
Sweetly, peacefully, he slumbers,
In the arms about him thrown.

And she gazes at him, thinking —
Not of all her dreary years —
Only of this isle of glory,
Reached with many doubts and fears,
Over love's frail bridge of rainbows
Fading in a mist of tears.

Then she nestles still more closely
To the heart so kind and dear,
Whispering, "Love me, love me, darling,
All my hope and rest is here,
And without thee, earth is nothing
But a desert cold and drear.

"O, that every night my slumbers
Might be so supremely blest,
Bounded by thy dear embraces,
Kissed from passion into rest;
I would ask no better heaven
Sheltered thus and thus caressed."

Fan them gently, odorous south wind,
And begone on pinions fleet!
Nothing in thy nightly journey
Shall thy wandering vision greet,
Half as perfect in fulfillment,
Satisfying and complete.

MARY LOUISE RITTER.

CLEOPATRA.

Here, Charmian, take my bracelets;
They bar with a purple stain
My arms; turn over my pillows, —
They are hot where I have lain:
Open the lattice wider,
A gauze o'er my bosom throw,
And let me inhale the odors
That over the garden blow.

I dreamed I was with my Antony
And in his arms I lay;
Ah me! the vision has vanished, —
The music has died away.
The flame and the perfume have perished —
As this spiced aromatic pastille
That wound the blue smoke of its odor,
Is now but an ashy hill.

Scatter upon me rose-leaves,
They cool me after my sleep,
And with sandal odors fan me
Till into my veins they creep;
Reach down the lute, and play me
A melancholy tune,
To rhyme with the dream that has vanished,
And the slumbering afternoon.

There, drowsing in golden sunlight,
Loiters the slow, smooth Nile,

Through slender papyri, that cover
The wary crocodile.
The lotus lolls on the water,
And opens its heart of gold,
And over its broad leaf pavement
Never a ripple is rolled.

The twilight breeze is too lazy
Those feathery palms to wave,
And yon little cloud is as motionless
As a stone above a grave.

Ah me! this lifeless nature
Oppresses my heart and brain!
O, for a storm and thunder,
For lightning and wild fierce rain!
Fling down that lute — I hate it!
Take rather his buckler and sword,
And crash them and clash them together
Till this sleeping world is stirred.

Hark! to my Indian beauty —
My cockatoo, creamy white,
With roses under his feathers —
That flashes across the light.
Look! listen! as backward and forward
To his hoop of gold he clings,
How he trembles, with crest uplifted,
And shrieks as he madly swings!

O cockatoo, shriek for Antony!
Cry, "Come, my love, come home!"
Shriek, "Antony! Antony! Antony!"
Till he hears you even in Rome.

There — leave me, and take from my chamber
That stupid little gazelle,
With its bright black eyes so meaningless,
And its silly tinkling bell!
Take him — my nerves he vexes —
The thing without blood or brain,
Or, by the body of Isis,
I 'll snap his neck in twain!

Leave me to gaze at the landscape
Mistily stretching away,
Where the afternoon's opaline tremors
O'er the mountains quivering play
Till the fiercer splendor of sunset
Pours from the west its fire,
And melted, as in a crucible,
Their earthly forms expire;

And the bald blear skull of the desert
With glowing mountains is crowned,
That, burning like molten jewels,
Circle its temples round.

I will lie and dream of the past time,
Æons of thought away,
And through the jungle of memory
Loosen my fancy to play;
When, a smooth and velvety tiger,
Ribbed with yellow and black,
Supple and cushion-footed,
I wandered where never the track
Of a human creature had rustled
The silence of mighty woods,
And, fierce in a tyrannous freedom,
I knew but the law of my moods.
The elephant, trumpeting, started
When he heard my footstep near,
And the spotted giraffes fled wildly
In a yellow cloud of fear.
I sucked in the noontide splendor
Quivering along the glade,
Or yawning, panting, and dreaming,
Basked in the tamarisk shade,
Till I heard my wild mate roaring,
As the shadows of night came on
To brood in the trees' thick branches,
And the shadow of sleep was gone;
Then I roused and roared in answer,
And unsheathed from my cushioned feet
My curving claws, and stretched me
And wandered my mate to greet.
We toyed in the amber moonlight,
Upon the warm flat sand,
And struck at each other our massive arms —
How powerful he was and grand!
His yellow eyes flashed fiercely
As he crouched and gazed at me,
And his quivering tail, like a serpent,
Twitched curving nervously;
Then like a storm he seized me,
With a wild, triumphant cry,
And we met as two clouds in heaven
When the thunders before them fly;
We grappled and struggled together,
For his love, like his rage, was rude;
And his teeth in the swelling folds of my neck
At times, in our play, drew blood.
Often another suitor —
For I was flexile and fair —
Fought for me in the moonlight,
While I lay crouching there,
Till his blood was drained by the desert;
And, ruffled with triumph and power,
He licked me and lay beside me
To breathe him a vast half-hour;
Then down to the fountain we loitered,
Where the antelopes came to drink, —
Like a bolt we sprang upon them,
Ere they had time to shrink.
We drank their blood and crushed them,
And tore them limb from limb,

And the hungriest lion doubted
  Ere he disputed with him.

That was a life to live for!
  Not this weak human life,
With its frivolous, bloodless passions,
  Its poor and petty strife!
Come to my arms, my hero,
  The shadows of twilight grow,
And the tiger's ancient fierceness
  In my veins begins to flow.
Come not cringing to sue me!
  Take me with triumph and power,
As a warrior storms a fortress!
  I will not shrink or cower.
Come as you came in the desert,
  Ere we were women and men,
When the tiger passions were in us,
  And love as you loved me then!

WILLIAM W. STORY.

SMILE AND NEVER HEED ME.

THOUGH, when other maids stand by,
I may deign thee no reply,
Turn not then away, and sigh, —
    Smile, and never heed me!
If our love, indeed, be such
As must thrill at every touch,
Why should others learn as much? —
    Smile, and never heed me!

Even if, with maiden pride,
I should bid thee quit my side,
Take this lesson for thy guide, —
    Smile, and never heed me!
But when stars and twilight meet,
And the dew is falling sweet,
And thou hear'st my coming feet, —
    Then thou — then — mayst heed me!

CHARLES SWAIN.

I ARISE FROM DREAMS OF THEE.

SERENADE.

I ARISE from dreams of thee
  In the first sweet sleep of night,
When the winds are breathing low,
  And the stars are shining bright.
I arise from dreams of thee,
  And a spirit in my feet
Has led me — who knows how? —
  To thy chamber-window, sweet!

The wandering airs they faint
  On the dark, the silent stream, —
The champak odors fail
  Like sweet thoughts in a dream;
The nightingale's complaint,
  It dies upon her heart,
As I must die on thine,
  O, belovèd as thou art!

O, lift me from the grass!
  I die, I faint, I fail!
Let thy love in kisses rain
  On my lips and eyelids pale.
My cheek is cold and white, alas!
  My heart beats loud and fast:
Oh! press it close to thine again,
  Where it will break at last!

PERCY BYSSHE SHELLEY.

SONNETS FROM THE PORTUGUESE.

Go from me. Yet I feel that I shall stand
Henceforward in thy shadow. Nevermore,
Alone upon the threshold of my door
Of individual life, I shall command
The uses of my soul, nor lift my hand
Serenely in the sunshine as before,
Without the sense of that which I forebore, . . .
Thy touch upon the palm. The widest land
Doom takes to part us, leaves thy heart in mine
With pulses that beat double. What I do
And what I dream include thee, as the wine
Must taste of its own grapes. And when I sue
God for myself, he hears that name of thine,
And sees within my eyes the tears of two.

THE face of all the world is changed, I think,
Since first I heard the footsteps of thy soul
Move still, O still, beside me, as they stole
Betwixt me and the dreadful outer brink
Of obvious death, where I, who thought to sink,
Was caught up into love, and taught the whole
Of life in a new rhythm. The cup of dole
God gave for baptism I am fain to drink,
And praise its sweetness, Sweet, with thee anear.
The names of country, heaven, are changed away
For where thou art or shall be, there or here;
And this, this lute and song, loved yesterday
(The singing angels know) are only dear,
Because thy name moves right in what they say.

INDEED, this very love which is my boast,
And which, when rising up from breast to brow,
Doth crown me with a ruby large enow
To draw men's eyes and prove the inner cost,
This love even, all my worth, to the uttermost,
I should not love withal, unless that thou
Hadst set me an example, shown me how,
When first thine earnest eyes with mine were crossed,

And love called love. And thus, I cannot speak
Of love even, as a good thing of my own.
Thy soul hath snatched up mine all faint and weak,
And placed it by thee on a golden throne, —
And that I love (O soul, we must be meek !)
Is by thee only, whom I love alone.

If thou must love me, let it be for naught
Except for love's sake only. Do not say,
"I love her for her smile, her look, her way
Of speaking gently, — for a trick of thought
That falls in well with mine, and certes brought
A sense of pleasant ease on such a day."
For these things in themselves, Belovèd, may
Be changed, or change for thee, — and love so wrought
May be unwrought so. Neither love me for
Thine own dear pity's wiping my cheeks dry, —
A creature might forget to weep, who bore
Thy comfort long, and lose thy love thereby.
But love me for love's sake, that evermore
Thou mayst love on, through love's eternity.

I never gave a lock of hair away
To a man, Dearest, except this to thee,
Which now upon my fingers thoughtfully
I ring out to the full brown length and say,
"Take it." My day of youth went yesterday;
My hair no longer bounds to my foot's glee.
Nor plant I it from rose or myrtle tree,
As girls do, any more. It only may
Now shade on two pale cheeks the mark of tears,
Taught drooping from the head that hangs aside
Through sorrow's trick. I thought the funeral-shears
Would take this first, but Love is justified, —
Take it thou, finding pure, from all those years,
The kiss my mother left here when she died.

The soul's Rialto hath its merchandise ;
I barter curl for curl upon that mart,
And from my poet's forehead to my heart
Receive this lock which outweighs argosies, —
As purely black, as erst, to Pindar's eyes,
The dim purpureal tresses gloomed athwart
The nine white Muse-brows. For this counterpart,
Thy bay-crown's shade, Belovèd, I surmise,
Still lingers on thy curl, it is so black !
Thus, with a fillet of smooth-kissing breath,
I tie the shadow safe from gliding back,
And lay the gift where nothing hindereth,
Here on my heart, as on thy brow, to lack
No natural heat till mine grows cold in death.

Say over again, and yet once over again,
That thou dost love me. Though the word repeated
Should seem "a cuckoo-song," as thou dost treat it,
Remember, never to the hill or plain,
Valley and wood, without her cuckoo-strain,
Comes the fresh spring in all her green completed.
Belovèd, I, amid the darkness greeted
By a doubtful spirit-voice, in that doubt's pain
Cry : "Speak once more — thou lovest !" Who can fear
Too many stars, though each in heaven shall roll, —
Too many flowers, though each shall crown the year?
Say thou dost love me, love me, love me, — toll
The silver iterance ! — only minding, dear,
To love me also in silence, with thy soul.

Is it indeed so? If I lay here dead,
Wouldst thou miss any life in losing mine?
And would the sun for thee more coldly shine,
Because of grave-damps falling round my head?
I marveled, my Belovèd, when I read
Thy thought so in the letter. I am thine —
But . . . *so* much to thee? Can I pour thy wine
While my hands tremble? Then my soul, instead
Of dreams of death, resumes life's lower range.
Then, love me, Love ! look on me . . . breathe on me !
As brighter ladies do not count it strange,
For love, to give up acres and degree,
I yield the grave for thy sake, and exchange
My near sweet view of Heaven, for earth with thee !

My letters ! all dead paper, mute and white ! —
And yet they seem alive and quivering
Against my tremulous hands which loose the string
And let them drop down on my knee to-night.
This said, he wished to have me in his sight
Once, as a friend : this fixed a day in spring
To come and touch my hand . . . a simple thing,
Yet I wept for it ! this . . . the paper's light . . .
Said, *Dear, I love thee ;* and I sank and quailed
As if God's future thundered on my past.
This said, *I am thine*, — and so its ink has paled
With lying at my heart that beat too fast.
And this . . . O Love, thy words have ill availed,
If what this said, I dared repeat at last !

I think of thee ! my thoughts do twine and bud
About thee, as wild vines about a tree,
Put out broad leaves, and soon there's naught to see
Except the straggling green which hides the wood.
Yet, O my palm-tree, be it understood
I will not have my thoughts instead of thee

Who art dearer, better! Rather instantly
Renew thy presence. As a strong tree should,
Rustle thy boughs and set thy trunk all bare,
And let these bands of greenery which insphere thee
Drop heavily down, burst, shattered, everywhere!
Because, in this deep joy to see and hear thee
And breathe within thy shadow a new air,
I do not think of thee, — I am too near thee.

The first time that the sun rose on thine oath
To love me, I looked forward to the moon
To slacken all those bonds which seemed too soon
And quickly tied to make a lasting troth.
Quick-loving hearts, I thought, may quickly loathe;
And, looking on myself, I seemed not one
For such man's love! — more like an out of tune
Worn viol, a good singer would be wroth
To spoil his song with, and which, snatched in haste
Is laid down at the first ill-sounding note.
I did not wrong myself so, but I placed
A wrong on *thee.* For perfect strains may float
Neath master-hands, from instruments defaced, —
And great souls, at one stroke, may do and doat.

First time he kissed me, he but only kissed
The fingers of this hand wherewith I write;
And, ever since, it grew more clean and white,
Slow to world-greetings, quick with its "O list!"
When the angels speak. A ring of amethyst
I could not wear here, plainer to my sight
Than that first kiss. The second passed in height
The first, and sought the forehead, and half missed,
Half falling on the hair. O, beyond meed!
That was the chrism of love, which love's own crown,
With sanctifying sweetness, did precede.
The third upon my lips was folded down
In perfect, purple state; since when, indeed,
I have been proud, and said, "My love, my own!"

How do I love thee? Let me count the ways.
I love thee to the depth and breadth and height
My soul can reach, when feeling out of sight
For the ends of Being and ideal Grace.
I love thee to the level of every day's
Most quiet need, by sun and candlelight.
I love thee freely, as men strive for Right;
I love thee purely, as they turn from Praise.
I love thee with the passion put to use
In my old griefs, and with my childhood's faith.
I love thee with a love I seemed to lose
With my lost saints, — I love thee with the breath,
Smiles, tears, of all my life! — and, if God choose,
I shall but love thee better after death.

Elizabeth Barrett Browning.

MY LITTLE SAINT.

I care not, though it be
By the preciser sort thought popery;
We poets can a license show
For everything we do.
Hear, then, my little saint! I 'll pray to thee.

If now thy happy mind,
Amidst its various joys, can leisure find
To attend to anything so low
As what I say or do,
Regard, and be — what thou wast ever — kind.

Let not the blest above
Engross thee quite, but sometimes hither rove:
Fain would I thy sweet image see,
And sit and talk with thee;
Nor is it curiosity, but love.

Ah! what delight 't would be,
Wouldst thou sometimes by stealth converse with me!
How should I thy sweet commune prize,
And other joys despise!
Come, then! I ne'er was yet denied by thee.

I would not long detain
Thy soul from bliss, nor keep thee here in pain;
Nor should thy fellow-saints e'er know
Of thy escape below:
Before thou 'rt missed, thou shouldst return again.

Sure, heaven must needs thy love,
As well as other qualities, improve:
Come, then! and recreate my sight
With rays of thy pure light;
'T will cheer my eyes more than the lamps above.

But if Fate 's so severe
As to confine thee to thy blissful sphere
(And by thy absence I shall know
Whether thy state be so),
Live happy, and be mindful of me there.

John Norris.

WAITING FOR THE GRAPES.

That I love thee, charming maid, I a thousand times have said,
And a thousand times more I have sworn it,
But 't is easy to be seen in the coldness of your mien
That you doubt my affection — or scorn it.
Ah me!

Not a single grain of sense is in the whole of these pretenses
For rejecting your lover's petitions;

Had I windows in my bosom, O, how gladly, I 'd expose 'em !
To undo your fantastic suspicions.
Ah me !

You repeat I 've known you long, and you hint I do you wrong,
In beginning so late to pursue ye ;
But 't is folly to look glum because people did not come
Up the stairs of your nursery to woo ye.
Ah me !

In a grapery one walks without looking at the stalks,
While the bunches are green that they 're bearing :
All the pretty little leaves that are dangling at the eaves
Scarce attract e'en a moment of staring.
Ah me !

But when time has swelled the grapes to a richer style of shapes,
And the sun has lent warmth to their blushes,
Then to cheer us and to gladden, to enchant us and to madden,
Is the ripe ruddy glory that rushes.
Ah me !

O, 't is then that mortals pant while they gaze on Bacchus' plant, —
O, 't is then, — will my simile serve ye ?
Should a damsel fair repine, though neglected like a vine ?
Both erelong shall turn heads topsy-turvy.
Ah me !

WILLIAM MAGINN.

BLACK AND BLUE EYES.

THE brilliant black eye
May in triumph let fly
All its darts without caring who feels 'em ;
But the soft eye of blue,
Though it scatter wounds too,
Is much better pleased when it heals 'em !
Dear Fanny !

The black eye may say,
"Come and worship my ray ;
By adoring, perhaps you may move me !"
But the blue eye, half hid,
Says, from under its lid,
"I love, and am yours, if you love me !"
Dear Fanny !

Then tell me, O why,
In that lovely blue eye,
Not a charm of its tint I discover ;
Or why should you wear
The only blue pair
That ever said "No" to a lover ?
Dear Fanny !

THOMAS MOORE.

ANSWER TO A CHILD'S QUESTION.

Do you ask what the birds say ? The sparrow, the dove,
The linnet, and thrush say, "I love, and I love !"
In the winter they 're silent, the wind is so strong ;
What it says I don't know, but it sings a loud song.
But green leaves, and blossoms, and sunny warm weather,
And singing and loving,—all come back together.
But the lark is so brimful of gladness and love,
The green fields below him, the blue sky above,
That he sings, and he sings, and forever sings he,
"I love my Love, and my Love loves me."

SAMUEL COLERIDGE.

THE LOVE-KNOT.

TYING her bonnet under her chin,
She tied her raven ringlets in.
But not alone in the silken snare
Did she catch her lovely floating hair,
For, tying her bonnet under her chin,
She tied a young man's heart within.

They were strolling together up the hill,
Where the wind came blowing merry and chill ;
And it blew the curls a frolicsome race,
All over the happy peach-colored face,
Till scolding and laughing, she tied them in,
Under her beautiful, dimpled chin.

And it blew a color, bright as the bloom
Of the pinkest fuchsia's tossing plume,
All over the cheeks of the prettiest girl
That ever imprisoned a romping curl,
Or, in tying her bonnet under her chin,
Tied a young man's heart within.

Steeper and steeper grew the hill,
Madder, merrier, chiller still,
The western wind blew down, and played
The wildest tricks with the little maid,
As, tying her bonnet under her chin,
She tied a young man's heart within.

O western wind, do you think it was fair
To play such tricks with her floating hair?
To gladly, gleefully, do your best
To blow her against the young man's breast,
Where he has gladly folded her in,
And kissed her mouth and dimpled chin?

O Ellery Vane, you little thought,
An hour ago, when you besought
This country lass to walk with you,
After the sun had dried the dew,
What terrible danger you 'd be in,
As she tied her bonnet under her chin.

NORA PERRY.

A GOLDEN GIRL.

LUCY is a golden girl;
  But a man, a *man*, should woo her!
They who seek her shrink aback,
  When they should, like storms, pursue her.

All her smiles are hid in light;
  All her hair is lost in splendor;
But she hath the eyes of Night
  And a heart that 's over-tender.

Yet the foolish suitors fly
  (Is 't excess of dread or duty?)
From the starlight of her eye,
  Leaving to neglect her beauty!

Men by fifty seasons taught
  Leave her to a young beginner,
Who, without a second thought,
  Whispers, woos, and straight must win her.

Lucy is a golden girl!
  Toast her in a goblet brimming!
May the man that wins her wear
  On his heart the Rose of Women!

BARRY CORNWALL.

PHILLIDA AND CORYDON.

IN the merry month of May,
In a morn by break of day,
With a troop of damsels playing
Forth I rode, forsooth, a-maying,
When anon by a woodside,
Where as May was in his pride,
I espièd, all alone,
Phillida and Corydon.

Much ado there was, God wot!
He would love and she would not:
She said, "Never man was true":
He says, "None was false to you."
He said he had loved her long:
She says, "Love should have no wrong."

Corydon he would kiss her then.
She says, "Maids must kiss no men
Till they do for good and all."
Then she made the shepherd call
All the heavens to witness, truth
Never loved a truer youth.

Thus, with many a pretty oath,
Yea and nay, and faith and troth, —
Such as silly shepherds use
When they will not love abuse, —
Love, which had been long deluded,
Was with kisses sweet concluded;
And Phillida, with garlands gay,
Was made the lady of the May,

NICHOLAS BRETON.

THE CHRONICLE.

MARGARITA first possessed,
If I remember well, my breast,
  Margarita first of all;
But when awhile the wanton maid
With my restless heart had played,
  Martha took the flying ball.

Martha soon did it resign
To the beauteous Catharine.
  Beauteous Catharine gave place
(Though loath and angry she to part
With the possession of my heart)
  To Eliza's conquering face.

Eliza till this hour might reign,
Had she not evil counsels ta'en;
  Fundamental laws she broke,
And still new favorites she chose,
Till up in arms my passions rose,
  And cast away her yoke.

Mary then, and gentle Anne,
Both to reign at once began;
  Alternately they swayed;
And sometimes Mary was the fair,
And sometimes Anne the crown did wear,
  And sometimes both I obeyed.

Another Mary then arose,
And did rigorous laws impose;
  A mighty tyrant she!
Long, alas! should I have been
Under that iron-sceptered queen,
  Had not Rebecca set me free.

When fair Rebecca set me free,
'T was then a golden time with me :
But soon those pleasures fled ;
For the gracious princess died
In her youth and beauty's pride,
And Judith reignèd in her stead.

One month, three days, and half an hour,
Judith held the sovereign power :
Wondrous beautiful her face !
But so weak and small her wit,
That she to govern was unfit,
And so Susanna took her place.

But when Isabella came,
Armed with a resistless flame,
And the artillery of her eye,
Whilst she proudly marched about,
Greater conquests to find out,
She beat out Susan, by the by.

But in her place I then obeyed
Black-eyed Bess, her viceroy-maid,
To whom ensued a vacancy :
Thousand worse passions then possessed
The interregnum of my breast ;
Bless me from such an anarchy !

Gentle Henrietta then,
And a third Mary next began ;
Then Joan and Jane, and Andria ;
And then a pretty Thomasine,
And then another Catharine,
And then a long *et cætera.*

But I will briefer with them be,
Since few of them were long with me.
An higher and a nobler strain
My present emperess does claim,
Heleonora, first of the name ;
Whom God grant long to reign !

ABRAHAM COWLEY.

GREEN GROW THE RASHES O!

GREEN grow the rashes O,
Green grow the rashes O ;
The sweetest hours that e'er I spend
Are spent amang the lasses O.

There 's naught but care on ev'ry han',
In every hour that passes O ;
What signifies the life o' man,
An' 't were na for the lasses O ?

The warly race may riches chase,
An' riches still may fly them O ;
An' though at last they catch them fast,
Their hearts can ne'er enjoy them O.

Gie me a canny hour at e'en,
My arms about my dearie O,
An' warly cares an' warly men
May all gae tapsalteerie O.

For you sae douce, ye sneer at this,
Ye 're naught but senseless asses O !
The wisest man the warl' e'er saw
He dearly lo'ed the lasses O.

Auld Nature swears the lovely dears
Her noblest work she classes O :
Her 'prentice han' she tried on man,
An' then she made the lasses O.

ROBERT BURNS.

TO CHLOE.

AN APOLOGY FOR GOING INTO THE COUNTRY.

CHLOE, we must not always be in heaven
Forever toying, ogling, kissing, billing ;
The joys for which I thousands would have given,
Will presently be scarcely worth a shilling.

Thy neck is fairer than the Alpine snows,
And, sweetly swelling, beats the down of doves,
Thy cheek of health, a rival to the rose ;
Thy pouting lips, the throne of all the loves ;
Yet, though thus beautiful beyond expression,
That beauty fadeth by too much possession.

Economy in love is peace to nature,
Much like economy in worldly matter ;
We should be prudent, never live too fast ;
Profusion will not, cannot always last.

Lovers are really spendthrifts —'t is a shame —
Nothing their thoughtless, wild career can tame,
Till penury stares them in the face ;
And when they find an empty purse,
Grown calmer, wiser, how the fault they curse,
And, limping, look with such a sneaking grace !
Job's war-horse fierce, his neck with thunder hung,
Sunk to an humble hack that carries dung.

Smell to the queen of flowers, the fragrant rose —
Smell twenty times — and then, my dear, thy nose
Will tell thee (not so much for scent athirst)
The twentieth drank less flavor than the *first.*

Love, doubtless, is the sweetest of all fellows ;
Yet often should the little god retire —
Absence, dear Chloe, is a pair of bellows,
That keeps alive the sacred fire.

DR. WOLCOT (PETER PINDAR.)

AN INUECTIUE AGAINST LOUE.

ALL is not golde that shineth bright in show,
Not euery floure good, as faire to sight,
The deepest streames aboue doe calmest flow,
And strongest poisons oft the taste delight.
The pleasant baite doth hide the harmfull hooke,
And false deceit can lend a friendly looke.

Loue is the gold whose outward hew doth passe,
Whose first beginnings goodly promise make
Of pleasures faire, and fresh as Sommer's grasse,
Which neither sunne can parch nor wind can shake;
But when the mould should in the fire be tride,
The gold is gone, the drosse doth still abide.

Beautie, the floure so fresh, so faire, so gay,
So sweet to smell, so soft to touch and tast;
As seemes it should endure by right for aye,
And neuer be with any storme defast;
But when the baleful southerne wind doth blow,
Gone is the glory which it erst did show.

Loue is the streame, whose waues so calmly flow
As might intice men's minds to wade therein;
Loue is the poison mixt with sugar so,
As might by outward sweetnesse liking win,
But as the deepe o'erflowing stops thy breath
So poyson once receiu'd brings certaine death.

Loue is the baite, whose taste the fish deceiues,
And makes them swallow down the choking hooke;
Loue is the face whose fairnesse iudgement reaues,
And makes thee trust a false and fainèd looke;
But as the hooke the foolish fish doth kill,
So flatt'ring lookes the lover's life doth spill.

ANONYMOUS.

A DOUBT.

FROM THE THIRD BOOK OF LAWES'S AYRES.

FAIN would I love, but that I fear
I quickly should the willow wear;
Fain would I marry, but men say
When love is tied he will away;
Then tell me, love, what shall I do
To cure these fears, whene'er I woo?

The fair one she 's a mark to all,
The brown each one doth lovely call,
The black 's a pearl in fair men's eyes,
The rest will stoop at any prize;
Then tell me, love, what shall I do
To cure these fears, whene'er I woo?

DR. R. HUGHES.

WISHES FOR THE SUPPOSED MISTRESS.

WHOE'ER she be,
That not impossible She
That shall command my heart and me;

Where'er she lie,
Locked up from mortal eye
In shady leaves of destiny:

Till that ripe birth
Of studied Fate stand forth,
And teach her fair steps to our earth;

Till that divine
Idea take a shrine
Of crystal flesh, through which to shine:

— Meet you her, my Wishes,
Bespeak her to my blisses,
And be ye called, my absent kisses.

I wish her beauty
That owes not all its duty
To gaudy tire, or glist'ring shoe-tie:

Something more than
Taffeta or tissue can,
Or rampant feather, or rich fan.

A face that 's best
By its own beauty drest,
And can alone command the rest:

A face made up
Out of no other shop
Than what Nature's white hand sets ope.

Sydneian showers
Of sweet discourse, whose powers
Can crown old Winter's head with flowers.

Whate'er delight
Can make day's forehead bright
Or give down to the wings of night.

Soft silken hours,
Open suns, shady bowers;
'Bove all, nothing within that lowers.

Days that need borrow
No part of their good morrow
From a fore-spent night of sorrow:

Days that, in spite
Of darkness, by the light
Of a clear mind, are day all night.

Life that dares send
A challenge to his end,
And, when it comes, say, "Welcome, friend."

I wish her store
Of worth may leave her poor
Of wishes; and I wish — no more.

— Now, if Time knows
That Her whose radiant brows
Weave them a garland of my vows;

Her that dares be
What these lines wish to see:
I seek no further, it is She.

'T is She, and here
Lo! I unclothe and clear
My wishes' cloudy character.

Such worth as this is
Shall fix my flying wishes,
And determine them to kisses.

Let her full glory,
My fancies, fly before ye;
Be ye my fictions, — but her story.

RICHARD CRASHAW.

AMY'S CRUELTY.

Fair Amy of the terraced house,
Assist me to discover
Why you who would not hurt a mouse
Can torture so your lover.

You give your coffee to the cat,
You stroke the dog for coming,
And all your face grows kinder at
The little brown bee's humming.

But when *he* haunts your door, — the town
Marks coming and marks going, —
You seem to have stitched your eyelids down
To that long piece of sewing!

You never give a look, not you,
Nor drop him a "Good morning,"
To keep his long day warm and blue,
So fretted by your scorning.

She shook her head: "The mouse and bee
For crumb or flower will linger;
The dog is happy at my knee,
The cat purrs at my finger.

"But *he* — to *him*, the least thing given
Means great things at a distance;
He wants my world, my sun, my heaven,
Soul, body, whole existence.

"They say love gives as well as takes;
But I 'm a simple maiden, —
My mother's first smile when she wakes
I still have smiled and prayed in.

"I only know my mother's love
Which gives all and asks nothing,
And this new loving sets the groove
Too much the way of loathing.

"Unless he gives me all in change,
I forfeit all things by him:
The risk is terrible and strange —
I tremble, doubt, — deny him.

"He 's sweetest friend, or hardest foe,
Best angel, or worst devil;
I either hate or — love him so,
I can't be merely civil!

"You trust a woman who puts forth
Her blossoms thick as summer's?
You think she dreams what love is worth,
Who casts it to new-comers?

"Such love 's a cowslip-ball to fling,
A moment's pretty pastime;
I give — all me, if anything,
The first time and the last time.

"Dear neighbor of the trellised house,
A man should murmur never,
Though treated worse than dog and mouse
Till doted on forever!"

ELIZABETH BARRETT BROWNING.

THE SHEPHERD'S RESOLUTION.

Shall I, wasting in despair,
Die because a woman 's fair?
Or make pale my cheeks with care
'Cause another's rosy are?
Be she fairer than the day,
Or the flowery meads in May,
If she be not so to me,
What care I how fair she be?

Shall my foolish heart be pined
'Cause I see a woman kind?
Or a well-disposèd nature
Joinèd with a lovely feature?
Be she meeker, kinder than
The turtle-dove or pelican,
If she be not so to me,
What care I how kind she be?

Shall a woman's virtues move
Me to perish for her love?
Or, her well-deservings known,
Make me quite forget mine own?
Be she with that goodness blest
Which may merit name of best,
If she be not such to me,
What care I how good she be?

'Cause her fortune seems too high,
Shall I play the fool and die?
Those that bear a noble mind
Where they want of riches find,
Think what with them they would do
That without them dare to woo;
And unless that mind I see,
What care I how great she be?

Great, or good, or kind, or fair,
I will ne'er the more despair:
If she love me, this believe, —
I will die ere she shall grieve.
If she slight me when I woo,
I can scorn and let her go;
For if she be not for me,
What care I for whom she be?

GEORGE WITHER.

ROSALIND'S COMPLAINT.

Love in my bosom, like a bee,
Doth suck his sweet;
Now with his wings he plays with me,
Now with his feet;
Within mine eyes he makes his nest,
His bed amidst my tender breast,
My kisses are his daily feast,
And yet he robs me of my rest:
Ah! wanton, will ye?

And if I sleep, then percheth he
With pretty flight,
And makes his pillow of my knee,
The livelong night;
Strike I my lute, he tunes the string;
He music plays, if I but sing:
He lends me every lovely thing,
Yet cruel, he my heart doth sting:
Whist! wanton, still you!

Else I with roses every day
Will whip you hence,
And bind you, when you long to play,
For your offense;
I'll shut my eyes to keep you in,
I'll make you fast it for your sin,
I'll count your power not worth a pin;
Alas! what hereby shall I win
If he gainsay me?

What if I beat the wanton boy
With many a rod?
He will repay me with annoy,
Because a god;
Then sit thou safely on my knee,
And let thy bower my bosom be;
Lurk in mine eyes, I like of thee,
O Cupid! so thou pity me,
Spare not, but play thee.

THOMAS LODGE.

CUPID AND CAMPASPE.

Cupid and my Campaspe played
At cards for kisses, — Cupid paid;
He stakes his quiver, bow, and arrows,
His mother's doves, and team of sparrows, —
Loses them too; then down he throws
The coral of his lip, the rose
Growing on's cheek (but none knows how);
With these the crystal on his brow,
And then the dimple of his chin, —
All these did my Campaspe win.
At last he set her both his eyes;
She won, and Cupid blind did rise.
O Love! hath she done this to thee?
What shall, alas! become of me?

JOHN LYLY.

DEATH AND CUPID.

Ah! who but oft hath marveled why
The gods, who rule above,
Should e'er permit the young to die,
The old to fall in love?

Ah! why should hapless human kind
Be punished out of season? —
Pray listen, and perhaps you'll find
My rhyme may give the reason.

Death, strolling out one summer's day,
Met Cupid, with his sparrows;
And, bantering in a merry way,
Proposed a change of arrows.

"Agreed!" quoth Cupid. "I foresee
The queerest game of errors;
For you the King of Hearts will be,
And I'll be King of Terrors!"

And so 't was done; — alas, the day
That multiplied their arts! —

Each from the other bore away
A portion of his darts.

And that explains the reason why,
Despite the gods above,
The young are often doomed to die,
The old to fall in love!

JOHN GODFREY SAXE.

LET NOT WOMAN E'ER COMPLAIN.

Let not woman e'er complain
Of inconstancy in love;
Let not woman e'er complain
Fickle man is apt to rove;
Look abroad through Nature's range,
Nature's mighty law is change;
Ladies, would it not be strange
Man should then a monster prove?

Mark the winds, and mark the skies;
Ocean's ebb and ocean's flow;
Sun and moon but set to rise,
Round and round the seasons go.
Why then ask of silly man,
To oppose great Nature's plan?
We 'll be constant while we can, —
You can be no more, you know.

ROBERT BURNS.

LOVE-LETTERS MADE OF FLOWERS.

An exquisite invention this,
Worthy of Love's most honeyed kiss, —
This art of writing *billet-doux*
In buds, and odors, and bright hues!
In saying all one feels and thinks
In clever daffodils and pinks;
In puns of tulips; and in phrases,
Charming for their truth, of daisies;
Uttering, as well as silence may,
The sweetest words the sweetest way.
How fit too for the lady's bosom!
The place where *billet-doux* repose 'em.
What delight in some sweet spot
Combining *love* with *garden* plot,
At once to cultivate one's flowers
And one's epistolary powers!
Growing one's own choice words and fancies
In orange tubs, and beds of pansies;
One's sighs, and passionate declarations,
In odorous rhetoric of carnations;
Seeing how far one's stocks will reach,
Taking due care one's flowers of speech
To guard from blight as well as bathos,
And watering every day one's pathos!
A letter comes, just gathered. We
Dote on its tender brilliancy,
Inhale its delicate expressions
Of balm and pea, and its confessions
Made with as sweet a *maiden's blush*
As ever morn bedewed on bush:
('T is in reply to one of ours,
Made of the most convincing flowers.)

Then, after we have kissed its wit,
And heart, in water putting it
(To keep its remarks fresh), go round
Our little eloquent plot of ground,
And with enchanted hands compose
Our answer, — all of lily and rose,
Of tuberose and of violet,
And *little darling* (mignonette);
Of *look at me* and *call me to you*
(Words that, while they greet, go through you);
Of *thoughts*, of *flames*, *forget-me-not*,
Bridewort, — in short, the whole blest lot
Of vouchers for a lifelong kiss, —
And literally, breathing bliss!

LEIGH HUNT.

THE GROOMSMAN TO HIS MISTRESS.

Every wedding, says the proverb,
Makes another, soon or late;
Never yet was any marriage
Entered in the book of fate,
But the names were also written
Of the patient pair that wait.

Blessings then upon the morning
When my friend, with fondest look,
By the solemn rites' permission,
To himself his mistress took,
And the destinies recorded
Other two within their book.

While the priest fulfilled his office,
Still the ground the lovers eyed,
And the parents and the kinsmen
Aimed their glances at the bride;
But the groomsmen eyed the virgins
Who were waiting at her side.

Three there were that stood beside her;
One was dark, and one was fair;
But nor fair nor dark the other,
Save her Arab eyes and hair;
Neither dark nor fair I call her,
Yet she was the fairest there.

While her groomsman — shall I own it?
Yes, to thee, and only thee —
Gazed upon this dark-eyed maiden
Who was fairest of the three,
Thus he thought: "How blest the bridal
Where the bride were such as she!"

Then I mused upon the adage,
Till my wisdom was perplexed,
And I wondered, as the churchman
Dwelt upon his holy text,
Which of all who heard his lesson
Should require the service next.

Whose will be the next occasion
For the flowers, the feast, the wine?
Thine, perchance, my dearest lady;
Or, who knows? — it may be mine;
What if 't were — forgive the fancy —
What if 't were — both mine and thine?

THOMAS WILLIAM PARSONS.

MY EYES! HOW I LOVE YOU.

MY eyes! how I love you,
You sweet little dove you!
There 's no one above you,
Most beautiful Kitty.

So glossy your hair is,
Like a sylph's or a fairy's;
And your neck, I declare, is
Exquisitely pretty!

Quite Grecian your nose is,
And your cheeks are like roses,
So delicious — O Moses!
Surpassingly sweet!

Not the beauty of tulips,
Nor the taste of mint-juleps,
Can compare with your two lips,
Most beautiful Kate!

Not the black eyes of Juno,
Nor Minerva's of blue, no,
Nor Venus's, you know,
Can equal your own!

O, how my heart prances,
And frolics and dances,
When its radiant glances
Upon me are thrown!

And now, dearest Kitty,
It 's not very pretty,
Indeed it 's a pity,
To keep me in sorrow!

So, if you 'll but chime in,
We 'll have done with our rhymin',
Swap Cupid for Hymen,
And be married to-morrow.

ANONYMOUS.

THE WHISTLE.

"YOU have heard," said a youth to his sweetheart, who stood,
While he sat on a corn-sheaf, at daylight's decline, —
"You have heard of the Danish boy's whistle of wood?
I wish that that Danish boy's whistle were mine."

"And what would you do with it? — tell me," she said,
While an arch smile played over her beautiful face.
"I would blow it," he answered; "and then my fair maid
Would fly to my side, and would here take her place."

"Is that all you wish it for? — That may be yours
Without any magic," the fair maiden cried:
"A favor so slight one's good-nature secures";
And she playfully seated herself by his side.

"I would blow it again," said the youth, "and the charm
Would work so, that not even Modesty's check
Would be able to keep from my neck your fine arm":
She smiled, — and she laid her fine arm round his neck.

"Yet once more would I blow, and the music divine
Would bring me the third time an exquisite bliss:
You would lay your fair cheek to this brown one of mine,
And your lips, stealing past it, would give me a kiss."

The maiden laughed out in her innocent glee, —
"What a fool of yourself with your whistle you 'd make!
For only consider, how silly 't would be,
To sit there and whistle for — what you might take."

ROBERT STORY.

WHEN THE SULTAN GOES TO ISPAHAN.

WHEN the Sultan Shah-Zaman
Goes to the city Ispahan,
Even before he gets so far
As the place where the clustered palm-trees are,
At the last of the thirty palace-gates,
The Pet of the Harem, *Rose in Bloom*,
Orders a feast in his favorite room, —

Glittering squares of colored ice,
Sweetened with syrop, tinctured with spice;
Creams, and cordials, and sugared dates;
Syrian apples, Othmanee quinces,
Limes, and citrons, and apricots;
And wines that are known to Eastern princes.
And Nubian slaves, with smoking pots
Of spicèd meats, and costliest fish,
And all that the curious palate could wish,
Pass in and out of the cedarn doors.

Scattered over mosaic floors
Are anemones, myrtles, and violets;
And a musical fountain throws its jets
Of a hundred colors into the air.
The dark Sultana loosens her hair,
And stains with the henna plant the tips
Of her pearly nails, and bites her lips
Till they bloom again; but alas, *that* rose
Not for the Sultan buds and blows!
Not for the Sultan Shah-Zaman
When he goes to the city Ispahan.

Then at a wave of her sunny hand,
The dancing girls of Samarcand
Float in like mists from Fairy-land!
And to the low voluptuous swoons
Of music, rise and fall the moons
Of their full brown bosoms. Orient blood
Runs in their veins, shines in their eyes;
And there in this Eastern paradise,
Filled with the fumes of sandal-wood,
And Khoten musk, and aloes, and myrrh,
Sits *Rose in Bloom* on a silk divan,
Sipping the wines of Astrakhan;
And her Arab lover sits with her.
That 's when the Sultan Shah-Zaman
Goes to the city Ispahan.

Now, when I see an extra light
Flaming, flickering on the night,
From my neighbor's casement opposite,
I know as well as I know to pray,
I know as well as a tongue can say,
That the innocent Sultan Shah-Zaman
Has gone to the city Ispahan.

THOMAS BAILEY ALDRICH.

CUPID SWALLOWED.

T' OTHER day, as I was twining
Roses for a crown to dine in,
What, of all things, midst the heap,
Should I light on, fast asleep,
But the little desperate elf,
The tiny traitor, — Love himself!
By the wings I pinched him up
Like a bee, and in a cup
Of my wine I plunged and sank him;
And what d' ye think I did?— I drank him!
Faith, I thought him dead. Not he!
There he lives with tenfold glee;
And now, this moment, with his wings
I feel him tickling my heart-strings.

LEIGH HUNT.

THE YOUNG MAY MOON.

THE young May moon is beaming, love,
The glow-worm's lamp is gleaming, love,
How sweet to rove
Through Morna's grove,
While the drowsy world is dreaming, love!
Then awake! — the heavens look bright, my dear!
'T is never too late for delight, my dear!
And the best of all ways
To lengthen our days
Is to steal a few hours from the night, my dear!

Now all the world is sleeping, love,
But the sage, his star-watch keeping, love,
And I, whose star,
More glorious far,
Is the eye from that casement peeping, love.
Then awake! — till rise of sun, my dear,
The sage's glass we 'll shun, my dear,
Or, in watching the flight
Of bodies of light,
He might happen to take thee for one, my dear!

THOMAS MOORE.

AH, SWEET KITTY NEIL!

"AH, sweet Kitty Neil! rise up from your wheel,
Your neat little foot will be weary from spinning;
Come, trip down with me to the sycamore-tree;
Half the parish is there, and the dance is beginning.
The sun is gone down; but the full harvest moon
Shines sweetly and cool on the dew-whitened valley;
While all the air rings with the soft, loving things
Each little bird sings in the green shaded alley."

With a blush and a smile, Kitty rose up the while,
Her eye in the glass, as she bound her hair, glancing;
'T is hard to refuse when a young lover sues,
So she could n't but choose to — go off to the dancing.
And now on the green the glad groups are seen, —
Each gay-hearted lad with the lass of his choosing;

And Pat, without fail, leads out sweet Kitty Neil, —
Somehow, when he asked, she ne'er thought of refusing.

Now Felix Magee puts his pipes to his knee,
And, with flourish so free, sets each couple in motion ;
With a cheer and a bound, the lads patter the ground,
The maids move around just like swans on the ocean.
Cheeks bright as the rose, — feet light as the doe's,
Now coyly retiring, now boldly advancing ;
Search the world all around from the sky to the ground,
No such sight can be found as an Irish lass dancing !

Sweet Kate ! who could view your bright eyes of deep blue,
Beaming humidly through their dark lashes so mildly,
Your fair-turned arm, heaving breast, rounded form,
Nor feel his heart warm, and his pulses throb wildly ?
Poor Pat feels his heart, as he gazes, depart,
Subdued by the smart of such painful yet sweet love ;
The sight leaves his eye as he cries with a sigh,
"Dance light, for my heart it lies under your feet, love !"

DENIS FLORENCE MACCARTHY.

DUNCAN GRAY CAM' HERE TO WOO.

DUNCAN GRAY cam' here to woo —
Ha, ha ! the wooing o't !
On blythe Yule night when we were fou —
Ha, ha ! the wooing o't !
Maggie coost her head fu' high,
Looked asklent and unco skeigh,
Gart poor Duncan stand abeigh —
Ha, ha ! the wooing o't !"

Duncan fleeched and Duncan prayed —
Ha, ha ! the wooing o't !
Meg was deaf as Ailsa craig —
Ha, ha ! the wooing o't !
Duncan sighed baith out and in,
Grat his een baith bleer't and blin',
Spak o' lowpin o'er a linn —
Ha, ha ! the wooing o't !

Time and chance are but a tide —
Ha, ha ! the wooing o't !
Slighted love is sair to bide —
Ha, ha ! the wooing o't !
Shall I, like a fool, quoth he,
For a haughty hizzie dee ?
She may gae to — France for me !
Ha, ha ! the wooing o't !

How it comes let doctors tell —
Ha, ha ! the wooing o't !
Meg grew sick as he grew heal —
Ha, ha ! the wooing o't !
Something in her bosom wrings, —
For relief a sigh she brings ;
And O, her een they speak sic things !
Ha, ha ! the wooing o't !

Duncan was a lad o' grace —
Ha, ha ! the wooing o't !
Maggie's was a piteous case —
Ha, ha ! the wooing o't !
Duncan could na be her death :
Swelling pity smoored his wrath.
Now they 're crouse and canty baith,
Ha, ha ! the wooing o't !

ROBERT BURNS.

RORY O'MORE ;

OR, GOOD OMENS.

YOUNG Rory O'More courted Kathleen Bawn ;
He was bold as the hawk, and she soft as the dawn ;
He wished in his heart pretty Kathleen to please,
And he thought the best way to do that was to tease.
"Now, Rory, be aisy," sweet Kathleen would cry,
Reproof on her lip, but a smile in her eye ;
"With your tricks, I don't know, in throth, what I 'm about ;
Faith you 've teazed till I 've put on my cloak inside out."
"Och ! jewel," says Rory, "that same is the way
You 've thrated my heart for this many a day ;
And 't is plazed that I am, and why not, to be sure ?
For 't is all for good luck," says bold Rory O'More.

"Indeed, then," says Kathleen, "don't think of the like,
For I half gave a promise to soothering Mike ;
The ground that I walk on he loves, I 'll be bound" —
"Faith !" says Rory, "I 'd rather love you than the ground."
"Now, Rory, I 'll cry if you don't let me go :
Sure I dream ev'ry night that I 'm hating you so !"
"Och !" says Rory, "that same I 'm delighted to hear,
For dhrames always go by conthraries, my dear.

Och! jewel, keep dhraming that same till you die,
And bright morning will give dirty night the black lie!
And 't is plazed that I am, and why not, to be sure?
Since 't is all for good luck," says bold Rory O'More.

"Arrah, Kathleen, my darlint, you 've teazed me enough;
Sure, I 've thrashed, for your sake, Dinny Grimes and Jim Duff;
And I 've made myself, drinking your health, quite a baste,
So I think, after that, I may talk to the priest."
Then Rory, the rogue, stole his arm round her neck,
So soft and so white, without freckle or speck;
And he looked in her eyes, that were beaming with light,
And he kissed her sweet lips — Don't you think he was right?
"Now, Rory, leave off, sir — you 'll hug me no more, —
That 's eight times to-day you have kissed me before."
"Then here goes another," says he, "to make sure,
For there 's luck in odd numbers," says Rory O'More.

SAMUEL LOVER.

THE CATALOGUE.

O, THAT 's what you mean now, a bit of a song,
Arrah, faith, then here goes, you sha'n't bother me long;
I require no teazing, no praying, nor stuff,
By my soul, if you wish it, I 'm ready enough
To give you no end; you shall have a beginning,
And, troth, though the music is not over fine,
'T is a bit of a thing that a body might sing
Just to set us a-going and season the wine.

O, I once was a lover, like some of you here,
And could feed a whole night on a sigh or a tear,
No sunshine I knew but from Kitty's black eye,
And the world was a desert when she was n't by;
But the devil knows how, I got fond of Miss Betty,
And Kitty slipt out of this bosom of mine.
'T is a bit of a thing that a body might sing
Just to set us a-going and season the wine.

Now Betty had eyes soft and blue as the sky,
And the lily was black when her bosom was nigh;
O, I vowed and I swore if she 'd not a kind eye
I 'd give up the whole world and in banishment die;
But Nancy came by, a round plump little creature,
And fixed in my heart quite another design.
'T is a bit of a thing that a body might sing
Just to set us a-going and season the wine.

Little Nance, like a Hebe, was buxom and gay,
Had a bloom like the rose and was fresher than May;
O, I felt if she frowned I would die by a rope,
And my bosom would burst if she slighted my hope;
But the slim, taper, elegant Fanny looked at me,
And, troth, I no longer for Nancy could pine.
'T is a bit of a thing that a body might sing
Just to set us a-going and season the wine.

Now Fanny's light frame was so slender and fine
That she skimmed in the air like a shadow divine.
Her motion bewitched, and to my loving eye
'T was an angel soft gliding 'twixt earth and the sky.
'T was all mighty well till I saw her fat sister,
And *that* gave a turn I could never define.
'T is a bit of a thing that a body might sing
Just to set us a-going and season the wine.

O, so I go on, ever constantly blest,
For I find I 've a great stock of love in my breast;
And it never grows less, for whenever I try
To get *one* in my heart, I get *two* in my eye.
To all kinds of beauty I bow with devotion,
And all kinds of liquor by turns I make mine;
So I 'll finish the thing that another may sing,
Just to keep us a-going and season the wine.

CAPT. MORRIS.*

THE AGE OF WISDOM.

Ho! pretty page, with the dimpled chin,
That never has known the barber's shear,
All your wish is woman to win;
This is the way that boys begin, —
Wait till you come to forty year.

Curly gold locks cover foolish brains;
Billing and cooing is all your cheer, —
Sighing, and singing of midnight strains,
Under Bonnybell's window-panes, —
Wait till you come to forty year.

Forty times over let Michaelmas pass;
Grizzling hair the brain doth clear;
Then you know a boy is an ass,
Then you know the worth of a lass, —
Once you have come to forty year.

* A boon companion of George, Prince Regent.

Pledge me round; I bid ye declare,
All good fellows whose beards are gray, —
Did not the fairest of the fair
Common grow and wearisome ere
Ever a month was past away?

The reddest lips that ever have kissed,
The brightest eyes that ever have shone,
May pray and whisper and we not list,
Or look away and never be missed, —
Ere yet ever a month is gone.

Gillian's dead! God rest her bier, —
How I loved her twenty years syne!
Marian's married; but I sit here,
Alone and merry at forty year,
Dipping my nose in the Gascon wine.

WILLIAM MAKEPEACE THACKERAY.

THE LOW-BACKED CAR.

When first I saw sweet Peggy,
'T was on a market-day:
A low-backed car she drove, and sat
Upon a truss of hay;
But when that hay was blooming grass,
And decked with flowers of spring,
No flower was there that could compare
With the blooming girl I sing.
As she sat in the low-backed car,
The man at the turnpike bar
Never asked for the toll,
But just rubbed his ould poll,
And looked after the low-backed car.

In battle's wild commotion,
The proud and mighty Mars
With hostile scythes demands his tithes
Of death in warlike cars;
While Peggy, peaceful goddess,
Has darts in her bright eye,
That knock men down in the market-town,
As right and left they fly;
While she sits in her low-backed car,
Than battle more dangerous far, —
For the doctor's art
Cannot cure the heart
That is hit from that low-backed car.

Sweet Peggy round her car, sir,
Has strings of ducks and geese,
But the scores of hearts she slaughters
By far outnumber these;
While she among her poultry sits,
Just like a turtle-dove,
Well worth the cage, I do engage,
Of the blooming god of Love!
While she sits in her low-backed car,
The lovers come, near and far,
And envy the chicken
That Peggy is pickin',
As she sits in her low-backed car.

I 'd rather own that car, sir,
With Peggy by my side,
Than a coach and four, and gold *galore*,
And a lady for my bride;
For the lady would sit forninst me,
On a cushion made with taste,
While Peggy would sit beside me,
With my arm around her waist,
While we drove in the low-backed car,
To be married by Father Mahar;
O, my heart would beat high
At her glance and her sigh, —
Though it beat in a low-backed car!

SAMUEL LOVER.

SALLY IN OUR ALLEY.

Of all the girls that are so smart,
There 's none like pretty Sally;
She is the darling of my heart,
And she lives in our alley.
There 's ne'er a lady in the land
That 's half so sweet as Sally;
She is the darling of my heart,
And she lives in our alley.

Her father he makes cabbage-nets,
And through the streets does cry 'em;
Her mother she sells laces long
To such as please to buy 'em;
But sure such folks could ne'er beget
So sweet a girl as Sally!
She is the darling of my heart,
And she lives in our alley.

When she is by I leave my work,
I love her so sincerely;
My master comes like any Turk,
And bangs me most severely.
But let him bang his bellyful, —
I 'll bear it all for Sally;
For she 's the darling of my heart,
And she lives in our alley.

Of all the days that 's in the week
I dearly love but one day,
And that 's the day that comes betwixt
A Saturday and Monday;
For then I 'm drest all in my best
To walk abroad with Sally;
She is the darling of my heart,
And she lives in our alley.

My master carries me to church,
And often am I blamèd
Because I leave him in the lurch
As soon as text is namèd :
I leave the church in sermon-time,
And slink away to Sally, —
She is the darling of my heart,
And she lives in our alley.

When Christmas comes about again,
O, then I shall have money !
I 'll hoard it up, and, box and all,
I 'll give it to my honey ;
And would it were ten thousand pound !
I 'd give it all to Sally ;
For she 's the darling of my heart,
And she lives in our alley.

My master and the neighbors all
Make game of me and Sally,
And but for she I 'd better be
A slave, and row a galley ;
But when my seven long years are out,
O, then I 'll marry Sally !
O, then we 'll wed, and then we 'll bed, —
But not in our alley !

HENRY CAREY.

LOVELY MARY DONNELLY.

O LOVELY Mary Donnelly, it 's you I love the best !
If fifty girls were round you, I 'd hardly see the rest ;
Be what it may the time of day, the place be where it will,
Sweet looks of Mary Donnelly, they bloom before me still.

Her eyes like mountain water that 's flowing on a rock,
How clear they are ! how dark they are ! and they give me many a shock ;
Red rowans warm in sunshine, and wetted with a shower,
Could ne'er express the charming lip that has me in its power.

Her nose is straight and handsome, her eyebrows lifted up,
Her chin is very neat and pert, and smooth like a china cup ;
Her hair 's the brag of Ireland, so weighty and so fine, —
It 's rolling down upon her neck, and gathered in a twine.

The dance o' last Whit-Monday night exceeded all before ;
No pretty girl for miles around was missing from the floor ;
But Mary kept the belt of love, and O, but she was gay ;
She danced a jig, she sung a song, and took my heart away !

When she stood up for dancing, her steps were so complete,
The music nearly killed itself, to listen to her feet ;
The fiddler mourned his blindness, he heard her so much praised,
But blessed himself he was n't deaf, when once her voice she raised.

And evermore I 'm whistling or lilting what you sung ;
Your smile is always in my heart, your name upon my tongue ;
But you 've as many sweethearts as you 'd count on both your hands,
And for myself there 's not a thumb or little finger stands.

O, you 're the flower of womankind, in country or in town ;
The higher I exalt you, the lower I 'm cast down.
If some great lord should come this way and see your beauty bright,
And you to be his lady, I 'd own it was but right.

O, might we live together in lofty palace hall,
Where joyful music rises, and where scarlet curtains fall ;
O, might we live together in a cottage mean and small,
With sods of grass the only roof, and mud the only wall !

O lovely Mary Donnelly, your beauty 's my distress ;
It 's far too glorious to be mine, but I 'll never wish it less ;
The proudest place would fit your face, and I am poor and low,
But blessings be about you, dear, wherever you may go !

WILLIAM ALLINGHAM.

THE FAITHFUL LOVERS.

I 'D been away from her three years, — about that,
And I returned to find my Mary true ;
And though I 'd question her, I did not doubt that
It was unnecessary so to do.

'T was by the chimney-corner we were sitting :
  "Mary," said I, "have you been always true?"
"Frankly," says she, just pausing in her knitting,
  "I don't think I 've unfaithful been to you :
But for the three years past I 'll tell you what
I 've done ; then say if I 've been true or not.

"When first you left my grief was uncontrollable ;
  Alone I mourned my miserable lot ;
And all who saw me thought me inconsolable,
  Till Captain Clifford came from Aldershott.
To flirt with him amused me while 't was new :
I don't count that unfaithfulness — do you ?

"The next — O! let me see — was Frankie Phipps ;
  I met him at my uncle's, Christmas-tide,
And 'neath the mistletoe, where lips meet lips,
  He gave me his first kiss—" And here she sighed.
"We stayed six weeks at uncle's — how time flew!
I don't count that unfaithfulness — do you ?

"Lord Cecil Fossmore — only twenty-one —
  Lent me his horse. O, how we rode and raced !
We scoured the downs — we rode to hounds — such fun !
  And often was his arm about my waist,—
That was to lift me up and down. But who
Would call just that unfaithfulness ? Would you ?

"Do you know Reggy Vere ? Ah, how he sings !
  We met, — 't was at a picnic. O, such weather !
He gave me, look, the first of these two rings
  When we were lost in Cliefden woods together.
Ah, what a happy time we spent, — we two !
I don't count that unfaithfulness to you.

"I 've yet another ring from him ; d' ye see
  The plain gold circlet that is shining here ?"
I took her hand : "O Mary ! can it be
  That you—" Quoth she, "that I am Mrs. Vere.
I don't call that unfaithfulness — do you ?"
"No," I replied, "for I am married too."

ANONYMOUS.

WIDOW MACHREE.

WIDOW machree, it 's no wonder you frown, —
    Och hone ! widow machree ;
Faith, it ruins your looks, that same dirty black gown,—
    Och hone ! widow machree.
  How altered your air,
  With that close cap you wear, —
  'T is destroying your hair,
    Which should be flowing free :
  Be no longer a churl
  Of its black silken curl, —
    Och hone ! widow machree !

Widow machree, now the summer is come, —
    Och hone ! widow machree,
When everything smiles, should a beauty look glum ?
    Och hone ! widow machree !
  See the birds go in pairs,
  And the rabbits and hares ;
  Why, even the bears
    Now in couples agree ;
  And the mute little fish,
  Though they can't spake, they wish, —
    Och hone ! widow machree !

Widow machree, and when winter comes in, —
    Och hone ! widow machree, —
To be poking the fire all alone is a sin,
    Och hone ! widow machree !
  Sure the shovel and tongs
  To each other belongs,
  And the kettle sings songs
    Full of family glee ;
  While alone with your cup
  Like a hermit you sup,
    Och hone ! widow machree !

And how do you know, with the comforts I 've towld, —
    Och hone ! widow machree, —
But you 're keeping some poor fellow out in the cowld ?
    Och hone ! widow machree !
  With such sins on your head,
  Sure your peace would be fled ;
  Could you sleep in your bed
    Without thinking to see
  Some ghost or some sprite,
  That would wake you each night,
    Crying "Och hone ! widow machree !"

Then take my advice, darling widow machree,—
    Och hone ! widow machree, —
And with my advice, faith, I wish you 'd take me,
    Och hone ! widow machree !
  You 'd have me to desire
  Then to stir up the fire ;
  And sure hope is no liar
    In whispering to me
  That the ghosts would depart
  When you 'd me near your heart, —
    Och hone ! widow machree !

SAMUEL LOVER.

THE LAIRD O' COCKPEN.

THE laird o' Cockpen he 's proud and he 's great,
His mind is ta'en up with the things o' the state ;
He wanted a wife his braw house to keep,
But favor wi' wooin' was fashious to seek.

Down by the dike-side a lady did dwell,
At his table-head he thought she 'd look well;
M'Lish's ae daughter o' Claverse-ha' Lee,
A penniless lass wi' a lang pedigree.

His wig was weel pouthered, and as gude as new;
His waistcoat was white, his coat it was blue;
He put on a ring, a sword, and coc̆ked hat,
And wha could refuse the Laird wi' a' that?

He took the gray mare, and rade cannily —
And rapped at the yett o' Claverse-ha' Lee:
"'Gae tell Mistress Jean to come speedily ben,
She 's wanted to speak to the Laird o' Cockpen."

Mistress Jean was makin' the elder-flower wine:
"And what brings the Laird at sic a like time?"
She put aff her apron, and on her silk gown,
Her mutch wi' red ribbons, and gaed awa' down.

And when she cam' ben, he bowèd fu' low,
And what was his errand he soon let her know;
Amazed was the Laird when the lady said "Na";
And wi' a laigh curtsey she turnèd awa'.

Dumbfoundered he was — nae sigh did he gie;
He mounted his mare — he rade cannily;
And aften he thought, as he gaed through the glen,
"She 's daft to refuse the Laird o' Cockpen."

And now that the Laird his exit had made,
Mistress Jean she reflected on what she had said;
"Oh! for ane I'll get better, it's waur I'll get ten,
I was daft to refuse the Laird o' Cockpen."

Next time that the Laird and the lady were seen,
They were gaun arm-in-arm to the kirk on the green.
Now she sits in the ha' like a weel-tappit hen —
But as yet there 's nae chickens appeared at Cockpen.

CAROLINA, BARONESS NAIRN.

UNSATISFACTORY.

"Have other lovers — say, my love —
Loved thus before to-day?"
"They may have, yes, they may, my love;
Not long ago they may."

"But, though they worshiped thee, my love,
Thy maiden heart was free?"
"Don't ask too much of me, my love;
Don't ask too much of me."

"Yet, now 't is you and I, my love,
Love's wings no more will fly?"
"If love could never die, my love,
Our love should never die."

"For shame! and is this so, my love,
And Love and I must go?"
"Indeed, I do not know, my love,
My life, I do not know."

"You will, you *must* be true, my love, —
Not look and love anew!"
"I'll see what I can do, my love,
I'll see what I can do."

ANONYMOUS.

COOKING AND COURTING.

FROM TOM TO NED.

Dear Ned, no doubt you 'll be surprised,
When you receive and read this letter.
I 've railed against the marriage state;
But then, you see, I knew no better.
I 've met a lovely girl out here;
Her manner is — well — very winning:
We 're soon to be — well, Ned, my dear,
I 'll tell you all, from the beginning.

I went to ask her out to ride
Last Wednesday — it was perfect weather.
She said she could n't possibly:
The servants had gone off together
(Hibernians always rush away,
At cousins' funerals to be looking);
Pies must be made, and she must stay,
She said, to do that branch of cooking.

"O, let me help you," then I cried:
"I 'll be a cooker too — how jolly!"
She laughed, and answered, with a smile,
"All right! but you 'll repent your folly;
For I shall be a tyrant, sir,
And good hard work you 'll have to grapple;
So sit down there, and don't you stir,
But take this knife, and pare that apple."

She rolled her sleeve above her arm, —
That lovely arm, so plump and rounded;
Outside, the morning sun shone bright;
Inside, the dough she deftly pounded.
Her little fingers sprinkled flour,
And rolled the pie-crust up in masses:
I passed the most delightful hour
Mid butter, sugar, and molasses.

With deep reflection her sweet eyes
Gazed on each pot and pan and kettle:
She sliced the apples, filled her pies,
And then the upper crust did settle.

Her rippling waves of golden hair
In one great coil were tightly twisted ;
But locks would break it, here and there,
And curl about where'er they listed.

And then her sleeve came down, and I
Fastened it up — her hands were doughy ;
O, it did take the longest time ! —
Her arm, Ned, was so round and snowy.
She blushed, and trembled, and looked shy ;
Somehow that made me all the bolder ;
Her arch lips looked so red that I —
Well — found her head upon my shoulder.

We 're to be married, Ned, next month ;
Come and attend the wedding revels.
I really think that bachelors
Are the most miserable devils !
You 'd better go for some girl's hand ;
And if you are uncertain whether
You dare to make a due demand,
Why, just try cooking pies together.

ANONYMOUS.

POSSESSION.

A Poet loved a Star,
And to it whispered nightly,
"Being so fair, why art thou, love, so far ?
Or why so coldly shine, who shinest so brightly ?
O Beauty wooed and unpossest !
O, might I to this beating breast
But clasp thee once, and then die blest !"
That Star her Poet's love,
So wildly warm, made human ;
And leaving, for his sake, her heaven above,
His Star stooped earthward, and became a Woman.
"Thou who hast wooed and hast possest,
My lover, answer : Which was best,
The Star's beam or the Woman's breast ?"
"I miss from heaven," the man replied,
"A light that drew my spirit to it."
And to the man the woman sighed,
"I miss from earth a poet."

OWEN MEREDITH (LORD LYTTON).

Poems
of
Home

Home, Sweet Home!

'Mid pleasures and palaces though we may roam
Be it ever so humble, there's no place like home!
A charm from the sky seems to hallow us there
Which, seek through the world, is ne'er met with elsewhere!

Home, home, – sweet, sweet home!
There's no place like home! there's no place like home!

John Howard Payne.

POEMS OF HOME.

MARRIAGE.

LOVE.

THERE are who say the lover's heart
  Is in the loved one's merged ;
O, never by love's own warm art
  So cold a plea was urged !
No !— hearts that love hath crowned or crossed
  Love fondly knits together ;
But not a thought or hue is lost
  That made a part of either.

. . . . .

It is an ill-told tale that tells
  Of "hearts by love made one":
He grows who near another's dwells
  More conscious of his own ;
In each spring up new thoughts and powers
  That, mid love's warm, clear weather,
Together tend like climbing flowers,
  And, turning, grow together.

Such fictions blink love's better part,
  Yield up its half of bliss ;
The wells are in the neighbor heart,
  When there is thirst in this :
There findeth love the passion-flowers
  On which it learns to thrive,
Makes honey in another's bowers,
  But brings it home to hive.

Love's life is in its own replies, —
  To each low beat it beats,
Smiles back the smiles, sighs back the sighs,
  And every throb repeats.
Then, since one loving heart still throws
  Two shadows in love's sun,
How should two loving hearts compose
  And mingle into one ?

THOMAS KIBBLE HERVEY.

THOU HAST SWORN BY THY GOD, MY JEANIE.

THOU hast sworn by thy God, my Jeanie,
  By that pretty white hand o' thine,
And by a' the lowing stars in heaven,
  That thou wad aye be mine !

And I hae sworn by my God, my Jeanie,
  And by that kind heart o' thine,
By a' the stars sown thick owre heaven,
  That thou shalt aye be mine !

Then foul fa' the hands that wad loose sic bands,
  And the heart that wad part sic luve !
But there 's nae hand can loose my band,
  But the finger o' Him abuve.
Though the wee, wee cot maun be my bield,
  And my claithing ne'er sae mean,
I wad lap me up rich i' the faulds o' luve, —
  Heaven's armfu' o' my Jean.

Her white arm wad be a pillow for me,
  Fu' safter than the down ;
And Luve wad winnow owre us his kind, kind wings,
  And sweetly I 'd sleep, and soun'.
Come here to me, thou lass o' my luve !
  Come here and kneel wi' me !
The morn is fu' o' the presence o' God,
  And I canna pray without thee.

The morn wind is sweet 'mang the beds o' new flowers,
  The wee birds sing kindlie and hie ;
Our gudeman leans owre his kale-yard dike,
  And a blythe auld bodie is he.
The Beuk maun be ta'en whan the carle comes hame,
  Wi' the holy psalmodie ;
And thou maun speak o' me to thy God,
  And I will speak o' thee.

ALLAN CUNNINGHAM.

UNTIL DEATH.

MAKE me no vows of constancy, dear friend,
  To love me, though I die, thy whole life long,
And love no other till thy days shall end, —
    Nay, it were rash and wrong.

If thou canst love another, be it so ;
  I would not reach out of my quiet grave

To bind thy heart, if it should choose to go; —
Love should not be a slave.

My placid ghost, I trust, will walk serene
In clearer light than gilds those earthly morns,
Above the jealousies and envies keen
Which sow this life with thorns.

Thou wouldst not feel my shadowy caress,
If, after death, my soul should linger here;
Men's hearts crave tangible, close tenderness,
Love's presence, warm and near.

It would not make me sleep more peacefully
That thou wert wasting all thy life in woe
For my poor sake; what love thou hast for me,
Bestow it ere I go!

Carve not upon a stone when I am dead
The praises which remorseful mourners give
To women's graves, — a tardy recompense, —
But speak them while I live.

Heap not the heavy marble on my head
To shut away the sunshine and the dew;
Let small blooms grow there, and let grasses wave,
And rain-drops filter through.

Thou wilt meet many fairer and more gay
Than I; but, trust me, thou canst never find
One who will love and serve thee night and day
With a more single mind.

Forget me when I die! The violets
Above my rest will blossom just as blue,
Nor miss thy tears; e'en Nature's self forgets; —
But while I live, be true!

ANONYMOUS.

ALICE.

FROM "ALICE AND UNA."

ALICE was a chieftain's daughter,
And though many suitors sought her,
She so loved Glengariff's water
That she let her lovers pine.
Her eye was beauty's palace,
And her cheek an ivory chalice,
Through which the blood of Alice
Gleamed soft as rosiest wine,
And her lips like lusmore blossoms which the fairies intertwine, —
And her heart a golden mine.

She was gentler and shyer
Than the light fawn which stood by her,
And her eyes emit a fire
Soft and tender as her soul;
Love's dewy light doth drown her,
And the braided locks that crown her
Than autumn's trees are browner,
When the golden shadows roll
Through the forests in the evening, when cathedral turrets toll,
And the purple sun advanceth to its goal.

Her cottage was a dwelling
All regal homes excelling,
But, ah! beyond the telling
Was the beauty round it spread, —
The wave and sunshine playing,
Like sisters each arraying,
Far down the sea-plants swaying
Upon their coral-bed,
And languid as the tresses on a sleeping maiden's head,
When the summer breeze is dead.

Need we say that Maurice loved her,
And that no blush reproved her,
When her throbbing bosom moved her
To give the heart she gave?
That by dawn-light and by twilight,
And, O blessed moon, by thy light, —
When the twinkling stars on high light
The wanderer o'er the wave, —
His steps unconscious led him where Glengariff's waters lave
Each mossy bank and cave.

. . . . . .

The sun his gold is flinging,
The happy birds are singing,
And bells are gayly ringing
Along Glengariff's sea;
And crowds in many a galley
To the happy marriage rally
Of the maiden of the valley
And the youth of Céim-an-eich;
Old eyes with joy are weeping, as all ask on bended knee,
A blessing, gentle Alice, upon thee.

DENIS FLORENCE MACCARTHY.

NUPTIALS OF ADAM AND EVE.

MINE eyes he closed, but open left the cell
Of fancy, my internal sight, by which
Abstract, as in a trance, methought I saw,
Though sleeping, where I lay, and saw the shape
Still glorious before whom awake I stood;
Who, stooping, opened my left side, and took
From thence a rib, with cordial spirits warm,
And life-blood streaming fresh; wide was the wound,

But suddenly with flesh filled up and healed :
The rib he formed and fashioned with his hands ;
Under his forming hands a creature grew,
Manlike, but different sex, so lovely fair,
That what seemed fair in all the world seemed now
Mean, or in her summed up, in her contained
And in her looks, which from that time infused
Sweetness into my heart, unfelt before,
And into all things from her air inspired
The spirit of love and amorous delight.
She disappeared, and left me dark ; I waked
To find her, or forever to deplore
Her loss, and other pleasures all abjure :
When out of hope, behold her, not far off,
Such as I saw her in my dream, adorned
With what all earth or Heaven could bestow
To make her amiable. On she came,
Led by her heavenly Maker, though unseen,
And guided by his voice, nor uninformed
Of nuptial sanctity and marriage rites :
Grace was in all her steps, Heaven in her eye,
In every gesture dignity and love.
I, overjoyed, could not forbear aloud :
"This turn hath made amends ; thou hast fulfilled
Thy words, Creator bounteous and benign,
Giver of all things fair, but fairest this
Of all thy gifts, nor enviest. I now see
Bone of my bone, flesh of my flesh, myself
Before me ; Woman is her name, of man
Extracted : for this cause he shall forego
Father and mother, and to his wife adhere ;
And they shall be one flesh, one heart, one soul."
She heard me thus, and though divinely brought,
Yet innocence and virgin modesty,
Her virtue and the conscience of her worth,
That would be wooed, and not unsought be won,
Not obvious, not obtrusive, but retired,
The more desirable ; or, to say all,
Nature herself, though pure of sinful thought,
Wrought in her so, that, seeing me, she turned :
I followed her ; she what was honor knew,
And with obsequious majesty approved
My pleaded reason. To the nuptial bower
I led her blushing like the morn : all Heaven,
And happy constellations on that hour
Shed their selectest influence ; the earth
Gave sign of gratulation, and each hill ;
Joyous the birds ; fresh gales and gentle airs
Whispered it to the woods, and from their wings
Flung rose, flung odors from the spicy shrub,
Disporting, till the amorous bird of night
Sung spousal, and bid haste the evening star
On his hill-top, to light the bridal lamp.

MILTON.

MY COTTAGE.

HERE have I found at last a home of peace
To hide me from the world ; far from its noise,
To feed that spirit, which, though sprung from earth,
And linked to human beings by the bond
Of earthly love, hath yet a loftier aim
Than perishable joy, and through the calm
That sleeps amid the mountain solitude,
Can hear the billows of eternity,
And hear delighted. . . .
There are thoughts
That slumber in the soul, like sweetest sounds
Amid the harp's loose strings, till airs from Heaven
On earth, at dewy nightfall, visitant,
Awake the sleeping melody ! Such thoughts,
My gentle Mary, I have owed to thee.
And if thy voice e'er melt into my soul
With a dear home-toned whisper, — if thy face
E'er brighten in the unsteady gleams of light
From our own cottage-hearth, — O Mary ! then
My overpowered spirit shall recline
Upon thy inmost heart, till it become,
Thou sinless seraph, almost worthy thee !

JOHN WILSON.

TO A LADY BEFORE MARRIAGE.

O, FORMED by Nature, and refined by Art,
With charms to win, and sense to fix the heart !
By thousands sought, Clotilda, canst thou free
Thy crowd of captives and descend to me,
Content in shades obscure to waste thy life,
A hidden beauty and a country wife ?
O, listen while thy summers are my theme !
Ah ! soothe thy partner in his waking dream !
In some small hamlet on the lonely plain,
Where Thames through meadows rolls his mazy train,
Or where high Windsor, thick with greens arrayed,
Waves his old oaks, and spreads his ample shade,
Fancy has figured out our calm retreat ;
Already round the visionary seat
Our limes begin to shoot, our flowers to spring,
The brooks to murmur, and the birds to sing.
Where dost thou lie, thou thinly peopled green,
Thou nameless lawn, and village yet unseen,
Where sons, contented with their native ground,
Ne'er traveled farther than ten furlongs round,
And the tanned peasant and his ruddy bride
Were born together, and together died,
Where early larks best tell the morning light,
And only Philomel disturbs the night ?
Midst gardens here my humble pile shall rise,
With sweets surrounded of ten thousand dyes ;

All savage where th' embroidered gardens end,
The haunt of echoes, shall my woods ascend;
And O, if Heaven th' ambitious thought approve,
A rill shall warble 'cross the gloomy grove, —
A little rill, o'er pebbly beds conveyed,
Gush down the steep, and glitter through the glade.
What cheering scents these bordering banks exhale!
How loud that heifer lows from yonder vale!
That thrush how shrill! his note so clear, so high,
He drowns each feathered minstrel of the sky.
Here let me trace beneath the purpled morn
The deep-mouthed beagle and the sprightly horn,
Or lure the trout with well-dissembled flies,
Or fetch the fluttering partridge from the skies.
Nor shall thy hand disdain to crop the vine,
The downy peach or flavored nectarine;
Or rob the beehive of its golden hoard,
And bear the unbought luxuriance to thy board.
Sometimes my books by day shall kill the hours,
While from thy needle rise the silken flowers,
And thou, by turns, to ease my feeble sight,
Resume the volume, and deceive the night.
O, when I mark thy twinkling eyes opprest,
Soft whispering, let me warn my love to rest;
Then watch thee, charmed, while sleep locks every sense,
And to sweet Heaven commend thy innocence.
Thus reigned our fathers o'er the rural fold,
Wise, hale, and honest, in the days of old;
Till courts arose, where substance pays for show,
And specious joys are bought with real woe.

THOMAS TICKELL.

THE EPITHALAMION.

WAKE now, my love, awake; for it is time;
The rosy Morn long since left Tithon's bed,
All ready to her silver coach to climb;
And Phœbus 'gins to show his glorious head.
Hark! now the cheerful birds do chant their lays,
And carol of Love's praise.
The merry lark her matins sings aloft;
The thrush replies; the mavis descant plays;
The ouzel shrills; the ruddock warbles soft;
So goodly all agree, with sweet consent,
To this day's merriment.
Ah! my dear love, why do you sleep thus long,
When meeter were that you should now awake,
T' await the coming of your joyous make,*
And hearken to the birds' love-learnèd song,
The dewy leaves among!
For they of joy and pleasance to you sing,
That all the woods them answer, and their echo ring.

* Mate.

My love is now awake out of her dream,
And her fair eyes like stars that dimmèd were
With darksome cloud, now show their goodly beams
More bright than Hesperus his head doth rear.
Come now, ye damsels, daughters of delight,
Help quickly her to dight;
But first come, ye fair Hours, which were begot,
In Jove's sweet paradise, of Day and Night;
Which do the seasons of the year allot,
And all, that ever in this world is fair,
Do make and still repair;
And ye three handmaids of the Cyprian Queen,
The which do still adorn her beauties' pride,
Help to adorn my beautifulest bride:
And, as ye her array, still throw between
Some graces to be seen;
And, as ye use to Venus, to her sing,
The whiles the woods shall answer, and your echo ring.

Now is my love all ready forth to come:
Let all the virgins therefore well await;
And ye, fresh boys, that tend upon her groom,
Prepare yourselves, for he is coming straight.
Set all your things in seemly good array,
Fit for so joyful day, —
The joyful'st day that ever sun did see.
Fair Sun! show forth thy favorable ray,
And let thy lifeful heat not fervent be,
For fear of burning her sunshiny face,
Her beauty to disgrace.
O fairest Phœbus! father of the Muse!
If ever I did honor thee aright,
Or sing the thing that might thy mind delight,
Do not thy servant's simple boon refuse,
But let this day, let this one day be mine;
Let all the rest be thine.
Then I thy sovereign praises loud will sing,
That all the woods shall answer, and their echo ring.

Lo! where she comes along with portly pace,
Like Phœbe, from her chamber of the east,
Arising forth to run her mighty race,
Clad all in white, that seems a virgin best.
So well it her beseems, that ye would ween
Some angel she had been.
Her long loose yellow locks, like golden wire,
Sprinkled with pearl, and pearling flowers atween,
Do like a golden mantle her attire;
And, being crownèd with a garland green,
Seem like some maiden queen.
Her modest eyes, abashèd to behold
So many gazers as on her do stare,
Upon the lowly ground affixèd are;
Ne dare lift up her countenance too bold,
But blush to hear her praises sung so loud,

So far from being proud.
Nathless do ye still loud her praises sing,
That all the woods may answer, and your echo ring.

Tell me, ye merchants' daughters, did ye see
So fair a creature in your town before?
So sweet, so lovely, and so mild as she,
Adorned with beauty's grace, and virtue's store;
Her goodly eyes like sapphires shining bright,
Her forehead ivory white,
Her cheeks like apples which the sun hath rudded,
Her lips like cherries charming men to bite,
Her breast like to a bowl of cream uncrudded.

. . . . .

Why stand ye still, ye virgins, in amaze,
Upon her so to gaze,
Whiles ye forget your former lay to sing,
To which the woods did answer, and your echo ring?

But if ye saw that which no eyes can see,
The inward beauty of her lively sprite,
Garnished with heavenly gifts of high degree,
Much more then would ye wonder at that sight,
And stand astonished like to those which red *
Medusa's mazeful head.
There dwells sweet Love, and constant Chastity,
Unspotted Faith, and comely Womanhood,
Regard of Honor, and mild Modesty;
There Virtue reigns as queen in royal throne,
And giveth laws alone,
The which the base affections do obey,
And yield their services unto her will;
Ne thought of things uncomely ever may
Thereto approach to tempt her mind to ill.
Had ye once seen these her celestial treasures,
And unrevealèd pleasures,
Then would ye wonder and her praises sing,
That all the woods should answer, and your echo ring.

Open the temple gates unto my love,
Open them wide that she may enter in,
And all the posts adorn as doth behove,
And all the pillars deck with garlands trim,
For to receive this saint with honor due,
That cometh in to you.
With trembling steps, and humble reverence,
She cometh in, before the Almighty's view:
Of her, ye virgins, learn obedience,
When so ye come into those holy places,
To humble your proud faces:
Bring her up to the high altar, that she may
The sacred ceremonies there partake,
The which do endless matrimony make;
And let the roaring organs loudly play

* Saw.

The praises of the Lord in lively notes;
The whiles, with hollow throats,
The choristers the joyous anthem sing,
That all the woods may answer, and their echo ring.

Behold, while she before the altar stands,
Hearing the holy priest that to her speaks,
And blesseth her with his two happy hands,
How the red roses flush up in her cheeks,
And the pure snow with goodly vermeil stain,
Like crimson dyed in grain;
That even the angels, which continually
About the sacred altar do remain,
Forget their service and about her fly,
Oft peeping in her face, that seems more fair,
The more they on it stare.
But her sad eyes, still fastened on the ground,
Are governèd with goodly modesty,
That suffers not a look to glance awry,
Which may let in a little thought unsound.
Why blush you, love, to give to me your hand,
The pledge of all our band?
Sing, ye sweet angels, Alleluia sing,
That all the woods may answer, and your echo ring.

EDMUND SPENSER.

LIKE A LAVEROCK IN THE LIFT.

It's we two, it's we two for aye,
All the world, and we two, and Heaven be our stay!
Like a laverock in the lift, sing, O bonny bride!
All the world was Adam once, with Eve by his side.

What's the world, my lass, my love! — what can it do?
I am thine, and thou art mine; life is sweet and new.
If the world have missed the mark, let it stand by;
For we two have gotten leave, and once more will try.

Like a laverock in the lift, sing, O bonny bride!
It's we two, it's we two, happy side by side.
Take a kiss from me, thy man; now the song begins:
"All is made afresh for us, and the brave heart wins."

When the darker days come, and no sun will shine,
Thou shalt dry my tears, lass, and I'll dry thine.
It's we two, it's we two, while the world's away,
Sitting by the golden sheaves on our wedding day.

JEAN INGELOW.

MAIRE BHAN ASTOR.*

IN a valley far away
  With my Maire bhan astór,
Short would be the summer-day,
  Ever loving more and more ;
Winter days would all grow long,
  With the light her heart would pour,
With her kisses and her song,
  And her loving mait go leór.
    Fond is Maire bhan astór,
    Fair is Maire bhan astór,
    Sweet as ripple on the shore,
    Sings my Maire bhan astór.

O, her sire is very proud,
  And her mother cold as stone ;
But her brother bravely vowed
  She should be my bride alone ;
For he knew I loved her well,
  And he knew she loved me too,
So he sought their pride to quell,
  But 't was all in vain to sue.
    True is Maire bhan astór,
    Tried is Maire bhan astór,
    Had I wings I 'd never soar
    From my Maire bhan astór.

There are lands where manly toil
  Surely reaps the crop it sows,
Glorious woods and teeming soil,
  Where the broad Missouri flows ;
Through the trees the smoke shall rise,
  From our hearth with mait go leór,
There shall shine the happy eyes
  Of my Maire bhan astór.
    Mild is Maire bhan astór,
    Mine is Maire bhan astór,
    Saints will watch about the door
    Of my Maire bhan astór.

THOMAS DAVIS.

* Fair Mary, my treasure.

THE BRIDE.

FROM "A BALLAD UPON A WEDDING."

THE maid, and thereby hangs a tale,
For such a maid no Whitsun-ale
  Could ever yet produce :
No grape that 's kindly ripe could be
So round, so plump, so soft as she,
  Nor half so full of juice.

Her finger was so small, the ring
Would not stay on which they did bring, —
  It was too wide a peck ;
And, to say truth, — for out it must, —
It looked like the great collar — just —
  About our young colt's neck.

Her feet beneath her petticoat,
Like little mice, stole in and out,
  As if they feared the light ;
But O, she dances such a way !
No sun upon an Easter-day
  Is half so fine a sight.

Her cheeks so rare a white was on,
No daisy makes comparison ;
  Who sees them is undone ;
For streaks of red were mingled there,
Such as are on a Cath'rine pear,
  The side that 's next the sun.

Her lips were red ; and one was thin,
Compared to that was next her chin.
  Some bee had stung it newly ;
But, Dick, her eyes so guard her face,
I durst no more upon them gaze,
  Than on the sun in July.

Her mouth so small, when she does speak,
Thou 'dst swear her teeth her words did break,
  That they might passage get ;
But she so handled still the matter,
They came as good as ours, or better,
  And are not spent a whit.

SIR JOHN SUCKLING.

HEBREW WEDDING.

To the sound of timbrels sweet
Moving slow our solemn feet,
We have borne thee on the road
To the virgin's blest abode ;
With thy yellow torches gleaming,
And thy scarlet mantle streaming,
And the canopy above
Swaying as we slowly move.

Thou hast left the joyous feast,
And the mirth and wine have ceased
And now we set thee down before
The jealously unclosing door,
That the favored youth admits
Where the veilèd virgin sits
In the bliss of maiden fear,
Waiting our soft tread to hear,
And the music's brisker din
At the bridegroom's entering in,
Entering in, a welcome guest,
To the chamber of his rest.

CHORUS OF MAIDENS.

Now the jocund song is thine,
Bride of David's kingly line;
How thy dove-like bosom trembleth,
And thy shrouded eye resembleth
Violets, when the dews of eve
A moist and tremulous glitter leave!

On the bashful sealèd lid.
Close within the bride-veil hid,
Motionless thou sitt'st and mute;
Save that at the soft salute
Of each entering maiden friend,
Thou dost rise and softly bend.

Hark! a brisker, merrier glee!
The door unfolds, — 't is he! 't is he!
Thus we lift our lamps to meet him,
Thus we touch our lutes to greet him.
Thou shalt give a fonder meeting,
Thou shalt give a tenderer greeting.

HENRY HART MILMAN.

MARRIAGE.

FROM "HUMAN LIFE."

THEN before All they stand, — the holy vow
And ring of gold, no fond illusions now,
Bind her as his. Across the threshold led,
And every tear kissed off as soon as shed,
His house she enters, — there to be a light,
Shining within, when all without is night;
A guardian angel o'er his life presiding,
Doubling his pleasures and his cares dividing,
Winning him back when mingling in the throng,
Back from a world we love, alas! too long,
To fireside happiness, to hours of ease,
Blest with that charm, the certainty to please.
How oft her eyes read his; her gentle mind
To all his wishes, all his thoughts inclined;
Still subject, — ever on the watch to borrow
Mirth of his mirth and sorrow of his sorrow!
The soul of music slumbers in the shell,
Till waked and kindled by the master's spell,
And feeling hearts — touch them but rightly — pour
A thousand melodies unheard before!

SAMUEL ROGERS.

SEVEN TIMES SIX.

GIVING IN MARRIAGE.

To bear, to nurse, to rear,
To watch, and then to lose:
To see my bright ones disappear,
Drawn up like morning dews; —
To bear, to nurse, to rear,
To watch, and then to lose:
This have I done when God drew near
Among his own to choose.

To hear, to heed, to wed,
And with thy lord depart
In tears that he, as soon as shed,
Will let no longer smart. —
To hear, to heed, to wed,
This while thou didst I smiled,
For now it was not God who said,
"Mother, give ME thy child."

O fond, O fool, and blind,
To God I gave with tears;
But when a man like grace would find,
My soul put by her fears.
O fond, O fool, and blind,
God guards in happier spheres;
That man will guard where he did bind
Is hope for unknown years.

To hear, to heed, to wed,
Fair lot that maidens choose,
Thy mother's tenderest words are said,
Thy face no more she views;
Thy mother's lot, my dear,
She doth in naught accuse;
Her lot to bear, to nurse, to rear,
To love — and then to lose.

JEAN INGELOW.

THE BANKS OF THE LEE.

O, THE banks of the Lee, the banks of the Lee,
And love in a cottage for Mary and me!
There 's not in the land a lovelier tide,
And I'm sure that there's no one so fair as my bride.
She 's modest and meek,
There 's a down on her cheek,
And her skin is as sleek
As a butterfly's wing;
Then her step would scarce show
On the fresh-fallen snow,
And her whisper is low,
But as clear as the spring.
O, the banks of the Lee, the banks of the Lee,
And love in a cottage for Mary and me!
I know not how love is happy elsewhere,
I know not how any but lovers are there.

O, so green is the grass, so clear is the stream,
So mild is the mist and so rich is the beam,
That beauty should never to other lands roam,
But make on the banks of our river its home!
When, dripping with dew,
The roses peep through,
'T is to look in at you

They are growing so fast;
While the scent of the flowers
Must be hoarded for hours,
'T is poured in such showers
When my Mary goes past.

O, the banks of the Lee, the banks of the Lee,
And love in a cottage for Mary and me!
O, Mary for me, Mary for me,
And 't is little I 'd sigh for the banks of the Lee!

THOMAS DAVIS.

HOME.

MY WIFE'S A WINSOME WEE THING.

SHE is a winsome wee thing,
She is a handsome wee thing,
She is a bonnie wee thing,
This sweet wee wife o' mine.

I never saw a fairer,
I never lo'ed a dearer,
And neist my heart I 'll wear her,
For fear my jewel tine.

She is a winsome wee thing,
She is a handsome wee thing,
She is a bonnie wee thing,
This sweet wee wife o' mine.

The warld's wrack we share o't,
The warstle and the care o't:
Wi' her I 'll blythely bear it,
And think my lot divine.

ROBERT BURNS.

SONNETS.

MY Love, I have no fear that thou shouldst die;
Albeit I ask no fairer life than this,
Whose numbering-clock is still thy gentle kiss,
While Time and Peace with hands unlockèd fly,—
Yet care I not where in Eternity
We live and love, well knowing that there is
No backward step for those who feel the bliss
Of Faith as their most lofty yearnings high:
Love hath so purified my being's core,
Meseems I scarcely should be startled, even,
To find, some morn, that thou hadst gone before;
Since, with thy love, this knowledge too was given,
Which each calm day doth strengthen more and more,
That they who love are but one step from Heaven.

I CANNOT think that thou shouldst pass away,
Whose life to mine is an eternal law,
A piece of nature that can have no flaw,
A new and certain sunrise every day;
But, if thou art to be another ray
About the Sun of Life, and art to live
Free from all of thee that was fugitive,
The debt of Love I will more fully pay,
Not downcast with the thought of thee so high,
But rather raised to be a nobler man,
And more divine in my humanity,
As knowing that the waiting eyes which scan
My life are lighted by a purer being,
And ask meek, calm-browed deeds, with it agreeing.

I THOUGHT our love at full, but I did err;
Joy's wreath drooped o'er mine eyes; I could not see
That sorrow in our happy world must be
Love's deepest spokesman and interpreter.
But, as a mother feels her child first stir
Under her heart, so felt I instantly
Deep in my soul another bond to thee
Thrill with that life we saw depart from her;
O mother of our angel child! twice dear!
Death knits as well as parts, and still, I wis,
Her tender radiance shall infold us here,
Even as the light, borne up by inward bliss,
Threads the void glooms of space without a fear,
To print on farthest stars her pitying kiss.

JAMES RUSSELL LOWELL.

ADAM TO EVE.

O FAIREST of creation, last and best
Of all God's works, creature in whom excelled
Whatever can to sight or thought be formed,
Holy, divine, good, amiable, or sweet!
How art thou lost, how on a sudden lost,
Defaced, deflowered, and now to death devote!
Rather, how hast thou yielded to transgress
The strict forbiddance, how to violate
The sacred fruit forbidden! Some cursèd fraud

Elizabeth Barrett Browning

J. B. FORD & Co. NEW YORK.

Of enemy hath beguiled thee, yet unknown,
And me with thee hath ruined, for with thee
Certain my resolution is to die.
How can I live without thee, how forego
Thy sweet converse, and love so dearly joined,
To live again in these wild woods forlorn?
Should God create another Eve, and I
Another rib afford, yet loss of thee
Would never from my heart; no, no, I feel
The link of nature draw me: flesh of flesh,
Bone of my bone thou art, and from thy state
Mine never shall be parted, bliss or woe.

. . . . .

However, I with thee have fixed my lot,
Certain to undergo like doom; if death
Consort with thee, death is to me as life;
So forcible within my heart I feel
The bond of nature draw me to my own,
My own in thee, for what thou art is mine;
Our state cannot be severed, we are one,
One flesh; to lose thee were to lose myself.

MILTON.

LORD WALTER'S WIFE.

"BUT why do you go?" said the lady, while both sate under the yew,
And her eyes were alive in their depth, as the kraken beneath the sea-blue.

"Because I fear you," he answered;— "because you are far too fair,
And able to strangle my soul in a mesh of your gold-colored hair."

"O that," she said, "is no reason! Such knots are quickly undone,
And too much beauty, I reckon, is nothing but too much sun."

"Yet farewell so," he answered;— "the sun-stroke 's fatal at times.
I value your husband, Lord Walter, whose gallop rings still from the limes."

"O, that," she said, "is no reason. You smell a rose through a fence:
If two should smell it, what matter? who grumbles, and where 's the pretense?"

"But I," he replied, "have promised another, when love was free,
To love her alone, alone, who alone and afar loves me."

"Why, that," she said, "is no reason. Love 's always free, I am told.
Will you vow to be safe from the headache on Tuesday, and think it will hold?"

"But you," he replied, "have a daughter, a young little child, who was laid
In your lap to be pure; so I leave you: the angels would make me afraid."

"O, that," she said, "is no reason. The angels keep out of the way;
And Dora, the child, observes nothing, although you should please me and stay."

At which he rose up in his anger,— "Why, now, you no longer are fair!
Why, now, you no longer are fatal, but ugly and hateful, I swear."

At which she laughed out in her scorn,— "These men! O, these men overnice,
Who are shocked if a color not virtuous is frankly put on by a vice."

Her eyes blazed upon him— "And *you!* You bring us your vices so near
That we smell them! you think in our presence a thought 't would defame us to hear!

"What reason had you, and what right,—I appeal to your soul from my life,—
To find me too fair as a woman? Why, sir, I am pure, and a wife.

"Is the day-star too fair up above you? It burns you not. Dare you imply
I brushed you more close than the star does, when Walter had set me as high?

"If a man finds a woman too fair, he means simply adapted too much
To uses unlawful and fatal. The praise!—shall I thank you for such?

"Too fair?—not unless you misuse us! and surely if, once in a while,
You attain to it, straightway you call us no longer too fair, but too vile.

"A moment,—I pray your attention!—I have a poor word in my head
I must utter, though womanly custom would set it down better unsaid.

"You grew, sir, pale to impertinence, once when I showed you a ring.
You kissed my fan when I dropped it. No matter! I 've broken the thing.

"You did me the honor, perhaps, to be moved at my side now and then
In the senses,—a vice, I have heard, which is common to beasts and some men.

"Love 's a virtue for heroes! — as white as the snow on high hills,
And immortal as every great soul is that struggles, endures, and fulfills.

"I love my Walter profoundly, — you, Maude, though you faltered a week,
For the sake of . . . what was it? an eyebrow? or, less still, a mole on a cheek?

"And since, when all 's said, you 're too noble to stoop to the frivolous cant
About crimes irresistible, virtues that swindle, betray, and supplant,

"I determined to prove to yourself that, whate'er you might dream or avow
By illusion, you wanted precisely no more of me than you have now.

"There! Look me full in the face! — in the face. Understand, if you can,
That the eyes of such women as I am are clean as the palm of a man.

"Drop his hand, you insult him. Avoid us for fear we should cost you a scar, —
You take us for harlots, I tell you, and not for the women we are.

"You wronged me: but then I considered . . . there 's Walter! And so at the end,
I vowed that he should not be mulcted, by me, in the hand of a friend.

"Have I hurt you indeed? We are quits then. Nay, friend of my Walter, be mine!
Come, Dora, my darling, my angel, and help me to ask him to dine."

ELIZABETH BARRETT BROWNING.

CONNUBIAL LIFE.

FROM "THE SEASONS."

But happy they, the happiest of their kind,
Whom gentler stars unite, and in one fate
Their hearts, their fortunes, and their beings blend.
'T is not the coarser tie of human laws,
Unnatural oft, and foreign to the mind,
That binds their peace, but harmony itself,
Attuning all their passions into love;
Where friendship full-exerts her softest power,
Perfect esteem enlivened by desire
Ineffable, and sympathy of soul;
Thought meeting thought, and will preventing will,
With boundless confidence: for naught but love
Can answer love, and render bliss secure.
Meantime a smiling offspring rises round,
And mingles both their graces. By degrees,
The human blossom blows; and every day,
Soft as it rolls along, shows some new charm,
The father's lustre and the mother's bloom.
Then infant reason grows apace, and calls
For the kind hand of an assiduous care.
Delightful task! to rear the tender thought,
To teach the young idea how to shoot,
To pour the fresh instruction o'er the mind,
To breathe the enlivening spirit, and to fix
The generous purpose in the glowing breast.
O, speak the joy! ye whom the sudden tear
Surprises often, while you look around,
And nothing strikes your eye but sights of bliss,
All various Nature pressing on the heart;
An elegant sufficiency, content,
Retirement, rural quiet, friendship, books,
Ease and alternate labor, useful life,
Progressive virtue, and approving Heaven.
These are the matchless joys of virtuous love;
And thus their moments fly. The Seasons thus,
As ceaseless round a jarring world they roll,
Still find them happy; and consenting Spring
Sheds her own rosy garland on their heads:
Till evening comes at last, serene and mild;
When, after the long vernal day of life,
Enamored more, as more remembrance swells
With many a proof of recollected love,
Together down they sink in social sleep;
Together freed, their gentle spirits fly
To scenes where love and bliss immortal reign.

JAMES THOMSON.

POSSESSION.

"It was our wedding-day
A month ago," dear heart, I hear you say.
If months, or years, or ages since have passed,
I know not: I have ceased to question Time.
I only know that once there pealed a chime
Of joyous bells, and then I held you fast,
And all stood back, and none my right denied,
And forth we walked: the world was free and wide
Before us. Since that day
I count my life: the Past is washed away.

It was no dream, that vow:
It was the voice that woke me from a dream, —
A happy dream, I think; but I am waking now,
And drink the splendor of a sun supreme
That turns the mist of former tears to gold.
Within these arms I hold
The fleeting promise, chased so long in vain:
Ah, weary bird! thou wilt not fly again:

Thy wings are clipped, thou canst no more depart, —
Thy nest is builded in my heart!

I was the crescent; thou
The silver phantom of the perfect sphere,
Held in its bosom: in one glory now
Our lives united shine, and many a year —
Not the sweet moon of bridal only — we
One luster, ever at the full, shall be:
One pure and rounded light, one planet whole,
One life developed, one completed soul!
For I in thee, and thou in me,
Unite our cloven halves of destiny.

God knew his chosen time.
He bade me slowly ripen to my prime,
And from my boughs withheld the promised fruit,
Till storm and sun gave vigor to the root.
Secure, O Love! secure
Thy blessing is: I have thee day and night:
Thou art become my blood, my life, my light:
God's mercy thou, and therefore shalt endure.

BAYARD TAYLOR.

THE DAY RETURNS, MY BOSOM BURNS.

THE day returns, my bosom burns,
The blissful day we twa did meet;
Though winter wild in tempest toiled,
Ne'er summer sun was half sae sweet.
Than a' the pride that loads the tide,
And crosses o'er the sultry line, —
Than kingly robes, and crowns and globes,
Heaven gave me more; it made thee mine.

While day and night can bring delight,
Or nature aught of pleasure give, —
While joys above my mind can move,
For thee and thee alone I live;
When that grim foe of life below
Comes in between to make us part,
The iron hand that breaks our band,
It breaks my bliss, — it breaks my heart.

ROBERT BURNS.

THE POET'S BRIDAL-DAY SONG.

O, MY love 's like the steadfast sun,
Or streams that deepen as they run;
Nor hoary hairs, nor forty years,
Nor moments between sighs and tears,
Nor nights of thought, nor days of pain,
Nor dreams of glory dreamed in vain,
Nor mirth, nor sweetest song that flows
To sober joys and soften woes,
Can make my heart or fancy flee,
One moment, my sweet wife, from thee.

Even while I muse, I see thee sit
In maiden bloom and matron wit;
Fair, gentle as when first I sued,
Ye seem, but of sedater mood;
Yet my heart leaps as fond for thee
As when, beneath Arbigland tree,
We stayed and wooed, and thought the moon
Set on the sea an hour too soon;
Or lingered mid the falling dew,
When looks were fond and words were few.

Though I see smiling at thy feet
Five sons, and ae fair daughter sweet,
And time, and care, and birthtime woes
Have dimmed thine eye and touched thy rose,
To thee, and thoughts of thee, belong
Whate'er charms me in tale or song.
When words descend like dews, unsought,
With gleams of deep, enthusiast thought,
And fancy in her heaven flies free,
They come, my love, they come from thee.

O, when more thought we gave, of old,
To silver, than some give to gold,
'T was sweet to sit and ponder o'er
How we should deck our humble bower;
'T was sweet to pull, in hope, with thee,
The golden fruit of fortune's tree;
And sweeter still to choose and twine
A garland for that brow of thine, —
A song-wreath which may grace my Jean,
While rivers flow, and woods grow green.

At times there come, as come there ought,
Grave moments of sedater thought,
When fortune frowns, nor lends our night
One gleam of her inconstant light;
And hope, that decks the peasant's bower,
Shines like a rainbow through the shower.
O, then I see, while seated nigh,
A mother's heart shine in thine eye,
And proud resolve, and purpose meek,
Speak of thee more than words can speak.
I think this wedded wife of mine,
The best of all that 's not divine.

ALLAN CUNNINGHAM.

AN ANGEL'S VISIT.

SHE stood in the harvest-field at noon,
And sang aloud for the joy of living.
She said: "'T is the sun that I drink like wine,
To my heart this gladness giving."

Rank upon rank the wheat fell slain;
The reapers ceased. "'T is sure the splendor
Of sloping sunset light that thrills
My breast with a bliss so tender."

Up and up the blazing hills
  Climbed the night from the misty meadows.
"Can they be stars, or living eyes
  That bend on me from the shadows?"

"Greeting!" - "And may you speak, indeed?"
  All in the dark her sense grew clearer;
She knew that she had, for company,
  All day an angel near her.

"May you tell us of the life divine,
  To us unknown, to angels given?"
"Count me your earthly joys, and I
  May teach you those of heaven."

"They say the pleasures of earth are vain;
  Delusions all, to lure from duty;
But while God hangs his bow in the rain,
  Can I help my joy in beauty?

"And while he quickens the air with song,
  My breaths with scent, my fruits with flavor,
Will he, dear angel, count as sin
  My life in sound and savor?

"See, at our feet the glow-worm shines,
  Lo! in the east a star arises;
And thought may climb from worm to world
  Forever through fresh surprises:

"And thought is joy. . . . And, hark! in the vale
  Music, and merry steps pursuing;
They leap in the dance, — a soul in my blood
  Cries out, Awake, be doing!

"Action is joy; or power at play,
  Or power at work in world or emprises:
Action is life; part from the deed,
  More from the doing rises."

"And are these all?" She flushed in the dark.
  "These are not all. I have a lover;
At sound of his voice, at touch of his hand,
  The cup of my life runs over.

"Once, unknowing, we looked and neared,
  And doubted, and neared, and rested never,
Till life seized life, as flame meets flame,
  To escape no more forever.

"Lover and husband; then was love
  The wine of my life, all life enhancing:
Now 't is my bread, too needful and sweet
  To be kept for feast-day chancing.

"I have a child." She seemed to change;
  The deep content of some brooding creature
Looked from her eyes. "O, sweet and strange!
  Angel, be thou my teacher:

"When He made us one in a babe,
  Was it for joy, or sorest proving?
For now I fear no heaven could win
  Our hearts from earthly loving.

"I have a friend. Howso I err,
  I see her uplifting love bend o'er me;
Howso I climb to my best, I know
  Her foot will be there before me.

"Howso parted, we must be nigh,
  Held by old years of every weather;
The best new love would be less than ours
  Who have lived our lives together.

"Now, lest forever I fail to see
  Right skies, through clouds so bright and tender,
Show me true joy." The angel's smile
  Lit all the night with splendor.

"Save that to Love and Learn and Do
  In wondrous measure to us is given;
Save that we see the face of God,
  You have named the joys of heaven."

ELIZA SPROAT TURNER.

WIFE, CHILDREN, AND FRIENDS.

WHEN the black-lettered list to the gods was presented
  (The list of what fate for each mortal intends),
At the long string of ills a kind goddess relented,
  And slipped in three blessings, — wife, children, and friends.

In vain surly Pluto maintained he was cheated,
  For justice divine could not compass its ends.
The scheme of man's penance he swore was defeated,
  For earth becomes heaven with — wife, children, and friends.

If the stock of our bliss is in stranger hands vested,
  The fund, ill secured, oft in bankruptcy ends;
But the heart issues bills which are never protested,
  When drawn on the firm of — wife, children, and friends.

The day-spring of youth, still unclouded by sorrow,
  Alone on itself for enjoyment depends;
But drear is the twilight of age if it borrow
  No warmth from the smile of — wife, children, and friends.

WILLIAM ROBERT SPENCER.

THE POET'S SONG TO HIS WIFE.

How many summers, love,
  Have I been thine?
How many days, thou dove,
  Hast thou been mine?
Time, like the wingèd wind
  When 't bends the flowers,
Hath left no mark behind,
  To count the hours!

Some weight of thought, though loath,
  On thee he leaves;
Some lines of care round both
  Perhaps he weaves;
Some fears, — a soft regret
  For joys scarce known;
Sweet looks we half forget; —
  All else is flown!

Ah! — With what thankless heart
  I mourn and sing!
Look, where our children start,
  Like sudden spring!
With tongues all sweet and low
  Like pleasant rhyme,
They tell how much I owe
  To thee and time!

BARRY CORNWALL.

IF THOU WERT BY MY SIDE, MY LOVE.

If thou wert by my side, my love,
  How fast would evening fail
In green Bengala's palmy grove,
  Listening the nightingale!

If thou, my love, wert by my side,
  My babies at my knee,
How gayly would our pinnace glide
  O'er Gunga's mimic sea!

I miss thee at the dawning gray,
  When, on our deck reclined,
In careless ease my limbs I lay
  And woo the cooler wind.

I miss thee when by Gunga's stream
  My twilight steps I guide,
But most beneath the lamp's pale beam
  I miss thee from my side.

I spread my books, my pencil try,
  The lingering noon to cheer,
But miss thy kind, approving eye,
  Thy meek, attentive ear.

But when at morn and eve the star
  Beholds me on my knee,
I feel, though thou art distant far,
  Thy prayers ascend for me.

Then on! then on! where duty leads,
  My course be onward still,
O'er broad Hindostan's sultry meads,
  O'er bleak Almorah's hill.

That course nor Delhi's kingly gates
  Nor mild Malwah detain;
For sweet the bliss us both awaits
  By yonder western main.

Thy towers, Bombay, gleam bright, they say,
  Across the dark blue sea;
But ne'er were hearts so light and gay
  As then shall meet in thee!

REGINALD HEBER.

TROTH-PLIGHT.

FOR THE GOLDEN WEDDING OF A HUSBAND THIRTY-SEVEN YEARS BLIND.

I BROUGHT her home, my bonny bride,
    Just fifty years ago;
Her eyes were bright,
Her step was light,
    Her voice was sweet and low.

In April was our wedding-day —
    The maiden month, you know,
Of tears and smiles,
And willful wiles,
    And flowers that spring from snow.

My love cast down her dear, dark eyes,
    As if she fain would hide
From my fond sight
Her own delight,
    Half shy, yet happy, bride.

But blushes told the tale, instead,
    As plain as words could speak,
In dainty red,
That overspread
    My darling's dainty cheek.

For twice six years and more I watched
    Her fairer grow each day;
My babes were blest
Upon her breast,
    And she was pure as they.

And then an angel touched my eyes,
And turned my day to night,
That fading charms
Or time's alarms
Might never vex my sight.

Thus sitting in the dark I see
My darling as of yore, —
With blushing face
And winsome grace,
Unchanged, forevermore.

Full fifty years of young and fair!
To her I pledge my vow
Whose spring-time grace
And April face
Have lasted until now.

LOUISE CHANDLER MOULTON.

O, LAY THY HAND IN MINE, DEAR!

O, LAY thy hand in mine, dear!
We 're growing old;
But Time hath brought no sign, dear,
That hearts grow cold.
'T is long, long since our new love
Made life divine;
But age enricheth true love,
Like noble wine.

And lay thy cheek to mine, dear,
And take thy rest;
Mine arms around thee twine, dear,
And make thy nest.
A many cares are pressing
On this dear head;
But Sorrow's hands in blessing
Are surely laid.

O, lean thy life on mine, dear!
'T will shelter thee.
Thou wert a winsome vine, dear,
On my young tree:
And so, till boughs are leafless,
And songbirds flown,
We 'll twine, then lay us, griefless,
Together down.

GERALD MASSEY.

THE WORN WEDDING-RING.

YOUR wedding-ring wears thin, dear wife; ah, summers not a few,
Since I put it on your finger first, have passed o'er me and you;
And, love, what changes we have seen, — what cares and pleasures, too, —
Since you became my own dear wife, when this old ring was new!

O, blessings on that happy day, the happiest of my life,
When, thanks to God, your low, sweet "Yes" made you my loving wife!
Your heart will say the same, I know; that day 's as dear to you, —
That day that made me yours, dear wife, when this old ring was new.

How well do I remember now your young sweet face that day!
How fair you were, how dear you were, my tongue could hardly say;
Nor how I doated on you; O, how proud I was of you!
But did I love you more than now, when this old ring was new?

No — no! no fairer were you then than at this hour to me;
And, dear as life to me this day, how could you dearer be?
As sweet your face might be that day as now it is, 't is true;
But did I know your heart as well when this old ring was new?

O partner of my gladness, wife, what care, what grief is there
For me you would not bravely face, with me you would not share?
O, what a weary want had every day, if wanting you,
Wanting the love that God made mine when this old ring was new!

Years bring fresh links to bind us, wife, — young voices that are here;
Young faces round our fire that make their mother's yet more dear;
Young loving hearts your care each day makes yet more like to you,
More like the loving heart made mine when this old ring was new.

And, blessed be God! all he has given are with us yet; around
Our table every precious life lent to us still is found.
Though cares we 've known, with hopeful hearts the worst we 've struggled through;
Blessed be his name for all his love since this old ring was new!

The past is dear, its sweetness still our memories treasure yet;
The griefs we 've borne, together borne, we would not now forget.
Whatever, wife, the future brings, heart unto heart still true,
We 'll share as we have shared all else since this old ring was new.

And if God spare us 'mongst our sons and daughters to grow old,
We know his goodness will not let your heart or mine grow cold.
Your aged eyes will see in mine all they 've still shown to you,
And mine in yours all they have seen since this old ring was new.

And O, when death shall come at last to bid me to my rest,
May I die looking in those eyes, and resting on that breast;
O, may my parting gaze be blessed with the dear sight of you,
Of those fond eyes, — fond as they were when this old ring was new!

WILLIAM COX BENNETT.

JOHN ANDERSON, MY JO.

JOHN ANDERSON, my jo, John,
When we were first acquent,
Your locks were like the raven,
Your bonnie brow was brent;
But now your brow is beld, John,
Your locks are like the snaw;
But blessings on your frosty pow,
John Anderson, my jo.

John Anderson, my jo, John,
We clamb the hill thegither;
And mony a canty day, John,
We 've had wi' ane anither.
Now we maun totter down, John,
But hand in hand we 'll go:
And sleep thegither at the foot,
John Anderson, my jo.

ROBERT BURNS.

FILIAL LOVE.

FROM "CHILDE HAROLD.

THERE is a dungeon in whose dim drear light
What do I gaze on? Nothing: look again!
Two forms are slowly shadowed on my sight, —
Two insulated phantoms of the brain:
It is not so; I see them full and plain, —
An old man and a female young and fair,
Fresh as a nursing mother, in whose vein
The blood is nectar: but what doth she there,
With her unmantled neck, and bosom white and bare?

Full swells the deep pure fountain of young life,
Where *on* the heart and *from* the heart we took
Our first and sweetest nurture, when the wife,
Blest into mother, in the innocent look,
Or even the piping cry of lips that brook
No pain and small suspense, a joy perceives
Man knows not, when from out its cradled nook
She sees her little bud put forth its leaves —
What may the fruit be yet? I know not — Cain was Eve's.

But here youth offers to old age the food,
The milk of his own gift: it is her sire
To whom she renders back the debt of blood
Born with her birth. No! he shall not expire
While in those warm and lovely veins the fire
Of health and holy feeling can provide
Great Nature's Nile, whose deep stream rises higher
Than Egypt's river; — from that gentle side
Drink, drink and live, old man! Heaven's realm holds no such tide.

The starry fable of the milky-way
Has not thy story's purity; it is
A constellation of a sweeter ray,
And sacred Nature triumphs more in this
Reverse of her decree, than in the abyss
Where sparkle distant worlds: — O, holiest nurse!
No drop of that clear stream its way shall miss
To thy sire's heart, replenishing its source
With life, as our freed souls rejoin the universe.

LORD BYRON.

ROCK ME TO SLEEP.

BACKWARD, turn backward, O Time, in your flight,
Make me a child again just for to-night!
Mother, come back from the echoless shore,
Take me again to your heart as of yore;
Kiss from my forehead the furrows of care,
Smooth the few silver threads out of my hair;
Over my slumbers your loving watch keep; —
Rock me to sleep, mother, — rock me to sleep!

Backward, flow backward, O tide of the years!
I am so weary of toil and of tears, —
Toil without recompense, tears all in vain, —
Take them, and give me my childhood again!

I have grown weary of dust and decay, —
Weary of flinging my soul-wealth away;
Weary of sowing for others to reap; —
Rock me to sleep, mother, — rock me to sleep!

Tired of the hollow, the base, the untrue,
Mother, O mother, my heart calls for you!
Many a summer the grass has grown green,
Blossomed, and faded our faces between,
Yet with strong yearning and passionate pain
Long I to-night for your presence again.
Come from the silence so long and so deep; —
Rock me to sleep, mother, — rock me to sleep!

Over my heart, in the days that are flown,
No love like mother-love ever has shone;
No other worship abides and endures, —
Faithful, unselfish, and patient like yours:
None like a mother can charm away pain
From the sick soul and the world-weary brain.
Slumber's soft calms o'er my heavy lids creep; —
Rock me to sleep, mother, — rock me to sleep!

Come, let your brown hair, just lighted with gold,
Fall on your shoulders again as of old;
Let it drop over my forehead to-night,
Shading my faint eyes away from the light;
For with its sunny-edged shadows once more
Haply will throng the sweet visions of yore;
Lovingly, softly, its bright billows sweep; —
Rock me to sleep, mother, — rock me to sleep!

Mother, dear mother, the years have been long
Since I last listened your lullaby song:
Sing, then, and unto my soul it shall seem
Womanhood's years have been only a dream.
Clasped to your heart in a loving embrace,
With your light lashes just sweeping my face,
Never hereafter to wake or to weep; —
Rock me to sleep, mother, — rock me to sleep!

ELIZABETH AKERS ALLEN
(FLORENCE PERCY).

TO AUGUSTA.

HIS SISTER, AUGUSTA LEIGH.

MY sister! my sweet sister! if a name
  Dearer and purer were, it should be thine.
Mountains and seas divide us, but I claim
  No tears, but tenderness to answer mine:
Go where I will, to me thou art the same, —
  A loved regret which I would not resign.
There yet are two things in my destiny, —
A world to roam through, and a home with thee.

The first were nothing, — had I still the last,
  It were the haven of my happiness;
But other claims and other ties thou hast,
  And mine is not the wish to make them less.
A strange doom is thy father's son's, and past
  Recalling, as it lies beyond redress;
Reversed for him our grandsire's fate of yore, —
He had no rest at sea, nor I on shore.

If my inheritance of storms hath been
  In other elements, and on the rocks
Of perils, overlooked or unforeseen,
  I have sustained my share of worldly shocks,
The fault was mine; nor do I seek to screen
  My errors with defensive paradox;
I have been cunning in mine overthrow,
The careful pilot of my proper woe.

Mine were my faults, and mine be their reward.
  My whole life was a contest, since the day
That gave me being gave me that which marred
  The gift, — a fate, or will, that walked astray:
And I at times have found the struggle hard,
  And thought of shaking off my bonds of clay:
But now I fain would for a time survive,
If but to see what next can well arrive.

Kingdoms and empires in my little day
  I have outlived, and yet I am not old;
And when I look on this, the petty spray
  Of my own years of trouble, which have rolled
Like a wild bay of breakers, melts away:
  Something — I know not what — does still uphold
A spirit of slight patience; — not in vain,
Even for its own sake, do we purchase pain.

Perhaps the workings of defiance stir
  Within me, — or perhaps of cold despair,
Brought on when ills habitually recur, —
  Perhaps a kinder clime, or purer air,
(For even to this may change of soul refer,
  And with light armor we may learn to bear,)
Have taught me a strange quiet, which was not
The chief companion of a calmer lot.

I feel almost at times as I have felt
  In happy childhood; trees, and flowers, and brooks,
Which do remember me of where I dwelt
  Ere my young mind was sacrificed to books,
Come as of yore upon me, and can melt
  My heart with recognition of their looks;
And even at moments I could think I see
Some living thing to love, — but none like thee.

Here are the Alpine landscapes which create
  A fund for contemplation; — to admire
Is a brief feeling of a trivial date;
  But something worthier do such scenes inspire.
Here to be lonely is not desolate,
  For much I view which I could most desire,

And, above all, a lake I can behold
Lovelier, not dearer, than our own of old.

O that thou wert but with me ! — but I grow
The fool of my own wishes, and forget
The solitude which I have vaunted so
Has lost its praise in this but one regret ;
There may be others which I less may show ;
I am not of the plaintive mood, and yet
I feel an ebb in my philosophy,
And the tide rising in my altered eye.

I did remind thee of our own dear Lake,
By the old Hall which may be mine no more.
Leman's is fair ? but think not I forsake
The sweet remembrance of a dearer shore ;
Sad havoc Time must with my memory make,
Ere *that* or *thou* can fade these eyes before ;
Though, like all things which I have loved, they are
Resigned forever, or divided far.

The world is all before me ; I but ask
Of Nature that with which she will comply, —
It is but in her summer's sun to bask,
To mingle with the quiet of her sky,
To see her gentle face without a mask,
And never gaze on it with apathy.
She was my early friend, and now shall be
My sister, — till I look again on thee.

I can reduce all feelings but this one ;
And that I would not ; for at length I see
Such scenes as those wherein my life begun.
The earliest, — even the only paths for me, —
Had I but sooner learnt the crowd to shun,
I had been better than I now can be ;
The passions which have torn me would have slept :
I had not suffered, and *thou* hadst not wept.

With false Ambition what had I to do ?
Little with Love, and least of all with Fame ;
And yet they came unsought, and with me grew,
And made me all which they can make, — a name.
Yet this was not the end I did pursue ;
Surely I once beheld a nobler aim.
But all is over ; I am one the more
To baffled millions which have gone before.

And for the future, this world's future may
From me demand but little of my care ;
I have outlived myself by many a day :
Having survived so many things that were ;
My years have been no slumber, but the prey
Of ceaseless vigils ; for I had the share
Of life which might have filled a century,
Before its fourth in time had passed me by.

And for the remnant which may be to come,
I am content ; and for the past I feel
Not thankless, — for within the crowded sum
Of struggles, happiness at times would steal,
And for the present, I would not benumb
My feelings farther. — Nor shall I conceal
That with all this I still can look around,
And worship Nature with a thought profound.

For thee, my own sweet sister, in thy heart
I know myself secure, as thou in mine :
We were and are — I am, even as thou art —
Beings who ne'er each other can resign ;
It is the same, together or apart,
From life's commencement to its slow decline
We are intwined, — let death come slow or fast,
The tie which bound the first endures the last !

LORD BYRON.

HOME.

CLING to thy home ! if there the meanest shed
Yield thee a hearth and shelter for thy head,
And some poor plot, with vegetables stored,
Be all that Heaven allots thee for thy board, —
Unsavory bread, and herbs that scattered grow
Wild on the river brink or mountain brow,
Yet e'en this cheerless mansion shall provide
More heart's repose than all the world beside.

From the Greek of LEONIDAS,
by ROBERT BLAND.

HOME, SWEET HOME.

FROM THE OPERA OF "CLARI, THE MAID OF MILAN."

MID pleasures and palaces though we may roam,
Be it ever so humble there 's no place like home !
A charm from the skies seems to hallow us there,
Which, seek through the world, is ne'er met with elsewhere.
Home ! home ! sweet, sweet home !
There 's no place like home !

An exile from home, splendor dazzles in vain :
O, give me my lowly thatched cottage again !
The birds singing gayly that came at my call ; —
Give me them, — and the peace of mind dearer than all !
Home ! home ! sweet, sweet home !
There 's no place like home !

JOHN HOWARD PAYNE.

A WISH.

MINE be a cot beside the hill ;
A beehive's hum shall soothe my ear ;
A willowy brook that turns a mill,
With many a fall shall linger near.

The swallow, oft, beneath my thatch
Shall twitter from her clay-built nest;
Oft shall the pilgrim lift the latch,
And share my meal, a welcome guest.

Around my ivied porch shall spring
Each fragrant flower that drinks the dew;
And Lucy, at her wheel, shall sing
In russet gown and apron blue.

The village-church among the trees,
Where first our marriage-vows were given,
With merry peals shall swell the breeze,
And point with taper spire to heaven.

SAMUEL ROGERS.

THE QUIET LIFE.

HAPPY the man, whose wish and care
A few paternal acres bound,
Content to breathe his native air
In his own ground.

Whose herds with milk, whose fields with bread,
Whose flocks supply him with attire;
Whose trees in summer yield him shade,
In winter, fire.

Blest, who can unconcern'dly find
Hours, days, and years slide soft away
In health of body, peace of mind,
Quiet by day,

Sound sleep by night; study and ease
Together mixed; sweet recreation,
And innocence, which most does please
With meditation.

Thus let me live, unseen, unknown;
Thus unlamented let me die;
Steal from the world, and not a stone
Tell where I lie.

ALEXANDER POPE.

A SONG FOR THE HEARTH AND HOME.

DARK is the night, and fitful and drearily
Rushes the wind like the waves of the sea:
Little care I, as here I sit cheerily,
Wife at my side and my baby on knee.
King, king, crown me the king:
Home is the kingdom, and Love is the king!

Flashes the firelight upon the dear faces,
Dearer and dearer as onward we go,
Forces the shadow behind us, and places
Brightness around us with warmth in the glow.
King, king, crown me the king:
Home is the kingdom, and Love is the king!

Flashes the lovelight, increasing the glory,
Beaming from bright eyes with warmth of the soul,
Telling of trust and content the sweet story,
Lifting the shadows that over us roll.
King, king, crown me the king:
Home is the kingdom, and Love is the king!

Richer than miser with perishing treasure,
Served with a service no conquest could bring;
Happy with fortune that words cannot measure,
Light-hearted I on the hearthstone can sing.
King, king, crown me the king:
Home is the kingdom, and Love is the king.

WILLIAM RANKIN DURYEA.

BY THE FIRESIDE.

WHAT is it fades and flickers in the fire,
Mutters and sighs, and yields reluctant breath,
As if in the red embers some desire,
Some word prophetic burned, defying death?

Lords of the forest, stalwart oak and pine,
Lie down for us in flames of martyrdom:
A human, household warmth, their death-fires shine;
Yet fragrant with high memories they come,

Bringing the mountain-winds that in their boughs
Sang of the torrent, and the plashy edge
Of storm-swept lakes; and echoes that arouse
The eagles from a splintered eyrie ledge;

And breath of violets sweet about their roots;
And earthy odors of the moss and fern;
And hum of rivulets; smell of ripening fruits;
And green leaves that to gold and crimson turn.

What clear Septembers fade out in a spark!
What rare Octobers drop with every coal!
Within these costly ashes, dumb and dark,
Are hid spring's budding hope, and summer's soul.

Pictures far lovelier smoulder in the fire,
Visions of friends who walked among these trees,
Whose presence, like the free air, could inspire
A wingèd life and boundless sympathies.

Eyes with a glow like that in the brown beech,
When sunset through its autumn beauty shines;
Or the blue gentian's look of silent speech,
To heaven appealing as earth's light declines;

Voices and steps forever fled away
  From the familiar glens, the haunted hills, —
Most pitiful and strange it is to stay
  Without you in a world your lost love fills.

Do you forget us, — under Eden trees,
  Or in full sunshine on the hills of God, —
Who miss you from the shadow and the breeze,
  And tints and perfumes of the woodland sod?

Dear for your sake the fireside where we sit
  Watching these sad, bright pictures come and go;
That waning years are with your memory lit,
  Is the one lonely comfort that we know.

Is it all memory? Lo, these forest-boughs
  Burst on the hearth into fresh leaf and bloom;
Waft a vague, far-off sweetness through the house,
  And give close walls the hillside's breathing-room.

A second life, more spiritual than the first,
  They find, — a life won only out of death.
O sainted souls, within you still is nursed
  For us a flame not fed by mortal breath!

Unseen, ye bring to us, who love and wait,
  Wafts from the heavenly hills, immortal air;
No flood can quench your hearts' warmth, or abate;
  Ye are our gladness, here and everywhere.

LUCY LARCOM.

A SHEPHERD'S LIFE.

FROM "THIRD PART OF HENRY VI."

KING HENRY. O God! methinks, it were a happy life,
To be no better than a homely swain;
To sit upon a hill, as I do now,
To carve out dials quaintly, point by point,
Thereby to see the minutes how they run;
How many make the hour full complete;
How many hours bring about the day;
How many days will finish up the year;
How many years a mortal man may live.
When this is known, then to divide the times,—
So many hours must I tend my flock;
So many hours must I take my rest;
So many hours must I contemplate;
So many hours must I sport myself;
So many days my ewes have been with young;
So many weeks ere the poor fools will yean;
So many years ere I shall shear the fleece:
So minutes, hours, days, weeks, months, and years,
Passed over to the end they were created,
Would bring white hairs unto a quiet grave.
Ah, what a life were this! how sweet! how lovely!
Gives not the hawthorn-bush a sweeter shade
To shepherds, looking on their silly sheep,
Than doth a rich embroidered canopy
To kings that fear their subjects' treachery?

SHAKESPEARE.

THE MEANS TO ATTAIN HAPPY LIFE.

MARTIAL, the things that do attain
  The happy life be these, I find, —
The riches left, not got with pain;
  The fruitful ground, the quiet mind,

The equal friend; no grudge, no strife;
  No charge of rule, nor governance;
Without disease, the healthful life;
  The household of continuance;

The mean diet, no delicate fare;
  True wisdom joined with simpleness;
The night dischargèd of all care,
  Where wine the wit may not oppress;

The faithful wife, without debate;
  Such sleeps as may beguile the night;
Contented with thine own estate,
  Ne wish for death, ne fear his might.

LORD SURREY.

THE FIRESIDE.

DEAR Chloe, while the busy crowd,
The vain, the wealthy, and the proud,
  In folly's maze advance;
Though singularity and pride
Be called our choice, we 'll step aside,
  Nor join the giddy dance.

From the gay world we 'll oft retire
To our own family and fire,
  Where love our hours employs;
No noisy neighbor enters here,
No intermeddling stranger near,
  To spoil our heartfelt joys.

If solid happiness we prize,
Within our breast this jewel lies,
  And they are fools who roam;
The world hath nothing to bestow, —
From our own selves our bliss must flow,
  And that dear hut, our home.

Our portion is not large, indeed;
But then how little do we need,
  For nature's calls are few;
In this the art of living lies,
To want no more than may suffice,
  And make that little do.

We 'll therefore relish with content
Whate'er kind Providence has sent,
Nor aim beyond our power;
For, if our stock be very small,
'T is prudence to enjoy it all,
Nor lose the present hour.

To be resigned when ills betide,
Patient when favors are denied,
And pleased with favors given, —
Dear Chloe, this is wisdom's part,
This is that incense of the heart,
Whose fragrance smells to heaven.

NATHANIEL COTTON.

AN ORDER FOR A PICTURE.

O GOOD painter, tell me true,
Has your hand the cunning to draw
Shapes of things that you never saw?
Ay? Well, here is an order for you.

Woods and cornfields, a little brown, —
The picture must not be over-bright, —
Yet all in the golden and gracious light
Of a cloud, when the summer sun is down.

Alway and alway, night and morn,
Woods upon woods, with fields of corn
Lying between them, not quite sere,
And not in the full, thick, leafy bloom,
When the wind can hardly find breathing-room
Under their tassels, — cattle near,
Biting shorter the short green grass,
And a hedge of sumach and sassafras,
With bluebirds twittering all around, —
(Ah, good painter, you can't paint sound!) —
These, and the house where I was born,
Low and little, and black and old,
With children, many as it can hold,
All at the windows, open wide, —
Heads and shoulders clear outside,
And fair young faces all ablush:
Perhaps you may have seen, some day,
Roses crowding the selfsame way,
Out of a wilding, wayside bush.

Listen closer. When you have done
With woods and cornfields and grazing herds,
A lady, the loveliest ever the sun
Looked down upon, you must paint for me;
O, if I only could make you see
The clear blue eyes, the tender smile,
The sovereign sweetness, the gentle grace,
The woman's soul, and the angel's face,
That are beaming on me all the while! —
I need not speak these foolish words:
Yet one word tells you all I would say, —
She is my mother: you will agree
That all the rest may be thrown away.

Two little urchins at her knee
You must paint, sir: one like me, —
The other with a clearer brow,
And the light of his adventurous eyes
Flashing with boldest enterprise:
At ten years old he went to sea, —
God knoweth if he be living now, —
He sailed in the good ship Commodore, —
Nobody ever crossed her track
To bring us news, and she never came back.
Ah, 't is twenty long years and more
Since that old ship went out of the bay
With my great-hearted brother on her deck;
I watched him till he shrank to a speck,
And his face was toward me all the way.

Bright his hair was, a golden brown,
The time we stood at our mother's knee:
That beauteous head, if it did go down,
Carried sunshine into the sea!

Out in the fields one summer night
We were together, half afraid
Of the corn-leaves' rustling, and of the shade
Of the high hills, stretching so still and far, —
Loitering till after the low little light
Of the candle shone through the open door,
And over the haystack's pointed top,
All of a tremble, and ready to drop,
The first half-hour, the great yellow star,
That we, with staring, ignorant eyes,
Had often and often watched to see
Propped and held in its place in the skies
By the fork of a tall red mulberry-tree,
Which close in the edge of our flax-field grew, —
Dead at the top, — just one branch full
Of leaves, notched round, and lined with wool,
From which it tenderly shook the dew
Over our heads, when we came to play
In its handbreadth of shadow, day after day: —
Afraid to go home, sir; for one of us bore
A nest full of speckled and thin-shelled eggs, —
The other, a bird, held fast by the legs,
Not so big as a straw of wheat:
The berries we gave her she would n't eat,
But cried and cried, till we held her bill,
So slim and shining, to keep her still.

At last we stood at our mother's knee.
Do you think, sir, if you try,
You can paint the look of a lie?
If you can, pray have the grace
To put it solely in the face
Of the urchin that is likest me:
I think 't was solely mine, indeed:

But that 's no matter, — paint it so ;
The eyes of our mother — take good heed —
Looking not on the nestful of eggs,
Nor the fluttering bird, held so fast by the legs,
But straight through our faces down to our lies,
And O, with such injured, reproachful surprise !
I felt my heart bleed where that glance went, as though
A sharp blade struck through it.
You, sir, know,
That you on the canvas are to repeat
Things that are fairest, things most sweet, —
Woods and cornfields and mulberry-tree, —
The mother, — the lads, with their bird, at her knee :
But, O, that look of reproachful woe !
High as the heavens your name I 'll shout,
If you paint me the picture, and leave that out.

ALICE CARY.

A WINTER'S EVENING HYMN TO MY FIRE.

O THOU of home the guardian Lar,
And when our earth hath wandered far
Into the cold, and deep snow covers
The walks of our New England lovers,
Their sweet secluded evening-star !
'T was with thy rays the English Muse
Ripened her mild domestic hues ;
'T was by thy flicker that she conned
The fireside wisdom that enrings
With light from heaven familiar things ;
By thee she found the homely faith
In whose mild eyes thy comfort stay'th,
When Death, extinguishing his torch,
Gropes for the latch-string in the porch ;
The love that wanders not beyond
His earliest nest, but sits and sings
While children smooth his patient wings.
Therefore with thee I love to read
Our brave old poets : at thy touch how stirs
Life in the withered words ! how swift recede
Time's shadows ! and how glows again
Through its dead mass the incandescent verse,
As when upon the anvils of the brain
It glittering lay, cyclopically wrought
By the fast-throbbing hammers of the poet's thought !
Thou murmurest, too, divinely stirred,
The aspirations unattained,
The rhythms so rathe and delicate,
They bent and strained
And broke, beneath the sombre weight
Of any airiest mortal word.

As who would say, " 'T is those, I ween,
Whom lifelong armor-chafe makes lean
That win the laurel " ;
While the gay snow-storm, held aloof,
To softest outline rounds the roof,
Or the rude North with baffled strain
Shoulders the frost-starred window-pane !
Now the kind nymph to Bacchus borne
By Morpheus' daughter, she that seems
Gifted upon her natal morn
By him with fire, by her with dreams,
Nicotia, dearer to the Muse
Than all the grapes' bewildering juice,
We worship, unforbid of thee ;
And, as her incense floats and curls
In airy spires and wayward whirls,
Or poises on its tremulous stalk
A flower of frailest revery,
So winds and loiters, idly free,
The current of unguided talk,
Now laughter-rippled, and now caught
In smooth dark pools of deeper thought.
Meanwhile thou mellowest every word,
A sweetly unobtrusive third :
For thou hast magic beyond wine,
To unlock natures each to each ;
The unspoken thought thou canst divine ;
Thou fillest the pauses of the speech
With whispers that to dream-land reach,
And frozen fancy-springs unchain
In Arctic outskirts of the brain.
Sun of all inmost confidences !
To thy rays doth the heart unclose
Its formal calyx of pretenses,
That close against rude day's offenses,
And open its shy midnight rose.

JAMES RUSSELL LOWELL.

HOME.

FROM "THE TRAVELER."

BUT where to find that happiest spot below,
Who can direct, when all pretend to know ?
The shudd'ring tenant of the frigid zone
Boldly proclaims that happiest spot his own ;
Extols the treasures of his stormy seas,
And his long nights of revelry and ease :
The naked negro, panting at the line,
Boasts of his golden sands and palmy wine,
Basks in the glare, or stems the tepid wave,
And thanks his gods for all the good they gave.
Such is the patriot's boast, where'er we roam,
His first, best country ever is at home.
And yet, perhaps, if countries we compare,
And estimate the blessings which they share,
Though patriots flatter, still shall wisdom find
An equal portion dealt to all mankind ;
As different good, by art or nature given,
To different nations makes their blessing even.

OLIVER GOLDSMITH.

THE HOMES OF ENGLAND.

THE stately Homes of England,
How beautiful they stand!
Amidst their tall ancestral trees,
O'er all the pleasant land;
The deer across their greensward bound
Through shade and sunny gleam,
And the swan glides past them with the sound
Of some rejoicing stream.

The merry Homes of England!
Around their hearths by night,
What gladsome looks of household love
Meet in the ruddy light.
There woman's voice flows forth in song,
Or childish tale is told;
Or lips move tunefully along
Some glorious page of old.

The blessed Homes of England!
How softly on their bowers
Is laid the holy quietness
That breathes from Sabbath hours!
Solemn, yet sweet, the church-bell's chime
Floats through their woods at morn;
All other sounds, in that still time,
Of breeze and leaf are born.

The cottage Homes of England!
By thousands on her plains,
They are smiling o'er the silvery brooks,
And round the hamlet-fanes.
Through glowing orchards forth they peep,
Each from its nook of leaves;
And fearless there the lowly sleep,
As the bird beneath their eaves.

The free, fair Homes of England!
Long, long in hut and hall,
May hearts of native proof be reared
To guard each hallowed wall!
And green forever be the groves,
And bright the flowery sod,
Where first the child's glad spirit loves
Its country and its God.

FELICIA HEMANS.

LOVE LIGHTENS LABOR.

A GOOD wife rose from her bed one morn,
And thought, with a nervous dread,
Of the piles of clothes to be washed, and more
Than a dozen mouths to be fed.
"There 's the meals to get for the men in the field,
And the children to fix away
To school, and the milk to be skimmed and churned;
And all to be done this day."

It had rained in the night, and all the wood
Was wet as it could be;
There were puddings and pies to bake, besides
A loaf of cake for tea.
And the day was hot, and her aching head
Throbbed wearily as she said,
"If *maidens* but knew what *good wives* know,
They would not be in haste to *wed!*"

"Jennie, what do you think I told Ben Brown?"
Called the farmer from the well;
And a flush crept up to his bronzèd brow,
And his eyes half-bashfully fell:
"It was this," he said, and coming near
He smiled, and stooping down,
Kissed her cheek—"'t was this, that you were the best
And the *dearest* wife in town!"

The farmer went back to the field, and the wife,
In a smiling, absent way,
Sang snatches of tender little songs
She 'd not sung for many a day.
And the pain in her head was gone, and the clothes
Were white as the foam of the sea;
Her bread was light, and her butter was sweet,
And as golden as it could be.

"Just think," the children all called in a breath,
"Tom Wood has run off to sea!
He would n't, I know, if he 'd only had
As happy a home as we."
The night came down, and the good wife smiled
To herself, as she softly said:
"'T is so sweet to labor for those we love,—
It 's *not* strange that *maids will wed!*"

ANONYMOUS.

THE TWO ANCHORS.

IT was a gallant sailor man,
Had just come from sea,
And, as I passed him in the town,
He sang "Ahoy!" to me.
I stopped, and saw I knew the man,—
Had known him from a boy;
And so I answered, sailor-like,
"Avast!" to his "Ahoy!"
I made a song for him one day,—
His ship was then in sight,—
"The little anchor on the left,
The great one on the right."

I gave his hand a hearty grip,
"So you are back again?
They say you have been pirating
Upon the Spanish Main;

Or was it some rich Indiaman
  You robbed of all her pearls?
Of course you have been breaking hearts
  Of poor Kanaka girls!"
"Wherever I have been," he said,
  "I kept my ship in sight, —
'The little anchor on the left,
  The great one on the right.'"

"I heard last night that you were in:
  I walked the wharves to-day,
But saw no ship that looked like yours.
  Where does the good ship lay?
I want to go on board of her."
  "And so you shall," said he;
"But there are many things to do
  When one comes home from sea.
You know the song you made for me?
  I sing it morn and night, —
'The little anchor on the left,
  The great one on the right.'"

"But how's your wife and little one?"
  "Come home with me," he said.
"Go on, go on: I follow you."
  I followed where he led.
He had a pleasant little house;
  The door was open wide,
And at the door the dearest face, —
  A dearer one inside.
He hugged his wife and child; he sang, —
  His spirits were so light, —
"The little anchor on the left,
  The great one on the right."

'T was supper-time, and we sat down, —
  The sailor's wife and child,
And he and I: he looked at them,
  And looked at me, and smiled.
"I think of this when I am tossed
  Upon the stormy foam,
And, though a thousand leagues away,
  Am anchored here at home."
Then, giving each a kiss, he said,
  "I see, in dreams at night,
This little anchor on my left,
  This great one on my right."

R. H. STODDARD.

THE CHILDREN.

When the lessons and tasks are all ended,
  And the school for the day is dismissed,
And the little ones gather around me,
  To bid me good night and be kissed;
O, the little white arms that encircle
  My neck in a tender embrace!
O, the smiles that are halos of heaven,
  Shedding sunshine of love on my face!

And when they are gone, I sit dreaming
  Of my childhood, too lovely to last;
Of love that my heart will remember
  When it wakes to the pulse of the past,
Ere the world and its wickedness made me
  A partner of sorrow and sin, —
When the glory of God was about me,
  And the glory of gladness within.

O, my heart grows weak as a woman's,
  And the fountains of feeling will flow,
When I think of the paths steep and stony,
  Where the feet of the dear ones must go;
Of the mountains of sin hanging o'er them,
  Of the tempest of Fate blowing wild;
O, there's nothing on earth half so holy
  As the innocent heart of a child!

They are idols of hearts and of households;
  They are angels of God in disguise;
His sunlight still sleeps in their tresses,
  His glory still gleams in their eyes;
O, these truants from home and from heaven,
  They have made me more manly and mild;
And I know how Jesus could liken
  The kingdom of God to a child.

I ask not a life for the dear ones,
  All radiant, as others have done,
But that life may have just enough shadow
  To temper the glare of the sun;
I would pray God to guard them from evil,
  But my prayer would bound back to myself;
Ah! a seraph may pray for a sinner,
  But a sinner must pray for himself.

The twig is so easily bended,
  I have banished the rule and the rod;
I have taught them the goodness of knowledge,
  They have taught *me* the goodness of God.
My heart is a dungeon of darkness,
  Where I shut them from breaking a rule;
My frown is sufficient correction,
  My love is the law of the school.

I shall leave the old house in the autumn,
  To traverse its threshold no more:
Ah! how shall I sigh for the dear ones
  That meet me each morn at the door!
I shall miss the "good nights" and the kisses,
  And the gush of their innocent glee,
The group on its green, and the flowers
  That are brought every morning to me.

I shall miss them at morn and at evening,
  Their song in the school and the street;
I shall miss the low hum of their voices,
  And the tramp of their delicate feet.
When the lessons and tasks are all ended,
  And death says, "The school is dismissed!"
May the little ones gather around me,
  To bid me good night and be kissed!

CHARLES DICKENS.

FAITH AND HOPE.

O, DON'T be sorrowful, darling!
  Now, don't be sorrowful, pray;
For, taking the year together, my dear,
  There is n't more night than day.
It 's rainy weather, my loved one;
  Time's wheels they heavily run;
But taking the year together, my dear,
  There is n't more cloud than sun.

We 're old folks now, companion, —
  Our heads they are growing gray;
But taking the year all round, my dear,
  You always will find the May.
We 've had our May, my darling,
  And our roses, long ago;
And the time of the year is come, my dear,
  For the long dark nights, and the snow.

But God is God, my faithful,
  Of night as well as of day;
And we feel and know that we can go
  Wherever he leads the way.
Ay, God of night, my darling!
  Of the night of death so grim;
And the gate that from life leads out, good wife,
  Is the gate that leads to Him.

REMBRANDT PEALE.

THE FAMILY MEETING.

We are all here,
Father, mother,
Sister, brother,
All who hold each other dear.
Each chair is filled; we 're all at home!
To-night let no cold stranger come.
It is not often thus around
Our old familiar hearth we 're found.
Bless, then, the meeting and the spot;
For once be every care forgot;
Let gentle peace assert her power,
And kind affection rule the hour.
We 're all — all here.

We 're not all here!
Some are away, — the dead ones dear,
Who thronged with us this ancient hearth,
And gave the hour to guileless mirth.
Fate, with a stern, relentless hand,
Looked in, and thinned our little band;
Some like a night-flash passed away,
And some sank lingering day by day;
The quiet graveyard, — some lie there, —
And cruel ocean has his share.
We 're not all here.

We are all here!
Even they, — the dead, — though dead, so dear, —
Fond memory, to her duty true,
Brings back their faded forms to view.
How lifelike, through the mist of years,
Each well-remembered face appears!
We see them, as in times long past;
From each to each kind looks are cast;
We hear their words, their smiles behold;
They 're round us, as they were of old.
We are all here.

We are all here,
Father, mother,
Sister, brother,
You that I love with love so dear.
This may not long of us be said;
Soon must we join the gathered dead,
And by the hearth we now sit round
Some other circle will be found.
O, then, that wisdom may we know,
Which yields a life of peace below;
So, in the world to follow this,
May each repeat in words of bliss,
We 're all — all here!

CHARLES SPRAGUE.

A PETITION TO TIME.

TOUCH us gently, Time!
  Let us glide adown thy stream
Gently, — as we sometimes glide
  Through a quiet dream!
Humble voyagers are we,
Husband, wife, and children three, —
(One is lost, — an angel, fled
To the azure overhead!)

Touch us gently, Time!
  We 've not proud nor soaring wings;
Our ambition, our content,
  Lies in simple things.
Humble voyagers are we,
O'er life's dim, unsounded sea,
Seeking only some calm clime; —
Touch us gently, gentle Time!

BRYAN WALLER PROCTER
(BARRY CORNWALL).

POEMS
of PARTING
& ABSENCE

Music — bid thy bugle play
No tunes of grief or sorrow,
Let them cheer the living brave to-day,
They may wail the dead to-morrow,

Fitz-Greene Halleck

'Twas ever thus! — Each hour that came,
Still unremitting, brought
Some newer form of grief or shame,
Some newer care for thought.

W. Gilmore Simms.

POEMS OF PARTING AND ABSENCE.

PARTING.

GOOD BYE.

"Farewell! farewell!" is often heard
From the lips of those who part:
'T is a whispered tone, — 't is a gentle word,
But it springs not from the heart.
It may serve for the lover's closing lay,
To be sung 'neath a summer sky;
But give to me the lips that say
The honest words, "Good bye!"

"Adieu! adieu!" may greet the ear,
In the guise of courtly speech:
But when we leave the kind and dear,
'T is not what the soul would teach.
Whene'er we grasp the hands of those
We would have forever nigh,
The flame of Friendship bursts and glows
In the warm, frank words, "Good bye."

The mother, sending forth her child
To meet with cares and strife,
Breathes through her tears her doubts and fears
For the loved one's future life.
No cold "adieu," no "farewell," lives
Within her choking sigh,
But the deepest sob of anguish gives,
"God bless thee, boy! Good bye!"

Go, watch the pale and dying one,
When the glance has lost its beam;
When the brow is cold as the marble stone,
And the world a passing dream;
And the latest pressure of the hand,
The look of the closing eye,
Yield what the heart *must* understand,
A long, a last Good bye.

Anonymous.

AS SHIPS BECALMED.

As ships becalmed at eve, that lay
With canvas drooping, side by side,
Two towers of sail, at dawn of day,
Are scarce long leagues apart descried.

When fell the night, up sprang the breeze,
And all the darkling hours they plied;
Nor dreamt but each the selfsame seas
By each was cleaving, side by side:

E'en so — but why the tale reveal
Of those whom, year by year unchanged,
Brief absence joined anew, to feel,
Astounded, soul from soul estranged?

At dead of night their sails were filled,
And onward each rejoicing steered;
Ah! neither blame, for neither willed
Or wist what first with dawn appeared.

To veer, how vain! On, onward strain,
Brave barks! — in light, in darkness too!
Through winds and tides one compass guides:
To that and your own selves be true.

But O blithe breeze! and O great seas!
Though ne'er that earliest parting past,
On your wide plain they join again,
Together lead them home at last.

One port, methought, alike they sought, —
One purpose hold where'er they fare;
O bounding breeze, O rushing seas,
At last, at last, unite them there!

Arthur Hugh Clough.

AE FOND KISS BEFORE WE PART.

Ae fond kiss and then we sever!
Ae fareweel, alas, forever!
Deep in heart-wrung tears I 'll pledge thee;
Warring sighs and groans I 'll wage thee.
Who shall say that fortune grieves him,
While the star of hope she leaves him?
Me, nae cheerfu' twinkle lights me;
Dark despair around benights me.

I 'll ne'er blame my partial fancy —
Naething could resist my Nancy:

But to see her was to love her,
Love but her, and love forever.
Had we never loved sae kindly,
Had we never loved sae blindly,
Never met — or never parted,
We had ne'er been broken-hearted.

Fare thee weel, thou first and fairest!
Fare thee weel, thou best and dearest!
Thine be ilka joy and treasure,
Peace, enjoyment, love, and pleasure!
Ae fond kiss, and then we sever!
Ae fareweel, alas, forever!
Deep in heart-wrung tears I 'll pledge thee;
Warring sighs and groans I 'll wage thee.

ROBERT BURNS.

THE VOW.

In holy night we made the vow;
And the same lamp which long before
Had seen our early passion grow
Was witness to the faith we swore.

Did I not swear to love her ever;
And have I ever dared to rove?
Did she not own a rival never
Should shake her faith, or steal her love?

Yet now she says those words were air,
Those vows were written all in water,
And by the lamp that saw her swear
Has yielded to the first that sought her.

From the Greek of MELEAGER,
by JOHN HERMAN MERIVALE.

THE KISS, DEAR MAID.

The kiss, dear maid! thy lip has left
Shall never part from mine,
Till happier hours restore the gift
Untainted back to thine.

Thy parting glance, which fondly beams,
An equal love may see:
The tear that from thine eyelid streams
Can weep no change in me.

I ask no pledge to make me blest
In gazing when alone;
Nor one memorial for a breast
Whose thoughts are all thine own.

Nor need I write — to tell the tale
My pen were doubly weak:
O, what can idle words avail,
Unless the heart could speak?

By day or night, in weal or woe,
That heart, no longer free,
Must bear the love it cannot show,
And silent, ache for thee.

LORD BYRON.

MAID OF ATHENS, ERE WE PART.

Ζώη μοῦ σάς ἀγαπῶ.*

Maid of Athens, ere we part,
Give, O, give me back my heart!
Or, since that has left my breast,
Keep it now, and take the rest!
Hear my vow before I go,
Ζώη μοῦ σάς ἀγαπῶ.

By those tresses unconfined,
Wooed by each Ægean wind;
By those lids whose jetty fringe
Kiss thy soft cheeks' blooming tinge;
By those wild eyes like the roe,
Ζώη μοῦ σάς ἀγαπῶ.

By that lip I long to taste;
By that zone-encircled waist;
By all the token-flowers that tell
What words can never speak so well;
By love's alternate joy and woe,
Ζώη μοῦ σάς ἀγαπῶ.

Maid of Athens! I am gone.
Think of me, sweet! when alone.
Though I fly to Istambol,
Athens holds my heart and soul:
Can I cease to love thee? No!
Ζώη μοῦ σάς ἀγαπῶ.

LORD BYRON.

* *Zoë mou, sas agapo*, — My life, I love thee.

THE HEATH THIS NIGHT MUST BE MY BED.

SONG OF THE YOUNG HIGHLANDER, SUMMONED FROM THE SIDE OF HIS BRIDE BY THE "FIERY CROSS" OF RODERICK DHU.

The heath this night must be my bed,
The bracken curtain for my head,
My lullaby the warder's tread,
Far, far from love and thee, Mary;
To-morrow eve, more stilly laid,
My couch may be my bloody plaid,
My vesper song, thy wail, sweet maid!
It will not waken me, Mary!

I may not, dare not, fancy now
The grief that clouds thy lovely brow,
I dare not think upon thy vow,
And all it promised me, Mary.

No fond regret must Norman know ;
When bursts Clan-Alpine on the foe,
His heart must be like bended bow,
His foot like arrow free, Mary.

A time will come with feeling fraught ;
For, if I fall in battle fought,
Thy hapless lover's dying thought
Shall be a thought on thee, Mary.
And if returned from conquered foes,
How blithely will the evening close,
How sweet the linnet sing repose,
To my young bride and me, Mary !

SIR WALTER SCOTT.

TO LUCASTA,

ON GOING TO THE WARS.

Tell me not, sweet, I am unkinde,
That from the nunnerie
Of thy chaste breast and quiet minde,
To warre and armes I flee.

True, a new mistresse now I chase, —
The first foe in the field ;
And with a stronger faith imbrace
A sword, a horse, a shield.

Yet this inconstancy is such
As you, too, should adore ;
I could not love thee, deare, so much,
Loved I not honor more.

RICHARD LOVELACE.

ADIEU, ADIEU! OUR DREAM OF LOVE —

Adieu, adieu ! our dream of love
Was far too sweet to linger long ;
Such hopes may bloom in bowers above,
But here they mock the fond and young.

We met in hope, we part in tears !
Yet O, 't is sadly sweet to know
That life, in all its future years,
Can reach us with no heavier blow ?

. . . . . .

The hour is come, the spell is past ;
Far, far from thee, my only love,
Youth's earliest hope, and manhood's last,
My darkened spirit turns to rove.

Adieu, adieu ! O, dull and dread
Sinks on the ear that parting knell !
Hope and the dreams of love lie dead, —
To them and thee, farewell, farewell !

THOMAS K. HERVEY.

BLACK-EYED SUSAN.

All in the Downs the fleet was moored,
The streamers waving in the wind,
When black-eyed Susan came aboard ;
"O, where shall I my true-love find ?
Tell me, ye jovial sailors, tell me true
If my sweet William sails among the crew."

William, who high upon the yard
Rocked with the billow to and fro,
Soon as her well-known voice he heard
He sighed, and cast his eyes below :
The cord slides swiftly through his glowing hands,
And quick as lightning on the deck he stands.

So the sweet lark, high poised in air,
Shuts close his pinions to his breast
If chance his mate's shrill call he hear,
And drops at once into her nest : —
The noblest captain in the British fleet
Might envy William's lip those kisses sweet.

"O Susan, Susan, lovely dear,
My vows shall ever true remain ;
Let me kiss off that falling tear ;
We only part to meet again.
Change as ye list, ye winds ; my heart shall be
The faithful compass that still points to thee.

"Believe not what the landmen say,
Who tempt with doubts thy constant mind :
They 'll tell thee sailors, when away,
In every port a mistress find :
Yes, yes, believe them when they tell thee so,
For thou art present wheresoe'er I go.

"If to fair India's coast we sail,
Thy eyes are seen in diamonds bright,
Thy breath is Afric's spicy gale,
Thy skin is ivory so white.
Thus every beauteous object that I view
Wakes in my soul some charm of lovely Sue.

"Though battle call me from thy arms,
Let not my pretty Susan mourn ;
Though cannons roar, yet safe from harms
William shall to his dear return.
Love turns aside the balls that round me fly,
Lest precious tears should drop from Susan's eye."

The boatswain gave the dreadful word,
The sails their swelling bosom spread ;
No longer must she stay aboard ;
They kissed, she sighed, he hung his head.
Her lessening boat unwilling rows to land ;
"Adieu !" she cries ; and waved her lily hand.

JOHN GAY.

HERO TO LEANDER.

O, GO not yet, my love,
The night is dark and vast;
The white moon is hid in her heaven above,
And the waves climb high and fast.
O, kiss me, kiss me, once again,
Lest thy kiss should be the last.
O kiss me ere we part;
Grow closer to my heart;
My heart is warmer surely than the bosom of the main.
O joy! O bliss of blisses!
My heart of hearts art thou.
Come, bathe me with thy kisses,
My eyelids and my brow.
Hark! how the wild rain hisses,
And the loud sea roars below.

Thy heart beats through thy rosy limbs,
So gladly doth it stir;
Thine eye in drops of gladness swims.
I have bathed thee with the pleasant myrrh;
Thy locks are dripping balm;
Thou shalt not wander hence to-night,
I 'll stay thee with my kisses.
To-night the roaring brine
Will rend thy golden tresses;
The ocean with the morrow light
Will be both blue and calm;
And the billow will embrace thee with a kiss as soft as mine.

No Western odors wander
On the black and moaning sea,
And when thou art dead, Leander,
My soul must follow thee!
O, go not yet, my love,
Thy voice is sweet and low;
The deep salt wave breaks in above
Those marble steps below.
The turret-stairs are wet
That lead into the sea.
Leander! go not yet!
The pleasant stars have set:
O, go not, go not yet,
Or I will follow thee.

ALFRED TENNYSON.

THE PARTING LOVERS.

SHE says, "The cock crows, — hark!"
He says, "No! still 't is dark."

She says, "The dawn grows bright,"
He says, "O no, my Light."

She says, "Stand up and say,
Gets not the heaven gray?"

He says, "The morning star
Climbs the horizon's bar."

She says, "Then quick depart:
Alas! you now must start;

"But give the cock a blow
Who did begin our woe!"

From the Chinese, by WILLIAM R. ALGER.

THE PARTING OF ROMEO AND JULIET.

JULIET. Wilt thou be gone? it is not yet near day:
It was the nightingale, and not the lark,
That pierced the fearful hollow of thine ear;
Nightly she sings on yon pomegranate-tree:
Believe me, love, it was the nightingale.
ROMEO. It was the lark, the herald of the morn,
No nightingale: look, love, what envious streaks
Do lace the severing clouds in yonder east:
Night's candles are burnt out, and jocund day
Stands tiptoe on the misty mountain-tops.
I must be gone and live, or stay and die.
JULIET. Yon light is not daylight, I know it, I:
It is some meteor, that the sun exhales,
To be to thee this night a torch-bearer,
And light thee on thy way to Mantua:
Therefore stay yet, — thou need'st not to be gone.
ROMEO. Let me be ta'en, let me be put to death;
I am content, so thou wilt have it so.
I 'll say, yon gray is not the morning's eye,
'T is but the pale reflex of Cynthia's brow;
Nor that is not the lark, whose notes do beat
The vaulty heaven so high above our heads:
I have more care to stay than will to go; —
Come, death, and welcome! Juliet wills it so. —
How is 't, my soul? let 's talk, it is not day.
JULIET. It is, it is; hie hence, be gone, away!
It is the lark that sings so out of tune,
Straining harsh discords, and unpleasing sharps.
Some say, the lark makes sweet division;
This doth not so, for she divideth us:
Some say, the lark and loathèd toad change eyes:
O, now I would they had changed voices too!
Since arm from arm that voice doth us affray,
Hunting thee hence, with hunts-up to the day.
O, now be gone; more light and light it grows.
ROMEO. More light and light, — more dark and dark our woes.
JULIET. Then, window, let day in, and let life out.

Jean Ingelow

J. B. FORD & Co. NEW YORK.

ROMEO. Farewell, farewell! one kiss, and I 'll descend. (*Descends.*)
JULIET. Art thou gone so? my love! my lord! my friend!
I must hear from thee every day i' the hour,
For in a minute there are many days:
O, by this count I shall be much in years,
Ere I again behold my Romeo.
ROMEO. Farewell! I will omit no opportunity
That may convey my greetings, love, to thee.
JULIET. O, think'st thou we shall ever meet again?
ROMEO. I doubt it not; and all these woes shall serve
For sweet discourses in our time to come.

SHAKESPEARE.

DIVIDED.

I.

AN empty sky, a world of heather,
Purple of foxglove, yellow of broom:
We two among them wading together,
Shaking out honey, treading perfume.

Crowds of bees are giddy with clover;
Crowds of grasshoppers skip at our feet;
Crowds of larks at their matins hang over,
Thanking the Lord for a life so sweet.

Flusheth the rise with her purple favor,
Gloweth the cleft with her golden ring,
'Twixt the two brown butterflies waver,
Lightly settle, and sleepily swing.

We two walk till the purple dieth,
And short dry grass under foot is brown;
But one little streak at a distance lieth
Green, like a ribbon, to prank the down.

II.

Over the grass we stepped unto it,
And God he knoweth how blithe we were!
Never a voice to bid us eschew it;
Hey the green ribbon that showed so fair!

Hey the green ribbon! we kneeled beside it,
We parted the grasses dewy and sheen;
Drop over drop there filtered and slided
A tiny bright beck that trickled between.

Tinkle, tinkle, sweetly it sung to us,
Light was our talk as of faëry bells —
Faëry wedding-bells faintly rung to us,
Down in their fortunate parallels.

Hand in hand, while the sun peered over,
We lapped the grass on that youngling spring,
Swept back its rushes, smoothed its clover,
And said, "Let us follow it westering."

III.

A dappled sky, a world of meadows;
Circling above us the black rooks fly,
Forward, backward: lo, their dark shadows
Flit on the blossoming tapestry —

Flit on the beck — for her long grass parteth,
As hair from a maid's bright eyes blown back;
And lo, the sun like a lover darteth
His flattering smile on her wayward track!

Sing on! we sing in the glorious weather,
Till one steps over the tiny strand,
So narrow, in sooth, that still together
On either brink we go hand in hand.

The beck grows wider, the hands must sever.
On either margin, our songs all done,
We move apart, while she singeth ever,
Taking the course of the stooping sun.

He prays, "Come over" — I may not follow;
I cry, "Return" — but he cannot come:
We speak, we laugh, but with voices hollow;
Our hands are hanging, our hearts are numb.

IV.

A breathing sigh — a sigh for answer;
A little talking of outward things:
The careless beck is a merry dancer,
Keeping sweet time to the air she sings.

A little pain when the beck grows wider —
"Cross to me now, for her wavelets swell":
"I may not cross" — and the voice beside her
Faintly reacheth, though heeded well.

No backward path; ah! no returning:
No second crossing that ripple's flow:
"Come to me now, for the west is burning:
Come ere it darkens." — "Ah, no! ah, no!"

Then cries of pain, and arms outreaching —
The beck grows wider and swift and deep;
Passionate words as of one beseeching —
The loud beck drowns them: we walk and weep.

V.

A yellow moon in splendor drooping,
A tired queen with her state oppressed,
Low by rushes and sword-grass stooping,
Lies she soft on the waves at rest.

The desert heavens have felt her sadness;
Her earth will weep her some dewy tears;
The wild beck ends her tune of gladness,
And goeth stilly as soul that fears.

We two walk on in our grassy places,
On either marge of the moonlit flood,
With the moon's own sadness in our faces,
Where joy is withered, blossom and bud.

VI.

A shady freshness, chafers whirring,
A little piping of leaf-hid birds;
A flutter of wings, a fitful stirring,
A cloud to the eastward snowy as curds.

Bare grassy slopes, where the kids are tethered;
Round valleys like nests all ferny-lined;
Round hills, with fluttering tree-tops feathered,
Swell high in their freckled robes behind.

A rose-flush tender, a thrill, a quiver,
When golden gleams to the tree-tops glide;
A flashing edge for the milk-white river,
The beck, a river — with still sleek tide.

Broad and white, and polished as silver,
On she goes under fruit-laden trees;
Sunk in leafage cooeth the culver,
And 'plaineth of love's disloyalties.

Glitters the dew, and shines the river;
Up comes the lily and dries her bell;
But two are walking apart forever,
And wave their hands for a mute farewell.

VII.

A braver swell, a swifter sliding;
The river hasteth, her banks recede;
Wing-like sails on her bosom gliding
Bear down the lily, and drown the reed.

Stately prows are rising and bowing —
(Shouts of mariners winnow the air) —
And level sands for banks endowing
The tiny green ribbon that showed so fair.

While, O my heart! as white sails shiver,
And crowds are passing, and banks stretch wide,
How hard to follow, with lips that quiver,
That moving speck on the far-off side!

Farther, farther — I see it — know it —
My eyes brim over, it melts away:
Only my heart to my heart shall show it,
As I walk desolate day by day.

VIII.

And yet I know past all doubting, truly, —
A knowledge greater than grief can dim —
I know, as he loved, he will love me duly —
Yea, better — e'en better than I love him;

And as I walk by the vast calm river,
The awful river so dread to see,
I say, "Thy breadth and thy depth forever
Are bridged by his thoughts that cross to me."

JEAN INGELOW.

PARTING LOVERS.

SIENNA, 1860.

I LOVE thee, love thee, Giulio!
Some call me cold, and some demure,
And if thou hast ever guessed that so
I love thee — well, — the proof was poor,
And no one could be sure.

Before thy song (with shifted rhymes
To suit my name) did I undo
The persian? If it moved sometimes,
Thou hast not seen a hand push through
A foolish flower or two.

My mother listening to my sleep
Heard nothing but a sigh at night, —
The short sigh rippling on the deep,
When hearts run out of breath and sight
Of men, to God's clear light.

When others named thee, — thought thy brows
Were straight, thy smile was tender, — "Here
He comes between the vineyard-rows!" —
I said not "Ay," — nor waited, dear,
To feel thee step too near.

I left such things to bolder girls,
Olivia or Clotilda. Nay,
When that Clotilda through her curls
Held both thine eyes in hers one day,
I marveled, let me say.

I could not try the woman's trick:
Between us straightway fell the blush
Which kept me separate, blind, and sick.
A wind came with thee in a flush,
As blown through Horeb's bush.

But now that Italy invokes
Her young men to go forth and chase
The foe or perish, — nothing chokes
My voice, or drives me from the place:
I look thee in the face.

I love thee! it is understood,
  Confest: I do not shrink or start.
No blushes: all my body's blood
  Has gone to greaten this poor heart,
  That, loving, we may part.

Our Italy invokes the youth
  To die if need be. Still there 's room,
Though earth is strained with dead, in truth:
  Since twice the lilies were in bloom
  They have not grudged a tomb.

And many a plighted maid and wife
  And mother, who can say since then
"My country," cannot say through life
  "My son," "my spouse," "my flower of men,"
  And not weep dumb again.

Heroic males the country bears,
  But daughters give up more than sons.
Flags wave, drums beat, and unawares
  You flash your souls out with the guns,
  And take your heaven at once!

But *we*, — we empty heart and home
  Of life's life, love! We bear to think
You 're gone, — to feel you may not come, —
  To hear the door-latch stir and clink
  Yet no more you, — nor sink.

Dear God! when Italy is one
  And perfected from bound to bound, —
Suppose (for my share) earth 's undone
  By one grave in 't! as one small wound
  May kill a man, 't is found!

What then? If love's delight must end,
  At least we 'll clear its truth from flaws.
I love thee, love thee, sweetest friend!
  Now take my sweetest without pause,
  To help the nation's cause.

And thus, of noble Italy
  We 'll both be worthy. Let her show
The future how we made her free,
  Not sparing life, nor Giulio,
  Nor this — this heart-break! Go!

ELIZABETH BARRETT BROWNING.

AS SLOW OUR SHIP.

As slow our ship her foamy track
  Against the wind was cleaving,
Her trembling pennant still looked back
  To that dear isle 't was leaving.
So loath we part from all we love,
  From all the links that bind us;
So turn our hearts, as on we rove,
  To those we 've left behind us!

When, round the bowl, of vanished years
  We talk with joyous seeming, —
With smiles that might as well be tears,
  So faint, so sad their beaming;
While memory brings us back again
  Each early tie that twined us,
O, sweet 's the cup that circles then
  To those we 've left behind us!

And when, in other climes, we meet
  Some isle or vale enchanting,
Where all looks flowery, wild, and sweet,
  And naught but love is wanting;
We think how great had been our bliss
  If Heaven had but assigned us
To live and die in scenes like this,
  With some we 've left behind us!

As travelers oft look back at eve
  When eastward darkly going,
To gaze upon that light they leave
  Still faint behind them glowing, —
So, when the close of pleasure's day
  To gloom hath near consigned us,
We turn to catch one fading ray
  Of joy that 's left behind us.

THOMAS MOORE.

LOCHABER NO MORE.

FAREWELL to Lochaber! and farewell, my Jean,
Where heartsome with thee I hae mony a day been!
For Lochaber no more, Lochaber no more,
We 'll maybe return to Lochaber no more!
These tears that I shed they are a' for my dear,
And no for the dangers attending on war,
Though borne on rough seas to a far bloody shore,
Maybe to return to Lochaber no more.

Though hurricanes rise, and rise every wind,
They 'll ne'er make a tempest like that in my mind;
Though loudest of thunders on louder waves roar,
That's naething like leaving my love on the shore.
To leave thee behind me my heart is sair pained;
By ease that 's inglorious no fame can be gained;
And beauty and love 's the reward of the brave,
And I maun deserve it before I can crave.

Then glory, my Jeany, maun plead my excuse;
Since honor commands me, how can I refuse?
Without it I ne'er can have merit for thee,
And without thy favor I 'd better not be.

I gae then, my lass, to win honor and fame,
And if I should luck to come gloriously hame,
I 'll bring a heart to thee with love running o'er,
And then I 'll leave thee and Lochaber no more.

ALLAN RAMSAY.

ADIEU, ADIEU! MY NATIVE SHORE.

Adieu, adieu! my native shore
  Fades o'er the waters blue;
The night-winds sigh, the breakers roar,
  And shrieks the wild sea-mew.
Yon sun that sets upon the sea
  We follow in his flight;
Farewell awhile to him and thee,
  My native land — Good Night!

A few short hours, and he will rise
  To give the morrow birth;
And I shall hail the main and skies,
  But not my mother earth.
Deserted is my own good hall,
  Its hearth is desolate;
Wild weeds are gathering on the wall;
  My dog howls at the gate.

LORD BYRON.

MY OLD KENTUCKY HOME.

NEGRO SONG.

The sun shines bright in our old Kentucky home;
  'T is summer, the darkies are gay;
The corn top 's ripe and the meadow 's in the bloom,
  While the birds make music all the day;
The young folks roll on the little cabin floor,
  All merry, all happy, all bright;
By'm-by hard times comes a knockin' at the door, —
  Then, my old Kentucky home, good night!

CHORUS.

Weep no more, my lady; O, weep no more to-day!
We 'll sing one song for my old Kentucky home,
For our old Kentucky home far away.

They hunt no more for the possum and the coon,
  On the meadow, the hill, and the shore;
They sing no more by the glimmer of the moon,
  On the bench by the old cabin-door;
The day goes by, like a shadow o'er the heart,
  With sorrow where all was delight;
The time has come, when the darkies have to part,
  Then, my old Kentucky home, good night!
    Weep no more, my lady, etc.

The head must bow, and the back will have to bend,
  Wherever the darky may go;
A few more days, and the troubles all will end,
  In the field where the sugar-cane grow;
A few more days to tote the weary load,
  No matter, it will never be light;
A few more days till we totter on the road,
  Then, my old Kentucky home, good night!
    Weep no more, my lady, etc.

STEPHEN C. FOSTER.

THE FAREWELL

OF A VIRGINIA SLAVE MOTHER TO HER DAUGHTERS SOLD INTO SOUTHERN BONDAGE.

Gone, gone, — sold and gone,
To the rice-swamp dank and lone.
Where the slave-whip ceaseless swings,
Where the noisome insect stings,
Where the fever demon strews
Poison with the falling dews,
Where the sickly sunbeams glare
Through the hot and misty air, —
Gone, gone, — sold and gone,
To the rice-swamp dank and lone,
From Virginia's hill and waters, —
Woe is me, my stolen daughters!

Gone, gone, — sold and gone,
To the rice-swamp dank and lone.
There no mother's eye is near them,
There no mother's ear can hear them;
Never, when the torturing lash
Seams their back with many a gash,
Shall a mother's kindness bless them,
Or a mother's arms caress them.
Gone, gone, — sold and gone,
To the rice-swamp dank and lone,
From Virginia's hills and waters, —
Woe is me, my stolen daughters!

Gone, gone, — sold and gone,
To the rice-swamp dank and lone.
O, when weary, sad, and slow,
From the fields at night they go,
Faint with toil, and racked with pain,
To their cheerless homes again,
There no brother's voice shall greet them, —
There no father's welcome meet them.
Gone, gone, — sold and gone,
To the rice-swamp dank and lone,
From Virginia's hills and waters, —
Woe is me, my stolen daughters!

Gone, gone, — sold and gone,
To the rice-swamp dank and lone,

From the tree whose shadow lay
On their childhood's place of play, —
From the cool spring where they drank, —
Rock, and hill, and rivulet bank, —
From the solemn house of prayer,
And the holy counsels there, —
Gone, gone, — sold and gone,
To the rice-swamp dank and lone,
From Virginia's hills and waters, —
Woe is me, my stolen daughters!

Gone, gone, — sold and gone,
To the rice-swamp dank and lone, —
Toiling through the weary day,
And at night the spoiler's prey.
O that they had earlier died,
Sleeping calmly, side by side,
Where the tyrant's power is o'er,
And the fetter galls no more!
Gone, gone, — sold and gone,
To the rice-swamp dank and lone,
From Virginia's hills and waters, —
Woe is me, my stolen daughters!

Gone, gone, — sold and gone,
To the rice-swamp dank and lone.
By the holy love He beareth, —
By the bruisèd reed He spareth, —
O, may He to whom alone
All their cruel wrongs are known
Still their hope and refuge prove,
With a more than mother's love!
Gone, gone, — sold and gone,
To the rice-swamp dank and lone,
From Virginia's hills and waters, —
Woe is me, my stolen daughters!

JOHN GREENLEAF WHITTIER.

COME, LET US KISSE AND PARTE.

SINCE there's no helpe, — come, let us kisse and parte!
Nay, I have done, — you get no more of me;
And I am glad, — yea, glad with all my hearte,
That thus so cleanly I myselfe can free.
Shake hands forever! — cancel all our vows;
And when we meet at any time againe,
Be it not seene in either of our brows,
That we one jot of former love retaine.

Now — at the last gaspe of Love's latest breath —
When, his pulse failing, Passion speechless lies;
When Faith is kneeling by his bed of death,
And Innocence is closing up his eyes,
Now! if thou wouldst — when all have given him over —
From death to life thou might'st him yet recover.

MICHAEL DRAYTON.

FAREWELL! THOU ART TOO DEAR.

FAREWELL! thou art too dear for my possessing,
And like enough thou know'st thy estimate:
The charter of thy worth gives thee releasing;
My bonds in thee are all determinate.
For how do I hold thee but by thy granting?
And for that riches where is my deserving?
The cause of this fair gift in me is wanting,
And so my patent back again is swerving.
Thyself thou gav'st, thy own worth then not knowing,
Or me, to whom thou gav'st it, else mistaking;
So thy great gift, upon misprision growing,
Comes home again, on better judgment making.
Thus have I had thee, as a dream doth flatter;
In sleep a king, but, waking, no such matter.

SHAKESPEARE.

AN EARNEST SUIT

TO HIS UNKIND MISTRESS NOT TO FORSAKE HIM.

AND wilt thou leave me thus?
Say nay! say nay! for shame!
To save thee from the blame
Of all my grief and grame.
And wilt thou leave me thus?
Say nay! say nay!

And wilt thou leave me thus,
That hath loved thee so long,
In wealth and woe among?
And is thy heart so strong
As for to leave me thus?
Say nay! say nay!

And wilt thou leave me thus,
That hath given thee my heart,
Never for to depart,
Neither for pain nor smart?
And wilt thou leave me thus?
Say nay! say nay!

And wilt thou leave me thus,
And have no more pity
Of him that loveth thee?
Alas! thy cruelty!
And wilt thou leave me thus?
Say nay! say nay!

SIR THOMAS WYATT.

WE PARTED IN SILENCE.

We parted in silence, we parted by night,
  On the banks of that lonely river;
Where the fragrant limes their boughs unite,
  We met — and we parted forever!
The night-bird sung, and the stars above
  Told many a touching story
Of friends long passed to the kingdom of love,
Where the soul wears its mantle of glory.

We parted in silence, — our cheeks were wet
  With the tears that were past controlling;
We vowed we would never, no, never forget,
  And those vows at the time were consoling;
But those lips that echoed the sounds of mine
  Are as cold as that lonely river;
And that eye, that beautiful spirit's shrine,
  Has shrouded its fires forever.

And now on the midnight sky I look,
  And my heart grows full of weeping;
Each star is to me a sealèd book,
  Some tale of that loved one keeping.
We parted in silence, — we parted in tears,
  On the banks of that lonely river:
But the odor and bloom of those bygone years
  Shall hang o'er its waters forever.

MRS. CRAWFORD.

PEACE! WHAT CAN TEARS AVAIL?

Peace! what can tears avail?
She lies all dumb and pale,
  And from her eye
The spirit of lovely life is fading, —
  And she must die!
Why looks the lover wroth, — the friend upbraiding?
  Reply, reply!

Hath she not dwelt too long
Midst pain, and grief, and wrong?
  Then why not die?
Why suffer again her doom of sorrow,
  And hopeless lie?
Why nurse the trembling dream until to-morrow?
  Reply, reply!

Death! Take her to thine arms,
In all her stainless charms!
  And with her fly
To heavenly haunts, where, clad in brightness,
  The angels lie!
Wilt bear her there, O death! in all her whiteness?
  Reply, reply?

BRYAN WALLER PROCTER (BARRY CORNWALL).

THE DYING GERTRUDE TO WALDEGRAVE.

FROM "GERTRUDE OF WYOMING."

Clasp me a little longer on the brink
Of fate! while I can feel thy dear caress;
And when this heart hath ceased to beat, — O, think,
And let it mitigate thy woe's excess,
That thou hast been to me all tenderness,
And friend to more than human friendship just.
O, by that retrospect of happiness,
And by the hopes of an immortal trust,
God shall assuage thy pangs, when I am laid in dust!

Go, Henry, go not back, when I depart,
The scene thy bursting tears too deep will move,
Where my dear father took thee to his heart,
And Gertrude thought it ecstasy to rove
With thee, as with an angel, through the grove
Of peace, imagining her lot was cast
In heaven; for ours was not like earthly love.
And must this parting be our very last?
No! I shall love thee still, when death itself is past.

Half could I bear, methinks, to leave this earth, —
And thee, more loved than aught beneath the sun,
If I had lived to smile but on the birth
Of one dear pledge; — but shall there then be none,
In future time, — no gentle little one,
To clasp thy neck, and look, resembling me?
Yet seems it, even while life's last pulses run,
A sweetness in the cup of death to be,
Lord of my bosom's love! to die beholding thee!

THOMAS CAMPBELL.

THE MOURNER.

Yes! there are real mourners, — I have seen
A fair sad girl, mild, suffering, and serene;
Attention (through the day) her duties claimed,
And to be useful as resigned she aimed;
Neatly she drest, nor vainly seemed t' expect
Pity for grief, or pardon for neglect;
But when her wearied parents sunk to sleep,
She sought her place to meditate and weep;
Then to her mind was all the past displayed,
That faithful memory brings to sorrow's aid:
For then she thought on one regretted youth,
Her tender trust, and his unquestioned truth;
In every place she wandered, where they 'd been,
And sadly-sacred held the parting scene,
Where last for sea he took his leave; that place
With double interest would she nightly trace!

Happy he sailed, and great the care she took
That he should softly sleep and smartly look;
White was his better linen, and his check
Was made more trim than any on the deck;
And every comfort men at sea can know
Was hers to buy, to make, and to bestow:
For he to Greenland sailed, and much she told,
How he should guard against the climate's cold;
Yet saw not danger; dangers he 'd withstood,
Nor could she trace the fever in his blood.
His messmates smiled at flushings on his cheek,
And he too smiled, but seldom would he speak;
For now he found the danger, felt the pain,
With grievous symptoms he could not explain.
He called his friend, and prefaced with a sigh
A lover's message, — "Thomas, I must die;
Would I could see my Sally, and could rest
My throbbing temples on her faithful breast,
And gazing go! — if not, this trifle take,
And say, till death I wore it for her sake:
Yes! I must die — blow on, sweet breeze, blow on!
Give me one look before my life be gone!
O, give me that, and let me not despair!
One last fond look! — and now repeat the prayer."
He had his wish, had more: I will not paint
The lovers' meeting; she beheld him faint, —
With tender fears, she took a nearer view,
Her terrors doubling as her hopes withdrew;
He tried to smile; and, half succeeding, said,
"Yes! I must die" — and hope forever fled.
Still, long she nursed him; tender thoughts meantime
Were interchanged, and hopes and views sublime.
To her he came to die, and every day
She took some portion of the dread away;
With him she prayed, to him his Bible read,
Soothed the faint heart, and held the aching head:
She came with smiles the hour of pain to cheer,
Apart she sighed; alone, she shed the tear;
Then, as if breaking from a cloud, she gave
Fresh light, and gilt the prospect of the grave.
One day he lighter seemed, and they forgot
The care, the dread, the anguish of their lot.
A sudden brightness in his look appeared,
A sudden vigor in his voice was heard; —
She had been reading in the Book of Prayer,
And led him forth, and placed him in his chair.
Lively he seemed, and spake of all he knew,
The friendly many, and the favorite few;
. . . . . . but then his hand she prest,
And fondly whispered, "Thou must go to rest."
"I go," he said; but as he spoke, she found
His hand more cold, and fluttering was the sound;
Then gazed affrighted; but she caught a last,
A dying look of love, and all was past!

She placed a decent stone his grave above,
Neatly engraved, — an offering of her love:
For that she wrought, for that forsook her bed,
Awake alike to duty and the dead;
She would have grieved, had friends presumed to spare
The least assistance, — 't was her proper care.
Here will she come, and on the grave will sit,
Folding her arms, in long abstracted fit:
But if observer pass, will take her round,
And careless seem, for she would not be found;
Then go again, and thus her hours employ,
While visions please her, and while woes destroy.

GEORGE CRABBE.

FAREWELL! BUT WHENEVER —

FAREWELL! — but whenever you welcome the hour
That awakens the night-song of mirth in your bower,
Then think of the friend who once welcomed it too,
And forgot his own griefs, to be happy with you.
His griefs may return — not a hope may remain
Of the few that have brightened his pathway of pain —
But he ne'er can forget the short vision that threw
Its enchantment around him while lingering with you!

And still on that evening when Pleasure fills up
To the highest top sparkle each heart and each cup,
Where'er my path lies, be it gloomy or bright,
My soul, happy friends! will be with you that night;
Shall join in your revels, your sports, and your wiles,
And return to me, beaming all o'er with your smiles! —
Too blest if it tell me that, mid the gay cheer,
Some kind voice has murmured, "I wish he were here!"

Let Fate do her worst, there are relics of joy,
Bright dreams of the past, which she cannot destroy;
Which come, in the night-time of sorrow and care,
And bring back the features which joy used to wear.
Long, long be my heart with such memories filled!
Like the vase in which roses have once been distilled —
You may break, you may ruin the vase, if you will,
But the scent of the roses will hang round it still.

THOMAS MOORE.

ABSENCE.

TO HER ABSENT SAILOR.

FROM "THE TENT ON THE BEACH."

Her window opens to the bay,
On glistening light or misty gray,
And there at dawn and set of day
In prayer she kneels:
"Dear Lord!" she saith, "to many a home
From wind and wave the wanderers come;
I only see the tossing foam
Of stranger keels.

"Blown out and in by summer gales,
The stately ships, with crowded sails,
And sailors leaning o'er their rails,
Before me glide;
They come, they go, but evermore,
Spice-laden from the Indian shore,
I see his swift-winged Isidore
The waves divide.

"O thou! with whom the night is day
And one the near and far away,
Look out on yon gray waste, and say
Where lingers he.
Alive, perchance, on some lone beach
Or thirsty isle beyond the reach
Of man, he hears the mocking speech
Of wind and sea.

"O dread and cruel deep, reveal
The secret which thy waves conceal,
And, ye wild sea-birds, hither wheel
And tell your tale!
Let winds that tossed his raven hair
A message from my lost one bear, —
Some thought of me, a last fond prayer
Or dying wail!

"Come, with your dreariest truth shut out
The fears that haunt me round about;
O God! I cannot bear this doubt
That stifles breath.
The worst is better than the dread;
Give me but leave to mourn my dead
Asleep in trust and hope, instead
Of life in death!"

It might have been the evening breeze
That whispered in the garden trees,
It might have been the sound of seas
That rose and fell;
But, with her heart, if not her ear,
The old loved voice she seemed to hear:
"I wait to meet thee: be of cheer,
For all is well!"

JOHN GREENLEAF WHITTIER.

TO LUCASTA.

If to be absent were to be
Away from thee;
Or that, when I am gone,
You or I were alone;
Then, my Lucasta, might I crave
Pity from blustering wind or swallowing wave.

But I'll not sigh one blast or gale
To swell my sail,
Or pay a tear to 'suage
The foaming blue-god's rage;
For, whether he will let me pass
Or no, I'm still as happy as I was.

Though seas and lands be 'twixt us both,
Our faith and troth,
Like separated souls,
All time and space controls:
Above the highest sphere we meet,
Unseen, unknown; and greet as angels greet.

So, then, we do anticipate
Our after-fate,
And are alive i' th' skies,
If thus our lips and eyes
Can speak like spirits unconfined
In heaven, — their earthly bodies left behind.

RICHARD LOVELACE.

OF A' THE AIRTS THE WIND CAN BLAW.

Of a' the airts the wind can blaw,
I dearly like the west;
For there the bonnie lassie lives,
The lassie I lo'e best.
There wild woods grow, and rivers row,
And monie a hill 's between;
But day and night my fancy's flight
Is ever wi' my Jean.

I see her in the dewy flowers,
I see her sweet and fair;

I hear her in the tunefu' birds,
  I hear her charm the air;
There 's not a bonnie flower that springs
  By fountain, shaw, or green, —
There 's not a bonnie bird that sings,
  But minds me of my Jean.

O, blaw ye westlin winds, blaw saft
  Amang the leafy trees;
Wi' gentle gale, fra muir and dale
  Bring hame the laden bees:
And bring the lassie back to me
  That 's aye sae neat and clean;
Ae look at her wad banish care,
  Sae lovely is my Jean.

ROBERT BURNS.

LOVE'S MEMORY.

FROM "ALL 'S WELL THAT ENDS WELL."

I AM undone: there is no living, none,
If Bertram be away. It were all one,
That I should love a bright particular star,
And think to wed it, he is so above me:
In his bright radiance and collateral light
Must I be comforted, not in his sphere.
The ambition in my love thus plagues itself:
The hind that would be mated by the lion
Must die for love. 'T was pretty, though a plague,
To see him ev'ry hour; to sit and draw
His archèd brows, his hawking eye, his curls,
In our heart's table, — heart too capable
Of every line and trick of his sweet favor:
But now he 's gone, and my idolatrous fancy
Must sanctify his relics.

SHAKESPEARE.

O, SAW YE BONNIE LESLEY?

O, SAW ye bonnie Lesley
  As she gaed o'er the border?
She 's gane, like Alexander,
  To spread her conquests farther.

To see her is to love her,
  And love but her forever;
For nature made her what she is,
  And ne'er made sic anither!

Thou art a queen, fair Lesley,
  Thy subjects we, before thee;
Thou art divine, fair Lesley,
  The hearts o' men adore thee.

The deil he could na scaith thee,
  Or aught that wad belang thee;
He 'd look into thy bonnie face,
  And say "I canna wrang thee!"

The powers aboon will tent thee;
  Misfortune sha' na steer thee;
Thou 'rt like themselves sae lovely
  That ill they 'll ne'er let near thee.

Return again, fair Lesley,
  Return to Caledonie!
That we may brag we hae a lass
  There 's nane again sae bonnie.

ROBERT BURNS.

JEANIE MORRISON.

I 'VE wandered east, I 've wandered west,
  Through mony a weary way;
But never, never can forget
  The luve o' life's young day!
The fire that 's blawn on Beltane e'en
  May weel be black gin Yule;
But blacker fa' awaits the heart
  Where first fond luve grows cule.

O dear, dear Jeanie Morrison,
  The thochts o' bygane years
Still fling their shadows ower my path,
  And blind my een wi' tears:
They blind my een wi' saut, saut tears,
  And sair and sick I pine,
As memory idly summons up
  The blithe blinks o' langsyne.

'T was then we luvit ilk ither weel,
  'T was then we twa did part;
Sweet time — sad time! twa bairns at scule,
  Twa bairns, and but ae heart!
'T was then we sat on ae laigh bink,
  To leir ilk ither lear;
And tones and looks and smiles were shed,
  Remembered evermair.

I wonder, Jeanie, aften yet,
  When sitting on that bink,
Cheek touchin' cheek, loof locked in loof,
  What our wee heads could think.
When baith bent doun ower ae braid page,
  Wi' ae buik on our knee,
Thy lips were on thy lesson, but
  My lesson was in thee.

O, mind ye how we hung our heads,
  How cheeks brent red wi' shame,
Whene'er the scule-weans, laughin', said
  We cleeked thegither hame?
And mind ye o' the Saturdays,
  (The scule then skail't at noon,)
When we ran aff to speel the braes, —
  The broomy braes o' June?

My head rins round and round about, —
My heart flows like a sea,
As ane by ane the thochts rush back
O' scule-time, and o' thee.
O mornin' life! O mornin' luve!
O lichtsome days and lang,
When hinnied hopes around our hearts
Like simmer blossoms sprang!

O, mind ye, luve, how aft we left
The deavin' dinsome toun,
To wander by the green burnside,
And hear its waters croon?
The simmer leaves hung ower our heads,
The flowers burst round our feet,
And in the gloamin' o' the wood
The throssil whusslit sweet;

The throssil whusslit in the wood,
The burn sang to the trees, —
And we, with nature's heart in tune,
Concerted harmonies;
And on the knowe abune the burn
For hours thegither sat
In the silentness o' joy, till baith
Wi' very gladness grat.

Ay, ay, dear Jeanie Morrison,
Tears trickled doun your cheek
Like dew-beads on a rose, yet nane
Had ony power to speak!
That was a time, a blessed time,
When hearts were fresh and young,
When freely gushed all feelings forth,
Unsyllabled — unsung!

I marvel, Jeanie Morrison,
Gin I hae been to thee
As closely twined wi' earliest thochts
As ye hae been to me.
O, tell me gin their music fills
Thine ear as it does mine!
O, say gin e'er your heart grows grit
Wi' dreamings o' langsyne!

I 've wandered east, I 've wandered west,
I 've borne a weary lot;
But in my wanderings, far or near,
Ye never were forgot.
The fount that first burst frae this heart
Still travels on its way;
And channels deeper, as it rins,
The luve o' life's young day.

O dear, dear Jeanie Morrison,
Since we were sindered young
I 've never seen your face nor heard
The music o' your tongue;
But I could hug all wretchedness,
And happy could I dee,
Did I but ken your heart still dreamed
O' bygone days and me!

WILLIAM MOTHERWELL.

"SHE TOUCHES A SAD STRING OF SOFT RECALL."

RETURN, return! all night my lamp is burning;
All night, like it, my wide eyes watch and burn;
Like it, I fade and pale, when day returning
Bears witness that the absent can return,
Return, return.

Like it, I lessen with a lengthening sadness;
Like it, I burn to waste and waste to burn;
Like it, I spend the golden oil of gladness
To feed the sorrowy signal for return,
Return, return.

Like it, like it, whene'er the east wind-sings,
I bend and shake; like it, I quake and yearn,
When Hope's late butterflies, with whispering wings,
Fly in out of the dark, to fall and burn —
Burn in the watchfire of return,
Return, return.

Like it, the very flame whereby I pine
Consumes me to its nature. While I mourn,
My soul becomes a better soul than mine,
And from its brightening beacon I discern
My starry love go forth from me, and shine
Across the seas a path for thy return,
Return, return.

Return, return! all night I see it burn,
All night it prays like me, and lifts a twin
Of palmèd praying hands that meet and yearn—
Yearn to the impleaded skies for thy return.
Day, like a golden fetter, locks them in,
And wans the light that withers, though it burn
As warmly still for thy return;
Still through the splendid load uplifts the thin
Pale, paler, palest patience that can learn
Naught but that votive sign for thy return,
That single suppliant sign for thy return,
Return, return.

Return, return! lest haply, love, or e'er
Thou touch the lamp the light have ceased to burn,
And thou, who through the window didst discern
The wonted flame, shalt reach the topmost stair
To find no wide eyes watching there,
No withered welcome waiting thy return!

A passing ghost, a smoke-wreath in the air,
The flameless ashes, and the soulless urn,
Warm with the famished fire that lived to burn—
Burn out its lingering life for thy return,
Its last of lingering life for thy return,
Its last of lingering life to light thy late return,
Return, return.

SIDNEY DOBELL.

LOVE.

FROM "THE TRIUMPH OF TIME."

THERE lived a singer in France of old
By the tideless, dolorous, midland sea.
In a land of sand and ruin and gold
There shone one woman, and none but she.
And finding life for her love's sake fail,
Being fain to see her, he bade set sail,
Touched land, and saw her as life grew cold,
And praised God, seeing; and so died he.

Died, praising God for his gift and grace:
For she bowed down to him weeping, and said,
"Live"; and her tears were shed on his face
Or ever the life in his face was shed.
The sharp tears fell through her hair, and stung
Once, and her close lips touched him and clung
Once, and grew one with his lips for a space;
And so drew back, and the man was dead.

O brother, the gods were good to you.
Sleep, and be glad while the world endures.
Be well content as the years wear through;
Give thanks for life, and the loves and lures;
Give thanks for life, O brother, and death,
For the sweet last sound of her feet, her breath,
For gifts she gave you, gracious and few,
Tears and kisses, that lady of yours.

Rest, and be glad of the gods; but I,
How shall I praise them, or how take rest?
There is not room under all the sky
For me that know not of worst or best,
Dream or desire of the days before,
Sweet things or bitterness, any more.
Love will not come to me now though I die,
As love came close to you, breast to breast.

I shall never be friends again with roses;
I shall loathe sweet tunes, where a note grown strong
Relents and recoils, and climbs and closes,
As a wave of the sea turned back by song.
There are sounds where the soul's delight takes fire,
Face to face with its own desire;
A delight that rebels, a desire that reposes;
I shall hate sweet music my whole life long.

The pulse of war and passion of wonder,
The heavens that murmur, the sounds that shine,
The stars that sing and the loves that thunder,
The music burning at heart like wine,
An armed archangel whose hands raise up
All senses mixed in the spirit's cup,
Till flesh and spirit are molten in sunder,—
These things are over, and no more mine.

These were a part of the playing I heard
Once, ere my love and my heart were at strife;
Love that sings and hath wings as a bird,
Balm of the wound and heft of the knife.
Fairer than earth is the sea, and sleep
Than overwatching of eyes that weep,
Now time has done with his one sweet word,
The wine and leaven of lovely life.

I shall go my ways, tread out my measure,
Fill the days of my daily breath
With fugitive things not good to treasure,
Do as the world doth, say as it saith;
But if we had loved each other—O sweet,
Had you felt, lying under the palms of your feet,
The heart of my heart, beating harder with pleasure
To feel you tread it to dust and death—

Ah, had I not taken my life up and given
All that life gives and the years let go,
The wine and money, the balm and leaven,
The dreams reared high and the hopes brought low,
Come life, come death, not a word be said;
Should I lose you living, and vex you dead?
I shall never tell you on earth; and in heaven,
If I cry to you then, will you hear or know?

ALGERNON CHARLES SWINBURNE.

DAY, IN MELTING PURPLE DYING.

DAY, in melting purple dying;
Blossoms, all around me sighing;
Fragrance, from the lilies straying;
Zephyr, with my ringlets playing;
Ye but waken my distress;
I am sick of loneliness!

Thou to whom I love to hearken,
Come, ere night around me darken;
Though thy softness but deceive me,
Say thou 'rt true, and I 'll believe thee;
Veil, if ill, thy soul's intent,
Let me think it innocent!

Save thy toiling, spare thy treasure;
All I ask is friendship's pleasure;
Let the shining ore lie darkling, —
Bring no gem in luster sparkling;
Gifts and gold are naught to me,
I would only look on thee!

Tell to thee the high-wrought feeling,
Ecstasy but in revealing;
Paint to thee the deep sensation,
Rapture in participation;
Yet but torture, if comprest
In a lone, unfriended breast.

Absent still! Ah! come and bless me!
Let these eyes again caress thee.
Once, in caution, I could fly thee;
Now, I nothing could deny thee.
In a look if death there be,
Come, and I will gaze on thee!

MARIA BROOKS.

THE ABSENT SOLDIER SON.

FROM "THE ROMAN."

Lord, I am weeping. As thou wilt, O Lord,
Do with him as thou wilt; but O my God,
Let him come back to die! Let not the fowls
O' the air defile the body of my child,
My own fair child, that when he was a babe,
I lift up in my arms and gave to thee!
Let not his garment, Lord, be vilely parted,
Nor the fine linen which these hands have spun
Fall to the stranger's lot! Shall the wild bird,
That would have pilfered of the ox, this year
Disdain the pens and stalls? Shall her blind young,
That on the fleck and moult of brutish beasts
Had been too happy, sleep in cloth of gold
Whereof each thread is to this beating heart
As a peculiar darling? Lo, the flies
Hum o'er him! Lo, a feather from the crow
Falls in his parted lips! Lo, his dead eyes
See not the raven! Lo, the worm, the worm
Creeps from his festering corse! My God! my God!

. . . . . .

O Lord, thou doest well. I am content.
If thou have need of him, he shall not stay.
But as one calleth to a servant, saying
"At such a time be with me," so, O Lord,
Call him to thee! O, bid him not in haste
Straight whence he standeth. Let him lay aside
The soilèd tools of labor. Let him wash
His hands of blood. Let him array himself
Meet for his Lord, pure from the sweat and fume
Of corporal travail! Lord, if he must die,
Let him die here. O, take him where thou gavest!
And even as once I held him in my womb
Till all things were fulfilled, and he came forth,
So, O Lord, let me hold him in my grave
Till the time come, and thou, who settest when
The hinds shall calve, ordain a better birth;
And as I looked and saw my son, and wept
For joy, I look again and see my son,
And weep again for joy of him and thee!

SIDNEY DOBELL.

HOMESICK.

Come to me, O my Mother! come to me,
Thine own son slowly dying far away!
Through the moist ways of the wide ocean, blown
By great invisible winds, come stately ships
To this calm bay for quiet anchorage;
They come, they rest awhile, they go away,
But, O my Mother, never comest thou!
The snow is round thy dwelling, the white snow,
That cold soft revelation pure as light,
And the pine-spire is mystically fringed,
Laced with incrusted silver. Here — ah me! —
The winter is decrepit, underborn,
A leper with no power but his disease.
Why am I from thee, Mother, far from thee?
Far from the frost enchantment, and the woods
Jeweled from bough to bough? O home, my home!
O river in the valley of my home,
With mazy-winding motion intricate,
Twisting thy deathless music underneath
The polished ice-work, — must I nevermore
Behold thee with familiar eyes, and watch
Thy beauty changing with the changeful day,
Thy beauty constant to the constant change?

DAVID GRAY.

THE RUSTIC LAD'S LAMENT IN THE TOWN.

O, wad that my time were owre but,
Wi' this wintry sleet and snaw,
That I might see our house again,
I' the bonnie birken shaw!
For this is no my ain life,
And I peak and pine away
Wi' the thochts o' hame and the young flowers,
In the glad green month of May.

I used to wauk in the morning
Wi' the loud sang o' the lark,
And the whistling o' the plowman lads,
As they gaed to their wark;
I used to wear the bit young lambs
Frae the tod and the roaring stream;
But the warld is changed, and a' thing now
To me seems like a dream.

There are busy crowds around me,
On ilka lang dull street;
Yet, though sae mony surround me,
I ken na ane I meet:
And I think o' kind kent faces,
And o' blithe an' cheery days,
When I wandered out wi' our ain folk,
Out owre the simmer braes.

Waes me, for my heart is breaking!
I think o' my brither sma',
And on my sister greeting,
When I cam frae hame awa.
And O, how my mither sobbit,
As she shook me by the hand,
When I left the door o' our auld house,
To come to this stranger land.

There 's nae hame like our ain hame —
O, I wush that I were there!
There 's nae hame like our ain hame
To be met wi' onywhere;
And O that I were back again,
To our farm and fields sae green;
And heard the tongues o' my ain folk,
And were what I hae been!

DAVID M. MOIR.

BY THE ALMA RIVER.

WILLIE, fold your little hands;
Let it drop, — that "soldier" toy;
Look where father's picture stands, —
Father, that here kissed his boy
Not a month since, — father kind,
Who this night may (never mind
Mother's sob, my Willie dear) —
Cry out loud that He may hear
Who is God of battles, — say
"God keep father safe this day
By the Alma River!"

Ask no more, child! Never heed
Either Russ, or Frank, or Turk;
Right of nations, trampled creed,
Chance-poised victory's bloody work;
Any flag i' the wind may roll
On thy heights, Sevastopol!
Willie, all to you and me
Is that spot, whate'er it be,
Where he stands — no other word —
Stands — God sure the child's prayers heard! —
Near the Alma River.

Willie, listen to the bells
Ringing in the town to-day;
That 's for victory. No knell swells
For the many swept away, —
Hundreds, thousands. Let us weep,
We who need not, — just to keep
Reason clear in thought and brain
Till the morning comes again;
Till the third dread morning tell
Who they were that fought and — *fell*
By the Alma River.

Come, — we 'll lay us down, my child;
Poor the bed is, — poor and hard;
But thy father, far exiled,
Sleeps upon the open sward,
Dreaming of us two at home;
Or, beneath the starry dome,
Digs out trenches in the dark,
Where he buries — Willie, mark! —
Where *he buries* those who died
Fighting — fighting at his side —
By the Alma River.

Willie, Willie, go to sleep;
God will help us, O my boy!
He will make the dull hours creep
Faster, and send news of joy;
When I need not shrink to meet
Those great placards in the street,
That for weeks will ghastly stare
In some eyes — child, say that prayer
Once again, — a different one, —
Say, "O God! thy will be done
By the Alma River."

DINAH MULOCK CRAIK.

THE WIFE TO HER HUSBAND.

LINGER not long. Home is not home without thee:
Its dearest tokens do but make me mourn.
O, let its memory, like a chain about thee,
Gently compel and hasten thy return!

Linger not long. Though crowds should woo thy staying,
Bethink thee, can the mirth of friends, though dear,
Compensate for the grief thy long delaying
Costs the fond heart that sighs to have thee here?

Linger not long. How shall I watch thy coming,
As evening shadows stretch o'er moor and dell;
When the wild bee hath ceased her busy humming,
And silence hangs on all things like a spell!

How shall I watch for thee, when fears grow stronger,
As night grows dark and darker on the hill!
How shall I weep, when I can watch no longer!
Ah! art thou absent, art thou absent still?

Yet I should grieve not, though the eye that seeth me
Gazeth through tears that make its splendor dull;
For O, I sometimes fear when thou art with me,
My cup of happiness is all too full.

Haste, haste thee home unto thy mountain dwelling,
Haste, as a bird unto its peaceful nest!
Haste, as a skiff, through tempests wide and swelling,
Flies to its haven of securest rest!

ANONYMOUS.

ABSENCE.

WHAT shall I do with all the days and hours
That must be counted ere I see thy face?
How shall I charm the interval that lowers
Between this time and that sweet time of grace?

Shall I in slumber steep each weary sense, —
Weary with longing? Shall I flee away
Into past days, and with some fond pretense
Cheat myself to forget the present day?

Shall love for thee lay on my soul the sin
Of casting from me God's great gift of time?
Shall I, these mists of memory locked within,
Leave and forget life's purposes sublime?

O, how or by what means may I contrive
To bring the hour that brings thee back more near?
How may I teach my drooping hope to live
Until that blessed time, and thou art here?

I 'll tell thee; for thy sake I will lay hold
Of all good aims, and consecrate to thee,
In worthy deeds, each moment that is told
While thou, belovèd one! art far from me.

For thee I will arouse my thoughts to try
All heavenward flights, all high and holy strains;
For thy dear sake, I will walk patiently
Through these long hours, nor call their minutes pains.

I will this dreary blank of absence make
A noble task-time; and will therein strive
To follow excellence, and to o'ertake
More good than I have won since yet I live.

So may this doomèd time build up in me
A thousand graces, which shall thus be thine;
So may my love and longing hallowed be,
And thy dear thought an influence divine.

FRANCES ANNE KEMBLE.

MY PLAYMATE.

THE pines were dark on Ramoth hill,
Their song was soft and low;
The blossoms in the sweet May wind
Were falling like the snow.

The blossoms drifted at our feet,
The orchard birds sang clear;
The sweetest and the saddest day
It seemed of all the year.

For, more to me than birds or flowers,
My playmate left her home,
And took with her the laughing spring,
The music and the bloom.

She kissed the lips of kith and kin,
She laid her hand in mine;
What more could ask the bashful boy
Who fed her father's kine?

She left us in the bloom of May;
The constant years told o'er
Their seasons with as sweet May morns,
But she came back no more.

I walk with noiseless feet the round
Of uneventful years;
Still o'er and o'er I sow the spring,
And reap the autumn ears.

She lives where all the golden year
Her summer roses blow;
The dusky children of the sun
Before her come and go.

There haply with her jeweled hands
She smooths her silken gown, —
No more the homespun lap wherein
I shook the walnuts down.

The wild grapes wait us by the brook,
The brown nuts on the hill,
And still the May-day flowers make sweet
The woods of Folly mill.

The lilies blossom in the pond,
The bird builds in the tree,
The dark pines sing on Ramoth hill
The slow song of the sea.

I wonder if she thinks of them,
And how the old time seems, —
If ever the pines of Ramoth wood
Are sounding in her dreams.

I see her face, I hear her voice:
Does she remember mine?

And what to her is now the boy
  Who fed her father's kine?

What cares she that the orioles build
  For other eyes than ours, —
That other hands with nuts are filled,
  And other laps with flowers?

O playmate in the golden time!
  Our mossy seat is green,
Its fringing violets blossom yet,
  The old trees o'er it lean.

The winds so sweet with birch and fern
  A sweeter memory blow;
And there in spring the veeries sing
  The song of long ago.

And still the pines of Ramoth wood
  Are moaning like the sea, —
The moaning of the sea of change
  Between myself and thee!

JOHN G. WHITTIER.

ON A PICTURE.

WHEN summer o'er her native hills
  A veil of beauty spread,
She sat and watched her gentle flocks
  And twined her flaxen thread.

The mountain daisies kissed her feet;
  The moss sprung greenest there;
The breath of summer fanned her cheek
  And tossed her wavy hair.

The heather and the yellow gorse
  Bloomed over hill and wold,
And clothed them in a royal robe
  Of purple and of gold.

There rose the skylark's gushing song,
  There hummed the laboring bee;
And merrily the mountain stream
  Ran singing to the sea.

But while she missed from those sweet sounds
  The voice she sighed to hear,
The song of bee and bird and stream
  Was discord to her ear.

Nor could the bright green world around
  A joy to her impart,
For still she missed the eyes that made
  The summer of her heart.

ANNE C. LYNCH (MRS. BOTTA).

THERE 'S NAE LUCK ABOUT THE HOUSE.

AND are ye sure the news is true?
  And are ye sure he 's weel?
Is this a time to think o' wark?
  Ye jades, lay by your wheel;
Is this the time to spin a thread,
  When Colin 's at the door?
Reach down my cloak, I 'll to the quay,
  And see him come ashore.
    For there 's nae luck about the house,
      There 's nae luck at a';
    There 's nae luck about the house
      When our gudeman 's awa'.

And gie to me my bigonet,
  My bishop's-satin gown;
For I maun tell the baillie's wife
  That Colin 's in the town.
My Turkey slippers maun gae on,
  My stockins pearly blue;
It 's a' to pleasure our gudeman,
  For he 's baith leal and true.

Rise, lass, and mak a clean fireside,
  Put on the muckle pot;
Gie little Kate her cotton gown,
  And Jock his Sunday coat;
And mak their shoon as black as slaes,
  Their hose as white as snaw;
It 's a' to please my ain gudeman,
  For he 's been long awa'.

There 's twa fat hens upo' the bauk,
  They 've fed this month and mair;
Mak haste and thraw their necks about,
  That Colin weel may fare;
And spread the table neat and clean,
  Gar ilka thing look braw,
For wha can tell how Colin fared
  When he was far awa'?

Sae true his heart, sae smooth his speech,
  His breath like caller air;
His very foot has music in 't
  As he comes up the stair, —
And will I see his face again?
  And will I hear him speak?
I 'm downright dizzy wi' the thought,
  In troth I 'm like to greet!

The cauld blasts o' the winter wind,
  That thirled through my heart,
They 're a' blown by, I hae him safe,
  Till death we 'll never part:
But what puts parting in my head?
  It may be far awa';
The present moment is our ain,
  The neist we never saw.

If Colin 's weel, and weel content,
  I hae nae mair to crave :
And gin I live to keep him sae
  I 'm blest aboon the lave :
And will I see his face again ?
  And will I hear him speak ?
I 'm downright dizzy wi' the thought,
  In troth I 'm like to greet.
    For there 's nae luck about the house,
      There 's nae luck at a' ;
    There 's little pleasure in the house
      When our gudeman 's awa'.

WILLIAM J. MICKLE.

ABSENCE.

WHEN I think on the happy days
  I spent wi' you, my dearie ;
And now what lands between us lie,
  How can I be but eerie !

How slow ye move, ye heavy hours,
  As ye were wae and weary !
It was na sae ye glinted by
  When I was wi' my dearie.

ANONYMOUS.

THE TERRACE AT BERNE.

TEN years ! — and to my waking eye
  Once more the roofs of Berne appear ;
The rocky banks, the terrace high,
  The stream, — and do I linger here ?

The clouds are on the Oberland,
  The Jungfrau snows look faint and far ;
But bright are those green fields at hand,
  And through those fields comes down the Aar,

And from the blue twin lakes it comes,
  Flows by the town, the churchyard fair,
And 'neath the garden-walk it hums,
  The house, — and is my Marguerite there ?

Ah, shall I see thee, while a flush
  Of startled pleasure floods thy brow,
Quick through the oleanders brush,
  And clap thy hands, and cry, '*T is thou?*

Or hast thou long since wandered back,
  Daughter of France ! to France, thy home ;
And flitted down the flowery track
  Where feet like thine too lightly come ?

Doth riotous laughter now replace
  Thy smile, and rouge, with stony glare,
Thy cheek's soft hue, and fluttering lace
  The kerchief that enwound thy hair ?

Or is it over ? — art thou dead ? —
  Dead ? — and no warning shiver ran
Across my heart, to say thy thread
  Of life was cut, and closed thy span !

Could from earth's ways that figure slight
  Be lost, and I not feel 't was so ?
Of that fresh voice the gay delight
  Fail from earth's air, and I not know ?

Or shall I find thee still, but changed,
  But not the Marguerite of thy prime ?
With all thy being rearranged,
  Passed through the crucible of time ;

With spirit vanished, beauty waned,
  And hardly yet a glance, a tone,
A gesture, — anything, — retained
  Of all that was my Marguerite's own ?

I will not know ! — for wherefore try,
  To things by mortal course that live,
A shadowy durability
  For which they were not meant, to give !

Like driftwood spars which meet and pass
  Upon the boundless ocean-plain,
So on the sea of life, alas !
  Man nears man, meets, and leaves again.

I knew it when my life was young,
  I feel it still, now youth is o'er !
The mists are on the mountain hung,
  And Marguerite I shall see no more.

MATTHEW ARNOLD.

THE BEAUTIFUL RIVER.

LIKE a foundling in slumber, the summer-day lay
  On the crimsoning threshold of even,
And I thought that the glow through the azure-arched way
  Was a glimpse of the coming of Heaven.
There together we sat by the beautiful stream ;
We had nothing to do but to love and to dream,
  In the days that have gone on before.
These are not the same days, though they bear the same name,
  With the ones I shall welcome no more.

But it may be that angels are calling them o'er,
  For a Sabbath and summer forever,
When the years shall forget the Decembers they wore,
  And the shroud shall be woven, no never !
In a twilight like that, Jennie June for a bride,

O, what more of the world could one wish for beside,
As we gazed on the river unrolled,
Till we heard, or we fancied, its musical tide,
When it flowed through the gateway of gold !

"Jennie June," then I said, "let us linger no more
On the banks of the beautiful river ;
Let the boat be unmoored, and be muffled the oar,
And we 'll steal into heaven together.
If the angel on duty our coming descries,
You have nothing to do but throw off the disguise
That you wore while you wandered with me,
And the sentry shall say, 'Welcome back to the skies,
We long have been waiting for thee.' "

Oh ! how sweetly she spoke, ere she uttered a word,
With that blush, partly hers, partly even's,
And a tone, like the dream of a song we once heard,
As she whispered, "*This* way is not heaven's:
For the River that runs by the realm of the blest
Has no song on its ripple, no star on its breast ;
Oh ! *that* river is nothing like this,
For it glides on in shadow beyond the world's west,
Till it breaks into beauty and bliss."

I am lingering yet, but I linger alone,
On the banks of the beautiful river ;
'T is the twin of that day, but the wave where it shone
Bears the willow-tree's shadow forever.

BENJAMIN F. TAYLOR.

ABSENT.

FROM you have I been absent in the spring,
When proud-pied April, dressed in all his trim,
Hath put a spirit of Youth in everything,
That heavy Saturn laughed and leaped with him.
Yet nor the lays of birds, nor the sweet smell
Of different flowers in odor and in hue,
Could make me any summer's story tell,
Or from their proud lap pluck them where they grew :
Nor did I wonder at the lilies white,
Nor praise the deep vermilion in the rose ;
They were but sweet, but figures of delight,
Drawn after you, you pattern of all those.
Yet seemed it winter still, and you away,
As with your shadow I with these did play.

SHAKESPEARE.

THE EMIGRANT'S WISH.

I WISH we were hame to our ain folk,
Our kind and our true-hearted ain folk,
Where the simple are weal, and the gentle are leal,
And the hames are the hames o' our ain folk.
We 've been wi' the gay, and the gude where we 've come,
We 're courtly wi' many, we 're couthy wi' some ;
But something 's still wantin' we never can find
Sin' the day that we left our auld neebors behind.

O, I wish we were hame to our ain folk,
Our kind and our true-hearted ain folk,
Where daffin and glee wi' the friendly and free
Made our hearts aye sae fond o' our ain folk.
Though *Spring* had its moils, and *Summer* its toils,
And *Autumn* craved pith ere we gathered its spoils,
Yet *Winter* repaid a' the toil that we took,
When ilk ane crawed crouse by his ain ingle nook.

O, I wish we were hame to our ain folk,
Our kind and our true-hearted ain folk,
Where maidens and men in hall and in glen
Still welcome us aye as their ain folk.
They told us in gowpens we 'd gather the gear,
Sae sune as we cam' to the rich Mailins here,
But what are the Mailins, or what are they worth,
If they be not enjoyed in the land o' our birth !

Then I wish we were hame to our ain folk,
Our kind and our true-hearted ain folk,
But deep are the howes and high are the knowes,
That keep us awa' frae our ain folk.
The seat by the door where our auld faithers sat,
To tell a' the news, their views, and a' that,
While down by the kailyard the burnie rowed clear,
'T was mair to my liking than aught that is here.

Then I wish we were hame to our ain folk,
Our kind and our true-hearted ain folk,
Where the wild thistles wave o'er th' abode o' the brave,
And the graves are the graves o' our ain folk.
But happy, gey lucky, we 'll trudge on our way,
Till our arm waxes weak and our haffets grow gray ;
And, tho' in this world our ain still we miss,
We 'll meet them at last in a world o' bliss.

And *then* we 'll be hame to our ain folk,
Our kind and our true-hearted ain folk,
Where far 'yont the moon in the heavens aboon
The hames are the hames o' our ain folk.

ANONYMOUS.

COME TO ME, DEAREST.

Come to me, dearest, I 'm lonely without thee,
Daytime and night-time, I 'm thinking about thee;
Night-time and daytime, in dreams I behold thee;
Unwelcome the waking which ceases to fold thee.
Come to me, darling, my sorrows to lighten,
Come in thy beauty to bless and to brighten;
Come in thy womanhood, meekly and lowly,
Come in thy lovingness, queenly and holy.

Swallows will flit round the desolate ruin,
Telling of spring and its joyous renewing;
And thoughts of thy love, and its manifold treasure,
Are circling my heart with a promise of pleasure.
O Spring of my spirit, O May of my bosom,
Shine out on my soul, till it bourgeon and blossom;
The waste of my life has a rose-root within it.
And thy fondness alone to the sunshine can win it.

Figure that moves like a song through the even;
Features lit up by a reflex of heaven;
Eyes like the skies of poor Erin, our mother,
Where shadow and sunshine are chasing each other;
Smiles coming seldom, but childlike and simple,
Planting in each rosy cheek a sweet dimple; —
O, thanks to the Saviour, that even thy seeming
Is left to the exile to brighten his dreaming.

You have been glad when you knew I was gladdened;
Dear, are you sad now to hear I am saddened?
Our hearts ever answer in tune and in time, love,
As octave to octave, and rhyme unto rhyme, love:
I cannot weep but your tears will be flowing,
You cannot smile but my cheek will be glowing;
I would not die without you at my side, love,
You will not linger when I shall have died, love.

Come to me, dear, ere I die of my sorrow,
Rise on my gloom like the sun of to-morrow;
Strong, swift, and fond as the words which I speak, love,
With a song on your lip and a smile on your cheek, love.
Come, for my heart in your absence is weary, —
Haste, for my spirit is sickened and dreary, —
Come to the arms which alone should caress thee,
Come to the heart that is throbbing to press thee!

JOSEPH BRENNAN.

POEMS OF
DISAPPOINTMENT AND ESTRANGEMENT

In Thee, I fondly hoped to clasp,
A Friend whom Death alone could sever
But Envy with malignant Grasp,
Has torn thee from my Breast forever

Byron

POEMS OF DISAPPOINTMENT AND ESTRANGEMENT.

THE BANKS O' DOON.

Ye banks and braes o' bonnie Doon,
  How can ye bloom sae fresh and fair?
How can ye chant, ye little birds,
  And I sae weary, fu' o' care?
Thou 'lt break my heart, thou warbling bird,
  That wantons through the flowering thorn;
Thou minds me o' departed joys,
  Departed — never to return.

Aft hae I roved by bonnie Doon,
  To see the rose and woodbine twine;
And ilka bird sang o' its luve,
  And, fondly, sae did I o' mine.
Wi' lightsome heart I pu'd a rose,
  Fu' sweet upon its thorny tree;
And my fause luver stole my rose,
  But ah! he left the thorn wi' me.

ROBERT BURNS.

AULD ROBIN GRAY.

When the sheep are in the fauld, and the kye 's come hame,
And a' the weary warld to rest are gane;
The waes o' my heart fa' in showers frae my ee,
Unkent by my gudeman wha sleeps sound by me.

Young Jamie lo'ed me weel, and socht me for his bride;
But, saving a crown piece, he had naething beside.
To make the crown a pound, my Jamie gaed to sea;
And the crown and the pound they were baith for me!

He hadna been gane awa a twelvemonth and a day,
When my father brake his arm, and the cow was stown awa;
My mither she fell sick, my young Jamie was at sea, —
And auld Robin Gray cam' a courting me.

My father cou'dna wark, — my mither cou'dna spin, —
I toiled day and night, but their bread I cou'dna win;
Auld Rob maintained them baith, and, wi' tears in his ee,
Said, "Jenny, O, for their sakes, will ye no marry me!"

My heart it said na, and I looked for Jamie back;
But hard blew the winds, and his ship was a wrack;
His ship was a wrack! Why didna Jamie die?
Or why am I spared to cry, Wae 's me?

My father urged me sair, — my mither didna speak,
But she looked in my face till my heart was like to break;
They gied him my hand, my heart was in the sea;
And so Robin Gray he was gudeman to me.

I hadna been his wife, a week but only four,
When, mournfully as I sat on the stane at my door,
I saw my Jamie's ghaist, for I cou'dna think it he,
Till he said, "I 'm come hame, love, to marry thee!"

O sair, sair did we greet, and mickle say of a',
I gied him ae kiss, and bade him gang awa',
I wish that I were dead, but I 'm na like to die;
For though my heart is broken, I 'm but young, wae 's me!

I gang like a ghaist, and I carena much to spin;
I darena think on Jamie, for that wad be a sin;
But I 'll do my best a gude wife to be,
For auld Robin Gray he is kind unto me.

LADY ANNE BARNARD.

THE COURSE OF TRUE LOVE.

FROM "MIDSUMMER NIGHT'S DREAM."

For aught that ever I could read,
Could ever hear by tale or history,
The course of true love never did run smooth:
But, either it was different in blood,
Or else misgraffèd in respect of years;
Or else it stood upon the choice of friends;
Or, if there were a sympathy in choice,
War, death, or sickness did lay siege to it,
Making it momentary as a sound,
Swift as a shadow, short as any dream;
Brief as the lightning in the collied night,
That, in a spleen, unfolds both heaven and earth,
And ere a man hath power to say, — Behold!
The jaws of darkness do devour it up:
So quick bright things come to confusion.

SHAKESPEARE.

BYRON'S LATEST VERSES.

[Missolonghi, January 23, 1824. On this day I completed my thirty-sixth year.]

'T is time this heart should be unmoved,
Since others it has ceased to move;
Yet, though I cannot be beloved,
Still let me love.

My days are in the yellow leaf,
The flowers and fruits of love are gone,
The worm, the canker, and the grief,
Are mine alone.

The fire that in my bosom preys
Is like to some volcanic isle,
No torch is kindled at its blaze,
A funeral pile.

The hope, the fear, the jealous care,
The exalted portion of the pain
And power of love, I cannot share,
But wear the chain.

But 't is not here, — it is not here,
Such thoughts should shake my soul, nor now,
Where glory seals the hero's bier,
Or binds his brow.

The sword, the banner, and the field,
Glory and Greece about us see;
The Spartan borne upon his shield
Was not more free.

Awake! not Greece, — she is awake!
Awake, my spirit! think through whom
My life-blood tastes its parent lake,
And then strike home!

Tread those reviving passions down,
Unworthy manhood! unto thee,
Indifferent should the smile or frown
Of beauty be.

If thou regrett'st thy youth, — why live?
The land of honorable death
Is here, — up to the field, and give
Away thy breath!

Seek out — less often sought than found —
A soldier's grave, for thee the best;
Then look around, and choose thy ground,
And take thy rest!

LORD BYRON.

CLAUDE MELNOTTE'S APOLOGY AND DEFENSE.

Pauline, by pride
Angels have fallen ere thy time; by pride, —
That sole alloy of thy most lovely mold, —
The evil spirit of a bitter love
And a revengeful heart had power upon thee.
From my first years my soul was filled with thee;
I saw thee midst the flowers the lowly boy
Tended, unmarked by thee, — a spirit of bloom,
And joy and freshness, as spring itself
Were made a living thing, and wore thy shape!
I saw thee, and the passionate heart of man
Entered the breast of the wild-dreaming boy;
And from that hour I grew — what to the last
I shall be — thine adorer! Well, this love,
Vain, frantic, — guilty, if thou wilt, became
A fountain of ambition and bright hope;
I thought of tales that by the winter hearth
Old gossips tell, — how maidens sprung from kings
Have stooped from their high sphere; how Love, like Death,
Levels all ranks, and lays the shepherd's crook
Beside the scepter. Thus I made my home
In the soft palace of a fairy Future!
My father died; and I, the peasant-born,
Was my own lord. Then did I seek to rise
Out of the prison of my mean estate;
And, with such jewels as the exploring mind
Brings from the caves of Knowledge, buy my ransom
From those twin jailers of the daring heart,
Low birth and iron fortune. Thy bright image,
Glassed in my soul, took all the hues of glory,
And lured me on to those inspiring toils
By which man masters men! For thee, I grew
A midnight student o'er the dreams of sages!
For thee, I sought to borrow from each Grace
And every Muse such attributes as lend
Ideal charms to Love. I thought of thee,

And passion taught me poesy, — of thee,
And on the painter's canvas grew the life
Of beauty! — Art became the shadow
Of the dear starlight of thy haunting eyes!
Men called me vain, — some, mad, — I heeded not;
But still toiled on, hoped on, — for it was sweet,
If not to win, to feel more worthy, thee!

. . . . .

At last, in one mad hour, I dared to pour
The thoughts that burst their channels into song,
And sent them to thee, — such a tribute, lady,
As beauty rarely scorns, even from the meanest.
The name — appended by the burning heart
That longed to show its idol what bright things
It had created — yea, the enthusiast's name,
That should have been thy triumph, was thy scorn!
That very hour — when passion, turned to wrath,
Resembled hatred most; when thy disdain
Made my whole soul a chaos — in that hour
The tempters found me a revengeful tool
For their revenge! Thou hadst trampled on the worm, —
It turned, and stung thee!

EDWARD BULWER (LORD LYTTON).

LEFT BEHIND.

It was the autumn of the year;
The strawberry-leaves were red and sear;
October's airs were fresh and chill,
When, pausing on the windy hill,
The hill that overlooks the sea,
You talked confidingly to me, —
Me whom your keen, artistic sight
Has not yet learned to read aright,
Since I have veiled my heart from you,
And loved you better than you knew.

You told me of your toilsome past;
The tardy honors won at last,
The trials borne, the conquests gained,
The longed-for boon of Fame attained;
I knew that every victory
But lifted you away from me,
That every step of high emprise
But left me lowlier in your eyes;
I watched the distance as it grew,
And loved you better than you knew.

You did not see the bitter trace
Of anguish sweep across my face;
You did not hear my proud heart beat,
Heavy and slow, beneath your feet;
You thought of triumph still unwon,
Of glorious deeds as yet undone;
And I, the while you talked to me,
I watched the gulls float lonesomely,
Till lost amid the hungry blue,
And loved you better than you knew.

You walk the sunny side of fate;
The wise world smiles, and calls you great;
The golden fruitage of success
Drops at your feet in plenteousness;
And you have blessings manifold:
Renown and power and friends and gold,
They build a wall between us twain,
Which may not be thrown down again,
Alas! for I, the long years through,
Have loved you better than you knew.

Your life's proud aim, your art's high truth,
Have kept the promise of your youth;
And while you won the crown, which now
Breaks into bloom upon your brow,
My soul cried strongly out to you
Across the ocean's yearning blue,
While, unremembered and afar,
I watched you, as I watch a star
Through darkness struggling into view,
And loved you better than you knew.

I used to dream in all these years
Of patient faith and silent tears,
That Love's strong hand would put aside
The barriers of place and pride,
Would reach the pathless darkness through,
And draw me softly up to you;
But that is past. If you should stray
Beside my grave, some future day,
Perchance the violets o'er my dust
Will half betray their buried trust,
And say, their blue eyes full of dew,
"She loved you better than you knew."

ELIZABETH AKERS ALLEN (FLORENCE PERCY).

LINDA TO HAFED.

FROM "THE FIRE-WORSHIPERS."

"How sweetly," said the trembling maid,
Of her own gentle voice afraid,
So long had they in silence stood,
Looking upon that moonlight flood, —
"How sweetly does the moonbeam smile
To-night upon yon leafy isle!
Oft in my fancy's wanderings,
I've wished that little isle had wings,
And we, within its fairy bowers,
Were wafted off to seas unknown,
Where not a pulse should beat but ours,
And we might live, love, die alone!

Far from the cruel and the cold, —
  Where the bright eyes of angels only
Should come around us, to behold
  A paradise so pure and lonely !
Would this be world enough for thee ?" —
Playful she turned, that he might see
  The passing smile her cheek put on ;
But when she marked how mournfully
  His eyes met hers, that smile was gone ;
And, bursting into heartfelt tears,
"Yes, yes," she cried, "my hourly fears,
My dreams, have boded all too right, —
We part — forever part — to-night !
I knew, I knew it *could* not last, —
'T was bright, 't was heavenly, but 't is past !
O, ever thus, from childhood's hour,
  I 've seen my fondest hopes decay ;
I never loved a tree or flower
  But 't was the first to fade away.
I never nursed a dear gazelle,
  To glad me with its soft black eye,
But when it came to know me well,
  And love me, it was sure to die !
Now, too, the joy most like divine
  Of all I ever dreamt or knew,
To see thee, hear thee, 'call thee mine, —
  O misery ! must I lose *that* too ?

THOMAS MOORE.

BERTHA IN THE LANE.

PUT the broidery-frame away,
  For my sewing is all done !
The last thread is used to-day,
  And I need not join it on.
  Though the clock stands at the noon,
  I am weary ! I have sewn,
  Sweet, for thee, a wedding-gown.

Sister, help me to the bed,
  And stand near me, dearest-sweet !
Do not shrink nor be afraid,
  Blushing with a sudden heat !
  No one standeth in the street ? —
  By God's love I go to meet,
  Love I thee with love complete.

Lean thy face down ! drop it in
  These two hands, that I may hold
'Twixt their palms thy cheek and chin,
  Stroking back the curls of gold.
  'T is a fair, fair face, in sooth, —
  Larger eyes and redder mouth
  Than mine were in my first youth !

Thou art younger by seven years —
  Ah ! so bashful at my gaze
That the lashes, hung with tears,
  Grow too heavy to upraise :
  I would wound thee by no touch
  Which thy shyness feels as such, —
  Dost thou mind me, dear, so much ?

Have I not been nigh a mother
  To thy sweetness, — tell me, dear ?
Have we not loved one another
  Tenderly, from year to year,
  Since our dying mother mild
  Said, with accents undefiled,
  "Child, be mother to this child ! "

Mother, mother, up in heaven,
  Stand up on the jasper sea,
And be witness I have given
  All the gifts required of me ; —
  Hope that blessed me, bliss that crowned,
  Love that left me with a wound,
  Life itself, that turneth round !

Mother, mother, thou art kind,
  Thou art standing in the room,
In a molten glory shrined,
  That rays off into the gloom !
  But thy smile is bright and bleak,
  Like cold waves, — I cannot speak ;
  I sob in it, and grow weak.

Ghostly mother, keep aloof
  One hour longer from my soul,
For I still am thinking of
  Earth's warm-beating joy and dole !
  On my finger is a ring
  Which I still see glittering,
  When the night hides everything.

Little sister, thou art pale !
  Ah, I have a wandering brain ;
But I lose that fever-bale,
  And my thoughts grow calm again.
  Lean down closer, closer still !
  I have words thine ear to fill,
  And would kiss thee at my will.

Dear, I heard thee in the spring,
  Thee and Robert, through the trees,
When we all went gathering
  Boughs of May-bloom for the bees.
  Do not start so ! think instead
  How the sunshine overhead
  Seemed to trickle through the shade.

What a day it was, that day !
  Hills and vales did openly
Seem to heave and throb away,
  At the sight of the great sky ;

And the silence, as it stood
In the glory's golden flood,
Audibly did bud, — and bud!

Through the winding hedge-rows green,
How we wandered, I and you, —
With the bowery tops shut in,
And the gates that showed the view;
How we talked there! thrushes soft
Sang our pauses out, or oft
Bleatings took them from the croft.

Till the pleasure, grown too strong,
Left me muter evermore;
And, the winding road being long,
I walked out of sight, before;
And so, wrapt in musings fond,
Issued (past the wayside pond)
On the meadow-lands beyond.

I sat down beneath the beech
Which leans over to the lane,
And the far sound of your speech
Did not promise any pain;
And I blessed you, full and free,
With a smile stooped tenderly
O'er the May-flowers on my knee.

But the sound grew into word
As the speakers drew more near —
Sweet, forgive me that I heard
What you wished me not to hear.
Do not weep so, do not shake —
O, I heard thee, Bertha, make
Good true answers for my sake.

Yes, and he too! let him stand
In thy thoughts, untouched by blame.
Could he help it, if my hand
He had claimed with hasty claim?
That was wrong perhaps, but then
Such things be — and will, again!
Women cannot judge for men.

Had he seen thee, when he swore
He would love but me alone?
Thou wert absent, — sent before
To our kin in Sidmouth town.
When he saw thee, who art best
Past compare, and loveliest,
He but judged thee as the rest.

Could we blame him with grave words,
Thou and I, dear, if we might?
Thy brown eyes have looks like birds
Flying straightway to the light;
Mine are older. — Hush! — look out —
Up the street! Is none without?
How the poplar swings about!

And that hour — beneath the beach —
When I listened in a dream,
And he said, in his deep speech,
That he owed me all *esteem* —
Each word swam in on my brain
With a dim, dilating pain,
Till it burst with that last strain.

I fell flooded with a dark,
In the silence of a swoon;
When I rose, still, cold and stark,
There was night, — I saw the moon;
And the stars, each in its place,
And the May-blooms on the grass,
Seemed to wonder what I was.

And I walked as if apart
From myself when I could stand,
And I pitied my own heart,
As if I held it in my hand
Somewhat coldly, with a sense
Of fulfilled benevolence,
And a "Poor thing" negligence.

And I answered coldly too,
When you met me at the door;
And I only *heard* the dew
Dripping from me to the floor;
And the flowers I bade you see
Were too withered for the bee, —
As my life, henceforth, for me.

Do not weep so — dear — heart-warm!
It was best as it befell!
If I say he did me harm,
I speak wild, — I am not well.
All his words were kind and good, —
He esteemed me! Only blood
Runs so faint in womanhood.

Then I always was too grave,
Liked the saddest ballads sung,
With that look, besides, we have
In our faces, who die young.
I had died, dear, all the same,
Life's long, joyous, jostling game
Is too loud for my meek shame.

We are so unlike each other,
Thou and I, that none could guess
We were children of one mother,
But for mutual tenderness.
Thou art rose-lined from the cold,
And meant, verily, to hold
Life's pure pleasures manifold.

I am pale as crocus grows
Close beside a rose-tree's root!

Whosoe'er would reach the rose,
Treads the crocus under foot;
I, like May-bloom on thorn-tree,
Thou, like merry summer-bee!
Fit that I be plucked for thee.

Yet who plucks me? — no one mourns;
I have lived my season out,
And now die of my own thorns,
Which I could not live without.
Sweet, be merry! How the light
Comes and goes! If it be night,
Keep the candles in my sight.

Are there footsteps at the door?
Look out quickly. Yea, or nay?
Some one might be waiting for
Some last word that I might say.
Nay? So best! — So angels would
Stand off clear from deathly road,
Not to cross the sight of God.

Colder grow my hands and feet, —
When I wear the shroud I made,
Let the folds lie straight and neat,
And the rosemary be spread,
That if any friend should come,
(To see *thee*, sweet!) all the room
May be lifted out of gloom.

And, dear Bertha, let me keep
On my hand this little ring,
Which at nights, when others sleep,
I can still see glittering.
Let me wear it out of sight,
In the grave, — where it will light
All the dark up, day and night.

On that grave drop not a tear!
Else, though fathom-deep the place,
Through the woolen shroud I wear
I shall feel it on my face.
Rather smile there, blessed one,
Thinking of me in the sun, —
Or forget me, smiling on!

Art thou near me? nearer? so!
Kiss me close upon the eyes,
That the earthly light may go
Sweetly as it used to rise,
When I watched the morning gray
Strike, betwixt the hills, the way
He was sure to come that day.

So — no more vain words be said!
The hosannas nearer roll —
Mother, smile now on thy dead, —
I am death-strong in my soul!

Mystic Dove alit on cross,
Guide the poor bird of the snows
Through the snow-wind above loss!

Jesus, victim, comprehending
Love's divine self-abnegation,
Cleanse my love in its self-spending,
And absorb the poor libation!
Wind my thread of life up higher,
Up through angels' hands of fire! —
I aspire while I expire! —

ELIZABETH BARRETT BROWNING.

UNREQUITED LOVE.

FROM "TWELFTH NIGHT."

VIOLA. Ay, but I know —
DUKE. What dost thou know?
VIOLA. Too well what love women to men may owe:
In faith, they are as true of heart as we.
My father had a daughter loved a man,
As it might be, perhaps, were I a woman,
I should your lordship.
DUKE. And what 's her history?
VIOLA. A blank, my lord. She never told her love,
But let concealment, like a worm i' the bud,
Feed on her damask cheek; she pined in thought;
And, with a green and yellow melancholy,
She sat like Patience on a monument,
Smiling at grief. Was not this love, indeed?
We men may say more, swear more: but, indeed,
Our shows are more than will; for still we prove
Much in our vows, but little in our love.

SHAKESPEARE.

DOROTHY IN THE GARRET.

In the low-raftered garret, stooping
Carefully over the creaking boards,
Old Maid Dorothy goes a-groping
Among its dusty and cobwebbed hoards;
Seeking some bundle of patches, hid
Far under the eaves, or bunch of sage,
Or satchel hung on its nail, amid
The heirlooms of a bygone age.

There is the ancient family chest,
There the ancestral cards and hatchel;
Dorothy, sighing, sinks down to rest,
Forgetful of patches, sage, and satchel.
Ghosts of faces peer from the gloom
Of the chimney, where, with swifts and reel,
And the long-disused, dismantled loom,
Stands the old-fashioned spinning-wheel.

She sees it back in the clean-swept kitchen,
A part of her girlhood's little world ;
Her mother is there by the window, stitching ;
Spindle buzzes, and reel is whirled
With many a click : on her little stool
She sits, a child, by the open door,
Watching, and dabbling her feet in the pool
Of sunshine spilled on the gilded floor.

Her sisters are spinning all day long ;
To her wakening sense the first sweet warning
Of daylight come is the cheerful song
To the hum of the wheel in the early morning.
Benjie, the gentle, red-cheeked boy,
On his way to school, peeps in at the gate ;
In neat white pinafore, pleased and coy,
She reaches a hand to her bashful mate ;

And under the elms, a prattling pair,
Together they go, through glimmer and gloom : —
It all comes back to her, dreaming there
In the low-raftered garret-room ;
The hum of the wheel, and the summer weather,
The heart's first trouble, and love's beginning,
Are all in her memory linked together ;
And now it is she herself that is spinning.

With the bloom of youth on cheek and lip,
Turning the spokes with the flashing pin,
Twisting the thread from the spindle-tip,
Stretching it out and winding it in,
To and fro, with a blithesome tread,
Singing she goes, and her heart is full,
And many a long-drawn golden thread
Of fancy is spun with the shining wool.

Her father sits in his favorite place,
Puffing his pipe by the chimney-side ;
Through curling clouds his kindly face
Glows upon her with love and pride.
Lulled by the wheel, in the old arm-chair
Her mother is musing, cat in lap,
With beautiful drooping head, and hair
Whitening under her snow-white cap.

One by one, to the grave, to the bridal,
They have followed her sisters from the door ;
Now they are old, and she is their idol : —
It all comes back on her heart once more.
In the autumn dusk the hearth gleams brightly,
The wheel is set by the shadowy wall, —
A hand at the latch, — 't is lifted lightly,
And in walks Benjie, manly and tall.

His chair is placed ; the old man tips
The pitcher, and brings his choicest fruit ;
Benjie basks in the blaze, and sips,
And tells his story, and joints his flute :

O, sweet the tunes, the talk, the laughter !
They fill the hour with a glowing tide ;
But sweeter the still, deep moments after,
When she is alone by Benjie's side.

But once with angry words they part :
O, then the weary, weary days !
Ever with restless, wretched heart,
Plying her task, she turns to gaze
Far up the road ; and early and late
She harks for a footstep at the door,
And starts at the gust that swings the gate,
And prays for Benjie, who comes no more.

Her fault ? O Benjie, and could you steel
Your thoughts toward one who loved you so ? —
Solace she seeks in the whirling wheel,
In duty and love that lighten woe ;
Striving with labor, not in vain,
To drive away the dull day's dreariness, —
Blessing the toil that blunts the pain
Of a deeper grief in the body's weariness.

Proud and petted and spoiled was she :
A word, and all her life is changed !
His wavering love too easily
In the great, gay city grows estranged :
One year : she sits in the old church pew ;
A rustle, a murmur, — O Dorothy ! hide
Your face and shut from your soul the view !
'T is Benjie leading a white-veiled bride !

Now father and mother have long been dead,
And the bride sleeps under a churchyard stone,
And a bent old man with grizzled head
Walks up the long dim aisle alone.
Years blur to a mist ; and Dorothy
Sits doubting betwixt the ghost she seems
And the phantom of youth, more real than she,
That meets her there in that haunt of dreams.

Bright young Dorothy, idolized daughter,
Sought by many a youthful adorer,
Life, like a new-risen dawn on the water,
Shining an endless vista before her !
Old Maid Dorothy, wrinkled and gray,
Groping under the farm-house eaves, —
And life is a brief November day
That sets on a world of withered leaves !

Yet faithfulness in the humblest part
Is better at last than proud success,
And patience and love in a chastened heart
Are pearls more precious than happiness ;
And in that morning when she shall wake
To the spring-time freshness of youth again,
All trouble will seem but a flying flake,
And lifelong sorrow a breath on the pane.

JOHN T. TROWBRIDGE.

MAKE BELIEVE.

Kiss me, though you make believe;
  Kiss me, though I almost know
You are kissing to deceive:
  Let the tide one moment flow
Backward ere it rise and break,
Only for poor pity's sake!

Give me of your flowers one leaf,
  Give me of your smiles one smile,
Backward roll this tide of grief
  Just a moment, though, the while,
I should feel and almost know
You are trifling with my woe.

Whisper to me sweet and low;
  Tell me how you sit and weave
Dreams about me, though I know
  It is only make believe!
Just a moment, though 't is plain
You are jesting with my pain.

ALICE CARY.

AN EXPERIENCE AND A MORAL.

I lent my love a book one day;
  She brought it back; I laid it by:
'T was little either had to say, —
  She was so strange, and I so shy.

But yet we loved indifferent things, —
  The sprouting buds, the birds in tune, —
And Time stood still and wreathed his wings
  With rosy links from June to June.

For her, what task to dare or do?
  What peril tempt? what hardship bear?
But with her — ah! she never knew
  My heart, and what was hidden there!

And she, with me, so cold and coy,
  Seemed a little maid bereft of sense;
But in the crowd, all life and joy,
  And full of blushful impudence.

She married, — well, — a woman needs
  A mate, her life and love to share, —
And little cares sprang up like weeds
  And played around her elbow-chair.

And years rolled by, — but I, content,
  Trimmed my own lamp, and kept it bright,
Till age's touch my hair besprent
  With rays and gleams of silver light.

And then it chanced I took the book
  Which she perused in days gone by;
And as I read, such passion shook
  My soul, — I needs must curse or cry.

For, here and there, her love was writ,
  In old, half-faded pencil-signs,
As if she yielded — bit by bit —
  Her heart in dots and underlines.

Ah, silvered fool, too late you look!
  I know it; let me here record
This maxim: *Lend no girl a book
  Unless you read it afterward!*

FREDERICK S. COZZENS.

A RELIC.

Only a woman's right-hand glove,
  Five and three quarters, Courvoisier's make, —
For all common purposes useless enough,
  Yet dearer for her sweet sake.

Dearer to me for her who filled
  Its empty place with a warm white hand, —
The hand I held ere her voice was stilled
  In the sleep of the silent land.

Only a glove! yet speaking to me
  Of the dear dead days now vanished and fled,
And the face that I never again shall see
  Till the grave give back its dead.

An empty glove! yet to me how full
  Of the fragrance of days that come no more,
Of memories that make us, and thoughts that rule
  Man's life in its inmost core!

The tone of her voice, the poise of her head, —
  All, all come back at the will's behest;
The music she loved, the books that she read, —
  Nay, the colors that suited her best.

And O, that night by the wild sea-shore,
  With its tears, and kisses, and vows of love,
When, as pledge of the parting promise we swore,
  Each gave a glove for a glove!

You laugh! but remember though only a glove,
  Which to you may no deeper meaning express,
To me it is changed by the light of that love
  To the one sweet thing I possess.

Our souls draw their nurture from many a ground,
  And faiths that are different in their roots,
Where the will is right, and the heart is sound,
  Are much the same in their fruits.

Men get at the truth by different roads,
  And must live the part of it each one sees:
You gather your guides out of orthodox codes,
  I mine out of trifles like these.

A trifle, no doubt, but, in such a case,
So bathed in the light of a love gone by,
It has entered the region and takes its place
With the things that cannot die.

This trifle to me is of heavenly birth;
No chance, as I take it, but purposely given
To help me to sit somewhat looser to earth,
And closer a little to heaven.

For it seems to bring me so near, O, so near
To the face of an angel watching above, —
That face of all others I held so dear,
With its yearning eyes of love!

J. B. S.

INTROSPECTION.

HAVE you sent her back her letters? have you given her back her ring?
Have you tried to forget the haunting songs that you loved to hear her sing?
Have you cursed the day you met her first, thanked God that you were free,
And said, in your inmost heart, as you thought, "She never was dear to me"?
You have cast her off; your pride is touched; you fancy that all is done;
That for you the world is bright again, and bravely shines the sun:
You have washed your hands of passion; you have whistled her down the wind, —
O Tom, old friend, this goes before, the sharpest comes behind!
Yes, the sharpest is yet to come, for love is a plant that never dies;
Its roots are deep as the earth itself, its branches wide as the skies;
And whenever once it has taken hold, it flourishes evermore,
Bearing a fruit that is fair outside, but bitter ashes at core.

You will learn this, Tom, hereafter; when anger has cooled, and you
Have time for introspection, you will find my words are true;
You will sit and gaze in your fire alone, and fancy that you can see
Her face, with its classic oval, her ringlets fluttering free,
Her soft blue eyes wide opened, her sweet red lips apart,
As she used to look, in the golden days when you fancied she had a heart:
Whatever you do, wherever you turn, you will see that glorious face
Coming with shadowy beauty, to haunt all time and space;
Those songs you wrote for her singing will sing themselves into your brain,
Till your life seems set to their rhythm, and your thoughts to their refrain;
Their old, old burden of love and grief, — the passion you have foresworn:
I tell you, Tom, it is not thrown off so well as you think, this morn.

But the worst, perhaps the worst of all, will be when the day has flown,
When darkness favors reflection, and your comrades leave you alone;
You will try to sleep, but the memories of unforgotten years
Will come with a storm of wild regret, — mayhap with a storm of tears;
Each look, each word, each playful tone, each timid little caress,
The golden gleam of her ringlets, the rustling of her dress,
The delicate touch of her ungloved hand, that woke such an exquisite thrill,
The flowers she gave you the night of the ball, — I think you treasure them still, —
All these will come, till you slumber, worn out by sheer despair,
And then you will hear vague echoes of song on the darkened air, —
Vague echoes rising and falling, of the voice you know so well,
Like the songs that were sung by the Lurlei maids, sweet with a deadly spell!

In dreams her heart will ever again be yours, and you will see
Fair glimpses of what might have been, — what now can never be;
And as she comes to meet you, with a sudden, wild unrest
You will stretch your arms forth lovingly to fold her to your breast;
But the Lurlei song will fade and die, and with its fading tone
You will wake to find you clasp the thin and empty air alone,
While the fire-bells' clanging dissonance, on the gusty night-wind borne,
Will seem an iron-tongued demon's voice, laughing your grief to scorn.
O Tom, you say it is over, — you talk of letters and rings, —
Do you think that Love's mighty spirit, then, is held by such trifling things?
No! if you once have truly loved, you will still love on, I know,
Till the churchyard myrtles blossom above, and you lie mute below.

How is it, I wonder, hereafter? Faith teaches us little, here,
Of the ones we have loved and lost on earth, — do you think they will still be dear?
Shall we live the lives we might have lead?— will those who are severed now
Remember the pledge of a lower sphere, and renew the broken vow?
It almost drives me wild to think of the gifts we throw away,
Unthinking whether or no we lose Life's honey and wine for aye!
But then, again, 't is a mighty joy — greater than I can tell —
To trust that the parted may some time meet, — that all may again be well.
However it be, I hold, that all the evil we know on earth
Finds in this violence done to Love its true and legitimate birth;
And the agonies we suffer, when the heart is left alone,
For every sin of Humanity should fully and well atone.

I see that you marvel greatly, Tom, to hear such words from me,
But, if you knew my inmost heart, 't would be no mystery.
Experience is bitter, but its teachings we retain:
It has taught me this, — who once has loved, loves never on earth again!
And I too have my closet, with a ghastly form inside, —
The skeleton of a perished love, killed by a cruel pride:
I sit by the fire at evening — as you will some time sit,
And watch, in the roseate half-light, the ghosts of happiness flit:
I too awaken at midnight, and stretch my arms to enfold
A vague and shadowy image, with tresses of brown and gold:
Experience is bitter indeed, — I have learned at a heavy cost
The secret of Love's persistency: I too have loved and lost!

George Arnold.

LOCKSLEY HALL.

Comrades, leave me here a little, while as yet 't is early morn, —
Leave me here, and when you want me, sound upon the bugle horn.

'T is the place, and all around it, as of old, the curlews call,
Dreary gleams about the moorland, flying over Locksley Hall:

Locksley Hall, that in the distance overlooks the sandy tracts,
And the hollow ocean-ridges roaring into cataracts.

Many a night from yonder ivied casement, ere I went to rest,
Did I look on great Orion sloping slowly to the west.

Many a night I saw the Pleiads, rising through the mellow shade,
Glitter like a swarm of fire-flies tangled in a silver braid.

Here about the beach I wandered, nourishing a youth sublime
With the fairy tales of science, and the long result of time;

When the centuries behind me like a fruitful land reposed;
When I clung to all the present for the promise that it closed;

When I dipt into the future far as human eye could see, —
Saw the vision of the world, and all the wonder that would be.

In the Spring a fuller crimson comes upon the robin's breast;
In the Spring the wanton lapwing gets himself another crest;

In the Spring a livelier iris changes on the burnished dove;
In the Spring a young man's fancy lightly turns to thoughts of love.

Then her cheek was pale and thinner than should be for one so young,
And her eyes on all my motions with a mute observance hung.

And I said, "My cousin Amy, speak, and speak the truth to me;
Trust me, cousin, all the current of my being sets to thee."

On her pallid cheek and forehead came a color and a light,
As I have seen the rosy red flushing in the northern night.

And she turned, — her bosom shaken with a sudden storm of sighs;
All the spirit deeply dawning in the dark of hazel eyes, —

Saying, "I have hid my feelings, fearing they should do me wrong";
Saying, "Dost thou love me, cousin?" weeping, "I have loved thee long."

Love took up the glass of time, and turned it in his glowing hands;
Every moment, lightly shaken, ran itself in golden sands.

Love took up the harp of Life, and smote on all the chords with might;
Smote the chord of Self, that, trembling, passed in music out of sight.

Many a morning on the moorland did we hear the copses ring,
And her whisper thronged my pulses with the fullness of the Spring.

Many an evening by the waters did we watch the stately ships,
And our spirits rushed together at the touching of the lips.

O my cousin, shallow-hearted! O my Amy, mine no more!
O, the dreary, dreary moorland! O, the barren, barren shore!

Falser than all fancy fathoms, falser than all songs have sung, —
Puppet to a father's threat, and servile to a shrewish tongue!

Is it well to wish thee happy? — having known me — to decline
On a range of lower feelings and a narrower heart than mine!

Yet it shall be: thou shalt lower to his level day by day,
What is fine within thee growing coarse to sympathize with clay.

As the husband is, the wife is; thou art mated with a clown,
And the grossness of his nature will have weight to drag thee down.

He will hold thee, when his passion shall have spent its novel force,
Something better than his dog, a little dearer than his horse.

What is this? his eyes are heavy, — think not they are glazed with wine.
Go to him; it is thy duty, — kiss him; take his hand in thine.

It may be my lord is weary, that his brain is overwrought, —
Soothe him with thy finer fancies, touch him with thy lighter thought.

He will answer to the purpose, easy things to understand, —
Better thou wert dead before me, though I slew thee with my hand!

Better thou and I were lying, hidden from the heart's disgrace,
Rolled in one another's arms, and silent in a last embrace.

Cursed be the social wants that sin against the strength of youth!
Cursed be the social lies that warp us from the living truth!

Cursed be the sickly forms that err from honest nature's rule!
Cursed be the gold that gilds the straitened forehead of the fool!

Well — 't is well that I should bluster! — Hadst thou less unworthy proved,
Would to God — for I had loved thee more than ever wife was loved.

Am I mad, that I should cherish that which bears but bitter fruit?
I will pluck it from my bosom, though my heart be at the root.

Never! though my mortal summers to such length of years should come
As the many-wintered crow that leads the clanging rookery home.

Where is comfort? in division of the records of the mind?
Can I part her from herself, and love her, as I knew her, kind?

I remember one that perished; sweetly did she speak and move;
Such a one do I remember, whom to look at was to love.

Can I think of her as dead, and love her for the love she bore?
No, — she never loved me truly; love is love forevermore.

Comfort? comfort scorned of devils! this is truth the poet sings,
That a sorrow's crown of sorrow is remembering happier things.

Drug thy memories, lest thou learn it, lest thy heart be put to proof,
In the dead, unhappy night, and when the rain is on the roof.

Like a dog, he hunts in dreams; and thou art staring at the wall,
Where the dying night-lamp flickers, and the shadows rise and fall.

Then a hand shall pass before thee, pointing to his drunken sleep,
To thy widowed marriage-pillows, to the tears that thou wilt weep.

Thou shalt hear the "Never, never," whispered by the phantom years,
And a song from out the distance in the ringing of thine ears;

And an eye shall vex thee, looking ancient kindness on thy pain.
Turn thee, turn thee on thy pillow; get thee to thy rest again.

Nay, but nature brings thee solace; for a tender voice will cry;
'T is a purer life than thine, a lip to drain thy trouble dry.

Baby lips will laugh me down; my latest rival brings thee rest, —
Baby fingers, waxen touches, press me from the mother's breast.

O, the child too clothes the father with a dearness not his due.
Half is thine and half is his: it will be worthy of the two.

O, I see thee old and formal, fitted to thy petty part,
With a little horde of maxims preaching down a daughter's heart.

"They were dangerous guides the feelings — she herself was not exempt —
Truly, she herself had suffered —" Perish in thy self-contempt!

Overlive it — lower yet — be happy! wherefore should I care?
I myself must mix with action, lest I wither by despair.

What is that which I should turn to, lighting upon days like these?
Every door is barred with gold, and opens but to golden keys.

Every gate is thronged with suitors, all the markets overflow.
I have but an angry fancy: what is that which I should do?

I had been content to perish, falling on the foeman's ground,
When the ranks are rolled in vapor, and the winds are laid with sound.

But the jingling of the guinea helps the hurt that honor feels,
And the nations do but murmur, snarling at each other's heels.

Can I but relive in sadness? I will turn that earlier page.
Hide me from my deep emotion, O thou wondrous mother-age!

Make me feel the wild pulsation that I felt before the strife,
When I heard my days before me, and the tumult of my life;

Yearning for the large excitement that the coming years would yield,
Eager-hearted as a boy when first he leaves his father's field,

And at night along the dusky highway near and nearer drawn,
Sees in heaven the light of London flaring like a dreary dawn;

And his spirit leaps within him to be gone before him then,
Underneath the light he looks at, in among the throngs of men;

Men, my brothers, men the workers, ever reaping something new:
That which they have done but earnest of the things that they shall do:

For I dipt into the future, far as human eye could see,
Saw the vision of the world, and all the wonder that would be;

Saw the heavens fill with commerce, argosies of magic sails,
Pilots of the purple twilight, dropping down with costly bales;

Eng^d by Geo E Perine New York.

A Tennyson

J. B. FORD & Co NEW YORK

Heard the heavens fill with shouting, and there rained a ghastly dew
From the nations' airy navies grappling in the central blue;

Far along the world-wide whisper of the south-wind rushing warm,
With the standards of the peoples plunging through the thunder-storm;

Till the war-drum throbbed no longer, and the battle-flags were furled
In the parliament of man, the federation of the world.

There the common sense of most shall hold a fretful realm in awe,
And the kindly earth shall slumber, lapt in universal law.

So I triumphed ere my passion sweeping through me left me dry,
Left me with the palsied heart, and left me with the jaundiced eye;

Eye, to which all order festers, all things here are out of joint.
Science moves, but slowly, slowly, creeping on from point to point:

Slowly comes a hungry people, as a lion, creeping nigher,
Glares at one that nods and winks behind a slowly dying fire.

Yet I doubt not through the ages one increasing purpose runs,
And the thoughts of men are widened with the process of the suns.

What is that to him that reaps not harvest of his youthful joys,
Though the deep heart of existence beat forever like a boy's?

Knowledge comes, but wisdom lingers; and I linger on the shore,
And the individual withers, and the world is more and more.

Knowledge comes, but wisdom lingers, and he bears a laden breast,
Full of sad experience moving toward the stillness of his rest.

Hark! my merry comrades call me, sounding on the bugle horn, —
They to whom my foolish passion were a target for their scorn;

Shall it not be scorn to me to harp on such a mouldered string?
I am shamed through all my nature to have loved so slight a thing.

Weakness to be wroth with weakness! woman's pleasure, woman's pain —
Nature made them blinder motions bounded in a shallower brain;

Woman is the lesser man, and all thy passions, matched with mine,
Are as moonlight unto sunlight, and as water unto wine —

Here at least, where nature sickens, nothing. Ah for some retreat
Deep in yonder shining Orient, where my life began to beat;

Where in wild Mahratta-battle fell my father, evil-starred;
I was left a trampled orphan, and a selfish uncle's ward.

Or to burst all links of habit, — there to wander far away,
On from island unto island at the gateways of the day, —

Larger constellations burning, mellow moons and happy skies,
Breadths of tropic shade and palms in cluster, knots of Paradise.

Never comes the trader, never floats an European flag, —
Slides the bird o'er lustrous woodland, swings the trailer from the crag, —

Droops the heavy-blossomed bower, hangs the heavy-fruited tree, —
Summer isles of Eden lying in dark-purple spheres of sea.

There, methinks, would be enjoyment more than in this march of mind —
In the steamship, in the railway, in the thoughts that shake mankind.

There the passions, cramped no longer, shall have scope and breathing-space;
I will take some savage woman, she shall rear my dusky race.

Iron-jointed, supple-sinewed, they shall dive, and they shall run,
Catch the wild goat by the hair, and hurl their lances in the sun,

Whistle back the parrot's call, and leap the rainbows of the brooks,
Not with blinded eyesight poring over miserable books —

Fool, again the dream, the fancy! but I know my words are wild,
But I count the gray barbarian lower than the Christian child.

I, to herd with narrow foreheads, vacant of our glorious gains,
Like a beast with lower pleasures, like a beast with lower pains!

Mated with a squalid savage, — what to me were sun or clime?
I, the heir of all the ages, in the foremost files of time, —

I, that rather held it better men should perish one by one,
Than that earth should stand at gaze like Joshua's moon in Ajalon!

Not in vain the distance beacons. Forward, forward let us range;
Let the great world spin forever down the ringing grooves of change.

Through the shadow of the globe we sweep into the younger day:
Better fifty years of Europe than a cycle of Cathay.

Mother-age (for mine I knew not), help me as when life begun, —
Rift the hills, and roll the waters, flash the lightnings, weigh the sun, —

O, I see the crescent promise of my spirit hath not set;
Ancient founts of inspiration well through all my fancy yet.

Howsoever these things be, a long farewell to Locksley Hall!
Now for me the woods may wither, now for me the roof-tree fall.

Comes a vapor from the margin, blackening over heath and holt,
Cramming all the blast before it, in its breast a thunderbolt.

Let it fall on Locksley Hall, with rain or hail, or fire or snow;
For the mighty wind arises, roaring seaward, and I go.

ALFRED TENNYSON.

ONLY A WOMAN.

"She loves with love that cannot tire:
And if, ah, woe! she loves alone,
Through passionate duty love flames higher,
As grass grows taller round a stone."

COVENTRY PATMORE.

So, the truth 's out. I 'll grasp it like a snake,—
It will not slay me. My heart shall not break
Awhile, if only for the children's sake.

For his, too, somewhat. Let him stand unblamed;
None say, he gave me less than honor claimed,
Except—one trifle scarcely worth being named—

The *heart*. That 's gone. The corrupt dead might be
As easily raised up, breathing, fair to see,
As he could bring his whole heart back to me.

I never sought him in coquettish sport,
Or courted him as silly maidens court,
And wonder when the longed-for prize falls short.

I only loved him, — any woman would:
But shut my love up till he came and sued,
Then poured it o'er his dry life like a flood.

I was so happy I could make him blest! —
So happy that I was his first and best,
As he mine, — when he took me to his breast.

Ah me! if only then he had been true!
If, for one little year, a month or two,
He had given me love for love, as was my due!

Or had he told me, ere the deed was done,
He only raised me to his heart's dear throne —
Poor substitute — because the queen was gone!

O, had he whispered, when his sweetest kiss
Was warm upon my mouth in fancied bliss,
He had kissed another woman even as this, —

It were less bitter! Sometimes I could weep
To be thus cheated, like a child asleep, —
Were not my anguish far too dry and deep.

So I built my house upon another's ground;
Mocked with a heart just caught at the rebound,—
A cankered thing that looked so firm and sound.

And when that heart grew colder, — colder still,
I, ignorant, tried all duties to fulfil,
Blaming my foolish pain, exacting will,

All, — anything but him. It was to be
The full draught others drink up carelessly
Was made this bitter Tantalus-cup for me.

I say again, — he gives me all I claimed,
I and my children never shall be shamed:
He is a just man, — he will live unblamed.

Only — O God, O God, to cry for bread,
And get a stone! Daily to lay my head
Upon a bosom where the old love 's dead!

Dead? — Fool! It never lived. It only stirred
Galvanic, like an hour-cold corpse. None heard:
So let me bury it without a word.

He 'll keep that other woman from my sight.
I know not if her face be foul or bright;
I only know that it was his delight —

As his was mine; I only know he stands
Pale, at the touch of their long-severed hands,
Then to a flickering smile his lips commands,

Lest I should grieve, or jealous anger show.
He need not. When the ship 's gone down, I trow,
We little reck whatever wind may blow.

And so my silent moan begins and ends:
No world's laugh or world's taunt, no pity of friends
Or sneer of foes, with this my torment blends.

None knows, — none heeds. I have a little pride;
Enough to stand up, wifelike, by his side,
With the same smile as when I was his bride.

And I shall take his children to my arms;
They will not miss these fading, worthless charms;
Their kiss — ah! unlike his — all pain disarms.

And haply as the solemn years go by,
He will think sometimes, with regretful sigh,
The other woman was less true than I.

DINAH MULOCK CRAIK.

HOME, WOUNDED.

WHEEL me into the sunshine,
Wheel me into the shadow,
There must be leaves on the woodbine,
Is the king-cup crowned in the meadow?

Wheel me down to the meadow,
Down to the little river,
In sun or in shadow
I shall not dazzle or shiver,
I shall be happy anywhere,
Every breath of the morning air
Makes me throb and quiver.

Stay wherever you will,
By the mount or under the hill,
Or down by the little river:
Stay as long as you please,
Give me only a bud from the trees,
Or a blade of grass in morning dew,
Or a cloudy violet clearing to blue,
I could look on it forever.

Wheel, wheel through the sunshine,
Wheel, wheel through the shadow;
There must be odors round the pine,
There must be balm of breathing kine,
Somewhere down in the meadow.
Must I choose? Then anchor me there
Beyond the beckoning poplars, where
The larch is snooding her flowery hair
With wreaths of morning shadow.

Among the thickest hazels of the brake
Perchance some nightingale doth shake
His feathers, and the air is full of song;
In those old days when I was young and strong,
He used to sing on yonder garden tree,
Beside the nursery.
Ah, I remember how I loved to wake,
And find him singing on the selfsame bough
(I know it even now)
Where, since the flit of bat,
In ceaseless voice he sat,
Trying the spring night over, like a tune,
Beneath the vernal moon;
And while I listed long,
Day rose, and still he sang,
And all his stanchless song,
As something falling unaware,
Fell out of the tall trees he sang among,
Fell ringing down the ringing morn, and rang, —
Rang like a golden jewel down a golden stair.

. . . . .

My soul lies out like a basking hound, —
A hound that dreams and dozes;
Along my life my length I lay,
I fill to-morrow and yesterday,
I am warm with the suns that have long since set,
I am warm with the summers that are not yet,
And like one who dreams and dozes
Softly afloat on a sunny sea,
Two worlds are whispering over me,
And there blows a wind of roses
From the backward shore to the shore before,
From the shore before to the backward shore,
And like two clouds that meet and pour
Each through each, till core in core
A single self reposes,
The nevermore with the evermore
Above me mingles and closes;
As my soul lies out like the basking hound,
And wherever it lies seems happy ground,

And when, awakened by some sweet sound,
A dreamy eye uncloses,
I see a blooming world around,
And I lie amid primroses, —
Years of sweet primroses,
Springs of fresh primroses,
Springs to be, and springs for me
Of distant dim primroses.

O, to lie a-dream, a-dream,
To feel I may dream and to know you deem
My work is done forever,
And the palpitating fever,
That gains and loses, loses and gains,
And beats the hurrying blood on the brunt of a thousand pains,
Cooled at once by that blood-let
Upon the parapet;
And all the tedious taskèd toil of the difficult long endeavor
Solved and quit by no more fine
Than these limbs of mine,
Spanned and measured once for all
By that right-hand I lost,
Bought up at so light a cost
As one bloody fall
On the soldier's bed,
And three days on the ruined wall
Among the thirstless dead.

O, to think my name is crost
From duty's muster-roll;
That I may slumber though the clarion call,
And live the joy of an embodied soul
Free as a liberated ghost.
O, to feel a life of deed
Was emptied out to feed
That fire of pain that burned so brief awhile, —
That fire from which I come, as the dead come
Forth from the irreparable tomb,
Or as a martyr on his funeral pile
Heaps up the burdens other men do bear
Through years of segregated care,
And takes the total load
Upon his shoulders broad,
And steps from earth to God.

. . .

And she,
Perhaps, O even she
May look as she looked when I knew her
In those old days of childish sooth,
Ere my boyhood dared to woo her.
I will not seek nor sue her,
For I 'm neither fonder nor truer
Than when she slighted my lovelorn youth,
My giftless, graceless, guinealess truth,
And I only lived to rue her.
But I 'll never love another,
And, in spite of her lovers and lands,
She shall love me yet, my brother!

As a child that holds by his mother,
While his mother speaks his praises,
Holds with eager hands,
And ruddy and silent stands
In the ruddy and silent daisies,
And hears her bless her boy,
And lifts a wondering joy,
So I 'll not seek nor sue her,
But I 'll leave my glory to woo her,
And I 'll stand like a child beside,
And from behind the purple pride
I 'll lift my eyes unto her,
And I shall not be denied.
And you will love her, brother dear,
And perhaps next year you 'll bring me here
All through the balmy April tide,
And she will trip like spring by my side,
And be all the birds to my ear.
And here all three we 'll sit in the sun,
And see the Aprils one by one,
Primrosed Aprils on and on,
Till the floating prospect closes
In golden glimmers that rise and rise,
And perhaps are gleams of Paradise,
And perhaps too far for mortal eyes,
New springs of fresh primroses,
Springs of earth's primroses,
Springs to be and springs for me
Of distant dim primroses.

SIDNEY DOBELL.

PERISHED.

CATSKILL MOUNTAIN HOUSE.

WAVE after wave of greenness rolling down
From mountain top to base, a whispering sea
Of affluent leaves through which the viewless breeze
Murmurs mysteriously.

And towering up amid the lesser throng,
A giant oak, so desolately grand,
Stretches its gray imploring arms to heaven
In agonized demand.

Smitten by lightning from a summer sky,
Or bearing in its heart a slow decay,
What matter, since inexorable fate
Is pitiless to slay.

Ah, wayward soul, hedged in and clothed about,
Doth not thy life's lost hope lift up its head,
And, dwarfing present joys, proclaim aloud, —
"Look on me, I am dead!"

MARY LOUISE RITTER.

PERISHED.

(A View in the Catskills.)

"Wave after wave of greenness rolling down
From mountain top to base . . .
And, towering up amid the lesser throng,
A giant oak, so desolately grand,
Stretches its gray imploring arms to Heaven."

DEATH OF THE WHITE FAWN.

The wanton troopers, riding by,
Have shot my fawn, and it will die.
Ungentle men! they cannot thrive
Who killed thee. Thou ne'er didst, alive,
Them any harm; alas! nor could
Thy death yet do them any good.
I 'm sure I never wished them ill, —
Nor do I for all this, nor will;
But if my simple prayers may yet
Prevail with Heaven to forget
Thy murder, I will join my tears,
Rather than fail. But, O my fears!
It cannot die so. Heaven's king
Keeps register of everything;
And nothing may we use in vain;
Even beasts must be with justice slain,—
Else men are made their deodands.
Though they should wash their guilty hands
In this warm life-blood, which doth part
From thine and wound me to the heart,
Yet could they not be clean, — their stain
Is dyed in such a purple grain;
There is not such another in
The world to offer for their sin.
Inconstant Sylvio, when yet
I had not found him counterfeit,
One morning (I remember well),
Tied in this silver chain and bell,
Gave it to me; nay, and I know
What he said then, — I 'm sure I do:
Said he, "Look how your huntsman here
Hath taught a fawn to hunt his dear!"
But Sylvio soon had me beguiled:
This waxed tame, while he grew wild;
And, quite regardless of my smart,
Left me his fawn, but took his heart.
Thenceforth I set myself to play
My solitary time away
With this; and, very well content,
Could so mine idle life have spent.
For it was full of sport, and light
Of foot and heart, and did invite
Me to its game. It seemed to bless
Itself in me; how could I less
Than love it? O, I cannot be
Unkind to a beast that loveth me!
Had it lived long, I do not know
Whether it, too, might have done so
As Sylvio did, — his gifts might be
Perhaps as false, or more, than he.
For I am sure, for aught that I
Could in so short a time espy,
Thy love was far more better than
The love of false and cruel man.
With sweetest milk and sugar, first
I it at mine own fingers nursed;
And as it grew, so every day
It waxed more white and sweet than they.
It had so sweet a breath! and oft
I blushed to see its foot more soft
And white — shall I say than my hand?
Nay, any lady's of the land.
It is a wondrous thing how fleet
'T was on those little silver feet.
With what a pretty, skipping grace
It oft would challenge me the race;
And when 't had left me far away,
'T would stay, and run again, and stay;
For it was nimbler much than hinds,
And trod as if on the four winds.
I have a garden of my own, —
But so with roses overgrown,
And lilies, that you would it guess
To be a little wilderness;
And all the springtime of the year
It only lovèd to be there.
Among the beds of lilies I
Have sought it oft, where it should lie;
Yet could not, till itself would rise,
Find it, although before mine eyes;
For in the flaxen lilies' shade
It like a bank of lilies laid.
Upon the roses it would feed,
Until its lips even seemed to bleed;
And then to me 't would boldly trip,
And print those roses on my lip.
But all its chief delight was still
On roses thus itself to fill;
And its pure virgin limbs to fold
In whitest sheets of lilies cold.
Had it lived long, it would have been
Lilies without, roses within.
O, help! O, help! I see it faint,
And die as calmly as a saint!
See how it weeps! the tears do come,
Sad, slowly, dropping like a gum.
So weeps the wounded balsam; so
The holy frankincense doth flow;
The brotherless Heliades
Melt in such amber tears as these.
I in a golden phial will
Keep these two crystal tears, and fill
It, till it do o'erflow with mine;
Then place it in Diana's shrine.
Now my sweet fawn is vanished to
Whither the swans and turtles go,
In fair Elysium to endure,
With milk-white lambs, and ermines pure.
O, do not run too fast! for I
Will but bespeak thy grave — and die.
First, my unhappy statue shall
Be cut in marble; and withal,
Let it be weeping too. But there
The engraver sure his art may spare;

For I so truly thee bemoan
That I shall weep, though I be stone,
Until my tears, still dropping, wear
My breast, themselves engraving there.
There at my feet shalt thou be laid,
Of purest alabaster made;
For I would have thine image be
White as I can, though not as thee.

ANDREW MARVELL.

IN A YEAR.

NEVER any more
While I live,
Need I hope to see his face
As before.
Once his love grown chill,
Mine may strive, —
Bitterly we re-embrace,
Single still.

Was it something said,
Something done,
Vexed him? was it touch of hand,
Turn of head?
Strange! that very way
Love begun.
I as little understand
Love's decay.

When I sewed or drew,
I recall
How he looked as if I sang
— Sweetly too.
If I spoke a word,
First of all
Up his cheek the color sprang,
Then he heard.

Sitting by my side,
At my feet,
So he breathed the air I breathed,
Satisfied!
I, too, at love's brim
Touched the sweet:
I would die if death bequeathed
Sweet to him.

"Speak, — I love thee best!"
He exclaimed.
"Let thy love my own foretell, —"
I confessed:
"Clasp my heart on thine
Now unblamed,
Since upon thy soul as well
Hangeth mine!"

Was it wrong to own,
Being truth?
Why should all the giving prove
His alone?
I had wealth and ease,
Beauty, youth, —
Since my lover gave me love,
I gave these.

That was all I meant,
— To be just,
And the passion I had raised
To content.
Since he chose to change
Gold for dust,
If I gave him what he praised,
Was it strange?

Would he loved me yet,
On and on,
While I found some way undreamed,
— Paid my debt!
Gave more life and more,
Till, all gone,
He should smile, "She never seemed
Mine before.

"What — she felt the while,
Must I think?
Love 's so different with us men,"
He should smile.
"Dying for my sake —
White and pink!
Can't we touch these bubbles then
But they break?"

Dear, the pang is brief.
Do thy part,
Have thy pleasure. How perplext
Grows belief!
Well, this cold clay clod
Was man's heart.
Crumble it, — and what comes next?
Is it God?

ROBERT BROWNING.

BLIGHTED LOVE.

FLOWERS are fresh, and bushes green,
Cheerily the linnets sing;
Winds are soft, and skies serene;
Time, however, soon shall throw
Winter's snow
O'er the buxom breast of Spring!

Hope, that buds in lover's heart,
Lives not through the scorn of years;

Time makes love itself depart;
Time and scorn congeal the mind, —
Looks unkind
Freeze affection's warmest tears.

Time shall make the bushes green;
Time dissolve the winter snow;
Winds be soft, and skies serene;
Linnets sing their wonted strain:
But again
Blighted love shall never blow!

From the Portuguese of LUIS DE CAMOENS,
by LORD STRANGFORD.

DISAPPOINTMENT.

FROM "ZOPHIEL, OR THE BRIDE OF SEVEN."

THE bard has sung, God never formed a soul
Without its own peculiar mate, to meet
Its wandering half, when ripe to crown the whole
Bright plan of bliss most heavenly, most complete.

But thousand evil things there are that hate
To look on happiness: these hurt, impede,
And leagued with time, space, circumstance and fate,
Keep kindred heart from heart, to pine, and pant, and bleed.

And as the dove to far Palmyra flying
From where her native founts of Antioch beam,
Weary, exhausted, longing, panting, sighing,
Lights sadly at the desert's bitter stream;

So many a soul, o'er life's drear desert faring,
Love's pure congenial spring unfound, unquaffed,
Suffers — recoils — then thirsty and despairing
Of what it would, descends and sips the nearest draught!

MARIA GOWEN BROOKS
(MARIA DEL OCCIDENTE).

SHIPS AT SEA.

I HAVE ships that went to sea
More than fifty years ago;
None have yet come home to me,
But are sailing to and fro.
I have seen them in my sleep,
Plunging through the shoreless deep,
With tattered sails and battered hulls,
While around them screamed the gulls,
Flying low, flying low.

I have wondered why they strayed
From me, sailing round the world;
And I 've said, "I 'm half afraid
That their sails will ne'er be furled."
Great the treasures that they hold,
Silks, and plumes, and bars of gold;
While the spices that they bear
Fill with fragrance all the air,
As they sail, as they sail.

Ah! each sailor in the port
Knows that I have ships at sea,
Of the waves and winds the sport,
And the sailors pity me.
Oft they come and with me walk,
Cheering me with hopeful talk,
Till I put my fears aside,
And, contented, watch the tide
Rise and fall, rise and fall.

I have waited on the piers,
Gazing for them down the bay,
Days and nights for many years,
Till I turned heart-sick away.
But the pilots, when they land,
Stop and take me by the hand,
Saying, "You will live to see
Your proud vessels come from sea,
One and all, one and all."

So I never quite despair,
Nor let hope or courage fail;
And some day, when skies are fair,
Up the bay my ships will sail.
I shall buy then all I need, —
Prints to look at, books to read,
Horses, wines, and works of art,
Everything — except a heart
That is lost, that is lost.

Once, when I was pure and young,
Richer, too, than I am now,
Ere a cloud was o'er me flung,
Or a wrinkle creased my brow,
There was one whose heart was mine;
But she 's something now divine,
And though come my ships from sea,
They can bring no heart to me
Evermore, evermore.

ROBERT B. COFFIN.

ENOCH ARDEN AT THE WINDOW.

BUT Enoch yearned to see her face again;
"If I might look on her sweet face again
And know that she is happy." So the thought
Haunted and harassed him, and drove him forth
At evening when the dull November day
Was growing duller twilight, to the hill.
There he sat down gazing on all below:

There did a thousand memories roll upon him,
Unspeakable for sadness. By and by
The ruddy square of comfortable light,
Far-blazing from the rear of Philip's house,
Allured him, as the beacon-blaze allures
The bird of passage, till he madly strikes
Against it, and beats out his weary life.

For Philip's dwelling fronted on the street,
The latest house to landward; but behind,
With one small gate that opened on the waste,
Flourished a little garden square and walled:
And in it throve an ancient evergreen,
A yew-tree, and all round it ran a walk
Of shingle, and a walk divided it:
But Enoch shunned the middle walk and stole
Up by the wall, behind the yew; and thence
That which he better might have shunned, if griefs
Like his have worse or better, Enoch saw.

For cups and silver on the burnished board
Sparkled and shone; so genial was the hearth;
And on the right hand of the hearth he saw
Philip, the slighted suitor of old times,
Stout, rosy, with his babe across his knees;
And o'er her second father stoopt a girl,
A later but a loftier Annie Lee,
Fair-haired and tall, and from her lifted hand
Dangled a length of ribbon and a ring
To tempt the babe, who reared his creasy arms,
Caught at and ever missed it, and they laughed:
And on the left hand of the hearth he saw
The mother glancing often toward her babe,
But turning now and then to speak with him,
Her son, who stood beside her tall and strong,
And saying that which pleased him, for he smiled.

Now when the dead man come to life beheld
His wife his wife no more, and saw the babe
Hers, yet not his, upon the father's knee,
And all the warmth, the peace, the happiness,
And his own children tall and beautiful,
And him, that other, reigning in his place,
Lord of his rights and of his children's love, —
Then he, though Miriam Lane had told him all,
Because things seen are mightier than things heard,
Staggered and shook, holding the branch, and feared
To send abroad a shrill and terrible cry,
Which in one moment, like the blast of doom,
Would shatter all the happiness of the hearth.

He therefore turning softly like a thief,
Lest the harsh shingle should grate under foot,
And feeling all along the garden-wall,
Lest he should swoon and tumble and be found,
Crept to the gate, and opened it, and closed,
As lightly as a sick man's chamber-door,
Behind him, and came out upon the waste.

And there he would have knelt, but that his knees
Were feeble, so that falling prone he dug
His fingers into the wet earth, and prayed.

ALFRED TENNYSON.

LOVE'S YOUNG DREAM.

O, THE days are gone when beauty bright
My heart's chain wove!
When my dream of life, from morn till night,
Was love, still love!
New hope may bloom,
And days may come,
Of milder, calmer beam,
But there 's nothing half so sweet in life
As love's young dream!
O, there 's nothing half so sweet in life
As love's young dream!

Though the bard to purer fame may soar,
When wild youth 's past;
Though he win the wise, who frowned before,
To smile at last;
He 'll never meet
A joy so sweet
In all his noon of fame
As when first he sung to woman's ear
His soul-felt flame,
And, at every close, she blushed to hear
The one loved name!

O, that hallowed form is ne'er forgot,
Which first love traced;
Still it lingering haunts the greenest spot
On memory's waste!
'T was odor fled
As soon as shed;
'T was morning's wingèd dream;
'T was a light that ne'er can shine again
On life's dull stream!
O, 't was light that ne'er can shine again
On life's dull stream!

THOMAS MOORE.

WHEN THE LAMP IS SHATTERED.

WHEN the lamp is shattered,
The light in the dust lies dead;
When the cloud is scattered,
The rainbow's glory is shed.
When the lute is broken,
Sweet tones are remembered not;
When the lips have spoken,
Loved accents are soon forgot.

As music and splendor
Survive not the lamp and the lute,
The heart's echoes render
No song when the spirit is mute, —
No song but sad dirges,
Like the wind through a ruined cell,
Or the mournful surges
That ring the dead seaman's knell.

When hearts have once mingled,
Love first leaves the well-built nest;
The weak one is singled
To endure what it once possest.
O Love! who bewailest
The frailty of all things here,
Why choose you the frailest
For your cradle, your home, and your bier?

Its passions will rock thee
As the storms rock the ravens on high;
Bright reason will mock thee,
Like the sun from a wintry sky.
From thy nest every rafter
Will rot, and thine eagle home
Leave thee naked to laughter,
When leaves fall and cold winds come.

PERCY BYSSHE SHELLEY.

TAKE, O, TAKE THOSE LIPS AWAY.

FROM "MEASURE FOR MEASURE."

TAKE, O, take those lips away,
  That so sweetly were forsworn;
And those eyes, the break of day,
  Lights that do mislead the morn;
But my kisses bring again,
Seals of love, but sealed in vain.

Hide, O, hide those hills of snow
  Which thy frozen bosom bears,
On whose tops the pinks that grow
  Are of those that April wears!
But first set my poor heart free,
Bound in those icy chains by thee.

SHAKESPEARE and JOHN FLETCHER.

I LOVED A LASS, A FAIR ONE.

I LOVED a lass, a fair one,
  As fair as e'er was seen;
She was indeed a rare one,
  Another Sheba Queen;
But fool as then I was,
  I thought she loved me too,
But now, alas! sh' 'as left me,
  Falero, lero, loo.

Her hair like gold did glister,
  Each eye was like a star,
She did surpass her sister
  Which past all others far;
She would me honey call,
  She 'd, O, she 'd kiss me too,
But now, alas! sh' 'as left me,
  Falero, lero, loo.

In summer time to Medley,
  My love and I would go, —
The boatmen there stood ready
  My love and I to row;
For cream there would we call,
  For cakes, and for prunes too,
But now, alas! sh' 'as left me,
  Falero, lero, loo.

Many a merry meeting
  My love and I have had;
She was my only sweeting,
  She made my heart full glad:
The tears stood in her eyes,
  Like to the morning dew,
But now, alas! sh' 'as left me,
  Falero, lero, loo.

And as abroad we walkèd,
  As lovers' fashion is,
Oft as we sweetly talkèd,
  The sun would steal a kiss;
The wind upon her lips
  Likewise most sweetly blew,
But now, alas! sh' 'as left me,
  Falero, lero, loo.

Her cheeks were like the cherry,
  Her skin as white as snow,
When she was blithe and merry,
  She angel-like did show;
Her waist exceeding small,
  The fives did fit her shoe,
But now, alas! sh' 'as left me,
  Falero, lero, loo.

In summer time or winter,
  She had her heart's desire;
I still did scorn to stint her,
  From sugar, sack, or fire;
The world went round about,
  No cares we ever knew,
But now, alas! sh' 'as left me,
  Falero, lero, loo.

As we walked home together
  At midnight through the town,
To keep away the weather,
  O'er her I 'd cast my gown;

No cold my love should feel,
Whate'er the heavens could do,
But now, alas! sh' 'as left me,
Falero, lero, loo.

Like doves we would be billing,
And clip and kiss so fast,
Yet she would be unwilling
That I should kiss the last;
They 're Judas kisses now,
Since that they proved untrue;
For now, alas! sh' 'as left me,
Falero, lero, loo.

To maiden's vows and swearing,
Henceforth no credit give,
You may give them the hearing, —
But never them believe;
They are as false as fair,
Unconstant, frail, untrue;
For mine, alas! hath left me,
Falero, lero, loo.

'T was I that paid for all things,
'T was other drank the wine;
I cannot now recall things,
Live but a fool to pine:
'T was I that beat the bush,
The birds to others flew,
For she, alas! hath left me,
Falero, lero, loo.

If ever that Dame Nature,
For this false lover's sake,
Another pleasing creature
Like unto her would make;
Let her remember this,
To make the other true,
For this, alas! hath left me,
Falero, lero, loo.

No riches now can raise me,
No want make me despair,
No misery amaze me,
Nor yet for want I care;
I have lost a world itself,
My earthly heaven, adieu!
Since she, alas! hath left me,
Falero, lero, loo.

GEORGE WITHER.

WHY SO PALE AND WAN?

WHY so pale and wan, fond lover?
Prythee, why so pale?—
Will, when looking well can't move her,
Looking ill prevail?
Prythee, why so pale?

Why so dull and mute, young sinner?
Prythee, why so mute?
Will, when speaking well can't win her,
Saying nothing do 't?
Prythee, why so mute?

Quit, quit, for shame! this will not move,
This cannot take her:
If of herself she will not love,
Nothing can make her:
The devil take her!

SIR JOHN SUCKLING.

THE DISAPPOINTED LOVER.

I WILL go back to the great sweet mother,
Mother and lover of men, the sea.
I will go down to her, I and none other,
Close with her, kiss her, and mix her with me;
Cling to her, strive with her, hold her fast.
O fair white mother, in days long past
Born without sister, born without brother,
Set free my soul as thy soul is free.

O fair green-girdled mother of mine,
Sea, that art clothed with the sun and the rain,
Thy sweet hard kisses are strong like wine,
Thy large embraces are keen like pain!
Save me and hide me with all thy waves,
Find me one grave of thy thousand graves,
Those pure cold populous graves of thine,
Wrought without hand in a world without stain.

I shall sleep, and move with the moving ships,
Change as the winds change, veer in the tide;
My lips will feast on the foam of thy lips,
I shall rise with thy rising, with thee subside;
Sleep, and not know if she be, if she were,
Filled full with life to the eyes and hair,
As a rose is fulfilled to the rose-leaf tips
With splendid summer and perfume and pride.

This woven raiment of nights and days,
Were it once cast off and unwound from me,
Naked and glad would I walk in thy ways,
Alive and aware of thy waves and thee;
Clear of the whole world, hidden at home,
Clothed with the green, and crowned with the foam,
A pulse of the life of thy straits and bays,
A vein in the heart of the streams of the sea.

ALGERNON CHARLES SWINBURNE.

OUTGROWN.

NAY, you wrong her, my friend, she 's not fickle;
her love she has simply outgrown:
One can read the whole matter, translating her
heart by the light of one's own.

Can you bear me to talk with you frankly? There is much that my heart would say;
And you know we were children together, have quarreled and "made up" in play.

And so, for the sake of old friendship, I venture to tell you the truth, —
As plainly, perhaps, and as bluntly, as I might in our earlier youth.

Five summers ago, when you wooed her, you stood on the selfsame plane,
Face to face, heart to heart, never dreaming your souls could be parted again.

She loved you at that time entirely, in the bloom of her life's early May;
And it is not her fault, I repeat it, that she does not love you to-day.

Nature never stands still, nor souls either: they ever go up or go down;
And hers has been steadily soaring, — but how has it been with your own?

She has struggled and yearned and aspired, — grown purer and wiser each year:
The stars are not farther above you in yon luminous atmosphere!

For she whom you crowned with fresh roses, down yonder, five summers ago,
Has learned that the first of our duties to God and ourselves is to grow.

Her eyes they are sweeter and calmer; but their vision is clearer as well:
Her voice has a tenderer cadence, but is pure as a silver bell.

Her face has the look worn by those who with God and his angels have talked:
The white robes she wears are less white than the spirits with whom she has walked.

And you? Have you aimed at the highest? Have you, too, aspired and prayed?
Have you looked upon evil unsullied? Have you conquered it undismayed?

Have you, too, grown purer and wiser, as the months and the years have rolled on?
Did you meet her this morning rejoicing in the triumph of victory won?

Nay, hear me! The truth cannot harm you. When to-day in her presence you stood,
Was the hand that you gave her as white and clean as that of her womanhood?

Go measure yourself by her standard. Look back on the years that have fled;
Then ask, if you need, why she tells you that the love of her girlhood is dead!

She cannot look down to her lover: her love like her soul, aspires;
He must stand by her side, or above her, who would kindle its holy fires.

Now farewell! For the sake of old friendship I have ventured to tell you the truth,
As plainly, perhaps, and as bluntly, as I might in our earlier youth.

JULIA C. R. DORR.

ALAS! HOW LIGHT A CAUSE MAY MOVE—

FROM "THE LIGHT OF THE HAREM."

ALAS! how light a cause may move
Dissension between hearts that love! —
Hearts that the world in vain has tried,
And sorrow but more closely tied;
That stood the storm when waves were rough,
Yet in a sunny hour fall off,
Like ships that have gone down at sea,
When heaven was all tranquillity!

A something light as air, — a look,
A word unkind or wrongly taken, —
O, love that tempests never shook,
A breath, a touch like this has shaken!
And ruder words will soon rush in
To spread the breach that words begin;
And eyes forget the gentle ray
They wore in courtship's smiling day;
And voices lose the tone that shed
A tenderness round all they said;
Till fast declining, one by one,
The sweetnesses of love are gone,
And hearts, so lately mingled, seem
Like broken clouds, — or like the stream,
That smiling left the mountain's brow,
As though its waters ne'er could sever,
Yet, ere it reach the plain below,
Breaks into floods that part forever.

O you, that have the charge of Love,
Keep him in rosy bondage bound,
As in the Fields of Bliss above
He sits, with flowerets fettered round; —
Loose not a tie that round him clings,
Nor ever let him use his wings;
For even an hour, a minute's flight
Will rob the plumes of half their light.
Like that celestial bird, — whose nest
Is found beneath far Eastern skies, —
Whose wings, though radiant when at rest,
Lose all their glory when he flies!

THOMAS MOORE.

AUX ITALIENS.

At Paris it was, at the opera there ;
 And she looked like a queen in a book that night,
With the wreath of pearl in her raven hair,
 And the brooch on her breast so bright.

Of all the operas that Verdi wrote,
 The best, to my taste, is the Trovatore ;
And Mario can soothe, with a tenor note,
 The souls in purgatory.

The moon on the tower slept soft as snow ;
 And who was not thrilled in the strangest way,
As we heard him sing, while the gas burned low,
 "*Non ti scordar di me*" ?

The emperor there, in his box of state,
 Looked grave ; as if he had just then seen
The red flag wave from the city gate,
 Where his eagles in bronze had been.

The empress, too, had a tear in her eye :
 You 'd have said that her fancy had gone back again,
For one moment, under the old blue sky,
 To the old glad life in Spain.

Well ! there in our front-row box we sat
 Together, my bride betrothed and I ;
My gaze was fixed on my opera hat,
 And hers on the stage hard by.

And both were silent, and both were sad ;—
 Like a queen she leaned on her full white arm,
With that regal, indolent air she had ;
 So confident of her charm !

I have not a doubt she was thinking then
 Of her former lord, good soul that he was,
Who died the richest and roundest of men,
 The Marquis of Carabas.

I hope that, to get to the kingdom of heaven,
 Through a needle's eye he had not to pass ;
I wish him well for the jointure given
 To my lady of Carabas.

Meanwhile, I was thinking of my first love
 As I had not been thinking of aught for years ;
Till over my eyes there began to move
 Something that felt like tears.

I thought of the dress that she wore last time,
 When we stood 'neath the cypress-trees together,
In that lost land, in that soft clime,
 In the crimson evening weather ;

Of that muslin dress (for the eve was hot) ;
 And her warm white neck in its golden chain ;
And her full soft hair, just tied in a knot,
 And falling loose again ;

And the jasmine flower in her fair young breast ;
 (O the faint, sweet smell of that jasmine flower !)
And the one bird singing alone to his nest ;
 And the one star over the tower.

I thought of our little quarrels and strife,
 And the letter that brought me back my ring ;
And it all seemed then, in the waste of life,
 Such a very little thing !

For I thought of her grave below the hill,
 Which the sentinel cypress-tree stands over :
And I thought, "Were she only living still,
 How I could forgive her and love her !"

And I swear, as I thought of her thus, in that hour,
 And of how, after all, old things are best,
That I smelt the smell of that jasmine flower
 Which she used to wear in her breast.

It smelt so faint, and it smelt so sweet,
 It made me creep, and it made me cold !
Like the scent that steals from the crumbling sheet
 Where a mummy is half unrolled.

And I turned and looked : she was sitting there,
 In a dim box over the stage ; and drest
In that muslin dress, with that full soft hair,
 And that jasmine in her breast !

I was here, and she was there ;
 And the glittering horseshoe curved between !—
From my bride betrothed, with her raven hair
 And her sumptuous scornful mien,

To my early love with her eyes downcast,
 And over her primrose face the shade,
(In short, from the future back to the past,)
 There was but a step to be made.

To my early love from my future bride
 One moment I looked. Then I stole to the door,
I traversed the passage ; and down at her side
 I was sitting, a moment more.

My thinking of her, or the music's strain,
 Or something which never will be exprest,
Had brought her back from the grave again,
 With the jasmine in her breast.

She is not dead, and she is not wed !
 But she loves me now, and she loved me then !
And the very first word that her sweet lips said,
 My heart grew youthful again.

The marchioness there, of Carabas,
  She is wealthy, and young, and handsome still;
And but for her — well, we 'll let that pass;
  She may marry whomever she will.

But I will marry my own first love,
  With her primrose face, for old things are best;
And the flower in her bosom, I prize it above
  The brooch in my lady's breast.

The world is filled with folly and sin,
  And love must cling where it can, I say:
For beauty is easy enough to win;
  But one is n't loved every day.

And I think, in the lives of most women and men,
  There 's a moment when all would go smooth and even,
If only the dead could find out when
  To come back and be forgiven.

But O, the smell of that jasmine flower!
  And O, that music! and O, the way
That voice rang out from the donjon tower,
  Non ti scordar di me,
    Non ti scordar di me!

ROBERT BULWER LYTTON.

THE BELLE OF THE BALL.

YEARS, years ago, ere yet my dreams
  Had been of being wise or witty,
Ere I had done with writing themes,
  Or yawned o'er this infernal Chitty, —
Years, years ago, while all my joys
  Were in my fowling-piece and filly, —
In short, while I was yet a boy,
  I fell in love with Laura Lilly.

I saw her at the county ball;
  There, when the sounds of flute and fiddle
Gave signal sweet in that old hall
  Of hands across and down the middle,
Hers was the subtlest spell by far
  Of all that sets young hearts romancing:
She was our queen, our rose, our star;
  And then she danced, — O Heaven! her dancing!

Dark was her hair; her hand was white,
  Her voice was exquisitely tender;
Her eyes were full of liquid light;
  I never saw a waist so slender;
Her every look, her every smile,
  Shot right and left a score of arrows;
I thought 't was Venus from her isle,
  And wondered where she 'd left her sparrows.

She talked of politics or prayers,
  Of Southey's prose or Wordsworth's sonnets,
Of danglers or of dancing bears,
  Of battles or the last new bonnets;
By candlelight, at twelve o'clock —
  To me it mattered not a tittle —
If those bright lips had quoted Locke,
  I might have thought they murmured Little.

Through sunny May, through sultry June,
  I loved her with a love eternal;
I spoke her praises to the moon,
  I wrote them to the Sunday Journal.
My mother laughed; I soon found out
  That ancient ladies have no feeling:
My father frowned; but how should gout
  See any happiness in kneeling?

She was the daughter of a dean, —
  Rich, fat, and rather apoplectic;
She had one brother just thirteen,
  Whose color was extremely hectic;
Her grandmother, for many a year,
  Had fed the parish with her bounty;
Her second-cousin was a peer,
  And lord-lieutenant of the county.

But titles and the three-per-cents,
  And mortgages, and great relations,
And India bonds, and tithes and rents,
  O, what are they to love's sensations?
Black eyes, fair forehead, clustering locks, —
  Such wealth, such honors Cupid chooses;
He cares as little for the stocks
  As Baron Rothschild for the muses.

She sketched; the vale, the wood, the beach,
  Grew lovelier from her pencil's shading:
She botanized; I envied each
  Young blossom in her boudoir fading:
She warbled Handel; it was grand, —
  She made the Catalina jealous:
She touched the organ; I could stand
  For hours and hours to blow the bellows.

She kept an album too, at home,
  Well filled with all an album's glories, —
Paintings of butterflies and Rome,
  Patterns for trimmings, Persian stories,
Soft songs to Julia's cockatoo,
  Fierce odes to famine and to slaughter,
And autographs of Prince Leeboo,
  And recipes for elder-water.

And she was flattered, worshiped, bored;
  Her steps were watched, her dress was noted;
Her poodle-dog was quite adored;
  Her sayings were extremely quoted.

She laughed, — and every heart was glad,
As if the taxes were abolished;
She frowned, — and every look was sad,
As if the opera were demolished.

She smiled on many just for fun, —
I knew that there was nothing in it;
I was the first, the only one
Her heart had thought of for a minute.
I knew it, for she told me so,
In phrase which was divinely molded;
She wrote a charming hand, — and O,
How sweetly all her notes were folded!

Our love was like most other loves, —
A little glow, a little shiver,
A rosebud and a pair of gloves,
And "Fly Not Yet," upon the river;
Some jealousy of some one's heir,
Some hopes of dying broken-hearted;
A miniature, a lock of hair,
The usual vows, — and then we parted.

We parted: months and years rolled by;
We met again four summers after.
Our parting was all sob and sigh,
Our meeting was all mirth and laughter!
For in my heart's most secret cell
There had been many other lodgers;
And she was not the ball-room's belle,
But only Mrs. — Something — Rogers!

WINTHROP MACKWORTH PRAED.

CHANGES.

WHOM first we love, you know, we seldom wed.
Time rules us all. And life, indeed, is not
The thing we planned it out ere hope was dead.
And then, we women cannot choose our lot.

Much must be borne which it is hard to bear;
Much given away which it were sweet to keep.
God help us all! who need, indeed, his care:
And yet, I know the Shepherd loves his sheep.

My little boy begins to babble now
Upon my knee his earliest infant prayer.
He has his father's eager eyes, I know;
And, they say, too, his mother's sunny hair.

But when he sleeps and smiles upon my knee,
And I can feel his light breath come and go,
I think of one (Heaven help and pity me!)
Who loved me, and whom I loved, long ago;

Who might have been — ah, what I dare not think!
We are all changed. God judges for us best.
God help us do our duty, and not shrink,
And trust in Heaven humbly for the rest.

But blame us women not, if some appear
Too cold at times; and some too gay and light.
Some griefs gnaw deep. Some woes are hard to bear.
Who knows the past? and who can judge us right?

Ah, were we judged by what we might have been,
And not by what we are — too apt to fall!
My little child — he sleeps and smiles between
These thoughts and me. In heaven we shall know all!

ROBERT BULWER LYTTON.

"COME NOT, WHEN I AM DEAD."

FROM "THE PRINCESS."

COME not, when I am dead,
To drop thy foolish tears upon my grave,
To trample round my fallen head,
And vex the unhappy dust thou wouldst not save.
There let the wind sweep and the plover cry;
But thou, go by!

Child, if it were thine error or thy crime
I care no longer, being all unblest:
Wed whom thou wilt, but I am sick of Time,
And I desire to rest.
Pass on, weak heart, and leave me where I lie:
Go by, go by!

ALFRED TENNYSON.

TRANSIENT BEAUTY.

FROM "THE GIAOUR."

As, rising on its purple wing,
The insect-queen of Eastern spring,
O'er emerald meadows of Kashmeer,
Invites the young pursuer near,
And leads him on from flower to flower,
A weary chase and wasted hour,
Then leaves him, as it soars on high,
With panting heart and tearful eye;
So Beauty lures the full-grown child,
With hue as bright, and wing as wild;
A chase of idle hopes and fears,
Begun in folly, closed in tears.
If won, to equal ills betrayed,
Woe waits the insect and the maid:
A life of pain, the loss of peace,
From infant's play and man's caprice;
The lovely toy, so fiercely sought,
Hath lost its charm by being caught;
For every touch that wooed its stay
Hath brushed its brighest hues away,
Till, charm and hue and beauty gone,
'T is left to fly or fall alone.
With wounded wing or bleeding breast,
Ah! where shall either victim rest?

Can this with faded pinion soar
From rose to tulip as before?
Or Beauty, blighted in an hour,
Find joy within her broken bower?
No; gayer insects fluttering by
Ne'er droop the wing o'er those that die,
And lovelier things have mercy shown
To every failing but their own,
And every woe a tear can claim,
Except an erring sister's shame.

LORD BYRON.

WOMAN'S INCONSTANCY.

I LOVED thee once, I 'll love no more,
Thine be the grief as is the blame;
Thou art not what thou wast before,
What reason I should be the same?
He that can love unloved again,
Hath better store of love than brain:
God send me love my debts to pay,
While unthrifts fool their love away.

Nothing could have my love o'erthrown,
If thou hadst still continued mine;
Yea, if thou hadst remained thy own,
I might perchance have yet been thine.
But thou thy freedom did recall,
That if thou might elsewhere inthrall;
And then how could I but disdain
A captive's captive to remain?

When new desires had conquered thee,
And changed the object of thy will,
It had been lethargy in me,
Not constancy, to love thee still.
Yea, it had been a sin to go
And prostitute affection so,
Since we are taught no prayers to say
To such as must to others pray.

Yet do thou glory in thy choice,
Thy choice of his good fortune boast;
I 'll neither grieve nor yet rejoice,
To see him gain what I have lost;
The height of my disdain shall be,
To laugh at him, to blush for thee;
To love thee still, but go no more
A begging to a beggar's door.

SIR ROBERT AYTON.

THE TRUE AND THE FALSE.

WHERE shall the lover rest
Whom the fates sever
From his true maiden's breast,
Parted forever?
Where, through groves deep and high
Sounds the far billow,
Where early violets die
Under the willow.
Eleu loro
Soft shall be his pillow.

There, through the summer day,
Cool streams are laving:
There, while the tempests sway,
Scarce are boughs waving;
There thy rest shalt thou take,
Parted forever,
Never again to wake
Never, O never!
Eleu loro
Never, O never!

Where shall the traitor rest,
He, the deceiver,
Who could win maiden's breast,
Ruin, and leave her?
In the lost battle,
Borne down by the flying,
Where mingles war's rattle
With groans of the dying;
Eleu loro
There shall he be lying.

Her wing shall the eagle flap
O'er the false-hearted;
His warm blood the wolf shall lap
Ere life be parted:
Shame and dishonor sit
By his grave ever;
Blessing shall hallow it
Never, O never!
Eleu loro
Never, O never!

SIR WALTER SCOTT.

LADY ANN BOTHWELL'S LAMENT.

A SCOTTISH SONG.

BALOW, my babe, ly stil and sleipe!
It grieves me sair to see thee weipe;
If thou 'st be silent, I 'se be glad,
Thy maining maks my heart ful sad.
Balow, my boy, thy mither's joy!
Thy father breides me great annoy.
Balow, my babe, ly stil and sleipe!
It grieves me sair to see thee weipe.

When he began to court my luve,
And with his sugred words to muve,
His faynings fals, and flattering cheire,
To me that time did not appeire:

But now I see, most cruell hee,
Cares neither for my babe nor mee.
Balow, my babe, ly stil and sleipe!
It grieves me sair to see thee weipe.

Ly stil, my darlinge, sleipe awhile,
And when thou wakest sweitly smile:
But smile not, as thy father did,
To cozen maids; nay, God forbid!
But yette I feire, thou wilt gae neire,
Thy fatheris hart and face to beire.
Balow, my babe, ly stil and sleipe!
It grieves me sair to see the weipe.

I cannae chuse, but ever will
Be luving to thy father stil:
Whair-eir he gae, whair-eir he ryde,
My luve with him maun stil abyde:
In weil or wae, whair-eir he gae,
Mine hart can neir depart him frae.
Balow, my babe, ly stil and sleipe!
It grieves me sair to see thee weipe.

But doe not, doe not, prettie mine,
To faynings fals thine hart incline;
Be loyal to thy luver trew,
And nevir change hir for a new;
If gude or faire, of hir have care,
For women's banning 's wonderous sair.
Balow, my babe, ly stil and sleipe!
It grieves me sair to see thee weipe.

Bairne, sin thy cruel father 's gane,
Thy winsome smiles maun eise my paine;
My babe and I 'll together live,
He 'll comfort me when cares doe grieve;
My babe and I right saft will ly,
And quite forget man's cruelty.
Balow, my babe, ly stil and sleipe!
It grieves me sair to see thee weipe.

Fareweil, fareweil, thou falsest youth
That ever kist a woman's mouth!
I wish all maids be warned by mee,
Nevir to trust man's curtesy;
For if we doe but chance to bow,
They 'll use us than they care not how.
Balow, my babe, ly stil and sleipe!
It grieves me sair to see thee weipe.

ANONYMOUS.

MY HEID IS LIKE TO REND, WILLIE.

My heid is like to rend, Willie,
My heart is like to break;
I 'm wearin' aff my feet, Willie,
I 'm dyin' for your sake!

O, lay your cheek to mine, Willie,
Your hand on my briest-bane, —
O, say ye 'll think on me, Willie,
When I am deid and gane!

It 's vain to comfort me, Willie,
Sair grief maun ha'e its will;
But let me rest upon your briest
To sab and greet my fill.
Let me sit on your knee, Willie,
Let me shed by your hair,
And look into the face, Willie,
I never sall see mair!

I 'm sittin' on your knee, Willie,
For the last time in my life, —
A puir heart-broken thing, Willie,
A mither, yet nae wife.
Ay, press your hand upon my heart,
And press it mair and mair,
Or it will burst the silken twine,
Sae strang is its despair.

O, wae 's me for the hour, Willie,
When we thegither met, —
O, wae 's me for the time, Willie,
That our first tryst was set!
O, wae 's me for the loanin' green
Where we were wont to gae, —
And wae 's me for the destinie
That gart me luve thee sae!

O, dinna mind my words, Willie,
I downa seek to blame;
But O, it 's hard to live, Willie,
And dree a warld's shame!
Het tears are hailin' ower your cheek,
And hailin' ower your chin:
Why weep ye sae for worthlessness,
For sorrow, and for sin?

I 'm weary o' this warld, Willie,
And sick wi' a' I see,
I canna live as I ha'e lived,
Or be as I should be.
But fauld unto your heart, Willie,
The heart that still is thine,
And kiss ance mair the white, white cheek
Ye said was red langsyne.

A stoun' gaes through my heid, Willie,
A sair stoun' through my heart;
O, haud me up and let me kiss
Thy brow ere we twa pairt.
Anither, and anither yet! —
How fast my life-strings break! —
Fareweel! fareweel! through yon kirk-yard
Step lichtly for my sake!

The lav'rock in the lift, Willie,
  That lilts far ower our heid,
Will sing the morn as merrilie
  Abune the clay-cauld deid;
And this green turf we 're sittin' on,
  Wi' dew-draps shimmerin' sheen,
Will hap the heart that luvit thee
  As warld has seldom seen.

But O, remember me, Willie,
  On land where'er ye be;
And O, think on the leal, leal heart,
  That ne'er luvit ane but thee!
And O, think on the cauld, cauld mools
  That file my yellow hair,
That kiss the cheek, and kiss the chin
  Ye never sall kiss mair!

WILLIAM MOTHERWELL.

MARIANA.

WITH blackest moss the flower-plots
  Were thickly crusted, one and all,
The rusted nails fell from the knots
  That held the peach to the garden-wall.
The broken sheds looked sad and strange,
  Unlifted was the clinking latch,
  Weeded and worn the ancient thatch
Upon the lonely moated grange.
    She only said, "My life is dreary,
      He cometh not," she said;
    She said, "I am aweary, aweary;
      I would that I were dead!"

Her tears fell with the dews at even;
  Her tears fell ere the dews were dried;
She could not look on the sweet heaven,
  Either at morn or eventide.
After the flitting of the bats,
  When thickest dark did trance the sky,
  She drew her casement-curtain by,
And glanced athwart the glooming flats.
    She only said, "The night is dreary,
      He cometh not," she said;
    She said, "I am aweary, aweary,
      I would that I were dead!"

Upon the middle of the night,
  Waking she heard the night-fowl crow;
The cock sung out an hour ere light:
  From the dark fen the oxen's low
Came to her: without hope of change,
  In sleep she seemed to walk forlorn,
  Till cold winds woke the gray-eyed morn
About the lonely moated grange.
    She only said, "The day is dreary,
      He cometh not," she said;
    She said, "I am aweary, aweary,
      And I would that I were dead!"

About a stone-cast from the wall
  A sluice with blackened waters slept,
And o'er it many, round and small,
  The clustered marish-mosses crept.
Hard by a poplar shook alway,
  All silver green with gnarlèd bark,
  For leagues no other tree did dark
The level waste, the rounding gray.
    She only said, "My life is dreary,
      He cometh not," she said;
    She said, "I am aweary, aweary,
      I would that I were dead!"

And ever when the moon was low,
  And the shrill winds were up and away,
In the white curtain, to and fro,
  She saw the gusty shadow sway.
But when the moon was very low,
  And wild winds bound within their cell,
  The shadow of the poplar fell
Upon her bed, across her brow.
    She only said, "The night is dreary,
      He cometh not," she said;
    She said, "I am aweary, aweary,
      I would that I were dead!"

All day within the dreamy house,
  The doors upon their hinges creaked,
The blue fly sung i' the pane; the mouse
  Behind the moldering wainscot shrieked,
Or from the crevice peered about.
  Old faces glimmered through the doors,
  Old footsteps trod the upper floors,
Old voices called her from without.
    She only said, "My life is dreary,
      He cometh not," she said;
    She said, "I am aweary, aweary,
      I would that I were dead!"

The sparrow's chirrup on the roof,
  The slow clock ticking, and the sound
Which to the wooing wind aloof
  The poplar made, did all confound
Her sense; but most she loathed the hour
  When the thick-moted sunbeam lay
  Athwart the chambers, and the day
Was sloping toward his western bower.
    Then, said she, "I am very dreary,
      He will not come," she said;
    She wept, "I am aweary, aweary,
      O God, that I were dead!"

ALFRED TENNYSON.

A WOMAN'S LOVE.

A SENTINEL angel, sitting high in glory,
Heard this shrill wail ring out from Purgatory:
"Have mercy, mighty angel, hear my story!

"I loved, — and, blind with passionate love, I fell.
Love brought me down to death, and death to Hell;
For God is just, and death for sin is well.

"I do not rage against his high decree,
Nor for myself do ask that grace shall be;
But for my love on earth who mourns for me.

"Great Spirit! Let me see my love again
And comfort him one hour, and I were fain
To pay a thousand years of fire and pain."

Then said the pitying angel, "Nay, repent
That wild vow! Look, the dial-finger 's bent
Down to the last hour of thy punishment!"

But still she wailed, "I pray thee, let me go!
I cannot rise to peace and leave him so.
O, let me soothe him in his bitter woe!"

The brazen gates ground sullenly ajar,
And upward, joyous, like a rising star,
She rose and vanished in the ether far.

But soon adown the dying sunset sailing,
And like a wounded bird her pinions trailing,
She fluttered back, with broken-hearted wailing.

She sobbed, "I found him by the summer sea
Reclined, his head upon a maiden's knee, —
She curled his hair and kissed him. Woe is me!"

She wept, "Now let my punishment begin!
I have been fond and foolish. Let me in
To expiate my sorrow and my sin."

The angel answered, "Nay, sad soul, go higher!
To be deceived in your true heart's desire
Was bitterer than a thousand years of fire!"

JOHN HAY.

DEATH AND THE YOUTH.

"NOT yet, the flowers are in my path,
The sun is in the sky;
Not yet, my heart is full of hope,
I cannot bear to die.

"Not yet, I never knew till now
How precious life could be;
My heart is full of love, O Death!
I cannot come with thee!"

But Love and Hope, enchanted twain,
Passed in their falsehood by;
Death came again, and then he said,
"I 'm ready now to die!"

LETITIA E. LANDON.

Poems of Sorrow and Death

One year, one year, one little year
And so much gone
And yet the even flow of life
Moves calmly on :

H B Stowe

Hark! to the tolling bells
In echoes deep and slow,
While on the breeze our banner floats
Draped in the weeds of woe.

L. Huntley Sigourney.

POEMS OF SORROW AND DEATH.

SORROW AND ADVERSITY.

RETROSPECTION.

FROM "THE PRINCESS."

TEARS, idle tears, I know not what they mean,
Tears from the depth of some divine despair
Rise in the heart, and gather to the eyes,
In looking on the happy autumn fields,
And thinking of the days that are no more.

Fresh as the first beam glittering on a sail,
That brings our friends up from the under world;
Sad as the last which reddens over one
That sinks with all we love below the verge, —
So sad, so fresh, the days that are no more.

Ah, sad and strange as in dark summer dawns
The earliest pipe of half-awakened birds
To dying ears, when unto dying eyes
The casement slowly grows a glimmering square;
So sad, so strange, the days that are no more.

Dear as remembered kisses after death,
And sweet as those by hopeless fancy feigned
On lips that are for others; deep as love,
Deep as first love, and wild with all regret, —
O Death in Life, the days that are no more.

ALFRED TENNYSON.

BREAK, BREAK, BREAK.

BREAK, break, break,
On thy cold gray stones, O sea!
And I would that my tongue could utter
The thoughts that arise in me.

O well for the fisherman's boy
That he shouts with his sister at play!
O well for the sailor lad
That he sings in his boat on the bay!

And the stately ships go on,
To the haven under the hill;
But O for the touch of a vanished hand,
And the sound of a voice that is still!

Break, break, break,
At the foot of thy crags, O sea!
But the tender grace of a day that is dead
Will never come back to me.

ALFRED TENNYSON.

MOAN, MOAN, YE DYING GALES.

MOAN, moan, ye dying gales!
The saddest of your tales
Is not so sad as life;
Nor have you e'er began
A theme so wild as man,
Or with such sorrow rife.

Fall, fall, thou withered leaf!
Autumn sears not like grief,
Nor kills such lovely flowers;
More terrible the storm,
More mournful the deform,
When dark misfortune lowers.

Hush! hush! thou trembling lyre,
Silence, ye vocal choir,
And thou, mellifluous lute,
For man soon breathes his last,
And all his hope is past,
And all his music mute.

Then, when the gale is sighing,
And when the leaves are dying,
And when the song is o'er,
O, let us think of those
Whose lives are lost in woes,
Whose cup of grief runs o'er.

HENRY NEELE.

HENCE, ALL YE VAIN DELIGHTS.

HENCE, all ye vain delights,
As short as are the nights
Wherein you spend your folly!
There 's naught in this life sweet,
If man were wise to see 't
But only melancholy,
O, sweetest melancholy!

Welcome, folded arms, and fixèd eyes,
A sigh that piercing mortifies,
A look that 's fastened to the ground,
A tongue chained up without a sound!

Fountain-heads and pathless groves,
Places which pale passion loves!
Moonlight walks, when all the fowls
Are warmly housed save bats and owls!
A midnight bell, a parting groan!
These are the sounds we feed upon;
Then stretch our bones in a still gloomy valley:
Nothing 's so dainty sweet as lovely melancholy.

BEAUMONT and FLETCHER.

BLOW, BLOW, THOU WINTER WIND.

FROM "AS YOU LIKE IT."

Blow, blow, thou winter wind,
Thou art not so unkind
As man's ingratitude;
Thy tooth is not so keen,
Because thou art not seen,
Although thy breath be rude.
Heigh-ho! sing heigh-ho! unto the green holly;
Most friendship is feigning, most loving mere folly:
Then, heigh-ho, the holly!
This life is most jolly!

Freeze, freeze, thou bitter sky,
Thou dost not bite so nigh
As benefits forgot:
Though thou the waters warp,
Thy sting is not so sharp
As friend remembered not.
Heigh-ho! sing heigh-ho! unto the green holly:
Most friendship is feigning, most loving mere folly:
Then, heigh-ho, the holly!
This life is most jolly!

SHAKESPEARE.

ODE TO A NIGHTINGALE.

[Written in the spring of 1819, when suffering from physical depression, the precursor of his death, which happened soon after.]

My heart aches, and a drowsy numbness pains
My sense, as though of hemlock I had drunk,
Or emptied some dull opiate to the drains
One minute past, and Lethe-ward had sunk.
'T is not through envy of thy happy lot,
But being too happy in thy happiness,
That thou, light-wingèd Dryad of the trees,
In some melodious plot
Of beechen green, and shadows numberless,
Singest of Summer in full-throated ease.

O for a draught of vintage
Cooled a long age in the deep-delvèd earth,
Tasting of Flora and the country green,
Dance, and Provençal song, and sunburnt mirth!
O for a beaker full of the warm South,
Full of the true, the blushful Hippocrene,
With beaded bubbles winking at the brim,
And purple-stainèd mouth,—
That I might drink, and leave the world unseen,
And with thee fade away into the forest dim;

Fade far away, dissolve, and quite forget
What thou among the leaves hast never known,
The weariness, the fever, and the fret,
Here, where men sit and hear each other groan;
Where palsy shakes a few sad, last gray hairs;
Where youth grows pale, and specter-thin, and dies;
Where but to think is to be full of sorrow
And leaden-eyed despairs;
Where Beauty cannot keep her lustrous eyes,
Or new Love pine at them beyond to-morrow.

Away! away! for I will fly to thee,
Not charioted by Bacchus and his pards,
But on the viewless wings of Poesy,
Though the dull brain perplexes and retards:
Already with thee! tender is the night,
And haply the queen-moon is on her throne,
Clustered around by all her starry fays;
But here there is no light,
Save what from heaven is with the breezes blown
Through verdurous glooms and winding mossy ways.

I cannot see what flowers are at my feet,
Nor what soft incense hangs upon the boughs;
But, in embalmèd darkness guess each sweet
Wherewith the seasonable month endows
The grass, the thicket, and the fruit-tree wild,
White hawthorn and the pastoral eglantine;
Fast-fading violets, covered up in leaves;
And mid-May's eldest child,
The coming musk-rose, full of dewy wine,
The murmurous haunt of flies on summer eves.

Darkling I listen; and for many a time
I have been half in love with easeful Death,
Called him soft names in many a musèd rhyme,
To take into the air my quiet breath;
Now, more than ever, seems it rich to die,
To cease upon the midnight, with no pain,
While thou art pouring forth thy soul abroad
In such an ecstasy!
Still wouldst thou sing, and I have ears in vain,—
To thy high requiem become a sod.

Thou wast not born for death, immortal bird!
No hungry generations tread thee down;

The voice I hear this passing night was heard
In ancient days by emperor and clown:
Perhaps the selfsame song that found a path
Through the sad heart of Ruth, when, sick for home,
She stood in tears amid the alien corn;
The same that ofttimes hath
Charmed magic casements opening on the foam
Of perilous seas, in faery lands forlorn.

Forlorn! the very word is like a bell,
To toll me back from thee to my sole self!
Adieu! the Fancy cannot cheat so well
As she is famed to do, deceiving elf.
Adieu! adieu! thy plaintive anthem fades
Past the near meadows, over the still stream,
Up the hillside; and now 't is buried deep
In the next valley-glades:
Was it a vision or a waking dream?
Fled is that music, — do I wake or sleep?

JOHN KEATS.

ROSALIE.

O, POUR upon my soul again
That sad, unearthly strain
That seems from other worlds to 'plain!
Thus falling, falling from afar,
As if some melancholy star
Had mingled with her light her sighs,
And dropped them from the skies.

No, never came from aught below
This melody of woe,
That makes my heart to overflow,
As from a thousand gushing springs
Unknown before; that with it brings
This nameless light — if light it be —
That veils the world I see.

For all I see around me wears
The hue of other spheres;
And something blent of smiles and tears
Comes from the very air I breathe.
O, nothing, sure, the stars beneath,
Can mould a sadness like to this, —
So like angelic bliss!

So, at that dreamy hour of day,
When the last lingering ray
Stops on the highest cloud to play, —
So thought the gentle Rosalie
As on her maiden revery
First fell the strain of him who stole
In music to her soul.

WASHINGTON ALLSTON.

OFT IN THE STILLY NIGHT.

OFT in the stilly night,
Ere slumber's chain has bound me,
Fond Memory brings the light
Of other days around me:
The smiles, the tears,
Of boyhood's years,
The words of love then spoken;
The eyes that shone,
Now dimmed and gone,
The cheerful hearts now broken.
Thus in the stilly night,
Ere slumber's chain has bound me,
Sad Memory brings the light
Of other days around me.

When I remember all
The friends so linked together
I 've seen around me fall,
Like leaves in wintry weather,
I feel like one
Who treads alone
Some banquet-hall deserted,
Whose lights are fled,
Whose garlands dead,
And all but he departed.
Thus in the stilly night,
Ere slumber's chain has bound me,
Sad Memory brings the light
Of other days around me.

THOMAS MOORE.

THOSE EVENING BELLS.

THOSE evening bells! those evening bells!
How many a tale their music tells
Of youth, and home, and that sweet time
When last I heard their soothing chime!

Those joyous hours are passed away;
And many a heart that then was gay
Within the tomb now darkly dwells,
And hears no more those evening bells.

And so 't will be when I am gone, —
That tuneful peal will still ring on;
While other bards shall walk these dells,
And sing your praise, sweet evening bells.

THOMAS MOORE.

THE SUN IS WARM, THE SKY IS CLEAR.

STANZAS WRITTEN IN DEJECTION NEAR NAPLES.

THE sun is warm, the sky is clear,
The waves are dancing fast and bright,
Blue isles and snowy mountains wear
The purple noon's transparent light:

The breath of the moist air is light
Around its unexpanded buds;
Like many a voice of one delight, —
The winds', the birds', the ocean-floods', —
The City's voice itself is soft like Solitude's.

I see the Deep's untrampled floor
With green and purple sea-weeds strown;
I see the waves upon the shore
Like light dissolved in star-showers thrown:
I sit upon the sands alone;
The lightning of the noontide ocean
Is flashing round me, and a tone
Arises from its measured motion, —
How sweet, did any heart now share in my emotion!

Alas! I have nor hope nor health,
Nor peace within nor calm around,
Nor that Content surpassing wealth
The sage in meditation found,
And walked with inward glory crowned, —
Nor fame, nor power, nor love, nor leisure.
Others I see whom these surround;
Smiling they live, and call life pleasure;
To me that cup has been dealt in another measure.

Yet now despair itself is mild
Even as the winds and waters are;
I could lie down like a tired child,
And weep away the life of care
Which I have borne, and yet must bear,
Till death like sleep might steal on me,
And I might feel in the warm air
My cheek grow cold, and hear the sea
Breathe o'er my dying brain its last monotony.

PERCY BYSSHE SHELLEY.

MY SHIP.

DOWN to the wharves, as the sun goes down,
And the daylight's tumult and dust and din
Are dying away in the busy town,
I go to see if my ship comes in.

I gaze far over the quiet sea,
Rosy with sunset, like mellow wine,
Where ships, like lilies, lie tranquilly,
Many and fair, — but I see not mine.

I question the sailors every night
Who over the bulwarks idly lean,
Noting the sails as they come in sight, —
"Have you seen my beautiful ship come in?"

"Whence does she come?" they ask of me;
"Who is her master, and what her name?"
And they smile upon me pityingly
When my answer is ever and ever the same.

O, mine was a vessel of strength and truth,
Her sails were white as a young lamb's fleece,
She sailed long since from the port of Youth, —
Her master was Love, and her name was Peace.

And like all beloved and beauteous things,
She faded in distance and doubt away, —
With only a tremble of snowy wings
She floated, swan-like, adown the bay,

Carrying with her a precious freight, —
All I had gathered by years of pain;
A tempting prize to the pirate, Fate, —
And still I watch for her back again; —

Watch from the earliest morning light
Till the pale stars grieve o'er the dying day,
To catch the gleam of her canvas white
Among the islands which gem the bay.

But she comes not yet, — she will never come
To gladden my eyes and my spirit more;
And my heart grows hopeless and faint and dumb,
As I wait and wait on the lonesome shore,

Knowing that tempest and time and storm
Have wrecked and shattered my beauteous bark;
Rank sea-weeds cover her wasting form,
And her sails are tattered and stained and dark.

But the tide comes up, and the tide goes down,
And the daylight follows the night's eclipse, —
And still with the sailors, tanned and brown,
I wait on the wharves and watch the ships.

And still with a patience that is not hope,
For vain and empty it long hath been,
I sit on the rough shore's rocky slope,
And watch to see if my ship comes in.

ELIZABETH AKERS ALLEN
(FLORENCE PERCY).

AFAR IN THE DESERT.

AFAR in the desert I love to ride,
With the silent Bush-boy alone by my side:
When the sorrows of life the soul o'ercast,
And, sick of the present, I cling to the past;
When the eye is suffused with regretful tears,
From the fond recollections of former years;
And shadows of things that have long since fled
Flit over the brain, like the ghosts of the dead, —
Bright visions of glory that vanished too soon;
Day-dreams, that departed ere manhood's noon;
Attachments by fate or falsehood reft;
Companions of early days lost or left;
And my native land, whose magical name
Thrills to the heart like electric flame;

The home of my childhood; the haunts of my prime;
All the passions and scenes of that rapturous time
When the feelings were young, and the world was new,
Like the fresh bowers of Eden unfolding to view;
All, all now forsaken, forgotten, foregone!
And I, a lone exile remembered of none,
My high aims abandoned, my good acts undone,
Aweary of all that is under the sun, —
With that sadness of heart which no stranger may scan,
I fly to the desert afar from man.

Afar in the desert I love to ride,
With the silent Bush-boy alone by my side!
When the wild turmoil of this wearisome life,
With its scenes of oppression, corruption, and strife,
The proud man's frown, and the base man's fear,
The scorner's laugh, and the sufferer's tear,
And malice, and meanness, and falsehood, and folly,
Dispose me to musing and dark melancholy;
When my bosom is full, and my thoughts are high,
And my soul is sick with the bondman's sigh,—
O, then there is feeedom, and joy, and pride,
Afar in the desert alone to ride!
There is rapture to vault on the champing steed,
And to bound away with the eagle's speed,
With the death-fraught firelock in my hand, —
The only law of the Desert Land!

Afar in the desert I love to ride,
With the silent Bush-boy alone by my side,
Away, away from the dwellings of men,
By the wild deer's haunt, by the buffalo's glen;
By valleys remote where the oribi plays,
Where the gnu, the gazelle, and the hartèbeest graze,
And the kudu and eland unhunted recline
By the skirts of gray forest o'erhung with wild vine;
Where the elephant browses at peace in his wood,
And the river-horse gambols unscared in the flood,
And the mighty rhinoceros wallows at will
In the fen where the wild ass is drinking his fill.

Afar in the desert I love ro ride,
With the silent Bush-boy alone by my side,
O'er the brown karroo, where the bleating cry
Of the springbok's fawn sounds plaintively;
And the timorous quagga's shrill whistling neigh
Is heard by the fountain at twilight gray;
Where the zebra wantonly tosses his mane,
With wild hoof scouring the desolate plain;
And the fleet-footed ostrich over the waste
Speeds like a horseman who travels in haste,
Hieing away to the home of her rest,
Where she and her mate have scooped their nest,
Far hid from the pitiless plunderer's view
In the pathless depths of the parched karroo.

Afar in the desert I love to ride,
With the silent Bush-boy alone by my side,
Away, away, in the wilderness vast
Where the white man's foot hath never passed,
And the quivered Coranna or Bechuan
Hath rarely crossed with his roving clan, —
A region of emptiness, howling and drear,
Which man hath abandoned from famine and fear;
Which the snake and the lizard inhabit alone,
With the twilight bat from the yawning stone;
Where grass, nor herb, nor shrub takes root,
Save poisonous thorns that pierce the foot;
And the bitter-melon, for food and drink,
Is the pilgrim's fare by the salt lake's brink;
A region of drought, where no river glides,
Nor rippling brook with osiered sides;
Where sedgy pool, nor bubbling fount,
Nor tree, nor cloud, nor misty mount,
Appears, to refresh the aching eye;
But the barren earth and the burning sky,
And the blank horizon, round and round,
Spread, — void of living sight or sound.
And here, while the night-winds round me sigh,
And the stars burn bright in the midnight sky,
As I sit apart by the desert stone,
Like Elijah at Horeb's cave, alone,
"A still small voice" comes through the wild
(Like a father consoling his fretful child),
Which banishes bitterness, wrath, and fear,
Saying, — Man is distant, but God is near!

THOMAS PRINGLE.

MAJESTY IN MISERY;

OR, AN IMPLORATION TO THE KING OF KINGS.

Great Monarch of the World, from whose Power Springs
The Potency and Power of Kings,
Record the Royal Woe my Suffering sings;

And teach my tongue, that ever did confine
Its faculties in Truth's Seraphic Line,
To track the Treasons of thy foes and mine.

Nature and law, by thy Divine Decree
(The only Root of Righteous Royaltie)
With this dim Diadem invested me:

With it the sacred Scepter, Purple Robe,
The Holy Unction, and the Royal Globe:
Yet am I levelled with the life of Job.

The fiercest Furies, that do daily tread
Upon my Grief, my Gray Dis-crownèd Head,
Are those that owe my Bounty for their Bread.

They raise a War, and Christen it *The Cause*,
Whilst sacrilegious hands have best applause,
Plunder and Murder are the Kingdom's Laws;

Tyranny bears the Title of *Taxation*,
Revenge and Robbery are *Reformation*,
Oppression gains the name of *Sequestration*.

My loyal Subjects, who in this bad season
Attend me (by the law of God and Reason),
They dare impeach and punish for High Treason.

Next at the Clergy do their Furies frown;
Pious Episcopacy must go down;
They will destroy the Crosier and the Crown.

Churchmen are chained and Schismaticks are free'd,
Mechanicks preach, and Holy Fathers bleed,
The Crown is crucifièd with the Creed.

The Church of England doth all factions foster,
The pulpit is usurped by each imposter,
Extempore excludes the *Pater Noster*.

The *Presbyter* and *Independent* seed
Springs with broad blades; to make Religion bleed,
Herod and Pontius Pilate are agreed.

The corner-stone 's misplaced by every Pavier:
With such a bloody method and behaviour
Their Ancestors did crucify our Saviour.

My Royal Consort, from whose fruitful Womb
So many Princes legally have come,
Is forced in Pilgrimage to seek a Tomb.

Great Britain's Heir is forcèd into France,
Whilst on his father's head his foes advance:
Poor child! He weeps at his Inheritance.

With my own Power my Majesty they wound
In the King's name the King himself 's uncrowned:
So doth the Dust destroy the Diamond.

With Propositions daily they enchant
My People's ears, such as do reason daunt,
And the Almighty will not let me grant.

They promise to erect my Royal Stem,
To make Me great, t' advance my Diadem,
If I will first fall down, and worship them.

But, for refusal, they devour my Thrones,
Distress my Children, and destroy my bones;
I fear they 'll force me to make bread of stones.

My Life they prize at such a slender rate
That in my absence they draw Bills of hate,
To prove the King a Traytor to the State.

Felons obtain more priviledge than I:
They are allowed to answer ere they die;
'T is death for me to ask the reason Why.

But, Sacred Saviour, with thy words I woo
Thee to forgive, and not be bitter to
Such as thou know'st do not know what they do.

For since they from their Lord are so disjointed
As to contemn those Edicts he appointed,
How can they prize the Power of his Anointed?

Augment my Patience, nullifie my Hate,
Preserve my Issue, and inspire my Mate:
Yet, though We perish, bless this Church and State.

CHARLES THE FIRST.

UNDER THE CROSS.

I CANNOT, cannot say,
Out of my bruised and breaking heart,
Storm-driven along a thorn-set way,
While blood-drops start
From every pore, as I drag on,
"Thy will, O God, be done!"

I thought, but yesterday,
My will was one with God's dear will;
And that it would be sweet to say,
Whatever ill
My happy state should smite upon,
"Thy will, my God, be done!"

But I was weak and wrong,
Both weak of soul and wrong of heart;
And Pride alone in me was strong,
With cunning art
To cheat me in the golden sun,
To say "God's will be done!"

O shadow drear and cold,
That frights me out of foolish pride;
O flood, that through my bosom rolled
Its billowy tide;
I said, till ye your power made known,
"God's will, not mine, be done!"

* Written during his captivity at Carisbrook castle, Anno Dom. 1648.

Jo. Milton

J. B. FORD & Co. NEW YORK

Now, faint and sore afraid,
Under my cross, heavy and rude,
My idols in the ashes laid,
Like ashes strewed,
The holy words my pale lips shun,
"O God, thy will be done!"

Pity my woes, O God,
And touch my will with thy warm breath;
Put in my trembling hand thy rod,
That quickens death;
That my dead faith may feel thy sun,
And say, "Thy will be done!"

WILLIAM CAREY RICHARDS.

LOVE NOT.

LOVE not, love not, ye hapless sons of clay!
Hope's gayest wreaths are made of earthly flowers, —
Things that are made to fade and fall away
Ere they have blossomed for a few short hours.
Love not!

Love not! the thing ye love may change;
The rosy lip may cease to smile on you,
The kindly-beaming eye grow cold and strange,
The heart still warmly beat, yet not be true.
Love not!

Love not! the thing you love may die, —
May perish from the gay and gladsome earth;
The silent stars, the blue and smiling sky,
Beam o'er its grave, as once upon its birth.
Love not!

Love not! O warning vainly said
In present hours as in years gone by!
Love flings a halo round the dear ones' head,
Faultless, immortal, till they change or die.
Love not!

CAROLINE E. NORTON.

SAMSON AGONISTES.

SAMSON.

A LITTLE onward lend thy guiding hand
To these dark steps, a little farther on;
For yonder bank hath choice of sun or shade:
There I am wont to sit, when any chance
Relieves me from my task of servile toil,
Daily in the common prison else enjoined me,
Where I a prisoner, chained, scarce freely draw
The air imprisoned also, close and damp,
Unwholesome draught; but here I feel amends,
The breath of heaven fresh blowing, pure and sweet,
With day-spring born: here leave me to respire.
This day a solemn feast the people hold
To Dagon, their sea-idol, and forbid
Laborious works: unwillingly this rest
Their superstition yields me; hence with leave
Retiring from the popular noise, I seek
This unfrequented place to find some ease, —
Ease to the body some, none to the mind
From restless thoughts, that, like a deadly swarm
Of hornets armed, no sooner found alone,
But rush upon me thronging, and present
Times past, what once I was, and what am now.
O, wherefore was my birth from Heaven foretold
Twice by an angel, who at last in sight
Of both my parents all in flames ascended
From off the altar, where an offering burned,
As in a fiery column, charioting
His godlike presence, and from some great act
Or benefit revealed to Abraham's race?
Why was my breeding ordered and prescribed
As of a person separate to God,
Designed for great exploits, if I must die
Betrayed, captived, and both my eyes put out,
Made of my enemies the scorn and gaze;
To grind in brazen fetters under task
With this Heaven-gifted strength? O glorious strength,
Put to the labor of a beast, debased
Lower than bondslave! Promise was that I
Should Israel from Philistian yoke deliver;
Ask for this great deliverer now, and find him
Eyeless in Gaza, at the mill with slaves,
Himself in bonds under Philistian yoke!

. . . . .

O loss of sight, of thee I most complain!
Blind among enemies, O, worse than chains,
Dungeon, or beggary, or decrepit age!
Light, the prime work of God, to me is extinct,
And all her various objects of delight
Annulled, which might in part my grief have eased.
Inferior to the vilest now become
Of man or worm; the vilest here excel me:
They creep, yet see; I, dark in light, exposed
To daily fraud, contempt, abuse, and wrong,
Within doors or without, still as a fool,
In power of others, never in my own;
Scarce half I seem to live, dead more than half.
O dark, dark, dark, amid the blaze of noon,
Irrecoverably dark, total eclipse,
Without all hope of day!

MILTON.

SELECTIONS FROM "PARADISE LOST."

EVE'S LAMENT.

O UNEXPECTED stroke, worse than of death!
Must I thus leave thee, Paradise? thus leave
Thee, native soil! these happy walks and shades,
Fit haunt of gods; where I had hope to spend,

Quiet, though sad, the respite of that day
That must be mortal to us both? O flowers,
That never will in other climate grow,
My early visitation, and my last
At even, which I bred up with tender hand
From the first opening bud, and gave ye names!
Who now shall rear ye to the sun, or rank
Your tribes, and water from the ambrosial fount?
Thee, lastly, nuptial bower! by me adorned
With what to sight or smell was sweet, from thee
How shall I part, and whither wander down
Into a lower world, to this obscure
And wild? how shall we breathe in other air
Less pure, accustomed to immortal fruits?

THE EXILE FROM PARADISE.

ADAM TO MICHAEL.

GENTLY hast thou told
Thy message, which might else in telling wound,
And in performing end us. What besides
Of sorrow, and dejection, and despair
Our frailty can sustain, thy tidings bring;
Departure from this happy place, our sweet
Recess, and only consolation left,
Familiar to our eyes, all places else
Inhospitable appear and desolate,
Nor knowing us nor known; and if by prayer
Incessant I could hope to change the will
Of Him who all things can, I would not cease
To weary him with my assiduous cries.
But prayer against his absolute decree
No more avails than breath against the wind,
Blown stifling back on him that breathes it forth;
Therefore to his great bidding I submit.
This most afflicts me, that, departing hence,
As from his face I shall be hid, deprived
His blessèd countenance, here I could frequent
With worship place by place where he vouchsafed
Presence divine, and to my sons relate,
On this mount he appeared; under this tree
Stood visible; among these pines his voice
I heard; here with him at this fountain talked:
So many grateful altars I would rear
Of grassy turf, and pile up every stone
Of luster from the brook, in memory
Or monument to ages, and thereon
Offer sweet-smelling gums, and fruits, and flowers.
In yonder nether world where shall I seek
His bright appearances, or footstep trace?
For though I fled him angry, yet, recalled
To life prolonged and promised race, I now
Gladly behold though but his utmost skirts
Of glory, and far off his steps adore.

. . . . . .

Henceforth I learn that to obey is best,
And love with fear the only God, to walk
As in his presence, ever to observe
His providence, and on him sole depend,
Merciful over all his works, with good
Still overcoming evil, and by small
Accomplishing great things, by things deemed
weak
Subverting worldly strong, and worldly wise
By simply meek; that suffering for truth's sake
Is fortitude to highest victory,
And to the faithful death the gate of life:
Taught this by his example, whom I now
Acknowledge my Redeemer ever blest.

EVE TO ADAM.

WITH sorrow and heart's distress
Wearied, I fell asleep. But now lead on;
In me is no delay; with thee to go,
Is to stay here; without thee here to stay,
Is to go hence unwilling; thou to me
Art all things under heaven, all places thou,
Who for my wilful crime art banished hence.
This further consolation, yet secure,
I carry hence; though all by me is lost,
Such favor I unworthy am vouchsafed,
By me the promised Seed shall all restore.

THE DEPARTURE.

IN either hand the hastening angel caught
Our lingering parents, and to the eastern gate
Led them direct, and down the cliff as fast
To the subjected plain; then disappeared.
They, looking back, all the eastern side beheld
Of Paradise, so late their happy seat,
Waved over by that flaming brand; the gate
With dreadful faces thronged and fiery arms.
Some natural tears they dropt, but wiped them
soon;
The world was all before them, where to choose
Their place of rest, and Providence their guide.
They, hand in hand, with wandering steps and
slow,
Through Eden took their solitary way.

MILTON.

WOOLSEY'S FALL.

FROM "HENRY VIII."

FAREWELL, a long farewell, to all my greatness!
This is the state of man: to-day he puts forth
The tender leaves of hope; to-morrow blossoms,
And bears his blushing honors thick upon him:
The third day comes a frost, a killing frost;
And — when he thinks, good easy man, full surely
His greatness is a ripening — nips his root,
And then he falls, as I do. I have ventured,
Like little wanton boys that swim on bladders,
This many summers in a sea of glory;
But far beyond my depth: my high-blown pride

At length broke under me; and now has left me,
Weary and old with service, to the mercy
Of a rude stream, that must forever hide me.
Vain pomp and glory of this world, I hate ye:
I feel my heart new opened. O, how wretched
Is that poor man that hangs on princes' favors!
There is, betwixt that smile we would aspire to,
That sweet aspéct of princes, and their ruin,
More pangs and fears than wars or women have:
And when he falls, he falls like Lucifer,
Never to hope again.

SHAKESPEARE.

CARDINAL WOLSEY'S SPEECH TO CROMWELL.

FROM "HENRY VIII."

CROMWELL, I did not think to shed a tear
In all my miseries; but thou hast forced me,
Out of thy honest truth, to play the woman.
Let 's dry our eyes: and thus far hear me, Cromwell;
And — when I am forgotten, as I shall be,
And sleep in dull, cold marble, where no mention
Of me more must be heard of — say, I taught thee,
Say, Wolsey — that once trod the ways of glory,
And sounded all the depths and shoals of honor —
Found thee a way, out of his wreck, to rise in;
A sure and safe one, though thy master missed it.
Mark but my fall, and that that ruined me.
Cromwell, I charge thee, fling away ambition:
By that sin fell the angels; how can man, then,
The image of his Maker, hope to win by 't?
Love thyself last: cherish those hearts that hate thee:
Corruption wins not more than honesty.
Still in thy right hand carry gentle peace,
To silence envious tongues. Be just, and fear not:
Let all the ends thou aim'st at be thy country's,
Thy God's, and truth's; then if thou fall'st, O Cromwell!
Thou fall'st a blessed martyr.
Serve the king; and — pr'ythee, lead me in:
There take an inventory of all I have,
To the last penny; 't is the king's: my robe,
And my integrity to heaven, is all
I dare now call mine own. O Cromwell, Cromwell!
Had I but served my God with half the zeal
I served my king, he would not in mine age
Have left me naked to mine enemies!

SHAKESPEARE.

THE LATE SPRING.

SHE stood alone amidst the April fields, —
Brown, sodden fields, all desolate and bare.
"The spring is late," she said, "the faithless spring,
That should have come to make the meadows fair.

"Their sweet South left too soon, among the trees
The birds, bewildered, flutter to and fro;
For them no green boughs wait, — their memories
Of last year's April had deceived them so."

She watched the homeless birds, the slow, sad spring,
The barren fields, and shivering, naked trees.
"Thus God has dealt with me, his child," she said;
"I wait my spring-time, and am cold like these.

"To them will come the fullness of their time;
Their spring, though late, will make the meadows fair;
Shall I, who wait like them, like them be blessed?
I am his own, — doth not my Father care?"

LOUISE CHANDLER MOULTON.

A LAMENT.

O WORLD! O Life! O Time!
On whose last steps I climb,
Trembling at that where I had stood before;
When will return the glory of your prime?
No more, — O nevermore!

Out of the day and night
A joy has taken flight:
Fresh spring, and summer, and winter hoar
Move my faint heart with grief, but with delight
No more, — O nevermore!

PERCY BYSSHE SHELLEY.

"WHAT CAN AN OLD MAN DO BUT DIE?"

SPRING it is cheery,
Winter is dreary,
Green leaves hang, but the brown must fly;
When he 's forsaken,
Withered and shaken,
What can an old man do but die?

Love will not clip him,
Maids will not lip him,
Maud and Marian pass him by;
Youth it is sunny,
Age has no honey, —
What can an old man do but die?

June it was jolly,
O for its folly!
A dancing leg and a laughing eye!
Youth may be silly,
Wisdom is chilly, —
What can an old man do but die?

Friends they are scanty,
Beggars are plenty,
If he has followers, I know why;
Gold's in his clutches
(Buying him crutches!) —
What can an old man do but die?

THOMAS HOOD.

WHEN SHALL WE ALL MEET AGAIN?

When shall we all meet again?
When shall we all meet again?
Oft shall glowing hope expire,
Oft shall wearied love retire,
Oft shall death and sorrow reign,
Ere we all shall meet again.

Though in distant lands we sigh,
Parched beneath a hostile sky;
Though the deep between us rolls,
Friendship shall unite our souls.
Still in Fancy's rich domain
Oft shall we all meet again.

When the dreams of life are fled,
When its wasted lamps are dead;
When in cold oblivion's shade,
Beauty, power, and fame are laid;
Where immortal spirits reign,
There shall we all meet again.

ANONYMOUS.

THE LAST LEAF.

I saw him once before,
As he passed by the door;
And again
The pavement-stones resound
As he totters o'er the ground
With his cane.

They say that in his prime,
Ere the pruning-knife of time
Cut him down,
Not a better man was found
By the crier on his round
Through the town.

But now he walks the streets,
And he looks at all he meets
So forlorn;
And he shakes his feeble head,
That it seems as if he said,
"They are gone."

The mossy marbles rest
On the lips that he has pressed
In their bloom;
And the names he loved to hear
Have been carved for many a year
On the tomb.

My grandmamma has said —
Poor old lady! she is dead
Long ago —
That he had a Roman nose,
And his cheek was like a rose
In the snow.

But now his nose is thin,
And it rests upon his chin
Like a staff;
And a crook is in his back,
And a melancholy crack
In his laugh.

I know it is a sin
For me to sit and grin
At him here,
But the old three-cornered hat,
And the breeches, — and all that,
Are so queer!

And if I should live to be
The last leaf upon the tree
In the spring,
Let them smile, as I do now,
At the old forsaken bough
Where I cling.

OLIVER WENDELL HOLMES.

THE APPROACH OF AGE.

FROM "TALES OF THE HALL."

Six years had passed, and forty ere the six,
When Time began to play his usual tricks:
The locks once comely in a virgin's sight,
Locks of pure brown, displayed the encroaching white;
The blood, once fervid, now to cool began,
And Time's strong pressure to subdue the man.
I rode or walked as I was wont before,
But now the bounding spirit was no more;
A moderate pace would now my body heat,
A walk of moderate length distress my feet.
I showed my stranger guest those hills sublime,
But said, "The view is poor, we need not climb."
At a friend's mansion I began to dread
The cold neat parlor and the gay glazed bed;
At home I felt a more decided taste,
And must have all things in my order placed.
I ceased to hunt; my horses pleased me less, —
My dinner more; I learned to play at chess.
I took my dog and gun, but saw the brute

Was disappointed that I did not shoot.
My morning walks I now could bear to lose,
And blessed the shower that gave me not to choose.
In fact, I felt a languor stealing on;
The active arm, the agile hand, were gone;
Small daily actions into habits grew,
And new dislike to forms and fashions new.
I loved my trees in order to dispose;
I numbered peaches, looked how stocks arose;
Told the same story oft, — in short, began to prose.

GEORGE CRABBE.

OLD.

By the wayside, on a mossy stone,
  Sat a hoary pilgrim, sadly musing;
Oft I marked him sitting there alone,
  All the landscape, like a page, perusing;
      Poor, unknown,
By the wayside, on a mossy stone.

Buckled knee and shoe, and broad-brimmed hat;
  Coat as ancient as the form 't was folding;
Silver buttons, queue, and crimped cravat;
  Oaken staff his feeble hand upholding;
      There he sat!
Buckled knee and shoe, and broad-brimmed hat.

Seemed it pitiful he should sit there,
  No one sympathizing, no one heeding,
None to love him for his thin gray hair,
  And the furrows all so mutely pleading
      Age and care:
Seemed it pitiful he should sit there.

It was summer, and we went to school,
  Dapper country lads and little maidens;
Taught the motto of the "Dunce's Stool," —
  Its grave import still my fancy ladens, —
      "Here 's a fool!"
It was summer, and we went to school.

When the stranger seemed to mark our play,
  Some of us were joyous, some sad-hearted,
I remember well, too well, that day!
  Oftentimes the tears unbidden started,
      Would not stay
When the stranger seemed to mark our play.

One sweet spirit broke the silent spell,
  O, to me her name was always Heaven!
She besought him all his grief to tell,
  (I was then thirteen, and she eleven,)
      Isabel!
One sweet spirit broke the silent spell.

"Angel," said he sadly, "I am old;
  Earthly hope no longer hath a morrow;
Yet, why I sit here thou shalt be told."
  Then his eye betrayed a pearl of sorrow,
      Down it rolled!
"Angel," said he sadly, "I am old.

"I have tottered here to look once more
  On the pleasant scene where I delighted
In the careless, happy days of yore,
  Ere the garden of my heart was blighted
      To the core:
I have tottered here to look once more.

"All the picture now to me how dear!
  E'en this gray old rock where I am seated,
Is a jewel worth my journey here;
  Ah that such a scene must be completed
      With a tear!
All the picture now to me how dear!

"Old stone school-house! — it is still the same;
  There 's the very step I so oft mounted;
There 's the window creaking in its frame,
  And the notches that I cut and counted
      For the game.
Old stone school-house, it is still the same.

"In the cottage yonder I was born;
  Long my happy home, that humble dwelling;
There the fields of clover, wheat, and corn;
  There the spring with limpid nectar swelling;
      Ah, forlorn!
In the cottage yonder I was born.

"Those two gateway sycamores you see
  Then were planted just so far asunder
That long well-pole from the path to free,
  And the wagon to pass safely under;
      Ninety-three!
Those two gateway sycamores you see.

"There 's the orchard where we used to climb
  When my mates and I were boys together,
Thinking nothing of the flight of time,
  Fearing naught but work and rainy weather;
      Past its prime!
There 's the orchard where we used to climb.

"There the rude, three-cornered chestnut-rails,
  Round the pasture where the flocks were grazing,
Where, so sly, I used to watch for quails
  In the crops of buckwheat we were raising;
      Traps and trails!
There the rude, three-cornered chestnut-rails.

"There 's the mill that ground our yellow grain;
  Pond and river still serenely flowing;

Cot there nestling in the shaded lane,
  Where the lily of my heart was blowing, —
    Mary Jane!
There 's the mill that ground our yellow grain.

"There 's the gate on which I used to swing,
  Brook, and bridge, and barn, and old red stable;
But alas! no more the morn shall bring
  That dear group around my father's table;
    Taken wing!
There 's the gate on which I used to swing.

"I am fleeing, — all I loved have fled.
  Yon green meadow was our place for playing;
That old tree can tell of sweet things said
  When around it Jane and I were straying;
    She is dead!
I am fleeing, — all I loved have fled.

"Yon white spire, a pencil on the sky,
  Tracing silently life's changeful story,
So familiar to my dim old eye,
  Points me to seven that are now in glory
    There on high!
Yon white spire, a pencil on the sky.

"Oft the aisle of that old church we trod,
  Guided thither by an angel mother;
Now she sleeps beneath its sacred sod;
  Sire and sisters, and my little brother,
    Gone to God!
Oft the aisle of that old church we trod.

"There I heard of Wisdom's pleasant ways;
  Bless the holy lesson! — but, ah, never
Shall I hear again those songs of praise,
  Those sweet voices silent now forever!
    Peaceful days!
There I heard of Wisdom's pleasant ways.

"There my Mary blest me with her hand
  When our souls drank in the nuptial blessing,
Ere she hastened to the spirit-land,
  Yonder turf her gentle bosom pressing;
    Broken band!
There my Mary blest me with her hand.

"I have come to see that grave once more,
  And the sacred place where we delighted,
Where we worshiped, in the days of yore,
  Ere the garden of my heart was blighted
    To the core!
I have come to see that grave once more.

"Angel," said he sadly, "I am old;
  Earthly hope no longer hath a morrow,
Now, why I sit here thou hast been told."
  In his eye another pearl of sorrow,
    Down it rolled!
"Angel," said he sadly, "I am old."

By the wayside, on a mossy stone,
  Sat the hoary pilgrim, sadly musing;
Still I marked him sitting there alone,
  All the landscape, like a page, perusing;
    Poor, unknown!
By the wayside, on a mossy stone.

RALPH HOYT.

THE WIDOW'S MITE.

A WIDOW — she had only one!
A puny and decrepit son;
  But, day and night,
Though fretful oft, and weak and small,
A loving child, he was her all —
  The Widow's Mite.

The Widow's Mite — ay, so sustained,
She battled onward, nor complained,
  Though friends were fewer:
And while she toiled for daily fare,
A little crutch upon the stair
  Was music to her.

I saw her then, — and now I see
That, though resigned and cheerful, she
  Has sorrowed much:
She has, He gave it tenderly,
Much faith; and carefully laid by,
  The little crutch.

FREDERICK LOCKER.

THE DREAMER.

FROM "POEMS BY A SEAMSTRESS."

  NOT in the laughing bowers,
Where by green swinging elms a pleasant shade
At summer's noon is made,
  And where swift-footed hours
  Steal the rich breath of enamored flowers,
Dream I. Nor where the golden glories be,
At sunset, laving o'er the flowing sea;
And to pure eyes the faculty is given
To trace a smooth ascent from Earth to Heaven!

  Not on a couch of ease,
With all the appliances of joy at hand, —
Soft light, sweet fragrance, beauty at command;
  Viands that might a godlike palate please,
  And music's soul-creative ecstasies,
Dream I. Nor gloating o'er a wide estate,
Till the full, self-complacent heart elate,

Well satisfied with bliss of mortal birth,
Sighs for an immortality on Earth!

But where the incessant din
Of iron hands, and roar of brazen throats,
Join their unmingled notes,
While the long summer day is pouring in,
Till day is gone, and darkness doth begin,
Dream I, — as in the corner where I lie,
On wintry nights, just covered from the sky! —
Such is my fate, — and, barren though it seem,
Yet, thou blind, soulless scorner, yet I dream!

And yet I dream, —
Dream what, were men more just, I might have been;
How strong, how fair, how kindly and serene,
Glowing of heart, and glorious of mien;
The conscious crown to Nature's blissful scene,
In just and equal brotherhood to glean,
With all mankind, exhaustless pleasure keen, —
Such is my dream!

And yet I dream, —
I, the despised of fortune, lift mine eyes,
Bright with the luster of integrity,
In unappealing wretchedness, on high,
And the last rage of Destiny defy;
Resolved alone to live, — alone to die,
Nor swell the tide of human misery!

And yet I dream, —
Dream of a sleep where dreams no more shall come,
My last, my first, my only welcome home!
Rest, unbeheld since Life's beginning stage,
Sole remnant of my glorious heritage,
Unalienable, I shall find thee yet,
And in thy soft embrace the past forget!
Thus do I dream!

ANONYMOUS.

A ROUGH RHYME ON A ROUGH MATTER.

THE ENGLISH GAME LAWS.

THE merry brown hares came leaping
Over the crest of the hill,
Where the clover and corn lay sleeping,
Under the moonlight still.

Leaping late and early,
Till under their bite and their tread,
The swedes, and the wheat, and the barley
Lay cankered, and trampled, and dead.

A poacher's widow sat sighing
On the side of the white chalk bank,
Where, under the gloomy fir-woods,
One spot in the lea throve rank.

She watched a long tuft of clover,
Where rabbit or hare never ran,
For its black sour haulm covered over
The blood of a murdered man.

She thought of the dark plantation,
And the hares, and her husband's blood,
And the voice of her indignation
Rose up to the throne of God:

"I am long past wailing and whining,
I have wept too much in my life:
I 've had twenty years of pining
As an English laborer's wife.

"A laborer in Christian England,
Where they cant of a Saviour's name,
And yet waste men's lives, like the vermin's,
For a few more brace of game.

"There's blood on your new foreign shrubs, squire,
There 's blood on your pointer's feet;
There 's blood on the game you sell, squire,
And there 's blood on the game you eat.

"You have sold the laboring man, squire,
Both body and soul to shame,
To pay for your seat in the House, squire,
And to pay for the feed of your game.

"You made him a poacher yourself, squire,
When you 'd give neither work nor meat,
And your barley-fed hares robbed the garden
At our starving children's feet;

"When, packed in one reeking chamber,
Man, maid, mother, and little ones lay;
While the rain pattered in on the rotten bride-bed,
And the walls let in the day;

"When we lay in the burning fever,
On the mud of the cold clay floor,
Till you parted us all for three months, squire,
At the cursèd workhouse door.

"We quarreled like brutes, and who wonders?
What self-respect could we keep,
Worse housed than your hacks and your pointers,
Worse fed than your hogs and your sheep?

"Our daughters, with base-born babies,
Have wandered away in their shame;
If your misses had slept, squire, where they did,
Your misses might do the same.

"Can your lady patch hearts that are breaking,
With handfuls of coals and rice,
Or by dealing out flannel and sheeting
A little below cost price?

"You may tire of the jail and the workhouse,
And take to allotments and schools,
But you 've run up a debt that will never
Be repaid us by penny-club rules.

"In the season of shame and sadness,
In the dark and dreary day,
When scrofula, gout, and madness
Are eating your race away;

"When to kennels and liveried varlets
You have cast your daughters' bread,
And, worn out with liquor and harlots,
Your heir at your feet lies dead;

"When your youngest, the mealy-mouthed rector,
Lets your soul rot asleep to the grave,
You will find in your God the protector
Of the freeman you fancied your slave."

She looked at the tuft of clover,
And wept till her heart grew light;
And at last, when her passion was over,
Went wandering into the night.

But the merry brown hares came leaping
Over the uplands still,
Where the clover and corn lay sleeping
On the side of the white chalk hill.

CHARLES KINGSLEY.

LOUIS XV.

THE king with all the kingly train had left his Pompadour behind,
And forth he rode in Senart's wood the royal beasts of chase to find.
That day by chance the monarch mused, and turning suddenly away,
He struck alone into a path that far from crowds and courtiers lay.

He saw the pale green shadows play upon the brown untrodden earth;
He saw the birds around him flit as if he were of peasant birth;
He saw the trees that know no king but him that bears a woodland ax;
He thought not, but he looked about like one who still in thinking lacks.

Then close to him a footstep fell, and glad of human sound was he,
For, truth to say, he found himself but melancholy company;
But that which he would ne'er have guessed before him now most plainly came;
The man upon his weary back a coffin bore of modest frame.

"Why, who art thou?" exclaimed the king, "and what is that I see thee bear?"
"I am a laborer in the wood, and 't is a coffin for Pierre.
Close by the royal hunting-lodge you may have often seen him toil;
But he will never work again, and I for him must dig the soil."

The laborer ne'er had seen the king, and this he thought was but a man,
Who made at first a moment's pause, and then anew his talk began;
"I think I do remember now, — he had a dark and glancing eye,
And I have seen his sturdy arm with wondrous strokes the pickax ply.

"Pray tell me, friend, what accident can thus have killed our good Pierre?"
"O, nothing more than usual, sir, he died of living upon air!
'T was hunger killed the poor good man, who long on empty hopes relied;
He could not pay *Gabelle* and tax, and feed his children, so he died."

The man stopped short, and then went on, — "It is, you know, a common story,
Our children's food is eaten up by courtiers, mistresses, and glory."
The king looked hard upon the man, and afterwards the coffin eyed,
Then spurred to ask of Pompadour, how came it that the peasants died.

JOHN WILSON
(CHRISTOPHER NORTH).

THE ORPHAN BOY'S TALE.

STAY, lady, stay, for mercy's sake,
And hear a helpless orphan's tale;
Ah, sure my looks must pity wake, —
'T is want that makes my cheek so pale;
Yet I was once a mother's pride,
And my brave father's hope and joy;
But in the Nile's proud fight he died,
And I am now an orphan boy!

Poor, foolish child! how pleased was I,
When news of Nelson's victory came,
Along the crowded streets to fly,
To see the lighted windows flame!

To force me home my mother sought, —
  She could not bear to hear my joy;
For with my father's life 't was bought, —
  And made me a poor orphan boy!

The people's shouts were long and loud;
  My mother, shuddering, closed her ears;
"*Rejoice!* REJOICE!" still cried the crowd, —
  My mother answered with her tears!
"O, why do tears steal down your cheek,"
  Cried I, "while others shout for joy?"
She kissed me; and in accents weak,
  She called me her poor orphan boy!

"What is an orphan boy?" I said;
  When suddenly she gasped for breath,
And her eyes closed! I shrieked for aid,
  But ah! her eyes were closed in death.
My hardships since I will not tell;
  But now, no more a parent's joy,
Ah! lady, I have learned *too* well
  What 't is to be an orphan boy!

O, were I by your bounty fed!
  Nay, gentle lady, do not chide;
Trust me, I mean to earn my bread, —
  The sailor's orphan boy has pride.
Lady, you weep; what is 't you say?
  You 'll give me clothing, food, employ?
Look down, dear parents! look and see
  Your happy, happy orphan boy!

AMELIA OPIE.

THE ORPHANS.

MY chaise the village inn did gain,
  Just as the setting sun's last ray
Tipped with refulgent gold the vane
  Of the old church across the way.

Across the way I silent sped,
  The time till supper to beguile,
In moralizing o'er the dead
  That moldered round the ancient pile.

There many a humble green grave showed
  Where want and pain and toil did rest;
And many a flattering stone I viewed
  O'er those who once had wealth possest.

A faded beech its shadow brown
  Threw o'er a grave where sorrow slept,
On which, though scarce with grass o'ergrown,
  Two ragged children sat and wept.

A piece of bread between them lay,
  Which neither seemed inclined to take,
And yet they looked so much a prey
  To want, it made my heart to ache.

"My little children, let me know
  Why you in such distress appear,
And why you wasteful from you throw
  That bread which many a one might cheer?"

The little boy, in accents sweet,
  Replied, while tears each other chased, —
"Lady! we 've not enough to eat,
  Ah! if we had, we should not waste.

"But Sister Mary 's naughty grown,
  And will not eat, whate'er I say,
Though sure I am the bread 's her own,
  For she has tasted none to-day."

"Indeed," the wan, starved Mary said,
  "Till Henry eats, I 'll eat no more,
For yesterday I got some bread,
  He 's had none since the day before."

My heart did swell, my bosom heave,
  I felt as though deprived of speech;
Silent I sat upon the grave,
  And clasped the clay-cold hand of each.

With looks of woe too sadly true,
  With looks that spoke a grateful heart,
The shivering boy then nearer drew,
  And did his simple tale impart:

"Before my father went away,
  Enticed by bad men o'er the sea,
Sister and I did naught but play, —
  We lived beside yon great ash-tree.

"But then poor mother did so cry,
  And looked so changed, I cannot tell;
She told us that she soon should die,
  And bade us love each other well.

"She said that when the war was o'er,
  Perhaps we might our father see;
But if we never saw him more,
  That God our father then would be!

"She kissed us both, and then she died,
  And we no more a mother have;
Here many a day we 've sat and cried
  Together at poor mother's grave.

"But when my father came not here,
  I thought if we could find the sea,
We should be sure to meet him there,
  And once again might happy be.

"We hand in hand went many a mile,
  And asked our way of all we met;
And some did sigh, and some did smile,
  And we of some did victuals get.

"But when we reached the sea and found
'T was one great water round us spread,
We thought that father must be drowned,
And cried, and wished we both were dead.

"So we returned to mother's grave,
And only longed with her to be;
For Goody, when this bread she gave,
Said father died beyond the sea.

"Then since no parent we have here,
We'll go and search for God around;
Lady, pray, can you tell us where
That God, our Father, may be found?

"He lives in heaven, our mother said,
And Goody says that mother's there;
So, if she knows we want his aid,
I think perhaps she'll send him here."

I clasped the prattlers to my breast,
And cried, "Come, both, and live with me;
I'll clothe you, feed you, give you rest,
And will a second mother be.

"And God shall be your Father still,
'T was he in mercy sent me here,
To teach you to obey his will,
Your steps to guide, your hearts to cheer."

ANONYMOUS.

LONDON CHURCHES.

I STOOD, one Sunday morning,
Before a large church door,
The congregation gathered
And carriages a score, —
From one out stepped a lady
I oft had seen before.

Her hand was on a prayer-book,
And held a vinaigrette;
The sign of man's redemption
Clear on the book was set, —
But above the Cross there glistened
A golden Coronet.

For her the obsequious beadle
The inner door flung wide;
Lightly, as up a ball-room,
Her footsteps seemed to glide, —
There might be good thoughts in her,
For all her evil pride.

But after her a woman
Peeped wistfully within,
On whose wan face was graven
Life's hardest discipline, —
The trace of the sad trinity
Of weakness, pain, and sin.

The few free-seats were crowded
Where she could rest and pray;
With her worn garb contrasted
Each side in fair array, —
"God's house holds no poor sinners,"
She sighed, and crept away.

RICHARD MONCKTON MILNES.

TWO WOMEN.

THE shadows lay along Broadway,
'T was near the twilight-tide,
And slowly there a lady fair
Was walking in her pride.
Alone walked she; but, viewlessly,
Walked spirits at her side.

Peace charmed the street beneath her feet,
And Honor charmed the air;
And all astir looked kind on her,
And called her good as fair, —
For all God ever gave to her
She kept with chary care.

She kept with care her beauties rare
From lovers warm and true,
For her heart was cold to all but gold,
And the rich came not to woo, —
But honored well are charms to sell
If priests the selling do.

Now walking there was one more fair, —
A slight girl, lily-pale;
And she had unseen company
To make the spirit quail, —
'Twixt Want and Scorn she walked forlorn,
And nothing could avail.

No mercy now can clear her brow
For this world's peace to pray;
For, as love's wild prayer dissolved in air,
Her woman's heart gave way! —
But the sin forgiven by Christ in heaven
By man is cursed alway!

NATHANIEL PARKER WILLIS.

BEAUTIFUL SNOW.

O THE snow, the beautiful snow,
Filling the sky and the earth below!
Over the house-tops, over the street,
Over the heads of the people you meet,
Dancing,
Flirting,
Skimming along.

Beautiful snow! it can do nothing wrong.
Flying to kiss a fair lady's cheek;
Clinging to lips in a frolicsome freak;
Beautiful snow, from the heavens above,
Pure as an angel and fickle as love!

O the snow, the beautiful snow!
How the flakes gather and laugh as they go!
Whirling about in its maddening fun,
It plays in its glee with every one.
Chasing,
Laughing,
Hurrying by,
It lights up the face and it sparkles the eye;
And even the dogs, with a bark and a bound,
Snap at the crystals that eddy around.
The town is alive, and its heart in a glow,
To welcome the coming of beautiful snow.

How the wild crowd go swaying along,
Hailing each other with humor and song!
How the gay sledges like meteors flash by, —
Bright for a moment, then lost to the eye!
Ringing,
Swinging,
Dashing they go
Over the crest of the beautiful snow:
Snow so pure when it falls from the sky,
To be trampled in mud by the crowd rushing by;
To be trampled and tracked by the thousands of feet
Till it blends with the horrible filth in the street.

Once I was pure as the snow, — but I fell:
Fell, like the snow-flakes, from heaven — to hell:
Fell, to be tramped as the filth of the street:
Fell, to be scoffed, to be spit on, and beat.
Pleading,
Cursing,
Dreading to die,
Selling my soul to whoever would buy,
Dealing in shame for a morsel of bread,
Hating the living and fearing the dead.
Merciful God! have I fallen so low?
And yet I was once like this beautiful snow!

Once I was fair as the beautiful snow,
With an eye like its crystals, a heart like its glow;
Once I was loved for my innocent grace, —
Flattered and sought for the charm of my face.
Father,
Mother,
Sisters all,
God, and myself, I have lost by my fall.
The veriest wretch that goes shivering by
Will take a wide sweep, lest I wander too nigh;
For of all that is on or about me, I know
There is nothing that 's pure but the beautiful snow.

How strange it should be that this beautiful snow
Should fall on a sinner with nowhere to go!
How strange it would be, when the night comes again,
If the snow and the ice struck my desperate brain!
Fainting,
Freezing,
Dying alone,
Too wicked for prayer, too weak for my moan
To be heard in the crash of the crazy town,
Gone mad in its joy at the snow's coming down;
To lie and to die in my terrible woe,
With a bed and a shroud of the beautiful snow!

JAMES W. WATSON.

THE BRIDGE OF SIGHS.

"Drowned! drowned!" — HAMLET.

ONE more unfortunate,
Weary of breath,
Rashly importunate,
Gone to her death!

Take her up tenderly,
Lift her with care!
Fashioned so slenderly,
Young, and so fair!

Look at her garments
Clinging like cerements,
Whilst the wave constantly
Drips from her clothing;
Take her up instantly,
Loving, not loathing!

Touch her not scornfully!
Think of her mournfully,
Gently and humanly, —
Not of the stains of her;
All that remains of her
Now is pure womanly.

Make no deep scrutiny
Into her mutiny,
Rash and undutiful;
Past all dishonor,
Death has left on her
Only the beautiful.

Still, for all slips of hers, —
One of Eve's family, —
Wipe those poor lips of hers,
Oozing so clammily.

Loop up her tresses
Escaped from the comb, —
Her fair auburn tresses, —
Whilst wonderment guesses
Where was her home?

Who was her father?
Who was her mother?
Had she a sister?
Had she a brother?
Or was there a dearer one
Still, and a nearer one
Yet, than all other?

Alas! for the rarity
Of Christian charity
Under the sun!
O, it was pitiful!
Near a whole city full,
Home she had none.

Sisterly, brotherly,
Fatherly, motherly
Feelings had changed, —
Love, by harsh evidence,
Thrown from its eminence;
Even God's providence
Seeming estranged.

Where the lamps quiver
So far in the river,
With many a light
From window and casement,
From garret to basement,
She stood, with amazement,
Houseless by night.

The bleak wind of March
Made her tremble and shiver;
But not the dark arch,
Or the black flowing river;
Mad from life's history,
Glad to death's mystery,
Swift to be hurled —
Anywhere, anywhere
Out of the world!

In she plunged boldly, —
No matter how coldly
The rough river ran —
Over the brink of it!
Picture it — think of it,
Dissolute man!
Lave in it, drink of it,
Then, if you can!

Take her up tenderly,
Lift her with care!
Fashioned so slenderly,
Young, and so fair!

Ere her limbs, frigidly,
Stiffen too rigidly,
Decently, kindly,
Smooth and compose them;
And her eyes, close them,
Staring so blindly!
Dreadfully staring
Through muddy impurity,
As when with the daring
Last look of despairing
Fixed on futurity.

Perishing gloomily,
Spurred by contumely,
Cold inhumanity,
Burning insanity,
Into her rest!
Cross her hands humbly,
As if praying dumbly,
Over her breast!

Owning her weakness,
Her evil behavior,
And leaving, with meekness,
Her sins to her Saviour!

THOMAS HOOD.

THE LITTLE MATCH-GIRL.

LITTLE Gretchen, little Gretchen wanders up and down the street;
The snow is on her yellow hair, the frost is on her feet.
The rows of long, dark houses without look cold and damp,
By the struggling of the moonbeam, by the flicker of the lamp.
The clouds ride fast as horses, the wind is from the north,
But no one cares for Gretchen, and no one looketh forth.
Within those dark, damp houses are merry faces bright,
And happy hearts are watching out the old year's latest night.

With the little box of matches she could not sell all day,
And the thin, tattered mantle the wind blows every way,
She clingeth to the railing, she shivers in the gloom, —
There are parents sitting snugly by the firelight in the room;

And children with grave faces are whispering one another
Of presents for the New Year, for father or for mother.
But no one talks to Gretchen, and no one hears her speak;
No breath of little whisperers comes warmly to her cheek.

. . . . .

Her home is cold and desolate; no smile, no food, no fire,
But children clamorous for bread, and an impatient sire.
So she sits down in an angle where two great houses meet,
And she curleth up beneath her for warmth her little feet;
And she looketh on the cold wall, and on the colder sky,
And wonders if the little stars are bright fires up on high.
She hears the clock strike slowly, up high in a church-tower,
With such a sad and solemn tone, telling the midnight hour.

She remembered her of stories her mother used to tell,
And of the cradle-songs she sang, when summer's twilight fell,
Of good men and of angels, and of the Holy Child,
Who was cradled in a manger when winter was most wild;
Who was poor, and cold, and hungry, and desolate and lone;
And she thought the song had told her he was ever with his own,
And all the poor and hungry and forsaken ones were his, —
"How good of him to look on me in such a place as this!"

Colder it grows and colder, but she does not feel it now,
For the pressure on her bosom, and the weight upon her brow;
But she struck one little match on the wall so cold and bare,
That she might look around her, and see if he was there.
The single match was kindled; and, by the light it threw,
It seemed to little Maggie that the wall was rent in two.
And she could see the room within, the room all warm and light,
With the fire-glow red and blazing, and the tapers burning bright.
And kindred there were gathered round the table richly spread,
With heaps of goodly viands, red wine, and pleasant bread.
She could smell the fragrant odor; she could hear them talk and play;
Then all was darkness once again — the match had burned away.
She struck another hastily, and now she seemed to see,
Within the same warm chamber a glorious Christmas-tree.
The branches all were laden down with things that children prize;
Bright gifts for boy and maiden they showed before her eyes.
And she almost seemed to touch them, and to join the welcome shout;
Then darkness fell around her, for the little match was out.
Another, yet another, she has tried, — they will not light;
Then all her little store she took, and struck with all her might.
And the whole place around her was lighted with the glare:
And lo! there hung a little Child before her in the air!
There were blood-drops on his forehead, a spear-wound in his side,
And cruel nail-prints in his feet, and in his hands spread wide.
And he looked upon her gently, and she felt that he had known
Pain, hunger, cold, and sorrow, — ay, equal to her own.

And he pointed to the laden board and to the Christmas-tree,
Then up to the cold sky, and said, "Will Gretchen come with me?"
The poor child felt her pulses fail, she felt her eyeballs swim,
And a ringing sound was in her ears, like her dead mother's hymn:
And she folded both her thin white hands and turned from that bright board,
And from the golden gifts, and said, "With thee, with thee, O Lord!"

The chilly winter morning breaks up in the dull skies
On the city wrapt in vapor, on the spot where Gretchen lies.
In her scant and tattered garments, with her back against the wall,
She sitteth cold and rigid, she answers to no call.

They lifted her up fearfully, and shuddered as they said,
"It was a bitter, bitter night! the child is frozen dead."
The angels sang their greeting for one more redeemed from sin;
Men said, "It was a bitter night; would no one let her in?"
And they shivered as they spoke of her, and sighed: they could not see
How much of happiness there was after that misery.

From the Danish of HANS CHRISTIAN ANDERSEN.

THE SONG OF THE SHIRT.

WITH fingers weary and worn,
With eyelids heavy and red,
A woman sat, in unwomanly rags,
Plying her needle and thread, —
Stitch! stitch! stitch!
In poverty, hunger, and dirt;
And still with a voice of dolorous pitch
She sang the "Song of the Shirt!"

"Work! work! work
While the cock is crowing aloof!
And work — work — work
Till the stars shine through the roof!
It 's, O, to be a slave
Along with the barbarous Turk,
Where woman has never a soul to save,
If this is Christian work!

"Work — work — work
Till the brain begins to swim!
Work — work — work
Till the eyes are heavy and dim!
Seam, and gusset, and band,
Band, and gusset, and seam, —
Till over the buttons I fall asleep,
And sew them on in a dream!

"O men with sisters dear!
O men with mothers and wives!
It is not linen you 're wearing out,
But human creatures' lives!
Stitch — stitch — stitch,
In poverty, hunger, and dirt, —
Sewing at once, with a double thread,
A shroud as well as a shirt!

"But why do I talk of death, —
That phantom of grisly bone?
I hardly fear his terrible shape,
It seems so like my own, —
It seems so like my own
Because of the fasts I keep;
O God! that bread should be so dear,
And flesh and blood so cheap!

"Work — work — work!
My labor never flags;
And what are its wages? A bed of straw,
A crust of bread — and rags,
That shattered roof — and this naked floor —
A table — a broken chair —
And a wall so blank my shadow I thank
For sometimes falling there!

"Work — work — work
From weary chime to chime!
Work — work — work
As prisoners work for crime!
Band, and gusset, and seam,
Seam, and gusset, and band, —
Till the heart is sick and the brain benumbed,
As well as the weary hand.

"Work — work — work
In the dull December light!
And work — work — work
When the weather is warm and bright!
While underneath the eaves
The brooding swallows cling,
As if to show me their sunny backs,
And twit me with the Spring.

"O, but to breathe the breath
Of the cowslip and primrose sweet, —
With the sky above my head,
And the grass beneath my feet!
For only one short hour
To feel as I used to feel,
Before I knew the woes of want
And the walk that costs a meal!

"O, but for one short hour, —
A respite, however brief!
No blessèd leisure for love or hope,
But only time for grief!
A little weeping would ease my heart;
But in their briny bed
My tears must stop, for every drop
Hinders needle and thread!"

With fingers weary and worn,
With eyelids heavy and red,
A woman sat, in unwomanly rags,
Plying her needle and thread, —
Stitch! stitch! stitch!
In poverty, hunger, and dirt;
And still with a voice of dolorous pitch —
Would that its tone could reach the rich! —
She sang this "Song of the Shirt!"

THOMAS HOOD.

GIVE ME THREE GRAINS OF CORN, MOTHER.

THE IRISH FAMINE.

Give me three grains of corn, mother, —
  Only three grains of corn;
It will keep the little life I have
  Till the coming of the morn.
I am dying of hunger and cold, mother, —
  Dying of hunger and cold;
And half the agony of such a death
  My lips have never told.

It has gnawed like a wolf, at my heart, mother, —
  A wolf that is fierce for blood;
All the livelong day, and the night beside,
  Gnawing for lack of food.
I dreamed of bread in my sleep, mother,
  And the sight was heaven to see;
I awoke with an eager, famishing lip,
  But you had no bread for me.

How could I look to you, mother, —
  How could I look to you
For bread to give to your starving boy,
  When you were starving too?
For I read the famine in your cheek,
  And in your eyes so wild,
And I felt it in your bony hand,
  As you laid it on your child.

The Queen has lands and gold, mother, —
  The Queen has lands and gold,
While you are forced to your empty breast
  A skeleton babe to hold, —
A babe that is dying of want, mother,
  As I am dying now,
With a ghastly look in its sunken eye,
  And famine upon its brow.

What has poor Ireland done, mother, —
  What has poor Ireland done,
That the world looks on, and sees us starve,
  Perishing one by one?
Do the men of England care not, mother, —
  The great men and the high, —
For the suffering sons of Erin's isle,
  Whether they live or die?

There is many a brave heart here, mother,
  Dying of want and cold,
While only across the Channel, mother,
  Are many that roll in gold;
There are rich and proud men there, mother,
  With wondrous wealth to view,
And the bread they fling to their dogs to-night
  Would give life to *me* and *you*.

Come nearer to my side, mother,
  Come nearer to my side,
And hold me fondly, as you held
  My father when *he* died;
Quick, for I cannot see you, mother,
  My breath is almost gone;
Mother! dear mother! ere I die,
  Give me three grains of corn.

Miss Edwards.

THE IDIOT BOY.

It had pleased God to form poor Ned
  A thing of idiot mind;
Yet to the poor, unreasoning boy
  God had not been unkind.

Old Sarah loved her helpless child,
  Whom helplessness made dear,
And life was everything to him
  Who knew no hope or fear.

She knew his wants, she understood
  Each half-articulate call,
For he was everything to her,
  And she to him was all.

And so for many a year they lived,
  Nor knew a wish beside;
But age at length on Sarah came,
  And she fell sick and died.

He tried in vain to waken her,
  He called her o'er and o'er;
They told him she was dead, — the word
  To him no import bore.

They closed her eyes and shrouded her,
  Whilst he stood wondering by,
And when they bore her to the grave
  He followed silently.

They laid her in the narrow house,
  And sung the funeral stave,
And when the mournful train dispersed
  He loitered by the grave.

The rabble boys that used to jeer
  Whene'er they saw poor Ned,
Now stood and watched him at the grave,
  And not a word was said.

They came and went and came again,
  And night at last drew on;
Yet still he lingered at the place
  Till every one had gone.

And when he found himself alone
  He quick removed the clay,

And raised the coffin in his arms
  And bore it quick away.

Straight went he to his mother's cot
  And laid it on the floor,
And with the eagerness of joy
  He barred the cottage door.

At once he placed his mother's corpse
  Upright within her chair,
And then he heaped the hearth and blew
  The kindling fire with care.

She now was in her wonted chair,
  It was her wonted place,
And bright the fire blazed and flashed,
  Reflected from her face.

Then, bending down, he 'd feel her hands,
  Anon her face behold ;
"Why, mother, do you look so pale,
  And why are you so cold ?"

And when the neighbors on next morn
  Had forced the cottage door,
Old Sarah's corpse was in the chair,
  And Ned's was on the floor.

It had pleased God from this poor boy
  His only friend to call ;
Yet God was not unkind to him,
  For death restored him all.

ROBERT SOUTHEY.

THE MANIAC.

STAY, jailer, stay, and hear my woe !
  She is not mad who kneels to thee ;
For what I 'm now too well I know,
  And what I was, and what should be.
I 'll rave no more in proud despair ;
  My language shall be mild, though sad ;
But yet I firmly, truly swear,
  I am not mad, I am not mad !

My tyrant husband forged the tale
  Which chains me in this dismal cell ;
My fate unknown my friends bewail, —
  O jailer, haste that fate to tell !
O, haste my father's heart to cheer !
  His heart at once 't will grieve and glad
To know, though kept a captive here,
  I am not mad, I am not mad !

He smiles in scorn, and turns the key ;
  He quits the grate ; I knelt in vain ;
His glimmering lamp still, still I see, —
  'T is gone ! and all is gloom again.

Cold, bitter cold ! — No warmth ! no light !
  Life, all thy comforts once I had ;
Yet here I 'm chained, this freezing night,
  Although not *mad ; no, no,— not mad !*

'T is sure some dream, some vision vain ;
  What ! *I*, the child of rank and wealth,—
Am *I* the wretch who clanks this chain,
  Bereft of freedom, friends, and health ?
Ah ! while I dwell on blessings fled,
  Which nevermore my heart must glad,
How aches my heart, how burns my head ;
  But 't is not *mad ; no, 't is not mad !*

Hast thou, my child, forgot, ere this,
  A mother's face, a mother's tongue ?
She 'll ne'er forget your parting kiss,
  Nor round her neck how fast you clung ;
Nor how with her you sued to stay ;
  Nor how that suit your sire forbade ;
Nor how — I 'll drive such thoughts away !
  They 'll *make* me mad, they 'll *make* me mad!

His rosy lips, how sweet they smiled !
  His mild blue eyes, how bright they shone !
None ever bore a lovelier child,
  And art thou now forever gone ?
And must I never see thee more,
  My pretty, pretty, pretty lad ?
I will be free ! unbar the door !
  I am not mad ; I am not mad !

O, hark ! what mean those yells and cries ?
  His chain some furious madman breaks ;
He comes, — I see his glaring eyes ;
  Now, now, my dungeon-grate he shakes.
Help ! Help ! — He 's gone ! — O, fearful woe,
  Such screams to hear, such sights to see !
My brain, my brain, — I know, I know
  I am *not* mad, but soon *shall* be.

Yes, soon ; — for, lo you ! while I speak, —
  Mark how yon demon's eyeballs glare !
He sees me ; now, with dreadful shriek,
  He whirls a serpent high in air.
Horror ! — the reptile strikes his tooth
  Deep in my heart, so crushed and sad ;
Ay, laugh, ye fiends ; — I feel the truth ;
  Your task is done, — I 'M MAD ! I 'M MAD !

MATTHEW GREGORY LEWIS.

THE PAUPER'S DEATH-BED.

TREAD softly, — bow the head, —
  In reverent silence bow, —
No passing-bell doth toll,
Yet an immortal soul
  Is passing now.

Stranger! however great,
With lowly reverence bow;
There 's one in that poor shed —
One by that paltry bed —
Greater than thou.

Beneath that beggar's roof,
Lo! Death doth keep his state.
Enter, no crowds attend;
Enter, no guards defend
This palace gate.

That pavement, damp and cold,
No smiling courtiers tread;
One silent woman stands,
Lifting with meager hands
A dying head.

No mingling voices sound, —
An infant wail alone;
A sob suppressed, — again
That short deep gasp, and then —
The parting groan.

O change! O wondrous change!
Burst are the prison bars, —
This moment, *there*, so low,
So agonized, and now, —
Beyond the stars.

O change! stupendous change!
There lies the soulless clod;
The sun eternal breaks,
The new immortal wakes, —
Wakes with his God!

CAROLINE ANNE BOWLES
(MRS. SOUTHEY).

THE PAUPER'S DRIVE.

THERE 's a grim one-horse hearse in a jolly round trot, —
To the churchyard a pauper is going, I wot;
The road it is rough, and the hearse has no springs;
And hark to the dirge which the mad driver sings:
Rattle his bones over the stones!
He 's only a pauper whom nobody owns!

O, where are the mourners? Alas! there are none;
He has left not a gap in the world, now he's gone, —
Not a tear in the eye of child, woman, or man;
To the grave with his carcass as fast as you can:
Rattle his bones over the stones!
He 's only a pauper whom nobody owns!

What a jolting, and creaking, and splashing, and din!
The whip, how it cracks! and the wheels, how they spin!
How the dirt, right and left, o'er the hedges is hurled! —
The pauper at length makes a noise in the world!
Rattle his bones over the stones!
He 's only a pauper whom nobody owns!

Poor pauper defunct! he has made some approach
To gentility, now that he 's stretched in a coach!
He 's taking a drive in his carriage at last;
But it will not be long, if he goes on so fast:
Rattle his bones over the stones!
He 's only a pauper whom nobody owns!

You bumpkins! who stare at your brother conveyed,
Behold what respect to a cloddy is paid!
And be joyful to think, when by death you 're laid low,
You 've a chance to the grave like a gemman to go!
Rattle his bones over the stones!
He 's only a pauper whom nobody owns!

But a truce to this strain; for my soul it is sad,
To think that a heart in humanity clad
Should make, like the brute, such a desolate end,
And depart from the light without leaving a friend!
Bear soft his bones over the stones!
Though a pauper, he 's one whom his Maker yet owns!

THOMAS NOEL.

FOR A' THAT AND A' THAT.

Is there for honest poverty
Wha hangs his head, and a' that?
The coward slave, we pass him by;
We dare be poor for a' that.
For a' that, and a' that,
Our toil's obscure, and a' that;
The rank is but the guinea's stamp, —
The man 's the gowd for a' that.

What though on hamely fare we dine,
Wear hoddin gray, and a' that?
Gie fools their silks, and knaves their wine, —
A man 's a man for a' that.
For a' that, and a' that,
Their tinsel show, and a' that;
The honest man, though e'er sae poor,
Is king o' men for a' that.

Ye see yon birkie ca'd a lord,
Wha struts, and stares, and a' that, —
Though hundreds worship at his word,
He 's but a coof for a' that;
For a' that, and a' that,
His riband, star, and a' that;
The man of independent mind,
He looks and laughs at a' that.

A prince can mak a belted knight,
  A marquis, duke, and a' that;
But an honest man 's aboon his might, —
  Guid faith, he maunna fa' that!
For a' that, and a' that;
  Their dignities, and a' that,
The pith o' sense, and pride o' worth,
  Are higher ranks than a' that.

Then let us pray that come it may, —
  As come it will for a' that, —
That sense and worth, o'er a' the earth,
  May bear the gree, and a' that.
For a' that, and a' that,
  It 's coming yet, for a' that, —
When man to man, the warld o'er,
  Shall brothers be for a' that!

ROBERT BURNS.

THE BLIND BOY.

O, SAY, what is that thing called Light,
  Which I must ne'er enjoy?
What are the blessings of the sight,
  O, tell your poor blind boy!

You talk of wondrous things you see,
  You say the sun shines bright;
I feel him warm, but how can he
  Or make it day or night?

My day or night myself I make
  Whene'er I sleep or play;
And could I ever keep awake
  With me 't were always day.

With heavy sighs I often hear
  You mourn my hapless woe;
But sure with patience I can bear
  A loss I ne'er can know.

Then let not what I cannot have
  My cheer of mind destroy:
Whilst thus I sing, I am a king,
  Although a poor blind boy.

COLLEY CIBBER.

DIVERSITIES OF FORTUNE.

FROM "MISS KILMANSEGG."

WHAT different dooms our birthdays bring!
For instance, one little manikin thing
  Survives to wear many a wrinkle;
While death forbids another to wake,
And a son that it took nine moons to make
  Expires without even a twinkle:

Into this world we come like ships,
Launched from the docks, and stocks, and slips,
  For fortune fair or fatal;
And one little craft is cast away
In its very first trip in Babbicome Bay,
  While another rides safe at Port Natal.

What different lots our stars accord!
This babe to be hailed and wooed as a lord,
  And that to be shunned like a leper!
One, to the world's wine, honey, and corn,
Another, like Colchester native, born
  To its vinegar only, and pepper.

One is littered under a roof
Neither wind nor water proof, —
  That 's the prose of Love in a cottage, —
A puny, naked, shivering wretch,
The whole of whose birthright would not fetch,
Though Robins himself drew up the sketch,
  The bid of "a mess of pottage."

Born of Fortunatus's kin,
Another comes tenderly ushered in
  To a prospect all bright and burnished:
No tenant he for life's back slums, —
He comes to the world as a gentleman comes
  To a lodging ready furnished.

And the other sex — the tender — the fair —
What wide reverses of fate are there!
Whilst Margaret, charmed by the Bulbul rare,
  In a garden of Gul reposes,
Poor Peggy hawks nosegays from street to street
Till — think of that, who find life so sweet! —
  She hates the smell of roses!

THOMAS HOOD.

THE END OF THE PLAY.

THE play is done, — the curtain drops,
  Slow falling to the prompter's bell;
A moment yet the actor stops,
  And looks around, to say farewell.
It is an irksome word and task;
  And, when he 's laughed and said his say,
He shows, as he removes the mask,
  A face that 's anything but gay.

One word, ere yet the evening ends, —
  Let 's close it with a parting rhyme;
And pledge a hand to all young friends,
  As fits the merry Christmas time;
On life's wide scene you, too, have parts
  That fate erelong shall bid you play;
Good night! — with honest, gentle hearts
  A kindly greeting go alway!

Good night! — I 'd say the griefs, the joys,
  Just hinted in this mimic page,
The triumphs and defeats of boys,
  Are but repeated in our age;
I 'd say your woes were not less keen,
  Your hopes more vain, than those of men, —
Your pangs or pleasures of fifteen
  At forty-five played o'er again.

I 'd say we suffer and we strive
  Not less nor more as men than boys, —
With grizzled beards at forty-five,
  As erst at twelve in corduroys;
And if, in time of sacred youth,
  We learned at home to love and pray,
Pray Heaven that early love and truth
  May never wholly pass away.

And in the world, as in the school,
  I 'd say how fate may change and shift, —
The prize be sometimes with the fool,
  The race not always to the swift:
The strong may yield, the good may fall,
  The great man be a vulgar clown,
The knave be lifted over all,
  The kind cast pitilessly down.

Who knows the inscrutable design?
  Blessèd be He who took and gave!
Why should your mother, Charles, not mine,
  Be weeping at her darling's grave;
We bow to Heaven that willed it so,
  That darkly rules the fate of all,
That sends the respite or the blow,
  That 's free to give or to recall.

This crowns his feast with wine and wit, —
  Who brought him to that mirth and state?
His betters, see, below him sit,
  Or hunger hopeless at the gate.
Who bade the mud from Dives' wheel
  To spurn the rags of Lazarus?
Come, brother, in that dust we 'll kneel,
  Confessing Heaven that ruled it thus.

So each shall mourn, in life's advance,
  Dear hopes, dear friends, untimely killed;
Shall grieve for many a forfeit chance
  And longing passion unfulfilled.
Amen! — whatever fate be sent,
  Pray God the heart may kindly glow,
Although the head with cares be bent,
  And whitened with the winter snow.

Come wealth or want, come good or ill,
  Let young and old accept their part,
And bow before the awful will,
  And bear it with an honest heart.
Who misses, or who wins the prize, —
  Go, lose or conquer as you can;
But if you fail, or if you rise,
  Be each, pray God, a gentleman.

A gentleman, or old or young!
  (Bear kindly with my humble lays;)
The sacred chorus first was sung
  Upon the first of Christmas days;
The shepherds heard it overhead, —
  The joyful angels raised it then:
Glory to Heaven on high, it said,
  And peace on earth to gentle men!

My song, save this, is little worth;
  I lay the weary pen aside,
And wish you health and love and mirth,
  As fits the solemn Christmas-tide.
As fits the holy Christmas birth,
  Be this, good friends, our carol still, —
Be peace on earth, be peace on earth,
  To men of gentle will.

WILLIAM MAKEPEACE THACKERAY.

BEREAVEMENT AND DEATH.

RESIGNATION.

There is no flock, however watched and tended,
But one dead lamb is there!
There is no fireside, howsoe'er defended,
But has one vacant chair!

The air is full of farewells to the dying,
And mournings for the dead;
The heart of Rachel, for her children crying,
Will not be comforted!

Let us be patient! These severe afflictions
Not from the ground arise,
But oftentimes celestial benedictions
Assume this dark disguise.

We see but dimly through the mists and vapors;
Amid these earthly damps
What seem to us but sad, funereal tapers
May be heaven's distant lamps.

There is no Death! What seems so is transition:
This life of mortal breath
Is but a suburb of the life elysian,
Whose portal we call Death.

She is not dead, — the child of our affection, —
But gone unto that school
Where she no longer needs our poor protection,
And Christ himself doth rule.

In that great cloister's stillness and seclusion,
By guardian angels led,
Safe from temptation, safe from sin's pollution,
She lives whom we call dead.

Day after day, we think what she is doing
In those bright realms of air;
Year after year, her tender steps pursuing,
Behold her grown more fair.

Thus do we walk with her, and keep unbroken
The bond which nature gives,
Thinking that our remembrance, though unspoken,
May reach her where she lives.

Not as a child shall we again behold her;
For when with raptures wild
In our embraces we again enfold her,
She will not be a child:

But a fair maiden, in her Father's mansion,
Clothed with celestial grace;
And beautiful with all the soul's expansion
Shall we behold her face.

And though, at times, impetuous with emotion
And anguish long suppressed,
The swelling heart heaves moaning like the ocean,
That cannot be at rest, —

We will be patient, and assuage the feeling
We may not wholly stay;
By silence sanctifying, not concealing,
The grief that must have way.

Henry Wadsworth Longfellow.

BURIED TO-DAY.

Buried to-day:
When the soft green buds are bursting out,
And up on the south-wind comes a shout
Of village boys and girls at play
In the mild spring evening gray.

Taken away,
Sturdy of heart and stout of limb,
From eyes that drew half their light from him,
And put low, low underneath the clay,
In his spring, — on this spring day.

Passes away
All the pride of boy-life begun,
All the hope of life yet to run;
Who dares to question when One saith "Nay."
Murmur not, — only pray.

Enters to-day
Another body in churchyard sod,
Another soul on the life in God.
His Christ was buried — and lives alway:
Trust Him, and go your way.

Dinah Mulock Craik.

GRIEF FOR THE DEAD.

O hearts that never cease to yearn!
O brimming tears that ne'er are dried!
The dead, though they depart, return
As though they had not died!

The living are the only dead;
The dead live, — nevermore to die;
And often, when we mourn them fled,
They never were so nigh!

And though they lie beneath the waves,
Or sleep within the churchyard dim,
(Ah! through how many different graves
God's children go to him!)

Yet every grave gives up its dead
Ere it is overgrown with grass;
Then why should hopeless tears be shed,
Or need we cry, "Alas"?

Or why should Memory, veiled with gloom,
And like a sorrowing mourner craped,
Sit weeping o'er an empty tomb,
Whose captives have escaped?

'T is but a mound, — and will be mossed
Whene'er the summer grass appears;
The loved, though wept, are never lost;
We only lose — our tears!

Nay, Hope may whisper with the dead
By bending forward where they are;
But Memory, with a backward tread,
Communes with them afar.

The joys we lose are but forecast,
And we shall find them all once more;
We look behind us for the Past,
But lo! 't is all before!

ANONYMOUS.

THE MOURNERS CAME AT BREAK OF DAY.

The mourners came at break of day,
Unto the garden sepulcher,
With saddened hearts to weep and pray
For him, the loved one, buried there.
What radiant light dispels the gloom?
An angel sits beside the tomb.

The earth doth mourn her treasures lost,
All sepulchered beneath the snow,
When wintry winds and chilling frost
Have laid her summer glories low;
The spring returns, the flowerets bloom, —
An angel sits beside the tomb.

Then mourn we not belovèd dead;
E'en while we come to weep and pray,
The happy spirit hath but fled
To brighter realms of heavenly day;
Immortal hope dispels the gloom, —
An angel sits beside the tomb.

SARAH F. ADAMS.

LINES

TO THE MEMORY OF "ANNIE," WHO DIED AT MILAN, JUNE 6, 1860.

"Jesus saith unto her, Woman, why weepest thou? whom seekest thou? She, supposing him to be the gardener, saith unto him, Sir, if thou have borne him hence, tell me where thou hast laid him." — *John* xx. 15.

In the fair gardens of celestial peace
Walketh a gardener in meekness clad;
Fair are the flowers that wreathe his dewy locks,
And his mysterious eyes are sweet and sad.

Fair are the silent foldings of his robes,
Falling with saintly calmness to his feet;
And when he walks, each floweret to his will
With living pulse of sweet accord doth beat.

Every green leaf thrills to its tender heart,
In the mild summer radiance of his eye;
No fear of storm, or cold, or bitter frost,
Shadows the flowerets when their sun is nigh.

And all our pleasant haunts of earthly love
Are nurseries to those gardens of the air;
And his far-darting eye, with starry beam,
Watches the growing of his treasures there.

We call them ours, o'erwept with selfish tears,
O'erwatched with restless longings night and day;
Forgetful of the high, mysterious right
He holds to bear our cherished plants away.

But when some sunny spot in those bright fields
Needs the fair presence of an added flower,
Down sweeps a starry angel in the night:
At morn the rose has vanished from our bower!

Where stood our tree, our flower, there is a grave!
Blank, silent, vacant; but in worlds above,
Like a new star outblossomed in the skies,
The angels hail an added flower of love.

Dear friend, no more upon that lonely mound,
Strewed with the red and yellow autumn leaf,
Drop thou the tear, but raise the fainting eye
Beyond the autumn mists of earthly grief.

Thy garden rosebud bore within its breast
Those mysteries of color, warm and bright,
That the bleak climate of this lower sphere
Could never waken into form and light.

Yes, the sweet Gardener hath borne her hence,
Nor must thou ask to take her thence away;
Thou shalt behold her, in some coming hour,
Full blossomed in his fields of cloudless day.

HARRIET BEECHER STOWE.

FOOTSTEPS OF ANGELS.

WHEN the hours of day are numbered,
  And the voices of the night
Wake the better soul that slumbered
  To a holy, calm delight;

Ere the evening lamps are lighted,
  And, like phantoms grim and tall,
Shadows from the fitful firelight
  Dance upon the parlor wall;

Then the forms of the departed
  Enter at the open door, —
The beloved ones, the true-hearted,
  Come to visit me once more:

He, the young and strong, who cherished
  Noble longings for the strife,
By the roadside fell and perished,
  Weary with the march of life!

They, the holy ones and weakly,
  Who the cross of suffering bore,
Folded their pale hands so meekly,
  Spake with us on earth no more!

And with them the being beauteous
  Who unto my youth was given,
More than all things else to love me,
  And is now a saint in heaven.

With a slow and noiseless footstep
  Comes that messenger divine,
Takes the vacant chair beside me,
  Lays her gentle hand in mine;

And she sits and gazes at me
  With those deep and tender eyes,
Like the stars, so still and saint-like,
  Looking downward from the skies.

Uttered not, yet comprehended,
  Is the spirit's voiceless prayer,
Soft rebukes, in blessings ended,
  Breathing from her lips of air.

O, though oft depressed and lonely,
  All my fears are laid aside
If I but remember only
  Such as these have lived and died!

HENRY WADSWORTH LONGFELLOW.

THE OLD FAMILIAR FACES.

I HAVE had playmates, I have had companions,
In my days of childhood, in my joyful school-days;
All, all are gone, the old familiar faces.

I have been laughing, I have been carousing,
Drinking late, sitting late, with my bosom cronies;
All, all are gone, the old familiar faces.

I loved a Love once, fairest among women:
Closed are her doors on me, I must not see her, —
All, all are gone, the old familiar faces.

I have a friend, a kinder friend has no man:
Like an ingrate, I left my friend abruptly;
Left him, to muse on the old familiar faces.

Ghost-like I paced round the haunts of my childhood,
Earth seemed a desert I was bound to traverse,
Seeking to find the old familiar faces.

Friend of my bosom, thou more than a brother,
Why wert not thou born in my father's dwelling?
So might we talk of the old familiar faces.

How some they have died, and some they have left me,
And some are taken from me; all are departed;
All, all are gone, the old familiar faces.

CHARLES LAMB.

THE BURIED FLOWER.

IN the silence of my chamber,
  When the night is still and deep,
And the drowsy heave of ocean
  Mutters in its charmèd sleep,

Oft I hear the angel voices
  That have thrilled me long ago, —
Voices of my lost companions,
  Lying deep beneath the snow.

Where are now the flowers we tended?
  Withered, broken, branch and stem;
Where are now the hopes we cherished?
  Scattered to the winds with them.

For ye, too, were flowers, ye dear ones!
  Nursed in hope and reared in love,
Looking fondly ever upward
  To the clear blue heaven above;

Smiling on the sun that cheered us,
  Rising lightly from the rain,
Never folding up your freshness
  Save to give it forth again.

. . . . . .

O, 't is sad to lie and reckon
  All the days of faded youth,
All the vows that we believed in,
  All the words we spoke in truth.

Severed, — were it severed only
  By an idle thought of strife,
Such as time may knit together;
  Not the broken chord of life!

. . . .

O, I fling my spirit backward,
  And I pass o'er years of pain;
All I loved is rising round me,
  All the lost returns again.

. . . .

Brighter, fairer far than living,
  With no trace of woe or pain,
Robed in everlasting beauty,
  Shall I see them once again,

By the light that never fadeth,
  Underneath eternal skies,
When the dawn of resurrection
  Breaks o'er deathless Paradise.

WILLIAM EDMONSTOWNE AYTOUN.

THE FUTURE LIFE.

How shall I know thee in the sphere which keeps
  The disembodied spirits of the dead,
When all of thee that time could wither sleeps
  And perishes among the dust we tread?

For I shall feel the sting of ceaseless pain
  If there I meet thy gentle presence not;
Nor hear the voice I love, nor read again
  In thy serenest eyes the tender thought.

Will not thy own meek heart demand me there?
  That heart whose fondest throbs to me were given;
My name on earth was ever in thy prayer,
  And wilt thou never utter it in heaven?

In meadows fanned by heaven's life-breathing wind,
  In the resplendence of that glorious sphere,
And larger movements of the unfettered mind,
  Wilt thou forget the love that joined us here?

The love that lived through all the stormy past,
  And meekly with my harsher nature bore,
And deeper grew, and tenderer to the last,
  Shall it expire with life, and be no more?

A happier lot than mine, and larger light,
  Await thee there; for thou hast bowed thy will
In cheerful homage to the rule of right,
  And lovest all, and renderest good for ill.

For me, the sordid cares in which I dwell,
  Shrink and consume my heart, as heat the scroll;
And wrath has left its scar — that fire of hell
  Has left its frightful scar upon my soul.

Yet though thou wear'st the glory of the sky,
  Wilt thou not keep the same belovèd name,
The same fair thoughtful brow, and gentle eye,
  Lovelier in heaven's sweet climate, yet the same?

Shalt thou not teach me, in that calmer home,
  The wisdom that I learned so ill in this —
The wisdom which is love — till I become
  Thy fit companion in that land of bliss?

WILLIAM CULLEN BRYANT.

THE ANGEL OF PATIENCE.

A FREE PARAPHRASE OF THE GERMAN.

To weary hearts, to mourning homes,
God's meekest Angel gently comes:
No power has he to banish pain,
Or give us back our lost again;
And yet in tenderest love our dear
And heavenly Father sends him here.

There's quiet in that Angel's glance,
There's rest in his still countenance!
He mocks no grief with idle cheer,
Nor wounds with words the mourner's ear;
But ills and woes he may not cure
He kindly trains us to endure.

Angel of Patience! sent to calm
Our feverish brows with cooling palm;
To lay the storms of hope and fear,
And reconcile life's smile and tear;
The throbs of wounded pride to still,
And make our own our Father's will!

O thou who mournest on thy way,
With longings for the close of day;
He walks with thee, that Angel kind,
And gently whispers, "Be resigned:
Bear up, bear on, the end shall tell
The dear Lord ordereth all things well!"

JOHN GREENLEAF WHITTIER.

FRIENDS DEPARTED.

THEY are all gone into the world of light,
  And I alone sit lingering here!
Their very memory is fair and bright,
    And my sad thoughts doth clear;

It glows and glitters in my cloudy breast,
  Like stars upon some gloomy grove,—
Or those faint beams in which this hill is drest
    After the sun's remove.

I see them walking in an air of glory,
Whose light doth trample on my days, —
My days which are at best but dull and hoary,
Mere glimmering and decays.

O holy hope! and high humility, —
High as the arching heavens above!
These are your walks, and you have showed them me,
To kindle my cold love.

Dear, beauteous death, — the jewel of the just, —
Shining nowhere but in the dark!
What mysteries do lie beyond thy dust,
Could man outlook that mark!

He that hath found some fledged bird's nest may know,
At first sight, if the bird be flown;
But what fair dell or grove he sings in now,
That is to him unknown.

And yet, as angels in some brighter dreams
Call to the soul when man doth sleep,
So some strange thoughts transcend our wonted themes,
And into glory peep.

If a star were confined into a tomb,
Her captive flames must needs burn there,
But when the hand that locked her up gives room,
She 'll shine through all the sphere.

O Father of eternal life, and all
Created glories under thee!
Resume thy spirit from this world of thrall
Into true liberty.

Either disperse these mists, which blot and fill
My pérspective still as they pass;
Or else remove me hence unto that hill
Where I shall need no glass.

HENRY VAUGHAN.

THE FIRST SNOW-FALL.

The snow had begun in the gloaming,
And busily all the night
Had been heaping field and highway
With a silence deep and white.

Every pine and fir and hemlock
Wore ermine too dear for an earl,
And the poorest twig on the elm-tree
Was ridged inch deep with pearl.

From sheds new-roofed with Carrara
Came Chanticleer's muffled crow,
The stiff rails were softened to swan's-down,
And still fluttered down the snow.

I stood and watched by the window
The noiseless work of the sky,
And the sudden flurries of snow-birds,
Like brown leaves whirling by.

I thought of a mound in sweet Auburn
Where a little headstone stood;
How the flakes were folding it gently,
As did robins the babes in the wood.

Up spoke our own little Mabel,
Saying, "Father, who makes it snow?"
And I told of the good All-father
Who cares for us here below.

Again I looked at the snow-fall,
And thought of the leaden sky
That arched o'er our first great sorrow,
When that mound was heaped so high.

I remembered the gradual patience
That fell from that cloud like snow,
Flake by flake, healing and hiding
The scar of our deep-plunged woe.

And again to the child I whispered,
"The snow that husheth all,
Darling, the merciful Father
Alone can make it fall!"

Then, with eyes that saw not, I kissed her;
And she, kissing back, could not know
That *my* kiss was given to her sister,
Folded close under deepening snow.

JAMES RUSSELL LOWELL.

THE REAPER AND THE FLOWERS.

There is a Reaper whose name is Death,
And, with his sickle keen,
He reaps the bearded grain at a breath,
And the flowers that grow between.

"Shall I have naught that is fair?" saith he;
"Have naught but the bearded grain?
Though the breath of these flowers is sweet to me,
I will give them all back again."

He gazed at the flowers with tearful eyes,
He kissed their drooping leaves;
It was for the Lord of Paradise
He bound them in his sheaves.

"My Lord has need of these flowerets gay,"
The Reaper said, and smiled;

Eng'd by Geo. E. Perine New York

Henry W. Longfellow

"Dear tokens of the earth are they,
  Where he was once a child.

"They shall all bloom in fields of light,
  Transplanted by my care,
And saints, upon their garments white,
  These sacred blossoms wear."

And the mother gave, in tears and pain,
  The flowers she most did love;
She knew she should find them all again
  In the fields of light above.

O, not in cruelty, not in wrath,
  The Reaper came that day;
'T was an angel visited the green earth,
  And took the flowers away.

HENRY WADSWORTH LONGFELLOW.

OVER THE RIVER.

Over the river they beckon to me,
  Loved ones who 've crossed to the farther side,
The gleam of their snowy robes I see,
  But their voices are lost in the dashing tide.
There 's one with ringlets of sunny gold,
  And eyes the reflection of heaven's own blue;
He crossed in the twilight gray and cold,
  And the pale mist hid him from mortal view.
We saw not the angels who met him there,
  The gates of the city we could not see:
Over the river, over the river,
  My brother stands waiting to welcome me.

Over the river the boatman pale
  Carried another, the household pet;
Her brown curls waved in the gentle gale,
  Darling Minnie! I see her yet.
She crossed on her bosom her dimpled hands,
  And fearlessly entered the phantom bark;
We felt it glide from the silver sands,
  And all our sunshine grew strangely dark;
We know she is safe on the farther side,
  Where all the ransomed and angels be:
Over the river, the mystic river,
  My childhood's idol is waiting for me.

For none return from those quiet shores,
  Who cross with the boatman cold and pale;
We hear the dip of the golden oars,
  And catch a gleam of the snowy sail;
And lo! they have passed from our yearning hearts,
  They cross the stream and are gone for aye.
We may not sunder the veil apart
  That hides from our vision the gates of day;
We only know that their barks no more
  May sail with us o'er life's stormy sea;
Yet somewhere, I know, on the unseen shore,
  They watch, and beckon, and wait for me.

And I sit and think, when the sunset's gold
  Is flushing river and hill and shore,
I shall one day stand by the water cold,
  And list for the sound of the boatman's oar;
I shall watch for a gleam of the flapping sail,
  I shall hear the boat as it gains the strand,
I shall pass from sight with the boatman pale,
  To the better shore of the spirit land.
I shall know the loved who have gone before,
  And joyfully sweet will the meeting be,
When over the river, the peaceful river,
  The angel of death shall carry me.

NANCY WOODBURY PRIEST.

THE TWO WAITINGS.

I.

Dear hearts, you were waiting a year ago
  For the glory to be revealed;
You were wondering deeply, with bated breath,
  What treasure the days concealed.

O, would it be this, or would it be that?
  Would it be girl or boy?
Would it look like father or mother most?
  And what should you do for joy?

And then, one day, when the time was full,
  And the spring was coming fast,
The trembling veil of the body was rent,
  And you saw your baby at last.

Was it or not what you had dreamed?
  It was, and yet it was not;
But O, it was better a thousand times
  Than ever you wished or thought.

II.

And now, dear hearts, you are waiting again,
  While the spring is coming fast;
For the baby that was a future dream
  Is now a dream of the past:

A dream of sunshine, and all that 's sweet;
  Of all that is pure and bright;
Of eyes that were blue as the sky by day,
  And as soft as the stars by night.

You are waiting again for the fullness of time,
  And the glory to be revealed;
You are wondering deeply with aching hearts
  What treasure is now concealed.

O, will she be this, or will she be that?
And what will there be in her face
That will tell you sure that she is your own,
When you meet in the heavenly place?

As it was before, it will be again,
Fashion your dream as you will;
When the veil is rent, and the glory is seen,
It will more than your hope fulfill.

JOHN WHITE CHADWICK.

ON AN INFANT'S DEATH.

A LITTLE life,
Five summer months of gladness
Without one cloud of sorrow, sin, or strife,
Cut short by sudden gloom and wintry sadness.

A little mound
By buttress gray defended,
Watered with tears and garlanded all round,
By loving hands affectionately tended.

A little cot,
Empty, forlorn, forsaken,
Silent remembrancer that he is not, —
Gone — past our voice to lull, or kiss to waken.

A little frock
He wore, a hat that shaded
His innocent brow, seen with a sudden shock
Of grief for that dear form so quickly faded.

A little flower,
Because he touched it cherished,
Fragile memorial of one happy hour
Before the beauty of our blossom perished.

A little hair,
Secured with trembling fingers,
All that is left us of our infant fair,
All we shall see of him while this life lingers.

A little name,
In parish records written,
A passing sympathy to claim
From other fathers for a father smitten.

But a great trust
Irradiates our sorrow,
That though to-day his name is writ in dust,
We shall behold it writ in heaven to-morrow.

And a great peace
Our troubled soul possesses,
That though to embrace him these poor arms must cease,
Our lamb lies folded in the Lord's caresses.

A little pain,
To point his life's brief story.
A few hours' mortal weariness, to gain
Unutterable rest and endless glory.

A little prayer,
By lips Divine once spoken,
"Thy will be done!" is breathed into the air
From hearts submissive, though with accents broken.

A little while,
And Time no more shall sever;
But we shall see him with his own sweet smile,
And clasp our darling in our arms forever!

ANONYMOUS.

FOR CHARLIE'S SAKE.

THE night is late, the house is still;
The angels of the hour fulfill
Their tender ministries, and move
From couch to couch in cares of love.
They drop into thy dreams, sweet wife,
The happiest smile of Charlie's life,
And lay on baby's lips a kiss,
Fresh from his angel-brother's bliss;
And, as they pass, they seem to make
A strange, dim hymn, "For Charlie's sake."

My listening heart takes up the strain,
And gives it to the night again,
Fitted with words of lowly praise,
And patience learned of mournful days,
And memories of the dead child's ways.

His will be done, His will be done!
Who gave and took away my son,
In "the far land" to shine and sing
Before the Beautiful, the King,
Who every day doth Christmas make,
All starred and belled for Charlie's sake.

For Charlie's sake I will arise;
I will anoint me where he lies,
And change my raiment, and go in
To the Lord's house, and leave my sin
Without, and seat me at his board,
Eat, and be glad, and praise the Lord.
For wherefore should I fast and weep,
And sullen moods of mourning keep?
I cannot bring him back, nor he,
For any calling, come to me.
The bond the angel Death did sign,
God sealed — for Charlie's sake, and mine.

JOHN WILLIAMSON PALMER.

"ONLY A YEAR."

ONE year ago, — a ringing voice,
A clear blue eye,
And clustering curls of sunny hair,
Too fair to die.

Only a year, — no voice, no smile,
No glance of eye,
No clustering curls of golden hair,
Fair but to die!

One year ago, — what loves, what schemes
Far into life!
What joyous hopes, what high resolves,
What generous strife!

The silent picture on the wall,
The burial-stone
Of all that beauty, life, and joy,
Remain alone!

One year, — one year, — one little year,
And so much gone!
And yet the even flow of life
Moves calmly on.

The grave grows green, the flowers bloom fair,
Above that head;
No sorrowing tint of leaf or spray
Says he is dead.

No pause or hush of merry birds
That sing above
Tells us how coldly sleeps below
The form we love.

Where hast thou been this year, beloved?
What hast thou seen, —
What visions fair, what glorious life,
Where thou hast been?

The veil! the veil! so thin, so strong!
'Twixt us and thee;
The mystic veil! when shall it fall,
That we may see?

Not dead, not sleeping, not even gone,
But present still,
And waiting for the coming hour
Of God's sweet will.

Lord of the living and the dead,
Our Saviour dear!
We lay in silence at thy feet
This sad, sad year.

HARRIET BEECHER STOWE.

MY CHILD.

I CANNOT make him dead!
His fair sunshiny head
Is ever bounding round my study chair;
Yet when my eyes, now dim
With tears, I turn to him,
The vision vanishes, — he is not there!

I walk my parlor floor,
And, through the open door,
I hear a footfall on the chamber stair;
I 'm stepping toward the hall
To give the boy a call;
And then bethink me that — he is not there!

I thread the crowded street;
A satcheled lad I meet,
With the same beaming eyes and colored hair;
And, as he 's running by,
Follow him with my eye,
Scarcely believing that — he is not there!

I know his face is hid
Under the coffin lid;
Closed are his eyes; cold is his forehead fair;
My hand that marble felt;
O'er it in prayer I knelt;
Yet my heart whispers that — he is not there!

I cannot make him dead!
When passing by the bed,
So long watched over with parental care,
My spirit and my eye
Seek him inquiringly,
Before the thought comes, that — he is not there!

When, at the cool gray break
Of day, from sleep I wake,
With my first breathing of the morning air
My soul goes up, with joy,
To Him who gave my boy;
Then comes the sad thought that — he is not there!

When at the day's calm close,
Before we seek repose,
I 'm with his mother, offering up our prayer;
Whate'er I may be saying,
I am in spirit praying
For our boy's spirit, though — he is not there!

Not there! — Where, then, is he?
The form I used to see
Was but the raiment that he used to wear.
The grave, that now doth press
Upon that cast-off dress,
Is but his wardrobe locked; — he is not there!

He lives! — In all the past
He lives; nor, to the last,
Of seeing him again will I despair;
In dreams I see him now;
And, on his angel brow,
I see it written, "Thou shalt see me *there!*"

Yes, we all live to God!
Father, thy chastening rod
So help us, thine afflicted ones, to bear,
That, in the spirit land,
Meeting at thy right hand,
'T will be our heaven to find that — he is there!

JOHN PIERPONT.

CASA WAPPY.

THE CHILD'S PET NAME, CHOSEN BY HIMSELF.

And hast thou sought thy heavenly home,
Our fond, dear boy, —
The realms where sorrow dare not come,
Where life is joy?
Pure at thy death as at thy birth,
Thy spirit caught no taint from earth;
Even by its bliss we mete our dearth,
Casa Wappy!

Despair was in our last farewell,
As closed thine eye;
Tears of our anguish may not tell
When thou didst die;
Words may not paint our grief for thee;
Sighs are but bubbles on the sea
Of our unfathomed agony;
Casa Wappy!

Thou wert a vision of delight,
To bless us given;
Beauty embodied to our sight,
A type of heaven!
So dear to us thou wert, thou art
Even less thine own self, than a part
Of mine, and of thy mother's heart,
Casa Wappy!

Thy bright, brief day knew no decline,
'T was cloudless joy;
Sunrise and night alone were thine,
Beloved boy!
This moon beheld thee blithe and gay;
That found thee prostrate in decay;
And ere a third shone, clay was clay,
Casa Wappy!

Gem of our hearth, our household pride,
Earth's undefiled,
Could love have saved, thou hadst not died,
Our dear, sweet child!
Humbly we bow to Fate's decree;
Yet had we hoped that Time should see
Thee mourn for us, not us for thee,
Casa Wappy!

. . . . . .

We mourn for thee when blind, blank night
The chamber fills;
We pine for thee when morn's first light
Reddens the hills:
The sun, the moon, the stars, the sea,
All — to the wallflower and wild pea —
Are changed; we saw the world through thee,
Casa Wappy!

And though, perchance, a smile may gleam
Of casual mirth,
It doth not own, whate'er may seem,
An inward birth;
We miss thy small step on the stair;
We miss thee at thine evening prayer;
All day we miss thee, — everywhere, —
Casa Wappy!

Snows muffled earth when thou didst go,
In life's spring-bloom,
Down to the appointed house below, —
The silent tomb.
But now the green leaves of the tree,
The cuckoo, and "the busy bee,"
Return, — but with them bring not thee,
Casa Wappy!

'T is so; but can it be — while flowers
Revive again —
Man's doom, in death that we and ours
For aye remain?
O, can it be, that o'er the grave
The grass renewed should yearly wave,
Yet God forget our child to save? —
Casa Wappy!

It cannot be; for were it so
Thus man could die,
Life were a mockery, thought were woe,
And truth a lie;
Heaven were a coinage of the brain;
Religion frenzy, virtue vain,
And all our hopes to meet again,
Casa Wappy!

Then be to us, O dear, lost child!
With beam of love,
A star, death's uncongenial wild
Smiling above!
Soon, soon thy little feet have trod
The skyward path, the seraph's road,
That led thee back from man to God,
Casa Wappy!

Yet 't is sweet balm to our despair,
Fond, fairest boy,
That heaven is God's, and thou art there,
With him in joy;
There past are death and all its woes;
There beauty's stream forever flows;
And pleasure's day no sunset knows,
Casa Wappy!

Farewell, then, — for a while, farewell, —
Pride of my heart!
It cannot be that long we dwell,
Thus torn apart.
Time's shadows like the shuttle flee;
And dark howe'er life's night may be,
Beyond the grave I 'll meet with thee,
Casa Wappy!

DAVID MACBETH MOIR.

TOMMY 'S DEAD.

You may give over plow, boys,
You may take the gear to the stead,
All the sweat o' your brow, boys,
Will never get beer and bread.
The seed 's waste, I know, boys,
There 's not a blade will grow, boys,
'T is cropped out, I trow, boys,
And Tommy 's dead.

Send the colt to fair, boys,
He 's going blind, as I said,
My old eyes can't bear, boys,
To see him in the shed;
The cow 's dry and spare, boys,
She 's neither here nor there, boys,
I doubt she 's badly bred;
Stop the mill to-morn, boys,
There 'll be no more corn, boys,
Neither white nor red;
There 's no sign of grass, boys,
You may sell the goat and the ass, boys,
The land 's not what it was, boys,
And the beasts must be fed:
You may turn Peg away, boys,
You may pay off old Ned,
We 've had a dull day, boys,
And Tommy 's dead.

Move my chair on the floor, boys,
Let me turn my head:
She 's standing there in the door, boys,
Your sister Winifred!
Take her away from me, boys,
Your sister Winifred!
Move me round in my place, boys,
Let me turn my head,
Take her away from me, boys,
As she lay on her death-bed,
The bones of her thin face, boys,
As she lay on her death-bed!
I don't know how it be, boys,
When all 's done and said,
But I see her looking at me, boys,
Wherever I turn my head;
Out of the big oak-tree, boys,
Out of the garden-bed,
And the lily as pale as she, boys,
And the rose that used to be red.

There 's something not right, boys,
But I think it 's not in my head,
I 've kept my precious sight, boys, —
The Lord be hallowèd!
Outside and in
The ground is cold to my tread,
The hills are wizen and thin,
The sky is shriveled and shred,
The hedges down by the loan
I can count them bone by bone,
The leaves are open and spread,
But I see the teeth of the land,
And hands like a dead man's hand,
And the eyes of a dead man's head.

There 's nothing but cinders and sand,
The rat and the mouse have fed,
And the summer 's empty and cold;
Over valley and wold
Wherever I turn my head
There 's a mildew and a mold,
The sun 's going out overhead,
And I 'm very old,
And Tommy 's dead.

What am I staying for, boys,
You 're all born and bred,
'T is fifty years and more, boys,
Since wife and I were wed,
And she 's gone before, boys,
And Tommy 's dead.

She was always sweet, boys,
Upon his curly head,
She knew she 'd never see 't, boys,
And she stole off to bed;
I 've been sitting up alone, boys,
For he 'd come home, he said,
But it 's time I was gone, boys,
For Tommy 's dead.

Put the shutters up, boys,
Bring out the beer and bread,
Make haste and sup, boys,
For my eyes are heavy as lead;

There 's something wrong i' the cup, boys,
There 's something ill wi' the bread,
I don't care to sup, boys,
And Tommy 's dead.

I 'm not right, I doubt, boys,
I 've such a sleepy head,
I shall nevermore be stout, boys,
You may carry me to bed.
What are you about, boys?
The prayers are all said,
The fire 's raked out, boys,
And Tommy 's dead.

The stairs are too steep, boys,
You may carry me to the head,
The night 's dark and deep, boys,
Your mother 's long in bed,
'T is time to go to sleep, boys,
And Tommy 's dead.

I 'm not used to kiss, boys,
You may shake my hand instead.
All things go amiss, boys,
You may lay me where she is, boys,
And I 'll rest my old head:
'T is a poor world, this, boys,
And Tommy 's dead.

SIDNEY DOBELL.

THE MERRY LARK.

THE merry, merry lark was up and singing,
And the hare was out and feeding on the lea,
And the merry, merry bells below were ringing,
When my child's laugh rang through me.
Now the hare is snared and dead beside the snowyard,
And the lark beside the dreary winter sea,
And my baby in his cradle in the churchyard
Waiteth there until the bells bring me.

CHARLES KINGSLEY.

THE MORNING-GLORY.

WE wreathed about our darling's head
The morning-glory bright;
Her little face looked out beneath
So full of life and light,
So lit as with a sunrise,
That we could only say,
"She is the morning-glory true,
And her poor types are they."

So always from that happy time
We called her by their name,
And very fitting did it seem, —
For sure as morning came,
Behind her cradle bars she smiled
To catch the first faint ray,
As from the trellis smiles the flower
And opens to the day.

But not so beautiful they rear
Their airy cups of blue,
As turned her sweet eyes to the light,
Brimmed with sleep's tender dew;
And not so close their tendrils fine
Round their supports are thrown,
As those dear arms whose outstretched plea
Clasped all hearts to her own.

We used to think how she had come,
Even as comes the flower,
The last and perfect added gift
To crown Love 's morning hour;
And how in her was imaged forth
The love we could not say,
As on the little dewdrops round
Shines back the heart of day.

. . . . .

The morning-glory's blossoming
Will soon be coming round, —
We see their rows of heart-shaped leaves
Upspringing from the ground;
The tender things the winter killed
Renew again their birth,
But the glory of our morning
Has passed away from earth.

O Earth! in vain our aching eyes
Stretch over thy green plain!
Too harsh thy dews, too gross thine air,
Her spirit to sustain;
But up in groves of Paradise
Full surely we shall see
Our morning-glory beautiful
Twine round our dear Lord's knee.

MARIA WHITE LOWELL.

ARE THE CHILDREN AT HOME?

EACH day, when the glow of sunset
Fades in the western sky,
And the wee ones, tired of playing,
Go tripping lightly by,
I steal away from my husband,
Asleep in his easy-chair,
And watch from the open doorway
Their faces fresh and fair.

Alone in the dear old homestead
That once was full of life,
Ringing with girlish laughter,
Echoing boyish strife,

We two are waiting together ;
And oft, as the shadows come,
With tremulous voice he calls me,
"It is night! are the children home?"

"Yes, love!" I answer him gently,
"They 're all home long ago"; —
And I sing, in my quivering treble,
A song so soft and low,
Till the old man drops to slumber,
With his head upon his hand,
And I tell to myself the number
At home in the better land.

At home, where never a sorrow
Shall dim their eyes with tears!
Where the smile of God is on them
Through all the summer years!
I know, — yet my arms are empty,
That fondly folded seven,
And the mother heart within me
Is almost starved for heaven.

Sometimes, in the dusk of evening,
I only shut my eyes,
And the children are all about me,
A vision from the skies:
The babes whose dimpled fingers
Lost the way to my breast,
And the beautiful ones, the angels,
Passed to the world of the blest.

With never a cloud upon them,
I see their radiant brows;
My boys that I gave to freedom, —
The red sword sealed their vows!
In a tangled Southern forest,
Twin brothers bold and brave,
They fell; and the flag they died for,
Thank God! floats over their grave.

A breath, and the vision is lifted
Away on wings of light,
And again we two are together,
All alone in the night.
They tell me his mind is failing,
But I smile at idle fears;
He is only back with the children,
In the dear and peaceful years.

And still, as the summer sunset
Fades away in the west,
And the wee ones, tired of playing,
Go trooping home to rest,
My husband calls from his corner,
"Say, love, have the children come?"
And I answer, with eyes uplifted,
"Yes, dear! they are all at home."

MRS. M. E. M. SANGSTER.

THE LOST SISTER.

THEY waked me from my sleep, I knew not why,
And bade me hasten where a midnight lamp
Gleamed from an inner chamber. There she lay,
With brow so pale, who yester-morn breathed forth
Through joyous smiles her superflux of bliss
Into the hearts of others. By her side
Her hoary sire, with speechless sorrow, gazed
Upon the stricken idol, — all dismayed
Beneath his God's rebuke. And she who nursed
That fair young creature at her gentle breast,
And oft those sunny locks had decked with buds
Of rose and jasmine, shuddering wiped the dews
Which death distills.
The sufferer just had given
Her long farewell, and for the last, *last* time
Touched with cold lips his cheek who led so late
Her footsteps to the altar, and received
In the deep transport of an ardent heart
Her vow of love. And she had striven to press
That golden circlet with her bloodless hand
Back on his finger, which he kneeling gave
At the bright bridal morn. So there she lay
In calm endurance, like the smitten lamb
Wounded in flowery pastures, from whose breast
The dreaded bitterness of death had passed.
— But a faint wail disturbed the silent scene,
And in its nurse's arms a new-born babe
Was borne in utter helplessness along,
Before that dying eye.
Its gathered film
Kindled one moment with a sudden glow
Of tearless agony, — and fearful pangs,
Racking the rigid features, told how strong
A mother's love doth root itself. One cry
Of bitter anguish, blent with fervent prayer,
Went up to Heaven, — and, as its cadence sank,
Her spirit entered there.
Morn after morn
Rose and retired; yet still as in a dream
I seemed to move. The certainty of loss
Fell not *at once* upon me. Then I wept
As weep the sisterless. — For thou wert fled,
My only, my beloved, my sainted one, —
Twin of my spirit! and my numbered days
Must wear the sable of that midnight hour
Which rent thee from me.

LYDIA H. SIGOURNEY.

GO TO THY REST.

Go to thy rest, fair child!
Go to thy dreamless bed,
While yet so gentle, undefiled,
With blessings on thy head.

Fresh roses in thy hand,
Buds on thy pillow laid,
Haste from this dark and fearful land,
Where flowers so quickly fade.

Ere sin has seared the breast,
Or sorrow waked the tear,
Rise to thy throne of changeless rest,
In yon celestial sphere!

Because thy smile was fair,
Thy lip and eye so bright,
Because thy loving cradle-care
Was such a dear delight,

Shall love, with weak embrace,
Thy upward wing detain?
No! gentle angel, seek thy place
Amid the cherub train.

ANONYMOUS.

"THEY ARE DEAR FISH TO ME."

THE farmer's wife sat at the door,
A pleasant sight to see;
And blithesome were the wee, wee bairns
That played around her knee.

When, bending 'neath her heavy creel,
A poor fish-wife came by,
And, turning from the toilsome road,
Unto the door drew nigh.

She laid her burden on the green,
And spread its scaly store;
With trembling hands and pleading words
She told them o'er and o'er.

But lightly laughed the young guidwife,
"We 're no sae scarce o' cheer;
Tak' up your creel, and gang your ways, —
I 'll buy nae fish sae dear."

Bending beneath her load again,
A weary sight to see;
Right sorely sighed the poor fish-wife,
"They are dear fish to me!

"Our boat was oot ae fearfu' night,
And when the storm blew o'er,
My husband, and my three brave sons,
Lay corpses on the shore.

"I 've been a wife for thirty years,
A childless widow three;
I maun buy them now to sell again, —
They are dear fish to me!"

The farmer's wife turned to the door, —
What was 't upon her cheek?
What was there rising in her breast,
That then she scarce could speak?

She thought upon her ain guidman,
Her lightsome laddies three;
The woman's words had pierced her heart, —
"They are dear fish to me!"

"Come back," she cried, with quivering voice,
And pity's gathering tear;
"Come in, come in, my poor woman,
Ye 're kindly welcome here.

"I kentna o' your aching heart,
Your weary lot to dree;
I 'll ne'er forget your sad, sad words:
'They are dear fish to me!'"

Ay, let the happy-hearted learn
To pause ere they deny
The meed of honest toil, and think
How much their gold may buy, —

How much of manhood's wasted strength,
What woman's misery, —
What breaking hearts might swell the cry:
"They are dear fish to me!"

ANONYMOUS.

CORONACH.

FROM "THE LADY OF THE LAKE."

HE is gone on the mountain,
He is lost to the forest,
Like a summer-dried fountain
When our need was the sorest.
The font, reappearing,
From the rain-drops shall borrow,
But to us comes no cheering,
To Duncan no morrow!

The hand of the reaper
Takes the ears that are hoary;
But the voice of the weeper
Wails manhood in glory.
The autumn winds rushing
Waft the leaves that are searest,
But our flower was in flushing
When blighting was nearest.

Fleet foot on the correi,
Sage counsel in cumber,
Red hand in the foray,
How sound is thy slumber!

Like the dew on the mountain,
Like the foam on the river,
Like the bubble on the fountain,
Thou art gone and forever!

SIR WALTER SCOTT.

IN HEAVEN.

"Their angels do always behold the face of my Father."

SILENCE filled the courts of heaven,
Hushed were seraphs' harp and tone,
When a little new-born cherub
Knelt before the Eternal Throne;
While its soft white hands were lifted,
Clasped as if in earnest prayer,
And its voice in dove-like murmurs
Rose like music on the ear.
Light from the full fount of glory
On his robe of whiteness glistened,
And the white-winged seraphs near him
Bowed their radiant heads and listened.

"Lord, from thy throne of glory here
My heart turns fondly to another;
O Lord my God, the Comforter,
Comfort, comfort my sweet mother!
Many sorrows hast thou sent her, —
Meekly has she drained the cup,
And the jewels thou hast lent her
Unrepining yielded up.
Comfort, comfort my sweet mother!

"Earth is growing lonely round her;
Friend and lover hast thou taken;
Let her not, though woes surround her,
Feel herself by thee forsaken.
Let her think, when faint and weary,
We are waiting for her *here;*
Let each loss that makes earth dreary
Make the hope of Heaven more dear.
Comfort, comfort my sweet mother!

"Thou who once, in nature human,
Dwelt on earth a little child,
Pillowed on the breast of woman,
Blessèd Mary undefiled;
Thou who, from the cross of suffering,
Marked thy mother's tearful face,
And bequeathed her to thy loved one,
Bidding him to fill thy place, —
Comfort, comfort my sweet mother!

"Thou who once, from heaven descending,
Tears and woes and conflicts won;
Thou who, nature's laws suspending,
Gav'st the widow back her son;
Thou who at the grave of Lazarus
Wept with those who wept their dead;
Thou who once in mortal anguish
Bowed thine own anointed head, —
Comfort, comfort my sweet mother!"

The dove-like murmurs died away
Upon the radiant air;
But still the little suppliant knelt
With hands still clasped in prayer.
Still were those mildly pleading eyes
Turned to the sapphire throne,
Till golden harp and angel voice
Rang forth in mingled tone.
And as the swelling numbers flowed,
By angel voices given,
Rich, sweet, and clear, the anthem rolled
Through all the courts of heaven:
"He is the widow's God," it said,
"Who spared not his OWN SON."
The infant cherub bowed its head:
"*Thy will, O Lord, be done!*"

THOMAS WESTWOOD.

MOTHER AND POET.*

TURIN, — AFTER NEWS FROM GAETA. 1861.

DEAD! one of them shot by the sea in the east,
And one of them shot in the west by the sea.
Dead! both my boys! When you sit at the feast
And are wanting a great song for Italy free,
Let none look at *me*!

Yet I was a poetess only last year,
And good at my art, for a woman, men said;
But this woman, this, who is agonized here,
The east sea and west sea rhyme on in her head
Forever instead.

What art can a woman be good at? O, vain!
What art is she good at, but hurting her breast
With the milk teeth of babes, and a smile at the pain?
Ah, boys, how you hurt! you were strong as you pressed,
And I proud, by that test.

What art 's for a woman? To hold on her knees
Both darlings! to feel all their arms round her throat
Cling, strangle a little! to sew by degrees
And 'broider the long-clothes and neat little coat;
To dream and to dote.

To teach them... It stings there! *I* made them indeed
Speak plain the word "country," *I* taught them, no doubt,

* This was Laura Savio of Turin, a poetess and patriot, whose sons were killed at Ancona and Gaeta.

That a country 's a thing men should die for at need.
I prated of liberty, rights, and about
The tyrant cast out.

And when their eyes flashed. . . O my beautiful eyes! . .
I exulted; nay, let them go forth at the wheels
Of the guns, and denied not. — But then the surprise,
When one sits quite alone! — Then one weeps, then one kneels!
— God! how the house feels!

At first, happy news came, in gay letters moiled
With my kisses, of camp-life, and glory, and how
They both loved me, and soon, coming home to be spoiled,
In return would fan off every fly from my brow
With their green laurel-bough.

Then was triumph at Turin: "Ancona was free!"
And some one came out of the cheers in the street
With a face pale as stone, to say something to me.
— My Guido was dead! — I fell down at his feet,
While they cheered in the street.

I bore it; — friends soothed me: my grief looked sublime
As the ransom of Italy. One boy remained
To be leant on and walked with, recalling the time
When the first grew immortal, while both of us strained
To the height he had gained.

And letters still came, — shorter, sadder, more strong,
Writ now but in one hand: "I was not to faint.
One loved me for two — would be with me ere long:
And 'Viva Italia' *he* died for, our saint,
Who forbids our complaint."

My Nanni would add "he was safe, and aware
Of a presence that turned off the balls — was imprest
It was Guido himself, who knew what I could bear,
And how 't was impossible, quite dispossessed,
To live on for the rest."

On which without pause up the telegraph line
Swept smoothly the next news from Gaeta: — "Shot.
Tell his mother." Ah, ah, "his" "their" mother; not "mine."
No voice says "*my* mother" again to me. What!
You think Guido forgot?

Are souls straight so happy that, dizzy with heaven,
They drop earth's affections, conceive not of woe?
I think not. Themselves were too lately forgiven
Through that Love and Sorrow which reconcilèd so
The above and below.

O Christ of the seven wounds, who look'dst through the dark
To the face of thy mother! consider, I pray,
How we common mothers stand desolate, mark,
Whose sons, not being Christs, die with eyes turned away,
And no last word to say!

Both boys dead! but that 's out of nature. We all
Have been patriots, yet each house must always keep one.
'T were imbecile, hewing out roads to a wall.
And when Italy 's made, for what end is it done
If we have not a son?

Ah, ah, ah! when Gaeta 's taken, what then?
When the fair wicked queen sits no more at her sport
Of the fire-balls of death crashing souls out of men,
When your guns at Cavalli with final retort
Have cut the game short, —

When Venice and Rome keep their new jubilee,
When your flag takes all heaven for its white, green, and red,
When you have your country from mountain to sea,
When King Victor has Italy's crown on his head,
(And I have my dead,) —

What then? Do not mock me. Ah, ring your bells low,
And burn your lights faintly! — *My* country is *there*,
Above the star pricked by the last peak of snow,
My Italy 's there, — with my brave civic pair,
To disfranchise despair!

Forgive me. Some women bear children in strength,
And bite back the cry of their pain in self-scorn.
But the birth-pangs of nations will wring us at length
Into such wail as this! — and we sit on forlorn
When the man-child is born.

Dead! one of them shot by the sea in the east,
And one of them shot in the west by the sea!
Both! both my boys! — If in keeping the feast
You want a great song for your Italy free,
Let none look at *me*!

ELIZABETH BARRETT BROWNING.

THE GOLDEN RINGLET.

HERE is a little golden tress
Of soft unbraided hair,
The all that 's left of loveliness
That once was thought so fair;
And yet, though time hath dimmed its sheen,
Though all beside hath fled,
I hold it here, a link between
My spirit and the dead.

Yes! from this shining ringlet still
A mournful memory springs,
That melts my heart, and sheds a thrill
Through all its trembling strings.
I think of her, the loved, the wept,
Upon whose forehead fair
For eighteen years, like sunshine, slept
This golden curl of hair.

O sunny tress! the joyous brow
Where thou didst lightly wave,
With all thy sister-tresses now
Lies cold within the grave;
That cheek is of its bloom bereft;
That eye no more is gay;
Of all her beauties thou art left,
A solitary ray.

AMELIA B. WELBY.

EVELYN HOPE.

BEAUTIFUL Evelyn Hope is dead!
Sit and watch by her side an hour.
That is her book-shelf, this her bed;
She plucked that piece of geranium-flower,
Beginning to die too, in the glass.
Little has yet been changed, I think;
The shutters are shut, — no light may pass
Save two long rays through the hinge's chink.

Sixteen years old when she died!
Perhaps she had scarcely heard my name, —
It was not her time to love; beside,
Her life had many a hope and aim,
Duties enough and little cares;
And now was quiet, now astir, —
Till God's hand beckoned unawares,
And the sweet white brow is all of her.

Is it too late, then, Evelyn Hope?
What! your soul was pure and true;
The good stars met in your horoscope,
Made you of spirit, fire, and dew;
And just because I was thrice as old,
And our paths in the world diverged so wide,
Each was naught to each, must I be told?
We were fellow-mortals, — naught beside?

No, indeed! for God above
Is great to grant as mighty to make,
And creates the love to reward the love;
I claim you still, for my own love's sake!
Delayed, it may be, for more lives yet,
Through worlds I shall traverse, not a few;
Much is to learn and much to forget
Ere the time be come for taking you.

But the time will come — at last it will —
When, Evelyn Hope, what meant, I shall say,
In the lower earth, — in the years long still, —
That body and soul so pure and gay?
Why your hair was amber I shall divine,
And your mouth of your own geranium's red, —
And what you would do with me, in fine,
In the new life come in the old one's stead.

I have lived, I shall say, so much since then,
Given up myself so many times,
Gained me the gains of various men,
Ransacked the ages, spoiled the climes;
Yet one thing — one — in my soul's full scope,
Either I missed or itself missed me, —
And I want and find you, Evelyn Hope!
What is the issue? let us see!

I loved you, Evelyn, all the while;
My heart seemed full as it could hold, —
There was place and to spare for the frank young smile,
And the red young mouth, and the hair's young gold.
So, hush! I will give you this leaf to keep;
See, I shut it inside the sweet, cold hand.
There, that is our secret! go to sleep;
You will wake, and remember, and understand.

ROBERT BROWNING.

ANNABEL LEE.

IT was many and many a year ago,
In a kingdom by the sea,
That a maiden lived, whom you may know
By the name of Annabel Lee;
And this maiden she lived with no other thought
Than to love, and be loved by me.

I was a child and she was a child,
In this kingdom by the sea;
But we loved with a love that was more than love,
I and my Annabel Lee, —
With a love that the wingèd seraphs of heaven
Coveted her and me.

And this was the reason that long ago,
In this kingdom by the sea,

A wind blew out of a cloud, chilling
  My beautiful Annabel Lee;
So that her high-born kinsman came,
  And bore her away from me,
To shut her up in a sepulcher,
  In his kingdom by the sea.

The angels, not so happy in heaven,
  Went envying her and me.
Yes! that was the reason (as all men know)
  In this kingdom by the sea,
That the wind came out of the cloud by night,
  Chilling and killing my Annabel Lee.

But our love it was stronger by far than the love
  Of those who were older than we,
  Of many far wiser than we;
And neither the angels in heaven above,
  Nor the demons down under the sea,
Can ever dissever my soul from the soul
  Of the beautiful Annabel Lee.

For the moon never beams without bringing me dreams
  Of the beautiful Annabel Lee,
And the stars never rise but I feel the bright eyes
  Of the beautiful Annabel Lee.
And so, all the night-tide, I lie down by the side
Of my darling, my darling, my life, and my bride,
  In her sepulcher there by the sea,
  In her tomb by the sounding sea.

EDGAR ALLEN POE.

FLORENCE VANE.

I LOVED thee long and dearly,
    Florence Vane;
My life's bright dream and early
    Hath come again;
I renew in my fond vision
    My heart's dear pain,
My hopes and thy derision,
    Florence Vane!

The ruin, lone and hoary,
    The ruin old,
Where thou didst hark my story,
    At even told, —
That spot, the hues elysian
    Of sky and plain,
I treasure in my vision,
    Florence Vane.

Thou wast lovelier than the roses
    In their prime;
Thy voice excelled the closes
    Of sweetest rhyme;
Thy heart was as a river
    Without a main,
Would I had loved thee never,
    Florence Vane!

But fairest, coldest wonder!
    Thy glorious clay
Lieth the green sod under;
    Alas the day!
And it boots not to remember
    Thy disdain,
To quicken love's pale ember,
    Florence Vane!

The lilies of the valley
    By young graves weep,
The daisies love to dally
    Where maidens sleep:
May their bloom, in beauty vying,
    Never wane
Where thine earthly part is lying,
    Florence Vane!

PHILIP P. COOKE.

FAIR HELEN OF KIRKCONNELL.

["A lady of the name of Helen Irving or Bell (for this is disputed by the two clans), daughter of the Laird of Kirkconnell, in Dumfriesshire, and celebrated for her beauty, was beloved by two gentlemen in the neighborhood. The name of the favored suitor was Adam Fleming of Kirkpatrick; that of the other has escaped tradition, although it has been alleged that he was a Bell of Blacket House. The addresses of the latter were, however, favored by the friends of the lady, and the lovers were therefore obliged to meet in secret, and by night, in the churchyard of Kirkconnell, a romantic spot surrounded by the river Kirtle. During one of these private interviews, the jealous and despised lover suddenly appeared on the opposite bank of the stream, and leveled his carabine at the breast of his rival. Helen threw herself before her lover, received in her bosom the bullet, and died in his arms. A desperate and mortal combat ensued between Fleming and the murderer, in which the latter was cut to pieces. Other accounts say that Fleming pursued his enemy to Spain, and slew him in the streets of Madrid." — SIR WALTER SCOTT.]

I WISH I were where Helen lies:
Night and day on me she cries;
O that I were where Helen lies,
  On fair Kirkconnell lea!

Curst be the heart that thought the thought,
And curst the hand that fired the shot,
When in my arms burd Helen dropt,
  And died to succor me!

O, think na but my heart was sair,
When my love dropt down and spake nae mair!
I laid her down wi' meikle care,
  On fair Kirkconnell lea.

As I went down to the water-side,
None but my foe to be my guide,
None but my foe to be my guide,
  On fair Kirkconnell lea, —

I lighted down, my sword did draw,
I hackèd him in pieces sma,
I hackèd him in pieces sma,
For her sake that died for me.

O Helen fair, beyond compare!
I 'll make a garland of thy hair
Shall bind my heart forevermair
Until the day I dee!

O that I were where Helen lies!
Night and day on me she cries;
Out of my bed she bids me rise,
Says, "Haste, and come to me!"

O Helen fair! O Helen chaste!
If I were with thee I were blest,
Where thou lies low, and takes thy rest,
On fair Kirkconnell lea.

I wish my grave were growing green;
A winding-sheet drawn ower my een,
And I in Helen's arms lying
On fair Kirkconnell lea.

I wish I were where Helen lies;
Night and day on me she cries,
And I am weary of the skies,
For her sake that died for me!

ANONYMOUS.

HIGHLAND MARY.

Ye banks and braes and streams around
The castle o' Montgomery,
Green be your woods, and fair your flowers,
Your waters never drumlie!
There simmer first unfauld her robes,
And there the langest tarry;
For there I took the last fareweel
O' my sweet Highland Mary.

How sweetly bloomed the gay green birk,
How rich the hawthorn's blossom,
As underneath their fragrant shade
I clasped her to my bosom!
The golden hours on angel wings
Flew o'er me and my dearie;
For dear to me as light and life
Was my sweet Highland Mary.

Wi' mony a vow and locked embrace
Our parting was fu' tender;
And pledging aft to meet again,
We tore oursels asunder;
But, O, fell death's untimely frost,
That nipt my flower sae early!
Now green 's the sod, and cauld 's the clay,
That wraps my Highland Mary!

O pale, pale now, those rosy lips,
I aft hae kissed sae fondly!
And closed for aye the sparkling glance
That dwelt on me sae kindly!
And moldering now in silent dust
That heart that lo'ed me dearly!
But still within my bosom's core
Shall live my Highland Mary.

ROBERT BURNS.

HIGH-TIDE ON THE COAST OF LINCOLNSHIRE.

The old mayor climbed the belfry tower,
The ringers rang by two, by three;
"Pull! if ye never pulled before;
Good ringers, pull your best," quoth he.
"Play uppe, play uppe, O Boston bells!
Ply all your changes, all your swells!
Play uppe *The Brides of Enderby!*"

Men say it was a "stolen tyde,"—
The Lord that sent it, he knows all,
But in myne ears doth still abide
The message that the bells let fall;
And there was naught of strange, beside
The flights of mews and peewits pied,
By millions crouched on the old sea-wall.

I sat and spun within the doore;
My thread brake off, I raised myne eyes:
The level sun, like ruddy ore,
Lay sinking in the barren skies;
And dark against day's golden death
She moved where Lindis wandereth,—
My sonne's faire wife, Elizabeth.

"Cusha! Cusha! Cusha!" calling,
Ere the early dews were falling,
Farre away I heard her song.
"Cusha! Cusha!" all along;
Where the reedy Lindis floweth,
Floweth, floweth,
From the meads where melick groweth,
Faintly came her milking-song.

"Cusha! Cusha! Cusha!" calling,
"For the dews will soone be falling;
Leave your meadow grasses mellow,
Mellow, mellow!
Quit your cowslips, cowslips yellow!
Come uppe, Whitefoot! come uppe, Lightfoot!
Quit the stalks of parsley hollow,
Hollow, hollow!
Come uppe, Jetty! rise and follow;
From the clovers lift your head!
Come uppe, Whitefoot! come uppe, Lightfoot!
Come uppe, Jetty! rise and follow,
Jetty, to the milking-shed."

If it be long — ay, long ago —
  When I beginne to think howe long,
Againe I hear the Lindis flow,
  Swift as an arrowe, sharpe and strong;
And all the aire, it seemeth mee,
Bin full of floating bells (sayth shee),
That ring the tune of *Enderby*.

Alle fresh the level pasture lay,
  And not a shadowe mote be seene,
Save where, full fyve good miles away,
  The steeple towered from out the greene.
And lo! the great bell farre and wide
Was heard in all the country side
That Saturday at eventide.

The swannerds, where their sedges are,
  Moved on in sunset's golden breath;
The shepherde lads I heard afarre,
  And my sonne's wife, Elizabeth;
Till, floating o'er the grassy sea,
Came downe that kyndly message free,
The Brides of Mavis Enderby.

Then some looked uppe into the sky,
  And all along where Lindis flows
To where the goodly vessels lie,
  And where the lordly steeple shows.
They sayde, "And why should this thing be,
What danger lowers by land or sea?
They ring the tune of *Enderby*.

"For evil news from Mablethorpe,
  Of pyrate galleys, warping down, —
For shippes ashore beyond the scorpe,
  They have not spared to wake the towne;
But while the west bin red to see,
And storms be none, and pyrates flee,
Why ring *The Brides of Enderby?*

I looked without, and lo! my sonne
  Came riding downe with might and main;
He raised a shout as he drew on,
  Till all the welkin rang again:
"Elizabeth! Elizabeth!"
(A sweeter woman ne'er drew breath
Than my sonne's wife, Elizabeth.)

"The olde sea-wall (he cryed) is downe!
  The rising tide comes on apace;
And boats adrift in yonder towne
  Go sailing uppe the market-place!"
He shook as one that looks on death:
"God save you, mother!" straight he sayth;
"Where is my wife, Elizabeth?"

"Good sonne, where Lindis winds away
  With her two bairns I marked her long;
And ere yon bells beganne to play,
  Afar I heard her milking-song."
He looked across the grassy sea,
To right, to left, *Ho, Enderby!*
They rang *The Brides of Enderby*.

With that he cried and beat his breast;
  For lo! along the river's bed
A mighty eygre reared his crest,
  And uppe the Lindis raging sped.
It swept with thunderous noises loud, —
Shaped like a curling snow-white cloud,
Or like a demon in a shroud.

And rearing Lindis, backward pressed,
  Shook all her trembling bankes amaine;
Then madly at the eygre's breast
  Flung uppe her weltering walls again.
Then bankes came downe with ruin and rout, —
Then beaten foam flew round about, —
Then all the mighty floods were out.

So farre, so fast, the eygre drave,
  The heart had hardly time to beat
Before a shallow seething wave
  Sobbed in the grasses at oure feet:
The feet had hardly time to flee
Before it brake against the knee, —
And all the world was in the sea.

Upon the roofe we sate that night;
  The noise of bells went sweeping by;
I marked the lofty beacon light
  Stream from the church tower, red and high, —
A lurid mark, and dread to see;
And awsome bells they were to mee,
That in the dark rang *Enderby*.

They rang the sailor lads to guide,
  From roofe to roofe who fearless rowed;
And I, — my sonne was at my side,
  And yet the ruddy beacon glowed;
And yet he moaned beneath his breath,
"O, come in life, or come in death!
O lost! my love, Elizabeth!"

And didst thou visit him no more?
  Thou didst, thou didst, my daughter deare!
The waters laid thee at his doore
  Ere yet the early dawn was clear;
Thy pretty bairns in fast embrace,
The lifted sun shone on thy face,
Downe drifted to thy dwelling-place.

That flow strewed wrecks about the grass,
  That ebbe swept out the flocks to sea, —
A fatal ebbe and flow, alas!
  To manye more than myne and mee;

But each will mourne his own (she sayth)
And sweeter women ne'er drew breath
Than my sonne's wife, Elizabeth.

I shall never hear her more
By the reedy Lindis shore,
"Cusha! Cusha! Cusha!" calling,
Ere the early dews be falling;
I shall never hear her song,
"Cusha! Cusha!" all along,
Where the sunny Lindis floweth,
Goeth, floweth,
From the meads where melick groweth,
Where the water, winding down,
Onward floweth to the town.

I shall never see her more,
Where the reeds and rushes quiver,
Shiver, quiver,
Stand beside the sobbing river, —
Sobbing, throbbing, in its falling,
To the sandy, lonesome shore;
I shall never hear her calling,
"Leave your meadow grasses mellow,
Mellow, mellow!
Quit your cowslips, cowslips yellow!
Come uppe, Whitefoot! come uppe, Lightfoot!
Quit your pipes of parsley hollow,
Hollow, hollow!
Come uppe, Lightfoot! rise and follow;
Lightfoot! Whitefoot!
From your clovers lift the head;
Come uppe, Jetty! follow, follow,
Jetty, to the milking-shed!"

JEAN INGELOW.

TO MARY IN HEAVEN.

[Composed by Burns, in September, 1789, on the anniversary of the day on which he heard of the death of his early love, Mary Campbell.]

THOU lingering star, with lessening ray,
That lov'st to greet the early morn,
Again thou usher'st in the day
My Mary from my soul was torn.
O Mary! dear departed shade!
Where is thy place of blissful rest?
See'st thou thy lover lowly laid?
Hear'st thou the groans that rend his breast?

That sacred hour can I forget, —
Can I forget the hallowed grove,
Where by the winding Ayr we met
To live one day of parting love?
Eternity will not efface
Those records dear of transports past;
Thy image at our last embrace;
Ah! little thought we 't was our last!

Ayr, gurgling, kissed his pebbled shore,
O'erhung with wild woods, thickening green;
The fragrant birch, and hawthorn hoar,
Twined amorous round the raptured scene;
The flowers sprang wanton to be prest,
The birds sang love on every spray, —
Till soon, too soon, the glowing west
Proclaimed the speed of wingèd day.

Still o'er these scenes my memory wakes,
And fondly broods with miser care!
Time but the impression stronger makes,
As streams their channels deeper wear.
My Mary! dear departed shade!
Where is thy place of blissful rest?
See'st thou thy lover lowly laid?
Hear'st thou the groans that rend his breast?

ROBERT BURNS.

O, SNATCHED AWAY IN BEAUTY'S BLOOM!

O, SNATCHED away in beauty's bloom!
On thee shall press no ponderous tomb!
But on thy turf shall roses rear
Their leaves, the earliest of the year,
And the wild cypress wave in tender gloom:
And oft by yon blue gushing stream
Shall Sorrow lean her drooping head,
And feed deep thought with many a dream,
And lingering pause and lightly tread;
Fond wretch! as if her step disturbed the dead!

Away! we know that tears are vain,
That Death nor heeds nor hears distress:
Will this unteach us to complain?
Or make one mourner weep the less?
And thou, who tell'st me to forget,
Thy looks are wan, thine eyes are wet.

LORD BYRON.

THE MAID'S LAMENT.

I LOVED him not; and yet, now he is gone,
I feel I am alone.
I checked him while he spoke; yet could he speak,
Alas! I would not check.
For reasons not to love him once I sought,
And wearied all my thought
To vex myself and him: I now would give
My love, could he but live
Who lately lived for me, and when he found
'T was vain, in holy ground
He hid his face amid the shades of death!
I waste for him my breath
Who wasted his for me; but mine returns,
And this lone bosom burns

With stifling heat, heaving it up in sleep,
And waking me to weep
Tears that had melted his soft heart: for years
Wept he as bitter tears!
"Merciful God!" such was his latest prayer,
"These may she never share!"
Quieter is his breath, his breast more cold
Than daisies in the mold,
Where children spell athwart the churchyard gate
His name and life's brief date.
Pray for him, gentle souls, whoe'er ye be,
And O, pray, too, for me!

WALTER SAVAGE LANDOR.

THY BRAES WERE BONNY.

THY braes were bonny, Yarrow stream,
When first on them I met my lover;
Thy braes how dreary, Yarrow stream,
When now thy waves his body cover.

Forever now, O Yarrow stream!
Thou art to me a stream of sorrow;
For never on thy banks shall I
Behold my love, the flower of Yarrow.

He promised me a milk-white steed,
To bear me to his father's bowers;
He promised me a little page,
To 'squire me to his father's towers;
He promised me a wedding-ring, —
The wedding-day was fixed to-morrow;
Now he is wedded to his grave,
Alas, his watery grave, in Yarrow!

Sweet were his words when last we met;
My passion I as freely told him:
Clasped in his arms, I little thought
That I should nevermore behold him!
Scarce was he gone, I saw his ghost;
It vanished with a shriek of sorrow;
Thrice did the water-wraith ascend,
And gave a doleful groan through Yarrow.

His mother from the window looked
With all the longing of a mother;
His little sister weeping walked
The greenwood path to meet her brother.
They sought him east, they sought him west,
They sought him all the forest thorough;
They only saw the cloud of night,
They only heard the roar of Yarrow!

No longer from thy window look,
Thou hast no son, thou tender mother!
No longer walk, thou lovely maid;
Alas, thou hast no more a brother!

No longer seek him east or west,
And search no more the forest thorough;
For, wandering in the night so dark,
He fell a lifeless corse in Yarrow.

The tear shall never leave my cheek,
No other youth shall be my marrow;
I 'll seek thy body in the stream,
And then with thee I 'll sleep in Yarrow.

JOHN LOGAN.

MARY'S DREAM.

THE moon had climbed the highest hill
Which rises o'er the source of Dee,
And from the eastern summit shed
Her silver light on tower and tree,
When Mary laid her down to sleep,
Her thoughts on Sandy far at sea,
When, soft and slow, a voice was heard
Say, "Mary, weep no more for me!"

She from her pillow gently raised
Her head, to ask who there might be,
And saw young Sandy shivering stand,
With visage pale, and hollow e'e.
"O Mary dear, cold is my clay;
It lies beneath a stormy sea.
Far, far from thee I sleep in death;
So, Mary, weep no more for me!

"Three stormy nights and stormy days
We tossed upon the raging main;
And long we strove our bark to save,
But all our striving was in vain.
Even then, when horror chilled my blood,
My heart was filled with love for thee:
The storm is past, and I at rest;
So, Mary, weep no more for me!

"O maiden dear, thyself prepare;
We soon shall meet upon that shore,
Where love is free from doubt and care,
And thou and I shall part no more!"
Loud crowed the cock, the shadow fled,
No more of Sandy could she see;
But soft the passing spirit said,
"Sweet Mary, weep no more for me!"

JOHN LOWE.

TOO LATE.

COULD ye come back to me, Douglas, Douglas,
In the old likeness that I knew,
I would be so faithful, so loving, Douglas,
Douglas, Douglas, tender and true.

Never a scornful word should grieve ye,
I 'd smile on ye sweet as the angels do; —

Sweet as your smile on me shone ever,
Douglas, Douglas, tender and true.

O to call back the days that are not!
My eyes were blinded, your words were few:
Do you know the truth now up in heaven,
Douglas, Douglas, tender and true?

I never was worthy of you, Douglas;
Not half worthy the like of you:
Now all men beside seem to me like shadows,—
I love *you*, Douglas, tender and true.

Stretch out your hand to me, Douglas, Douglas,
Drop forgiveness from heaven like dew;
As I lay my heart on your dead heart, Douglas,
Douglas, Douglas, tender and true.

DINAH MULOCH CRAIK.

FIRST SPRING FLOWERS.

I AM watching for the early buds to wake
Under the snow:
From little beds the soft white covering take,
And, nestling, lo!
They lie, with pink lips parted, all aglow!

O darlings! open wide your tender eyes;
See! I am here—
Have been here, waiting under winter skies
Till you appear—
You, just come up from where *he* lies so near.

Tell me, dear flowers, is he gently laid,
Wrapped round from cold;
Has spring about him fair green garments made,
Fold over fold;
Are sweet things growing with him in the mold?

Has he found quiet resting-place at last,
After the fight?
What message did he send me, as you passed
Him in the night,
Eagerly pushing upward toward the light?

I will not pluck you, lest *his* hand should be
Close clasping you:
These slender fibers which so cling to me
Do grasp *him* too—
What gave these delicate veins their blood-red hue?

One kiss I press, dear little bud, half shut,
On your sweet eyes;
For when the April rain falls at your foot,
And April sun yearns downward to your root
From soft spring skies,
It, too, may reach him, where he sleeping lies.

MRS. HOWLAND.

AN APRIL VIOLET.

UNDER the larch, with its tassels wet,
While the early sunbeams lingered yet,
In the rosy dawn my love I met.

Under the larch, when the sun was set,
He came with an April violet:
Forty years—and I have it yet.

Out of life, with its fond regret,
What have love and memory yet?
Only an April violet.

ANONYMOUS.

A SIGH.

IT was nothing but a rose I gave her,
Nothing but a rose
Any wind might rob of half its savor,
Any wind that blows.

When she took it from my trembling fingers
With a hand as chill—
Ah, the flying touch upon them lingers,
Stays, and thrills them still!

Withered, faded, pressed between the pages,
Crumpled fold on fold,—
Once it lay upon her breast, and ages
Cannot make it old!

ANONYMOUS.

MINSTREL'S SONG.

O, SING unto my roundelay!
O, drop the briny tear with me!
Dance no more at holiday;
Like a running river be;
My love is dead,
Gone to his death-bed,
All under the willow-tree.

Black his hair as the winter night,
White his neck as summer snow,
Ruddy his face as the morning light;
Cold he lies in the grave below:
My love is dead, etc.

Sweet his tongue as the throstle's note;
Quick in dance as thought can be;
Deft his tabor, cudgel stout;
O, he lies by the willow-tree!
My love is dead, etc.

Hark! the raven flaps his wing
In the briered dell below;

Hark! the death-owl loud doth sing
To the nightmares as they go.
My love is dead, etc.

See! the white moon shines on high;
Whiter is my true-love's shroud,
Whiter than the morning sky,
Whiter than the evening cloud.
My love is dead, etc.

Here, upon my true-love's grave
Shall the barren flowers be laid,
Nor one holy saint to save
All the coldness of a maid.
My love is dead, etc.

With my hands I 'll bind the briers
Round his holy corse to gre;
Elfin-fairy, light your fires;
Here my body still shall be.
My love is dead, etc.

Come, with acorn-cup and thorn,
Drain my heart's blood all away;
Life and all its good I scorn,
Dance by night, or feast by day.
My love is dead, etc.

Water-witches, crowned with reytes,
Bear me to your lethal tide.
I die! I come! my true-love waits.
Thus the damsel spake, and died.

THOMAS CHATTERTON.

LAMENT FOR BION.

O FOREST dells and streams! O Dorian tide!
Groan with my grief, since lovely Bion died:
Ye plants and copses, now his loss bewail:
Flowers, from your tufts a sad perfume exhale:
Anemones and roses, mournful show
Your crimson leaves and wear a blush of woe:
And hyacinth, now more than ever spread
The woeful "ah," that marks thy petaled head
With lettered grief: the beauteous minstrel 's dead!

Sicilian Muses, pour the dirge of woe:
Ye nightingales, whose plaintive warblings flow
From the thick leaves of some embowering wood,
Tell the sad loss to Arethusa's flood:
The shepherd Bion dies: with him is dead
The life of song: the Doric Muse is fled.

. . . . . .

Sicilian Muses, pour the dirge of woe:
The herds no more that chant melodious know:
No more beneath the lonely oak he sings,
But breathes his strains to Lethe's sullen springs:
The mountains now are mute: the heifers pass
Slow-wandering by, nor browse the tender grass.

Sicilian Muses, pour the dirge of woe:
For thee, O Bion! in the grave laid low,
Apollo weeps: dark palls the sylvan's shroud;
Fauns ask thy wonted song, and wail aloud:
Each fountain-nymph disconsolate appears,
And all her waters turn to trickling tears:—
Mute Echo pines the silent rocks around,
And mourns those lips that waked their sweetest sound.

. . . . . .

Sicilian Muses, pour the dirge of woe:
But retribution sure will deal the blow:
I, in this trance of grief, still drop the tear,
And mourn forever o'er thy livid bier:—
O that, as Orpheus, in the days of yore,
Ulysses, or Alcides, passed before,
I could descend to Pluto's house of night,
And mark if thou wouldst Pluto's ear delight,
And listen to the song: O then rehearse
Some sweet Sicilian strain, bucolic verse,
To soothe the maid of Enna's vale, who sang
These Doric songs, while Ætna's upland rang.
Not unrewarded should thy ditties prove:
As the sweet harper, Orpheus, erst could move
Her breast to yield his dear departed wife,
Treading the backward road from death to life,
So should he melt to Bion's Dorian strain,
And send him joyous to his hills again.
O, could my touch command the stops like thee,
I too would seek the dead, and sing thee free!

From the Greek of MOSCHUS,
by CHARLES ABRAHAM ELTON.

LYCIDAS.

[In memory of a young clerical friend of the poet's, drowned A. D. 1637.]

YET once more, O ye laurels, and once more,
Ye myrtles brown, with ivy never sere,
I come to pluck your berries harsh and crude;
And, with forced fingers rude,
Shatter your leaves before the mellowing year.
Bitter constraint, and sad occasion dear,
Compels me to disturb your season due:
For Lycidas is dead, dead ere his prime,
Young Lycidas, and hath not left his peer.
Who would not sing for Lycidas? he knew
Himself to sing, and build the lofty rhyme.
He must not float upon his watery bier
Unwept, and welter to the parching wind,
Without the meed of some melodious tear.
Begin, then, sisters of the sacred well
That from beneath the seat of Jove doth spring;
Begin, and somewhat loudly sweep the string.
Hence with denial vain, and coy excuse:

So may some gentle Muse
With lucky words favor my destined urn;
And, as he passes, turn,
And bid fair peace be to my sable shroud.
For we were nursed upon the selfsame hill,
Fed the same flock by fountain, shade, and rill;
Together both, ere the high lawns appeared
Under the opening eyelids of the morn,
We drove afield, and both together heard
What time the gray fly winds her sultry horn,
Battening our flocks with the fresh dews of night,
Oft till the star, that rose at evening bright,
Towards heaven's descent had sloped his westering wheel.
Meanwhile the rural ditties were not mute,
Tempered to the oaten flute;
Rough Satyrs danced, and Fauns with cloven heel
From the glad sound would not be absent long;
And old Damœtas loved to hear our song.
But, O the heavy change now thou art gone,
Now thou art gone, and never must return!
Thee, shepherd, thee the woods, and desert caves,
With wild thyme and the gadding vine o'ergrown,
And all their echoes, mourn.
The willows, and the hazel copses green,
Shall now no more be seen
Fanning their joyous leaves to thy soft lays.
As killing as the canker to the rose,
Or taint-worm to the weanling herds that graze,
Or frost to flowers, that their gay wardrobe wear,
When first the white-thorn blows;
Such, Lycidas, thy loss to shepherds' ear.
Where were ye, nymphs, when the remorseless deep
Closed o'er the head of your loved Lycidas?
For neither were ye playing on the steep,
Where your old bards, the famous Druids, lie,
Nor on the shaggy top of Mona high,
Nor yet where Deva spreads her wizard stream:
Ay me! I fondly dream,
Had ye been there: for what could that have done?
What could the Muse herself that Orpheus bore,
The Muse herself, for her enchanting son,
Whom universal nature did lament,
When, by the rout that made the hideous roar,
His gory visage down the stream was sent,
Down the swift Hebrus to the Lesbian shore?
Alas! what boots it with incessant care
To tend the homely, slighted shepherd's trade,
And strictly meditate the thankless Muse?
Were it not better done, as others use,
To sport with Amaryllis in the shade,
Or with the tangles of Neæra's hair?
Fame is the spur that the clear spirit doth raise
(That last infirmity of noble minds)
To scorn delights, and live laborious days;
But the fair guerdon when we hope to find,
And think to burst out into sudden blaze,
Comes the blind Fury with the abhorrèd shears,
And slits the thin-spun life. "But not the praise,"
Phœbus replied, and touched my trembling ears;
"Fame is no plant that grows on mortal soil,
Nor in the glistering foil
Set off to the world, nor in broad rumor lies:
But lives and spreads aloft by those pure eyes,
And perfect witness of all-judging Jove;
As he pronounces lastly on each deed,
Of so much fame in heaven expect thy meed!"
O fountain Arethuse, and thou honored flood,
Smooth-sliding Mincius, crowned with vocal reeds!
That strain I heard was of a higher mood:
But now my oat proceeds,
And listens to the herald of the sea
That came in Neptune's plea;
He asked the waves, and asked the felon winds,
What hard mishap hath doomed this gentle swain?
And questioned every gust of rugged wings,
That blows from off each beakèd promontory:
They knew not of his story;
And sage Hippotades their answer brings,
That not a blast was from his dungeon strayed:
The air was calm, and on the level brine
Sleek Panope with all her sisters played.
It was that fatal and perfidious bark,
Built in the eclipse, and rigged with curses dark,
That sunk so low that sacred head of thine.
Next Camus, reverend sire, went footing slow,
His mantle hairy, and his bonnet sedge,
Inwrought with figures dim, and on the edge
Like to that sanguine flower inscribed with woe.
"Ah! who hath reft," quoth he, "my dearest pledge?"
Last came, and last did go,
The pilot of the Galilean lake:
Two massy keys he bore of metals twain,
(The golden opes, the iron shuts amain,)
He shook his mitered locks, and stern bespake:
"How well could I have spared for thee, young swain,
Enow of such, as for their bellies' sake,
Creep, and intrude, and climb into the fold!
Of other care they little reckoning make,
Than how to scramble at the shearers' feast,
And shove away the worthy bidden guest;
Blind mouths! that scarce themselves know how to hold
A sheep-hook, or have learned aught else the least
That to the faithful herdsman's art belongs!
What recks it them? What need they? They are sped;
And when they list, their lean and flashy songs
Grate on their scrannel pipes of wretched straw;
The hungry sheep look up, and are not fed,
But, swoll'n with wind and the rank mist they draw,
Rot inwardly, and foul contagion spread:

Besides what the grim wolf with privy paw
Daily devours apace, and nothing said:
But that two-handed engine at the door
Stands ready to smite once, and smite no more.
Return, Alpheus, the dread voice is past,
That shrunk thy streams; return, Sicilian Muse,
And call the vales, and bid them hither cast
Their bells, and flowerets of a thousand hues.
Ye valleys low, where the mild whispers use
Of shades, and wanton winds, and gushing brooks
On whose fresh lap the swart-star sparely looks;
Throw hither all your quaint enameled eyes,
That on the green turf suck the honeyed showers,
And purple all the ground with vernal flowers.
Bring the rathe primrose that forsaken dies,
The tufted crow-toe, and pale jessamine,
The white pink, and the pansy freaked with jet,
The glowing violet,
The musk-rose, and the well-attired woodbine,
With cowslips wan that hang the pensive head,
And every flower that sad embroidery wears:
Bid Amaranthus all his beauty shed,
And daffadillies fill their cups with tears,
To strew the laureate hearse where Lycid lies.
For, so to interpose a little ease,
Let our frail thoughts dally with false surmise;
Ay me! whilst thee the shores and sounding seas
Wash far away, where'er thy bones are hurled,
Whether beyond the stormy Hebrides,
Where thou, perhaps, under the whelming tide,
Visit'st the bottom of the monstrous world;
Or whether thou, to our moist vows denied,
Sleep'st by the fable of Bellerus old,
Where the great vision of the guarded mount
Looks toward Namancos and Bayona's hold;
Look homeward, angel, now, and melt with ruth:
And, O ye dolphins, waft the hapless youth.
Weep no more, woful shepherds, weep no more;
For Lycidas your sorrow is not dead,
Sunk though he be beneath the watery floor;
So sinks the day-star in the ocean bed,
And yet anon repairs his drooping head,
And tricks his beams, and with new-spangled ore
Flames in the forehead of the morning sky:
So Lycidas sunk low, but mounted high,
Through the dear might of Him that walked the waves;
Where, other groves and other streams along,
With nectar pure his oozy locks he laves,
And hears the unexpressive nuptial song,
In the blest kingdoms meek of joy and love.
There entertain him all the saints above,
In solemn troops, and sweet societies,
That sing, and, singing, in their glory move,
And wipe the tears forever from his eyes.
Now, Lycidas, the shepherds weep no more;
Henceforth thou art the Genius of the shore,
In thy large recompense, and shalt be good
To all that wander in that perilous flood.
Thus sang the uncouth swain to the oaks and rills,
While the still morn went out with sandals gray;
He touched the tender stops of various quills,
With eager thought warbling his Doric lay:
And now the sun had stretched out all the hills,
And now was dropt into the western bay:
At last he rose, and twitched his mantle blue:
To-morrow to fresh woods, and pastures new.

JOHN MILTON.

SELECTIONS FROM "IN MEMORIAM."

[ARTHUR HENRY HALLAM, OB. 1833.]

GRIEF UNSPEAKABLE.

I SOMETIMES hold it half a sin
To put in words the grief I feel;
For words, like Nature, half reveal
And half conceal the Soul within.

But, for the unquiet heart and brain,
A use in measured language lies;
The sad mechanic exercise,
Like dull narcotics, numbing pain.

In words, like weeds, I 'll wrap me o'er,
Like coarsest clothes against the cold;
But that large grief which these enfold
Is given in outline and no more.

DEAD, IN A FOREIGN LAND.

FAIR ship, that from the Italian shore
Sailest the placid ocean-plains
With my lost Arthur's loved remains,
Spread thy full wings, and waft him o'er!

So draw him home to those that mourn
In vain; a favorable speed
Ruffle thy mirrored mast, and lead
Through prosperous floods his holy urn!

All night no ruder air perplex
Thy sliding keel, till Phosphor, bright
As our pure love, through early light
Shall glimmer on the dewy decks!

Sphere all your lights around, above;
Sleep, gentle heavens, before the prow;
Sleep, gentle winds, as he sleeps now,
My friend, the brother of my love;

My Arthur, whom I shall not see
Till all my widowed race be run;
Dear as the mother to the son,
More than my brothers are to me!

THE PEACE OF SORROW.

Calm is the morn, without a sound,
  Calm as to suit a calmer grief,
  And only through the faded leaf
The chestnut pattering to the ground :

Calm and deep peace on this high wold
  And on these dews that drench the furze,
  And all the silvery gossamers
That twinkle into green and gold :

Calm and still light on yon great plain
  That sweeps with all its autumn bowers,
  And crowded farms and lessening towers,
To mingle with the bounding main :

Calm and deep peace in this wide air,
  These leaves that redden to the fall ;
  And in my heart, if calm at all,
If any calm, a calm despair :

Calm on the seas, and silver sleep,
  And waves that sway themselves in rest,
  And dead calm in that noble breast
Which heaves but with the heaving deep.

TIME AND ETERNITY.

If Sleep and Death be truly one,
  And every spirit's folded bloom
  Through all its intervital gloom
In some long trance should slumber on ;

Unconscious of the sliding hour,
  Bare of the body, might it last,
  And silent traces of the past
Be all the color of the flower :

So then were nothing lost to man ;
  So that still garden of the souls
  In many a figured leaf enrolls
The total world since life began ;

And love will last as pure and whole
  As when he loved me here in Time,
  And at the spiritual prime
Rewaken with the dawning soul.

PERSONAL RESURRECTION.

That each, who seems a separate whole,
  Should move his rounds, and fusing all
  The skirts of self again, should fall
Remerging in the general Soul,

Is faith as vague as all unsweet :
  Eternal form shall still divide
  The eternal soul from all beside ;
And I shall know him when we meet :

And we shall sit at endless feast,
  Enjoying each the other's good :
  What vaster dream can hit the mood
Of Love on earth ? He seeks at least

Upon the last and sharpest height,
  Before the spirits fade away,
  Some landing-place to clasp and say,
"Farewell! We lose ourselves in light."

SPIRITUAL COMPANIONSHIP.

Do we indeed desire the dead
  Should still be near us at our side ?
  Is there no baseness we would hide ?
No inner vileness that we dread ?

Shall he for whose applause I strove,
  I had such reverence for his blame,
  See with clear eye some hidden shame,
And I be lessened in his love ?

I wrong the grave with fears untrue :
  Shall love be blamed for want of faith ?
  There must be wisdom with great Death :
The dead shall look me through and through.

Be near us when we climb or fall :
  Ye watch, like God, the rolling hours
  With larger other eyes than ours,
To make allowance for us all.

MOONLIGHT MUSINGS.

When on my bed the moonlight falls,
  I know that in thy place of rest,
  By that broad water of the west,
There comes a glory on the walls ;

Thy marble bright in dark appears,
  As slowly steals a silver flame
  Along the letters of thy name,
And o'er the number of thy years.

The mystic glory swims away ;
  From off my bed the moonlight dies :
  And, closing eaves of wearied eyes,
I sleep till dusk is dipt in gray :

And then I know the mist is drawn
  A lucid vale from coast to coast,
  And in the dark church, like a ghost,
Thy tablet glimmers to the dawn.

DEATH IN LIFE'S PRIME.

So many worlds, so much to do,
  So little done, such things to be,
  How know I what had need of thee ?
For thou wert strong as thou wert true.

The fame is quenched that I foresaw,
  The head hath missed an earthly wreath:
  I curse not nature, no, nor death;
For nothing is that errs from law.

We pass; the path that each man trod
  Is dim, or will be dim, with weeds:
  What fame is left for human deeds
In endless age? It rests with God.

O hollow wraith of dying fame,
  Fade wholly, while the soul exults,
  And self-enfolds the large results
Of force that would have forged a name.

THE POET'S TRIBUTE.

WHAT hope is here for modern rhyme
  To him who turns a musing eye
  On songs, and deeds, and lives, that lie
Foreshortened in the tract of time?

These mortal lullabies of pain
  May bind a book, may line a box,
  May serve to curl a maiden's locks:
Or, when a thousand moons shall wane,

A man upon a stall may find,
  And, passing, turn the page that tells
  A grief, then changed to something else,
Sung by a long-forgotten mind.

But what of that? My darkened ways
  Shall ring with music all the same;
  To breathe my loss is more than fame,
To utter love more sweet than praise.

ALFRED TENNYSON.

THE PASSAGE.

MANY a year is in its grave
Since I crossed this restless wave:
And the evening, fair as ever,
Shines on ruin, rock, and river.

Then in this same boat beside,
Sat two comrades old and tried, —
One with all a father's truth,
One with all the fire of youth.

One on earth in silence wrought,
And his grave in silence sought;
But the younger, brighter form
Passed in battle and in storm.

So, whene'er I turn mine eye
Back upon the days gone by,
Saddening thoughts of friends come o'er me,
Friends that closed their course before me.

But what binds us, friend to friend,
But that soul with soul can blend?
Soul-like were those hours of yore;
Let us walk in soul once more.

Take, O boatman, thrice thy fee,
Take, I give it willingly;
For invisible to thee,
Spirits twain have crossed with me.

From the German of LUDWIG UHLAND,
by H. W. LONGFELLOW.

HOME THEY BROUGHT HER WARRIOR DEAD.

FROM "THE PRINCESS."

HOME they brought her warrior dead:
  She nor swooned, nor uttered cry;
All her maidens, watching, said,
  "She must weep or she will die."

Then they praised him, soft and low,
  Called him worthy to be loved,
Truest friend and noblest foe;
  Yet she neither spoke nor moved.

Stole a maiden from her place,
  Lightly to the warrior stept,
Took the face-cloth from the face,
  Yet she neither moved nor wept.

Rose a nurse of ninety years,
  Set his child upon her knee, —
Like summer tempest came her tears, —
  "Sweet my child, I live for thee."

ALFRED TENNYSON.

THE FLOWER OF FINAE.

A BRIGADE BALLAD.

[Early in the eighteenth century, the flower of the Catholic youth of Ireland were drawn away to recruit the ranks of the Irish Brigade in the service of the King of France. These recruits were popularly known as "Wild Geese." Few returned.]

BRIGHT red is the sun on the waves of Lough
    Sheelin,
A cool gentle breeze from the mountain is stealing,
While fair round its islets the small ripples play,
But fairer than all is the Flower of Finae.

Her hair is like night, and her eyes like grey
    morning,
She trips on the heather as if its touch scorning,
Yet her heart and her lips are as mild as May day,
Sweet Eily MacMahon, the Flower of Finae.

But who down the hillside than red deer runs
    fleeter?
And who on the lakeside is hastening to greet her?

Who but Fergus O'Farrell, the fiery and gay,
The darling and pride of the Flower of Finae?

One kiss and one clasp, and one wild look of gladness;
Ah! why do they change on a sudden to sadness, —
He has told his hard fortune, normore can he stay,
He must leave his poor Eily to pine at Finae.

For Fergus O'Farrell was true to his sire-land,
And the dark hand of tyranny drove him from Ireland;
He joins the Brigade, in the wars far away,
But he vows he'll come back to the Flower of Finae.

He fought at Cremona, — she hears of his story;
He fought at Cassano, — she's proud of his glory.
Yet sadly she sings "Shule Aroon" all the day,
"O, come, come, my darling, come home to Finae."

Eight long years have passed, till she's nigh broken-hearted,
Her reel, and her rock, and her flax she has parted;
She sails with the "Wild Geese" to Flanders away,
And leaves her sad parents alone in Finae.

Lord Clare on the field of Ramillies is charging,
Before him the Sassanach squadrons enlarging, —
Behind him the Cravats their sections display, —
Beside him rides Fergus and shouts for Finae.

On the slopes of La Judoigne the Frenchmen are flying,
Lord Clare and his squadrons, the foe still defying,
Outnumbered, and wounded, retreat in array;
And bleeding rides Fergus and thinks of Finae.

. . . . . .

In the cloisters of Ypres a banner is swaying,
And by it a pale weeping maiden is praying;
That flag's the sole trophy of Ramillies' fray,
This nun is poor Eily, the Flower of Finae.

THOMAS DAVIS.

ELEONORA.

ELEGY ON THE COUNTESS OF ABINGDON.

No single virtue we could most commend,
Whether the wife, the mother, or the friend;
For she was all, in that supreme degree,
That, as no one prevailed, so all was she.
The several parts lay hidden in the piece;
The occasion but exerted that, or this.
A wife as tender, and as true withal,
As the first woman was before her fall:
Made for the man, of whom she was a part;
Made to attract his eyes, and keep his heart.
A second Eve, but by no crime accursed;
As beauteous, not as brittle, as the first.
Had she been first, still Paradise had been,
And death had found no entrance by her sin.
So she not only had preserved from ill
Her sex and ours, but lived their pattern still.
Love and obedience to her lord she bore;
She much obeyed him, but she loved him more:
Not awed to duty by superior sway,
But taught by his indulgence to obey.
Thus we love God, as author of our good.

. . . . . .

Yet unemployed no minute slipped away;
Moments were precious in so short a stay.
The haste of Heaven to have her was so great
That some were single acts, though each complete;
But every act stood ready to repeat.
Her fellow-saints with busy care will look
For her blest name in fate's eternal book;
And, pleased to be outdone, with joy will see
Numberless virtues, endless charity:
But more will wonder at so short an age,
To find a blank beyond the thirtieth page;
And with a pious fear begin to doubt
The piece imperfect, and the rest torn out.
But 't was her Saviour's time; and could there be
A copy near the original, 't was she.
As precious gums are not for lasting fire,
They but perfume the temple, and expire;
So was she soon exhaled, and vanished hence, —
A short sweet odor, of a vast expense.
She vanished, we can scarcely say she died;
For but a now did heaven and earth divide:
She passed serenely with a single breath;
This moment perfect health, the next was death:
One sigh did her eternal bliss assure;
So little penance needs, when souls are almost pure.
As gentle dreams our waking thoughts pursue;
Or, one dream passed, we slide into a new;
So close they follow, such wild order keep,
We think ourselves awake, and are asleep:
So softly death succeeded life in her:
She did but dream of heaven, and she was there.
No pains she suffered, nor expired with noise;
Her soul was whispered out with God's still voice;
As an old friend is beckoned to a feast,
And treated like a long-familiar guest.
He took her as he found, but found her so,
As one in hourly readiness to go:
E'en on that day, in all her trim prepared;
As early notice she from heaven had heard,
And some descending courier from above
Had given her timely warning to remove;
Or counseled her to dress the nuptial room,
For on that night the bridegroom was to come.
He kept his hour, and found her where she lay
Clothed all in white, the livery of the day.

JOHN DRYDEN.

LAMENT OF THE IRISH EMIGRANT.

I'M sittin' on the stile, Mary,
Where we sat side by side
On a bright May mornin' long ago,
When first you were my bride;
The corn was springin' fresh and green,
And the lark sang loud and high;
And the red was on your lip, Mary,
And the love-light in your eye.

The place is little changed, Mary;
The day is bright as then;
The lark's loud song is in my ear,
And the corn is green again;
But I miss the soft clasp of your hand,
And your breath, warm on my cheek;
And I still keep list'nin' for the words
You nevermore will speak.

'T is but a step down yonder lane,
And the little church stands near, —
The church where we were wed, Mary;
I see the spire from here.
But the graveyard lies between, Mary,
And my step might break your rest, —
For I 've laid you, darling, down to sleep,
With your baby on your breast.

I 'm very lonely now, Mary,
For the poor make no new friends;
But, O, they love the better still
The few our Father sends!
And you were all I had, Mary, —
My blessin' and my pride;
There 's nothing left to care for now,
Since my poor Mary died.

Yours was the good, brave heart, Mary,
That still kept hoping on,
When the trust in God had left my soul,
And my arm's young strength was gone;
There was comfort ever on your lip, —
And the kind look on your brow, —
I bless you, Mary, for that same,
Though you cannot hear me now.

I thank you for the patient smile
When your heart was fit to break, —
When the hunger pain was gnawin' there,
And you hid it for my sake;
I bless you for the pleasant word,
When your heart was sad and sore, —
O, I 'm thankful you are gone, Mary,
Where grief can't reach you more!

I 'm biddin' you a long farewell,
My Mary — kind and true!
But I 'll not forget you, darling,
In the land I 'm goin' to;
They say there 's bread and work for all,
And the sun shines always there, —
But I 'll not forget old Ireland,
Were it fifty times as fair!

And often in those grand old woods
I 'll sit, and shut my eyes,
And my heart will travel back again
To the place where Mary lies;
And I 'll think I see the little stile
Where we sat side by side,
And the springin' corn and the bright May morn,
When first you were my bride.

LADY DUFFERIN
(Formerly the HON. MRS. BLACKWOOD).

THE KING OF DENMARK'S RIDE.

WORD was brought to the Danish king
(Hurry!)
That the love of his heart lay suffering,
And pined for the comfort his voice would bring;
(O, ride as though you were flying!)
Better he loves each golden curl
On the brow of that Scandinavian girl
Than his rich crown jewels of ruby and pearl:
And his rose of the isles is dying!

Thirty nobles saddled with speed;
(Hurry!)
Each one mounting a gallant steed
Which he kept for battle and days of need;
(O, ride as though you were flying!)
Spurs were struck in the foaming flank;
Worn-out chargers staggered and sank;
Bridles were slackened, and girths were burst;
But, ride as they would, the king rode first,
For his rose of the isles lay dying!

His nobles are beaten, one by one;
(Hurry!)
They have fainted, and faltered, and homeward gone;
His little fair page now follows alone,
For strength and for courage trying!
The king looked back at that faithful child;
Wan was the face that answering smiled;
They passed the drawbridge with clattering din,
Then he dropped; and only the king rode in
Where his rose of the isles lay dying!

The king blew a blast on his bugle-horn;
(Silence!)
No answer came; but faint and forlorn
An echo returned on the cold gray morn,
Like the breath of a spirit sighing.
The castle portal stood grimly wide;
None welcomed the king from that weary ride;

For dead, in the light of the dawning day,
The pale sweet form of the welcomer lay,
  Who had yearned for his voice while dying!

The panting steed, with a drooping crest,
    Stood weary.
The king returned from her chamber of rest,
The thick sobs choking in his breast;
    And, that dumb companion eying,
The tears gushed forth which he strove to check;
He bowed his head on his charger's neck:
"O steed, that every nerve didst strain,
Dear steed, our ride hath been in vain
  To the halls where my love lay dying!"

CAROLINE E. NORTON.

LAMENT OF THE BORDER WIDOW.

[This ballad relates to the execution of Cockburne of Henderland, a border freebooter, hanged over the gate of his own tower by James V. in his famous expedition, in 1529, against the marauders of the border. In a deserted burial-place near the ruins of the castle, the monument of Cockburne and his lady is still shown. The following inscription is still legible, though defaced: "HERE LYES PERYS OF COKBURNE AND HIS WYFE MARJORY."—*Sir Walter Scott.*]

My love he built me a bonnie bower,
And clad it a' wi' lily flower;
A brawer bower ye ne'er did see,
Than my true-love he built for me.

There came a man, by middle day,
He spied his sport, and went away;
And brought the king that very night,
Who brake my bower, and slew my knight.

He slew my knight, to me sae dear;
He slew my knight, and poin'd his gear:
My servants all for life did flee,
And left me in extremitie.

I sewed his sheet, making my mane;
I watched the corpse mysell alane;
I watched his body night and day;
No living creature came that way.

I took his body on my back,
And whiles I gaed, and whiles I sat;
I digged a grave, and laid him in,
And happed him with the sod sae green.

But think na ye my heart was sair,
When I laid the moul' on his yellow hair?
O, think na ye my heart was wae,
When I turned about, away to gae?

Nae living man I 'll love again,
Since that my lively knight is slain;
Wi' ae lock o' his yellow hair
I 'll chain my heart forevermair.

ANONYMOUS.

FAREWELL TO THEE, ARABY'S DAUGHTER.

FROM "THE FIRE-WORSHIPERS."

FAREWELL,—farewell to thee, Araby's daughter!
  (Thus warbled a Peri beneath the dark sea;)
No pearl ever lay under Oman's green water
  More pure in its shell than thy spirit in thee.

O, fair as the sea-flower close to thee growing,
  How light was thy heart till love's witchery came,
Like the wind of the south o'er a summer lute blowing,
  And hushed all its music and withered its frame!

But long, upon Araby's green sunny highlands,
  Shall maids and their lovers remember the doom
Of her who lies sleeping among the Pearl Islands,
  With naught but the sea-star to light up her tomb.

And still, when the merry date-season is burning,
  And calls to the palm-groves the young and the old,
The happiest there, from their pastime returning
  At sunset, will weep when thy story is told.

The young village maid, when with flowers she dresses
  Her dark-flowing hair for some festival day,
Will think of thy fate, till neglecting her tresses,
  She mournfully turns from the mirror away.

Nor shall Iran, beloved of her hero, forget thee,—
  Though tyrants watch over her tears as they start,
Close, close by the side of that hero she 'll set thee,
  Embalmed in the innermost shrine of her heart.

Farewell!—be it ours to embellish thy pillow
  With everything beauteous that grows in the deep;
Each flower of the rock and each gem of the billow
  Shall sweeten thy bed and illumine thy sleep.

Around thee shall glisten the loveliest amber
  That ever the sorrowing sea-bird has wept;
With many a shell, in whose hollow-wreathed chamber,
  We, Peris of ocean, by moonlight have slept.

We'll dive where the gardens of coral lie darkling,
  And plant all the rosiest stems at thy head;
We 'll seek where the sands of the Caspian are sparkling,
  And gather their gold to strew over thy bed.

Farewell! — farewell! — until pity's sweet fountain
Is lost in the hearts of the fair and the brave,
They 'll weep for the chieftain who died on that mountain,
They 'll weep for the maiden who sleeps in the wave.

THOMAS MOORE.

GRIEF.

FROM "HAMLET, PRINCE OF DENMARK."

QUEEN. Good Hamlet, cast thy nighted color off,
And let thine eye look like a friend on Denmark.
Do not, forever, with thy veilèd lids
Seek for thy noble father in the dust:
Thou know'st 't is common, — all that live must die,
Passing through nature to eternity.
HAMLET. Ay, madam, it is common.
QUEEN. If it be,
Why seems it so particular with thee?
HAM. Seems, madam! nay, it is; I know not seems.
'T is not alone my inky cloak, good mother,
Nor customary suits of solemn black,
Nor windy suspiration of forced breath,
No, nor the fruitful river in the eye,
Nor the dejected havior of the visage,
Together with all forms, modes, shows of grief,
That can denote me truly: these, indeed, seem,
For they are actions that a man might play:
But I have that within, which passeth show;
These but the trappings and the suits of woe.

SHAKESPEARE.

ON THE DEATH OF A BEAUTIFUL WIFE.

SLEEP on, my love, in thy cold bed,
Never to be disquieted.
My last "Good Night!" Thou wilt not wake
Till I thy fate shall overtake;
Till age, or grief, or sickness must
Marry my body to that dust
It so much loves, and fill the room
My heart keeps empty in thy tomb.

Stay for me there: I will not fail
To meet thee in that hollow vale;
And think not much of my delay,
I am already on the way;
And follow thee with all the speed
Desire can make or sorrows breed.
Each minute is a short degree,
And every hour a step toward thee.
At night, when I betake to rest,
Next morn I rise nearer my west
Of life, almost by eight hours' sail,
Than when sleep breathed his drowsy gale.

HENRY KING.

TO DEATH.

METHINKS it were no pain to die
On such an eve, when such a sky
O'er-canopies the west;
To gaze my fill on yon calm deep,
And, like an infant, fall asleep
On Earth, my mother's breast.

There 's peace and welcome in yon sea
Of endless blue tranquillity:
These clouds are living things:
I trace their veins of liquid gold,
I see them solemnly unfold
Their soft and fleecy wings.

These be the angels that convey
Us weary children of a day —
Life's tedious nothing o'er —
Where neither passions come, nor woes,
To vex the genius of repose
On Death's majestic shore.

No darkness there divides the sway
With startling dawn and dazzling day;
But gloriously serene
Are the interminable plains:
One fixed, eternal sunset reigns
O'er the wide silent scene.

I cannot doff all human fear;
I know thy greeting is severe
To this poor shell of clay:
Yet come, O Death! thy freezing kiss
Emancipates! thy rest is bliss!
I would I were away!

From the German of GLUCK.

INDIAN DEATH-SONG.

THE sun sets in night, and the stars shun the day;
But glory remains when their lights fade away.
Begin, ye tormentors! your threats are in vain,
For the son of Alknomook will never complain.

Remember the arrows he shot from his bow;
Remember your chiefs by his hatchet laid low!
Why so slow? do you wait till I shrink from the pain?
No! the son of Alknomook shall never complain.

Remember the wood where in ambush we lay,
And the scalps which we bore from your nation away!
Now the flame rises fast, you exult in my pain;
But the son of Alknomook can never complain.

I go to the land where my father is gone;
His ghost shall rejoice in the fame of his son.
Death comes, like a friend, to relieve me from pain;
And thy son, O Alknomook! has scorned to complain.

ANNE HOME HUNTER.

NOW AND AFTERWARDS.

"Two hands upon the breast, and labor is past."
RUSSIAN PROVERB.

"Two hands upon the breast,
And labor 's done;
Two pale feet crossed in rest, —
The race is won;
Two eyes with coin-weights shut,
And all tears cease;
Two lips where grief is mute,
Anger at peace":
So pray we oftentimes, mourning our lot;
God in his kindness answereth not.

"Two hands to work addrest
Aye for his praise;
Two feet that never rest
Walking his ways;
Two eyes that look above
Through all their tears;
Two lips still breathing love,
Not wrath, nor fears":
So pray we afterwards, low on our knees;
Pardon those erring prayers! Father, hear these!

DINAH MULOCK CRAIK.

FAREWELL, LIFE.

WRITTEN DURING SICKNESS, APRIL, 1845.

FAREWELL, life! my senses swim,
And the world is growing dim;
Thronging shadows cloud the light,
Like the advent of the night, —
Colder, colder, colder still,
Upward steals a vapor chill;
Strong the earthy odor grows, —
I smell the mold above the rose!

Welcome, life! the spirit strives!
Strength returns and hope revives;
Cloudy fears and shapes forlorn
Fly like shadows at the morn, —
O'er the earth there comes a bloom;
Sunny light for sullen gloom,
Warm perfume for vapor cold, —
I smell the rose above the mold!

THOMAS HOOD.

REST.

LINES FOUND UNDER THE PILLOW OF A SOLDIER WHO DIED IN HOSPITAL AT PORT ROYAL, VA.

I LAY me down to sleep,
With little care
Whether my waking find
Me here, or there.

A bowing, burdened head
That only asks to rest,
Unquestioning, upon
A loving breast.

My good right-hand forgets
Its cunning now;
To march the weary march
I know not how.

I am not eager, bold,
Nor strong, — all that is past;
I am ready not to do,
At last, at last.

My half-day's work is done,
And this is all my part, —
I give a patient God
My patient heart;

And grasp his banner still,
Though all the blue be dim;
These stripes as well as stars
Lead after him.

ANONYMOUS.

HANG UP HIS HARP; HE'LL WAKE NO MORE!

HIS young bride stood beside his bed,
Her weeping watch to keep;
Hush! hush! he stirred not, — was he dead,
Or did he only sleep?

His brow was calm, no change was there,
No sigh had filled his breath;
O, did he wear that smile so fair
In slumber or in death?

"Reach down his harp," she wildly cried,
"And if one spark remain,
Let him but hear 'Loch Erroch's Side';
He'll kindle at the strain.

"That tune e'er held his soul in thrall;
It never breathed in vain;
He'll waken as its echoes fall,
Or never wake again."

The strings were swept. 'T was sad to hear
Sweet music floating there;
For every note called forth a tear
Of anguish and despair.

"See! see!" she cried, "the tune is o'er:
No opening eye, no breath;
Hang up his harp; he 'll wake no more;
He sleeps the sleep of death."

ELIZA COOK.

BEYOND THE SMILING AND THE WEEPING.

BEYOND the smiling and the weeping
I shall be soon;
Beyond the waking and the sleeping,
Beyond the sowing and the reaping,
I shall be soon.
Love, rest, and home!
Sweet hope!
Lord, tarry not, but come.

Beyond the blooming and the fading
I shall be soon;
Beyond the shining and the shading,
Beyond the hoping and the dreading,
I shall be soon.
Love, rest, and home! etc.

Beyond the rising and the setting
I shall be soon;
Beyond the calming and the fretting,
Beyond remembering and forgetting,
I shall be soon.
Love, rest, and home! etc.

Beyond the gathering and the strowing
I shall be soon;
Beyond the ebbing and the flowing,
Beyond the coming and the going,
I shall be soon.
Love, rest, and home! etc.

Beyond the parting and the meeting
I shall be soon;
Beyond the farewell and the greeting,
Beyond this pulse's fever beating,
I shall be soon.
Love, rest, and home! etc.

Beyond the frost chain and the fever
I shall be soon;
Beyond the rock waste and the river,
Beyond the ever and the never,
I shall be soon.
Love, rest, and home!
Sweet hope!
Lord, tarry not, but come.

HORATIUS BONAR.

THE LAND O' THE LEAL.

I'M wearing awa', Jean,
Like snaw when it 's thaw, Jean;
I'm wearing awa'
To the land o' the leal.
There 's nae sorrow there, Jean,
There 's neither cauld nor care, Jean,
The day is aye fair
In the land o' the leal.

Ye were aye leal and true, Jean;
Your task 's ended noo, Jean,
And I'll welcome you
To the land o' the leal.
Our bonnie bairn 's there, Jean,
She was baith guid and fair, Jean:
O, we grudged her right sair
To the land o' the leal!

Then dry that tearfu' e'e, Jean,
My soul langs to be free, Jean,
And angels wait on me
To the land o' the leal!
Now fare ye weel, my ain Jean,
This warld's care is vain, Jean;
We 'll meet and aye be fain
In the land o' the leal.

CAROLINA, BARONESS NAIRN.

SOFTLY WOO AWAY HER BREATH.

SOFTLY woo away her breath,
Gentle death!
Let her leave thee with no strife,
Tender, mournful, murmuring life!
She hath seen her happy day, —
She hath had her bud and blossom;
Now she pales and shrinks away,
Earth, into thy gentle bosom!

She hath done her bidding here,
Angels dear!
Bear her perfect soul above,
Seraph of the skies, — sweet love!
Good she was, and fair in youth;
And her mind was seen to soar,
And her heart was wed to truth:
Take her, then, forevermore, —
Forever — evermore!

BRYAN WALLER PROCTER
(BARRY CORNWALL.)

ON THE DEATH OF A DAUGHTER.

'T IS o'er, — in that long sigh she past —
Th' enfranchised spirit soars at last!

And now I gaze with tearless eye
On what to view was agony.
That panting heart is tranquil now,
And heavenly calm that ruffled brow,
And those pale lips which feebly strove
To force one parting smile of love,
Retain it yet, — soft, placid, mild,
As when it graced my living child.

O, I have watched with fondest care
To see my opening flow'ret blow,
And felt the joy which parents share,
The pride which fathers only know.

And I have sat the long, long night,
And marked that tender flower decay;
Not torn abruptly from the sight,
But slowly, sadly, waste away!
The spoiler came, yet paused, as though
So meek a victim checked his arm,
Half gave and half withheld the blow,
As forced to strike, yet loath to harm.

We saw that fair cheek's fading bloom
The ceaseless canker-worm consume,
And gazed on hopelessly,
Till the mute suffering pictured there
Wrung from the father's lip a prayer,
O God! the prayer his child might die.

Ay, from his lip — the doting heart
E'en then refused to bear its part.

But the sad conflict 's past, — 't is o'er;
That gentle bosom throbs no more!
The spirit 's freed, — through realms of light
Faith's eagle-glance pursues her flight
To other worlds, to happier skies;
Hope dries the tear which sorrow weepeth,
No mortal sound, the voice which cries,
"The damsel is not dead, but sleepeth!"

RICHARD HARRIS BARHAM
(THOMAS INGOLDSBY).

WE WATCHED HER BREATHING.

WE watched her breathing through the night,
Her breathing soft and low,
As in her breast the wave of life
Kept heaving to and fro.

So silently we seemed to speak,
So slowly moved about,
As we had lent her half our powers
To eke her living out.

Our very hopes belied our fears,
Our fears our hopes belied, —
We thought her dying when she slept,
And sleeping when she died.

For when the morn came dim and sad,
And chill with early showers,
Her quiet eyelids closed, — she had
Another morn than ours.

THOMAS HOOD.

A DEATH-BED.

HER suffering ended with the day;
Yet lived she at its close,
And breathed the long, long night away
In statue-like repose.

But when the sun, in all his state,
Illumed the eastern skies,
She passed through glory's morning-gate,
And walked in Paradise!

JAMES ALDRICH.

ANTONY AND CLEOPATRA.

WRITTEN IN HOSPITAL, WHILE LYING MORTALLY WOUNDED AT CHICAMAUGA.

"I am dying, Egypt, dying." — SHAKESPEARE.

I AM dying, Egypt, dying,
Ebbs the crimson life-tide fast,
And the dark, Plutonian shadows
Gather on the evening blast.
Let thine arm, O Queen, support me!
Hush thy sobs, and bow thine ear!
Hearken to the great heart secrets
Thou, and thou alone, must hear.

Though my scarred and veteran legions
Bear their eagles high no more,
And my wrecked and scattered galleys
Strew dark Actium's fatal shore;
Though no glittering guards surround me,
Prompt to do their master's will,
I must perish like a Roman,
Die the great triumvir still.

Let not Cæsar's servile minions
Mock the lion thus laid low;
'T was no foeman's hand that slew him,
'T was his own that struck the blow.
Hear, then, pillowed on thy bosom,
Ere his star fades quite away,
Him, who, drunk with thy caresses,
Madly flung a world away!

Should the base plebeian rabble
Dare assail my fame at Rome,
Where the noble spouse, Octavia,
Weeps within her widowed home,
Seek her, say the gods have told me,
Altars, augurs, circling wings,
That her blood, with mine commingled,
Yet shall mount the throne of kings.

And for thee, star-eyed Egyptian!
Glorious sorceress of the Nile!
Light the path to Stygian horrors
With the splendors of thy smile;
Give the Cæsar crowns and arches,
Let his brow the laurel twine,
I can scorn the Senate's triumphs,
Triumphing in love like thine.

I am dying, Egypt, dying;
Hark! the insulting foeman's cry!
They are coming — quick, my falchion!
Let me front them ere I die.
Ah! no more amid the battle
Shall my heart exulting swell!
Isis and Osiris guard thee,
Cleopatra! Rome! — farewell!

WILLIAM H. LYTLE.

LIGHT.

THE night has a thousand eyes,
The day but one;
Yet the light of the bright world dies
With the dying sun.

The mind has a thousand eyes,
And the heart but one;
Yet the light of a whole life dies
When its day is done.

BOURDILLON.

THRENODY.

MY heart is there,
Where, on eternal hills, my loved one dwells,
Among the lilies and the asphodels;
Clad in the brightness of the Great White Throne,
Glad in the smile of Him who sits thereon;
The glory gilding all his wealth of hair,
And making his immortal face more fair;
There is my treasure, and my heart is there.

My heart is there;
With him who made all earthly life so sweet;
So fit to live, and yet to die so meet;
So meek, so grand, so gentle, and so brave,
So ready to forgive, so strong to save;
His fair, pure spirit makes the heavens more fair,
And thither rises all my longing prayer;
There is my treasure, and my heart is there.

ANONYMOUS.

WHEN I AM DEAD.

TOLL not the bell of death for me
When I am dead;
Strew not the flowery wreath o'er me,
On my cold bed.

Let friendship's sacred tear
On my fresh grave appear,
Gemming with pearls my bier —
When I am dead.

No dazzling, proud array
Of pageantry display,
My fate to spread;
Let not the busy crowd be near,
When I am dead,

Fanning with unfelt sighs my bier,
Sighs quickly sped.
Deep let the impression rest
On some fond female breast;
Then were my memory blest,
When I am dead.

Let not the day be writ;
Love will remember it
Untold, unsaid.

ANONYMOUS.

THE FEMALE CONVICT.

SHE shrank from all, and her silent mood
Made her wish only for solitude:
Her eye sought the ground, as it could not brook,
For innermost shame, on another's to look;
And the cheerings of comfort fell on her ear
Like deadliest words, that were curses to hear! —
She still was young, and she had been fair;
But weather-stains, hunger, toil, and care,
That frost and fever that wear the heart,
Had made the colors of youth depart
From the sallow cheek, save over it came
The burning flush of the spirit's shame.

They were sailing over the salt sea-foam,
Far from her country, far from her home;
And all she had left for her friends to keep
Was a name to hide and a memory to weep!
And her future held forth but the felon's lot, —
To live forsaken, to die forgot!

She could not weep, and she could not pray,
But she wasted and withered from day to day,
Till you might have counted each sunken vein,
When her wrist was prest by the iron chain;
And sometimes I thought her large dark eye
Had the glisten of red insanity.

She called me once to her sleeping-place,
A strange, wild look was upon her face,
Her eye flashed over her cheek so white,
Like a gravestone seen in the pale moonlight,
And she spoke in a low, unearthly tone, —
The sound from mine ear hath never gone! —
"I had last night the loveliest dream:
My own land shone in the summer beam,
I saw the fields of the golden grain,
I heard the reaper's harvest strain;
There stood on the hills the green pine-tree,
And the thrush and the lark sang merrily.
A long and a weary way I had come;
But I stopped, methought, by mine own sweet home.
I stood by the hearth, and my father sat there,
With pale, thin face, and snow-white hair!
The Bible lay open upon his knee,
But he closed the book to welcome me.
He led me next where my mother lay,
And together we knelt by her grave to pray,
And heard a hymn it was heaven to hear,
For it echoed one to my young days dear.
This dream has waked feelings long, long since fled,
And hopes which I deemed in my heart were dead!
— We have not spoken, but still I have hung
On the Northern accents that dwell on thy tongue.
To me they are music, to me they recall
The things long hidden by Memory's pall!
Take this long curl of yellow hair,
And give it my father, and tell him my prayer,
My dying prayer, was for him." . . . .

Next day
Upon the deck a coffin lay;
They raised it up, and like a dirge
The heavy gale swept over the surge;
The corpse was cast to the wind and wave, —
The convict has found in the green sea a grave.

LETITIA ELIZABETH LANDON.

SOLILOQUY ON DEATH.

FROM "HAMLET, PRINCE OF DENMARK."

HAMLET. To be, or not to be, — that is the question: —
Whether 't is nobler in the mind to suffer
The slings and arrows of outrageous fortune,
Or to take arms against a sea of troubles,
And, by opposing, end them? — To die, — to sleep; —
No more; and, by a sleep, to say we end
The heart-ache, and the thousand natural shocks
That flesh is heir to, — 't is a consummation
Devoutly to be wished. To die, — to sleep; —
To sleep! perchance to dream: — ay, there 's the rub;
For in that sleep of death what dreams may come,
When we have shuffled off this mortal coil,
Must give us pause: there 's the respect
That makes calamity of so long life;
For who would bear the whips and scorns of time,
The oppressor's wrong, the proud man's contumely,
The pangs of déspised love, the law's delay,
The insolence of office, and the spurns
That patient merit of the unworthy takes,
When he himself might his quietus make
With a bare bodkin? who would fardels bear,
To grunt and sweat under a weary life,
But that the dread of something after death, —
That undiscovered country, from whose bourn
No traveler returns, — puzzles the will,
And makes us rather bear those ills we have,
Than fly to others that we know not of?
Thus conscience does make cowards of us all;
And thus the native hue of resolution
Is sicklied o'er with the pale cast of thought;
And enterprises of great pith and moment,
With this regard, their currents turn awry,
And lose the name of action.

SHAKESPEARE.

THE SECRET OF DEATH.

"SHE is dead!" they said to him. "Come away;
Kiss her and leave her, — thy love is clay!"

They smoothed her tresses of dark brown hair;
On her forehead of stone they laid it fair;

Over her eyes, which gazed too much,
They drew the lids with a gentle touch;

With a tender touch they closed up well
The sweet, thin lips that had secrets to tell;

About her brows and beautiful face
They tied her veil and her marriage-lace,

And drew on her white feet the white silk shoes, —
Which were the whitest no eye could choose!

And over her bosom they crossed her hands, —
"Come away," they said, "God understands!"

But there was a silence, and nothing there
But silence, and scents of eglantere,

And jasmine, and roses, and rosemary,
And they said, "As a lady should lie, lies she."

And they held their breath as they left the room
With a shudder, to glance at its stillness and gloom.

But he who loved her too well to dread
The sweet, the stately, and beautiful dead,

He lit his lamp and took the key
And turned it. Alone again — he and she!

He and she; yet she would not speak,
Though he kissed, in the old place, the quiet cheek.

He and she; yet she would not smile,
Though he called her the name she loved erewhile.

He and she; still she did not move
To any passionate whisper of love.

Then he said: "Cold lips, and breast without breath!
Is there no voice, no language of death,

"Dumb to the ear and still to the sense,
But to heart and soul distinct, intense?

"See now; I will listen with soul, not ear;
What was the secret of dying, dear?

"Was it the infinite wonder of all
That you ever could let life's flower fall?

"Or was it a greater marvel to feel
The perfect calm o'er the agony steal?

"Was the miracle deeper to find how deep,
Beyond all dreams, sank downward that sleep?

"Did life roll back its record, dear,
And show, as they say it does, past things clear?

"O perfect dead! O dead most dear!
I hold the breath of my soul to hear!

"I listen as deep as to horrible hell,
As high as to heaven, and you do not tell!

"There must be a pleasure in dying, sweet,
To make you so placid from head to feet.

"I would tell you, darling, if I were dead,
And 't were your hot tears upon my brow shed;

"I would say, though the angel of death had laid
His sword on my lips to keep it unsaid.

"You should not ask vainly, with streaming eyes,
Which of all death's was the chief surprise;

"The very strangest and suddenest thing,
Of all the surprises that dying must bring."

Ah, foolish world! O, most kind dead!
Though he told me, who will believe it was said?

Who will believe what he heard her say,
With a sweet, soft voice, in the dear old way?

"The utmost wonder is this, — I hear,
And see you, and love you, and kiss you, dear;

"And am your angel, who was your bride,
And know that, though dead, I have never died."

ANONYMOUS.

ONLY THE CLOTHES SHE WORE.

There is the hat
With the blue veil thrown 'round it, just as they found it,
Spotted and soiled, stained and all spoiled —
Do you recognize that?

The gloves, too, lie there,
And in them still lingers the shape of her fingers,
That some one has pressed, perhaps, and caressed,
So slender and fair.

There are the shoes,
With their long silken laces, still bearing traces,
To the toe's dainty tip, of the mud of the slip,
The slime and the ooze.

There is the dress,
Like the blue veil, all dabbled, discolored, and drabbled —
This you should know without doubt, and, if so,
All else you may guess.

There is the shawl,
With the striped border, hung next in order,
Soiled hardly less than the white muslin dress,
And — that is all.

Ah, here is a ring
We were forgetting, with a pearl setting;
There was only this one—name or date?—none?
A frail, pretty thing;

A keepsake, maybe,
The gift of another, perhaps a brother,
Or lover, who knows? him her heart chose,
Or was she heart-free?

Does the hat there,
With the blue veil around it, the same as they found it,
Summon up a fair face with just a trace
Of gold in the hair?

Or does the shawl,
Mutely appealing to some hidden feeling,
A form, young and slight, to your mind's sight
Clearly recall?

A month now has passed,
And her sad history remains yet a mystery,
But these we keep still, and shall keep them until
Hope dies at last.

Was she a prey
Of some deep sorrow clouding the morrow,
Hiding from view the sky's happy blue?
Or was there foul play?

Alas! who may tell?
Some one or other, perhaps a fond mother,
May recognize these when her child's clothes she sees;
Then—will it be well?

N. G. SHEPHERD.

UNCLE JO.

I HAVE in memory a little story,
That few indeed would rhyme about but me;
'T is not of love, nor fame, nor yet of glory,
Although a little colored with the three, —
In very truth, I think, as much, perchance,
As most tales disembodied from romance.

Jo lived about the village, and was neighbor
To every one who had hard work to do;
If he possessed a genius, 't was for labor
Most people thought, but there were one or two
Who sometimes said, when he arose to go,
"Come in again and see us, Uncle Jo!"

The "Uncle" was a courtesy they gave, —
And felt they could afford to give to him, —
Just as the master makes of some good slave
An Aunt Jemima, or an Uncle Jim;
And of this dubious kindness Jo was glad, —
Poor fellow, it was all he ever had!

A mile or so away, he had a brother, —
A rich, proud man that people did n't hire;
But Jo had neither sister, wife, nor mother,
And baked his corncake at his cabin fire
After the day's work, hard for you or me,
But he was never tired, — how could he be?

They called him dull, but he had eyes of quickness
For everybody that he could befriend;
Said one and all, "How kind he is in sickness,"
But there, of course, his goodness had an end.
Another praise there was might have been given,
For one or more days out of every seven —

With his old pickax swung across his shoulder,
And downcast eyes, and slow and sober tread —
He sought the place of graves, and each beholder
Wondered and asked some other who was dead;
But when he digged all day, nobody thought
That he had done a whit more than he ought.

At length, one winter when the sunbeams slanted
Faintly and cold across the churchyard snow,
The bell tolled out, — alas! a grave was wanted,
And all looked anxiously for Uncle Jo;
His spade stood there against his own roof-tree,
There was his pickax too, but where was he?

They called and called again, but no replying;
Smooth at the window, and about the door,
The snow in cold and heavy drifts was lying, —
He did not need the daylight any more.
One shook him roughly, and another said,
"As true as preaching, Uncle Jo is dead!"

And when they wrapped him in the linen, fairer
And finer, too, than he had worn till then,
They found a picture, — haply of the sharer
Of sunny hope some time, or where or when,
They did not care to know, but closed his eyes
And placed it in the coffin where he lies!

None wrote his epitaph, nor saw the beauty
Of the pure love that reached into the grave,
Nor how in unobtrusive ways of duty
He kept, despite the dark; but men less brave
Have left great names, while not a willow bends
Above his dust, — poor Jo, he had no friends!

ALICE CARY.

FOR ANNIE.

THANK Heaven! the crisis, —
The danger is past,
And the lingering illness
Is over at last, —
And the fever called "Living"
Is conquered at last.

Sadly, I know,
I am shorn of my strength,
And no muscle I move
As I lie at full length, —
But no matter! — I feel
I am better at length.

And I rest so composedly
Now, in my bed,
That any beholder
Might fancy me dead, —
Might start at beholding me,
Thinking me dead.

The moaning and groaning,
The sighing and sobbing,
Are quieted now,
With that horrible throbbing
At heart, — ah, that horrible,
Horrible throbbing!

The sickness, the nausea,
The pitiless pain,
Have ceased, with the fever
That maddened my brain, —
With the fever called "Living"
That burned in my brain.

And O, of all tortures
That torture the worst
Has abated, — the terrible
Torture of thirst
For the naphthaline river
Of Passion accurst!
I have drunk of a water
That quenches all thirst, —

Of a water that flows,
With a lullaby sound,
From a spring but a very few
Feet under ground, —
From a cavern not very far
Down under ground.

And ah! let it never
Be foolishly said
That my room it is gloomy
And narrow my bed;
For man never slept
In a different bed, —
And, to *sleep*, you must slumber
In just such a bed.

My tantalized spirit
Here blandly reposes,
Forgetting, or never
Regretting, its roses, —
Its old agitations
Of myrtles and roses:

For now, while so quietly
Lying, it fancies
A holier odor
About it, of pansies, —
A rosemary odor,
Commingled with pansies,
With rue and the beautiful
Puritan pansies.

And so it lies happily,
Bathing in many
A dream of the truth
And the beauty of Annie, —
Drowned in a bath
Of the tresses of Annie.

She tenderly kissed me,
She fondly caressed,
And then I fell gently
To sleep on her breast, —
Deeply to sleep
From the heaven of her breast.

When the light was extinguished,
She covered me warm,
And she prayed to the angels
To keep me from harm, —
To the queen of the angels
To shield me from harm.

And I lie so composedly
Now in my bed,
(Knowing her love,)
That you fancy me dead; —
And I rest so contentedly
Now in my bed,
(With her love at my breast,)
That you fancy me dead, —
That you shudder to look at me,
Thinking me dead:

But my heart it is brighter
Than all of the many
Stars in the sky;
For it sparkles with Annie, —
It glows with the light
Of the love of my Annie,
With the thought of the light
Of the eyes of my Annie.

EDGAR ALLAN POE.

THE LYKE-WAKE DIRGE.

AN ANCIENT FUNERAL CHANT OF THE "NORTH COUNTRY," ENGLAND.

THIS ae nighte, this ae nighte,
Every nighte and alle:
Fire and fleet and candle-light,
And Christe receive thy saule.

When thou from hence away art paste,
Every nighte and alle:

To Whinny-muir thou comes at laste,
And Christe receive thy saule.

If ever thou gave either hosen or shoon,
Every nighte and alle :
Sit thee down and put them on,
And Christe receive thy saule.

But if hosen or shoon thou never gave neean,
Every nighte and alle :
The whinnes shall prick thee to the bare beean,
And Christe receive thy saule.

From Whinny-muir when thou may passe,
Every nighte and alle :
To Brig o' Dread thou comes at laste,
And Christe receive thy saule.

. . . . . .

From Brig o' Dread when thou art paste,
Every nighte and alle :
To Purgatory Fire thou comes at laste,
And Christe receive thy saule.

If ever thou gave either meat or drinke,
Every nighte and alle :
The fire shall never make thee shrinke,
And Christe receive thy saule.

But if milke or drinke thou never gave neean,
Every nighte and alle :
The fire shall burn thee to the bare beean,
And Christe receive thy saule.

ANONYMOUS.

DE PROFUNDIS.

THE face which, duly as the sun,
Rose up for me with life begun,
To mark all bright hours of the day
With hourly love, is dimmed away, —
And yet my days go on, go on.

The tongue which, like a stream, could run
Smooth music from the roughest stone,
And every morning with "Good day"
Make each day good, is hushed away, —
And yet my days go on, go on.

The heart which, like a staff, was one
For mine to lean and rest upon,
The strongest on the longest day
With steadfast love, is caught away, —
And yet my days go on, go on.

And cold before my summer's done,
And deaf in Nature's general tune,
And fallen too low for special fear,
And here, with hope no longer here, —
While the tears drop, my days go on.

The world goes whispering to its own,
"This anguish pierces to the bone";
And tender friends go sighing round,
"What love can ever cure this wound?"
My days go on, my days go on.

The past rolls forward on the sun
And makes all night. O dreams begun,
Not to be ended! Ended bliss,
And life that will not end in this!
My days go on, my days go on.

Breath freezes on my lips to moan:
As one alone, once not alone,
I sit and knock at Nature's door,
Heartbare, heart-hungry, very poor,
Whose desolate days go on.

I knock and cry, — Undone, undone!
Is there no help, no comfort, — none?
No gleaning in the wide wheat-plains
Where others drive their loaded wains?
My vacant days go on, go on.

This Nature, though the snows be down,
Thinks kindly of the bird of June:
The little red hip on the tree
Is ripe for such. What is for me,
Whose days so winterly go on?

No bird am I, to sing in June,
And dare not ask an equal boon.
Good nests and berries red are Nature's
To give away to better creatures, —
And yet my days go on, go on.

I ask less kindness to be done, —
Only to loose these pilgrim-shoon,
(Too early worn and grimed) with sweet
Cool deathly touch to these tired feet,
Till days go out which now go on.

. . . . . .

From gracious Nature have I won
Such liberal bounty? may I run
So, lizard-like, within her side,
And there be safe, who now am tried
By days that painfully go on?

— A Voice reproves me thereupon,
More sweet than Nature's when the drone
Of bees is sweetest, and more deep
Than when the rivers overleap
The shuddering pines, and thunder on.

God's Voice, not Nature's. Night and noon
He sits upon the great white throne
And listens for the creatures' praise.
What babble we of days and days?
The Day-spring he, whose days go on.

He reigns above, he reigns alone;
Systems burn out and leave his throne:
Fair mists of seraphs melt and fall
Around him, changeless amid all, —
Ancient of Days, whose days go on.

He reigns below, he reigns alone,
And, having life in love foregone
Beneath the crown of sovran thorns,
He reigns the jealous God. Who mourns
Or rules with him, while days go on?

By anguish which made pale the sun,
I hear him charge his saints that none
Among his creatures anywhere
Blaspheme against him with despair,
However darkly days go on.

Take from my head the thorn-wreath brown!
No mortal grief deserves that crown.
O súpreme Love, chief Misery,
The sharp regalia are for THEE,
Whose days eternally go on!

For us, — whatever 's undergone,
Thou knowest, willest what is done.
Grief may be joy misunderstood;
Only the Good discerns the good,
I trust thee while my days go on.

Whatever 's lost, it first was won:
We will not struggle nor impugn.
Perhaps the cup was broken here,
That Heaven's new wine might show more clear.
I praise thee while my days go on.

I praise thee while my days go on;
I love thee while my days go on;
Through dark and dearth, through fire and frost,
With emptied arms and treasure lost,
I thank thee while my days go on.

ELIZABETH BARRETT BROWNING.

THE FAIREST THING IN MORTAL EYES.

[Addressed to his deceased wife, who died in childbed at the age of twenty-two.]

To make my lady's obsequies
My love a minster wrought,
And, in the chantry, service there
Was sung by doleful thought;
The tapers were of burning sighs,
That light and odor gave:
And sorrows, painted o'er with tears,
Enluminèd her grave;
And round about, in quaintest guise,
Was carved: "Within this tomb there lies
The fairest thing in mortal eyes."

Above her lieth spread a tomb
Of gold and sapphires blue:
The gold doth show her blessedness,
The sapphires mark her true;
For blessedness and truth in her
Were livelily portrayed,
When gracious God with both his hands
Her goodly substance made.
He framed her in such wondrous wise,
She was, to speak without disguise,
The fairest thing in mortal eyes.

No more, no more! my heart doth faint
When I the life recall
Of her who lived so free from taint,
So virtuous deemed by all, —
That in herself was so complete
I think that she was ta'en
By God to deck his paradise,
And with his saints to reign;
Whom while on earth each one did prize
The fairest thing in mortal eyes.

But naught our tears avail, or cries;
All soon or late in death shall sleep;
Nor living wight long time may keep
The fairest thing in mortal eyes.

From the French of CHARLES DUKE OF ORLEANS, by HENRY FRANCIS CARY.

DIRGE FOR A YOUNG GIRL.

UNDERNEATH the sod low-lying,
Dark and drear,
Sleepeth one who left, in dying,
Sorrow here.

Yes, they 're ever bending o'er her
Eyes that weep;
Forms, that to the cold grave bore her,
Vigils keep.

When the summer moon is shining
Soft and fair,
Friends she loved in tears are twining
Chaplets there.

Rest in peace, thou gentle spirit,
Throned above, —
Souls like thine with God inherit
Life and love!

JAMES T. FIELDS.

FEAR NO MORE THE HEAT O' THE SUN.

FROM "CYMBELINE."

Fear no more the heat o' the sun,
Nor the furious winter's rages;
Thou thy worldly task hast done,
Home art gone, and ta'en thy wages:
Golden lads and girls all must,
As chimney-sweepers, come to dust.

Fear no more the frown o' the great,
Thou art past the tyrant's stroke;
Care no more to clothe, and eat;
To thee the reed is as the oak:
The scepter, learning, physic, must
All follow this and come to dust.

Fear no more the lightning flash
Nor the all-dreaded thunder-stone;
Fear not slander, censure rash;
Thou hast finished joy and moan:
All lovers young, all lovers must
Consign to thee, and come to dust.

SHAKESPEARE.

DEATH THE LEVELER.

[These verses are said to have "chilled the heart" of Oliver Cromwell.]

The glories of our birth and state
Are shadows, not substantial things;
There is no armor against fate, —
Death lays his icy hand on kings;
Scepter and crown
Must tumble down,
And in the dust be equal made
With the poor crookéd scythe and spade.

Some men with swords may reap the field,
And plant fresh laurels where they kill;
But their strong nerves at last must yield, —
They tame but one another still;
Early or late
They stoop to fate,
And must give up their murmuring breath,
When they, pale captives, creep to death.

The garlands wither on your brow, —
Then boast no more your mighty deeds;
Upon death's purple altar, now
See where the victor victim bleeds!
All heads must come
To the cold tomb, —
Only the actions of the just
Smell sweet, and blossom in the dust.

JAMES SHIRLEY.

SIC VITA.

Like to the falling of a star,
Or as the flights of eagles are,
Or like the fresh spring's gaudy hue,
Or silver drops of morning dew,
Or like a wind that chafes the flood,
Or bubbles which on water stood, —
E'en such is man, whose borrowed light
Is straight called in, and paid to-night.
The wind blows out, the bubble dies,
The spring entombed in autumn lies,
The dew dries up, the star is shot,
The flight is past, — and man forgot!

HENRY KING.

O, WHY SHOULD THE SPIRIT OF MORTAL BE PROUD?

[The following poem was a particular favorite with Abraham Lincoln. It was first shown to him when a young man by a friend, and afterwards he cut it from a newspaper and learned it by heart. He said to a friend, "I would give a great deal to know who wrote it, but have never been able to ascertain."]

O, why should the spirit of mortal be proud?
Like a swift-fleeting meteor, a fast-flying cloud,
A flash of the lightning, a break of the wave,
Man passes from life to his rest in the grave.

The leaves of the oak and the willow shall fade,
Be scattered around and together be laid;
And the young and the old, and the low and the high,
Shall molder to dust and together shall lie.

The infant a mother attended and loved,
The mother that infant's affection who proved;
The husband that mother and infant who blessed,
Each, all, are away to their dwellings of rest.

The maid on whose cheek, on whose brow, in whose eye,
Shone beauty and pleasure,—her triumphs are by;
And the memory of those who loved her and praised,
Are alike from the minds of the living erased.

The hand of the king that the scepter hath borne,
The brow of the priest that the miter hath worn,
The eye of the sage, and the heart of the brave,
Are hidden and lost in the depths of the grave.

The peasant whose lot was to sow and to reap,
The herdsman who climbed with his goats up the steep,
The beggar who wandered in search of his bread,
Have faded away like the grass that we tread.

The saint who enjoyed the communion of heaven,
The sinner who dared to remain unforgiven,

The wise and the foolish, the guilty and just,
Have quietly mingled their bones in the dust.

So the multitude goes, like the flower and the weed
That wither away to let others succeed;
So the multitude comes, even those we behold,
To repeat every tale that has often been told.

For we are the same that our fathers have been;
We see the same sights that our fathers have seen,—
We drink the same stream and view the same sun,
And run the same course that our fathers have run.

The thoughts we are thinking our fathers would think;
From the death we are shrinking from, they too would shrink,
To the life we are clinging to, they too would cling;
But it speeds from the earth, like a bird on the wing.

They loved, but their story we cannot unfold;
They scorned, but the heart of the haughty is cold;
They grieved, but no wail from their slumbers will come;
They joyed, but the voice of their gladness is dumb.

They died,—ay! they died: and we things that are now,
Who walk on the turf that lies over their brow,
Who make in their dwelling a transient abode,
Meet the changes they met on their pilgrimage road.

Yea! hope and despondency, pleasure and pain,
Are mingled together in sunshine and rain;
And the smile and the tear, the song and the dirge,
Still follow each other, like surge upon surge.

'T is the twink of an eye, 't is the draught of a breath,
From the blossom of health to the paleness of death,
From the gilded saloon to the bier and the shroud,—
O, why should the spirit of mortal be proud?

WILLIAM KNOX.

VIRTUE IMMORTAL.

SWEET day, so cool, so calm, so bright,
The bridall of the earth and skie:
The dew shall weep thy fall to-night;
For thou must die.

Sweet rose, whose hue angrie and brave
Bids the rash gazer wipe his eye,
Thy root is ever in its grave,
And thou must die.

Sweet spring, full of sweet dayes and roses,
A box where sweets compacted lie,
My musick shows ye have your closes,
And all must die.

Onely a sweet and vertuous soul,
Like seasoned timber, never gives;
But, though the whole world turn to coal,
Then chiefly lives.

GEORGE HERBERT.

MAN'S MORTALITY.

LIKE as the damask rose you see,
Or like the blossom on the tree,
Or like the dainty flower in May,
Or like the morning of the day,
Or like the sun, or like the shade,
Or like the gourd which Jonas had,—
E'en such is man; whose thread is spun,
Drawn out, and cut, and so is done.—
The rose withers, the blossom blasteth,
The flower fades, the morning hasteth,
The sun sets, the shadow flies,
The gourd consumes,—and man he dies!

Like to the grass that 's newly sprung,
Or like a tale that 's new begun,
Or like the bird that 's here to-day,
Or like the pearlèd dew of May,
Or like an hour, or like a span,
Or like the singing of a swan,—
E'en such is man;—who lives by breath,
Is here, now there, in life and death.—
The grass withers, the tale is ended,
The bird is flown, the dew 's ascended,
The hour is short, the span is long,
The swan 's near death,—man's life is done!

SIMON WASTELL.

IF THOU WILT EASE THINE HEART.

DIRGE.

IF thou wilt ease thine heart
Of love, and all its smart,—
Then sleep, dear, sleep!
And not a sorrow
Hang any tear on your eyelashes;
Lie still and deep,
Sad soul, until the sea-wave washes
The rim o' the sun to-morrow,
In eastern sky.

But wilt thou cure thine heart
Of love, and all its smart,—
Then die, dear, die!
'T is deeper, sweeter,

Than on a rose bank to lie dreaming
With folded eye;
And then alone, amid the beaming
Of love's stars, thou 'lt meet her
In eastern sky.

THOMAS LOVELL BEDDOES.

DEATH.

FROM "THE GIAOUR."

He who hath bent him o'er the dead
Ere the first day of death is fled,
The first dark day of nothingness,
The last of danger and distress,
(Before Decay's effacing fingers
Have swept the lines where beauty lingers,)
And marked the mild angelic air,
The rapture of repose, that 's there,
The fixed yet tender traits that streak
The languor of the placid cheek,
And — but for that sad shrouded eye,
That fires not, wins not, weeps not now,
And but for that chill, changeless brow,
Where cold Obstruction's apathy
Appalls the gazing mourner's heart,
As if to him it could impart
The doom he dreads, yet dwells upon;
Yes, but for these and these alone,
Some moments, ay, one treacherous hour,
He still might doubt the tyrant's power;
So fair, so calm, so softly sealed,
The first, last look by death revealed!
Such is the aspect of this shore;
'T is Greece, but living Greece no more!
So coldly sweet, so deadly fair,
We start, for soul is wanting there.
Hers is the loveliness in death,
That parts not quite with parting breath;
But beauty with that fearful bloom,
That hue which haunts it to the tomb,
Expression's last receding ray,
A gilded halo hovering round decay,
The farewell beam of Feeling past away;
Spark of that flame, perchance of heavenly birth,
Which gleams, but warms no more its cherished earth!

LORD BYRON.

THE DIRGE.

What is the existence of man's life
But open war, or slumbered strife?
Where sickness to his sense presents
The combat of the elements;
And never feels a perfect peace,
Till Death's cold hand signs his release?

It is a storm — where the hot blood
Outvies in rage the boiling flood;
And each loud passion of the mind
Is like a furious gust of wind,
Which beats his bark with many a wave,
Till he casts anchor in the grave.

It is a flower — which buds and grows
And withers as the leaves disclose;
Whose spring and fall faint seasons keep,
Like fits of waking before sleep;
Then shrinks into that fatal mold
Where its first being was enrolled.

It is a dream — whose seeming truth
Is moralized in age and youth;
Where all the comforts he can share
As wandering as his fancies are;
Till in the mist of dark decay
The dreamer vanish quite away.

It is a dial — which points out
The sunset as it moves about;
And shadows out in lines of night
The subtle stages of Time's flight,
Till all-obscuring earth hath laid
The body in perpetual shade.

It is a weary interlude —
Which doth short joys, long woes, include;
The world the stage, the prologue tears,
The acts vain hopes and varied fears;
The scene shuts up with loss of breath,
And leaves no epilogue but death.

HENRY KING.

THE HUSBAND AND WIFE'S GRAVE.

Husband and wife! no converse now ye hold,
As once ye did in your young days of love,
On its alarms, its anxious hours, delays,
Its silent meditations and glad hopes,
Its fears, impatience, quiet sympathies;
Nor do ye speak of joy assured, and bliss
Full, certain, and possessed. Domestic cares
Call you not now together. Earnest talk
On what your children may be moves you not.
Ye lie in silence, and an awful silence;
Not like to that in which ye rested once
Most happy, — silence eloquent, when heart
With heart held speech, and your mysterious frames,
Harmonious, sensitive, at every beat
Touched the soft notes of love.

A stillness deep,
Insensible, unheeding, folds you round,
And darkness, as a stone, has sealed you in;

Away from all the living, here ye rest,
In all the nearness of the narrow tomb,
Yet feel ye not each other's presence now; —
Dread fellowship! — together, yet alone.
Is this thy prison-house, thy grave, then, Love?
And doth death cancel the great bond that holds
Commingling spirits? Are thoughts that know no bounds,
But, self-inspired, rise upward, searching out
The Eternal Mind, the Father of all thought, —
Are they become mere tenants of a tomb? —
Dwellers in darkness, who the illuminate realms
Of uncreated light have visited, and lived? —
Lived in the dreadful splendor of that throne
Which One, with gentle hand the veil of flesh
Lifting that hung 'twixt man and it, revealed
In glory? — throne before which even now
Our souls, moved by prophetic power, bow down
Rejoicing, yet at their own natures awed? —
Souls that thee know by a mysterious sense,
Thou awful unseen Presence, — are they quenched?
Or burn they on, hid from our mortal eyes
By that bright day which ends not; as the sun
His robe of light flings round the glittering stars?
And do our loves all perish with our frames?
Do those that took their root and put forth buds,
And then soft leaves unfolded in the warmth
Of mutual hearts, grow up and live in beauty,
Then fade and fall, like fair, unconscious flowers?
Are thoughts and passions that to the tongue give speech,
And make it send forth winning harmonies,
That to the cheek do give its living glow,
And vision in the eye the soul intense
With that for which there is no utterance, —
Are these the body's accidents, no more?
To live in it, and when that dies go out
Like the burnt taper's flame?

O listen, man!
A voice within us speaks the startling word,
"Man, thou shalt never die!" Celestial voices
Hymn it around our souls; according harps,
By angel fingers touched when the mild stars
Of morning sang together, sound forth still
The song of our great immortality;
Thick-clustering orbs, and this our fair domain,
The tall, dark mountains and the deep-toned seas,
Join in this solemn, universal song.
O listen, ye, our spirits! drink it in
From all the air! 'T is in the gentle moonlight;
Is floating in day's setting glories; Night,
Wrapped in her sable robe, with silent step
Comes to our bed and breathes it in our ears; —
Night and the dawn, bright day and thoughtful eve,
All time, all bounds, the limitless expanse,
As one vast mystic instrument, are touched
By an unseen, living Hand, and conscious chords
Quiver with joy in this great jubilee.
The dying hear it; and, as sounds of earth
Grow dull and distant, wake their passing souls
To mingle in this heavenly harmony.

Why is it that I linger round this tomb?
What holds it? Dust that cumbered those I mourn.
They shook it off, and laid aside earth's robes,
And put on those of light. They 're gone to dwell
In love, — their God's and angels'! Mutual love,
That bound them here, no longer needs a speech
For full communion; nor sensations strong,
Within the breast, their prison, strive in vain
To be set free, and meet their kind in joy.
Changed to celestials, thoughts that rise in each
By natures new impart themselves, though silent.
Each quickening sense, each throb of holy love,
Affections sanctified, and the full glow
Of being, which expand and gladden one,
By union all mysterious, thrill and live
In both immortal frames; — sensation all,
And thought, pervading, mingling sense and thought!
Ye paired, yet one! wrapt in a consciousness
Twofold, yet single, — this is love, this life!
Why call we, then, the square-built monument,
The upright column, and the low-laid slab
Tokens of death, memorials of decay?
Stand in this solemn, still assembly, man,
And learn thy proper nature; for thou seest
In these shaped stones and lettered tables figures
Of life. Then be they to thy soul as those
Which he who talked on Sinai's mount with God
Brought to the old Judeans, — types are these
Of thine eternity.

I thank thee, Father,
That at this simple grave on which the dawn
Is breaking, emblem of that day which hath
No close, thou kindly unto my dark mind
Hast sent a sacred light, and that away
From this green hillock, whither I had come
In sorrow, thou art leading me in joy.

RICHARD HENRY DANA.

THE ENDS OF LIFE.

A GOOD that never satisfies the mind,
A beauty fading like the April flowers,
A sweet with floods of gall that runs combined,
A pleasure passing ere in thought made ours,
An honor that more fickle is than wind,
A glory at opinion's frown that lowers,
A treasury which bankrupt time devours,
A knowledge than grave ignorance more blind,
A vain delight our equals to command,

A style of greatness, in effect a dream,
A swelling thought of holding sea and land,
A servile lot, decked with a pompous name, —
Are the strange ends we toil for here below,
Till wisest death make us our errors know.

WILLIAM DRUMMOND.

THE GRAVES OF A HOUSEHOLD.

THEY grew in beauty, side by side,
They filled one home with glee; —
Their graves are severed far and wide,
By mount and stream and sea.

The same fond mother bent at night
O'er each fair sleeping brow;
She had each folded flower in sight, —
Where are those dreamers now?

One midst the forest of the West,
By a dark stream is laid, —
The Indian knows his place of rest,
Far in the cedar shade.

The sea, the blue lone sea, hath one, —
He lies where pearls lie deep;
He was the loved of all, yet none
O'er his low bed may weep.

One sleeps where Southern vines are drest,
Above the noble slain;
He wrapt his colors round his breast
On a blood-red field of Spain.

And one—o'er *her* the myrtle showers
Its leaves, by soft winds fanned;
She faded midst Italian flowers, —
The last of that bright band.

And parted thus they rest, who played
Beneath the same green tree;
Whose voices mingled as they prayed
Around one parent knee!

They that with smiles lit up the hall,
And cheered with song the hearth—
Alas! for love, if *thou* wert all,
And naught beyond, O earth!

FELICIA HEMANS.

GREENWOOD CEMETERY.

How calm they sleep beneath the shade
Who once were weary of the strife,
And bent, like us, beneath the load
Of human life!

The willow hangs with sheltering grace
And benediction o'er their sod,
And Nature, hushed, assures the soul
They rest in God.

O weary hearts, what rest is here,
From all that curses yonder town!
So deep the peace, I almost long
To lay me down.

For, O, it will be blest to sleep,
Nor dream, nor move, that silent night,
Till wakened in immortal strength
And heavenly light!

CRAMMOND KENNEDY.

GOD'S-ACRE.

I LIKE that ancient Saxon phrase which calls
The burial-ground God's-Acre! It is just;
It consecrates each grave within its walls,
And breathes a benison o'er the sleeping dust.

God's-Acre! Yes, that blessed name imparts
Comfort to those who in the grave have sown
The seed that they had garnered in their hearts,
Their bread of life, alas! no more their own.

Into its furrows shall we all be cast,
In the sure faith that we shall rise again
At the great harvest, when the archangel's blast
Shall winnow, like a fan, the chaff and grain.

Then shall the good stand in immortal bloom,
In the fair gardens of that second birth;
And each bright blossom mingle its perfume
With that of flowers which never bloomed on earth.

With thy rude plowshare, Death, turn up the sod,
And spread the furrow for the seed we sow;
This is the field and Acre of our God,
This is the place where human harvests grow!

HENRY WADSWORTH LONGFELLOW.

THE OLD BURYING-GROUND.

PLUMED ranks of tall wild-cherry
And birch surround
The half-hid, solitary
Old burying-ground.

All the low wall is crumbled
And overgrown,
And in the turf lies tumbled
Stone upon stone.

Only the school-boy, scrambling
After his arrow
Or lost ball, — searching, trampling
The tufts of yarrow,

Of milkweed and slim mullein, —
The place disturbs;
Or bowed wise-woman, culling
Her magic herbs.

No more the melancholy
Dark trains draw near;
The dead possess it wholly
This many a year.

The headstones lean, winds whistle,
The long grass waves,
Rank grow the dock and thistle
Over the graves;

And all is waste, deserted,
And drear, as though
Even the ghosts departed
Long years ago!

The squirrels start forth and chatter
To see me pass;
Grasshoppers leap and patter
In the dry grass.

I hear the drowsy drumming
Of woodpeckers,
And suddenly at my coming
The quick grouse whirs.

Untouched through all mutation
Of times and skies,
A bygone generation
Around me lies;

Of high and low condition,
Just and unjust,
The patient and physician,
All turned to dust.

Suns, snows, drouth, cold, birds, blossoms,
Visit the spot;
Rains drench the quiet bosoms
Which heed them not.

Under an aged willow,
The earth my bed,
A mossy mound my pillow,
I lean my head.

Babe of this mother, dying
A fresh young bride,
That old, old man is lying
Here by her side!

I muse: above me hovers
A haze of dreams:
Bright maids and laughing lovers,
Life's morning gleams;

The past with all its passions,
Its toils and wiles,
Its ancient follies, fashions,
And tears and smiles;

With thirsts and fever-rages,
And ceaseless pains,
Hoarding as for the ages
Its little gains!

Fair lives that bloom and wither,
Their summer done;
Loved forms with heart-break hither
Borne one by one.

Wife, husband, child, and mother,
Now reck no more
Which mourned on earth the other,
Or went before.

The soul, risen from its embers,
In its blest state
Perchance not even remembers
Its earthly fate;

Nor heeds, in the duration
Of spheres sublime,
This pebble of creation,
This wave of time.

For a swift moment only
Such dreams arise;
Then, turning from this lonely,
Tossed field, my eyes

Through clumps of whortleberry
And brier look down
Toward yonder cemetery,
And modern town,

Where still men build, and marry,
And strive, and mourn,
And now the dark pall carry,
And now are borne.

JOHN T. TROWBRIDGE.

ELEGY WRITTEN IN A COUNTRY CHURCH-YARD.

The curfew tolls the knell of parting day;
The lowing herd winds slowly o'er the lea;
The plowman homeward plods his weary way,
And leaves the world to darkness and to me.

GOD'S-ACRE.

"I like that ancient Saxon phrase which calls
The burial-ground GOD'S-ACRE! *It is just;*
It consecrates each grave within its walls,
And breathes a benison o'er the sleeping dust."

Now fades the glimmering landscape on the sight,
  And all the air a solemn stillness holds,
Save where the beetle wheels his droning flight,
  And drowsy tinklings lull the distant folds;

Save that, from yonder ivy-mantled tower,
  The moping owl does to the moon complain
Of such as, wandering near her secret bower,
  Molest her ancient, solitary reign.

[Hark! how the holy calm that breathes around
  Bids every fierce tumultuous passion cease;
In still small accents whispering from the ground
  The grateful earnest of eternal peace.] *

Beneath those rugged elms, that yew-tree's shade,
  Where heaves the turf in many a moldering heap,
Each in his narrow cell forever laid,
  The rude forefathers of the hamlet sleep.

The breezy call of incense-breathing morn,
  The swallow twittering from the straw-built shed,
The cock's shrill clarion, or the echoing horn,
  No more shall rouse them from their lowly bed.

For them no more the blazing hearth shall burn,
  Or busy housewife ply her evening care;
No children run to lisp their sire's return,
  Or climb his knees the envied kiss to share.

Oft did the harvest to their sickle yield,
  Their furrow oft the stubborn glebe has broke;
How jocund did they drive their team afield!
  How bowed the woods beneath their sturdy stroke!

Let not ambition mock their useful toil,
  Their homely joys, and destiny obscure;
Nor grandeur hear with a disdainful smile
  The short and simple annals of the poor.

The boast of heraldry, the pomp of power,
  And all that beauty, all that wealth e'er gave,
Await alike the inevitable hour;
  The paths of glory lead but to the grave.

Nor you, ye proud, impute to these the fault,
  If memory o'er their tomb no trophies raise,
Where, through the long-drawn aisle and fretted vault,
  The pealing anthem swells the note of praise.

Can storied urn, or animated bust,
  Back to its mansion call the fleeting breath?
Can honor's voice provoke the silent dust,
  Or flattery soothe the dull, cold ear of death?

* Removed by the author from the original poem.

Perhaps in this neglected spot is laid
  Some heart once pregnant with celestial fire;
Hands that the rod of empire might have swayed,
  Or waked to ecstasy the living lyre;

But knowledge to their eyes her ample page,
  Rich with the spoils of time, did ne'er unroll;
Chill penury repressed their noble rage,
  And froze the genial current of the soul.

Full many a gem of purest ray serene
  The dark, unfathomed caves of ocean bear;
Full many a flower is born to blush unseen,
  And waste its sweetness on the desert air.

Some village Hampden, that, with dauntless breast,
  The little tyrant of his fields withstood;
Some mute, inglorious Milton here may rest;
  Some Cromwell, guiltless of his country's blood.

The applause of listening senates to command,
  The threats of pain and ruin to despise,
To scatter plenty o'er a smiling land,
  And read their history in a nation's eyes,

Their lot forbade: nor circumscribed alone
  Their growing virtues, but their crimes confined;
Forbade to wade through slaughter to a throne,
  And shut the gates of mercy on mankind;

The struggling pangs of conscious truth to hide,
  To quench the blushes of ingenuous shame,
Or heap the shrine of luxury and pride
  With incense kindled at the muse's flame.

Far from the madding crowd's ignoble strife,
  Their sober wishes never learned to stray;
Along the cool, sequestered vale of life
  They kept the noiseless tenor of their way.

Yet even these bones from insult to protect,
  Some frail memorial still erected nigh,
With uncouth rhymes and shapeless sculpture decked,
  Implores the passing tribute of a sigh.

Their name, their years, spelt by the unlettered muse,
  The place of fame and elegy supply;
And many a holy text around she strews,
  That teach the rustic moralist to die.

For who, to dumb forgetfulness a prey,
  This pleasing, anxious being e'er resigned,
Left the warm precincts of the cheerful day,
  Nor cast one longing, lingering look behind?

On some fond breast the parting soul relies,
  Some pious drops the closing eye requires;

E'en from the tomb the voice of Nature cries,
  E'en in our ashes live their wonted fires.

For thee, who, mindful of the unhonored dead,
  Dost in these lines their artless tale relate;
If chance, by lonely contemplation led,
  Some kindred spirit shall inquire thy fate,

Haply some hoary-headed swain may say: —
  "Oft have we seen him, at the peep of dawn,
Brushing with hasty steps the dews away,
  To meet the sun upon the upland lawn.

"There at the foot of yonder nodding beech,
  That wreathes its old, fantastic roots so high,
His listless length at noontide would he stretch,
  And pore upon the brook that babbles by.

"Hard by yon wood, now smiling as in scorn,
  Muttering his wayward fancies, he would rove;
Now drooping, woful-wan, like one forlorn,
  Or crazed with care, or crossed in hopeless love.

"One morn I missed him on the customed hill,
  Along the heath, and near his favorite tree;
Another came, — nor yet beside the rill,
  Nor up the lawn, nor at the wood was he;

"The next, with dirges due, in sad array,
  Slow through the church-way path we saw him borne; —
Approach and read (for thou canst read) the lay
  Graved on the stone beneath yon aged thorn."

THE EPITAPH.

Here rests his head upon the lap of earth,
  A youth to fortune and to fame unknown;
Fair science frowned not on his humble birth,
  And melancholy marked him for her own.

Large was his bounty, and his soul sincere;
  Heaven did a recompense as largely send;
He gave to misery (all he had) a tear,
  He gained from heaven ('t was all he wished) a friend.

No further seek his merits to disclose,
  Or draw his frailties from their dread abode, —
(There they alike in trembling hope repose,)
  The bosom of his Father and his God.

THOMAS GRAY.

INSCRIPTION ON MELROSE ABBEY.

THE earth goes on the earth glittering in gold,
The earth goes to the earth sooner than it wold;
The earth builds on the earth castles and towers,
The earth says to the earth — All this is ours.

THANATOPSIS.

To him who, in the love of Nature, holds
Communion with her visible forms, she speaks
A various language: for his gayer hours
She has a voice of gladness, and a smile
And eloquence of beauty; and she glides
Into his darker musings with a mild
And healing sympathy, that steals away
Their sharpness, ere he is aware. When thoughts
Of the last bitter hour come like a blight
Over thy spirit, and sad images
Of the stern agony, and shroud, and pall,
And breathless darkness, and the narrow house,
Make thee to shudder, and grow sick at heart,
Go forth under the open sky, and list
To Nature's teachings, while from all around —
Earth and her waters, and the depths of air —
Comes a still voice: — Yet a few days, and thee
The all-beholding sun shall see no more
In all his course; nor yet in the cold ground,
Where thy pale form was laid, with many tears,
Nor in the embrace of ocean, shall exist
Thy image. Earth, that nourished thee, shall claim
Thy growth, to be resolved to earth again;
And, lost each human trace, surrendering up
Thine individual being, shalt thou go
To mix forever with the elements;
To be a brother to the insensible rock,
And to the sluggish clod, which the rude swain
Turns with his share, and treads upon. The oak
Shall send his roots abroad, and pierce thy mold.
  Yet not to thine eternal resting-place
Shalt thou retire alone, — nor couldst thou wish
Couch more magnificent. Thou shalt lie down
With patriarchs of the infant world, — with kings,
The powerful of the earth, — the wise, the good,
Fair forms, and hoary seers of ages past,
All in one mighty sepulcher. The hills,
Rock-ribbed, and ancient as the sun; the vales
Stretching in pensive quietness between;
The venerable woods; rivers that move
In majesty, and the complaining brooks,
That make the meadows green; and, poured round all,
Old ocean's gray and melancholy waste, —
Are but the solemn decorations all
Of the great tomb of man! The golden sun,
The planets, all the infinite host of heaven,
Are shining on the sad abodes of death,
Through the still lapse of ages. All that tread
The globe are but a handful to the tribes
That slumber in its bosom. Take the wings
Of morning, pierce the Barcan wilderness,
Or lose thyself in the continuous woods
Where rolls the Oregon, and hears no sound
Save his own dashings, — yet the dead are there!
And millions in those solitudes, since first

The flight of years began, have laid them down
In their last sleep, — the dead reign there alone!
So shalt thou rest; and what if thou withdraw
In silence from the living, and no friend
Take note of thy departure? All that breathe
Will share thy destiny. The gay will laugh
When thou art gone, the solemn brood of care
Plod on, and each one, as before, will chase
His favorite phantom; yet all these shall leave
Their mirth and their employments, and shall come
And make their bed with thee. As the long train
Of ages glide away, the sons of men —
The youth in life's green spring, and he who goes
In the full strength of years, matron and maid,
The speechless babe, and the gray-headed man —
Shall, one by one, be gathered to thy side
By those who in their turn shall follow them.

So live, that when thy summons comes to join
The innumerable caravan that moves
To that mysterious realm, where each shall take
His chamber in the silent halls of death,
Thou go not, like the quarry-slave at night,
Scourged to his dungeon, but, sustained and soothed
By an unfaltering trust, approach thy grave
Like one who wraps the drapery of his couch
About him, and lies down to pleasant dreams.

WILLIAM CULLEN BRYANT.

THE COMMON LOT.

ONCE, in the flight of ages past,
There lived a Man; — and WHO WAS HE?
— Mortal! howe'er thy lot be cast,
That Man resembled thee.

Unknown the region of his birth,
The land in which he died unknown:
His name has perished from the earth,
This truth survives alone: —

That joy and grief, and hope and fear,
Alternate triumphed in his breast:
His bliss and woe — a smile, a tear!
— Oblivion hides the rest.

The bounding pulse, the languid limb,
The changing spirit's rise and fall, —
We know that these were felt by him,
For these are felt by all.

He suffered, — but his pangs are o'er;
Enjoyed, — but his delights are fled;
Had friends, — his friends are now no more;
And foes, — his foes are dead.

He loved, — but whom he loved, the grave
Hath lost in its unconscious womb:
O, she was fair, — but naught could save
Her beauty from the tomb.

He saw whatever thou hast seen;
Encountered all that troubles thee;
He was — whatever thou hast been;
He is — what thou shalt be.

The rolling seasons, day and night,
Sun, moon, and stars, the earth and main,
Erewhile his portion, life and light,
To him exist in vain.

The clouds and sunbeams, o'er his eye
That once their shades and glory threw,
Have left in yonder silent sky
No vestige where they flew.

The annals of the human race,
Their ruins, since the world began,
Of *him* afford no other race
Than this, — THERE LIVED A MAN.

JAMES MONTGOMERY.

LINES WRITTEN IN RICHMOND CHURCH-YARD, YORKSHIRE.

"It is good for us to be here; it thou wilt, let us make here three tabernacles; one for thee, and one for Moses, and one for Elias." — *Matt.* xvii. 4.

METHINKS it is good to be here;
If thou wilt, let us build — but for whom?
Nor Elias nor Moses appear,
But the shadows of eve that encompass the gloom,
The abode of the dead and the place of the tomb.

Shall we build to Ambition? O, no!
Affrighted, he shrinketh away;
For, see! they would pin him below,
In a small narrow cave, and, begirt with cold clay,
To the meanest of reptiles a peer and a prey.

To Beauty? ah, no! — she forgets
The charms which she wielded before —
Nor knows the foul worm that he frets
The skin which but yesterday fools could adore
For the smoothness it held, or the tint which it wore.

Shall we build to the purple of Pride —
The trappings which dizen the proud?
Alas! they are all laid aside;
And here 's neither dress nor adornment allowed,
But the long winding-sheet and the fringe of the shroud.

To Riches? alas! 't is in vain;
Who hid, in their turn have been hid:

The treasures are squandered again ;
And here in the grave are all metals forbid,
But the tinsel that shines on the dark coffin-lid.

To the pleasures which Mirth can afford, —
The revel, the laugh, and the jeer ?
Ah ! here is a plentiful board !
But the guests are all mute as their pitiful cheer,
And none but the worm is a reveler here.

Shall we build to Affection and Love ?
Ah, no ! they have withered and died,
Or fled with the spirit above ;
Friends, brothers, and sisters are laid side by side,
Yet none have saluted, and none have replied.

Unto Sorrow ? — The dead cannot grieve ;
Not a sob, not a sigh meets mine ear,
Which compassion itself could relieve !
Ah ! sweetly they slumber, nor hope, love, nor fear, —
Peace, peace is the watchword, the only one here !

Unto Death, to whom monarchs must bow ?
Ah, no ! for his empire is known,
And here there are trophies enow !
Beneath — the cold dead, and around — the dark stone,
Are the signs of a scepter that none may disown.

The first tabernacle to Hope we will build,
And look for the sleepers around us to rise ;
The second to Faith, which insures it fulfilled ;
And the third to the Lamb of the great sacrifice,
Who bequeathed us them both when he rose to the skies.

HERBERT KNOWLES.

Poems
of
Religion
I
II
III
IIII
V
VI
VII
VIII
IX
X

In the beauty of the lilies Christ was born
across the sea,
With a glory in his bosom that transfigures you
and me;
As he died to make men holy, let us die to
make men free
While God is marching on.

Julia Ward Howe.

POEMS OF RELIGION.

THE CELESTIAL COUNTRY.

[The poem *De Contemptu Mundi* was written in dactylic hexameter Latin verse by Bernard de Morlaix, Monk of Cluni who lived in the earlier half of the twelfth century. It contained three thousand lines divided into three books. The poem commences:—

Hora novissima, tempora pessima
  Sunt, vigilemus.
Ecce minaciter imminet arbiter
  Ille supremus.
Imminet, imminet et mala terminet,
  Æqua coronet,
Recta remuneret, anxia liberet,
  Æthera donet,
Auferat aspera duraque pondera
  Mentes onustæ
Sobria muniat, improba puniat,
  Utraque juste.

Which have been rendered:—

Hours of the latest! times of the basest!
  Our vigil before us!
Judgment eternal of Being supernal
  Now hanging o'er us!
Evil to terminate, equity vindicate,
  Cometh the Kingly;
Righteousness seeing, anxious hearts freeing,
  Crowning each singly.
Bearing life's weariness, tasting life's bitterness,
  Life as it must be
Th' righteous retaining, sinners arraigning,
  Judging all justly.

The translation following is of a portion of the poem distinguished by the sub-title "LAUS PATRIÆ CŒLESTIS."

THE world is very evil,
  The times are waxing late;
Be sober and keep vigil,
  The Judge is at the gate,—
The Judge that comes in mercy,
  The Judge that comes with might,
To terminate the evil,
  To diadem the right.
When the just and gentle Monarch
  Shall summon from the tomb,
Let man, the guilty, tremble,
  For Man, the God, shall doom!

Arise, arise, good Christian,
  Let right to wrong succeed;
Let penitential sorrow
  To heavenly gladness lead,—
To the light that hath no evening,
  That knows nor moon nor sun,
The light so new and golden,
  The light that is but one.

And when the Sole-Begotten
  Shall render up once more
The kingdom to the FATHER,
  Whose own it was before,
Then glory yet unheard of
  Shall shed abroad its ray,
Resolving all enigmas,
  An endless Sabbath-day.

For thee, O dear, dear Country!
  Mine eyes their vigils keep;
For very love, beholding
  Thy happy name, they weep.
The mention of thy glory
  Is unction to the breast,
And medicine in sickness,
  And love, and life, and rest.

O one, O only Mansion!
  O Paradise of Joy,
Where tears are ever banished,
  And smiles have no alloy!
Beside thy living waters
  All plants are, great and small,
The cedar of the forest,
  The hyssop of the wall;
With jaspers glow thy bulwarks,
  Thy streets with emeralds blaze,
The sardius and the topaz
  Unite in thee their rays;
Thine ageless walls are bonded
  With amethyst unpriced;
Thy Saints build up its fabric,
  And the corner-stone is CHRIST.

The Cross is all thy splendor,
  The Crucified thy praise;
His laud and benediction
  Thy ransomed people raise:
"Jesus, the Gem of Beauty,
  True God and Man," they sing,
"The never-failing Garden,
  The ever-golden Ring;

The Door, the Pledge, the Husband,
  The Guardian of his Court;
The Day-star of Salvation,
  The Porter and the Port!"

Thou hast no shore, fair ocean!
  Thou hast no time, bright day!
Dear fountain of refreshment
  To pilgrims far away!
Upon the Rock of Ages
  They raise thy holy tower;
Thine is the victor's laurel,
  And thine the golden dower!

Thou feel'st in mystic rapture,
  O Bride that know'st no guile,
The Prince's sweetest kisses,
  The Prince's loveliest smile;
Unfading lilies, bracelets
  Of living pearl thine own;
The Lamb is ever near thee,
  The Bridegroom thine alone.
The Crown is he to guerdon,
  The Buckler to protect,
And he himself the Mansion,
  And he the Architect.

The only art thou needest —
  Thanksgiving for thy lot;
The only joy thou seekest —
  The Life where Death is not.
And all thine endless leisure,
  In sweetest accents, sings
The ill that was thy merit,
  The wealth that is thy King's!

Jerusalem the golden,
  With milk and honey blest,
Beneath thy contemplation
  Sink heart and voice oppressed.
I know not, O I know not,
  What social joys are there!
What radiancy of glory,
  What light beyond compare!

And when I fain would sing them,
  My spirit fails and faints;
And vainly would it image
  The assembly of the Saints.

They stand, those halls of Zion,
  Conjubilant with song,
And bright with many an angel,
  And all the martyr throng;
The Prince is ever in them,
  The daylight is serene;
The pastures of the Blessèd
  Are decked in glorious sheen.

There is the Throne of David,
  And there, from care released,
The song of them that triumph,
  The shout of them that feast;
And they who, with their Leader,
  Have conquered in the fight,
Forever and forever
  Are clad in robes of white!

O holy, placid harp-notes
  Of that eternal hymn!
O sacred, sweet reflection,
  And peace of Seraphim!
O thirst, forever ardent,
  Yet evermore content!
O true peculiar vision
  Of God cunctipotent!
Ye know the many mansions
  For many a glorious name,
And divers retributions
  That divers merits claim;
For midst the constellations
  That deck our earthly sky,
This star than that is brighter —
  And so it is on high.

Jerusalem the glorious!
  The glory of the Elect!
O dear and future vision
  That eager hearts expect!
Even now by faith I see thee,
  Even here thy walls discern;
To thee my thoughts are kindled,
  And strive, and pant, and yearn.

Jerusalem the only,
  That look'st from heaven below,
In thee is all my glory,
  In me is all my woe;
And though my body may not,
  My spirit seeks thee fain,
Till flesh and earth return me
  To earth and flesh again.

O none can tell thy bulwarks,
  How gloriously they rise!
O none can tell thy capitals
  Of beautiful device!
Thy loveliness oppresses
  All human thought and heart;
And none, O peace, O Zion,
  Can sing thee as thou art!

New mansion of new people,
  Whom God's own love and light
Promote, increase, make holy,
  Identify, unite!

Thou City of the Angels!
  Thou City of the Lord!
Whose everlasting music
  Is the glorious decachord!

And there the band of Prophets
  United praise ascribes,
And there the twelvefold chorus
  Of Israel's ransomed tribes,
The lily-beds of virgins,
  The roses' martyr-glow,
The cohort of the Fathers
  Who kept the faith below.

And there the Sole-Begotten
  Is Lord in regal state, —
He, Judah's mystic Lion,
  He, Lamb Immaculate.
O fields that know no sorrow!
  O state that fears no strife!
O princely bowers! O land of flowers!
  O realm and home of Life!

Jerusalem, exulting
  On that securest shore,
I hope thee, wish thee, sing thee,
  And love thee evermore!
I ask not for my merit,
  I seek not to deny
My merit is destruction,
  A child of wrath am I;
But yet with faith I venture
  And hope upon my way;
For those perennial guerdons
  I labor night and day.

The best and dearest FATHER,
  Who made me and who saved,
Bore with me in defilement,
  And from defilement laved,
When in his strength I struggle,
  For very joy I leap,
When in my sin I totter,
  I weep, or try to weep:
Then grace, sweet grace celestial,
  Shall all its love display,
And David's Royal Fountain
  Purge every sin away.

O mine, my golden Zion!
  O lovelier far than gold,
With laurel-girt battalions,
  And safe victorious fold!
O sweet and blessed Country,
  Shall I ever see thy face?
O sweet and blessed Country,
  Shall I ever win thy grace?
I have the hope within me
  To comfort and to bless!
Shall I ever win the prize itself?
  O tell me, tell me, Yes!

Exult! O dust and ashes!
  The Lord shall be thy part;
His only, his forever,
  Thou shalt be, and thou art!
Exult, O dust and ashes!
  The Lord shall be thy part;
His only, his forever,
  Thou shalt be, and thou art!

Translated from the Latin of BERNARD DE MORLAIX,
by JOHN MASON NEALE.

DIES IRÆ.

[A Latin poem by Thomas of Celano (a Neapolitan village), about A. D. 1250. Perhaps no poem has been more frequently translated. A German collector published eighty-seven versions in German. Dr. Coles, of Newark, N. J., has made thirteen. Seven are given in the "Seven Great Hymns of the Mediæval Church," Randolph & Co., N. Y. The version here given preserves the measure of the original.]

DIES IRÆ, DIES ILLA, *dies tribulationis et angustiæ, dies calamitatis et miseriæ, dies tenebrarum et caliginis, dies nebulæ et turbinis, dies tubæ et clangoris super civitatis munitas, et super angulos excelsos!* — Sophonias i. 15, 16.

THAT DAY, A DAY OF WRATH, *a day of trouble and distress, a day of wasteness and desolation, a day of darkness and gloominess, a day of clouds and thick darkness, a day of the trumpet and alarm against the fenced cities, and against the high towers!* — Zephaniah i. 15, 16.

I.

DIES iræ, dies illa!
Solvet sæclum in favillâ,
Teste David cum Sybillâ.

1.

DAY of vengeance, without morrow!
Earth shall end in flame and sorrow,
As from Saint and Seer we borrow.

II.

Quantus tremor est futurus,
Quando Judex est venturus,
Cuncta stricte discussurus!

2.

Ah! what terror is impending,
When the Judge is seen descending,
And each secret veil is rending!

III.

Tuba mirum spargens sonum
Per sepulcra regionum,
Coget omnes ante thronum.

3.

To the throne, the trumpet sounding,
Through the sepulchers resounding,
Summons all, with voice astounding.

IV.

Mors stupebit, et natura,
Quum resurget creatura,
Judicanti responsura.

4.

Death and Nature, mazed, are quaking,
When, the grave's long slumber breaking,
Man to judgment is awaking.

V.

Liber scriptus proferetur,
In quo totum continetur,
Unde mundus judicetur.

5.

On the written Volume's pages,
Life is shown in all its stages —
Judgment-record of past ages.

VI.

Judex ergo cum sedebit,
Quidquid latet, apparebit:
Nil inultum remanebit.

6.

Sits the Judge, the raised arraigning,
Darkest mysteries explaining,
Nothing unavenged remaining.

VII.

Quid sum, miser! tunc dicturus,
Quem patronum rogaturus,
Quum vix justus sit securus?

7.

What shall I then say, unfriended,
By no advocate attended,
When the just are scarce defended?

VIII.

Rex tremendæ majestatis,
Qui salvandos salvas gratis,
Salva me, fons pietatis!

8.

King of majesty tremendous,
By thy saving grace defend us,
Fount of pity, safety send us!

IX.

Recordare, Jesu pie,
Quod sum causa tuæ viæ;
Ne me perdas illâ die!

9.

Holy JESUS, meek, forbearing,
For my sins the death-crown wearing,
Save me, in that day, despairing!

X.

Quærens me, sedisti lassus,
Redemisti, crucem passus:
Tantus labor non sit cassus!

10.

Worn and weary, thou hast sought me;
By thy cross and passion bought me —
Spare the hope thy labors brought me!

XI.

Juste Judex ultionis,
Donum fac remissionis
Ante diem rationis!

11.

Righteous Judge of retribution,
Give, O give me absolution
Ere the day of dissolution!

XII.

Ingemisco tanquam reus,
Culpâ rubet vultus meus;
Supplicanti parce, Deus!

12.

As a guilty culprit groaning,
Flushed my face, my errors owning,
Hear, O God, my spirit's moaning!

XIII.

Qui Mariam absolvisti,
Et latronem exaudisti,
Mihi quoque spem dedisti.

13.

Thou to Mary gav'st remission,
Heard'st the dying thief's petition,
Bad'st me hope in my contrition.

XIV.

Preces meæ non sunt dignæ,
Sed tu bonus fac benigne
Ne perenni cremer igne!

14.

In my prayers no grace discerning,
Yet on me thy favor turning,
Save my soul from endless burning!

XV.

Inter oves locum præsta,
Et ab hædis me sequestra,
Statuens in parte dextrâ.

15.

Give me, when thy sheep confiding
Thou art from the goats dividing,
On thy right a place abiding!

XVI.

Confutatis maledictis,
Flammis acribus addictis,
Voca me cum benedictis!

16.

When the wicked are confounded,
And by bitter flames surrounded,
Be my joyful pardon sounded!

XVII.

Oro supplex et acclinis,
Cor contritum quasi cinis,
Gere curam mei finis!

17.

Prostrate, all my guilt discerning,
Heart as though to ashes turning;
Save, O save me from the burning!

XVIII.

Lacrymosa dies illa,
Qua resurget ex favillâ
Judicandus homo reus;
Huic ergo parce, Deus!

THOMAS À CELANO.

18.

Day of weeping, when from ashes
Man shall rise mid lightning flashes, —
Guilty, trembling with contrition,
Save him, Father, from perdition!

JOHN A. DIX.

STABAT MATER DOLOROSA.

[A Latin poem, written in the thirteenth century by Jacopone, a Franciscan friar, of Umbria. Of this and the two preceding poems Dr. Neale says: "The *De Contemptu* is the most lovely, the *Dies Iræ* the most sublime, and the *Stabat Mater* the most pathetic, of mediæval poems."]

I.

STABAT Mater dolorosa
Juxta crucem lacrymosa,
Dum pendebat filius;
Cujus animam gementem,
Contristatam et dolentem,
Pertransivit gladius.

1.

STOOD the afflicted mother weeping,
Near the cross her station keeping
Whereon hung her Son and Lord;
Through whose spirit sympathizing,
Sorrowing and agonizing,
Also passed the cruel sword.

II.

O quam tristis et afflicta,
Fuit illa benedicta
Mater unigeniti,
Quæ mœrebat et dolebat,
Pia mater, dum videbat
Nati pœnas inclyti!

2.

Oh! how mournful and distressèd
Was that favored and most blessèd
Mother of the only Son,
Trembling, grieving, bosom heaving,
While perceiving, scarce believing,
Pains of that Illustrious One!

III.

Quis est homo qui non fleret,
Christi matrem si videret
In tanto supplicio?
Quis non posset contristari
Piam matrem contemplari
Dolentem cum filio?

3.

Who the man, who, called a brother,
Would not weep, saw he Christ's mother
In such deep distress and wild?
Who could not sad tribute render
Witnessing that mother tender
Agonizing with her child?

IV.

Pro peccatis suæ gentis,
Vidit Jesum in tormentis,
    Et flagellis subditum.
Vidit suum dulcem natum,
Morientem, desolatum,
    Dum emisit spiritum.

4.

For his people's sins atoning,
Him she saw in torments groaning,
    Given to the scourger's rod;
Saw her darling offspring dying,
Desolate, forsaken, crying,
    Yield his spirit up to God.

V.

Eia mater, fons amoris,
Me sentire vim doloris
    Fac, ut tecum lugeam.
Fac ut ardeat cor meum
In amando Christum Deum,
    Ut illi complaceam.

5.

Make me feel thy sorrow's power,
That with thee I tears may shower,
    Tender mother, fount of love!
Make my heart with love unceasing
Burn toward Christ the Lord, that pleasing
    I may be to him above.

VI.

Sancta Mater, istud agas,
Crucifixi fige plagas
    Cordi meo valide.
Tui nati vulnerati,
Tam dignati pro me pati,
    Pœnas mecum divide.

6.

Holy mother, this be granted,
That the slain one's wounds be planted
    Firmly in my heart to bide.
Of him wounded, all astounded —
Depths unbounded for me sounded —
    All the pangs with me divide.

VII.

Fac me vere tecum flere,
Crucifixo condolere,
    Donec ego vixero;
Juxta crucem tecum stare,
Et tibi me sociare
    In planctu desidero.

7.

Make me weep with thee in union;
With the Crucified, communion
    In his grief and suffering give;
Near the cross, with tears unfailing,
I would join thee in thy wailing
    Here as long as I shall live.

VIII.

Virgo virginum præclara,
Mihi jam non sis amara;
    Fac me tecum plangere;
Fac ut portem Christi mortem,
Passionis fac consortem,
    Et plagas recolere.

8.

Maid of maidens, all excelling!
Be not bitter, me repelling;
    Make thou me a mourner too;
Make me bear about Christ's dying,
Share his passion, shame defying;
    All his wounds in me renew.

IX.

Fac me plagis vulnerari,
Cruce hac inebriari,
    Et cruore filii;
Inflammatus et accensus,
Per te, Virgo, sim defensus
    In die judicii.

9.

Wound for wound be there created;
With the cross intoxicated
    For thy Son's dear sake, I pray —
May I, fired with pure affection,
Virgin, have through thee protection
    In the solemn Judgment Day.

X.

Fac me cruce custodiri,
Morte Christi præmuniri,
    Confoveri gratia.
Quando corpus morietur,
Fac ut animæ donetur
    Paradisi gloria.

FRA JACOPONE.

10.

Let me by the cross be warded,
By the death of Christ be guarded,
    Nourished by divine supplies.
When the body death hath riven,
Grant that to the soul be given
    Glories bright of Paradise.

ABRAHAM COLES.

VENI SANCTE SPIRITUS.

[This hymn was written in the tenth century by Robert II., the gentle son of Hugh Capet. It is often mentioned as second in rank to the *Dies Iræ*.]

I.

VENI, Sancte Spiritus,
Et emitte cœlitus
Lucis tuæ radium.

II.

Veni, pater pauperum,
Veni, dator munerum,
Veni, lumen cordium.

III.

Consolator optime,
Dulcis hospes animæ,
Dulce refrigerium.

IV.

In labore requies,
In æstu temperies,
In fletu solatium.

V.

O lux beatissima!
Reple cordis intima,
Tuorum fidelium.

VI.

Sine tuo numine,
Nihil est in homine,
Nihil est innoxium.

VII.

Lava quod est sordidum,
Riga quod est aridum,
Sana quod est saucium.

VIII.

Flecte quod est rigidum,
Fove quod est frigidum,
Rege quod est devium.

IX.

Da tuis fidelibus,
In te confidentibus,
Sacrum septenarium;

X.

Da virtutis meritum,
Da salutis exitum,
Da perenne gaudium!

ROBERT II., OF FRANCE.

1.

COME, Holy Ghost! thou fire divine!
From highest heaven on us down shine!
Comforter, be thy comfort mine!

2.

Come, Father of the poor, to earth;
Come, with thy gifts of precious worth;
Come, Light of all of mortal birth!

3.

Thou rich in comfort! Ever blest
The heart where thou art constant guest,
Who giv'st the heavy-laden rest.

4.

Come, thou in whom our toil is sweet,
Our shadow in the noon-day heat,
Before whom mourning flieth fleet.

5.

Bright Sun of Grace! thy sunshine dart
On all who cry to thee apart,
And fill with gladness every heart.

6.

Whate'er without thy aid is wrought,
Or skillful deed, or wisest thought,
God counts it vain and merely naught.

7.

O cleanse us that we sin no more,
O'er parchèd souls thy waters pour;
Heal the sad heart that acheth sore.

8.

Thy will be ours in all our ways;
O melt the frozen with thy rays;
Call home the lost in error's maze.

9.

And grant us, LORD, who cry to thee,
And hold the Faith in unity,
Thy precious gifts of charity;

10.

That we may live in holiness,
And find in death our happiness,
And dwell with thee in lasting bliss!

CATHARINE WINKWORTH.

VENI CREATOR SPIRITUS.

[This hymn, one of the most important in the service of the Latin Church, has been sometimes attributed to the Emperor Charlemagne. The better opinion, however, inclines to Pope Gregory I., called the Great, as the author, and fixes its origin somewhere in the Sixth Century.]

I.

Veni, Creator Spiritus,
Mentes tuorum visita,
Imple superna gratia,
Quæ tu creasti pectora.

II.

Qui diceris Paraclitus,
Altissimi donum Dei,
Fons vivus, ignis, caritas,
Et spiritalis unctio.

III.

Tu septiformis munere,
Dextræ Dei tu digitus
Tu rite promissum Patris,
Sermone ditans guttura.

IV.

Accende lumen sensibus,
Infunde amorem cordibus,
Infirma nostri corporis
Virtute firmans perpeti.

V.

Hostem repellas longius,
Pacemque dones protinus:
Ductore sic te prævio
Vitemus omne noxium.

VI.

Per te sciamus da Patrem,
Noscamus atque Filium;
Te utriusque Spiritum
Credamus omni tempore.

VII.

Deo Patri sit gloria
Et Filio qui a mortuis
Surrexit, ac Paraclito,
In sæculorum sæcula.

St. Gregory the Great.

1.

Creator Spirit, by whose aid
The world's foundations first were laid,
Come visit every pious mind,
Come pour thy joys on human kind;
From sin and sorrow set us free,
And make thy temples worthy thee.

2.

O source of uncreated light,
The Father's promised Paraclete!
Thrice holy fount, thrice holy fire,
Our hearts with heavenly love inspire;
Come, and thy sacred unction bring,
To sanctify us while we sing.

3.

Plenteous of grace, descend from high,
Rich in thy seven-fold energy!
Thou strength of his almighty hand,
Whose power does heaven and earth command!
Proceeding Spirit, our defense,
Who dost the gifts of tongues dispense,
And crown'st thy gift with eloquence!

4.

Refine and purge our earthly parts;
But, O, inflame and fire our hearts!
Our frailties help, our vice control,
Submit the senses to the soul;
And when rebellious they are grown,
Then lay thy hand and hold 'em down.

5.

Chase from our minds th' infernal foe,
And peace, the fruit of love, bestow;
And, lest our feet should step astray,
Protect and guide us on the way.

6.

Make us eternal truths receive,
And practice all that we believe;
Give us thyself, that we may see
The Father and the Son by thee.

7.

Immortal honor, endless fame,
Attend the Almighty Father's name;
The Saviour Son be glorified,
Who for lost man's redemption died;
And equal adoration be,
Eternal Paraclete, to thee.

John Dryden.

VEXILLA REGIS.

THE Royal Banners forward go;
The cross shines forth in mystic glow;
Where He in flesh, our flesh who made,
Our sentence bore, our ransom paid;

Where deep for us the spear was dyed,
Life's torrent rushing from his side,
To wash us in that precious flood
Where mingled water flowed, and blood.

Fulfilled is all that David told
In true prophetic song of old;
Amidst the nations GOD, saith he,
Hath reigned and triumphed from the tree.

O Tree of Beauty! Tree of Light!
O Tree with royal purple dight!
Elect on whose triumphal breast
Those holy limbs should find their rest;

On whose dear arms, so widely flung,
The weight of this world's ransom hung,
The price of human kind to pay,
And spoil the Spoiler of his prey!

O Cross, our one reliance, hail!
This holy Passion-tide, avail
To give fresh merit to the saint,
And pardon to the penitent.

To thee, eternal Three in One,
Let homage meet by all be done;
Whom by the Cross thou dost restore,
Preserve and govern evermore!

From the Latin of VENANTIUS FORTUNATUS,
by JOHN MASON NEALE.

LITANY.

SAVIOUR, when in dust to thee
Low we bend the adoring knee;
When, repentant, to the skies
Scarce we lift our weeping eyes, —
O, by all thy pains and woe
Suffered once for man below,
Bending from thy throne on high,
Hear our solemn litany!

By thy helpless infant years;
By thy life of want and tears;
By thy days of sore distress
In the savage wilderness;
By the dread mysterious hour
Of the insulting tempter's power, —
Turn, O, turn a favoring eye,
Hear our solemn litany!

By the sacred griefs that wept
O'er the grave where Lazarus slept;
By the boding tears that flowed
Over Salem's loved abode;
By the anguished sigh that told
Treachery lurked within thy fold, —
From thy seat above thy sky
Hear our solemn litany!

By thine hour of dire despair;
By thine agony of prayer;
By the cross, the nail, the thorn,
Piercing spear, and torturing scorn;
By the gloom that veiled the skies
O'er the dreadful sacrifice, —
Listen to our humble cry,
Hear our solemn litany!

By thy deep expiring groan;
By the sad sepulchral stone;
By the vault whose dark abode
Held in vain the rising God!
O, from earth to heaven restored,
Mighty, reascended Lord, —
Listen, listen to the cry
Of our solemn litany!

SIR ROBERT GRANT.

THE HOLY SPIRIT.

IN the hour of my distress,
When temptations me oppress,
And when I my sins confess,
Sweet Spirit, comfort me!

When I lie within my bed,
Sick at heart, and sick in head,
And with doubts discomforted,
Sweet Spirit, comfort me!

When the house doth sigh and weep,
And the world is drowned in sleep,
Yet mine eyes the watch do keep,
Sweet Spirit, comfort me!

When the artless doctor sees
No one hope but of his fees,
And his skill runs on the lees,
Sweet Spirit, comfort me!

When his potion and his pill
Has or none or little skill,
Meet for nothing but to kill, —
Sweet Spirit, comfort me!

When the passing-bell doth toll,
And the Furies, in a shoal,
Come to fright a parting soul,
Sweet Spirit, comfort me!

When the tapers now burn blue,
And the comforters are few,
And that number more than true,
Sweet Spirit, comfort me!

When the priest his last hath prayed,
And I nod to what is said
Because my speech is now decayed,
Sweet Spirit, comfort me!

When, God knows, I'm tost about
Either with despair or doubt,
Yet before the glass be out,
Sweet Spirit, comfort me!

When the tempter me pursu'th
With the sins of all my youth,
And half damns me with untruth,
Sweet Spirit, comfort me!

When the flames and hellish cries
Fright mine ears, and fright mine eyes,
And all terrors me surprise,
Sweet Spirit, comfort me!

When the judgment is revealed,
And that opened which was sealed, —
When to thee I have appealed,
Sweet Spirit, comfort me!

ROBERT HERRICK.

GOD.

O THOU eternal One! whose presence bright
All space doth occupy, all motion guide;
Unchanged through time's all-devastating flight;
Thou only God! There is no God beside!
Being above all beings! Three in one!
Whom none can comprehend, and none explore;
Who fill'st existence with *thyself* alone;
Embracing all, supporting, ruling o'er! —
Being whom we call God — and know no more!
In its sublime research, philosophy
May measure out the ocean deep, — may count
The sands or the sun's rays, — but God! for thee
There is no weight nor measure; — none can mount
Up to thy mysteries. Reason's brightest spark,
Though kindled by thy light, in vain would try
To trace thy counsels, infinite and dark;
And thought is lost ere thought can soar so high, —
E'en like past moments in eternity.
Thou from primeval nothingness didst call,
First chaos, then existence; — Lord! on thee
Eternity had its foundation; — all
Sprung forth from thee, of light, joy, harmony,
Sole origin; — all life, all beauty, thine.
Thy word created all, and doth create;
Thy splendor fills all space with rays divine;
Thou art, and wert, and shalt be! Glorious,
Light-giving, life-sustaining Potentate!
Thy chains the unmeasured universe surround;
Upheld by thee, by thee inspired with breath!
Thou the beginning with the end hast bound,
And beautifully mingled life and death!
As sparks mount upward from the fiery blaze,
So suns are born, so worlds spring forth from thee,
And as the spangles in the sunny rays
Shine round the silver snow, the pageantry
Of heaven's bright army glitters in thy praise.
A million torches, lighted by thy hand,
Wander unwearied through the blue abyss:
They own thy power, accomplish thy command,
All gay with life, all eloquent with bliss.
What shall we call them? Pyres of crystal light,
A glorious company of golden streams,
Lamps of celestial ether burning bright,
Suns lighting systems with their joyful beams?
But thou to these art as the noon to night.
Yes! as a drop of water in the sea,
All this magnificence in thee is lost; —
What are ten thousand worlds compared to thee?
And what am *I* then? Heaven's unnumbered host,
Though multiplied by myriads, and arrayed
In all the glory of sublimest thought,
Is but an atom in the balance weighed
Against thy greatness, — is a cipher brought
Against infinity! What am *I* then? Naught!
Naught! But the effluence of thy light divine,
Pervading worlds, hath reached my bosom too;
Yes, in my spirit doth thy spirit shine,
As shines the sunbeam in a drop of dew.
Naught? but I live, and on hope's pinions fly
Eager toward thy presence; for in thee
I live, and breathe, and dwell; aspiring high
Even to the throne of thy divinity.
I am, O God! and surely *thou* must be!
Thou art! directing, guiding all, thou art!
Direct my understanding then to thee;
Control my spirit, guide my wandering heart;
Though but an atom midst immensity,
Still I am something, fashioned by thy hand.
I hold a middle rank, 'twixt heaven and earth,
On the last verge of mortal being stand,
Close to the realm where angels have their birth,
Just on the boundaries of the spirit land!
The chain of being is complete in me;
In me is matter's last gradation lost,
And the next step is spirit — Deity!

I can command the lightning, and am dust!
A monarch, and a slave; a worm, a god!
Whence came I here, and how? so marvelously
Constructed and conceived? Unknown! this clod
Lives surely through some higher energy;
For from itself alone it could not be!
Creator, yes! Thy wisdom and thy word
Created *me!* Thou source of life and good!
Thou spirit of my spirit, and my Lord!
Thy light, thy love, in the bright plenitude,
Filled me with an immortal soul, to spring
Over the abyss of death, and bade it wear
The garments of eternal day, and wing
Its heavenly flight beyond the little sphere
Even to its source, — to thee, its author there.
O thoughts ineffable! O visions blest!
Though worthless our conception all of thee,
Yet shall thy shadowed image fill our breast,
And waft its homage to thy Deity.
God! thus alone my lonely thoughts can soar;
Thus seek thy presence, Being wise and good;
Midst thy vast works admire, obey, adore;
And, when the tongue is eloquent no more,
The soul shall speak in tears of gratitude.

From the Russian of DERZHAVIN,
by DR. BOWRING.

DESIRE.

THOU, who dost dwell alone;
Thou, who dost know thine own;
Thou, to whom all are known,
From the cradle to the grave, —
Save, O, save!

From the world's temptations;
From tribulations;
From that fierce anguish
Wherein we languish;
From that torpor deep
Wherein we lie asleep,
Heavy as death, cold as the grave, —
Save, O, save!

When the soul, growing clearer,
Sees God no nearer;
When the soul, mounting higher,
To God comes no nigher;
But the arch-fiend Pride
Mounts at her side,
Foiling her high emprize,
Sealing her eagle eyes,
And, when she fain would soar,
Makes idols to adore;
Changing the pure emotion
Of her high devotion,
To a skin-deep sense
Of her own eloquence;
Strong to deceive, strong to enslave, —
Save, O, save!

From the ingrained fashion
Of this earthly nature
That mars thy creature;
From grief, that is but passion;
From mirth, that is but feigning;
From tears, that bring no healing;
From wild and weak complaining; —
Thine old strength revealing,
Save, O save!

From doubt, where all is double,
Where wise men are not strong;
Where comfort turns to trouble;
Where just men suffer wrong;
Where sorrow treads on joy;
Where sweet things soonest cloy;
Where faiths are built on dust;
Where love is half mistrust,
Hungry, and barren, and sharp as the sea;
O, set us free!

O, let the false dream fly
Where our sick souls do lie,
Tossing continually.
O, where thy voice doth come,
Let all doubts be dumb;
Let all words be mild;
All strife be reconciled;
All pains beguiled.
Light bring no blindness;
Love no unkindness;
Knowledge no ruin;
Fear no undoing,
From the cradle to the grave, —
Save, O, save!

MATTHEW ARNOLD.

MY GOD, I LOVE THEE.

MY God, I love thee! not because
I hope for heaven thereby;
Nor because those who love thee not
Must burn eternally.

Thou, O my Jesus, thou didst me
Upon the cross embrace!
For me didst bear the nails and spear,
And manifold disgrace,

And griefs and torments numberless,
And sweat of agony,
Yea, death itself, — and all for one
That was thine enemy.

Then why, O blessed Jesus Christ,
  Should I not love thee well?
Not for the hope of winning heaven,
  Nor of escaping hell;

Not with the hope of gaining aught,
  Not seeking a reward;
But as thyself hast lovèd me,
  O everlasting Lord!

E'en so I love thee, and will love,
  And in thy praise will sing, —
Solely because thou art my God,
  And my eternal King.

From the Latin of ST. FRANCIS XAVIER,
by EDWARD CASWALL.

THE NEW JERUSALEM.

[Founded on a Latin hymn of the eighth century, obscurely traced, as to its original conception, to St. Augustine.]

O MOTHER dear, Jerusalem,
  When shall I come to thee?
When shall my sorrows have an end, —
  Thy joys when shall I see?

O happy harbor of God's saints!
  O sweet and pleasant soil!
In thee no sorrow can be found,
  Nor grief, nor care, nor toil.

No dimly cloud o'ershadows thee,
  Nor gloom, nor darksome night;
But every soul shines as the sun,
  For God himself gives light.

Thy walls are made of precious stone,
  Thy bulwarks diamond-square,
Thy gates are all of orient pearl, —
  O God! if I were there!

O my sweet home, Jerusalem!
  Thy joys when shall I see? —
The King sitting upon thy throne,
  And thy felicity?

Thy gardens and thy goodly walks
  Continually are green,
Where grow such sweet and pleasant flowers
  As nowhere else are seen.

Quite through the streets with pleasing sound
  The flood of life doth flow;
And on the banks, on every side,
  The trees of life do grow.

Those trees each month yield ripened fruit;
  Forevermore they spring,
And all the nations of the earth
  To thee their honors bring.

Jerusalem, God's dwelling-place
  Full sore I long to see;
O that my sorrows had an end,
  That I might dwell in thee!

I long to see Jerusalem,
  The comfort of us all;
For thou art fair and beautiful, —
  None ill can thee befall.

No candle needs, no moon to shine,
  No glittering star to light;
For Christ the King of Righteousness
  Forever shineth bright.

O, passing happy were my state,
  Might I be worthy found
To wait upon my God and King,
  His praises there to sound!

Jerusalem! Jerusalem!
  Thy joys fain would I see;
Come quickly, Lord, and end my grief,
  And take me home to thee!

DAVID DICKSON.

DROP, DROP, SLOW TEARS.

DROP, drop, slow tears,
  And bathe those beauteous feet
Which brought from heaven
  The news and prince of peace!
Cease not, wet eyes,
  His mercies to entreat;
To cry for vengeance
  Sin doth never cease;
In your deep floods
  Drown all my faults and fears;
Nor let his eye
  See sin but through my tears.

PHINEAS FLETCHER.

DARKNESS IS THINNING.

DARKNESS is thinning; shadows are retreating;
Morning and light are coming in their beauty;
Suppliant seek we, with an earnest outcry,
    God the Almighty!

So that our Master, having mercy on us,
May repel languor, may bestow salvation,
Granting us, Father, of thy loving-kindness
    Glory hereafter!

This, of his mercy, ever-blessèd Godhead,
Father, and Son, and Holy Spirit, give us, —
Whom through the wide world celebrate forever
Blessing and glory!

From the Latin of ST. GREGORY THE GREAT, by J. M. NEALE.

DELIGHT IN GOD.

I LOVE, and have some cause to love, the earth, —
She is my Maker's creature, therefore good;
She is my mother, for she gave me birth;
She is my tender nurse, she gives me food:
But what 's a creature, Lord, compared with thee?
Or what 's my mother or my nurse to me?

I love the air, — her dainty sweets refresh
My drooping soul, and to new sweets invite me;
Her shrill-mouthed choir sustain me with their flesh,
And with their polyphonian notes delight me:
But what 's the air, or all the sweets that she
Can bless my soul withal, compared to thee?

I love the sea, — she is my fellow-creature,
My careful purveyor; she provides me store;
She walls me round; she makes my diet greater;
She wafts my treasure from a foreign shore:
But, Lord of oceans, when compared with thee,
What is the ocean or her wealth to me?

To heaven's high city I direct my journey,
Whose spangled suburbs entertain mine eye;
Mine eye, by contemplation's great attorney,
Transcends the crystal pavement of the sky:
But what is heaven, great God, compared to thee?
Without thy presence, heaven 's no heaven to me.

Without thy presence, earth gives no refection;
Without thy presence, sea affords no treasure;
Without thy presence, air 's a rank infection;
Without thy presence, heaven 's itself no pleasure:
If not possessed, if not enjoyed in thee,
What 's earth, or sea, or air, or heaven to me?

The highest honors that the world can boast
Are subjects far too low for my desire;
The brightest beams of glory are, at most,
But dying sparkles of thy living fire;
The loudest flames that earth can kindle be
But nightly glow-worms, if compared to thee.

Without thy presence, wealth is bags of cares;
Wisdom but folly; joy, disquiet — sadness;
Friendship is treason, and delights are snares;
Pleasures but pain, and mirth but pleasing madness;
Without thee, Lord, things be not what they be,
Nor have their being, when compared with thee.

In having all things, and not thee, what have I?
Not having thee, what have my labors got?
Let me enjoy but thee, what further crave I?
And having thee alone, what have I not?
I wish nor sea nor land; nor would I be
Possessed of heaven, heaven unpossessed of thee!

FRANCIS QUARLES.

A THANKSGIVING FOR HIS HOUSE.

LORD, thou hast given me a cell,
Wherein to dwell;
A little house, whose humble roof
Is weather-proof,
Under the spars of which I lie
Both soft and dry;
Where thou, my chamber for to ward,
Hast set a guard
Of harmless thoughts, to watch and keep
Me while I sleep.
Low is my porch, as is my fate,
Both void of state;
And yet the threshold of my door
Is worn by the poor,
Who hither come, and freely get
Good words or meat.
Like as my parlor, so my hall,
And kitchen small;
A little buttery, and therein
A little bin,
Which keeps my little loaf of bread
Unchipt, unflead.
Some brittle sticks of thorn or brier
Make me a fire,
Close by whose living coal I sit,
And glow like it.
Lord, I confess, too, when I dine,
The pulse is thine,
And all those other bits that be
There placed by thee.
The worts, the purslain, and the mess
Of water-cress,
Which of thy kindness thou hast sent:
And my content
Makes those, and my belovèd beet,
To be more sweet.
'T is thou that crown'st my glittering hearth
With guiltless mirth;
And giv'st me wassail bowls to drink,
Spiced to the brink.

Lord, 't is thy plenty-dropping hand
    That sows my land :
All this, and better, dost thou send
    Me for this end :
That I should render for my part
    A thankful heart,
Which, fired with incense, I resign
    As wholly thine :
But the acceptance — that must be,
    O Lord, by thee.

ROBERT HERRICK.

"WITH WHOM IS NO VARIABLENESS, NEITHER SHADOW OF TURNING."

IT fortifies my soul to know
That, though I perish, Truth is so
That, howsoe'er I stray and range,
Whate'er I do, Thou dost not change.
I steadier step when I recall
That, if I slip, Thou dost not fall.

ARTHUR HUGH CLOUGH.

TWO WENT UP TO THE TEMPLE TO PRAY.

Two went to pray ? O, rather say,
One went to brag, the other to pray ;

One stands up close and treads on high,
Where the other dares not lend his eye ;

One nearer to God's altar trod,
The other to the altar's God.

RICHARD CRASHAW.

THE PILGRIMAGE.

GIVE me my scallop-shell of quiet,
  My staff of faith to walk upon ;
My scrip of joy, immortal diet ;
  My bottle of salvation ;
My gown of glory, hope's true gauge,
And thus I 'll take my pilgrimage !
Blood must be my body's 'balmer,
No other balm will there be given ;
Whilst my soul, like quiet palmer,
Traveleth towards the land of Heaven,
Over the silver mountains
Where spring the nectar fountains.
There will I kiss the bowl of bliss,
And drink mine everlasting fill
Upon every milken hill.
My soul will be a-dry before,
But after, it will thirst no more.
Then by that happy, blissful day,
More peaceful pilgrims I shall see,
That have cast off their rags of clay,
And walk appareled fresh like me.
I 'll take them first to quench their thirst,
And taste of nectar's suckets
At those clear wells where sweetness dwells
Drawn up by saints in crystal buckets.
And when our bottles and all we
Are filled with immortality,
Then the blest paths we 'll travel,
Strewed with rubies thick as gravel, —
Ceilings of diamonds, sapphire floors,
High walls of coral, and pearly bowers.
From thence to Heaven's bribeless hall,
Where no corrupted voices brawl ;
No conscience molten into gold,
No forged accuser, bought or sold,
No cause deferred, no vain-spent journey,
For there Christ is the King's Attorney ;
Who pleads for all without degrees,
And he hath angels, but no fees ;
And when the grand twelve-million jury
Of our sins, with direful fury,
'Gainst our souls black verdicts give,
Christ pleads his death, and then we live.
Be thou my speaker, taintless pleader,
Unblotted lawyer, true proceeder !
Thou giv'st salvation even for alms, —
Not with a bribèd lawyer's palms.
And this is mine eternal plea
To Him that made heaven, earth, and sea,
That, since my flesh must die so soon,
And want a head to dine next noon,
Just at the stroke when my veins start and spread,
Set on my soul an everlasting head :
Then am I, like a palmer, fit
To tread those blest paths which before I writ.
Of death and judgment, heaven and hell,
Who oft doth think, must needs die well.

SIR WALTER RALEIGH.

A TRUE LENT.

Is this a fast, — to keep
    The larder lean,
        And clean
From fat of veals and sheep ?

Is it to quit the dish
    Of flesh, yet still
        To fill
The platter high with fish ?

Is it to fast an hour,
    Or rag'd to go,
        Or show
A downcast look, and sour ?

No! 't is a fast to dole
Thy sheaf of wheat,
And meat,
Unto the hungry soul.

It is to fast from strife,
From old debate
And hate, —
To circumcise thy life.

To show a heart grief-rent;
To starve thy sin,
Not bin, —
And that 's to keep thy Lent.

ROBERT HERRICK.

A PASSAGE IN THE LIFE OF ST. AUGUSTINE.

LONG pored St. Austin o'er the sacred page,
And doubt and darkness overspread his mind;
On God's mysterious being thought the Sage,
The Triple Person in one Godhead joined.
The more he thought, the harder did he find
To solve the various doubts which fast arose;
And as a ship, caught by imperious wind,
Tosses where chance its shattered body throws,
So tossed his troubled soul and nowhere found repose.

Heated and feverish, then he closed his tome,
And went to wander by the ocean-side,
Where the cool breeze at evening loved to come,
Murmuring responsive to the murmuring tide;
And as Augustine o'er its margent wide
Strayed, deeply pondering the puzzling theme,
A little child before him he espied:
In earnest labor did the urchin seem,
Working with heart intent close by the sounding stream.

He looked, and saw the child a hole had scooped,
Shallow and narrow in the shining sand,
O'er which at work the laboring infant stooped,
Still pouring water in with busy hand.
The saint addressed the child in accents bland:
"Fair boy," quoth he, "I pray what toil is thine?
Let me its end and purpose understand."
The boy replied: "An easy task is mine,
To sweep into this hole all the wide ocean's brine."

"O foolish boy!" the saint exclaimed, "to hope
That the broad ocean in that hole should lie!"
"O foolish saint!" exclaimed the boy; "thy scope
Is still more hopeless than the toil I ply,
Who think'st to comprehend God's nature high
In the small compass of thine human wit!
Sooner, Augustine, sooner far, shall I
Confine the ocean in this tiny pit,
Than finite minds conceive God's nature infinite!"

ANONYMOUS.

I WOULD I WERE AN EXCELLENT DIVINE—

I WOULD I were an excellent divine
That had the Bible at my fingers' ends;
That men might hear out of this mouth of mine
How God doth make his enemies his friends;
Rather than with a thundering and long prayer
Be led into presumption, or despair.

This would I be, and would none other be,
But a religious servant of my God;
And know there is none other God but he,
And willingly to suffer mercy's rod, —
Joy in his grace, and live but in his love,
And seek my bliss but in the world above.

And I would frame a kind of faithful prayer,
For all estates within the state of grace,
That careful love might never know despair,
Nor servile fear might faithful love deface;
And this would I both day and night devise
To make my humble spirit's exercise.

And I would read the rules of sacred life;
Persuade the troubled soul to patience;
The husband care, and comfort to the wife,
To child and servant due obedience;
Faith to the friend, and to the neighbor peace,
That love might live, and quarrels all might cease.

Prayer for the health of all that are diseased,
Confession unto all that are convicted,
And patience unto all that are displeased,
And comfort unto all that are afflicted,
And mercy unto all that have offended,
And grace to all, that all may be amended.

NICHOLAS BRETON.

DUM VIVIMUS, VIVAMUS.

"LIVE while you live!" the epicure would say,
"And seize the pleasures of the present day!"
"Live while you live!" the sacred Preacher cries,
"And give to God each moment as it flies!"
Lord, in my view let both united be,
I live in pleasure while I live to thee.

PHILIP DODDRIDGE.

ADAM'S MORNING HYMN IN PARADISE.

THESE are thy glorious works, Parent of good,
Almighty, thine this universal frame,
Thus wondrous fair; thyself how wondrous then
Unspeakable, who sitt'st above these heavens
To us invisible, or dimly seen
In these thy lowest works; yet these declare
Thy goodness beyond thought, and power divine.

Speak, ye who best can tell, ye sons of light,
Angels; for ye behold him, and with songs
And choral symphonies, day without night,
Circle his throne rejoicing; ye in Heaven,
On earth join, all ye creatures, to extol
Him first, him last, him midst, and without end.
Fairest of stars, last in the train of night,
If better thou belong not to the dawn,
Sure pledge of day, that crown'st the smiling morn
With thy bright circlet, praise him in thy sphere,
While day arises, that sweet hour of prime.
Thou sun, of this great world both eye and soul,
Acknowledge him thy greater; sound his praise
In thy eternal course, both when thou climb'st,
And when high noon hast gained, and when thou fall'st.
Moon, that now meets the orient sun, now fliest,
With the fixed stars, fixed in their orb that flies,
And ye five other wandering fires that move
In mystic dance not without song, resound
His praise, who out of darkness called up light.
Air, and ye elements, the eldest birth
Of Nature's womb, that in quaternion run
Perpetual circle, multiform, and mix
And nourish all things, let your ceaseless change
Vary to our great Maker still new praise.
Ye mists and exhalations, that now rise
From hill or steaming lake, dusky or gray,
Till the sun paint your fleecy skirts with gold,
In honor to the world's great Author rise,
Whether to deck with clouds the uncolored sky,
Or wet the thirsty earth with falling showers,
Rising or falling, still advance his praise.
His praise, ye winds, that from four quarters blow,
Breathe soft or loud; and wave your tops, ye pines,
With every plant, in sign of worship wave.
Fountains, and ye that warble, as ye flow,
Melodious murmurs, warbling tune his praise.
Join voices, all ye living souls; ye birds,
That singing up to Heaven-gate ascend,
Bear on your wings and in your notes his praise.
Ye that in waters glide, and ye that walk
The earth, and stately tread, or lowly creep,
Witness if I be silent, morn or even,
To hill or valley, fountain or fresh shade,
Made vocal by my song, and taught his praise.
Hail, universal Lord! be bounteous still
To give us only good; and if the night
Have gathered aught of evil, or concealed,
Disperse it, as now light dispels the dark.

MILTON.

PRAISE.

To write a verse or two is all the praise
That I can raise;
Mend my estate in any wayes,
Thou shalt have more.

I go to church; help me to wings, and I
Will thither flie;
Or, if I mount unto the skie,
I will do more.

Man is all weaknesse: there is no such thing
As Prince or King:
His arm is short; yet with a sling
He may do more.

A herb destilled, and drunk, may dwell next doore,
On the same floore,
To a brave soul: Exalt the poore,
They can do more.

O, raise me then! poore bees, that work all day,
Sting my delay,
Who have a work, as well as they,
And much, much more.

GEORGE HERBERT.

UP HILL.

DOES the road wind up hill all the way?
Yes, to the very end.
Will the day's journey take the whole long day?
From morn to night, my friend.

But is there for the night a resting-place?
A roof for when the slow dark hours begin?
May not the darkness hide it from my face?
You cannot miss that inn.

Shall I meet other wayfarers at night?
Those who have gone before.
Then must I knock, or call when just in sight?
They will not keep you standing at that door.

Shall I find comfort, travel-sore and weak?
Of labor you shall find the sum.
Will there be beds for me and all who seek?
Yea, beds for all who come.

CHRISTINA G. ROSSETTI.

THE PILLAR OF THE CLOUD.

LEAD, kindly Light, amid the encircling gloom,
Lead thou me on!
The night is dark, and I am far from home, —
Lead thou me on!
Keep thou my feet; I do not ask to see
The distant scene, — one step enough for me.

I was not ever thus, nor prayed that thou
Shouldst lead me on:
I loved to choose and see my path, but now
Lead thou me on!

I loved the garish day, and, spite of fears,
Pride ruled my will: remember not past years.

So long thy power hath blessed me, sure it still
Will lead me on;
O'er moor and fen, o'er crag and torrent, till
The night is gone;
And with the morn those angel faces smile
Which I have loved long since, and lost awhile.

JOHN HENRY NEWMAN.

THE CHURCH PORCH.

THOU whose sweet youth and early hopes enhance
Thy rate and price, and mark thee for a treasure,
Hearken unto a Verser, who may chance
Rhyme thee to good, and make a bait of pleasure:
A verse may find him who a sermon flies
And turn delight into a sacrifice.

When thou dost purpose aught (within thy power),
Be sure to doe it, though it be but small;
Constancie knits the bones, and make us stowre,
When wanton pleasures beckon us to thrall.
Who breaks his own bond, forfeiteth himself:
What nature made a ship, he makes a shelf.

By all means use sometimes to be alone.
Salute thyself: see what thy soul doth wear.
Dare to look in thy chest; for 't is thine own:
And tumble up and down what thou find'st there.
Who cannot rest till he good fellows finde,
He breaks up house, turns out of doores his minde.

In clothes, cheap handsomenesse doth bear the bell.
Wisdome 's a trimmer thing than shop e'er gave.
Say not then, This with that lace will do well;
But, This with my discretion will be brave.
Much curiousnesse is a perpetual wooing;
Nothing, with labor; folly, long a doing.

When once thy foot enters the church, be bare.
God is more there than thou; for thou art there
Only by his permission. Then beware,
And make thyself all reverence and fear.
Kneeling ne'er spoiled silk stockings; quit thy state;
All equal are within the church's gate.

Resort to sermons, but to prayers most:
Praying 's the end of preaching. O, be drest!
Stay not for th' other pin: why thou hast lost
A joy for it worth worlds. Thus hell doth jest
Away thy blessings, and extremely flout thee,
Thy clothes being fast, but thy soul loose about thee.

Judge not the preacher; for he is thy judge:
If thou mislike him, thou conceiv'st him not.
God calleth preaching folly. Do not grudge
To pick out treasures from an earthen pot.
The worst speak something good: if *all* want sense,
God takes a text, and preacheth patience.

GEORGE HERBERT.

ANCIENT HYMN.

ART thou weary, art thou languid, art thou sore distrest?
"Come to me," saith One — and, "coming, Be at rest!"
Hath he mark to lead me to him — if he be my guide?
In his feet and hands are wound-prints,
And his side.
Is there diadem, as monarch, that his brow adorns?
Yea; a crown, in very surety, —
But of thorns!
If I find him, if I follow, what his guerdon here?
Many a sorrow, many a labor,
Many a tear!
If I still hold closely to him, what hath he at last?
Sorrow vanquished, labor ended,
Jordan passed!
If I ask him to receive me, will he say me nay?
Not till earth, and not till heaven,
Pass away!
Tending, following, keeping, struggling, is he sure to bless?
Angels, martyrs, prophets, pilgrims,
Answer "Yes!"

ANONYMOUS.

TO HEAVEN APPROACHED A SUFI SAINT.

To heaven approached a Sufi Saint,
From groping in the darkness late,
And, tapping timidly and faint,
Besought admission at God's gate.

Said God, "Who seeks to enter here?"
"'T is I, dear Friend," the Saint replied,
And trembling much with hope and fear.
"If it be *thou*, without abide."

Sadly to earth the poor Saint turned,
To bear the scourging of life's rods;
But aye his heart within him yearned
To mix and lose its love in God's.

He roamed alone through weary years,
By cruel men still scorned and mocked,
Until from faith's pure fires and tears
Again he rose, and modest knocked.

Asked God, "Who now is at the door?"
"It is thyself, belovèd Lord,"
Answered the Saint, in doubt no more,
But clasped and rapt in his reward.

From the Persian of DSCHELLALEDDIN RUMI, by WILLIAM R. ALGER.

THE DYING CHRISTIAN TO HIS SOUL.

VITAL spark of heavenly flame!
Quit, O, quit this mortal frame!
Trembling, hoping, lingering, flying,
O, the pain, the bliss of dying!
Cease, fond nature, cease thy strife,
And let me languish into life!

Hark! they whisper; angels say,
Sister spirit, come away!
What is this absorbs me quite?
Steals my senses, shuts my sight,
Drowns my spirits, draws my breath?
Tell me, my soul, can this be death?

The world recedes; it disappears!
Heaven opens on my eyes! my ears
With sounds seraphic ring:
Lend, lend your wings! I mount! I fly!
O Grave! where is thy victory?
O Death! where is thy sting?

ALEXANDER POPE.

PRAYER.

O GOD! though sorrow be my fate,
And the world's hate
For my heart's faith pursue me,
My peace they cannot take away;
From day to day
Thou dost anew imbue me;
Thou art not far; a little while
Thou hid'st thy face with brighter smile
Thy father-love to show me.

Lord, not my will, but thine, be done;
If I sink down
When men to terrors leave me,
Thy father-love still warms my breast;
All 's for the best;
Shall man have power to grieve me,
When bliss eternal is my goal,
And thou the keeper of my soul,
Who never will deceive me?

Thou art my shield, as saith the Word.
Christ Jesus, Lord,
Thou standest pitying by me,
And lookest on each grief of mine
And if 't were thine:
What, then, though foes may try me,
Though thorns be in my path concealed?
World, do thy worst! God is my shield!
And will be ever nigh me.

Translated from MARY, QUEEN OF HUNGARY.

PER PACEM AD LUCEM.

I DO not ask, O Lord, that life may be
A pleasant road;
I do not ask that thou wouldst take from me
Aught of its load:

I do not ask that flowers should always spring
Beneath my feet;
I know too well the poison and the sting
Of things too sweet.

For one thing only, Lord, dear Lord, I plead,
Lead me aright—
Though strength should falter and though heart should bleed—
Through Peace to Light.

I do not ask, O Lord, that thou shouldst shed
Full radiance here;
Give but a ray of peace, that I may tread
Without a fear.

I do not ask my cross to understand,
My way to see;
Better in darkness just to feel thy hand,
And follow thee.

Joy is like restless day; but peace divine
Like quiet night;
Lead me, O Lord—till perfect day shall shine—
Through Peace to Light.

ADELAIDE A. PROCTER.

THE MARTYRS' HYMN.

FLUNG to the heedless winds,
Or on the waters cast,
The martyrs' ashes, watched,
Shall gathered be at last;
And from that scattered dust,
Around us and abroad,
Shall spring a plenteous seed
Of witnesses for God.

The Father hath received
Their latest living breath;
And vain is Satan's boast
Of victory in their death;

Still, still, though dead, they speak,
  And, trumpet-tongued, proclaim
To many a wakening land
  The one availing name.

From the German of MARTIN LUTHER,
by W. J. FOX.

THE FIGHT OF FAITH.

[The author of this poem, one of the victims of the persecuting Henry VIII., was burnt to death at Smithfield in 1546. It was made and sung by her while a prisoner in Newgate.]

LIKE as the armèd Knighte,
Appointed to the fielde,
With this world wil I fight,
And faith shal be my shilde.

Faith is that weapon stronge,
Which wil not faile at nede;
My foes therefore amonge,
Therewith wil I procede.

As it is had in strengthe,
And forces of Christes waye,
It wil prevaile at lengthe,
Though all the devils saye *naye.*

Faithe of the fathers olde
Obtainèd right witness,
Which makes me verye bolde
To fear no worldes distress.

I now rejoice in harte,
And hope bides me do so;
For Christ wil take my part,
And ease me of my wo.

Thou sayst, Lord, whoso knocke,
To them wilt thou attende;
Undo, therefore, the locke,
And thy stronge power sende.

More enemies now I have
Than heeres upon my head;
Let them not me deprave,
But fight thou in my steade.

On thee my care I cast,
For all their cruell spight;
I set not by their hast,
For thou art my delight.

I am not she that list
My anker to let fall
For every drislinge mist;
My shippe's substancial.

Not oft I use to wright
In prose, nor yet in ryme;
Yet wil I shewe one sight,
That I sawe in my time:

I sawe a royall throne,
Where Justice shulde have sitte;
But in her steade was One
Of moody cruell witte.

Absorpt was rightwisness,
As by the raginge floude;
Sathan, in his excess,
Sucte up the guiltlesse bloude.

Then thought I, — Jesus, Lorde,
When thou shalt judge us all,
Harde is it to recorde
On these men what will fall.

Yet, Lorde, I thee desire,
For that they doe to me,
Let them not taste the hire
Of their iniquitie.

ANNE ASKEWE.

HOW LONG?

MY God, it is not fretfulness
  That makes me say, "How long?"
It is not heaviness of heart
  That hinders me in song;
'T is not despair of truth and right,
  Nor coward dread of wrong.

But how can I, with such a hope
  Of glory and of home,
With such a joy before my eyes,
  Not wish the time were come, —
Of years the jubilee, of days
  The Sabbath and the sum?

These years, what ages they have been!
  This life, how long it seems!
And how can I, in evil days,
  Mid unknown hills and streams,
But sigh for those of home and heart,
  And visit them in dreams?

Yet peace, my heart, and hush, my tongue;
  Be calm, my troubled breast;
Each restless hour is hastening on
  The everlasting rest:
Thou knowest that the time thy God
  Appoints for thee is best.

Let faith, not fear, nor fretfulness,
  Awake the cry, "How long?"
Let no faint-heartedness of soul
  Damp thy aspiring song:
Right comes, truth dawns, the night departs
  Of error and of wrong.

HORATIUS BONAR.

ON HIS BLINDNESS.

When I consider how my light is spent
Ere half my days, in this dark world and wide,
And that one talent, which is death to hide,
Lodged with me useless, though my soul more bent
To serve therewith my Maker, and present
My true account, lest he returning chide;
"Doth God exact day-labor, light denied?"
I fondly ask. But Patience, to prevent
That murmur, soon replies, "God doth not need
Either man's work or his own gifts; who best
Bear his mild yoke, they serve him best: his state
Is kingly; thousands at his bidding speed,
And post o'er land and ocean without rest;
They also serve who only stand and wait."

MILTON.

SAID I NOT SO?

Said I not so, — that I would sin no more?
Witness, my God, I did;
Yet I am run again upon the score:
My faults cannot be hid.

What shall I do? — Make vows and break them still?
'T will be but labor lost;
My good cannot prevail against mine ill:
The business will be crost.

O, say not so; thou canst not tell what strength
Thy God may give thee at the length.
Renew thy vows, and if thou keep the last,
Thy God will pardon all that 's past.
Vow while thou canst; while thou canst vow, thou mayst
Perhaps perform it when thou thinkest least.

Thy God hath not denied thee all,
Whilst he permits thee but to call.
Call to thy God for grace to keep
Thy vows; and if thou break them, weep.
Weep for thy broken vows, and vow again:
Vows made with tears cannot be still in vain.
Then once again
I vow to mend my ways;
Lord, say Amen,
And thine be all the praise.

GEORGE HERBERT.

HEAVEN.

O beauteous God! uncircumscribèd treasure
Of an eternal pleasure!
Thy throne is seated far
Above the highest star,
Where thou preparest a glorious place,
Within the brightness of thy face,
For every spirit
To inherit
That builds his hopes upon thy merit,
And loves thee with a holy charity.
What ravished heart, seraphic tongue, or eyes
Clear as the morning rise,
Can speak, or think, or see
That bright eternity,
Where the great King's transparent throne
Is of an entire jasper stone?
There the eye
O' the chrysolite,
And a sky
Of diamonds, rubies, chrysoprase, —
And above all thy holy face, —
Makes an eternal charity.
When thou thy jewels up dost bind, that day
Remember us, we pray, —
That where the beryl lies,
And the crystal 'bove the skies,
There thou mayest appoint us place
Within the brightness of thy face, —
And our soul
In the scroll
Of life and blissfulness enroll,
That we may praise thee to eternity. Allelujah!

JEREMY TAYLOR.

"ROCK OF AGES."

"Such hymns are never forgotten. They cling to us through our whole life. We carry them with us upon our journey. We sing them in the forest. The workman follows the plow with sacred songs. Children catch them, and singing only for the joy it gives them now, are yet laying up for all their life food of the sweetest joy." — HENRY WARD BEECHER.

"Rock of ages, cleft for me,"
Thoughtlessly the maiden sung.
Fell the words unconsciously
From her girlish, gleeful tongue;
Sang as little children sing;
Sang as sing the birds in June;
Fell the words like light leaves down
On the current of the tune, —
"Rock of ages, cleft for me,
Let me hide myself in thee."

"Let me hide myself in thee." —
Felt her soul no need to hide, —
Sweet the song as song could be,
And she had no thought beside;
All the words unheedingly
Fell from lips untouched by care,
Dreaming not that they might be
On some other lips a prayer, —
"Rock of ages, cleft for me,
Let me hide myself in thee."

MILTON ON HIS BLINDNESS.

"Doth God exact day-labor, light denied?"
I fondly ask: But Patience, to prevent
That murmur, soon replies, ...
"They also serve who only stand and wait."

"Rock of ages, cleft for me,"
'T was a woman sung them now,
Pleadingly and prayerfully;
Every word her heart did know.
Rose the song as storm-tossed bird
Beats with weary wing the air,
Every note with sorrow stirred,
Every syllable a prayer, —
"Rock of ages, cleft for me,
Let me hide myself in thee."

"Rock of ages, cleft for me,"—
Lips grown aged sung the hymn
Trustingly and tenderly,
Voice grown weak and eyes grown dim, —
"Let me hide myself in Thee."
Trembling though the voice and low,
Rose the sweet strain peacefully
Like a river in its flow;
Sung as only they can sing
Who life's thorny path have passed;
Sung as only they can sing
Who behold the promised rest, —
"Rock of ages, cleft for me,
Let me hide myself in thee."

"Rock of ages, cleft for me,"
Sung above a coffin lid;
Underneath, all restfully,
All life's joys and sorrows hid.
Nevermore, O storm-tossed soul!
Nevermore from wind or tide,
Nevermore from billow's roll,
Wilt thou need thyself to hide.
Could the sightless, sunken eyes,
Closed beneath the soft gray hair,
Could the mute and stiffened lips
Move again in pleading prayer,
Still, aye still, the words would be, —
"Let me hide myself in Thee."

ANONYMOUS.

THE SPIRIT-LAND.

FATHER! thy wonders do not singly stand,
Nor far removed where feet have seldom strayed;
Around us ever lies the enchanted land,
In marvels rich to thine own sons displayed.
In finding thee are all things round us found;
In losing thee are all things lost beside;
Ears have we, but in vain strange voices sound;
And to our eyes the vision is denied.
We wander in the country far remote,
Mid tombs and ruined piles in death to dwell;
Or on the records of past greatness dote,
And for a buried soul the living sell;
While on our path bewildered falls the night
That ne'er returns us to the fields of light.

JONES VERY.

HEAVEN.

BEYOND these chilling winds and gloomy skies,
Beyond death's cloudy portal,
There is a land where beauty never dies,
Where love becomes immortal;

A land whose life is never dimmed by shade,
Whose fields are ever vernal;
Where nothing beautiful can ever fade,
But blooms for aye eternal.

We may not know how sweet its balmy air,
How bright and fair its flowers;
We may not hear the songs that echo there,
Through those enchanted bowers.

The city's shining towers we may not see
With our dim earthly vision,
For Death, the silent warder, keeps the key
That opes the gates elysian.

But sometimes, when adown the western sky
A fiery sunset lingers,
Its golden gates swing inward noiselessly,
Unlocked by unseen fingers.

And while they stand a moment half ajar,
Gleams from the inner glory
Stream brightly through the azure vault afar
And half reveal the story.

O land unknown! O land of love divine!
Father, all-wise, eternal!
O, guide these wandering, wayworn feet of mine
Into those pastures vernal!

NANCY A. W. PRIEST.

"ONLY WAITING."

[A very aged man in an almshouse was asked what he was doing now. He replied, "Only waiting."]

ONLY waiting till the shadows
Are a little longer grown,
Only waiting till the glimmer
Of the day's last beam is flown;
Till the night of earth is faded
From the heart, once full of day;
Till the stars of heaven are breaking
Through the twilight soft and gray.

Only waiting till the reapers
Have the last sheaf gathered home,
For the summer time is faded,
And the autumn winds have come.
Quickly, reapers! gather quickly
The last ripe hours of my heart,
For the bloom of life is withered,
And I hasten to depart.

Only waiting till the angels
  Open wide the mystic gate,
At whose feet I long have lingered,
  Weary, poor, and desolate.
Even now I hear the footsteps,
  And their voices far away;
If they call me, I am waiting,
  Only waiting to obey.

Only waiting till the shadows
  Are a little longer grown,
Only waiting till the glimmer
  Of the day's last beam is flown.
Then from out the gathered darkness,
  Holy, deathless stars shall rise,
By whose light my soul shall gladly
  Tread its pathway to the skies.

ADELAIDE ANNE PROCTER.

THE SOUL.

COME, Brother, turn with me from pining thought
And all the inward ills that sin has wrought;
Come, send abroad a love for all who live,
And feel the deep content in turn they give.
Kind wishes and good deeds, — they make not poor;
They'll home again, full laden, to thy door;
The streams of love flow back where they begin,
For springs of outward joys lie deep within.
  Even let them flow, and make the places glad
Where dwell thy fellow-men. Shouldst thou be sad,
And earth seem bare, and hours, once happy, press
Upon thy thoughts, and make thy loneliness
More lonely for the past, thou then shalt hear
The music of those waters running near;
And thy faint spirit drink the cooling stream,
And thine eye gladden with the playing beam
That now upon the water dances, now
Leaps up and dances in the hanging bough.
  Is it not lovely? Tell me, where doth dwell
The power that wrought so beautiful a spell?
In thine own bosom, Brother? Then as thine
Guard with a reverent fear this power divine.
  And if, indeed, 't is not the outward state,
But temper of the soul by which we rate
Sadness or joy, even let thy bosom move
With noble thoughts and wake thee into love;
And let each feeling in thy breast be given
An honest aim, which, sanctified by Heaven,
And springing into act, new life imparts,
Till beats thy frame as with a thousand hearts.
  Sin clouds the mind's clear vision;
Around the self-starved soul has spread a dearth.
The earth is full of life; the living Hand
Touched it with life; and all its forms expand
With principles of being made to suit
Man's varied powers and raise him from the brute.
And shall the earth of higher ends be full, —
Earth which thou tread'st, — and thy poor mind be dull?
Thou talk of life, with half thy soul asleep?
Thou "living dead man," let thy spirit leap
Forth to the day, and let the fresh air blow
Through thy soul's shut-up mansion. Wouldst thou know
Something of what is life, shake off this death;
Have thy soul feel the universal breath
With which all nature's quick, and learn to be
Sharer in all that thou dost touch or see;
Break from thy body's grasp, thy spirit's trance;
Give thy soul air, thy faculties expanse;
Love, joy, even sorrow, — yield thyself to all!
They make thy freedom, groveler, not thy thrall.
Knock off the shackles which thy spirit bind
To dust and sense, and set at large the mind!
Then move in sympathy with God's great whole,
And be like man at first, a *living soul*.

RICHARD HENRY DANA.

SIT DOWN, SAD SOUL.

SIT down, sad soul, and count
  The moments flying;
Come, tell the sweet amount
  That's lost by sighing!
How many smiles? — a score?
Then laugh, and count no more;
    For day is dying!

Lie down, sad soul, and sleep,
  And no more measure
The flight of time, nor weep
  The loss of leisure;
But here, by this lone stream,
Lie down with us, and dream
    Of starry treasure!

We dream; do thou the same;
  We love, — forever;
We laugh, yet few we shame, —
  The gentle never.
Stay, then, till sorrow dies:
Then — hope and happy skies
    Are thine forever!

BARRY CORNWALL.

TELL ME, YE WINGED WINDS.

TELL me, ye wingèd winds,
  That round my pathway roar,
Do ye not know some spot
  Where mortals weep no more?

Some lone and pleasant dell,
Some valley in the west,
Where, free from toil and pain,
The weary soul may rest?
The loud wind dwindled to a whisper low,
And sighed for pity as it answered, — "No."

Tell me, thou mighty deep,
Whose billows round me play,
Know'st thou some favored spot,
Some island far away,
Where weary man may find
The bliss for which he sighs, —
Where sorrow never lives,
And friendship never dies?
The loud waves, rolling in perpetual flow,
Stopped for a while, and sighed to answer, —
"No."

And thou, serenest moon,
That, with such lovely face,
Dost look upon the earth,
Asleep in night's embrace;
Tell me, in all thy round
Hast thou not seen some spot
Where miserable man
May find a happier lot!
Behind a cloud the moon withdrew in woe,
And a voice, sweet but sad, responded, — "No."

Tell me, my secret soul,
O, tell me, Hope and Faith,
Is there no resting-place
From sorrow, sin, and death?
Is there no happy spot
Where mortals may be blest,
Where grief may find a balm,
And weariness a rest?
Faith, Hope, and Love, best boons to mortals given,
Waved their bright wings, and whispered, —
"Yes, in heaven!"

CHARLES MACKAY.

NOTHING BUT LEAVES.

NOTHING but leaves; the spirit grieves
Over a wasted life;
Sin committed while conscience slept,
Promises made, but never kept,
Hatred, battle, and strife;
Nothing but leaves!

Nothing but leaves; no garnered sheaves
Of life's fair, ripened grain;
Words, idle words, for earnest deeds;
We sow our seeds, — lo! tares and weeds:
We reap, with toil and pain,
Nothing but leaves!

Nothing but leaves; memory weaves
No veil to screen the past:
As we retrace our weary way,
Counting each lost and misspent day,
We find, sadly, at last,
Nothing but leaves!

And shall we meet the Master so,
Bearing our withered leaves?
The Saviour looks for perfect fruit;
We stand before him, humbled, mute;
Waiting the words he breathes, —
"*Nothing but leaves?*"

LUCY E. AKERMAN.

THE UNIVERSAL PRAYER.

FATHER of all! in every age,
In every clime adored,
By saint, by savage, and by sage,
Jehovah, Jove, or Lord!

Thou great First Cause, least understood,
Who all my sense confined
To know but this, that thou art good,
And that myself am blind;

Yet gave me, in this dark estate,
To see the good from ill;
And, binding nature fast in fate,
Left free the human will:

What conscience dictates to be done,
Or warns me not to do,
This, teach me more than hell to shun,
That, more than heaven pursue.

What blessings thy free bounty gives
Let me not cast away;
For God is paid when man receives,
To enjoy is to obey.

Yet not to earth's contracted span
Thy goodness let me bound,
Or think thee Lord alone of man,
When thousand worlds are round:

Let not this weak, unknowing hand
Presume thy bolts to throw,
And deal damnation round the land
On each I judge thy foe.

If I am right, thy grace impart
Still in the right to stay;
If I am wrong, O, teach my heart
To find that better way!

Save me alike from foolish pride
  And impious discontent
At aught thy wisdom has denied,
  Or aught thy goodness lent.

Teach me to feel another's woe,
  To hide the fault I see;
That mercy I to others show,
  That mercy show to me.

Mean though I am, not wholly so,
  Since quickened by thy breath;
O, lead me whereso'er I go,
  Through this day's life or death!

This day be bread and peace my lot;
  All else beneath the sun,
Thou know'st if best bestowed or not,
  And let thy will be done.

To thee, whose temple is all space,
  Whose altar, earth, sea, skies,
One chorus let all Being raise,
  All Nature's incense rise!

ALEXANDER POPE.

WRESTLING JACOB.

FIRST PART.

COME, O thou Traveler unknown,
  Whom still I hold, but cannot see;
My company before is gone,
  And I am left alone with thee;
With thee all night I mean to stay,
And wrestle till the break of day.

I need not tell thee who I am;
  My sin and misery declare;
Thyself hast called me by my name;
  Look on thy hands, and read it there;
But who, I ask thee, who art thou?
Tell me thy name, and tell me now.

In vain thou strugglest to get free;
  I never will unloose my hold:
Art thou the Man that died for me?
  The secret of thy love unfold;
Wrestling, I will not let thee go
Till I thy name, thy nature know.

Wilt thou not yet to me reveal
  Thy new, unutterable name?
Tell me, I still beseech thee, tell;
  To know it now resolved I am;
Wrestling, I will not let thee go
Till I thy name, thy nature know.

What though my shrinking flesh complain
  And murmur to contend so long,
I rise superior to my pain;
  When I am weak, then am I strong!
And when my all of strength shall fail,
I shall with the God-man prevail.

SECOND PART.

YIELD to me now, for I am weak,
  But confident in self-despair;
Speak to my heart, in blessings speak;
  Be conquered by my instant prayer;
Speak, or thou never hence shalt move,
And tell me if thy name be Love.

'T is Love! 't is Love! Thou diedst for me;
  I hear thy whisper in my heart;
The morning breaks, the shadows flee;
  Pure, universal Love thou art;
To me, to all, thy bowels move;
Thy nature and thy name is Love.

My prayer hath power with God; the grace
  Unspeakable I now receive;
Through faith I see thee face to face;
  I see thee face to face and live!
In vain I have not wept and strove;
Thy nature and thy name is Love.

I know thee, Saviour, who thou art,
  Jesus, the feeble sinner's friend;
Nor wilt thou with the night depart,
  But stay and love me to the end;
Thy mercies never shall remove;
Thy nature and thy name is Love.

The Sun of Righteousness on me
  Hath risen, with healing in his wings;
Withered my nature's strength; from thee
  My soul its life and succor brings;
My help is all laid up above;
Thy nature and thy name is Love.

Contented now upon my thigh
  I halt till life's short journey end;
All helplessness, all weakness, I
  On thee alone for strength depend;
Nor have I power from thee to move;
Thy nature and thy name is Love.

Lame as I am, I take the prey;
  Hell, earth, and sin with ease o'ercome;
I leap for joy, pursue my way,
  And, as a bounding hart, fly home;
Through all eternity to prove
Thy nature and thy name is Love.

CHARLES WESLEY.

"I WILL THAT MEN PRAY EVERYWHERE."

To prayer! to prayer!—for the morning breaks,
And earth in her Maker's smile awakes.
His light is on all, below and above,—
The light of gladness and life and love.
O, then on the breath of this early air,
Send upward the incense of grateful prayer.

To prayer!—for the glorious sun has gone,
And the gathering darkness of night comes on.
Like a curtain from God's kind hand it flows,
To shade the couch where his children repose.
Then kneel, while the watching stars are bright,
And give your last thoughts to the Guardian of night.

To prayer! for the day that God has blest,
Comes tranquilly on with its welcome rest.
It speaks of creation's early bloom,
It speaks of the Prince who burst the tomb.
Then summon the spirit's exalted powers,
And devote to Heaven the hallowed hours.

There are smiles and tears in the mother's eyes,
For her new-born infant beside her lies.
O, hour of bliss! when the heart o'erflows
With rapture a mother only knows;—
Let it gush forth in words of fervent prayer;
Let it swell up to Heaven for her precious care.

There are smiles and tears in that gathering band,
Where the heart is pledged with the trembling hand.
What trying thoughts in her bosom swell,
As the bride bids parents and home farewell!
Kneel down by the side of the tearful fair,
And strengthen the perilous hour with prayer.

Kneel down by the dying sinner's side,
And pray for his soul, through Him who died.
Large drops of anguish are thick on his brow:—
O, what are earth and its pleasures now?
And what shall assuage his dark despair
But the penitent cry of humble prayer?

Kneel down at the couch of departing faith,
And hear the last words the believer saith.
He has bidden adieu to his earthly friends:
There is peace in his eye that upward bends;
There is peace in his calm confiding air:
For his last thoughts are God's,—his last words, prayer.

The voice of prayer at the sable bier!—
A voice to sustain, to soothe, and to cheer.
It commends the spirit to God who gave;
It lifts the thoughts from the cold dark grave;
It points to the glory where He shall reign,
Who whispered, "Thy brother shall rise again."

The voice of prayer in the world of bliss!—
But gladder, purer, than rose from this.
The ransomed shout to their glorious King,
When no sorrow shades the soul as they sing;
But a sinless and joyous song they raise,
And their voice of prayer is eternal praise.

Awake! awake! and gird up thy strength
To join that holy band at length.
To Him who unceasing love displays,
Whom the powers of nature unceasingly praise,
To Him thy heart and thy hours be given;
For a life of prayer is the life of Heaven.

HENRY WARE, JR.

A MIGHTY FORTRESS IS OUR GOD.

Ein' feste burg ist unser Gott.

A MIGHTY fortress is our God,
A bulwark never failing;
Our helper he amid the flood
Of mortal ills prevailing.
For still our ancient foe
Doth seek to work us woe;
His craft and power are great,
And, armed with equal hate,
On earth is not his equal.

Did we in our own strength confide,
Our striving would be losing;
Were not the right man on our side,
The man of God's own choosing.
Dost ask who that may be?
Christ Jesus, it is he,
Lord Sabaoth his name,
From age to age the same,
And he must win the battle.

From the German of MARTIN LUTHER,
by F. H. HEDGE.

IT KINDLES ALL MY SOUL.

Urit me Patriæ decor.

IT kindles all my soul,
My country's loveliness! Those starry choirs
That watch around the pole,
And the moon's tender light, and heavenly fires
Through golden halls that roll.
O chorus of the night! O planets, sworn
The music of the spheres
To follow! Lovely watchers, that think scorn
To rest till day appears!
Me, for celestial homes of glory born,

Why here, O, why so long,
Do ye behold an exile from on high?
Here, O ye shining throng,
With lilies spread the mound where I shall lie:
Here let me drop my chain,
And dust to dust returning, cast away
The trammels that remain;
The rest of me shall spring to endless day!

From the Latin of CASIMIR OF POLAND.

JEWISH HYMN IN JERUSALEM.

GOD of the thunder! from whose cloudy seat
The fiery winds of Desolation flow;
Father of vengeance! that with purple feet
Like a full wine-press tread'st the world below;
The embattled armies wait thy sign to slay,
Nor springs the beast of havoc on his prey,
Nor withering Famine walks his blasted way,
Till thou hast marked the guilty land for woe.

God of the rainbow! at whose gracious sign
The billows of the proud their rage suppress;
Father of mercies! at one word of thine
An Eden blooms in the waste wilderness,
And fountains sparkle in the arid sands,
And timbrels ring in maidens' glancing hands,
And marble cities crown the laughing lands,
And pillared temples rise thy name to bless.

O'er Judah's land thy thunders broke, O Lord!
The chariots rattled o'er her sunken gate,
Her sons were wasted by the Assyrian's sword,
Even her foes wept to see her fallen state;
And heaps her ivory palaces became,
Her princes wore the captive's garb of shame,
Her temples sank amid the smoldering flame,
For thou didst ride the tempest cloud of fate.

O'er Judah's land thy rainbow, Lord, shall beam,
And the sad City lift her crownless head,
And songs shall wake and dancing footsteps gleam
In streets where broods the silence of the dead.
The sun shall shine on Salem's gilded towers,
On Carmel's side our maidens cull the flowers
To deck at blushing eve their bridal bowers,
And angel feet the glittering Sion tread.

Thy vengeance gave us to the stranger's hand,
And Abraham's children were led forth for slaves.
With fettered steps we left our pleasant land,
Envying our fathers in their peaceful graves.
The strangers' bread with bitter tears we steep,
And when our weary eyes should sink to sleep,
In the mute midnight we steal forth to weep,
Where the pale willows shade Euphrates' waves.

The born in sorrow shall bring forth in joy;
Thy mercy, Lord, shall lead thy children home;
He that went forth a tender prattling boy
Yet, ere he die, to Salem's streets shall come;
And Canaan's vines for us their fruit shall bear,
And Hermon's bees their honeyed stores prepare,
And we shall kneel again in thankful prayer,
Where o'er the cherub-seated God full blazed
the irradiate throne.

HENRY HART MILMAN.

THE DYING SAVIOUR.

O SACRED Head, now wounded,
With grief and shame weighed down;
Now scornfully surrounded
With thorns, thy only crown;
O sacred Head, what glory,
What bliss, till now was thine!
Yet, though despised and gory,
I joy to call thee mine.

O noblest brow and dearest,
In other days the world
All feared when thou appearedst;
What shame on thee is hurled!
How art thou pale with anguish,
With sore abuse and scorn!
How does that visage languish
Which once was bright as morn!

What language shall I borrow,
To thank thee, dearest Friend,
For this thy dying sorrow,
Thy pity without end!
O, make me thine forever,
And should I fainting be,
Lord, let me never, never,
Outlive my love to thee.

If I, a wretch, should leave thee,
O Jesus, leave not me!
In faith may I receive thee,
When death shall set me free.
When strength and comfort languish,
And I must hence depart,
Release me then from anguish,
By thine own wounded heart.

Be near when I am dying,
O, show thy cross to me!
And for my succor flying,
Come, Lord, to set me free.
These eyes new faith receiving,
From Jesus shall not move;
For he who dies believing
Dies safely — through thy love.

PAUL GERHARDT.

THE MINISTRY OF ANGELS.

AND is there care in heaven? And is there love
In heavenly spirits to these creatures base,
That may compassion of their evils move?
There is:— else much more wretched were the case
Of men than beasts: but O the exceeding grace
Of Highest God! that loves his creatures so,
And all his workes with mercy doth embrace,
That blessed angels he sends to and fro,
To serve to wicked man, to serve his wicked foe!

How oft do they their silver bowers leave,
To come to succour us that succour want!
How oft do they with golden pinions cleave
The flitting skyes, like flying pursuivant,
Against fowle feendes to ayd us militant!
They for us fight, they watch, and dewly ward,
And their bright squadrons round about us plant;
And all for love, and nothing for reward;
O, why should heavenly God to men have such regard!

EDMUND SPENSER.

NEARER, MY GOD, TO THEE.

NEARER, my God, to thee,
Nearer to thee!
E'en though it be a cross
That raiseth me;
Still all my song shall be,—
Nearer, my God, to thee,
Nearer to thee!

Though, like the wanderer,
The sun gone down,
Darkness be over me,
My rest a stone;
Yet in my dreams I 'd be
Nearer, my God, to thee,
Nearer to thee!

There let the way appear
Steps unto heaven;
All that thou sendest me
In mercy given;
Angels to beckon me
Nearer, my God, to thee,
Nearer to thee!

Then with my waking thoughts,
Bright with thy praise,
Out of my stony griefs
Bethel I 'll raise;
So by my woes to be
Nearer, my God, to thee,
Nearer to thee!

Or if on joyful wing
Cleaving the sky,
Sun, moon, and stars forgot,
Upward I fly;
Still all my song shall be,—
Nearer, my God, to thee,
Nearer to thee.

SARAH FLOWER ADAMS.

FROM THE RECESSES OF A LOWLY SPIRIT.

FROM the recesses of a lowly spirit,
Our humble prayer ascends; O Father! hear it.
Upsoaring on the wings of awe and meekness,
Forgive its weakness!

We see thy hand,—it leads us, it supports us;
We hear thy voice,—it counsels and it courts us;
And then we turn away; and still thy kindness
Forgives our blindness.

O, how long-suffering, Lord! but thou delightest
To win with love the wandering: thou invitest,
By smiles of mercy, not by frowns or terrors,
Man from his errors.

Father and Saviour! plant within each bosom
The seeds of holiness, and bid them blossom
In fragrance and in beauty bright and vernal,
And spring eternal.

JOHN BOWRING.

NEARER HOME.

ONE sweetly solemn thought
Comes to me o'er and o'er;
I 'm nearer my home to-day
Than I ever have been before;

Nearer my Father's house,
Where the many mansions be;
Nearer the great white throne,
Nearer the crystal sea;

Nearer the bound of life,
Where we lay our burdens down;
Nearer leaving the cross,
Nearer gaining the crown!

But the waves of that silent sea
Roll dark before my sight
That brightly the other side
Break on a shore of light.

O, if my mortal feet
Have almost gained the brink;

If it be I am nearer home
  Even to-day than I think, —

Father, perfect my trust!
  Let my spirit feel, in death,
That her feet are firmly set
  On the Rock of a living faith!

PHŒBE CARY.

THE SPACIOUS FIRMAMENT ON HIGH.

The spacious firmament on high,
With all the blue ethereal sky,
And spangled heavens, a shining frame,
Their great Original proclaim;
The unwearied sun, from day to day,
Does his Creator's power display,
And publishes to every land
The work of an Almighty hand.

Soon as the evening shades prevail,
The moon takes up the wondrous tale,
And nightly to the listening earth
Repeats the story of her birth;
While all the stars that round her burn,
And all the planets in their turn,
Confirm the tidings as they roll,
And spread the truth from pole to pole.

What though, in solemn silence, all
Move round the dark terrestrial ball?
What though no real voice or sound
Amid their radiant orbs be found?
In Reason's ear they all rejoice,
And utter forth a glorious voice,
Forever singing, as they shine,
"*The Hand that made us is divine!*"

JOSEPH ADDISON.

LORD! WHEN THOSE GLORIOUS LIGHTS I SEE —

HYMN AND PRAYER FOR THE USE OF BELIEVERS.

Lord! when those glorious lights I see
  With which thou hast adorned the skies,
Observing how they movèd be,
  And how their splendor fills mine eyes,
Methinks it is too large a grace,
  But that thy love ordained it so, —
That creatures in so high a place
  Should servants be to man below.

The meanest lamp now shining there
  In size and lustre doth exceed
The noblest of thy creatures here,
  And of our friendship hath no need.
Yet these upon mankind attend
  For secret aid or public light;
And from the world's extremest end
  Repair unto us every night.

O, had that stamp been undefaced
  Which first on us thy hand had set,
How highly should we have been graced,
  Since we are so much honored yet!
Good God, for what but for the sake
  Of thy beloved and only Son,
Who did on him our nature take,
  Were these exceeding favors done?

As we by him have honored been,
  Let us to him due honors give;
Let his uprightness hide our sin,
  And let us worth from him receive.
Yea, so let us by grace improve
  What thou by nature doth bestow,
That to thy dwelling-place above
  We may be raisèd from below.

GEORGE WITHER.

HYMN

BEFORE SUNRISE, IN THE VALE OF CHAMOUNI.

Hast thou a charm to stay the morning-star
In his steep course? So long he seems to pause
On thy bald, awful head, O sovereign Blanc!
The Arve and Arveiron at thy base
Rave ceaselessly; but thou, most awful Form,
Risest from forth thy silent sea of pines
How silently! Around thee and above,
Deep is the air and dark, substantial, black, —
An ebon mass. Methinks thou piercest it,
As with a wedge! But when I look again,
It is thine own calm home, thy crystal shrine,
Thy habitation from eternity!
O dread and silent Mount! I gazed upon thee,
Till thou, still present to the bodily sense,
Didst vanish from my thought. Entranced in prayer
I worshiped the Invisible alone.

  Yet, like some sweet beguiling melody,
So sweet we know not we are listening to it,
Thou, the mean while, wast blending with my thought, —
Yea, with my life and life's own secret joy, —
Till the dilating soul, enrapt, transfused,
Into the mighty vision passing, there,
As in her natural form, swelled vast to Heaven!

  Awake, my soul! not only passive praise
Thou owest! not alone these swelling tears,
Mute thanks, and secret ecstasy! Awake,

S. T. Coleridge

J. B. FORD & Co NEW YORK

Voice of sweet song! Awake, my heart, awake!
Green vales and icy cliffs, all join my hymn.

Thou first and chief, sole sovereign of the vale!
O, struggling with the darkness all the night,
And visited all night by troops of stars,
Or when they climb the sky or when they sink,
Companion of the morning-star at dawn,
Thyself Earth's rosy star, and of the dawn
Co-herald, — wake, O, wake, and utter praise!
Who sank thy sunless pillars deep in earth?
Who filled thy countenance with rosy light?
Who made thee parent of perpetual streams?

And you, ye five wild torrents fiercely glad!
Who called you forth from night and utter death,
From dark and icy caverns called you forth,
Down those precipitous, black, jagged rocks,
Forever shattered and the same forever?
Who gave you your invulnerable life,
Your strength, your speed, your fury, and your joy,
Unceasing thunder and eternal foam?
And who commanded (and the silence came),
Here let the billows stiffen, and have rest?

Ye ice-falls! ye that from the mountain's brow
Adown enormous ravines slope amain, —
Torrents, methinks, that heard a mighty voice,
And stopped at once amid their maddest plunge!
Motionless torrents! silent cataracts!
Who made you glorious as the gates of Heaven
Beneath the keen full moon? Who bade the sun
Clothe you with rainbows? Who, with living flowers
Of loveliest blue, spread garlands at your feet?
God! — let the torrents, like a shout of nations,
Answer! and let the ice-plains echo, God!
God! sing, ye meadow-streams, with gladsome voice!
Ye pine-groves, with your soft and soul-like sounds!
And they too have a voice, yon piles of snow,
And in their perilous fall shall thunder, God!
Ye living flowers that skirt the eternal frost!
Ye wild goats sporting round the eagle's nest!
Ye eagles, playmates of the mountain-storm!
Ye lightnings, the dread arrows of the clouds!
Ye signs and wonders of the elements!
Utter forth God, and fill the hills with praise!

Thou, too, hoar Mount! with thy sky-pointing peaks,
Oft from whose feet the avalanche, unheard,
Shoots downward, glittering through the pure serene,
Into the depth of clouds that veil thy breast, —
Thou too again, stupendous Mountain! thou
That, as I raise my head, awhile bowed low
In adoration, upward from thy base
Slow traveling with dim eyes suffused with tears,
Solemnly seemest, like a vapory cloud,
To rise before me, — Rise, O, ever rise!
Rise like a cloud of incense, from the Earth!
Thou kingly Spirit throned among the hills,
Thou dread ambassador from Earth to Heaven,
Great Hierarch! tell thou the silent sky,
And tell the stars, and tell yon rising sun,
Earth, with her thousand voices, praises God.

SAMUEL TAYLOR COLERIDGE.

AMAZING, BEAUTEOUS CHANGE!

AMAZING, beauteous change!
A world created new!
My thoughts with transport range,
The lovely scene to view;
In all I trace,
Saviour divine,
The work is thine, —
Be thine the praise!

See crystal fountains play
Amidst the burning sands;
The river's winding way
Shines through the thirsty lands;
New grass is seen,
And o'er the meads
Its carpet spreads
Of living green.

Where pointed brambles grew,
Intwined with horrid thorn,
Gay flowers, forever new,
The painted fields adorn, —
The blushing rose
And lily there,
In union fair,
Their sweets disclose.

Where the bleak mountain stood
All bare and disarrayed,
See the wide-branching wood
Diffuse its grateful shade;
Tall cedars nod,
And oaks and pines,
And elms and vines
Confess the God.

The tyrants of the plain
Their savage chase give o'er, —
No more they rend the slain,
And thirst for blood no more;
But infant hands
Fierce tigers stroke,
And lions yoke
In flowery bands.

O, when, Almighty Lord!
Shall these glad scenes arise,
To verify thy word,
And bless our wondering eyes?
That earth may raise,
With all its tongues,
United songs
Of ardent praise.

PHILIP DODDRIDGE.

THE SABBATH.

How still the morning of the hallowed day!
Mute is the voice of rural labor, hushed
The plowboy's whistle and the milkmaid's song.
The scythe lies glittering in the dewy wreath
Of tedded grass, mingled with fading flowers,
That yestermorn bloomed waving in the breeze;
Sounds the most faint attract the ear, — the hum
Of early bee, the trickling of the dew,
The distant bleating, midway up the hill.
Calmness sits throned on yon unmoving cloud.
To him who wanders o'er the upland leas
The blackbird's note comes mellower from the dale;
And sweeter from the sky the gladsome lark
Warbles his heaven-tuned song; the lulling brook
Murmurs more gently down the deep-worn glen;
While from yon lowly roof, whose circling smoke
O'ermounts the mist, is heard at intervals
The voice of psalms, the simple song of praise.
With dovelike wings Peace o'er yon village broods;
The dizzying mill-wheel rests; the anvil's din
Hath ceased; all, all around is quietness.
Less fearful on this day, the limping hare
Stops, and looks back, and stops, and looks on man,
Her deadliest foe. The toil-worn horse, set free,
Unheedful of the pasture, roams at large;
And as his stiff, unwieldy bulk he rolls,
His iron-armed hoofs gleam in the morning ray.

JAMES GRAHAME.

THE MEETING.

The elder folk shook hands at last,
Down seat by seat the signal passed.
To simple ways like ours unused,
Half solemnized and half amused,
With long-drawn breath and shrug, my guest
His sense of glad relief expressed.
Outside, the hills lay warm in sun;
The cattle in the meadow-run
Stood half-leg deep; a single bird
The green repose above us stirred.
"What part or lot have you," he said,
"In these dull rites of drowsy-head?
Is silence worship? Seek it where
It soothes with dreams the summer air;
Not in this close and rude-benched hall,
But where soft lights and shadows fall,
And all the slow, sleep-walking hours
Glide soundless over grass and flowers!
From time and place and form apart,
Its holy ground the human heart,
Nor ritual-bound nor templeward
Walks the free spirit of the Lord!
Our common Master did not pen
His followers up from other men;
His service liberty indeed,
He built no church, he framed no creed;
But while the saintly Pharisee
Made broader his phylactery,
As from the synagogue was seen
The dusty-sandaled Nazarene
Through ripening cornfields lead the way
Upon the awful Sabbath day,
His sermons were the healthful talk
That shorter made the mountain-walk,
His wayside texts were flowers and birds,
Where mingled with his gracious words
The rustle of the tamarisk-tree
And ripple-wash of Galilee."

"Thy words are well, O friend," I said;
"Unmeasured and unlimited,
With noiseless slide of stone to stone,
The mystic Church of God has grown.
Invisible and silent stands
The temple never made with hands,
Unheard the voices still and small
Of its unseen confessional.
He needs no special place of prayer
Whose hearing ear is everywhere;
He brings not back the childish days
That ringed the earth with stones of praise,
Roofed Karnak's hall of gods, and laid
The plinths of Philæ's colonnade.
Still less he owns the selfish good
And sickly growth of solitude, —
The worthless grace that, out of sight,
Flowers in the desert anchorite;
Dissevered from the suffering whole,
Love hath no power to save a soul.
Not out of Self, the origin
And native air and soil of sin,
The living waters spring and flow,
The trees with leaves of healing grow.

"Dream not, O friend, because I seek
This quiet shelter twice a week,
I better deem its pine-laid floor
Than breezy hill or sea-sung shore;

But nature is not solitude;
She crowds us with her thronging wood;
Her many hands reach out to us,
Her many tongues are garrulous;
Perpetual riddles of surprise
She offers to our ears and eyes;
She will not leave our senses still,
But drags them captive at her will;
And, making earth too great for heaven,
She hides the Giver in the given.

"And so I find it well to come
For deeper rest to this still room,
For here the habit of the soul
Feels less the outer world's control;
The strength of mutual purpose pleads
More earnestly our common needs;
And from the silence multiplied
By these still forms on either side,
The world that time and sense have known
Falls off and leaves us God alone.

"Yet rarely through the charmed repose
Unmixed the stream of motive flows,
A flavor of its many springs,
The tints of earth and sky it brings;
In the still waters needs must be
Some shade of human sympathy;
And here, in its accustomed place,
I look on memory's dearest face;
The blind by-sitter guesseth not
What shadow haunts that vacant spot;
No eyes save mine alone can see
The love wherewith it welcomes me!
And still, with those alone my kin,
In doubt and weakness, want and sin,
I bow my head, my heart I bare
As when that face was living there,
And strive (too oft, alas! in vain)
The peace of simple trust to gain,
Fold fancy's restless wings, and lay
The idols of my heart away.

"Welcome the silence all unbroken,
Nor less the words of fitness spoken, —
Such golden words as hers for whom
Our autumn flowers have just made room;
Whose hopeful utterance through and through
The freshness of the morning blew;
Who loved not less the earth that light
Fell on it from the heavens in sight,
But saw in all fair forms more fair
The Eternal beauty mirrored there.
Whose eighty years but added grace
And saintlier meaning to her face, —
The look of one who bore away
Glad tidings from the hills of day,
While all our hearts went forth to meet
The coming of her beautiful feet!
Or haply hers whose pilgrim tread
Is in the paths where Jesus led;
Who dreams her childhood's sabbath dream
By Jordan's willow-shaded stream,
And, of the hymns of hope and faith,
Sung by the monks of Nazareth,
Hears pious echoes, in the call
To prayer, from Moslem minarets fall,
Repeating where His works were wrought
The lesson that her Master taught,
Of whom an elder Sibyl gave,
The prophesies of Cumæ's cave!

"I ask no organ's soulless breath
To drone the themes of life and death,
No altar candle-lit by day,
No ornate wordsman's rhetoric-play,
No cool philosophy to teach
Its bland audacities of speech
To doubled-tasked idolaters,
Themselves their gods and worshipers,
No pulpit hammered by the fist
Of loud-asserting dogmatist,
Who borrows for the hand of love
The smoking thunderbolts of Jove.
I know how well the fathers taught,
What work the later schoolmen wrought;
I reverence old-time faith and men,
But God is near us now as then;
His force of love is still unspent,
His hate of sin as imminent;
And still the measure of our needs
Outgrows the cramping bounds of creeds;
The manna gathered yesterday
Already savors of decay;
Doubts to the world's child-heart unknown
Question us now from star and stone;
Too little or too much we know,
And sight is swift and faith is slow;
The power is lost to self-deceive
With shallow forms of make-believe.
We walk at high noon, and the bells
Call to a thousand oracles,
But the sound deafens, and the light
Is stronger than our dazzled sight;
The letters of the sacred Book
Glimmer and swim beneath our look;
Still struggles in the Age's breast
With deepening agony of quest
The old entreaty: 'Art thou He,
Or look we for the Christ to be?'

"God should be most where man is least;
So, where is neither church nor priest,
And never rag of form or creed
To clothe the nakedness of need, —
Where farmer-folk in silence meet, —

I turn my bell-unsummoned feet;
I lay the critic's glass aside,
I tread upon my lettered pride,
And, lowest-seated, testify
To the oneness of humanity;
Confess the universal want,
And share whatever Heaven may grant.
He findeth not who seeks his own,
The soul is lost that's saved alone.
Not on one favored forehead fell
Of old the fire-tongued miracle,
But flamed o'er all the thronging host
The baptism of the Holy Ghost;
Heart answers heart: in one desire
The blending lines of prayer aspire;
'Where, in my name, meet two or three,
Our Lord hath said, 'I there will be!'

"So sometimes comes to soul and sense
The feeling which is evidence
That very near about us lies
The realm of spiritual mysteries.
The sphere of the supernal powers
Impinges on this world of ours.
The low and dark horizon lifts,
To light the scenic terror shifts;
The breath of a diviner air
Blows down the answer of a prayer: —
That all our sorrow, pain, and doubt
A great compassion clasps about,
And law and goodness, love and force,
Are wedded fast beyond divorce.
Then duty leaves to love its task,
The beggar Self forgets to ask;
With smile of trust and folded hands,
The passive soul in waiting stands
To feel, as flowers the sun and dew,
The One true Life its own renew.

"So, to the calmly gathered thought
The innermost of truth is taught,
The mystery dimly understood,
That love of God is love of good,
And, chiefly, its divinest trace
In Him of Nazareth's holy face;
That to be saved is only this, —
Salvation from our selfishness,
From more than elemental fire,
The soul's unsanctified desire,
From sin itself, and not the pain
That warns us of its chafing chain;
That worship's deeper meaning lies
In mercy, and not sacrifice,
Not proud humilities of sense
And posturing of penitence,
But love's unforced obedience;
That Book and Church and Day are given
For man, not God, — for earth, not heaven, —
The blessèd means to holiest ends,
Not masters, but benignant friends;
That the dear Christ dwells not afar,
The king of some remoter star,
But flamed o'er all the thronging host
The baptism of the Holy Ghost;
Heart answers heart: in one desire
The blending lines of prayer aspire;
'Where, in my name, meet two or three,'
Our Lord hath said, 'I there will be!'"

JOHN GREENLEAF WHITTIER.

A PRAYER FOR LIFE.

O FATHER, let me not die young!
Earth's beauty asks a heart and tongue
To give true love and praises to her worth;
Her sins and judgment-sufferings call
For fearless martyrs to redeem thy Earth
From her disastrous fall.
For though her summer hills and vales might seem
The fair creation of a poet's dream, —
Ay, of the Highest Poet,
Whose wordless rhythms are chanted by the gyres
Of constellate star-choirs,
That with deep melody flow and overflow it, —
The sweet Earth, — very sweet, despite
The rank grave-smell forever drifting in
Among the odors from her censers white
Of wave-swung lilies and of wind-swung roses, —
The Earth sad-sweet is deeply attaint with sin!
The pure air, which encloses
Her and her starry kin,
Still shudders with the unspent palpitating
Of a great Curse, that to its utmost shore
Thrills with a deadly shiver
Which has not ceased to quiver
Down all the ages, nathless the strong beating
Of Angel-wings, and the defiant roar
Of Earth's Titanic thunders.

Fair and sad,
In sin and beauty, our belovèd Earth
Has need of all her sons to make her glad;
Has need of martyrs to refire the hearth
Of her quenched altars, — of heroic men
With freedom's sword, or Truth's supernal pen,
To shape the worn-out mold of nobleness again.
And she has need of Poets who can string
Their harps with steel to catch the lightning's fire,
And pour her thunders from the clanging wire,
To cheer the hero, mingling with his cheer,
Arouse the laggard in the battle's rear,

Daunt the stern wicked, and from discord wring
Prevailing harmony, while the humblest soul
Who keeps the tune the warder angels sing
In golden choirs above,
And only wears, for crown and aureole,
The glow-worm light of lowliest human love,
Shall fill with low, sweet undertones the chasms
Of silence, 'twixt the booming thunder-spasms.
And Earth has need of Prophets fiery-lipped
And deep-souled, to announce the glorious dooms
Writ on the silent heavens in starry script,
And flashing fitfully from her shuddering tombs, —
Commissioned Angels of the new-born Faith,
To teach the immortality of Good,
The soul's God-likeness, Sin's coeval death,
And Man's indissoluble Brotherhood.

Yet never an age, when God has need of him,
Shall want its Man, predestined by that need,
To pour his life in fiery word or deed, —
The strong Archangel of the Elohim!
Earth's hollow want is prophet of his coming:
In the low murmur of her famished cry,
And heavy sobs breathed up despairingly,
Ye hear the near invisible humming
Of his wide wings that fan the lurid sky
Into cool ripples of new life and hope,
While far in its dissolving ether ope
Deeps beyond deeps, of sapphire calm, to cheer
With Sabbath gleams the troubled Now and Here.

Father! thy will be done!
Holy and righteous One!
Though the reluctant years
May never crown my throbbing brows with white,
Nor round my shoulders turn the golden light
Of my thick locks to wisdom's royal ermine:
Yet by the solitary tears,
Deeper than joy or sorrow, — by the thrill,
Higher than hope or terror, whose quick germin,
In those hot tears to sudden vigor sprung,
Sheds, even now, the fruits of graver age, —
By the long wrestle in which inward ill
Fell like a trampled viper to the ground, —
By all that lifts me o'er my outward peers
To that supernal stage
Where soul dissolves the bonds by Nature bound, —
Fall when I may, by pale disease unstrung,
Or by the hand of fratricidal rage,
I cannot now die young!

ANONYMOUS.

WHEN.

If I were told that I must die to-morrow,
That the next sun
Which sinks should bear me past all fear and sorrow
For any one,
All the fight fought, all the short journey through,
What should I do?

I do not think that I should shrink or falter,
But just go on,
Doing my work, nor change nor seek to alter
Aught that is gone;
But rise and move and love and smile and pray
For one more day.

And, lying down at night for a last sleeping,
Say in that ear
Which hearkens ever: "Lord, within thy keeping
How should I fear?
And when to-morrow brings thee nearer still,
Do thou thy will."

I might not sleep for awe; but peaceful, tender,
My soul would lie
All the night long; and when the morning splendor
Flushed o'er the sky,
I think that I could smile — could calmly say,
"It is his day."

But if a wondrous hand from the blue yonder
Held out a scroll,
On which my life was writ, and I with wonder
Beheld unroll
To a long century's end its mystic clue,
What should I do?
What *could* I do, O blessed Guide and Master,

Other than this;
Still to go on as now, not slower, faster,
Nor fear to miss
The road, although so very long it be,
While led by thee?

Step after step, feeling thee close beside me,
Although unseen,
Through thorns, through flowers, whether the tempest hide thee,
Or heavens serene,
Assured thy faithfulness cannot betray,
Thy love decay.

I may not know; my God, no hand revealeth
Thy counsels wise;
Along the path a deepening shadow stealeth,
No voice replies
To all my questioning thought, the time to tell;
And it is well.

Let me keep on, abiding and unfearing
Thy will always,
Through a long century's ripening fruition
Or a short day's;
Thou canst not come too soon; and I can wait
If thou come late.

SUSAN COOLIDGE.

THE FLIGHT INTO EGYPT.

A BALLAD.

There 's a legend that 's told of a gypsy who dwelt
In the lands where the pyramids be;
And her robe was embroidered with stars, and her belt
With devices right wondrous to see;
And she lived in the days when our Lord was a child
On his mother's immaculate breast;
When he fled from his foes, — when to Egypt exiled,
He went down with St. Joseph the blest.

This Egyptian held converse with magic, methinks,
And the future was given to her gaze;
For an obelisk marked her abode, and a sphinx
On her threshold kept vigil always.
She was pensive and ever alone, nor was seen
In the haunts of the dissolute crowd;
But communed with the ghosts of the Pharaohs, I ween,
Or with visitors wrapped in a shroud.

And there came an old man from the desert one day,
With a maid on a mule by that road;
And a child on her bosom reclined, and the way
Led them straight to the gypsy's abode;
And they seemed to have traveled a wearisome path,
From thence many, many a league, —
From a tyrant's pursuit, from an enemy's wrath,
Spent with toil and o'ercome with fatigue.

And the gypsy came forth from her dwelling, and prayed
That the pilgrims would rest them awhile;
And she offered her couch to that delicate maid,
Who had come many, many a mile.
And she fondled the babe with affection's caress,
And she begged the old man would repose;
"Here the stranger," she said, "ever finds free access,
And the wanderer balm for his woes."

Then her guests from the glare of the noonday she led
To a seat in her grotto so cool;
Where she spread them a banquet of fruits, and a shed,
With a manger, was found for the mule;
With the wine of the palm-tree, with dates newly culled,
All the toil of the day she beguiled;
And with song in a language mysterious she lulled
On her bosom the wayfaring child.

When the gypsy anon in her Ethiop hand
Took the infant's diminutive palm,
O, 'twas fearful to see how the features she scanned
Of the babe in his slumbers so calm!
Well she noted each mark and each furrow that crossed
O'er the tracings of destiny's line:
"Whence came ye?" she cried, in astonishment lost,
"For this Child is of lineage Divine!"

"From the village of Nazareth," Joseph replied,
"Where we dwelt in the land of the Jew,
We have fled from a tyrant whose garment is dyed
In the gore of the children he slew:
We were told to remain till an angel's command
Should appoint us the hour to return;
But till then we inhabit the foreigners' land,
And in Egypt we make our sojourn."

"Then ye tarry with me," cried the gypsy in joy,
"And ye make of my dwelling your home;
Many years have I prayed that the Israelite boy
(Blessed hope of the Gentiles!) would come."
And she kissed both the feet of the infant and knelt,
And adored him at once; then a smile
Lit the face of his mother, who cheerfully dwelt
With her host on the banks of the Nile.

FRANCIS MAHONY (FATHER PROUT).

BURIAL OF MOSES.

"And he buried him in a valley in the land of Moab, over against Beth-peor; but no man knoweth of his sepulcher unto this day." — *Deut.* xxxiv. 6.

By Nebo's lonely mountain,
On this side Jordan's wave,
In a vale in the land of Moab,
There lies a lonely grave;
But no man built that sepulcher,
And no man saw it e'er;
For the angels of God upturned the sod,
And laid the dead man there.

That was the grandest funeral
That ever passed on earth;
Yet no man heard the trampling,
Or saw the train go forth:
Noiselessly as the daylight
Comes when the night is done,
And the crimson streak on ocean's cheek
Grows into the great sun;

Noiselessly as the spring-time
Her crown of verdure weaves,
And all the trees on all the hills
Unfold their thousand leaves :
So without sound of music
Or voice of them that wept,
Silently down from the mountain's crown
The great procession swept.

Perchance the bald old eagle
On gray Beth-peor's height
Out of his rocky eyry
Looked on the wondrous sight ;
Perchance the lion stalking
Still shuns that hallowed spot ;
For beast and bird have seen and heard
That which man knoweth not.

But, when the warrior dieth,
His comrades of the war,
With arms reversed and muffled drums,
Follow the funeral car :
They show the banners taken ;
They tell his battles won ;
And after him lead his masterless steed,
While peals the minute-gun.

Amid the noblest of the land
Men lay the sage to rest,
And give the bard an honored place,
With costly marbles drest,
In the great minster transept
Where lights like glories fall,
And the sweet choir sings, and the organ rings
Along the emblazoned hall.

This was the bravest warrior
That ever buckled sword ;
This the most gifted poet
That ever breathed a word ;
And never earth's philosopher
Traced with his golden pen
On the deathless page truths half so sage
As he wrote down for men.

And had he not high honor ? —
The hillside for a pall !
To lie in state while angels wait,
With stars for tapers tall !
And the dark rock-pines, like tossing plumes,
Over his bier to wave,
And God's own hand, in that lonely land,
To lay him in his grave ! —

In that strange grave without a name,
Whence his uncoffined clay
Shall break again — O wondrous thought ! —
Before the judgment-day,
And stand, with glory wrapped around,
On the hills he never trod,
And speak of the strife that won our life
With the incarnate Son of God.

O lonely tomb in Moab's land !
O dark Beth-peor's hill !
Speak to these curious hearts of ours,
And teach them to be still :
God hath his mysteries of grace,
Ways that we cannot tell,
He hides them deep, like the secret sleep
Of him he loved so well.

CECIL FRANCES ALEXANDER.

THE GREENWOOD SHRIFT.

GEORGE III. AND A DYING WOMAN IN WINDSOR FOREST.

OUTSTRETCHED beneath the leafy shade
Of Windsor forest's deepest glade,
A dying woman lay ;
Three little children round her stood,
And there went up from the greenwood
A woful wail that day.

"O mother !" was the mingled cry,
"O mother, mother ! do not die,
And leave us all alone."
"My blessèd babes !" she tried to say,
But the faint accents died away
In a low sobbing moan.

And then, life struggled hard with death,
And fast and strong she drew her breath,
And up she raised her head ;
And, peering through the deep wood maze
With a long, sharp, unearthly gaze,
"Will she not come ?" she said.

Just then, the parting boughs between,
A little maid's light form was seen,
All breathless with her speed ;
And, following close, a man came on
(A portly man to look upon),
Who led a panting steed.

"Mother !" the little maiden cried,
Or e'er she reached the woman's side,
And kissed her clay-cold cheek, —
"I have not idled in the town,
But long went wandering up and down,
The minister to seek.

"They told me here, they told me there, —
I think they mocked me everywhere ;
And when I found his home,

And begged him on my bended knee
To bring his book and come with me,
Mother! he would not come.

"I told him how you dying lay,
And could not go in peace away
Without the minister;
I begged him, for dear Christ his sake,
But O, my heart was fit to break, —
Mother! he would not stir.

"So, though my tears were blinding me,
I ran back, fast as fast could be,
To come again to you;
And here — close by — this squire I met,
Who asked (so mild) what made me fret;
And when I told him true, —

"'I will go with you, child,' he said,
'God sends me to this dying bed,' —
Mother, he 's here, hard by."
While thus the little maiden spoke,
The man, his back against an oak,
Looked on with glistening eye.

The bridle on his neck hung free,
With quivering flank and trembling knee,
Pressed close his bonny bay;
A statelier man, a statelier steed,
Never on greensward paced, I rede,
Than those stood there that day.

So, while the little maiden spoke,
The man, his back against an oak,
Looked on with glistening eye
And folded arms, and in his look
Something that, like a sermon-book,
Preached, — "All is vanity."

But when the dying woman's face
Turned toward him with a wishful gaze,
He stepped to where she lay;
And, kneeling down, bent over her,
Saying, "I am a minister,
My sister! let us pray."

And well, withouten book or stole,
(God's words were printed on his soul!)
Into the dying ear
He breathed, as 't were an angel's strain,
The things that unto life pertain,
And death's dark shadows clear.

He spoke of sinners' lost estate,
In Christ renewed, regenerate, —
Of God's most blest decree,
That not a single soul should die
Who turns repentant, with the cry
"Be merciful to me."

He spoke of trouble, pain, and toil,
Endured but for a little while
In patience, faith, and love, —
Sure, in God's own good time, to be
Exchanged for an eternity
Of happiness above.

Then, as the spirit ebbed away,
He raised his hands and eyes to pray
That peaceful it might pass;
And then — the orphans' sobs alone
Were heard, and they knelt, every one,
Close round on the green grass.

Such was the sight their wandering eyes
Beheld, in heart-struck, mute surprise,
Who reined their coursers back,
Just as they found the long astray,
Who, in the heat of chase that day,
Had wandered from their track.

But each man reined his pawing steed,
And lighted down, as if agreed,
In silence at his side;
And there, uncovered all, they stood, —
It was a wholesome sight and good
That day for mortal pride.

For of the noblest of the land
Was that deep-hushed, bareheaded band;
And, central in the ring,
By that dead pauper on the ground,
Her ragged orphans clinging round,
Knelt their anointed king.

ROBERT and CAROLINE SOUTHEY.

THE RELIGION OF HUDIBRAS.

He was of that stubborn crew
Of errant saints, whom all men grant
To be the true church militant;
Such as do build their faith upon
The holy text of pike and gun;
Decide all controversies by
Infallible artillery,
And prove their doctrine orthodox
By apostolic blows and knocks;
Call fire, and sword, and desolation
A godly, thorough Reformation,
Which always must be carried on
And still be doing, never done;
As if religion were intended
For nothing else but to be mended.
A sect whose chief devotion lies
In odd perverse antipathies;
In falling out with that or this,
And finding somewhat still amiss;

More peevish, cross, and splenetic,
Than dog distract, or monkey sick;
That with more care keep holiday
The wrong than others the right way;
Compound for sins they are inclined to,
By damning those they have no mind to;
Still so perverse and opposite,
As if they worshiped God for spite;
The selfsame thing they will abhor
One way, and long another for.

SAMUEL BUTLER.

THE FAITHFUL ANGEL.

FROM "PARADISE LOST."

The seraph Abdiel, faithful found
Among the faithless, faithful only he;
Among innumerable false, unmoved,
Unshaken, unseduced, unterrified,
His loyalty he kept, his love, his zeal;
Nor number, nor example with him wrought
To swerve from truth, or change his constant mind,
Though single. From amidst them forth he passed,
Long way through hostile scorn, which he sustained
Superior, nor of violence feared aught;
And with retorted scorn his back he turned
On those proud towers to swift destruction doomed.

MILTON.

THE REAPER'S DREAM.

The road was lone; the grass was dank
With night-dews on the briery bank
Whereon a weary reaper sank.
His garb was old; his visage tanned;
The rusty sickle in his hand
Could find no work in all the land.

He saw the evening's chilly star
Above his native vale afar;
A moment on the horizon's bar
It hung, then sank, as with a sigh;
And there the crescent moon went by,
An empty sickle down the sky.

To soothe his pain, Sleep's tender palm
Laid on his brow its touch of balm;
His brain received the slumberous calm;
And soon that angel without name,
Her robe a dream, her face the same,
The giver of sweet visions came.

She touched his eyes; no longer sealed,
They saw a troop of reapers wield
Their swift blades in a ripened field.
At each thrust of their snowy sleeves
A thrill ran through the future sheaves
Rustling like rain on forest leaves.

They were not brawny men who bowed,
With harvest-voices rough and loud,
But spirits, moving as a cloud.
Like little lightnings in their hold,
The silver sickles manifold
Slid musically through the gold.

O, bid the morning stars combine
To match the chorus clear and fine,
That rippled lightly down the line, —
A cadence of celestial rhyme,
The language of that cloudless clime,
To which their shining hands kept time!

Behind them lay the gleaming rows,
Like those long clouds the sunset shows
On amber meadows of repose;
But, like a wind, the binders bright
Soon followed in their mirthful might,
And swept them into sheaves of light.

Doubling the splendor of the plain,
There rolled the great celestial wain,
To gather in the fallen grain.
Its frame was built of golden bars;
Its glowing wheels were lit with stars;
The royal Harvest's car of cars.

The snowy yoke that drew the load,
On gleaming hoofs of silver trode;
And music was its only goad.
To no command of word or beck
It moved, and felt no other check
Than one white arm laid on the neck, —

The neck, whose light was overwound
With bells of lilies, ringing round
Their odors till the air was drowned:
The starry foreheads meekly borne,
With garlands looped from horn to horn,
Shone like the many-colored morn.

The field was cleared. Home went the bands,
Like children, linking happy hands,
While singing through their father's lands;
Or, arms about each other thrown,
With amber tresses backward blown,
They moved as they were music's own.

The vision brightening more and more,
He saw the garner's glowing door,
And sheaves, like sunshine, strew the floor, —
The floor was jasper, — golden flails,
Swift-sailing as a whirlwind sails,
Throbbed mellow music down the vales.

He saw the mansion, — all repose, —
Great corridors and porticoes,
Propped with the columns, shining rows;
And these — for beauty was the rule —
The polished pavements, hard and cool,
Redoubled, like a crystal pool.

And there the odorous feast was spread;
The fruity fragrance, widely shed,
Seemed to the floating music wed.
Seven angels, like the Pleiad seven,
Their lips to silver clarions given,
Blew welcome round the walls of heaven.

In skyey garments, silky thin,
The glad retainers floated in
A thousand forms, and yet no din:
And from the visage of the Lord,
Like splendor from the Orient poured,
A smile illumined all the board.

Far flew the music's circling sound;
Then floated back, with soft rebound,
To join, not mar, the converse round, —
Sweet notes, that, melting, still increased,
Such as ne'er cheered the bridal feast
Of king in the enchanted East.

Did any great door ope or close,
It seemed the birth-time of repose,
The faint sound died where it arose;
And they who passed from door to door,
Their soft feet on the polished floor
Met their soft shadows, — nothing more.

Then once again the groups were drawn
Through corridors, or down the lawn,
Which bloomed in beauty like a dawn:
Where countless fountains leapt alway,
Veiling their silver heights in spray,
The choral people held their way.

There, midst the brightest, brightly shone
Dear forms he loved in years agone, —
The earliest loved, — the earliest flown.
He heard a mother's sainted tongue,
A sister's voice, who vanished young,
While one still dearer sweetly sung!

No further might the scene unfold;
The gazer's voice could not withhold;
The very rapture made him bold:
He cried aloud, with claspèd hands,
"O happy fields! O happy bands,
Who reap the never-failing lands!

"O master of these broad estates,
Behold, before your very gates
A worn and wanting laborer waits!
Let me but toil amid your grain,
Or be a gleaner on the plain,
So I may leave these fields of pain!

"A gleaner, I will follow far,
With never look or word to mar,
Behind the Harvest's yellow car;
All day my hand shall constant be,
And every happy eve shall see
The precious burden borne to thee!"

At morn some reapers neared the place,
Strong men, whose feet recoiled apace;
Then, gathering round the upturned face,
They saw the lines of pain and care,
Yet read in the expression there
The look as of an answered prayer.

THOMAS BUCHANAN READ.

THE COTTER'S SATURDAY NIGHT.

INSCRIBED TO R. AIKEN, ESQ.

"Let not ambition mock their useful toil,
Their homely joys and destiny obscure;
Nor grandeur hear, with a disdainful smile,
The short but simple annals of the poor." — GRAY.

My loved, my honored, much-respected friend,
No mercenary bard his homage pays:
With honest pride I scorn each selfish end;
My dearest meed, a friend's esteem and praise.
To you I sing, in simple Scottish lays,
The lowly train in life's sequestered scene;
The native feelings strong, the guileless ways;
What Aiken in a cottage would have been;
Ah! though his worth unknown, far happier there, I ween.

November chill blaws loud wi' angry sugh;
The shortening winter-day is near a close;
The miry beasts retreating frae the pleugh,
The blackening trains o' craws to their repose;
The toilworn cotter frae his labor goes, —
This night his weekly moil is at an end, —
Collects his spades, his mattocks, and his hoes,
Hoping the morn in ease and rest to spend,
And weary, o'er the moor, his course does hameward bend.

At length his lonely cot appears in view,
Beneath the shelter of an aged tree;
Th' expectant wee things, toddlin', stacher through
To meet their dad, wi' flichterin' noise an' glee.
His wee bit ingle, blinking bonnily,
His clean hearthstane, his thriftie wifie's smile,

Eng^d by Geo E. Perine, New York.

Robert Burns

J. B. FORD & C° NEW YORK.

The lisping infant prattling on his knee,
Does a' his weary carking cares beguile,
And makes him quite forget his labor and his toil.

Belyve the elder bairns come drapping in,
At service out amang the farmers roun';
Some ca' the pleugh, some herd, some tentie rin
A cannie errand to a neibor town;
Their eldest hope, their Jenny, woman grown,
In youthfu' bloom, love sparkling in her e'e,
Comes hame, perha'ps, to shew a bra' new gown,
Or deposit her sair-won penny-fee,
To help her parents dear, if they in hardship be.

Wi' joy unfeigned brothers and sisters meet,
An' each for other's weelfare kindly spiers:
The social hours, swift-winged, unnoticed fleet;
Each tells the uncos that he sees or hears;
The parents, partial, eye their hopeful years;
Anticipation forward points the view:
The mother, wi' her needle an' her shears,
Gars auld claes look amaist as weel 's the new;
The father mixes a' wi' admonition due.

Their master's an' their mistress's command,
The younkers a' are warnèd to obey;
And mind their labors wi' an eydent hand,
And ne'er, though out o' sight, to jauk or play;
"An' O, be sure to fear the Lord alway!
An' mind your duty, duly, morn an' night!
Lest in temptation's path ye gang astray,
Implore his counsel and assisting might;
They never sought in vain that sought the Lord aright!"

But, hark! a rap comes gently to the door.
Jenny, wha kens the meaning o' the same,
Tells how a neibor lad cam o'er the moor,
To do some errands and convoy her hame.
The wily mother sees the conscious flame
Sparkle in Jenny's e'e, and flush her cheek;
Wi' heart-struck anxious care inquires his name,
While Jenny hafflins is afraid to speak;
Weel pleased the mother hears it 's nae wild, worthless rake.

Wi' kindly welcome, Jenny brings him ben;
A strappin' youth; he taks the mother's e'e;
Blithe Jenny sees the visit 's no ill ta'en;
The father cracks of horses, pleughs, and kye.
The youngster's artless heart o'erflows wi' joy,
But blate and lathefu', scarce can weel behave;
The mother, wi' a woman's wiles, can spy
What makes the youth sae bashfu' an' sae grave;
Weel pleased to think her bairn 's respected like the lave.

O happy love! where love like this is found!
O heartfelt raptures! bliss beyond compare!
I 've pacèd much this weary mortal round,
And sage experience bids me this declare:—
If Heaven a draught of heavenly pleasure spare,
One cordial in this melancholy vale,
'T is when a youthful, loving, modest pair
In other's arms breathe out the tender tale,
Beneath the milk-white thorn that scents the evening gale.

Is there, in human form, that bears a heart,
A wretch, a villain, lost to love and truth,
That can, with studied, sly, ensnaring art,
Betray sweet Jenny's unsuspecting youth?
Curse on his perjured arts! dissembling smooth!
Are honor, virtue, conscience, all exiled?
Is there no pity, no relenting ruth,
Points to the parents fondling o'er their child,
Then paints the ruined maid, and their distraction wild?

But now the supper crowns their simple board,
The halesome parritch, chief o' Scotia's food;
The soupe their only hawkie does afford,
That 'yont the hallan snugly chows her cood;
The dame brings forth, in complimental mood,
To grace the lad, her weel-hained kebbuck fell,
An' aft he 's prest, an' aft he ca's it guid;
The frugal wifie, garrulous, will tell,
How 't was a towmond auld, sin' lint was i' the bell.

The cheerfu' supper done, wi' serious face,
They, round the ingle, form a circle wide;
The sire turns o'er, wi' patriarchal grace,
The big ha'-Bible, ance his father's pride;
His bonnet reverently is laid aside,
His lyart haffets wearing thin an' bare:
Those strains that once did sweet in Zion glide,
He wales a portion with judicious care;
And "Let us worship God!" he says with solemn air.

They chant their artless notes in simple guise;
They tune their hearts, by far the noblest aim:
Perhaps "Dundee's" wild-warbling measures rise,
Or plaintive "Martyrs," worthy of the name;
Or noble "Elgin" beets the heavenward flame,
The sweetest far of Scotia's holy lays:
Compared with these, Italian trills are tame;
The tickled ears no heartfelt raptures raise;
Nae unison hae they with our Creator's praise.

The priest-like father reads the sacred page,—
How Abram was the friend of God on high;

Or Moses bade eternal warfare wage
With Amalek's ungracious progeny,
Or how the royal bard did groaning lie
Beneath the stroke of Heaven's avenging ire;
Or Job's pathetic plaint, and wailing cry;
Or rapt Isaiah's wild, seraphic fire;
Or other holy seers that tune the sacred lyre.

Perhaps the Christian volume is the theme,—
How guiltless blood for guilty man was shed;
How He, who bore in heaven the second name,
Had not on earth whereon to lay his head:
How his first followers and servants sped;
The precepts sage they wrote to many a land;
How he, who lone in Patmos banishèd,
Saw in the sun a mighty angel stand,
And heard great Bab'lon's doom pronounced by Heaven's command.

Then, kneeling down, to heaven's eternal King,
The saint, the father, and the husband prays:
Hope "springs exulting on triumphant wing,"
That thus they all shall meet in future days;
There ever bask in uncreated rays,
No more to sigh, or shed the bitter tear,
Together hymning their Creator's praise,
In such society, yet still more dear;
While circling Time moves round in an eternal sphere.

Compared with this, how poor Religion's pride,
In all the pomp of method and of art,
When men display to congregations wide,
Devotion's every grace, except the heart!
The Power, incensed, the pageant will desert,
The pompous strain, the sacerdotal stole;
But, haply, in some cottage far apart,
May hear, well pleased, the language of the soul;
And in his Book of Life the inmates poor enroll.

Then homeward all take off their several way;
The youngling cottagers retire to rest:
The parent-pair their secret homage pay,
And proffer up to Heaven the warm request,
That He who stills the raven's clamorous nest,
And decks the lily fair in flowery pride,
Would, in the way his wisdom sees the best,
For them and for their little ones provide;
But, chiefly, in their hearts with grace divine preside.

From scenes like these old Scotia's grandeur springs,
That makes her loved at home, revered abroad;
Princes and lords are but the breath of kings,
"An honest man's the noblest work of God!"
And certes, in fair Virtue's heavenly road,
The cottage leaves the palace far behind:
What is a lordling's pomp?—a cumbrous load,
Disguising oft the wretch of human kind,
Studied in arts of hell, in wickedness refined!

O Scotia! my dear, my native soil!
For whom my warmest wish to Heaven is sent,
Long may thy hardy sons of rustic toil
Be blest with health, and peace, and sweet content!
And, O, may Heaven their simple lives prevent
From luxury's contagion, weak and vile!
Then, howe'er crowns and coronets be rent,
A virtuous populace may rise the while,
And stand a wall of fire around their much-loved isle.

O Thou! who poured the patriotic tide,
That streamed through Wallace's undaunted heart;
Who dared to nobly stem tyrannic pride,
Or nobly die, the second glorious part,
(The patriot's God peculiarly thou art,
His friend, inspirer, guardian, and reward!)
O, never, never Scotia's realm desert;
But still the patriot and the patriot bard
In bright succession raise, her ornament and guard!

ROBERT BURNS.

THE OTHER WORLD.

It lies around us like a cloud, —
A world we do not see;
Yet the sweet closing of an eye
May bring us there to be.

Its gentle breezes fan our cheek;
Amid our worldly cares
Its gentle voices whisper love,
And mingle with our prayers.

Sweet hearts around us throb and beat,
Sweet helping hands are stirred,
And palpitates the veil between
With breathings almost heard.

The silence — awful, sweet, and calm —
They have no power to break;
For mortal words are not for them
To utter or partake.

So thin, so soft, so sweet they glide,
So near to press they seem, —
They seem to lull us to our rest,
And melt into our dream.

And in the hush of rest they bring
'T is easy now to see
How lovely and how sweet a pass
The hour of death may be.

To close the eye, and close the ear,
Wrapped in a trance of bliss,
And gently dream in loving arms
To swoon to that — from this.

Scarce knowing if we wake or sleep,
Scarce asking where we are,
To feel all evil sink away,
All sorrow and all care.

Sweet souls around us! watch us still,
Press nearer to our side,
Into our thoughts, into our prayers,
With gentle helpings glide.

Let death between us be as naught,
A dried and vanished stream;
Your joy be the reality,
Our suffering life the dream.

HARRIET BEECHER STOWE.

THE LOVE OF GOD.

All things that are on earth shall wholly pass away,
Except the love of God, which shall live and last for aye.
The forms of men shall be as they had never been;
The blasted groves shall lose their fresh and tender green;
The birds of the thicket shall end their pleasant song,
And the nightingale shall cease to chant the evening long.
The kine of the pasture shall feel the dart that kills,
And all the fair white flocks shall perish from the hills.
The goat and antlered stag, the wolf and the fox,
The wild boar of the wood, and the chamois of the rocks,
And the strong and fearless bear, in the trodden dust shall lie;
And the dolphin of the sea, and the mighty whale, shall die.
And realms shall be dissolved, and empires be no more,
And they shall bow to death, who ruled from shore to shore;
And the great globe itself, so the holy writings tell,
With the rolling firmament, where the starry armies dwell,
Shall melt with fervent heat — they shall all pass away,
Except the love of God, which shall live and last for aye.

From the Provençal of BERNARD RASCAS, by WILLIAM CULLEN BRYANT.

THE MASTER'S TOUCH.

In the still air the music lies unheard;
In the rough marble beauty hides unseen:
To make the music and the beauty, needs
The master's touch, the sculptor's chisel keen.

Great Master, touch us with thy skillful hand;
Let not the music that is in us die!
Great Sculptor, hew and polish us; nor let,
Hidden and lost, thy form within us lie!

Spare not the stroke! do with us as thou wilt!
Let there be naught unfinished, broken, marred;
Complete thy purpose, that we may become
Thy perfect image, thou our God and Lord!

HORATIUS BONAR.

ALL 'S WELL.

The day is ended. Ere I sink to sleep,
My weary spirit seeks repose in thine!
Father, forgive my trespasses, and keep
This little life of mine!

With loving kindness curtain thou my bed,
And cool in rest my burning pilgrim feet;
Thy pardon be the pillow for my head:
So shall my rest be sweet.

At peace with all the world, dear Lord, and thee,
No fears my soul's unwavering faith can shake!
All 's well, whichever side the grave for me
The morning light may break.

ANONYMOUS.

CANA.

Dear Friend! whose presence in the house,
Whose gracious word benign,
Could once, at Cana's wedding feast,
Change water into wine;

Come, visit us! and when dull work
Grows weary, line on line,
Revive our souls, and let us see
Life's water turned to wine.

Gay mirth shall deepen into joy,
Earth's hopes grow half divine,
When Jesus visits us, to make
Life's water glow as wine.

The social talk, the evening fire,
  The homely household shrine,
Grow bright with angel visits, when
  The Lord pours out the wine.

For when self-seeking turns to love,
  Not knowing mine nor thine,
The miracle again is wrought,
  And water turned to wine.

JAMES FREEMAN CLARKE.

QUIET FROM GOD.

QUIET from God! It cometh not to still
  The vast and high aspirings of the soul,
The deep emotions which the spirit fill,
  And speed its purpose onward to the goal;
    It dims not youth's bright eye,
      Bends not joy's lofty brow,
    No guiltless ecstasy
      Need in its presence bow.

It comes not in a sullen form, to place
  Life's greatest good in an inglorious rest;
Through a dull, beaten track its way to trace,
  And to lethargic slumber lull the breast;
    Action may be its sphere,
      Mountain paths, boundless fields,
    O'er billows its career:
      This is the power it yields:

To sojourn in the world, and yet apart;
  To dwell with God, yet still with man to feel;
To bear about forever in the heart
  The gladness which his spirit doth reveal;
    Not to deem evil gone
      From every earthly scene;
    To see the storm come on,
      But feel his shield between.

It giveth not a strength to human kind,
  To leave all suffering powerless at its feet,
But keeps within the temple of the mind
  A golden altar, and a mercy-seat;
    A spiritual ark,
      Bearing the peace of God
    Above the waters dark,
      And o'er the desert's sod.

How beautiful within our souls to keep
  This treasure, the All-Merciful hath given;
To feel, when we awake, and when we sleep,
  Its incense round us, like a breeze from heaven!
    Quiet at hearth and home,
      Where the heart's joys begin;
    Quiet where'er we roam,
      Quiet around, within.

Who shall make trouble? — not the evil minds
  Which like a shadow o'er creation lower;
The spirit peace hath so attunèd, finds
  There feelings that may own the Calmer's power;
    What may she not confer,
      E'en where she must condemn?
    They take not peace from her,
      She may speak peace to them!

ANONYMOUS.

THE WAY, THE TRUTH, AND THE LIFE.

O THOU, great Friend to all the sons of men,
  Who once appeared in humblest guise below,
Sin to rebuke, to break the captive's chain,
  And call thy brethren forth from want and
    woe, —

We look to thee! thy truth is still the Light
  Which guides the nations, groping on their way,
Stumbling and falling in disastrous night,
  Yet hoping ever for the perfect day.

Yes; thou art still the Life, thou art the Way
  The holiest know; Light, Life, the Way of
    heaven!
And they who dearest hope and deepest pray,
  Toil by the Light, Life, Way, which thou hast
    given.

THEODORE PARKER.

THERE WAS SILENCE IN HEAVEN.

CAN angel spirits need repose
  In the full sunlight of the sky?
And can the veil of slumber close
  A cherub's bright and blazing eye?

Have seraphim a weary brow,
  A fainting heart, an aching breast?
No, far too high their pulses flow
  To languish with inglorious rest.

O, not the death-like calm of sleep
  Could hush the everlasting song;
No fairy dream or slumber deep
  Entrance the rapt and holy throng.

Yet not the lightest tone was heard
  From angel voice or angel hand;
And not one plumèd pinion stirred
  Among the pure and blissful band.

For there was silence in the sky,
  A joy not angel tongues could tell,
As from its mystic fount on high
  The peace of God in stillness fell.

O, what is silence here below?
The fruit of a concealed despair;
The pause of pain, the dream of woe; —
It is the rest of rapture there.

And to the wayworn pilgrim here,
More kindred seems that perfect peace,
Than the full chants of joy to hear
Roll on, and never, never cease.

From earthly agonies set free,
Tired with the path too slowly trod,
May such a silence welcome me
Into the palace of my God.

ANONYMOUS.

FOREVER WITH THE LORD.

FOREVER with the Lord!
Amen! so let it be!
Life from the dead is in that word,
And immortality.

Here in the body pent,
Absent from him I roam,
Yet nightly pitch my moving tent
A day's march nearer home.

My Father's house on high,
Home of my soul! how near,
At times, to faith's foreseeing eye
Thy golden gates appear!

Ah! then my spirit faints
To reach the land I love,
The bright inheritance of saints,
Jerusalem above!

Yet clouds will intervene,
And all my prospect flies;
Like Noah's dove, I flit between
Rough seas and stormy skies.

Anon the clouds depart,
The winds and waters cease;
While sweetly o'er my gladdened heart
Expands the bow of peace!

Beneath its glowing arch,
Along the hallowed ground,
I see cherubic armies march,
A camp of fire around.

I hear at morn and even,
At noon and midnight hour,
The choral harmonies of heaven
Earth's Babel tongues o'erpower.

Then, then I feel that he,
Remembered or forgot,
The Lord, is never far from me,
Though I perceive him not.

In darkness as in light,
Hidden alike from view,
I sleep, I wake, as in his sight
Who looks all nature through.

All that I am, have been,
All that I yet may be,
He sees at once, as he hath seen,
And shall forever see.

"Forever with the Lord":
Father, if 't is thy will,
The promise of that faithful word
Unto thy child fulfill!

So, when my latest breath
Shall rend the veil in twain,
By death I shall escape from death,
And life eternal gain.

JAMES MONTGOMERY.

THE SABBATH OF THE SOUL.

SLEEP, sleep to-day, tormenting cares,
Of earth and folly born;
Ye shall not dim the light that streams
From this celestial morn.

To-morrow will be time enough
To feel your harsh control;
Ye shall not violate, this day,
The Sabbath of my soul.

Sleep, sleep forever, guilty thoughts;
Let fires of vengeance die;
And, purged from sin, may I behold
A God of purity!

ANNA L. BARBAULD.

SEARCH AFTER GOD.

I SOUGHT thee round about, O thou my God!
In thine abode.
I said unto the earth, "Speak, art thou he?"
She answered me,
"I am not." I inquired of creatures all,
In general,
Contained therein. They with one voice proclaim
That none amongst them challenged such a name.

I asked the seas and all the deeps below,
My God to know;
I asked the reptiles and whatever is
In the abyss, —

Even from the shrimp to the leviathan
Inquiry ran;
But in those deserts which no line can sound,
The God I sought for was not to be found.

I asked the air if that were he; but lo!
It told me "No."
I from the towering eagle to the wren
Demanded then
If any feathered fowl 'mongst them were such;
But they all, much
Offended with my question, in full choir,
Answered, "To find thy God thou must look higher."

I asked the heavens, sun, moon, and stars; but they
Said, "We obey
The God thou seekest." I asked what eye or ear
Could see or hear, —
What in the world I might descry or know
Above, below;
With an unanimous voice, all these things said,
"We are not God, but we by him were made."

I asked the world's great universal mass
If that God was;
Which with a mighty and strong voice replied,
As stupefied, —
"I am not he, O man! for know that I
By him on high
Was fashioned first of nothing; thus instated
And swayed by him by whom I was created."

I sought the court; but smooth-tongued flattery there
Deceived each ear;
In the thronged city there was selling, buying,
Swearing, and lying;
I' the country, craft in simpleness arrayed,
And then I said, —
"Vain is my search, although my pains be great;
Where my God is there can be no deceit."

A scrutiny within myself I then
Even thus began:
"O man, what art thou?" What more could I say
Than dust and clay, —
Frail, mortal, fading, a mere puff, a blast,
That cannot last;
Enthroned to-day, to-morrow in an urn,
Formed from that earth to which I must return?

I asked myself what this great God might be
That fashioned me.
I answered: The all-potent, sole, immense,
Surpassing sense;
Unspeakable, inscrutable, eternal,
Lord over all;
The only terrible, strong, just, and true,
Who hath no end, and no beginning knew.

He is the well of life, for he doth give
To all that live
Both breath and being; he is the Creator
Both of the water,
Earth, air, and fire. Of all things that subsist
He hath the list, —
Of all the heavenly host, or what earth claims,
He keeps the scroll, and calls them by their names.

And now, my God, by thine illumining grace,
Thy glorious face
(So far forth as it may discovered be)
Methinks I see;
And though invisible and infinite,
To human sight
Thou, in thy mercy, justice, truth, appearest,
In which, to our weak sense, thou comest nearest.

O, make us apt to seek and quick to find,
Thou, God, most kind!
Give us love, hope, and faith, in thee to trust,
Thou, God, most just!
Remit all our offenses, we entreat,
Most good! most great!
Grant that our willing, though unworthy quest
May, through thy grace, admit us 'mongst the blest.

THOMAS HEYWOOD.

HUMILITY.

The bird that soars on highest wing
Builds on the ground her lowly nest;
And she that doth most sweetly sing,
Sings in the shade when all things rest:
In lark and nightingale we see,
What honor hath Humility.

When Mary chose the better part,
She meekly sat at Jesus' feet;
And Lydia's gently opened heart
Was made for God's own temple meet.
Fairest and best adorned is she
Whose clothing is Humility.

The saint that wears heaven's brightest crown,
In deepest adoration bends;
The weight of glory bears him down
The most when most his soul ascends.
Nearest the throne itself must be
The footstool of Humility.

ANONYMOUS.

EDWIN AND PAULINUS:

THE CONVERSION OF NORTHUMBRIA.

THE black-haired gaunt Paulinus
By ruddy Edwin stood: —
"Bow down, O king of Deira,
Before the blessèd Rood!
Cast out thy heathen idols,
And worship Christ our Lord."
— But Edwin looked and pondered,
And answered not a word.

Again the gaunt Paulinus
To ruddy Edwin spake:
"God offers life immortal
For his dear Son's own sake!
Wilt thou not hear his message,
Who bears the keys and sword?"
— But Edwin looked and pondered,
And answered not a word.

Rose then a sage old warrior
Was fivescore winters old;
Whose beard from chin to girdle
Like one long snow-wreath rolled: —
"At Yule-time in our chamber
We sit in warmth and light,
While cold and howling round us
Lies the black land of Night.

"Athwart the room a sparrow
Darts from the open door:
Within the happy hearth-light
One red flash, — and no more!
We see it come from darkness,
And into darkness go: —
So is our life, King Edwin!
Alas, that it is so!

"But if this pale Paulinus
Have somewhat more to tell;
Some news of Whence and Whither,
And where the soul will dwell; —
If on that outer darkness
The sun of Hope may shine; —
He makes life worth the living!
I take his God for mine!"

So spake the wise old warrior;
And all about him cried,
"Paulinus' God hath conquered!
And he shall be our guide: —
For he makes life worth living
Who brings this message plain,
When our brief days are over,
That we shall live again."

ANONYMOUS.

THE LOVE OF GOD SUPREME.

THOU hidden love of God, whose height,
Whose depth unfathomed no man knows,
I see from far thy beauteous light,
Inly I sigh for thy repose.
My heart is pained, nor can it be
At rest till it finds rest in thee.

Thy secret voice invites me still
The sweetness of thy yoke to prove,
And fain I would; but though my will
Be fixt, yet wide my passions rove.
Yet hindrances strew all the way;
I aim at thee, yet from thee stray.

"'T is mercy all that thou hast brought
My mind to seek her peace in thee.
Yet while I seek but find thee not
No peace my wand'ring soul shall see.
Oh! when shall all my wand'rings end,
And all my steps to-thee-ward tend?

Is there a thing beneath the sun
That strives with thee my heart to share?
Ah! tear it thence and reign alone,
The Lord of every motion there.
Then shall my heart from earth be free,
When it has found repose in thee.

Oh! hide this self from me, that I
No more, but Christ in me, may live.
My vile affections crucify,
Nor let one darling lust survive.
In all things nothing may I see,
Nothing desire or seek but thee.

O Love, thy sovereign aid impart,
To save me from low-thoughted care;
Chase this self-will through all my heart,
Through all its latent mazes there.
Make me thy duteous child, that I
Ceaseless may Abba, Father, cry.

Ah! no; ne'er will I backward turn:
Thine wholly, thine alone I am.
Thrice happy he who views with scorn
Earth's toys, for thee his constant flame.
Oh! help, that I may never move
From the blest footsteps of thy love.

Each moment draw from earth away
My heart, that lowly waits thy call.
Speak to my inmost soul, and say,
"I am thy Love, thy God, thy All."
To feel thy power, to hear thy voice,
To taste thy love is all my choice.

JOHN WESLEY.

THE STAR OF BETHLEHEM.

As shadows cast by cloud and sun
  Flit o'er the summer grass,
So, in thy sight, Almighty One,
  Earth's generations pass.

And while the years, an endless host,
  Come pressing swiftly on,
The brightest names that earth can boast
  Just glisten and are gone.

Yet doth the Star of Bethlehem shed
  A luster pure and sweet,
And still it leads, as once it led,
  To the Messiah's feet.

O Father, may that holy star
  Grow every year more bright,
And send its glorious beams afar
  To fill the world with light.

WILLIAM CULLEN BRYANT.

THE RIGHT MUST WIN.

O, IT is hard to work for God,
  To rise and take his part
Upon this battle-field of earth,
  And not sometimes lose heart!

He hides himself so wondrously,
  As though there were no God;
He is least seen when all the powers
  Of ill are most abroad.

Or he deserts us at the hour
  The fight is all but lost;
And seems to leave us to ourselves
  Just when we need him most.

Ill masters good, good seems to change
  To ill with greatest ease;
And, worst of all, the good with good
  Is at cross-purposes.

Ah! God is other than we think;
  His ways are far above,
Far beyond reason's height, and reached
  Only by childlike love.

Workman of God! O, lose not heart,
  But learn what God is like;
And in the darkest battle-field
  Thou shalt know where to strike.

Thrice blest is he to whom is given
  The instinct that can tell
That God is on the field when he
  Is most invisible.

Blest, too, is he who can divine
  Where real right doth lie,
And dares to take the side that seems
  Wrong to man's blindfold eye.

For right is right, since God is God;
  And right the day must win;
To doubt would be disloyalty,
  To falter would be sin!

FREDERIC WILLIAM FABER.

A DYING HYMN.

EARTH, with its dark and dreadful ills,
  Recedes and fades away;
Lift up your heads, ye heavenly hills;
  Ye gates of death, give way!

My soul is full of whispered song, —
  My blindness is my sight;
The shadows that I feared so long
  Are full of life and light.

The while my pulses fainter beat,
  My faith doth so abound;
I feel grow firm beneath my feet
  The green, immortal ground.

That faith to me a courage gives
  Low as the grave to go:
I know that my Redeemer lives, —
  That I shall live I know.

The palace walls I almost see
  Where dwells my Lord and King!
O grave, where is thy victory?
  O death, where is thy sting?

ALICE CARY.

HOPEFULLY WAITING.

"Blessed are they who are homesick, for they shall come at last to their Father's house." — HEINRICH STILLING.

NOT as you meant, O learned man, and good!
  Do I accept thy words of truth and rest;
  God, knowing all, knows what for me is best,
And gives me what I need, not what he could,
      Nor always as I would!
I shall go to the Father's house, and see
  Him and the Elder Brother face to face, —
What day or hour I know not. Let me be
  Steadfast in work, and earnest in the race,
    Not as a homesick child who all day long
    Whines at its play, and seldom speaks in song.

If for a time some loved one goes away,
And leaves us our appointed work to do,
Can we to him or to ourselves be true
In mourning his departure day by day,
And so our work delay?
Nay, if we love and honor, we shall make
The absence brief by doing well our task, —
Not for ourselves, but for the dear One's sake.
And at his coming only of him ask
Approval of the work, which most was done,
Not for ourselves, but our Belovèd One.

Our Father's house, I know, is broad and grand;
In it how many, many mansions are!
And far beyond the light of sun or star,
Four little ones of mine through that fair land
Are walking hand in hand!
Think you I love not, or that I forget
These of my loins? Still this world is fair,
And I am singing while my eyes are wet
With weeping in this balmy summer air:
Yet I 'm not homesick, and the children *here*
Have need of me, and so my way is clear.

I would be joyful as my days go by,
Counting God's mercies to me. He who bore
Life's heaviest cross is mine forevermore,
And I who wait his coming, shall not I
On his sure word rely?
And if sometimes the way be rough and steep,
Be heavy for the grief he sends to me,
Or at my waking I would only weep,
Let me remember these are things to be,
To work his blessed will until he come
To take my hand, and lead me safely home.

A. D. F. RANDOLPH.

WHY THUS LONGING?

WHY thus longing, thus forever sighing
For the far off, unattained, and dim,
While the beautiful, all round thee lying,
Offers up its low perpetual hymn?

Wouldst thou listen to its gentle teaching,
All thy restless yearnings it would still,
Leaf and flower and laden bee are preaching
Thine own sphere, though humble, first to fill.

Poor indeed thou must be, if around thee
Thou no ray of light and joy canst throw,
If no silken chord of love hath bound thee
To some little world through weal and woe;

If no dear eyes thy fond love can brighten,
No fond voices answer to thine own,
If no brother's sorrow thou canst lighten
By daily sympathy and gentle tone.

Not by deeds that gain the world's applauses,
Not by works that win thee world-renown,
Not by martyrdom or vaunted crosses,
Canst thou win and wear the immortal crown.

Daily struggling, though unloved and lonely,
Every day a rich reward will give;
Thou wilt find by hearty striving only,
And truly loving, thou canst truly live.

Dost thou revel in the rosy morning
When all nature hails the Lord of light,
And his smile, nor low nor lofty scorning,
Gladdens hall and hovel, vale and height?

Other hands may grasp the field and forest,
Proud proprietors in pomp may shine,
But with fervent love if thou adorest,
Thou art wealthier, — all the world is thine.

Yet if through earth's wide domains thou rovest,
Sighing that they are not thine alone,
Not those fair fields, but thyself thou lovest,
And their beauty and thy wealth are gone.

HARRIET WINSLOW SEWALL.

THE LOVE OF GOD.

THOU Grace Divine, encircling all,
A soundless, shoreless sea!
Wherein at last our souls must fall,
O Love of God most free!

When over dizzy heights we go,
One soft hand blinds our eyes,
The other leads us, safe and slow,
O Love of God most wise!

And though we turn us from thy face,
And wander wide and long,
Thou hold'st us still in thine embrace,
O Love of God most strong!

The saddened heart, the restless soul,
The toilworn frame and mind,
Alike confess thy sweet control,
O Love of God most kind!

But not alone thy care we claim,
Our wayward steps to win;
We know thee by a dearer name,
O Love of God within!

And filled and quickened by thy breath,
Our souls are strong and free
To rise o'er sin and fear and death,
O Love of God, to thee!

ELIZA SCUDDER.

MY TIMES ARE IN THY HAND.

FATHER, I know that all my life
  Is portioned out for me,
And the changes that will surely come,
  I do not fear to see;
But I ask thee for a present mind
  Intent on pleasing thee.

I ask thee for a thoughtful love,
  Through constant watching wise,
To meet the glad with joyful smiles,
  And to wipe the weeping eyes;
And a heart at leisure from itself,
  To soothe and sympathize.

I would not have the restless will
  That hurries to and fro,
Seeking for some great thing to do,
  Or secret thing to know;
I would be treated as a child,
  And guided where I go.

Wherever in the world I am,
  In whatsoe'er estate,
I have a fellowship with hearts
  To keep and cultivate;
And a work of lowly love to do,
  For the Lord on whom I wait.

So I ask thee for the daily strength,
  To none that ask denied;
And a mind to blend with outward life,
  While keeping at thy side,
Content to fill a little space,
  If thou be glorified.

And if some things I do not ask
  In my cup of blessing be,
I would have my spirit filled the more
  With grateful love to thee;
And careful, less to serve thee much
  Than to please thee perfectly.

There are briers besetting every path,
  Which call for patient care;
There is a cross in every lot,
  And an earnest need for prayer;
But a lowly heart that leans on thee
  Is happy anywhere.

In a service which thy love appoints,
  There are no bonds for me;
For my secret heart is taught "the truth"
  That makes thy children "free";
And a life of self-renouncing love
  Is a life of liberty.

ANNA L. WARING.

THE SOUL'S DEFIANCE.

I SAID to Sorrow's awful storm
  That beat against my breast,
Rage on, — thou mayst destroy this form,
  And lay it low at rest;
But still the spirit that now brooks
  Thy tempest, raging high,
Undaunted on its fury looks,
  With steadfast eye.

I said to Penury's meager train,
  Come on, — your threats I brave;
My last poor life-drop you may drain,
  And crush me to the grave;
Yet still the spirit that endures
  Shall mock your force the while,
And meet each cold, cold grasp of yours
  With bitter smile.

I said to cold Neglect and Scorn,
  Pass on, — I heed you not;
Ye may pursue me till my form
  And being are forgot;
Yet still the spirit, which you see
  Undaunted by your wiles,
Draws from its own nobility
  Its highborn smiles.

I said to Friendship's menaced blow,
  Strike deep, — my heart shall bear;
Thou canst but add one bitter woe
  To those already there;
Yet still the spirit that sustains
  This last severe distress
Shall smile upon its keenest pains,
  And scorn redress.

I said to Death's uplifted dart,
  Aim sure, — O, why delay?
Thou wilt not find a fearful heart,
  A weak, reluctant prey;
For still the spirit, firm and free,
  Unruffled by this last dismay,
Wrapt in its own eternity,
  Shall pass away.

LAVINIA STODDARD.

I SAW THEE.

"When thou wast under the fig-tree, I saw thee."

I SAW thee when, as twilight fell,
And evening lit her fairest star,
Thy footsteps sought yon quiet dell,
The world's confusion left afar.

I saw thee when thou stoodst alone,
Where drooping branches thick o'erhung,

Thy still retreat to all unknown,
Hid in deep shadows darkly flung.

I saw thee when, as died each sound
Of bleating flock or woodland bird,
Kneeling, as if on holy ground,
Thy voice the listening silence heard.

I saw thy calm uplifted eyes,
And marked the heaving of thy breast,
When rose to heaven thy heartfelt sighs
For purer life, for perfect rest.

I saw the light that o'er thy face
Stole with a soft, suffusing glow,
As if, within, celestial grace
Breathed the same bliss that angels know.

I saw — what thou didst not — above
Thy lowly head an open heaven;
And tokens of thy Father's love
With smiles to thy rapt spirit given.

I saw thee from that sacred spot
With firm and peaceful soul depart;
I, Jesus, saw thee, — doubt it not, —
And read the secrets of thy heart!

RAY PALMER.

FROM "SAINT PAUL."

CHRIST! I am Christ's! and let the name suffice you,
Ay, for me too he greatly hath sufficed:
Lo, with no winning words I would entice you,
Paul has no honor and no friend but Christ.

Yes, without cheer of sister or of daughter,
Yes, without stay of father or of son,
Lone on the land and homeless on the water,
Pass I in patience till the work be done.

Yet not in solitude if Christ anear me
Waketh him workers for the great employ,
O, not in solitude, if souls that hear me
Catch from my joyance the surprise of joy.

Hearts I have won of sister or of brother,
Quick on the earth or hidden in the sod,
Lo, every heart awaiteth me, another
Friend in the blameless family of God.

What was their sweet desire and subtle yearning,
Lovers, and ladies whom their song enrolls?
Faint to the flame which in my breast is burning,
Less than the love with which I ache for souls.

. . . . .

Then with a ripple and a radiance through me
Rise and be manifest, O Morning Star!
Flow on my soul, thou Spirit, and renew me,
Fill with thyself, and let the rest be far.

Safe to the hidden house of thine abiding
Carry the weak knees and the heart that faints;
Shield from the scorn and cover from the chiding;
Give the world joy, but patience to the saints.

Saints, did I say? with your remembered faces,
Dear men and women, whom I sought and slew!
Ah, when we mingle in the heavenly places,
How will I weep to Stephen and to you!

O for the strain that rang to our reviling
Still, when the bruised limbs sank upon the sod;
O for the eyes that looked their last in smiling,
Last on this world here, but their first on God!

. . . . .

O, could I tell, ye surely would believe it!
O, could I only say what I have seen!
How should I tell or how can ye receive it,
How, till He bringeth you where I have been?

Therefore, O Lord, I will not fail or falter;
Nay, but I ask it, nay, but I desire;
Lay on my lips thine embers of the altar,
Seal with the sting and furnish with the fire;

Give me a voice, a cry and a complaining, —
O, let my sound be stormy in their ears!
Throat that would shout but cannot stay for straining,
Eyes that would weep but cannot wait for tears.

Quick in a moment, infinite forever,
Send an arousal better than I pray;
Give me a grace upon the faint endeavor,
Souls for my hire and Pentecost to-day!

. . . . .

Hark what a sound, and too divine for hearing,
Stirs on the earth and trembles in the air!
Is it the thunder of the Lord's appearing?
Is it the music of his people's prayer?

Surely he cometh, and a thousand voices
Shout to the saints and to the deaf are dumb;
Surely he cometh, and the earth rejoices,
Glad in his coming who hath sworn, I come.

This hath he done, and shall we not adore him?
This shall he do, and can we still despair?
Come, let us quickly fling ourselves before him,
Cast at his feet the burden of our care,

Flash from our eyes the glow of our thanksgiving,
Glad and regretful, confident and calm;
Then through all life and what is after living
Thrill to the tireless music of a psalm.

Yea, through life, death, through sorrow and through sinning,
He shall suffice me, for he hath sufficed:
Christ is the end, for Christ was the beginning,
Christ the beginning, for the end is Christ.

FREDERIC W. H. MYERS.

THE CHRISTIAN CALLING.

THY night is dark; behold, the shade was deeper
In the old garden of Gethsemane,
When that calm voice awoke the weary sleeper:
"Couldst thou not watch one hour alone with me?"

O thou, so weary of thy self-denials!
And so impatient of thy little cross,
Is it so hard to bear thy daily trials,
To count all earthly things a gainful loss?

What if thou *always* suffer tribulation,
And if thy Christian warfare never cease;
The gaining of the quiet habitation
Shall gather thee to everlasting peace.

But here we all must suffer, walking lonely
The path that Jesus once himself hath gone:
Watch thou in patience through the dark hour only,
This one dark hour, — before the eternal dawn.

The captive's oar may pause upon the galley,
The soldier sleep beneath his plumèd crest,
And Peace may fold her wing o'er hill and valley,
But thou, O Christian! must not take thy rest.

Thou must walk on, however man upbraid thee,
With Him who trod the wine-press all alone;
Thou wilt not find one human hand to aid thee,
One human soul to comprehend thine own.

Heed not the images forever thronging
From out the foregone life thou liv'st no more;
Faint-hearted mariner! still art thou longing
For the dim line of the receding shore.

Canst thou forget thy Christian supersciption,
"Behold, we count them happy which endure"?
What treasure wouldst thou, in the land Egyptian,
Repass the stormy water to secure?

Poor, wandering soul! I know that thou art seeking
Some easier way, as all have sought before,
To silence the reproachful inward speaking, —
Some landward path unto an island shore.

O, that thy faithless soul, one great hour only,
Would comprehend the Christian's perfect life;
Despised with Jesus, sorrowful and lonely,
Yet calmly looking upward in its strife.

In meek obedience to the heavenly Teacher,
Thy weary soul can find its only peace;
Seeking no aid from any human creature, —
Looking to God alone for his release.

And he will come in his own time and power
To set his earnest-hearted children free:
Watch only through this dark and painful hour,
And the bright morning yet will break for thee.

ANONYMOUS.

THE SOUL'S CRY.

"I cry unto Thee daily." — Ps. lxxxvi. 3.

O, EVER from the deeps
Within my soul, oft as I muse alone,
Comes forth a voice that pleads in tender tone;
As when one long unblest
Sighs ever after rest;
Or as the wind perpetual murmuring keeps.

I hear it when the day
Fades o'er the hills, or 'cross the shimmering sea;
In the soft twilight, as is wont to be,
Without my wish or will,
While all is hushed and still,
Like a sad, plaintive cry heard far away.

Not even the noisy crowd,
That like some mighty torrent rushing down
Sweeps clamoring on, this cry of want can drown;
But ever in my heart
Afresh the echoes start;
I hear them still amidst the tumult loud.

Each waking morn anew
The sense of many a need returns again;
I feel myself a child, helpless as when
I watched my mother's eye,
As the slow hours went by,
And from her glance my being took its hue.

I cannot shape my way
Where nameless perils ever may betide,
O'er slippery steeps whereon my feet may slide;
Some mighty hand I crave,
To hold and help and save,
And guide me ever when my steps would stray.

There is but One, I know,
That all my hourly, endless wants can meet;
Can shield from harm, recall my wandering feet;
My God, thy hand can feed
And day by day can lead
Where the sweet streams of peace and safety flow.

RAY PALMER.

POEMS
of
NATURE

Tears, idle tears, I know not what they mean,
Tears from the depth of some divine despair
Rise in the heart & gather to the eyes
In looking on the happy Autumn fields,
And thinking on the days that are no more.

A Tennyson

They turned to the Earth, but she frowns on her child;
They turned to the Sea, and he smiled as of old:
Sweeter was the peril of the breakers white and wild,
Sweeter than the land, with its bondage and gold!

Bayard Taylor

POEMS OF NATURE.

WORLDLINESS.

THE World is too much with us ; late and soon,
Getting and spending, we lay waste our powers ;
Little we see in nature that is ours ;
We have given our hearts away, a sordid boon !

This sea that bares her bosom to the moon,
The winds that will be howling at all hours
And are up-gathered now like sleeping flowers,
For this, for everything, we are out of tune ;

It moves us not. — Great God ! I 'd rather be
A Pagan suckled in a creed outworn, —
So might I, standing on this pleasant lea,
Have glimpses that would make me less forlorn ;
Have sight of Proteus rising from the sea ;
Or hear old Triton blow his wreathèd horn.

WILLIAM WORDSWORTH.

NATURE.

THE bubbling brook doth leap when I come by,
Because my feet find measure with its call ;
The birds know when the friend they love is nigh,
For I am known to them, both great and small.
The flower that on the lonely hillside grows
Expects me there when spring its bloom has given ;
And many a tree and bush my wanderings knows
And e'en the clouds and silent stars of heaven ;
For he who with his Maker walks aright,
Shall be their lord as Adam was before ;
His ear shall catch each sound with new delight,
Each object wear the dress that then it wore ;
And he, as when erect in soul he stood,
Hear from his Father's lips that all is good.

JONES VERY.

TINTERN ABBEY.

I HAVE learned
To look on nature, not as in the hour
Of thoughtless youth, but hearing oftentimes
The still, sad music of humanity,
Not harsh nor grating, though of ample power
To chasten and subdue. And I have felt
A presence that disturbs me with the joy
Of elevated thoughts ; a sense sublime
Of something far more deeply interfused,
Whose dwelling is the light of setting suns,
And the round ocean, and the living air,
And the blue sky, and, in the mind of man,
A motion and a spirit that impels
All thinking things, all objects of all thought,
And rolls through all things. Therefore am I still
A lover of the meadows, and the woods,
And mountains, and of all that we behold
From this green earth ; of all the mighty world
Of eye and ear, both what they half create
And what perceive ; well pleased to recognize
In nature and the language of the sense
The anchor of my purest thoughts.

WILLIAM WORDSWORTH.

CORRESPONDENCES.

HEXAMETERS AND PENTAMETERS.

ALL things in nature are beautiful types to the soul that reads them ;
Nothing exists upon earth but for unspeakable ends ;
Every object that speaks to the senses was meant for the spirit ;
Nature is but a scroll ; God's handwriting thereon.
Ages ago, when man was pure, ere the flood overwhelmed him,
While in the image of God every soul yet lived,
Everything stood as a letter or word of a language familiar,
Telling of truths which now only the angels can read.
Lost to man was the key of those sacred hieroglyphics,
Stolen away by sin, till Heaven restored it ;
Now with infinite pains we here and there spell out a letter,
Here and there will the sense feebly shine through the dark.

When we perceive the light that breaks through the visible symbol,
What exultation is ours! We the discovery have made,
Yet is the meaning the same as when Adam lived sinless in Eden,
Only long hidden it slept, and now again is revealed.
Man unconsciously uses figures of speech every moment,
Little dreaming the cause why to such terms he is prone,
Little dreaming that everything here has its own correspondence
Folded within its form, as in the body the soul.
Gleams of the mystery fall on us still, though much is forgotten,
And through our commonest speech illumine the path of our thoughts.
Thus doth the lordly sun shine forth a type of God-head;
Wisdom and love the beams that stream on a darkened world.
Thus do the sparkling waters flow, giving joy to the desert,
And the fountain of life opens itself to the thirst.
Thus doth the word of God distill like the rain and the dew-drops;
Thus doth the warm wind breathe like to the spirit of God;
And the green grass and the flowers are signs of the regeneration.

O thou Spirit of Truth, visit our minds once more;
Give us to read in letters of light the language celestial,
Written all over the earth, written all over the sky, —
Thus may we bring our hearts once more to know our Creator,
Seeing in all things around, types of the Infinite Mind.

CHRISTOPHER P. CRANCH.

NATURE'S CHAIN.

FROM "THE ESSAY ON MAN."

LOOK round our world; behold the chain of love
Combining all below and all above,
See plastic nature working to this end,
The single atoms each to other tend,
Attract, attracted to, the next in place,
Formed and impelled its neighbor to embrace.
See matter next, with various life endued,
Press to one center still, the general good.
See dying vegetables life sustain,
See life dissolving vegetate again:
All forms that perish other forms supply
(By turns we catch the vital breath, and die);
Like bubbles on the sea of matter borne,
They rise, they break, and to that sea return.
Nothing is foreign; parts relate to whole;
One all-extending, all-preserving Soul
Connects each being, greatest with the least;
Made beast in aid of man, and man of beast;
All served, all serving; nothing stands alone;
The chain holds on, and where it ends, unknown.
Has God, thou fool! worked solely for thy good,
Thy joy, thy pastime, thy attire, thy food?
Who for thy table feeds the wanton fawn,
For him as kindly spreads the flowery lawn.
Is it for thee the lark ascends and sings?
Joy tunes his voice, joy elevates his wings.
Is it for thee the linnet pours his throat?
Loves of his own and raptures swell the note.
The bounding steed you pompously bestride
Shares with his lord the pleasure and the pride.
Is thine alone the seed that strews the plain?
The birds of heaven shall vindicate their grain.
Thine the full harvest of the golden year?
Part pays, and justly, the deserving steer:
The hog that plows not, nor obeys thy call,
Lives on the labors of this lord of all.
Know, Nature's children all divide her care;
The fur that warms a monarch warmed a bear.
While man exclaims, "See all things for my use!"
"See man for mine!" replies a pampered goose:
And just as short of reason he must fall
Who thinks all made for one, not one for all.
Grant that the powerful still the weak control;
Be man the wit and tyrant of the whole:
Nature that tyrant checks; he only knows,
And helps, another creature's wants and woes.
Say, will the falcon, stooping from above,
Smit with her varying plumage, spare the dove?
Admires the jay the insect's gilded wings?
Or hears the hawk when Philomela sings?
Man cares for all: to birds he gives his woods,
To beasts his pastures, and to fish his floods;
For some his interest prompts him to provide,
For more his pleasure, yet for more his pride:
All feed on one vain patron, and enjoy
The extensive blessing of his luxury.
That very life his learnèd hunger craves,
He saves from famine, from the savage saves;
Nay, feasts the animal he dooms his feast,
And, till he ends the being, makes it blest;
Which sees no more the stroke, or feels the pain,
Than favored man by touch ethereal slain.
The creature had his feast of life before;
Thou too must perish when thy feast is o'er!

ALEXANDER POPE.

THE IDLER.

WHEN days are long and skies are bright,
  When woods are green and fields are breezy,
I take my fill of air and light,
  And take — yes, take things rather easy.

You men of figures sneer, I know, —
  Call me an idle, dreamy fellow;
But my chief business here below
  Is, like the apple, to grow mellow.

I coax the fish in cove or creek;
  My light skiff rocks on rocking billow;
Or, weary, in some shade I seek
  A mossy hummock for my pillow.

There, stretched upon the checkered grass,
  Above the bare, brown margin growing,
I watch the still, soft shadows pass,
  Lulled by the hum of warm airs blowing.

On bending spray of tallest tree
  The brown thrush balanced takes his station,
And now in jest, now soberly,
  Holds forth, half song and half oration.

The red-capped workman on a limb,
  Up, down, in circles briskly hopping,
Nods to the helpmeet calling him,
  With knowing air his sage head dropping.

At times, by plashy shore, the still
  White-belted watchman springs his rattle,
While faintly from the distant hill
  Come tinkling bells and low of cattle.

The waves in long procession tread
  Upon the beach in solemn motion,
Fringed with white breakers; overhead,
  Cloud-islands dot the upper ocean.

I know you solid men will sneer;
  Call me a thriftless, idle fellow;
But, as I said, my business here
  Is, like the apples, to grow mellow.

And since the summer will not stay,
  And since the winter follows fleetly,
To fitly use the passing day
  Requires my time and thought completely.

But, if of life I get the best,
  The use of wealth without its fetters,
Am I more idle than the rest,
  Or wiser than the money-getters?

H. E. WARNER.

CREATION.

FROM "PARADISE LOST."

THE earth was formed, but in the womb as yet
Of waters, embryon immature involved,
Appeared not; over all the face of earth
Main ocean flowed, not idle; but, with warm
Prolific humor softening all her globe,
Fermented the great mother to conceive,
Satiate with genial moisture; when God said,
"Be gathered now, ye waters under heaven,
Into one place, and let dry land appear."
Immediately the mountains huge appear
Emergent, and their broad bare backs upheave
Into the clouds; their tops ascend the sky:
So high as heaved the tumid hills, so low
Down sunk a hollow bottom broad and deep,
Capacious bed of waters: thither they
Hasted with glad precipitance, uprolled,
As drops on dust conglobing from the dry:
Part rise in crystal wall, or ridge direct,
For haste; such flight the great command impressed
On the swift floods; as armies at the call
Of trumpet (for of armies thou hast heard)
Troop to their standard; so the watery throng,
Wave rolling after wave, where way they found,
If steep, with torrent rapture, if through plain,
Soft ebbing; nor withstood them rock or hill;
But they, or under ground, or circuit wide
With serpent error wandering, found their way,
And on the washy ooze deep channels wore;
Easy, ere God had bid the ground be dry,
All but within those banks, where rivers now
Stream, and perpetual draw their humid train.
The dry land, Earth; and the great receptacle
Of congregated waters, he called Seas;
And saw that it was good: and said, "Let the earth
Put forth the verdant grass, herb yielding seed,
And fruit-tree yielding fruit after her kind,
Whose seed is in herself upon the earth."
He scarce had said, when the bare earth, till then
Desert and bare, unsightly, unadorned,
Brought forth the tender grass, whose verdure clad
Her universal face with pleasant green;
Then herbs of every leaf, that sudden flowered
Opening their various colors, and made gay
Her bosom, smelling sweet: and, these scarce blown,
Forth flourished thick the clustering vine, forth crept
The swelling gourd, up stood the corny reed
Embattled in her field, and the humble shrub,
And bush with frizzled hair implicit: last
Rose, as in dance, the stately trees, and spread
Their branches hung with copious fruit, or gemmed

Their blossoms : with high woods the fields were crowned,
With tufts the valleys, and each fountain-side ;
With borders long the rivers : that earth now
Seemed like to heaven, a seat where gods might dwell,
Or wander with delight, and love to haunt
Her sacred shades : though God had yet not rained
Upon the earth, and man to till the ground
None was ; but from the earth a dewy mist
Went up, and watered all the ground, and each
Plant of the field ; which, ere it was in the earth,
God made, and every herb, before it grew
On the green stem : God saw that it was good :
So even and morn recorded the third day.
Again the Almighty spake, "Let there be lights
High in the expanse of heaven, to divide
The day from night ; and let them be for signs,
For seasons, and for days, and circling years ;
And let them be for lights, as I ordain
Their office in the firmament of heaven,
To give light on the earth" ; and it was so.
And God made two great lights, great for their use
To man, the greater to have rule by day,
The less by night, altern ; and made the stars,
And set them in the firmament of heaven
To illuminate the earth, and rule the day,
In their vicissitude, and rule the night,
And light from darkness to divide. God saw,
Surveying his great work, that it was good :
For of celestial bodies first the sun
A mighty sphere he framed, unlightsome first,
Though of ethereal mold ; then formed the moon
Globose, and every magnitude of stars,
And sowed with stars the heaven, thick as a field :
Of light by far the greater part he took,
Transplanted from her cloudy shrine, and placed
In the sun's orb, made porous to receive
And drink the liquid light ; firm to retain
Her gathered beams, great palace now of light.
Hither, as to their fountain, other stars
Repairing, in their golden urns drew light,
And hence the morning planet gilds her horns ;
By tincture or reflection they augment
Their small peculiar, though from human sight
So far remote, with diminution seen.
First in his east the glorious lamp was seen,
Regent of day, and all the horizon round
Invested with bright rays, jocund to run
His longitude through heaven's high road ; the gray
Dawn, and the Pleiades, before him danced,
Shedding sweet influence : less bright the moon,
But opposite in leveled west was set,
His mirror, with full face borrowing her light
From him ; for other light she needed none
In that aspéct, and still that distance keeps
Till night ; then in the east her turn she shines,
Revolved on heaven's great axle, and her reign
With thousand lesser lights dividual holds,
With thousand thousand stars, that then appeared
Spangling the hemisphere : then first adorned
With their bright luminaries that set and rose,
Glad evening and glad morn crowned the fourth day.
And God said, "Let the waters generate
Reptile with spawn abundant, living soul :
And let fowl fly above the earth, with wings
Displayed on the open firmament of heaven."
And God created the great whales, and each
Soul living, each that crept, which plenteously
The waters generated by their kinds ;
And every bird of wing after his kind ;
And saw that it was good, and blessed them, saying,
"Be fruitful, multiply, and in the seas,
And lakes, and running streams, the waters fill ;
And let the fowl be multiplied on the earth."
Forthwith the sounds and seas, each creek and bay
With fry innumerable swarm, and shoals
Of fish that with their fins, and shining scales,
Glide under the green wave, in sculls that oft
Bank the mid sea : part single, or with mate,
Graze the sea-weed their pasture, and through groves
Of coral stray ; or sporting with quick glance,
Show to the sun their waved coats dropt with gold ;
Or, in their pearly shells at ease, attend
Moist nutriment : or under rocks their food
In jointed armor watch : on smooth the seal
And bended dolphins play : part huge of bulk,
Wallowing unwieldy, enormous in their gait,
Tempest the ocean : there leviathan,
Hugest of living creatures, on the deep
Stretched like a promontory, sleeps or swims,
And seems a moving land ; and at his gills
Draws in, and at his trunk spouts out, a sea.
Meanwhile the tepid caves, and fens, and shores,
Their brood as numerous hatch, from the egg that soon
Bursting with kindly rupture forth disclosed
Their callow young ; but feathered soon and fledge
They summed their pens ; and, soaring the air sublime,
With clang despised the ground, under a cloud
In prospect : there the eagle and the stork
On cliffs and cedar-tops their eyries build ;
Part loosely wing the region, part more wise
In common, ranged in figure, wedge their way,
Intelligent of seasons, and set forth
Their aëry caravan, high over seas
Flying, and over lands, with mutual wing
Easing their flight ; so steers the prudent crane
Her annual voyage, borne on winds ; the air

Floats as they pass, fanned with unnumbered plumes;
From branch to branch the smaller birds with songs
Solaced the woods, and spread their painted wings
Till even; nor then the solemn nightingale
Ceased warbling, but all night tuned her soft lays:
Others, on silver lakes and rivers, bathed
Their downy breast; the swan with archèd neck,
Between her white wings mantling proudly, rows
Her state with oary feet; yet oft they quit
The dank, and, rising on stiff pennons, tower
The mid aërial sky: others on ground
Walked firm; the crested cock whose clarion sounds
The silent hours, and the other whose gay train
Adorns him, colored with the florid hue
Of rainbows and starry eyes. The waters thus
With fish replenished, and the air with fowl,
Evening and morn solemnized the fifth day.
The sixth, and of creation last, arose
With evening harps and matin; when God said,
"Let the earth bring forth soul living in her kind,
Cattle, and creeping things, and beast of the earth,
Each in their kind." The earth obeyed, and straight
Opening her fertile womb, teemed at a birth
Innumerous living creatures, perfect forms,
Limbed and full grown: out of the ground up rose,
As from his lair, the wild beast, where he wons
In forest wild, in thicket, brake, or den;
Among the trees in pairs they rose, they walked:
The cattle in the fields and meadows green;
Those rare and solitary, these in flocks
Pasturing at once, and in broad herds upsprung.
The grassy clods now calved; now half appeared
The tawny lion, pawing to get free
His hinder parts, then springs, as broke from bonds,
And rampant shakes his brinded mane; the ounce,
The libbard, and the tiger, as the mole
Rising, the crumbled earth above them threw
In hillocks: the swift stag from under ground
Bore up his branching head: scarce from his mold
Behemoth, biggest born of earth, upheaved
His vastness: fleeced the flocks and bleating rose,
As plants: ambiguous between sea and land
The river-horse, and scaly crocodile.
At once came forth whatever creeps the ground,
Insect or worm: those waved their limber fans
For wings, and smallest lineaments exact
In all the liveries decked of summer's pride,
With spots of gold and purple, azure and green;
These as a line their long dimension drew,
Streaking the ground with sinuous trace; not all
Minims of nature; some of serpent-kind,
Wondrous in length and corpulence, involved
Their snaky folds, and added wings. First crept
The parsimonious emmet, provident
Of future; in small room large heart enclosed;
Pattern of just equality perhaps
Hereafter, joined in her popular tribes
Of commonalty: swarming next appeared
The female bee, that feeds her husband drone
Deliciously, and builds her waxen cells
With honey stored: the rest are numberless,
And thou their natures knowest, and gavest them names,
Needless to thee repeated; nor unknown
The serpent, subtlest beast of all the field,
Of huge extent sometimes, with brazen eyes
And hairy mane terrific, though to thee
Not noxious, but obedient at thy call.

MILTON.

EACH AND ALL.

LITTLE thinks, in the field, yon red-cloaked clown,
Of thee from the hill-top looking down;
The heifer that lows in the upland farm,
Far-heard, lows not thine ear to charm;
The sexton, tolling his bell at noon,
Deems not that great Napoleon
Stops his horse, and lists with delight,
Whilst his files sweep round yon Alpine height;
Nor knowest thou what argument
Thy life to thy neighbor's creed has lent.
All are needed by each one;
Nothing is fair or good alone.
I thought the sparrow's note from heaven,
Singing at dawn on the alder bough;
I brought him home, in his nest, at even;
He sings the song, but it pleases not now,
For I did not bring home the river and sky;—
He sang to my ear, — they sang to my eye.
The delicate shells lay on the shore;
The bubbles of the latest wave
Fresh pearls to their enamel gave;
And the bellowing of the savage sea
Greeted their safe escape to me.
I wiped away the weeds and foam,
I fetched my sea-born treasures home;
But the poor, unsightly, noisome things
Had left their beauty on the shore,
With the sun and the sand and the wild uproar.
The lover watched his graceful maid,
As mid the virgin train she strayed,
Nor knew her beauty's best attire
Was woven still by the snow-white choir.
At last she came to his hermitage,
Like the bird from the woodlands to the cage;—
The gay enchantment was undone,

A gentle wife, but fairy none.
Then I said, "I covet truth;
Beauty is unripe childhood's cheat;
I leave it behind with the games of youth."—
As I spoke, beneath my feet
The ground-pine curled its pretty wreath,
Running over the club-moss burrs;
I inhaled the violet's breath;
Around me stood the oaks and firs;
Pine-cones and acorns lay on the ground;
Over me soared the eternal sky,
Full of light and of deity;
Again I saw, again I heard,
The rolling river, the morning bird;—
Beauty through my senses stole;
I yielded myself to the perfect whole.

RALPH WALDO EMERSON.

RETIREMENT.

INSCRIPTION IN A HERMITAGE.

Beneath this stony roof reclined,
I soothe to peace my pensive mind;
And while, to shade my lowly cave,
Embowering elms their umbrage wave,
And while the maple dish is mine,—
The beechen cup, unstained with wine,—
I scorn the gay licentious crowd,
Nor heed the toys that deck the proud.

Within my limits, lone and still,
The blackbird pipes in artless trill;
Fast by my couch, congenial guest,
The wren has wove her mossy nest:
From busy scenes and brighter skies,
To lurk with innocence, she flies,
Here hopes in safe repose to dwell,
Nor aught suspects the sylvan cell.

At morn I take my customed round,
To mark how buds yon shrubby mound,
And every opening primrose count,
That trimly paints my blooming mount;
Or o'er the sculptures, quaint and rude,
That grace my gloomy solitude,
I teach in winding wreaths to stray
Fantastic ivy's gadding spray.

At eve, within yon studious nook,
I ope my brass-embossèd book,
Portrayed with many a holy deed
Of martyrs, crowned with heavenly meed;
Then, as my taper waxes dim,
Chant, ere I sleep, my measured hymn,
And, at the close, the gleams behold
Of parting wings, bedropt with gold.

While such pure joys my bliss create,
Who but would smile at guilty state?
Who but would wish his holy lot
In calm oblivion's humble grot?
Who but would cast his pomp away,
To take my staff, and amice gray;
And to the world's tumultuous stage
Prefer the blameless hermitage?

THOMAS WARTON.

COME TO THESE SCENES OF PEACE.

Come to these scenes of peace,
Where, to rivers murmuring,
The sweet birds all the summer sing,
Where cares and toil and sadness cease!
Stranger, does thy heart deplore
Friends whom thou wilt see no more?
Does thy wounded spirit prove
Pangs of hopeless, severed love?
Thee the stream that gushes clear,
Thee the birds that carol near
Shall soothe, as silent thou dost lie
And dream of their wild lullaby;
Come to bless these scenes of peace,
Where cares and toil and sadness cease.

WILLIAM LISLE BOWLES.

SEE, O SEE!

See, O see!
How every tree,
Every bower,
Every flower,
A new life gives to others' joys;
While that I
Grief-stricken lie,
Nor can meet
With any sweet
But what faster mine destroys.
What are all the senses' pleasures
When the mind has lost all measures?

Hear, O hear!
How sweet and clear
The nightingale
And water's fall
In concert join for others' ear;
While to me,
For harmony,
Every air
Echoes despair,
And every drop provokes a tear.
What are all the senses' pleasures
When the soul has lost all measures?

JOHN DIGBY, EARL OF BRISTOL.

ON A BEAUTIFUL DAY.

O UNSEEN Spirit! now a calm divine
  Comes forth from thee, rejoicing earth and air!
Trees, hills, and houses, all distinctly shine,
  And thy great ocean slumbers everywhere.

The mountain ridge against the purple sky
  Stands clear and strong, with darkened rocks and dells,
And cloudless brightness opens wide and high
  A home aërial, where thy presence dwells.

The chime of bells remote, the murmuring sea,
  The song of birds in whispering copse and wood,
The distant voice of children's thoughtless glee,
  And maiden's song, are all one voice of good.

Amid the leaves' green mass a sunny play
  Of flash and shadow stirs like inward life;
The ship's white sail glides onward far away,
  Unhaunted by a dream of storm or strife.

JOHN STERLING.

INVOCATION TO LIGHT.

FROM "PARADISE LOST."

HAIL, holy Light, offspring of Heaven first-born!
Or of the Eternal coeternal beam
May I express thee unblamed? since God is light,
And never but in unapproachèd light
Dwelt from eternity, dwelt then in thee,
Bright effluence of bright essence increate!
Or hear'st thou rather pure ethereal stream,
Whose fountain who shall tell? Before the sun,
Before the heavens, thou wert, and at the voice
Of God, as with a mantle, didst invest
The rising world of waters dark and deep,
Won from the void and formless infinite.
Thee I revisit now with bolder wing,
Escaped the Stygian pool, though long detained
In that obscure sojourn, while in my flight
Through utter and through middle darkness borne,
With other notes than to the Orphean lyre,
I sung of Chaos and eternal Night,
Taught by the heavenly Muse to venture down
The dark descent, and up to re-ascend,
Though hard and rare: thee I revisit safe,
And feel thy sovereign vital lamp; but thou
Revisitest not these eyes, that roll in vain
To find thy piercing ray, and find no dawn;
So thick a drop serene hath quenched their orbs,
Or dim suffusion veiled. Yet not the more
Cease I to wander where the Muses haunt
Clear spring, or shady grove, or sunny hill,
Smit with the love of sacred song; but chief
Thee, Sion, and the flowery brooks beneath,
That wash thy hallowed feet, and warbling flow,
Nightly I visit: nor sometimes forget
Those other two equaled with me in fate,
So were I equaled with them in renown,
Blind Thamyris and blind Mæonides,
And Tiresias and Phineus, prophets old:
Then feed on thoughts that voluntary move
Harmonious numbers; as the wakeful bird
Sings darkling, and in shadiest covert hid
Tunes her nocturnal note. Thus with the year
Seasons return, but not to me returns
Day, or the sweet approach of even or morn,
Or sight of vernal bloom, or summer's rose,
Or flocks, or herds, or human face divine;
But cloud, instead, and ever-during dark,
Surrounds me, from the cheerful ways of men
Cut off, and for the book of knowledge fair
Presented with a universal blank
Of nature's works, to me expunged and rased,
And wisdom at one entrance quite shut out.
So much the rather thou, celestial Light,
Shine inward, and the mind through all her powers
Irradiate; there plant eyes, all mist from thence
Purge and disperse, that I may see and tell
Of things invisible to mortal sight.

MILTON.

FROM THE "HYMN TO LIGHT."

SAY, from what golden quivers of the sky
    Do all thy wingèd arrows fly?
    Swiftness and Power by birth are thine:
From thy great sire they came, thy sire, the Word Divine.

Thou in the Moon's bright chariot, proud and gay,
    Dost thy bright wood of stars survey;
    And all the year dost with thee bring
Of thousand flowery lights thine own nocturnal spring.

Thou, Scythian-like, dost round thy lands above
    The Sun's gilt tent forever move,
    And still, as thou in pomp dost go,
The shining pageants of the world attend thy show.

Nor amidst all these triumphs dost thou scorn
    The humble glow-worms to adorn,
    And with those living spangles gild
(O greatness without pride!) the bushes of the field.

Night and her ugly subjects thou dost fright,
    And Sleep, the lazy owl of night;
    Ashamed, and fearful to appear,
They screen their horrid shapes with the black hemisphere.

At thy appearance, Grief itself is said
    To shake his wings, and rouse his head:

And cloudy Care has often took
A gentle beamy smile, reflected from thy look.

When, goddess, thou lift'st up thy wakened head
Out of the morning's purple bed,
Thy quire of birds about thee play,
And all the joyful world salutes the rising day.

All the world's bravery, that delights our eyes,
Is but thy several liveries;
Thou the rich dye on them bestow'st,
Thy nimble pencil paints this landscape as thou go'st.

A crimson garment in the rose thou wear'st;
A crown of studded gold thou bear'st;
The virgin-lilies, in their white,
Are clad but with the lawn of almost naked light.

The violet, Spring's little infant, stands
Girt in thy purple swaddling-bands;
On the fair tulip thou dost dote;
Thou cloth'st it in a gay and party-colored coat.

Through the soft ways of Heaven, and air, and sea,
Which open all their pores to thee,
Like a clear river thou dost glide,
And with thy living stream through the close channels slide.

But the vast ocean of unbounded day,
In th' empyrean Heaven does stay.
Thy rivers, lakes, and springs, below,
From thence took first their rise, thither at last must flow.

ABRAHAM COWLEY.

DAYBREAK.

A WIND came up out of the sea,
And said, "O mists, make room for me!"

It hailed the ships, and cried, "Sail on,
Ye mariners, the night is gone!"

And hurried landward far away,
Crying, "Awake! it is the day!"

It said unto the forest, "Shout!
Hang all your leafy banners out!"

It touched the wood-bird's folded wing,
And said, "O bird, awake and sing!"

And o'er the farms, "O chanticleer,
Your clarion blow; the day is near!"

It whispered to the fields of corn,
"Bow down, and hail the coming morn!"

It shouted through the belfry-tower,
"Awake, O bell! proclaim the hour."

It crossed the churchyard with a sigh,
And said, "Not yet! in quiet lie."

HENRY WADSWORTH LONGFELLOW.

UP! QUIT THY BOWER!

UP! quit thy bower! late wears the hour,
Long have the rooks cawed round the tower;
O'er flower and tree loud hums the bee,
And the wild kid sports merrily.
The sun is bright, the sky is clear;
Wake, lady, wake! and hasten here.

Up, maiden fair! and bind thy hair,
And rouse thee in the breezy air!
The lulling stream that soothed thy dream
Is dancing in the sunny beam.
Waste not these hours, so fresh, so gay:
Leave thy soft couch and haste away!

Up! Time will tell the morning bell
Its service-sound has chimèd well;
The aged crone keeps house alone,
The reapers to the fields are gone.
Lose not these hours, so cool, so gay:
Lo! while thou sleep'st they haste away!

JOANNA BAILLIE.

MORNING.

IN the barn the tenant cock,
Close to partlet perched on high,
Briskly crows (the shepherd's clock!)
Jocund that the morning 's nigh.

Swiftly from the mountain's brow,
Shadows, nursed by night, retire:
And the peeping sunbeam now,
Paints with gold the village spire.

Philomel forsakes the thorn,
Plaintive where she prates at night;
And the lark, to meet the morn,
Soars beyond the shepherd's sight.

From the low-roofed cottage ridge,
See the chattering swallow spring;
Darting through the one-arched bridge,
Quick she dips her dappled wing.

Now the pine-tree's waving top
Gently greets the morning gale:
Kidlings now begin to crop
Daisies, on the dewy dale.

From the balmy sweets, uncloyed
(Restless till her task be done),
Now the busy bee 's employed
Sipping dew before the sun.

Trickling through the creviced rock,
Where the limpid stream distills,
Sweet refreshment waits the flock
When 't is sun-drove from the hills.

Colin 's for the promised corn
(Ere the harvest hopes are ripe)
Anxious ; — whilst the huntsman's horn,
Boldly sounding, drowns his pipe.

Sweet, O sweet, the warbling throng,
On the white emblossomed spray !
Nature's universal song
Echoes to the rising day.

JOHN CUNNINGHAM.

THE NORTHERN LIGHTS.

To claim the Arctic came the sun
With banners of the burning zone.
Unrolled upon their airy spars,
They froze beneath the light of stars ;
And there they float, those streamers old,
Those Northern Lights, forever cold !

BENJAMIN F. TAYLOR.

DAWN.

THE night was dark, though sometimes a faint star
A little while a little space made bright.
The night was long and like an iron bar
Lay heavy on the land : till o'er the sea
Slowly, within the East, there grew a light
Which half was starlight, and half seemed to be
The herald of a greater. The pale white
Turned slowly to pale rose, and up the height
Of heaven slowly climbed. The gray sea grew
Rose-colored like the sky. A white gull flew
Straight toward the utmost boundary of the East,
Where slowly the rose gathered and increased.
It was as on the opening of a door
By one that in his hand a lamp doth hold,
Whose flame is hidden by the garment's fold, —
The still air moves, the wide room is less dim.

More bright the East became, the ocean turned
Dark and more dark against the brightening sky, —
Sharper against the sky the long sea line.
The hollows of the breakers on the shore
Were green like leaves whereon no sun doth shine,
Though white the outer branches of the tree.
From rose to red the level heaven burned ;
Then sudden, as if a sword fell from on high,
A blade of gold flashed on the horizon's rim.

RICHARD W. GILDER.

PACK CLOUDS AWAY.

PACK clouds away, and welcome day,
With night we banish sorrow ;
Sweet air, blow soft ; mount, lark, aloft,
To give my love good morrow.
Wings from the wind to please her mind,
Notes from the lark I 'll borrow :
Bird, prune thy wing ; nightingale, sing,
To give my love good morrow.
To give my love good morrow,
Notes from them all I 'll borrow.

Wake from thy nest, robin redbreast,
Sing, birds, in every furrow ;
And from each hill let music shrill
Give my fair love good morrow.
Blackbird and thrush in every bush,
Stare, linnet, and cock-sparrow,
You petty elves, amongst yourselves,
Sing my fair love good morrow.
To give my love good morrow,
Sing, birds, in every furrow.

THOMAS HEYWOOD.

MORNING.

FROM "THE MINSTREL."

BUT who the melodies of morn can tell ?
The wild brook babbling down the mountain-side ;
The lowing herd ; the sheepfold's simple bell ;
The pipe of early shepherd dim descried
In the lone valley ; echoing far and wide
The clamorous horn along the cliffs above ;
The hollow murmur of the ocean-tide ;
The hum of bees, the linnet's lay of love,
And the full choir that wakes the universal grove.

The cottage curs at early pilgrim bark ;
Crowned with her pail the tripping milkmaid sings ;
The whistling plowman stalks afield ; and, hark !
Down the rough slope the ponderous wagon rings ;
Through rustling corn the hare astonished springs ;
Slow tolls the village-clock the drowsy hour ;
The partridge bursts away on whirring wings ;
Deep mourns the turtle in sequestered bower,
And shrill lark carols clear from her aërial tower.

JAMES BEATTIE.

THE SABBATH MORNING.

With silent awe I hail the sacred morn,
That slowly wakes while all the fields are still!
A soothing calm on every breeze is borne;
A graver murmur gurgles from the rill;
And echo answers softer from the hill;
And sweeter sings the linnet from the thorn:
The skylark warbles in a tone less shrill.
Hail, light serene! hail, sacred Sabbath morn!
The rooks float silent by in airy drove;
The sun a placid yellow luster throws;
The gales that lately sighed along the grove
Have hushed their downy wings in dead repose;
The hovering rack of clouds forgets to move, —
So smiled the day when the first morn arose!

JOHN LEYDEN.

RÊVE DU MIDI.

When o'er the mountain steeps
The hazy noontide creeps,
And the shrill cricket sleeps
Under the grass;
When soft the shadows lie,
And clouds sail o'er the sky,
And the idle winds go by,
With the heavy scent of blossoms as they pass, —

Then, when the silent stream
Lapses as in a dream,
And the water-lilies gleam
Up to the sun;
When the hot and burdened day
Rests on its downward way,
When the moth forgets to play,
And the plodding ant may dream her work is done, —

Then, from the noise of war
And the din of earth afar,
Like some forgotten star
Dropt from the sky, —
The sounds of love and fear,
All voices sad and clear,
Banished to silence drear, —
The willing thrall of trances sweet I lie.

Some melancholy gale
Breathes its mysterious tale,
Till the rose's lips grow pale
With her sighs;
And o'er my thoughts are cast
Tints of the vanished past,
Glories that faded fast,
Renewed to splendor in my dreaming eyes.

As poised on vibrant wings,
Where its sweet treasure swings,
The honey-lover clings
To the red flowers, —
So, lost in vivid light,
So, rapt from day and night,
I linger in delight,
Enraptured o'er the vision-freighted hours.

ROSE TERRY COOKE.

A SUMMER NOON.

Who has not dreamed a world of bliss
On a bright sunny noon like this,
Couched by his native brook's green maze,
With comrade of his boyish days,
While all around them seemed to be
Just as in joyous infancy?
Who has not loved at such an hour,
Upon that heath, in birchen bower,
Lulled in the poet's dreamy mood,
Its wild and sunny solitude?
While o'er the waste of purple ling
You mark a sultry glimmering;
Silence herself there seems to sleep,
Wrapped in a slumber long and deep,
Where slowly stray those lonely sheep
Through the tall foxglove's crimson bloom,
And gleaming of the scattered broom.
Love you not, then, to list and hear
The crackling of the gorse-flowers near,
Pouring an orange-scented tide
Of fragrance o'er the desert wide?
To hear the buzzard's whimpering shrill,
Hovering above you high and still?
The twittering of the bird that dwells
Among the heath's delicious bells?
While round your bed, o'er fern and blade,
Insects in green and gold arrayed,
The sun's gay tribes have lightly strayed;
And sweeter sound their humming wings
Than the proud minstrel's echoing strings.

WILLIAM HOWITT.

NOONTIDE.

Beneath a shivering canopy reclined,
Of aspen-leaves that wave without a wind,
I love to lie, when lulling breezes stir
The spiry cones that tremble on the fir;
Or wander mid the dark-green fields of broom,
When peers in scattered tufts the yellow bloom;
Or trace the path with tangling furze o'errun,
When bursting seed-bells crackle in the sun,
And pittering grasshoppers, confus'dly shrill,
Pipe giddily along the glowing hill:

Sweet grasshopper, who lov'st at noon to lie
Serenely in the green-ribbed clover's eye,
To sun thy filmy wings and emerald vest,
Unseen thy form, and undisturbed thy rest,
Oft have I listening mused the sultry day,
And wondered what thy chirping song might say,
When naught was heard along the blossomed lea,
To join thy music, save the listless bee.

JOHN LEYDEN.

THE MIDGES DANCE ABOON THE BURN.

THE midges dance aboon the burn ;
The dews begin to fa' ;
The pairtricks down the rushy holm
Set up their e'ening ca'.
Now loud and clear the blackbird's sang
Rings through the briery shaw,
While, flitting gay, the swallows play
Around the castle wa'.

Beneath the golden gloamin' sky
The mavis mends her lay ;
The redbreast pours his sweetest strains
To charm the lingering day ;
While weary yeldrins seem to wail
Their little nestlings torn,
The merry wren, frae den to den,
Gaes jinking through the thorn.

The roses fauld their silken leaves,
The foxglove shuts its bell ;
The honeysuckle and the birk
Spread fragrance through the dell.
Let others crowd the giddy court
Of mirth and revelry,
The simple joys that nature yields
Are dearer far to me.

ROBERT TANNAHILL.

THE EVENING WIND.

SPIRIT that breathest through my lattice : thou
That cool'st the twilight of the sultry day !
Gratefully flows thy freshness round my brow ;
Thou hast been out upon the deep at play,
Riding all day the wild blue waves till now,
Roughening their crests, and scattering high their spray,
And swelling the white sail. I welcome thee
To the scorched land, thou wanderer of the sea !

Nor I alone, — a thousand bosoms round
Inhale thee in the fullness of delight ;
And languid forms rise up, and pulses bound
Livelier, at coming of the wind of night ;
And languishing to hear thy welcome sound,
Lies the vast inland, stretched beyond the sight.
Go forth into the gathering shade ; go forth, —
God's blessing breathed upon the fainting earth !

Go, rock the little wood-bird in his nest ;
Curl the still waters, bright with stars ; and rouse
The wide old wood from his majestic rest,
Summoning, from the innumerable boughs,
The strange deep harmonies that haunt his breast.
Pleasant shall be thy way where meekly bows
The shutting flower, and darkling waters pass,
And where the o'ershadowing branches sweep the grass.

Stoop o'er the place of graves, and softly sway
The sighing herbage by the gleaming stone,
That they who near the churchyard willows stray,
And listen in the deepening gloom, alone,
May think of gentle souls that passed away,
Like thy pure breath, into the vast unknown,
Sent forth from heaven among the sons of men,
And gone into the boundless heaven again.

The faint old man shall lean his silver head
To feel thee ; thou shalt kiss the child asleep,
And dry the moistened curls that overspread
His temples, while his breathing grows more deep ;
And they who stand about the sick man's bed
Shall joy to listen to thy distant sweep,
And softly part his curtains to allow
Thy visit, grateful to his burning brow.

Go, — but the circle of eternal change,
Which is the life of nature, shall restore,
With sounds and scents from all thy mighty range,
Thee to thy birthplace of the deep once more.
Sweet odors in the sea air, sweet and strange,
Shall tell the homesick mariner of the shore ;
And, listening to thy murmur, he shall deem
He hears the rustling leaf and running stream.

WILLIAM CULLEN BRYANT.

THE EVENING STAR.

STAR that bringest home the bee,
And sett'st the weary laborer free !
If any star shed peace, 't is thou,
That send'st it from above,
Appearing when heaven's breath and brow
Are sweet as hers we love.

Come to the luxuriant skies,
Whilst the landscape's odors rise,
Whilst far-off lowing herds are heard,
And songs, when toil is done,

From cottages whose smoke unstirred
Curls yellow in the sun.

Star of love's soft interviews,
Parted lovers on thee muse;
Their remembrancer in heaven
Of thrilling vows thou art,
Too delicious to be riven
By absence from the heart.

THOMAS CAMPBELL.

CAPE-COTTAGE AT SUNSET.

WE stood upon the ragged rocks,
When the long day was nearly done;
The waves had ceased their sullen shocks,
And lapped our feet with murmuring tone,
And o'er the bay in streaming locks
Blew the red tresses of the sun.

Along the west the golden bars
Still to a deeper glory grew;
Above our heads the faint, few stars
Looked out from the unfathomed blue;
And the fair city's clamorous jars
Seemed melted in that evening hue.

O sunset sky! O purple tide!
O friends to friends that closer pressed!
Those glories have in darkness died,
And ye have left my longing breast.
I could not keep you by my side,
Nor fix that radiance in the west.

WILLIAM BELCHER GLAZIER.

SUNSET.

IF solitude hath ever led thy steps
To the wild ocean's echoing shore,
And thou hast lingered there
Until the sun's broad orb
Seemed resting on the burnished wave,
Thou must have marked the lines
Of purple gold that motionless
Hung o'er the sinking sphere:
Thou must have marked the billowy clouds,
Edged with intolerable radiancy,
Towering like rocks of jet
Crowned with a diamond wreath.
And yet there is a moment,
When the sun's highest point
Peeps like a star o'er ocean's western edge,
When those far clouds of feathery gold,
Shaded with deepest purple, gleam
Like islands on a dark-blue sea;
Then has thy fancy soared above the earth,
And furled its wearied wing
Within the Fairy's fane.

Yet not the golden islands
Gleaming in yon flood of light,
Nor the feathery curtains
Stretching o'er the sun's bright couch,
Nor the burnished ocean's waves
Paving that gorgeous dome,
So fair, so wonderful a sight
As Mab's ethereal palace could afford.
Yet likest evening's vault, that fairy Hall!
Heaven, low resting on the wave, it spread
Its floors of flashing light,
Its vast and azure dome,
Its fertile golden islands
Floating on a silver sea;
Whilst suns their mingling beamings darted
Through clouds of circumambient darkness,
And pearly battlements around
Looked o'er the immense of heaven.

PERCY BYSSHE SHELLEY.

NIGHTFALL: A PICTURE.

Low burns the summer afternoon;
A mellow luster lights the scene;
And from its smiling beauty soon
The purpling shade will chase the sheen.

The old, quaint homestead's windows blaze;
The cedars long, black pictures show;
And broadly slopes one path of rays
Within the barn, and makes it glow.

The loft stares out — the cat intent,
Like carving, on some gnawing rat —
With sun-bathed hay and rafters bent,
Nooked, cobwebbed homes of wasp and bat.

The harness, bridle, saddle, dart
Gleams from the lower, rough expanse;
At either side the stooping cart,
Pitchfork and plow cast looks askance.

White Dobbin through the stable-doors
Shows his round shape; faint color coats
The manger, where the farmer pours,
With rustling rush, the glancing oats.

A sun-haze streaks the dusky shed;
Makes spears of seams and gems of chinks:
In mottled gloss the straw is spread;
And the gray grindstone dully blinks.

The sun salutes the lowest west
With gorgeous tints around it drawn;
A beacon on the mountain's breast,
A crescent, shred, a star — and gone.

The landscape now prepares for night :
  A gauzy mist slow settles round ;
Eve shows her hues in every sight,
  And blends her voice with every sound.

The sheep stream rippling down the dell,
  Their smooth, sharp faces pointed straight;
The pacing kine, with tinkling bell,
  Come grazing through the pasture-gate.

The ducks are grouped, and talk in fits :
  One yawns with stretch of leg and wing ;
One rears and fans, then, settling, sits ;
  One at a moth makes awkward spring.

The geese march grave in Indian file,
  The ragged patriarch at the head ;
Then, screaming, flutter off awhile,
  Fold up, and once more stately tread.

Brave chanticleer shows haughtiest air ;
  Hurls his shrill vaunt with lofty bend ;
Lifts foot, glares round, then follows where
  His scratching, picking partlets wend.

Staid Towser scents the glittering ground ;
  Then, yawning, draws a crescent deep,
Wheels his head-drooping frame around
  And sinks with fore-paws stretched for sleep.

The oxen, loosened from the plow,
  Rest by the pear-tree's crooked trunk ;
Tim, standing with yoke-burdened brow,
  Trim, in a mound beside him sunk.

One of the kine upon the bank
  Heaves her face-lifting, wheezy roar ;
One smooths, with lapping tongue, her flank ;
  With ponderous droop one finds the floor.

Freed Dobbin through the soft, clear dark
  Glimmers across the pillared scene,
With the grouped geese, — a pallid mark, —
  And scattered bushes black between.

The fire-flies freckle every spot
  With fickle light that gleams and dies ;
The bat, a wavering, soundless blot,
  The cat, a pair of prowling eyes.

Still the sweet, fragrant dark o'erflows
  The deepening air and darkening ground ;
By its rich scent I trace the rose,
  The viewless beetle by its sound.

The cricket scrapes its rib-like bars ;
  The tree-toad purrs in whirring tone ;
And now the heavens are set with stars,
  And night and quiet reign alone.

ALFRED B. STREET.

EVENING.

FROM "DON JUAN."

AVE Maria ! o'er the earth and sea,
That heavenliest hour of heaven is worthiest thee !

Ave Maria ! blessed be the hour,
  The time, the clime, the spot, where I so oft
Have felt that moment in its fullest power
  Sink o'er the earth so beautiful and soft,
While swung the deep bell in the distant tower
  Or the faint dying day hymn stole aloft,
And not a breath crept through the rosy air,
And yet the forest leaves seemed stirred with prayer.

Ave Maria ! 't is the hour of prayer !
  Ave Maria ! 't is the hour of love !
Ave Maria ! may our spirits dare
  Look up to thine and to thy Son's above !
Ave Maria ! O that face so fair !
  Those downcast eyes beneath the Almighty dove, —
What though 't is but a pictured image ? — strike, —
That painting is no idol, — 't is too like.

Sweet hour of twilight ! in the solitude
  Of the pine forest, and the silent shore
Which bounds Ravenna's immemorial wood,
  Rooted where once the Adrian wave flowed o'er
To where the last Cæsarean fortress stood,
  Evergreen forest ; which Boccaccio's lore
And Dryden's lay made haunted ground to me,
How have I loved the twilight hour and thee !

The shrill cicalas, people of the pine,
  Making their summer lives one ceaseless song,
Were the sole echoes, save my steed's and mine,
  And vesper bells that rose the boughs along ;
The specter huntsman of Onesti's line,
  His hell-dogs, and their chase, and the fair throng
Which learned from this example not to fly
From a true lover, — shadowed my mind's eye.

O Hesperus ! thou bringest all good things, —
  Home to the weary, to the hungry cheer,
To the young bird the parent's brooding wings,
  The welcome stall to the o'erlabored steer ;
Whate'er of peace about our hearthstone clings,
  Whate'er our household gods protect of dear,
Are gathered round us by thy look of rest ;
Thou bring'st the child, too, to the mother's breast.

Soft hour ! which wakes the wish and melts the heart
  Of those who sail the seas, on the first day
When they from their sweet friends are torn apart ;
  Or fills with love the pilgrim on his way,

As the far bell of vesper makes him start,
Seeming to weep the dying day's decay :
Is this a fancy which our reason scorns ?
Ah ! surely nothing dies but something mourns.

LORD BYRON.

ODE TO EVENING.

If aught of oaten stop or pastoral song
May hope, chaste Eve, to soothe thy modest ear,
Like thy own solemn springs,
Thy springs, and dying gales, —

O nymph reserved, while now the bright-haired Sun
Sits in yon western tent, whose cloudy skirts,
With braid ethereal wove,
O'erhang his wavy bed :

Now air is hushed, save where the weak-eyed bat,
With short, shrill shriek flits by on leathern wing ;
Or where the beetle winds
His small but sullen horn,

As oft he rises midst the twilight path,
Against the pilgrim borne in heedless hum ;
Now teach me, maid composed,
To breathe some softened strain,

Whose numbers, stealing through thy darkening vale,
May not unseemly with its stillness suit ;
As, musing slow, I hail
Thy genial, loved return !

For when thy folding-star arising shows
His paly circlet, at his warning lamp,
The fragrant Hours, and Elves
Who slept in buds the day,

And many a Nymph who wreathes her brows with sedge,
And sheds the freshening dew, and, lovelier still,
The pensive Pleasures sweet,
Prepare thy shadowy car.

Then let me rove some wild and heathy scene ;
Or find some ruin midst its dreary dells,
Whose walls more awful nod
By thy religious gleams.

Or, if chill, blustering winds, or driving rain,
Prevent my willing feet, be mine the hut
That from the mountain's side
Views wilds, and swelling floods,

And hamlets brown, and dim-discovered spires ;
And hears their simple bell, and marks o'er all
Thy dewy fingers draw
The gradual, dusky veil.

While Spring shall pour his showers, as oft he wont,
And bathe thy breathing tresses, meekest Eve !
While Summer loves to sport
Beneath thy lingering light ;

While sallow Autumn fills thy lap with leaves ;
Or Winter, yelling through the troublous air,
Affrights thy shrinking train,
And rudely rends thy robes, —

So long, regardful of thy quiet rule,
Shall Fancy, Friendship, Science, smiling Peace,
Thy gentlest influence own,
And love thy favorite name !

WILLIAM COLLINS.

SUNSET.

FROM "CHILDE HAROLD."

The moon is up, and yet it is not night:
Sunset divides the sky with her ; a sea
Of glory streams along the Alpine height
Of blue Friuli's mountains ; heaven is free
From clouds, but of all colors seems to be
Melted to one vast Iris of the west,
Where the day joins the past eternity ;
While, on the other hand, meek Dian's crest
Floats through the azure air, an island of the blest.

A single star is at her side, and reigns
With her o'er half the lovely heaven ; but still
Yon sunny sea heaves brightly, and remains
Rolled o'er the peak of the far Rhœtian hill,
As day and night contending were until
Nature reclaimed her order : gently flows
The deep-dyed Brenta, where their hues instill
The odorous purple of a new-born rose,
Which streams upon her stream, and glassed within it glows,

Filled with the face of heaven, which, from afar,
Comes down upon the waters ; all its hues,
From the rich sunset to the rising star,
Their magical variety diffuse :
And now they change ; a paler shadow strews
Its mantle o'er the mountains : parting day
Dies like the dolphin, whom each pang imbues
With a new color as it gasps away,
The last still loveliest, till 't is gone — and all is gray.

LORD BYRON.

EVENING.

"Now air is hushed, save where the weak-eyed bat,
With short, shrill shriek flits by on leathern wing."

EVENING IN PARADISE.

Now came still evening on, and twilight gray
Had in her sober livery all things clad;
Silence accompanied; for beast and bird,
They to their grassy couch, these to their nests,
Were slunk, all but the wakeful nightingale;
She all night long her amorous descant sung.
Silence was pleased: now glowed the firmament
With living sapphires; Hesperus, that led
The starry host, rode brightest, till the moon,
Rising in clouded majesty, at length
Apparent queen, unveiled her peerless light,
And o'er the dark her silver mantle threw.
When Adam thus to Eve: "Fair consort, the hour
Of night, and all things now retired to rest,
Mind us of like repose, since God hath set
Labor and rest, as day and night, to men
Successive; and the timely dew of sleep,
Now falling with soft slumberous weight, inclines
Our eyelids. Other creatures all day long
Rove idle, unemployed, and less need rest;
Man hath his daily work of body or mind
Appointed, which declares his dignity,
And the regard of Heaven on all his ways;
While other animals unactive range,
And of their doings God takes no account.
To-morrow, ere fresh morning streak the east
With first approach of light, we must be risen,
And at our pleasant labor, to reform
Yon flowery arbors, yonder alleys green,
Our walk at noon, with branches overgrown,
That mock our scant manuring, and require
More hands than ours to lop their wanton growth.
Those blossoms also, and those dropping gums,
That lie bestrewn, unsightly and unsmooth,
Ask riddance, if we mean to tread with ease;
Meanwhile, as Nature wills, night bids us rest."
To whom thus Eve with perfect beauty adorned:
"My author and disposer, what thou bidd'st
Unargued I obey; so God ordains;
God is thy law, thou mine; to know no more
Is woman's happiest knowledge and her praise.
With thee conversing I forget all time;
All seasons and their change, all please alike.
Sweet is the breath of morn, her rising sweet,
With charm of earliest birds; pleasant the sun,
When first on this delightful land he spreads
His orient beams, on herb, tree, fruit, and flower,
Glistering with dew; fragrant the fertile earth
After soft showers; and sweet the coming on
Of grateful evening mild; then silent night,
With this her solemn bird, and this fair moon,
And these the gems of heaven, her starry train:
But neither breath of morn, when she ascends
With charms of earliest birds; nor rising sun
On this delightful land; nor herb, fruit, flower,
Glistering with dew; nor fragrance after showers,
Nor grateful evening mild; nor silent night
With this her solemn bird, nor walk by moon,
Or glittering starlight, without thee is sweet."
Thus talking, hand in hand alone they passed
On to their blissful bower.

MILTON.

TO NIGHT.

SWIFTLY walk over the western wave,
Spirit of Night!
Out of the misty eastern cave,
Where, all the long and lone daylight,
Thou wovest dreams of joy and fear
Which make thee terrible and dear, —
Swift be thy flight!

Wrap thy form in a mantle gray,
Star-inwrought;
Blind with thine hair the eyes of Day,
Kiss her until she be wearied out;
Then wander o'er city and sea and land,
Touching all with thine opiate wand, —
Come, long-sought!

When I arose and saw the dawn,
I sighed for thee;
When light rode high, and the dew was gone,
And noon lay heavy on flower and tree,
And the weary Day turned to her rest,
Lingering like an unloved guest,
I sighed for thee!

Thy brother Death came, and cried,
"Wouldst thou me?"
Thy sweet child Sleep, the filmy-eyed,
Murmured like a noontide bee,
"Shall I nestle near thy side?
Wouldst thou me?"—And I replied,
"No, not thee!"

Death will come when thou art dead,
Soon, too soon, —
Sleep will come when thou art fled;
Of neither would I ask the boon
I ask of thee, belovèd Night, —
Swift be thine approaching flight,
Come soon, soon!

PERCY BYSSHE SHELLEY.

NIGHT.

MYSTERIOUS Night! when our first parent knew
Thee, from report divine, and heard thy name,
Did he not tremble for this lovely frame, —
This glorious canopy of light and blue?

Yet, 'neath a curtain of translucent dew,
Bathed in the rays of the great setting flame,
Hesperus, with the host of heaven, came,
And lo! creation widened in man's view.
Who could have thought such darkness lay concealed
Within thy beams, O Sun! or who could find,
Whilst fly and leaf and insect stood revealed,
That to such countless orbs thou mad'st us blind!
Why do we then shun death with anxious strife?
If light can thus deceive, wherefore not life?

JOSEPH BLANCO WHITE.

NIGHT.

FROM "CHILDE HAROLD."

'T is night, when Meditation bids us feel
We once have loved, though love is at an end:
The heart, lone mourner of its baffled zeal,
Though friendless now, will dream it had a friend.
Who with the weight of years would wish to bend,
When Youth itself survives young Love and joy?
Alas! when mingling souls forget to blend,
Death hath but little left him to destroy!
Ah! happy years! once more who would not be a boy?

Thus bending o'er the vessel's laving side,
To gaze on Dian's wave-reflected sphere,
The soul forgets her schemes of Hope and Pride,
And flies unconscious o'er each backward year.
None are so desolate but something dear,
Dearer than self, possesses or possessed
A thought, and claims the homage of a tear;
A flashing pang! of which the weary breast
Would still, albeit in vain, the heavy heart divest.

To sit on rocks, to muse o'er flood and fell,
To slowly trace the forest's shady scene,
Where things that own not man's dominion dwell,
And mortal foot hath ne'er or rarely been;
To climb the trackless mountain all unseen,
With the wild flock that never needs a fold;
Alone o'er steeps and foaming falls to lean,—
This is not solitude; 't is but to hold
Converse with Nature's charms, and view her stores unrolled.

But midst the crowd, the hum, the shock of men
To hear to see, to feel, and to possess,
And roam along, the world's tired denizen,
With none who bless us, none whom we can bless;
Minions of splendor shrinking from distress!
None that, with kindred consciousness endued,
If we were not, would seem to smile the less
Of all that flattered, followed, sought, and sued;
This is to be alone; this, this is solitude!

LORD BYRON.

NIGHT.

How beautiful this night! the balmiest sigh
Which vernal zephyrs breathe in evening's ear
Were discord to the speaking quietude
That wraps this moveless scene. Heaven's ebon vault,
Studded with stars unutterably bright,
Through which the moon's unclouded grandeur rolls,
Seems like a canopy which love has spread
To curtain her sleeping world. Yon gentle hills,
Robed in a garment of untrodden snow;
Yon darksome rocks, whence icicles depend,
So stainless that their white and glittering spires
Tinge not the moon's pure beam; yon castle steep,
Whose banner hangeth o'er the timeworn tower
So idly that rapt fancy deemeth it
A metaphor of peace — all form a scene
Where musing solitude might love to lift
Her soul above this sphere of earthliness;
Where silence undisturbed might watch alone,
So cold, so bright, so still.

The orb of day
In southern climes o'er ocean's waveless field
Sinks sweetly smiling: not the faintest breath
Steals o'er the unruffled deep; the clouds of eve
Reflect unmoved the lingering beam of day;
And vesper's image on the western main
Is beautifully still. To-morrow comes:
Cloud upon cloud, in dark and deepening mass,
Rolls o'er the blackened waters; the deep roar
Of distant thunder mutters awfully;
Tempest unfolds its pinion o'er the gloom
That shrouds the boiling surge; the pitiless fiend,
With all his winds and lightnings, tracks his prey;
The torn deep yawns, — the vessel finds a grave
Beneath its jagged gulf.

PERCY BYSSHE SHELLEY.

NIGHT.

Night is the time for rest:
How sweet, when labors close,
To gather round an aching breast
The curtain of repose,
Stretch the tired limbs, and lay the head
Down on our own delightful bed!

Night is the time for dreams:
The gay romance of life,
When truth that is, and truth that seems,
Mix in fantastic strife;
Ah! visions, less beguiling far
Than waking dreams by daylight are!

Night is the time for toil:
To plow the classic field,
Intent to find the buried spoil
Its wealthy furrows yield;
Till all is ours that sages taught,
That poets sang, and heroes wrought.

Night is the time to weep:
To wet with unseen tears
Those graves of Memory, where sleep
The joys of other years;
Hopes, that were Angels at their birth,
But died when young, like things of earth.

Night is the time to watch:
O'er ocean's dark expanse,
To hail the Pleiades, or catch
The full moon's earliest glance,
That brings into the homesick mind
All we have loved and left behind.

Night is the time for care:
Brooding on hours misspent,
To see the specter of Despair
Come to our lonely tent;
Like Brutus, midst his slumbering host,
Summoned to die by Cæsar's ghost.

Night is the time to think:
When, from the eye, the soul
Takes flight; and on the utmost brink
Of yonder starry pole
Discerns beyond the abyss of night
The dawn of uncreated light.

Night is the time to pray:
Our Saviour oft withdrew
To desert mountains far away;
So will his follower do, —
Steal from the throng to haunts untrod,
And commune there alone with God.

Night is the time for Death:
When all around is peace,
Calmly to yield the weary breath,
From sin and suffering cease,
Think of heaven's bliss, and give the sign
To parting friends; — such death be mine.

JAMES MONTGOMERY.

HYMN TO THE NIGHT.

'Ασπασίη, τρίλλιστος.

I HEARD the trailing garments of the Night
Sweep through her marble halls!
I saw her sable skirts all fringed with light
From the celestial walls!

I felt her presence, by its spell of might,
Stoop o'er me from above;
The calm, majestic presence of the Night,
As of the one I love.

I heard the sounds of sorrow and delight,
The manifold, soft chimes,
That fill the haunted chambers of the Night,
Like some old poet's rhymes.

From the cool cisterns of the midnight air
My spirit drank repose;
The fountain of perpetual peace flows there, —
From those deep cisterns flows.

O holy Night! from thee I learn to bear
What man has borne before!
Thou layest thy finger on the lips of Care,
And they complain no more.

Peace! Peace! Orestes-like I breathe this prayer!
Descend with broad-winged flight,
The welcome, the thrice-prayed for, the most fair,
The best-belovèd Night!

HENRY WADSWORTH LONGFELLOW.

HYMN.

FROM "THE SEASONS."

THESE, as they change, Almighty Father, these
Are but the varied God. The rolling year
Is full of thee. Forth in the pleasing spring
Thy beauty walks, thy tenderness and love.
Wide flush the fields; the softening air is balm;
Echo the mountains round; the forest smiles;
And every sense and every heart is joy.
Then comes thy glory in the summer months,
With light and heat refulgent. Then thy sun
Shoots full perfection through the swelling year;
And oft thy voice in dreadful thunder speaks,
And oft at dawn, deep noon, or falling eve,
By brooks and groves in hollow-whispering gales.
Thy bounty shines in autumn unconfined,
And spreads a common feast for all that lives.
In winter awful thou! with clouds and storms
Around thee thrown, tempest o'er tempest rolled,
Majestic darkness! on the whirlwind's wing
Riding sublime, thou bid'st the world adore,
And humblest nature with thy northern blast.
Mysterious round! what skill, what force divine,
Deep felt, in these appear! a simple train,

Yet so delightful mixed, with such kind art,
Such beauty and beneficence combined;
Shade, unperceived, so softening into shade;
And all so forming an harmonious whole,
That, as they still succeed, they ravish still.
But wandering oft, with brute unconscious gaze,
Man marks not thee, marks not the mighty hand,
That, ever busy, wheels the silent spheres;
Works in the secret deep; shoots, steaming, thence
The fair profusion that o'erspreads the spring;
Flings from the sun direct the flaming day;
Feeds every creature; hurls the tempest forth;
And, as on earth this grateful change revolves,
With transport touches all the springs of life.
Nature, attend! join every living soul,
Beneath the spacious temple of the sky,
In adoration join; and, ardent, raise
One general song! To Him, ye vocal gales,
Breathe soft, whose spirit in your freshness breathes:
O, talk of him in solitary glooms;
Where, o'er the rock, the scarcely waving pine
Fills the brown shade with a religious awe.
And ye whose bolder note is heard afar,
Who shake the astonished world, lift high to Heaven
The impetuous song, and say from whom you rage.
His praise, ye brooks, attune, ye trembling rills;
And let me catch it as I muse along.
Ye headlong torrents, rapid, and profound;
Ye softer floods, that lead the humid maze
Along the vale; and thou, majestic main,
A secret world of wonders in thyself,
Sound his stupendous praise, — whose greater voice
Or bids you roar, or bids your roarings fall.
Soft roll your incense, herbs, and fruits, and flowers,
In mingled clouds to him, — whose sun exalts,
Whose breath perfumes you, and whose pencil paints.
Ye forests bend, ye harvests wave, to him;
Breathe your still song into the reaper's heart,
As home he goes beneath the joyous moon.
Ye that keep watch in heaven, as earth asleep
Unconscious lies, effuse your mildest beams,
Ye constellations, while your angels strike,
Amid the spangled sky, the silver lyre.
Great source of day! best image here below
Of thy Creator, ever pouring wide,
From world to world, the vital ocean round,
On Nature write with every beam his praise.
The thunder rolls: be hushed the prostrate world;
While cloud to cloud returns the solemn hymn.
Bleat out afresh, ye hills; ye mossy rocks,
Retain the sound; the broad responsive low,
Ye valleys, raise; for the great Shepherd reigns,
And his unsuffering kingdom yet will come.
Ye woodlands all, awake: a boundless song
Burst from the groves; and when the restless day,
Expiring, lays the warbling world asleep,
Sweetest of birds! sweet Philomela, charm
The listening shades, and teach the night his praise.
Ye chief, for whom the whole creation smiles,
At once the head, the heart, and tongue of all,
Crown the great hymn! in swarming cities vast,
Assembled men to the deep organ join
The long-resounding voice, oft breaking clear,
At solemn pauses, through the swelling bass;
And, as each mingling flame increases each,
In one united ardor rise to heaven.
Or if you rather choose the rural shade,
And find a fane in every sacred grove,
There let the shepherd's flute, the virgin's lay,
The prompting seraph, and the poet's lyre,
Still sing the God of seasons as they roll.
For me, when I forget the darling theme,
Whether the blossom blows, the summer ray
Russets the plain, inspiring autumn gleams,
Or winter rises in the blackening east, —
Be my tongue mute, my fancy paint no more,
And, dead to joy, forget my heart to beat!
Should fate command me to the farthest verge
Of the green earth, to distant barbarous climes,
Rivers unknown to song, — where first the sun
Gilds Indian mountains, or his setting beam
Flames on the Atlantic isles, — 't is naught to me:
Since God is ever present, ever felt,
In the void waste as in the city full;
And where he vital breathes there must be joy.
When even at last the solemn hour shall come,
And wing my mystic flight to future worlds,
I cheerful will obey; there, with new powers,
Will rising wonders sing: I cannot go
Where Universal Love not smiles around,
Sustaining all yon orbs, and all their suns;
From seeming evil still educing good,
And better thence again, and better still,
In infinite progression. But I lose
Myself in him, in light ineffable!
Come, then, expressive Silence, muse his praise.

JAMES THOMSON.

THE FOUR SEASONS.

SPRINGE is ycomen in,
Dappled larke singe;
Snowe melteth,
Runnell pelteth,
Smelleth winde of newe buddinge.

Summer is ycomen in,
Loude singe cucku;

Groweth seede,
Bloweth meade,
And springeth the weede newe.

Autumne is ycomen in,
Ceres filleth horne;
Reaper swinketh,
Farmer drinketh,
Creaketh waine with newe corne.

Winter is ycomen in
With stormy sadde cheere;
In the paddocke,
Whistle ruddock,
Brighte sparke in the dead yeare.

ANONYMOUS.

EPIGÆA ASLEEP.

Arbutus lies beneath the snows,
While Winter waits her brief repose,
And says, "No fairer flower grows!"

Of sunny April days she dreams,
Of robins' notes and murmuring streams,
And smiling in her sleep she seems.

She thinks her rosy buds expand
Beneath the touch of childhood's hand,
And beauty breathes throughout the land.

The arching elders bending o'er
The silent river's sandy shore,
Their golden tresses trim once more.

The pussy-willows in their play
Their varnished caps have flung away,
And hung their furs on every spray.

The toads their cheery music chant,
The squirrel seeks his summer haunt,
And life revives in every plant.

"I must awake! I hear the bee!
The butterfly I long to see!
The buds are bursting on the tree!"

Ah! blossom, thou art dreaming, dear,
The wild winds howl about thee here,
—The dirges of the dying year!

Thy gentle eyes with tears are wet;
In sweeter sleep these pains forget;
Thy merry morning comes not yet!

WILLIAM WHITMAN BAILEY.

MARCH.

Slayer of winter, art thou here again?
O welcome, thou that bring'st the summer nigh!
The bitter wind makes not thy victory vain,
Nor will we mock thee for thy faint blue sky.
Welcome, O March! whose kindly days and dry
Make April ready for the throstle's song,
Thou first redresser of the winter's wrong!

Yea, welcome, March! and though I die ere June,
Yet for the hope of life I give thee praise,
Striving to swell the burden of the tune
That even now I hear thy brown birds raise,
Unmindful of the past or coming days;
Who sing, "O joy! a new year is begun!
What happiness to look upon the sun!"

O, what begetteth all this storm of bliss,
But Death himself, who, crying solemnly,
Even from the heart of sweet Forgetfulness,
Bids us, "Rejoice! lest pleasureless ye die.
Within a little time must ye go by.
Stretch forth your open hands, and, while ye live,
Take all the gifts that Death and Life may give"?

WILLIAM MORRIS.

SPRING.

FROM "IN MEMORIAM.

Dip down upon the northern shore,
O sweet new-year, delaying long:
Thou doest expectant Nature wrong;
Delaying long, delay no more.

What stays thee from the clouded noons,
Thy sweetness from its proper place?
Can trouble live with April days,
Or sadness in the summer moons?

Bring orchis, bring the foxglove spire,
The little speedwell's darling blue,
Deep tulips dashed with fiery dew,
Laburnums, dropping-wells of fire.

O thou, new-year, delaying long,
Delayest the sorrow in my blood,
That longs to burst a frozen bud,
And flood a fresher throat with song.

. . . . .

Now fades the last long streak of snow;
Now bourgeons every maze of quick
About the flowering squares, and thick
By ashen roots the violets blow.

Now rings the woodland loud and long,
The distance takes a lovelier hue,
And drowned in yonder living blue
The lark becomes a sightless song.

Now dance the lights on lawn and lea,
The flocks are whiter down the vale,
And milkier every milky sail
On winding stream or distant sea;

Where now the sea-mew pipes, or dives
In yonder greening gleam, and fly
The happy birds, that change their sky
To build and brood, that live their lives

From land to land; and in my breast
Spring wakens too; and my regret
Becomes an April violet,
And buds and blossoms like the rest.

ALFRED TENNYSON.

DIE DOWN, O DISMAL DAY!

Die down, O dismal day, and let me live;
And come, blue deeps, magnificently strewn
With colored clouds, — large, light, and fugitive, —
By upper winds through pompous motions blown.
Now it is death in life, — a vapor dense
Creeps round my window, till I cannot see
The far snow-shining mountains, and the glens
Shagging the mountain-tops. O God! make free
This barren shackled earth, so deadly cold, —
Breathe gently forth thy spring, till winter flies
In rude amazement, fearful and yet bold,
While she performs her customed charities;
I weigh the loaded hours till life is bare, —
O God, for one clear day, a snowdrop, and sweet air!

DAVID GRAY.

SUMMER LONGINGS.

Ah! my heart is weary waiting,
Waiting for the May, —
Waiting for the pleasant rambles
Where the fragrant hawthorn-brambles,
With the woodbine alternating,
Scent the dewy way.
Ah! my heart is weary waiting,
Waiting for the May.

Ah! my heart is sick with longing,
Longing for the May, —
Longing to escape from study
To the young face fair and ruddy,
And the thousand charms belonging
To the summer's day.
Ah! my heart is sick with longing,
Longing for the May.

Ah! my heart is sore with sighing,
Sighing for the May, —
Sighing for their sure returning,
When the summer beams are burning,
Hopes and flowers that, dead or dying,
All the winter lay.
Ah! my heart is sore with sighing,
Sighing for the May.

Ah! my heart is pained with throbbing,
Throbbing for the May, —
Throbbing for the seaside billows,
Or the water-wooing willows;
Where, in laughing and in sobbing,
Glide the streams away.
Ah! my heart, my heart is throbbing,
Throbbing for the May.

Waiting sad, dejected, weary,
Waiting for the May:
Spring goes by with wasted warnings, —
Moonlit evenings, sunbright mornings, —
Summer comes, yet dark and dreary
Life still ebbs away;
Man is ever weary, weary,
Waiting for the May!

DENIS FLORENCE MAC-CARTHY.

WHEN THE HOUNDS OF SPRING.

When the hounds of spring are on winter's traces,
The mother of months in meadow or plain
Fills the shadows and windy places
With lisp of leaves and ripple of rain;
And the brown bright nightingale amorous
Is half assuaged for Itylus,
For the Thracian ships and the foreign faces;
The tongueless vigil, and all the pain.

Come with bows bent and with emptying of quivers,
Maiden most perfect, lady of light,
With a noise of winds and many rivers,
With a clamor of waters, and with might;
Bind on thy sandals, O thou most fleet,
Over the splendor and speed of thy feet!
For the faint east quickens, the wan west shivers,
Round the feet of the day and the feet of the night.

Where shall we find her, how shall we sing to her,
Fold our hands round her knees and cling?
O that man's heart were as fire and could spring to her,
Fire, or the strength of the streams that spring!
For the stars and the winds are unto her
As raiment, as songs of the harp-player;
For the risen stars and the fallen cling to her,
And the southwest-wind and the west-wind sing.

For winter's rains and ruins are over,
And all the season of snows and sins;

The days dividing lover and lover,
The light that loses, the night that wins;
And time remembered is grief forgotten,
And frosts are slain and flowers begotten,
And in green underwood and cover
Blossom by blossom the spring begins.

The full streams feed on flower of rushes,
Ripe grasses trammel a traveling foot,
The faint fresh flame of the young year flushes
From leaf to flower and flower to fruit;
And fruit and leaf are as gold and fire,
And the oat is heard above the lyre,
And the hoofèd heel of a satyr crushes
The chestnut-husk at the chestnut-root.

And Pan by noon and Bacchus by night,
Fleeter of foot than the fleet-foot kid,
Follows with dancing and fills with delight
The Mænad and the Bassarid;
And soft as lips that laugh and hide,
The laughing leaves of the trees divide,
And screen from seeing and leave in sight
The god pursuing, the maiden hid.

The ivy falls with the Bacchanal's hair
Over her eyebrows shading her eyes;
The wild vine slipping down leaves bare
Her bright breast shortening into sighs;
The wild vine slips with the weight of its leaves,
But the berried ivy catches and cleaves
To the limbs that glitter, the feet that scare
The wolf that follows, the fawn that flies.

ALGERNON CHARLES SWINBURNE.

THE WINTER BEING OVER.

The winter being over,
In order comes the spring,
Which doth green herbs discover,
And cause the birds to sing.
The night also expired,
Then comes the morning bright,
Which is so much desired
By all that love the light.
This may learn
Them that mourn
To put their grief to flight:
The spring succeedeth winter,
And day must follow night.

He therefore that sustaineth
Affliction or distress
Which every member paineth,
And findeth no release, —
Let such therefore despair not,
But on firm hope depend,
Whose griefs immortal are not,
And therefore must have end.
They that faint
With complaint
Therefore are to blame;
They add to their afflictions,
And amplify the same.

For if they could with patience
Awhile possess the mind,
By inward consolations
They might refreshing find,
To sweeten all their crosses
That little time they 'dure;
So might they gain by losses,
And sharp would sweet procure.
But if the mind
Be inclined
To unquietness,
That only may be called
The worst of all distress.

He that is melancholy,
Detesting all delight,
His wits by sottish folly
Are ruinated quite.
Sad discontent and murmurs
To him are incident;
Were he possessed of honors,
He could not be content.
Sparks of joy
Fly away;
Floods of care arise;
And all delightful motion
In the conception dies.

But those that are contented
However things do fall,
Much anguish is prevented,
And they soon freed from all.
They finish all their labors
With much felicity;
Their joy in trouble savors
Of perfect piety.
Cheerfulness
Doth express
A settled pious mind,
Which is not prone to grudging,
From murmuring refined.

ANNE COLLINS.

SPRING.

WRITTEN WHILE A PRISONER IN ENGLAND.

The Time hath laid his mantle by
Of wind and rain and icy chill,
And dons a rich embroidery
Of sunlight poured on lake and hill.

No beast or bird in earth or sky,
Whose voice doth not with gladness thrill,
For Time hath laid his mantle by
Of wind and rain and icy chill.

River and fountain, brook and rill,
Bespangled o'er with livery gay
Of silver droplets, wind their way.
All in their new apparel vie,
For Time hath laid his mantle by.

CHARLES OF ORLEANS.

RETURN OF SPRING.

God shield ye, heralds of the spring!
Ye faithful swallows, fleet of wing,
Houps, cuckoos, nightingales,
Turtles, and every wilder bird,
That make your hundred chirpings heard
Through the green woods and dales.

God shield ye, Easter daisies all,
Fair roses, buds, and blossoms small,
And he whom erst the gore
Of Ajax and Narciss did print,
Ye wild thyme, anise, balm, and mint,
I welcome ye once more!

God shield ye, bright embroidered train
Of butterflies, that on the plain
Of each sweet herblet sip;
And ye, new swarms of bees, that go
Where the pink flowers and yellow grow
To kiss them with your lip!

A hundred thousand times I call
A hearty welcome on ye all!
This season how I love —
This merry din on every shore —
For winds and storms, whose sullen roar
Forbade my steps to rove.

From the French of PIERRE RONSARD.

MARCH.

The cock is crowing,
The stream is flowing,
The small birds twitter,
The lake doth glitter,
The green field sleeps in the sun;
The oldest and youngest
Are at work with the strongest;
The cattle are grazing,
Their heads never raising;
There are forty feeding like one?

Like an army defeated
The snow hath retreated,
And now doth fare ill
On the top of the bare hill;
The plowboy is whooping — anon — anon!
There's joy on the mountains;
There's life in the fountains;
Small clouds are sailing,
Blue sky prevailing;
The rain is over and gone!

WILLIAM WORDSWORTH.

SONG OF SPRING.

Laud the first spring daisies;
Chant aloud their praises;
Send the children up
To the high hill's top;
Tax not the strength of their young hands
To increase your lands.
Gather the primroses,
Make handfuls into posies;
Take them to the little girls who are at work in mills:
Pluck the violets blue, —
Ah, pluck not a few!
Knowest thou what good thoughts from Heaven the violet instills?

Give the children holidays,
(And let these be jolly days,)
Grant freedom to the children in this joyous spring;
Better men, hereafter,
Shall we have, for laughter
Freely shouted to the woods, till all the echoes ring.
Send the children up
To the high hill's top,
Or deep into the wood's recesses,
To woo spring's caresses.

See, the birds together,
In this splendid weather,
Worship God (for he is God of birds as well as men);
And each feathered neighbor
Enters on his labor, —
Sparrow, robin, redpole, finch, the linnet, and the wren.
As the year advances,
Trees their naked branches
Clothe, and seek your pleasure in their green apparel.
Insect and wild beast
Keep no Lent, but feast;
Spring breathes upon the earth, and their joy's increased,
And the rejoicing birds break forth in one loud carol.

Ah, come and woo the spring;
List to the birds that sing;
Pluck the primroses; pluck the violets:
Pluck the daisies,
Sing their praises;
Friendship with the flowers some noble thought begets.
Come forth and gather these sweet elves
(More witching are they than the fays of old),
Come forth and gather them yourselves;
Learn of these gentle flowers whose worth is more than gold.

Come, come into the wood;
Pierce into the bowers
Of these gentle flowers,
Which not in solitude
Dwell, but with each other keep society:
And with a simple piety,
Are ready to be woven into garlands for the good.
Or, upon summer earth,
To die, in virgin worth;
Or to be strewn before the bride,
And the bridegroom by her side.

Come forth on Sundays;
Come forth on Mondays;
Come forth on any day;
Children, come forth to play: —
Worship the God of Nature in your childhood;
Worship him at your tasks with best endeavor;
Worship him in your sports; worship him ever;
Worship him in the wildwood;
Worship him amidst the flowers;
In the greenwood bowers;
Pluck the buttercups, and raise
Your voices in his praise!

EDWARD YOUL.

SPRING.

AGAIN the violet of our early days
Drinks beauteous azure from the golden sun,
And kindles into fragrance at his blaze;
The streams, rejoiced that winter's work is done,
Talk of to-morrow's cowslips, as they run.
Wild apple, thou art blushing into bloom!
Thy leaves are coming, snowy-blossomed thorn!
Wake, buried lily! spirit, quit thy tomb!
And thou shade-loving hyacinth, be born!
Then, haste, sweet rose! sweet woodbine, hymn the morn,
Whose dewdrops shall illume with pearly light
Each grassy blade that thick embattled stands
From sea to sea, while daisies infinite
Uplift in praise their little glowing hands,
O'er every hill that under heaven expands.

EBENEZER ELLIOTT.

SWEETLY BREATHING, VERNAL AIR.

SWEETLY breathing, vernal air,
That with kind warmth doth repair
Winter's ruins; from whose breast
All the gums and spice of the East
Borrow their perfumes; whose eye
Gilds the morn, and clears the sky;
Whose disheveled tresses shed
Pearls upon the violet bed;
On whose brow, with calm smiles drest
The halcyon sits and builds her nest;
Beauty, youth, and endless spring
Dwell upon thy rosy wing!

Thou, if stormy Boreas throws
Down whole forests when he blows,
With a pregnant, flowery birth,
Canst refresh the teeming earth.
If he nip the early bud,
If he blast what 's fair or good,
If he scatter our choice flowers,
If he shake our halls or bowers,
If his rude breath threaten us,
Thou canst stroke great Æolus,
And from him the grace obtain,
To bind him in an iron chain.

THOMAS CAREW.

SPRING.

Lo! where the rosy-bosomed Hours,
  Fair Venus' train, appear,
Disclose the long-expecting flowers
  And wake the purple year!
The Attic warbler pours her throat
Responsive to the cuckoo's note,
The untaught harmony of spring:
While, whispering pleasure as they fly,
Cool zephyrs through the clear blue sky
  Their gathered fragrance fling.

Where'er the oak's thick branches stretch
  A broader, browner shade,
Where'er the rude and moss-grown beech
  O'er-canopies the glade,
Beside some water's rushy brink
With me the Muse shall sit, and think
(At ease reclined in rustic state)
How vain the ardor of the crowd,
How low, how little are the proud,
  How indigent the great!

Still is the toiling hand of care;
  The panting herds repose:
Yet hark, how through the peopled air
  The busy murmur glows!

The insect youth are on the wing,
Eager to taste the honeyed spring
And float amid the liquid noon:
Some lightly o'er the current skim,
Some show their gayly gilded trim
Quick-glancing to the sun.

To Contemplation's sober eye
Such is the race of man;
And they that creep, and they that fly,
Shall end where they began.
Alike the busy and the gay
But flutter through life's little day,
In Fortune's varying colors drest:
Brushed by the hand of rough mischance
Or chilled by age, their airy dance
They leave, in dust to rest.

Methinks I hear in accents low
The sportive kind reply:
Poor moralist! and what art thou?
A solitary fly!
Thy joys no glittering female meets,
No hive hast thou of hoarded sweets,
No painted plumage to display;
On hasty wings thy youth is flown;
Thy sun is set, thy spring is gone, —
We frolic while 't is May.

THOMAS GRAY.

SPRING, THE SWEET SPRING.

SPRING, the sweet spring, is the year's pleasant king;
Then blooms each thing, then maids dance in a ring,
Cold doth not sting, the pretty birds do sing,
Cuckoo, jug-jug, pu-we, to-witta-woo!

The palm and may make country houses gay,
Lambs frisk and play, the shepherds pipe all day,
And we hear aye birds tune this merry lay,
Cuckoo, jug-jug, pu-we, to-witta-woo!

The fields breathe sweet, the daisies kiss our feet,
Young lovers meet, old wives a sunning sit,
In every street these tunes our ears do greet,
Cuckoo, jug-jug, pu-we, to-witta-woo!
Spring! the sweet spring!

THOMAS NASH.

SPRING.

BEHOLD the young, the rosy Spring
Gives to the breeze her scented wing,
While virgin graces, warm with May,
Fling roses o'er her dewy way.
The murmuring billows of the deep
Have languished into silent sleep;
And mark! the flitting sea-birds lave
Their plumes in the reflecting wave;
While cranes from hoary winter fly
To flutter in a kinder sky.
Now the genial star of day
Dissolves the murky clouds away,
And cultured field and winding stream
Are freshly glittering in his beam.
Now the earth prolific swells
With leafy buds and flowery bells;
Gemming shoots the olive twine;
Clusters bright festoon the vine;
All along the branches creeping,
Through the velvet foliage peeping,
Little infant fruits we see
Nursing into luxury.

From the Greek of ANACREON,
by THOMAS MOORE.

MAY MORNING.

Now the bright morning star, day's harbinger,
Comes dancing from the east, and leads with her
The flowery May, who from her green lap throws
The yellow cowslip and the pale primrose.
Hail, bounteous May! that doth inspire
Mirth and youth and warm desire;
Woods and groves are of thy dressing,
Hill and dale doth boast thy blessing.
Thus we salute thee with our early song,
And welcome thee, and wish thee long.

MILTON.

TO AURELIA.

SEE, the flowery spring is blown,
Let us leave the smoky town;
From the mall, and from the ring,
Every one has taken wing;
Chloe, Strephon, Corydon,
To the meadows all are gone.
What is left you worth your stay?
Come, Aurelia, come away.

Come, Aurelia, come and see
What a lodge I 've dressed for thee;
But the seat you cannot see,
'T is so hid with jessamy,
With the vine that o'er the walls,
And in every window crawls;
Let us there be blithe and gay!
Come, Aurelia, come away.

Come with all thy sweetest wiles,
With thy graces and thy smiles;
Come, and we will merry be,
Who shall be so blest as we?

We will frolic all the day,
Haste, Aurelia, while we may:
Ay! and should not life be gay?
Yes, Aurelia, — come away.

JOHN DYER.

MAY.

MAY, thou month of rosy beauty,
Month when pleasure is a duty;
Month of maids that milk the kine,
Bosom rich, and health divine;
Month of bees and month of flowers,
Month of blossom-laden bowers:
Month of little hands with daisies,
Lovers' love, and poets' praises;
O thou merry month complete,
May, the very name is sweet!
May was MAID in olden times,
And is still in Scottish rhymes —
May 's the month that 's laughing now.
I no sooner write the word,
Than it seems as though it heard,
And looks up and laughs at me,
Like a sweet face, rosily, —
Flushing from the paper's white;
Like a bride that knows her power,
Startled in a summer bower.

If the rains that do us wrong
Come to keep the winter long
And deny us thy sweet looks,
I can love thee, sweet, in books,
Love thee in the poets' pages,
Where they keep thee green for ages;
Love and read thee as a lover
Reads his lady's letters over,
Breathing blessings on the art
Which commingles those that part.

There is May in books forever:
May will part from Spencer never;
May 's in Milton, May 's in Prior,
May 's in Chaucer, Thomson, Byer;
May 's in all the Italian books;
She has old and modern nooks,
Where she sleeps with nymphs and elves
In happy places they call shelves,
And will rise and dress your rooms
With a drapery thick with blooms.

Come, ye rains, then, if ye will,
May 's at home and with me still;
But come rather, thou good weather,
And find us in the fields together.

LEIGH HUNT.

MAY.

I FEEL a newer life in every gale;
The winds that fan the flowers,
And with their welcome breathings fill the sail,
Tell of serener hours, —
Of hours that glide unfelt away
Beneath the sky of May.

The spirit of the gentle south-wind calls
From his blue throne of air,
And where his whispering voice in music falls,
Beauty is budding there;
The bright ones of the valley break
Their slumbers, and awake.

The waving verdure rolls along the plain,
And the wide forest weaves,
To welcome back its playful mates again,
A canopy of leaves;
And from its darkening shadow floats
A gush of trembling notes.

Fairer and brighter spreads the reign of May;
The tresses of the woods
With the light dallying of the west-wind play;
And the full-brimming floods,
As gladly to their goal they run,
Hail the returning sun.

JAMES GATES PERCIVAL.

THEY COME! THE MERRY SUMMER MONTHS.

THEY come! the merry summer months of beauty, song, and flowers;
They come! the gladsome months that bring thick leafiness to bowers.
Up, up, my heart! and walk abroad; fling cark and care aside;
Seek silent hills, or rest thyself where peaceful waters glide;
Or, underneath the shadow vast of patriarchal tree,
Scan through its leaves the cloudless sky in rapt tranquillity.

The grass is soft, its velvet touch is grateful to the hand;
And, like the kiss of maiden love, the breeze is sweet and bland;
The daisy and the buttercup are nodding courteously;
It stirs their blood with kindest love, to bless and welcome thee;
And mark how with thine own thin locks — they now are silvery gray —
That blissful breeze is wantoning, and whispering, "Be gay!"

There is no cloud that sails along the ocean of yon sky
But hath its own winged mariners to give it melody;
Thou seest their glittering fans outspread, all gleaming like red gold;
And hark! with shrill pipe musical, their merry course they hold.
God bless them all, those little ones, who, far above this earth,
Can make a scoff of its mean joys, and vent a nobler mirth.

But soft! mine ear upcaught a sound, — from yonder wood it came!
The spirit of the dim green glade did breathe his own glad name; —
Yes, it is he! the hermit bird, that, apart from all his kind,
Slow spells his beads monotonous to the soft western wind;
Cuckoo! Cuckoo! he sings again, — his notes are void of art;
But simplest strains do soonest sound the deep founts of the heart.

Good Lord! it is a gracious boon for thought-crazed wight like me,
To smell again these summer flowers beneath this summer tree!
To suck once more in every breath their little souls away,
And feed my fancy with fond dreams of youth's bright summer day,
When, rushing forth like untamed colt, the reckless, truant boy
Wandered through greenwoods all day long, a mighty heart of joy!

I'm sadder now, — I have had cause; but O, I'm proud to think
That each pure joy-fount, loved of yore, I yet delight to drink; —
Leaf, blossom, blade, hill, valley, stream, the calm, unclouded sky,
Still mingle music with my dreams, as in the days gone by.
When summer's loveliness and light fall round me dark and cold,
I'll bear indeed life's heaviest curse, — a heart that hath waxed old!

WILLIAM MOTHERWELL.

JUNE.

FROM "THE VISION OF SIR LAUNFAL."

Earth gets its price for what Earth gives us;
The beggar is taxed for a corner to die in,
The priest hath his fee who comes and shrives us,
We bargain for the graves we lie in;
At the Devil's booth are all things sold,
Each ounce of dross costs its ounce of gold;
For a cap and bells our lives we pay,
Bubbles we earn with a whole soul's tasking:
'T is heaven alone that is given away,
'T is only God may be had for the asking;
There is no price set on the lavish summer,
And June may be had by the poorest comer.

And what is so rare as a day in June?
Then, if ever, come perfect days;
Then Heaven tries the earth if it be in tune,
And over it softly her warm ear lays:
Whether we look, or whether we listen,
We hear life murmur, or see it glisten;
Every clod feels a stir of might,
An instinct within it that reaches and towers
And, grasping blindly above it for light,
Climbs to a soul in grass and flowers;
The flush of life may well be seen
Thrilling back over hills and valleys;
The cowslip startles in meadows green,
The buttercup catches the sun in its chalice,
And there's never a leaf or a blade too mean
To be some happy creature's palace;
The little bird sits at his door in the sun,
A-tilt like a blossom among the leaves,
And lets his illumined being o'errun
With the deluge of summer it receives;
His mate feels the eggs beneath her wings,
And the heart in her dumb breast flutters and sings;
He sings to the wide world, and she to her nest, —
In the nice ear of Nature, which song is the best?

Now is the high-tide of the year,
And whatever of life hath ebbed away
Comes flooding back, with a ripply cheer,
Into every bare inlet and creek and bay;
Now the heart is so full that a drop overfills it,
We are happy now because God so wills it;
No matter how barren the past may have been,
'T is enough for us now that the leaves are green;
We sit in the warm shade and feel right well
How the sap creeps up and the blossoms swell;
We may shut our eyes, but we cannot help knowing
That skies are clear and grass is growing;
The breeze comes whispering in our ear,
That dandelions are blossoming near,
That maize has sprouted, that streams are flowing,
That the river is bluer than the sky,
That the robin is plastering his house hard by;
And if the breeze kept the good news back,
For other couriers we should not lack;
We could guess it all by yon heifer's lowing, —

And hark! how clear bold chanticleer,
Warmed with the new wine of the year,
Tells all in his lusty crowing!
Joy comes, grief goes, we know not how;
Everything is happy now,
Everything is upward striving;
'T is as easy now for the heart to be true
As for grass to be green or skies to be blue, —
'T is the natural way of living:
Who knows whither the clouds have fled?
In the unscarred heaven they leave no wake,
And the eyes forget the tears they have shed,
The heart forgets its sorrow and ache;
The soul partakes the season's youth,
And the sulphurous rifts of passion and woe
Lie deep 'neath a silence pure and smooth,
Like burnt-out craters healed with snow.

JAMES RUSSELL LOWELL.

THE CHILD'S WISH IN JUNE.

MOTHER, mother, the winds are at play,
Prithee, let me be idle to-day.
Look, dear mother, the flowers all lie
Languidly under the bright blue sky.
See, how slowly the streamlet glides;
Look, how the violet roguishly hides;
Even the butterfly rests on the rose,
And scarcely sips the sweets as he goes.
Poor Tray is asleep in the noonday sun,
And the flies go about him one by one;
And pussy sits near with a sleepy grace,
Without ever thinking of washing her face.
There flies a bird to a neighboring tree,
But very lazily flieth he,
And he sits and twitters a gentle note,
That scarcely ruffles his little throat.

You bid me be busy; but, mother, hear
How the humdrum grasshopper soundeth near,
And the soft west-wind is so light in its play,
It scarcely moves a leaf on the spray.

I wish, O, I wish I was yonder cloud,
That sails about with its misty shroud;
Books and work I no more should see,
And I 'd come and float, dear mother, o'er thee.

CAROLINE GILMAN.

IN SUMMER TIME.

O LINDEN-TREES! whose branches high
Shut out the noontide's sultry sky,
Throwing a shadow cool and dim
Along the meadow's grassy rim,
How sweet in dreamy rest to lie,
Unheeding how the moments fly;
While woodland odors, faint and rare,
Of fern and wild rose scent the air, —
And hear the light winds play around
From leaf to leaf with rustling sound, —
And trill of bird, and insect's hum,
And all the lulling tones that come
In summer time.

O Linden-trees! so mossy-old,
What pleasant memories you hold
Of early childhood, and its days
Of frolic, sport, and guileless ways;
A time of joyance, bright and fair,
Beneath a mother's tender care.
And ever on, till manhood brought
Maturer aims and deeper thought, —
And Love arose, and life became
All radiant with his quenchless flame,
As here, within your shelter wide,
We met and lingered side by side,
In summer time.

O Linden-trees! as now once more
I live those happy moments o'er,
And, stretched at ease upon the grass,
See picture after picture pass,
Another, brighter vision stays
My backward thoughts and fills my gaze;
For look! where down yon shaded walk
A merry troop, in cheerful talk,
And gleeful laugh, and shout and song,
Maud and the children pass along!
O Lindens! tell me what could be
More sweet to hear, or fair to see,
In summer time?

W. W. CALDWELL.

SUMMER MORNING.

FROM "THE SEASONS."

SHORT is the doubtful empire of the night;
And soon, observant of approaching day,
The meek-eyed morn appears, mother of dews,
At first faint gleaming in the dappled east, —
Till far o'er ether spreads the widening glow,
And, from before the luster of her face,
White break the clouds away. With quickened step,
Brown night retires. Young day pours in apace,
And opens all the lawny prospect wide.
The dripping rock, the mountain's misty top,
Swell on the sight, and brighten with the dawn.
Blue, through the dusk, the smoking currents shine;
And from the bladed field the fearful hare

Limps, awkward; while along the forest glade
The wild deer trip, and often turning gaze
At early passenger. Music awakes,
The native voice of undissembled joy;
And thick around the woodland hymns arise.
Roused by the cock, the soon-clad shepherd leaves
His mossy cottage, where with peace he dwells;
And from the crowded fold, in order, drives
His flock, to taste the verdure of the morn.

JAMES THOMSON.

SONG OF THE SUMMER WINDS.

Up the dale and down the bourne,
  O'er the meadow swift we fly;
Now we sing, and now we mourn,
  Now we whistle, now we sigh.

By the grassy-fringèd river,
  Through the murmuring reeds we sweep;
Mid the lily-leaves we quiver,
  To their very hearts we creep.

Now the maiden rose is blushing
  At the frolic things we say,
While aside her cheek we 're rushing,
  Like some truant bees at play.

Through the blooming groves we rustle,
  Kissing every bud we pass, —
As we did it in the bustle,
  Scarcely knowing how it was.

Down the glen, across the mountain,
  O'er the yellow heath we roam,
Whirling round about the fountain,
  Till its little breakers foam.

Bending down the weeping willows,
  While our vesper hymn we sigh;
Then unto our rosy pillows
  On our weary wings we hie.

There of idlenesses dreaming,
  Scarce from waking we refrain,
Moments long as ages deeming
  Till we 're at our play again.

GEORGE DARLEY.

THE STORY OF A SUMMER DAY.

O PERFECT Light, which shaid away
  The darkness from the light,
And set a ruler o'er the day,
  Another o'er the night;

Thy glory, when the day forth flies,
  More vively does appear,
Than at midday unto our eyes
  The shining sun is clear.

The shadow of the earth anon
  Removes and drawis by,
While in the east, when it is gone,
  Appears a clearer sky.

Which soon perceive the little larks,
  The lapwing and the snipe,
And time their songs, like Nature's clerks,
  O'er meadow, muir, and stripe.

Our hemisphere is polished clean,
  And lightened more and more;
While everything is clearly seen,
  Which seemèd dim before;

Except, the glistening astres bright,
  Which all the night were clear,
Offuskèd with a greater light,
  No longer do appear.

The golden globe incontinent
  Sets up his shining head,
And o'er the earth and firmament
  Displays his beams abread.

For joy the birds with boulden throats
  Against his visage sheen
Take up their kindly music notes
  In woods and gardens green.

The dew upon the tender crops,
  Like pearles white and round,
Or like to melted silver drops,
  Refreshes all the ground.

The misty reek, the clouds of rain
  From tops of mountains skails,
Clear are the highest hills and plain,
  The vapors take the vales.

The ample heaven, of fabric sure,
  In cleanness does surpass
The crystal and the silver pure,
  Or clearest polished glass.

The time so tranquil is and still,
  That nowhere shall ye find,
Save on a high and barren hill,
  The air of peeping wind.

All trees and simples, great and small,
  That balmy leaf do bear,
Than they were painted on a wall,
  No more they move or steir.

Calm is the deep and purple sea,
  Yea, smoother than the sand ;
The waves, that weltering wont to be,
  Are stable like the land.

So silent is the cessile air,
  That every cry and call,
The hills and dales and forest fair
  Again repeats them all.

The flourishes and fragrant flowers,
  Through Phœbus' fostering heat,
Refreshed with dew and silver showers,
  Cast up an odor sweet.

The cloggèd, busy humming-bees,
  That never think to drone,
On flowers and flourishes of trees,
  Collect their liquor brown.

The sun, most like a speedy post,
  With ardent course ascends ;
The beauty of the heavenly host
  Up to our zenith tends ;

Not guided by a Phaëthon,
  Not trainèd in a chair,
But by the high and holy One,
  Who does all where empíre.

The burning beams down from his face
  So fervently can beat,
That man and beast now seek a place
  To save them from the heat.

The herds beneath some leafy tree,
  Amidst the flowers they lie ;
The stable ships upon the sea
  Tend up their sails to dry.

With gilded eyes and open wings,
  The cock his courage shows ;
With claps of joy his breast he dings,
  And twenty times he crows.

The dove with whistling wings so blue,
  The winds can fast collect,
Her purple pens turn many a hue
  Against the sun direct.

Now noon is went ; gone is midday,
  The heat does slake at last,
The sun descends down west away,
  For three o'clock is past.

The rayons of the sun we see
  Diminish in their strength,
The shade of every tower and tree
  Extended is in length.

Great is the calm, for everywhere
  The wind is settling down,
The reek throws right up in the air
  From every tower and town.

The gloaming comes, the day is spent,
  The sun goes out of sight,
And painted is the occident
  With purple sanguine bright.

The scarlet nor the golden thread,
  Who would their beauty try,
Are nothing like the color red
  And beauty of the sky.

Our west horizon circular,
  From time the sun be set,
Is all with rubies, as it were,
  Or roses red o'erfret.

What pleasure were to walk and see,
  Endlong a river clear,
The perfect form of every tree
  Within the deep appear.

O, then it were a seemly thing,
  While all is still and calm,
The praise of God to play and sing
  With cornet and with shalm !

All laborers draw home at even,
  And can to other say,
Thanks to the gracious God of heaven,
  Which sent this summer day !

ALEXANDER HUME.

SIGNS OF RAIN.

FORTY REASONS FOR NOT ACCEPTING AN INVITATION OF A FRIEND TO MAKE AN EXCURSION WITH HIM.

1 The hollow winds begin to blow ;
2 The clouds look black, the glass is low,
3 The soot falls down, the spaniels sleep,
4 And spiders from their cobwebs peep.
5 Last night the sun went pale to bed,
6 The moon in halos hid her head ;
7 The boding shepherd heaves a sigh,
8 For see, a rainbow spans the sky !
9 The walls are damp, the ditches smell,
10 Closed is the pink-eyed pimpernel.
11 Hark how the chairs and tables crack !
12 Old Betty's nerves are on the rack ;
13 Loud quacks the duck, the peacocks cry,
14 The distant hills are seeming nigh.
15 How restless are the snorting swine !
16 The busy flies disturb the kine,
17 Low o'er the grass the swallow wings,
18 The cricket, too, how sharp he sings !
19 Puss on the hearth, with velvet paws,

20 Sits wiping o'er her whiskered jaws;
21 Through the clear streams the fishes rise,
22 And nimbly catch the incautious flies.
23 The glowworms, numerous and light,
24 Illumed the dewy dell last night;
25 At dusk the squalid toad was seen,
26 Hopping and crawling o'er the green;
27 The whirling dust the wind obeys,
28 And in the rapid eddy plays;
29 The frog has changed his yellow vest,
30 And in a russet coat is dressed.
31 Though June, the air is cold and still,
32 The mellow blackbird's voice is shrill;
33 My dog, so altered in his taste,
34 Quits mutton-bones on grass to feast;
35 And see yon rooks, how odd their flight!
36 They imitate the gliding kite,
37 And seem precipitate to fall,
38 As if they felt the piercing ball.
39 'T will surely rain; I see with sorrow,
40 Our jaunt must be put off to-morrow.

DR. EDWARD JENNER.

SUMMER MOODS.

I LOVE at eventide to walk alone,
Down narrow glens, o'erhung with dewy thorn,
Where from the long grass underneath, the snail,
Jet black, creeps out, and sprouts his timid horn.
I love to muse o'er meadows newly mown,
Where withering grass perfumes the sultry air;
Where bees search round, with sad and weary drone,
In vain, for flowers that bloomed but newly there;
While in the juicy corn the hidden quail
Cries, "Wet my foot"; and, hid as thoughts unborn,
The fairy-like and seldom-seen land-rail
Utters "Craik, craik," like voices underground,
Right glad to meet the evening's dewy veil,
And see the light fade into gloom around.

JOHN CLARE.

RAIN IN SUMMER.

How beautiful is the rain!
After the dust and heat,
In the broad and fiery street,
In the narrow lane,
How beautiful is the rain!

How it clatters along the roofs,
Like the tramp of hoofs!
How it gushes and struggles out
From the throat of the overflowing spout!
Across the window-pane
It pours and pours;
And swift and wide,
With a muddy tide,
Like a river down the gutter roars
The rain, the welcome rain!

The sick man from his chamber looks
At the twisted brooks;
He can feel the cool
Breath of each little pool;
His fevered brain
Grows calm again,
And he breathes a blessing on the rain.

From the neighboring school
Come the boys,
With more than their wonted noise
And commotion;
And down the wet streets
Sail their mimic fleets,
Till the treacherous pool
Ingulfs them in its whirling
And turbulent ocean.

In the country, on every side,
Where far and wide,
Like a leopard's tawny and spotted hide,
Stretches the plain,
To the dry grass and the drier grain
How welcome is the rain!

In the furrowed land
The toilsome and patient oxen stand;
Lifting the yoke-encumbered head,
With their dilated nostrils spread,
They silently inhale
The clover-scented gale,
And the vapors that arise
From the well-watered and smoking soil.
For this rest in the furrow after toil
Their large and lustrous eyes
Seem to thank the Lord,
More than man's spoken word.

Near at hand,
From under the sheltering trees,
The farmer sees
His pastures, and his fields of grain,
As they bend their tops
To the numberless beating drops
Of the incessant rain.
He counts it as no sin
That he sees therein
Only his own thrift and gain.

These, and far more than these,
The Poet sees!
He can behold
Aquarius old
Walking the fenceless fields of air;

Engraved by Geo. E. Perine

J. B. FORD & C° NEW YORK.

And from each ample fold
Of the clouds about him rolled
Scattering everywhere
The showery rain,
As the farmer scatters his grain.

He can behold
Things manifold
That have not yet been wholly told, —
Have not been wholly sung or said.
For his thought, that never stops,
Follows the water-drops
Down to the graves of the dead,
Down through chasms and gulfs profound,
To the dreary fountain-head
Of lakes and rivers underground;
And sees them, when the rain is done,
On the bridge of colors seven
Climbing up once more to heaven,
Opposite the setting sun.

Thus the Seer,
With vision clear,
Sees forms appear and disappear,
In the perpetual round of strange,
Mysterious change
From birth to death, from death to birth,
From earth to heaven, from heaven to earth;
Till glimpses more sublime
Of things, unseen before,
Unto his wondering eyes reveal
The Universe, as an immeasurable wheel
Turning forevermore
In the rapid and rushing river of Time.

HENRY WADSWORTH LONGFELLOW.

SUMMER STORM.

UNTREMULOUS in the river clear,
Toward the sky's image, hangs the imaged bridge;
So still the air that I can hear
The slender clarion of the unseen midge;
Out of the stillness, with a gathering creep,
Like rising wind in leaves, which now decreases,
Now lulls, now swells, and all the while increases.
The huddling trample of a drove of sheep
Tilts the loose planks, and then as gradually ceases
In dust on the other side; life's emblem deep,
A confused noise between two silences,
Finding at last in dust precarious peace.
On the wide marsh, the purple-blossomed grasses
Soak up the sunshine; sleeps the brimming tide
Save when the wedge-shaped wake in silence passes
Of some slow water-rat, whose sinuous glide
Wavers the long green sedge's shade from side to side;
But up the west, like a rock-shivered surge,
Climbs a great cloud edged with sun-whitened spray;
Huge whirls of foam boil toppling o'er its verge,
And falling still it seems, and yet it climbs alway.

Suddenly all the sky is hid
As with the shutting of a lid,
One by one great drops are falling
Doubtful and slow;
Down the pane they are crookedly crawling,
And the wind breathes low;
Slowly the circles widen on the river,
Widen and mingle, one and all;
Here and there the slenderer flowers shiver,
Struck by an icy rain-drop's fall.

Now on the hills I hear the thunder mutter,
The wind is gathering in the west;
The upturned leaves first whiten and flutter,
Then droop to a fitful rest;
Up from the stream with sluggish flap
Struggles the gull and floats away;
Nearer and nearer rolls the thunder-clap, —
We shall not see the sun go down to-day:
Now leaps the wind on the sleepy marsh,
And tramples the grass with terrified feet,
The startled river turns leaden and harsh,
You can hear the quick heart of the tempest beat.

Look! look! that livid flash!
And instantly follows the rattling thunder,
As if some cloud-crag, split asunder,
Fell, splintering with a ruinous crash,
On the Earth, which crouches in silence under;
And now a solid gray wall of rain
Shuts off the landscape, mile by mile;
For a breath's space I see the blue wood again,
And, ere the next heart-beat, the wind-hurled pile,
That seemed but now a league aloof,
Bursts crackling o'er the sun-parched roof;
Against the windows the storm comes dashing,
Through tattered foliage the hail tears crashing,
The blue lightning flashes,
The rapid hail clashes,
The white waves are tumbling,
And, in one baffled roar,
Like the toothless sea mumbling
A rock-bristled shore,
The thunder is rumbling
And crashing and crumbling, —
Will silence return nevermore?

Hush! Still as death,
The tempest holds his breath
As from a sudden will;
The rain stops short, but from the eaves
You see it drop, and hear it from the leaves,
All is so bodingly still;

Again, now, now, again
Plashes the rain in heavy gouts,
The crinkled lightning
Seems ever brightening,
And loud and long
Again the thunder shouts
His battle-song, —
One quivering flash,
One wildering crash,
Followed by silence dead and dull,
As if the cloud, let go,
Leapt bodily below
To whelm the earth in one mad overthrow,
And then a total lull.

Gone, gone, so soon!
No more my half-crazed fancy there
Can shape a giant in the air,
No more I see his streaming hair,
The writhing portent of his form; —
The pale and quiet moon
Makes her calm forehead bare,
And the last fragments of the storm,
Like shattered rigging from a fight at sea,
Silent and few, are drifting over me.

JAMES RUSSELL LOWELL.

THE STORM.

FROM "LEONORE."

WHILE yet the feeble accents hung
Unfinished on his faltering tongue,
Through the tall arches flashing came
A broad and livid sheet of flame,
Playing with fearful radiance o'er
The upraised features of Leonore,
The shrinking form of her trembling sire,
The bridegroom's face of scowling ire,
And the folded hands and heaving breast,
And prophet-like mien of the aged priest!

'T was a breathless pause, — but a moment more,
And that fierce, unnatural beam was o'er,
And a stunning crash, as if earth were driven
On thundering wheels to the gates of heaven,
Burst, pealed, and muttered long and deep,
Then sinking, growled itself to sleep,
And all was still.

MARGARET DAVIDSON.

AFTER A SUMMER SHOWER.

THE rain is o'er. How dense and bright
Yon pearly clouds reposing lie!
Cloud above cloud, a glorious sight,
Contrasting with the dark blue sky!

In grateful silence earth receives
The general blessing; fresh and fair,
Each flower expands its little leaves,
As glad the common joy to share.

The softened sunbeams pour around
A fairy light, uncertain, pale;
The wind flows cool; the scented ground
Is breathing odors on the gale.

Mid yon rich clouds' voluptuous pile,
Methinks some spirit of the air
Might rest, to gaze below awhile,
Then turn to bathe and revel there.

The sun breaks forth; from off the scene
Its floating veil of mist is flung;
And all the wilderness of green
With trembling drops of light is hung.

Now gaze on Nature, — yet the same, —
Glowing with life, by breezes fanned,
Luxuriant, lovely, as she came,
Fresh in her youth, from God's own hand.

Hear the rich music of that voice,
Which sounds from all below, above;
She calls her children to rejoice,
And round them throws her arms of love.

Drink in her influence; low-born care,
And all the train of mean desire,
Refuse to breathe this holy air,
And mid this living light expire.

ANDREWS NORTON.

A DROP OF DEW.

SEE how the orient dew,
Shed from the bosom of the morn
Into the blowing roses,
(Yet careless of its mansion new
For the clear region where 't was born)
Round in itself encloses,
And in its little globe's extent
Frames, as it can, its native element.
How it the purple flower does slight,
Scarce touching where it lies;
But gazing back upon the skies,
Shines with a mournful light,
Like its own tear,
Because so long divided from the sphere;
Restless it rolls, and unsecure,
Trembling, lest it grow impure,
Till the warm sun pities its pain,
And to the skies exhales it back again.
So the soul, that drop, that ray

Of the clear fountain of eternal day,
Could it within the human flower be seen,
Remembering still its former height,
Shuns the sweet leaves and blossoms green,
And, recollecting its own light,
Does, in its pure and circling thoughts, express
The greater heaven in a heaven less.
In how coy a figure wound,
Every way it turns away;
So the world excluding round,
Yet receiving in the day.
Dark beneath, but bright above;
Here disdaining, there in love.
How loose and easy hence to go!
How girt and ready to ascend!
Moving but on a point below,
It all about does upwards bend.
Such did the manna's sacred dew distill,
White and entire, although congealed and chill,—
Congealed on earth, but does, dissolving, run
Into the glories of the Almighty sun.

ANDREW MARVELL.

A SUMMER EVENING'S MEDITATION.

"One sun by day, by night ten thousand shine."—YOUNG.

'T IS past, — the sultry tyrant of the South
Has spent his short-lived rage; more grateful hours
Move silent on; the skies no more repel
The dazzled sight, but, with mild maiden beams
Of tempered luster, court the cherished eye
To wander o'er their sphere; where, hung aloft,
Dian's bright crescent, like a silver bow,
New strung in heaven, lifts its beamy horns
Impatient for the night, and seems to push
Her brother down the sky. Fair Venus shines
Even in the eye of day; with sweetest beam
Propitious shines, and shakes a trembling flood
Of softened radiance with her dewy locks.
The shadows spread apace; while meekened Eve,
Her cheek yet warm with blushes, slow retires
Through the Hesperian gardens of the West,
And shuts the gates of Day. 'T is now the hour
When Contemplation, from her sunless haunts,
The cool damp grotto, or the lonely depth
Of unpierced woods, where rapt in solid shade
She mused away the gaudy hours of noon,
And fed on thoughts unripened by the sun,
Moves forward and with radiant finger points
To yon blue concave swelled by breath divine,
Where, one by one, the living eyes of heaven
Awake, quick kindling o'er the face of ether
One boundless blaze; ten thousand trembling fires,
And dancing lusters, where the unsteady eye,
Restless and dazzled, wanders unconfined
O'er all this field of glories; spacious field,
And worthy of the Master, — He whose hand
With hieroglyphics elder than the Nile
Inscribed the mystic tablet, hung on high
To public gaze, and said, Adore, O man!
The finger of thy God. From what pure wells
Of milky light, what soft o'erflowing urn,
Are all these lamps so filled? — these friendly lamps,
Forever streaming o'er the azure deep
To point our path, and light us to our home.
How soft they slide along their lucid spheres,
And, silent as the foot of Time, fulfill
Their destined courses! Nature's self is hushed,
And but a scattered leaf, which rustles through
The thick-wove foliage, not a sound is heard
To break the midnight air; though the raised ear,
Intently listening, drinks in every breath.
How deep the silence, yet how loud the praise!
But are they silent all? or is there not
A tongue in every star that talks with man,
And wooes him to be wise? nor wooes in vain:
This dead of midnight is the noon of thought,
And Wisdom mounts her zenith with the stars.
At this still hour the self-collected soul
Turns inward, and beholds a stranger there
Of high descent, and more than mortal rank;
An embryo God; a spark of fire divine,
Which must burn on for ages, when the sun
(Fair transitory creature of a day!)
Has closed his golden eye, and, wrapt in shades,
Forgets his wonted journey through the East.
Ye citadels of light, and seats of gods!
Perhaps my future home, from whence the soul,
Revolving periods past, may oft look back,
With recollected tenderness, on all
The various busy scenes she left below,
Its deep-laid projects and its strange events,
As on some fond and doting tale that soothed
Her infant hours, — O, be it lawful now
To tread the hallowed circle of your courts,
And with mute wonder and delighted awe
Approach your burning confines! Seized in thought,
On Fancy's wild and roving wing I sail,
From the green borders of the peopled earth,
And the pale moon, her duteous, fair attendant;
From solitary Mars; from the vast orb
Of Jupiter, whose huge gigantic bulk
Dances in ether like the lightest leaf,
To the dim verge, the suburbs of the system,
Where cheerless Saturn midst his watery moons
Girt with a lucid zone, in gloomy pomp,
Sits like an exiled monarch: fearless thence
I launch into the trackless deeps of space,
Where, burning round, ten thousand suns appear,
Of elder beam, which ask no leave to shine
Of our terrestrial star, nor borrow light
From the proud regent of our scanty day;

Sons of the morning, first-born of creation,
And only less than Him who marks their track
And guides their fiery wheels. Here must I stop,
Or is there aught beyond? What hand unseen
Impels me onward through the glowing orbs
Of habitable nature, far remote,
To the dread confines of eternal night,
To solitudes of waste unpeopled space,
The deserts of creation, wide and wild;
Where embryo systems and unkindled suns
Sleep in the womb of chaos? Fancy droops,
And Thought, astonished, stops her bold career.
But, O thou mighty Mind! whose powerful word
Said, "Thus let all things be," and thus they were,
Where shall I seek thy presence? how unblamed
Invoke thy dread perfection?
Have the broad eyelids of the morn beheld thee?
Or does the beamy shoulder of Orion
Support thy throne? O, look with pity down
On erring, guilty man; not in thy names
Of terror clad; not with those thunders armed
That conscious Sinai felt, when fear appalled
The scattered tribes; thou hast a gentler voice,
That whispers comfort to the swelling heart,
Abashed, yet longing to behold her Maker!
But now my soul, unused to stretch her powers
In flight so daring, drops her weary wing,
And seeks again the known accustomed spot,
Drest up with sun and shade and lawns and streams,
A mansion fair and spacious for its guests,
And all replete with wonders. Let me here,
Content and grateful, wait the appointed time,
And ripen for the skies: the hour will come
When all these splendors bursting on my sight
Shall stand unveiled, and to my ravished sense
Unlock the glories of the world unknown.

ANNA LETITIA BARBAULD.

A SUMMER EVENING.

How fine has the day been! how bright was the sun!
How lovely and joyful the course that he run,
Though he rose in a mist when his race he begun,
And there followed some droppings of rain!
But now the fair traveler's come to the west,
His rays are all gold, and his beauties are best:
He paints the sky gay as he sinks to his rest,
And foretells a bright rising again.

Just such is the Christian; his course he begins,
Like the sun in a mist, when he mourns for his sins,
And melts into tears; then he breaks out and shines,
And travels his heavenly way:
But when he comes nearer to finish his race,
Like a fine setting sun, he looks richer in grace,
And gives a sure hope, at the end of his days,
Of rising in brighter array.

ISAAC WATTS.

THE RAINBOW.

My heart leaps up when I behold
A rainbow in the sky;
So was it when my life began,
So is it now I am a man,
So be it when I shall grow old,
Or let me die!
The Child is father of the Man;
And I could wish my days to be
Bound each to each by natural piety.

WILLIAM WORDSWORTH.

MOONLIGHT IN SUMMER.

Low on the utmost boundary of the sight,
The rising vapors catch the silver light;
Thence fancy measures, as they parting fly,
Which first will throw its shadow on the eye,
Passing the source of light; and thence away,
Succeeded quick by brighter still than they.
For yet above these wafted clouds are seen
(In a remoter sky still more serene)
Others, detached in ranges through the air,
Spotless as snow, and countless as they 're fair;
Scattered immensely wide from east to west,
The beauteous semblance of a flock at rest.
These, to the raptured mind, aloud proclaim
Their mighty Shepherd's everlasting name;
And thus the loiterer's utmost stretch of soul
Climbs the still clouds, or passes those that roll,
And loosed imagination soaring goes
High o'er his home and all his little woes.

ROBERT BLOOMFIELD.

SEPTEMBER.

Sweet is the voice that calls
From babbling waterfalls
In meadows where the downy seeds are flying;
And soft the breezes blow,
And eddying come and go
In faded gardens where the rose is dying.

Among the stubbled corn
The blithe quail pipes at morn,
The merry partridge drums in hidden places,
And glittering insects gleam
Above the reedy stream,
Where busy spiders spin their filmy laces.

At eve, cool shadows fall
Across the garden wall,
And on the clustered grapes to purple turning;
And pearly vapors lie
Along the eastern sky,
Where the broad harvest moon is redly burning.

Ah, soon on field and hill
The wind shall whistle chill,
And patriarch swallows call their flocks together,
To fly from frost and snow,
And seek for lands where blow
The fairer blossoms of a balmier weather.

The cricket chirps all day,
"O fairest summer, stay!
The squirrel eyes askance the chestnuts browning;
The wild fowl fly afar
Above the foamy bar,
And hasten southward ere the skies are frowning.

Now comes a fragrant breeze
Through the dark cedar-trees,
And round about my temples fondly lingers,
In gentle playfulness,
Like to the soft caress
Bestowed in happier days by loving fingers.

Yet, though a sense of grief
Comes with the falling leaf,
And memory makes the summer doubly pleasant,
In all my autumn dreams
A future summer gleams,
Passing the fairest glories of the present!

GEORGE ARNOLD.

AUTUMN.

A DIRGE.

THE autumn is old;
The sear leaves are flying;
He hath gathered up gold,
And now he is dying:
Old age, begin sighing!

The vintage is ripe;
The harvest is heaping;
But some that have sowed
Have no riches for reaping:—
Poor wretch, fall a-weeping!

The year 's in the wane;
There is nothing adorning;
The night has no eve,
And the day has no morning;
Cold winter gives warning.

The rivers run chill;
The red sun is sinking;
And I am grown old,
And life is fast shrinking;
Here 's enow for sad thinking!

THOMAS HOOD.

THE LATTER RAIN.

THE latter rain, — it falls in anxious haste
Upon the sun-dried fields and branches bare,
Loosening with searching drops the rigid waste
As if it would each root's lost strength repair;
But not a blade grows green as in the spring;
No swelling twig puts forth its thickening leaves;
The robins only mid the harvests sing,
Pecking the grain that scatters from the sheaves;
The rain falls still, — the fruit all ripened drops,
It pierces chestnut-burr and walnut-shell;
The furrowed fields disclose the yellow crops;
Each bursting pod of talents used can tell;
And all that once received the early rain
Declare to man it was not sent in vain.

JONES VERY.

AUTUMN.

THE warm sun is failing; the bleak wind is wailing;
The bare boughs are sighing; the pale flowers are dying;
And the Year
On the earth, her death-bed, in shroud of leaves dead,
Is lying.
Come, months, come away,
From November to May;
In your saddest array
Follow the bier
Of the dead, cold Year,
And like dim shadows watch by her sepulcher.

The chill rain is falling; the nipt worm is crawling;
The rivers are swelling; the thunder is knelling
For the Year;
The blithe swallows are flown, and the lizards each gone
To his dwelling;
Come, months, come away;
Put on white, black, and gray;
Let your light sisters play, —
Ye, follow the bier
Of the dead, cold Year,
And make her grave green with tear on tear.

PERCY BYSSHE SHELLEY.

THE AUTUMN.

THE autumn time is with us! Its approach
Was heralded, not many days ago,
By hazy skies that veiled the brazen sun,
And sea-like murmurs from the rustling corn,
And low-voiced brooks that wandered drowsily
By purpling clusters of the juicy grape,
Swinging upon the vine. And now, 't is here,
And what a change hath passed upon the face
Of Nature, where thy waving forests spread,
Then robed in deepest green! All through the night
The subtle frost hath plied its mystic art,
And in the day the golden sun hath wrought
True wonders; and the wings of morn and even
Have touched with magic breath the changing leaves.
And now, as wanders the dilating eye
Athwart the varied landscape circling far,
What gorgeousness, what blazonry, what pomp
Of colors, bursts upon the ravished sight!
Here, where the maple rears its yellow crest,
A golden glory; yonder, where the oak
Stands monarch of the forest, and the ash
Is girt with flame-like parasite, and broad
The dog-wood spreads beneath a rolling field
Of deepest crimson; and afar, where looms
The gnarlèd gum, a cloud of bloodiest red!

WILLIAM D. GALLAGHER.

INDIAN SUMMER.

THERE is a time, just when the frost
Begins to pave old Winter's way,
When Autumn, in a revery lost,
The mellow daytime dreams away;

When Summer comes, in musing mind,
To gaze once more on hill and dell,
To mark how many sheaves they bind,
And see if all are ripened well.

With balmy breath she whispers low;
The dying flowers look up and give
Their sweetest incense ere they go,
For her who made their beauties live.

She enters 'neath the woodland shade,
Her zephyrs lift the lingering leaf,
And bear it gently where are laid
The loved and lost ones of its grief.

At last, old Autumn, rising, takes
Again his scepter and his throne;
With boisterous hand the tree he shakes,
Intent on gathering all his own.

Sweet Summer, sighing, flies the plain,
And waiting Winter, gaunt and grim,
Sees miser Autumn hoard his grain,
And smiles to think it 's all for him.

ANONYMOUS.

INDIAN SUMMER.

FROM gold to gray
Our mild sweet day
Of Indian summer fades too soon;
But tenderly
Above the sea
Hangs, white and calm, the hunter's moon.

In its pale fire,
The village spire
Shows like the zodiac's spectral lance;
The painted walls
Whereon it falls
Transfigured stand in marble trance!

JOHN GREENLEAF WHITTIER.

INDIAN SUMMER.

WHEN leaves grow sear all things take somber hue;
The wild winds waltz no more the woodside through,
And all the faded grass is wet with dew.

A gauzy nebula films the pensive sky,
The golden bee supinely buzzes by,
In silent flocks the bluebirds southward fly.

The forest's cheeks are crimsoned o'er with shame,
The cynic frost enlaces every lane,
The ground with scarlet blushes is aflame!

The one we love grows lustrous-eyed and sad,
With sympathy too thoughtful to be glad,
While all the colors round are running mad.

The sunbeams kiss askant the somber hill,
The naked woodbine climbs the window-sill,
The breaths that noon exhales are faint and chill.

The ripened nuts drop downward day by day,
Sounding the hollow tocsin of decay,
And bandit squirrels smuggle them away.

Vague sighs and scents pervade the atmosphere,
Sounds of invisible stirrings hum the ear,
The morning's lash reveals a frozen tear.

The hermit mountains gird themselves with mail,
Mocking the threshers with an echo flail,
The while the afternoons grow crisp and pale.

Inconstant Summer to the tropics flees,
And, as her rose-sails catch the amorous breeze,
Lo! bare, brown Autumn trembles to her knees!

The stealthy nights encroach upon the days,
The earth with sudden whiteness is ablaze,
And all her paths are lost in crystal maze!

Tread lightly where the dainty violets blew,
Where the spring winds their soft eyes open flew;
Safely they sleep the churlish winter through.

Though all life's portals are indiced with woe,
And frozen pearls are all the world can show,
Feel! Nature's breath is warm beneath the snow.

Look up, dear mourners! Still the blue expanse,
Serenely tender, bends to catch thy glance;
Within thy tears sibyllic sunbeams dance!

With blooms full-sapped again will smile the land:
The fall is but the folding of His hand,
Anon with fuller glories to expand.

The dumb heart hid beneath the pulseless tree
Will throb again; and then the torpid bee
Upon the ear will drone his drowsy glee.

So shall the truant bluebirds backward fly,
And all loved things that vanish or that die
Return to us in some sweet By-and-By.

ANONYMOUS.

WINTER SONG.

SUMMER joys are o'er;
Flowerets bloom no more,
Wintry winds are sweeping;
Through the snow-drifts peeping,
Cheerful evergreen
Rarely now is seen.

Now no plumèd throng
Charms the wood with song;
Ice-bound trees are glittering;
Merry snow-birds, twittering,
Fondly strive to cheer
Scenes so cold and drear.

Winter, still I see
Many charms in thee, —
Love thy chilly greeting,
Snow-storms fiercely beating,
And the dear delights
Of the long, long nights.

From the German of LUDWIG HÖLTY,
by CHARLES T. BROOKS.

NO!

No sun — no moon!
No morn — no noon —
No dawn — no dust — no proper time of day —
No sky — no earthly view —
No distance looking blue —
No road — no street — no "t' other side the way" —
No end to any Row —
No indications where the Crescents go —
No top to any steeple —
No recognitions of familiar people —
No courtesies for showing 'em —
No knowing 'em!
No traveling at all — no locomotion,
No inkling of the way — no notion —
"No go" — by land or ocean —
No mail — no post —
No news from any foreign coast —
No park — no ring — no afternoon gentility —
No company — no nobility —
No warmth, no cheerfulness, no healthful ease,
No comfortable feel in any member —
No shade, no shine, no butterflies, no bees,
No fruits, no flowers, no leaves, no birds,
November!

THOMAS HOOD.

WINTER.

FROM "THE WINTER MORNING WALK."

'T is morning; and the sun, with ruddy orb
Ascending, fires the horizon; while the clouds,
That crowd away before the driving wind,
More ardent as the disk emerges more,
Resemble most some city in a blaze,
Seen through the leafless wood. His slanting ray
Slides ineffectual down the snowy vale,
And, tingeing all with his own rosy hue,
From every herb and every spiry blade
Stretches a length of shadow o'er the field.
Mine, spindling into longitude immense,
In spite of gravity, and sage remark
That I myself am but a fleeting shade,
Provokes me to a smile. With eye askance
I view the muscular proportioned limb
Transformed to a lean shank. The shapeless pair,
As they designed to mock me, at my side
Take step for step; and, as I near approach
The cottage, walk along the plastered wall,
Preposterous sight! the legs without the man.
The verdure of the plain lies buried deep
Beneath the dazzling deluge; and the bents,
And coarser grass, upspearing o'er the rest,

Of late unsightly and unseen, now shine
Conspicuous, and in bright apparel clad,
And, fledged with icy feathers, nod superb.
The cattle mourn in corners, where the fence
Screens them, and seem half petrified to sleep
In unrecumbent sadness. There they wait
Their wonted fodder ; not, like hungering man,
Fretful if unsupplied ; but silent, meek,
And patient of the slow-paced swain's delay.
He from the stack carves out the accustomed load,
Deep plunging, and again deep plunging oft,
His broad keen knife into the solid mass :
Smooth as a wall the upright remnant stands,
With such undeviating and even force
He severs it away : no needless care
Lest storms should overset the leaning pile
Deciduous, or its own unbalanced weight.
Forth goes the woodman, leaving unconcerned
The cheerful haunts of men, — to wield the ax
And drive the wedge in yonder forest drear,
From morn to eve his solitary task.
Shaggy and lean and shrewd with pointed ears,
And tail cropped short, half lurcher and half cur,
His dog attends him. Close behind his heel
Now creeps he slow ; and now, with many a frisk
Wide-scampering, snatches up the drifted snow
With ivory teeth, or plows it with his snout ;
Then shakes his powdered coat, and barks for joy.

. . . . .

Now from the roost, or from the neighboring pale,
Where, diligent to catch the first faint gleam
Of smiling day, they gossiped side by side,
Come trooping at the housewife's well-known call
The feathered tribes domestic. Half on wing,
And half on foot, they brush the fleecy flood,
Conscious and fearful of too deep a plunge.
The sparrows peep, and quit the sheltering eaves
To seize the fair occasion. Well they eye
The scattered grain, and, thievishly resolved
To escape the impending famine, often scared
As oft return, a pert voracious kind.
Clean riddance quickly made, one only care
Remains to each, the search of sunny nook,
Or shed impervious to the blast. Resigned
To sad necessity, the cock foregoes
His wonted strut, and, wading at their head
With well-considered steps, seems to resent
His altered gait and stateliness retrenched.
How find the myriads, that in summer cheer
The hills and valleys with their ceaseless songs,
Due sustenance, or where subsist they now ?
Earth yields them naught ; the imprisoned worm is safe
Beneath the frozen clod ; all seeds of herbs
Lie covered close ; and berry-bearing thorns,
That feed the thrush (whatever some suppose),
Afford the smaller minstrels no supply.
The long protracted rigor of the year
Thins all their numerous flocks. In chinks and holes
Ten thousand seek an unmolested end,
As instinct prompts ; self-buried ere they die.

WILLIAM COWPER.

NEW ENGLAND IN WINTER.

FROM "SNOW-BOUND."

THE sun that brief December day
Rose cheerless over hills of gray,
And, darkly circled, gave at noon
A sadder light than waning moon.
Slow tracing down the thickening sky
Its mute and ominous prophecy,
A portent seeming less than threat,
It sank from sight before it set.
A chill no coat, however stout,
Of homespun stuff could quite shut out,
A hard, dull bitterness of cold,
That checked, mid-vein, the circling race
Of life-blood in the sharpened face,
The coming of the snow-storm told.
The wind blew east : we heard the roar
Of Ocean on his wintry shore,
And felt the strong pulse throbbing there
Beat with low rhythm our inland air.

Meanwhile we did our nightly chores, —
Brought in the wood from out of doors,
Littered the stalls, and from the mows
Raked down the herd's-grass for the cows ;
Heard the horse whinnying for his corn ;
And, sharply clashing horn on horn,
Impatient down the stanchion rows
The cattle shake their walnut bows ;
While, peering from his early perch
Upon the scaffold's pole of birch,
The cock his crested helmet bent
And down his querulous challenge sent.

Unwarmed by any sunset light
The gray day darkened into night,
A night made hoary with the swarm
And whirl-dance of the blinding storm,
As zigzag wavering to and fro
Crossed and recrossed the wingèd snow :
And ere the early bedtime came
The white drift piled the window-frame,
And through the glass the clothes-line posts
Looked in like tall and sheeted ghosts.

So all night long the storm roared on :
The morning broke without a sun ;
In tiny spherule traced with lines
Of Nature's geometric signs,
In starry flake, and pellicle,
All day the hoary meteor fell ;

And, when the second morning shone,
We looked upon a world unknown,
On nothing we could call our own.
Around the glistening wonder bent
The blue walls of the firmament,
No cloud above, no earth below, —
A universe of sky and snow!
The old familiar sights of ours
Took marvelous shapes; strange domes and towers
Rose up where sty or corn-crib stood,
Or garden wall, or belt of wood;
A smooth white mound the brush-pile showed,
A fenceless drift what once was road;
The bridle-post an old man sat
With loose-flung coat and high cocked hat;
The well-curb had a Chinese roof;
And even the long sweep, high aloof,
In its slant splendor, seemed to tell
Of Pisa's leaning miracle.

A prompt, decisive man, no breath
Our father wasted: "Boys, a path!"
Well pleased, (for when did farmer boy
Count such a summons less than joy?)
Our buskins on our feet we drew;
With mittened hands, and caps drawn low,
To guard our necks and ears from snow,
We cut the solid whiteness through.
And, where the drift was deepest, made
A tunnel walled and overlaid
With dazzling crystal: we had read
Of rare Aladdin's wondrous cave,
And to our own his name we gave,
With many a wish the luck were ours
To test his lamp's supernal powers.
We reached the barn with merry din,
And roused the prisoned brutes within.
The old horse thrust his long head out,
And grave with wonder gazed about;
The cock his lusty greeting said,
And forth his speckled harem led;
The oxen lashed their tails, and hooked,
And mild reproach of hunger looked;
The hornèd patriarch of the sheep,
Like Egypt's Amun roused from sleep,
Shook his sage head with gesture mute,
And emphasized with stamp of foot.

All day the gusty north-wind bore
The loosening drift its breath before;
Low circling round its southern zone,
The sun through dazzling snow-mist shone.
No church-bell lent its Christian tone
To the savage air, no social smoke
Curled over woods of snow-hung oak.
A solitude made more intense
By dreary-voicèd elements,
The shrieking of the mindless wind,
The moaning tree-boughs swaying blind,
And on the glass the unmeaning beat
Of ghostly finger-tips of sleet.
Beyond the circle of our hearth
No welcome sound of toil or mirth
Unbound the spell, and testified
Of human life and thought outside.
We minded that the sharpest ear
The buried brooklet could not hear,
The music of whose liquid lip
Had been to us companionship,
And, in our lonely life, had grown
To have an almost human tone.
As night drew on, and, from the crest
Of wooded knolls that ridged the west,
The sun, a snow-blown traveler, sank
From sight beneath the smothering bank,
We piled, with care, our nightly stack
Of wood against the chimney-back, —
The oaken log, green, huge, and thick,
And on its top the stout back-stick;
The knotty forestick laid apart,
And filled between with curious art
The ragged brush; then, hovering near,
We watched the first red blaze appear,
Heard the sharp crackle, caught the gleam
On whitewashed wall and sagging beam,
Until the old, rude-furnished room
Burst, flower-like, into rosy bloom;
While radiant with a mimic flame
Outside the sparkling drift became,
And through the bare-boughed lilac-tree
Our own warm hearth seemed blazing free.
The crane and pendent trammels showed;
The Turks' heads on the andirons glowed;
While childish fancy, prompt to tell
The meaning of the miracle,
Whispered the old rhyme: "*Under the tree,*
When fire outdoors burns merrily,
There the witches are making tea."

The moon above the eastern wood
Shone at its full; the hill-range stood
Transfigured in the silver flood,
Its blown snows flashing cold and keen,
Dead white, save where some sharp ravine
Took shadow, or the somber green
Of hemlocks turned to pitchy black
Against the whiteness at their back.
For such a world and such a night
Most fitting that unwarming light,
Which only seemed where'er it fell
To make the coldness visible.

Shut in from all the world without,
We sat the clean-winged hearth about.
Content to let the north-wind roar
In baffled rage at pane and door,

While the red logs before us beat
The frost-line back with tropic heat;
And ever, when a louder blast
Shook beam and rafter as it passed,
The merrier up its roaring draught
The great throat of the chimney laughed;
The house-dog on his paws outspread
Laid to the fire his drowsy head,
The cat's dark silhouette on the wall
A couchant tiger's seemed to fall;
And, for the winter fireside meet,
Between the andirons' straddling feet,
The mug of cider simmered slow,
The apples sputtered in a row,
And, close at hand, the basket stood
With nuts from brown October's wood.

JOHN GREENLEAF WHITTIER.

WINTER WALK AT NOON.

THE night was winter in his roughest mood,
The morning sharp and clear. But now at noon
Upon the southern side of the slant hills,
And where the woods fence off the northern blast,
The season smiles, resigning all its rage,
And has the warmth of May. The vault is blue
Without a cloud, and white without a speck
The dazzling splendor of the scene below.
Again the harmony comes o'er the vale;
And through the trees I view the embattled tower,
Whence all the music. I again perceive
The soothing influence of the wafted strains,
And settle in soft musings as I tread
The walk, still verdant, under oaks and elms,
Whose outspread branches overarch the glade.

. . . . .

No noise is here, or none that hinders thought.
The redbreast warbles still, but is content
With slender notes, and more than half suppressed:
Pleased with his solitude, and flitting light
From spray to spray, where'er he rests he shakes
From many a twig the pendent drops of ice,
That tinkle in the withered leaves below.
Stillness, accompanied with sounds so soft,
Charms more than silence. Meditation here
May think down hours to moments. Here the heart
May give a useful lesson to the head,
And Learning wiser grow without his books.

WILLIAM COWPER.

WINTER.

THE day had been a calm and sunny day,
And tinged with amber was the sky at even;
The fleecy clouds at length had rolled away,
And lay in furrows on the eastern heaven;—
The moon arose and shed a glimmering ray,
And round her orb a misty circle lay.

The hoar-frost glittered on the naked heath,
The roar of distant winds was loud and deep,
The dry leaves rustled in each passing breath,
And the gay world was lost in quiet sleep.
Such was the time when, on the landscape brown,
Through a December air the snow came down.

The morning came, the dreary morn, at last,
And showed the whitened waste. The shivering herd
Lowed on the hoary meadow-ground, and fast
Fell the light flakes upon the earth unstirred;
The forest firs with glittering snows o'erlaid
Stood like hoar priests in robes of white arrayed.

JOHN H. BRYANT.

WINTER PICTURES.

FROM "THE VISION OF SIR LAUNFAL."

DOWN swept the chill wind from the mountain peak,
From the snow five thousand summers old;
On open wold and hill-top bleak
It had gathered all the cold,
And whirled it like sleet on the wanderer's cheek;
It carried a shiver everywhere
From the unleafed boughs and pastures bare;
The little brook heard it and built a roof
'Neath which he could house him, winter-proof;
All night by the white stars' frosty gleams
He groined his arches and matched his beams;
Slender and clear were his crystal spars
As the lashes of light that trim the stars:
He sculptured every summer delight
In his halls and chambers out of sight;
Sometimes his tinkling waters slipt
Down through a frost-leaved forest-crypt,
Long, sparkling aisles of steel-stemmed trees
Bending to counterfeit a breeze;
Sometimes the roof no fretwork knew
But silvery mosses that downward grew;
Sometimes it was carved in sharp relief
With quaint arabesques of ice-fern leaf;
Sometimes it was simply smooth and clear
For the gladness of heaven to shine through, and here
He had caught the nodding bulrush-tops
And hung them thickly with diamond drops,
Which crystaled the beams of moon and sun,
And made a star of every one:
No mortal builder's most rare device
Could match this winter-palace of ice;
'T was as if every image that mirrored lay
In his depths serene through the summer day,

Each flitting shadow of earth and sky,
  Lest the happy model should be lost,
Had been mimicked in fairy masonry
  By the elfin builders of the frost.

Within the hall are song and laughter,
  The cheeks of Christmas glow red and jolly,
And sprouting is every corbel and rafter
  With the lightsome green of ivy and holly;
Through the deep gulf of the chimney wide
Wallows the Yule-log's roaring tide;
The broad flame-pennons droop and flap
  And belly and tug as a flag in the wind;
Like a locust shrills the imprisoned sap,
  Hunted to death in its galleries blind;
And swift little troops of silent sparks,
  Now pausing, now scattering away as in fear,
Go threading the soot-forest's tangled darks
  Like herds of startled deer.

But the wind without was eager and sharp,
Of Sir Launfal's gray hair it makes a harp,
    And rattles and wrings
    The icy strings,
  Singing, in dreary monotone,
  A Christmas carol of its own,
  Whose burden still, as he might guess,
  Was — "Shelterless, shelterless, shelterless!"
The voice of the seneschal flared like a torch
As he shouted the wanderer away from the porch,
And he sat in the gateway and saw all night
  The great hall-fire, so cheery and bold,
  Through the window-slits of the castle old,
Build out its piers of ruddy light
  Against the drift of the cold.

. . . . . .

There was never a leaf on bush or tree,
The bare boughs rattled shudderingly;
The river was dumb and could not speak,
  For the frost's swift shuttles its shroud had spun;
A single crow on the tree-top bleak
  From his shining feathers shed off the cold sun;
Again it was morning, but shrunk and cold,
As if her veins were sapless and old,
And she rose up decrepitly
For a last dim look at earth and sea.

JAMES RUSSELL LOWELL.

WINTER SCENES.

THE keener tempests rise; and fuming dun
From all the livid east, or piercing north,
Thick clouds ascend; in whose capacious womb
A vapory deluge lies, to snow congealed.
Heavy they roll their fleecy world along;
And the sky saddens with the gathered storm.
Through the hushed air the whitening shower descends
At first thin wavering; till at last the flakes
Fall broad and wide and fast, dimming the day
With a continual flow. The cherished fields
Put on their winter robe of purest white.
'T is brightness all; save where the new snow melts
Along the mazy current. Low the woods
Bow their hoar head; and, ere the languid sun
Faint from the west emits his evening ray,
Earth's universal face, deep hid and chill,
Is one wide dazzling waste, that buries wide
The works of man. Drooping, the laborer-ox
Stands covered o'er with snow, and then demands
The fruit of all his toil. The fowls of heaven,
Tamed by the cruel season, crowd around
The winnowing store, and claim the little boon
Which Providence assigns them. One alone,
The redbreast, sacred to the household gods,
Wisely regardful of the embroiling sky,
In joyless fields and thorny thickets leaves
His shivering mates, and pays to trusted man
His annual visit. Half afraid, he first
Against the window beats; then, brisk, alights
On the warm hearth; then, hopping o'er the floor,
Eyes all the smiling family askance,
And pecks, and starts, and wonders where he is:
Till, more familiar grown, the table-crumbs
Attract his slender feet. The foodless wilds
Pour forth their brown inhabitants. The hare,
Though timorous of heart, and hard beset
By death in various forms, dark snares, and dogs,
And more unpitying man, the garden seeks,
Urged on by fearless want. The bleating kind
Eye the bleak heaven, and next the glistening earth,
With looks of dumb despair; then, sad dispersed,
Dig for the withered herb through heaps of snow.

JAMES THOMSON.

WHEN ICICLES HANG BY THE WALL.

FROM "LOVE'S LABOR'S LOST."

WHEN icicles hang by the wall,
  And Dick the shepherd blows his nail,
And Tom bears logs into the hall,
  And milk comes frozen home in pail,
When blood is nipped, and ways be foul,
Then nightly sings the staring owl,
    To-who;
To-whit, to-who, a merry note,
While greasy Joan doth keel the pot.

When all aloud the wind doth blow,
  And coughing drowns the parson's saw,
And birds sit brooding in the snow,
  And Marian's nose looks red and raw,

When roasted crabs hiss in the bowl,
Then nightly sings the staring owl,
To-who;
To-whit, to-who, a merry note,
While greasy Joan doth keel the pot.

SHAKESPEARE.

THE SNOW-STORM.

ANNOUNCED by all the trumpets of the sky,
Arrives the snow; and, driving o'er the fields,
Seems nowhere to alight; the whited air
Hides hills and woods, the river, and the heaven,
And veils the farm-house at the garden's end.
The sled and traveler stopped, the courier's feet
Delayed, all friends shut out, the housemates sit
Around the radiant fireplace, enclosed
In a tumultuous privacy of storm.
Come see the north-wind's masonry!
Out of an unseen quarry, evermore
Furnished with tile, the fierce artificer
Curves his white bastions with projected roof
Round every windward stake or tree or door;
Speeding, the myriad-handed, his wild work
So fanciful, so savage; naught cares he
For number or proportion. Mockingly,
On coop or kennel he hangs Parian wreaths;
A swan-like form invests the hidden thorn;
Fills up the farmer's lane from wall to wall,
Mauger the farmer's sighs; and at the gate
A tapering turret overtops the work.
And when his hours are numbered, and the world
Is all his own, retiring as he were not,
Leaves, when the sun appears, astonished Art
To mimic in slow structures, stone by stone,
Built in an age, the mad wind's night-work,
The frolic architecture of the snow.

RALPH WALDO EMERSON.

THE SNOW-SHOWER.

STAND here by my side and turn, I pray,
On the lake below thy gentle eyes;
The clouds hang over it, heavy and gray,
And dark and silent the water lies;
And out of that frozen mist the snow
In wavering flakes begins to flow;
Flake after flake
They sink in the dark and silent lake.

See how in a living swarm they come
From the chambers beyond that misty veil;
Some hover awhile in air, and some
Rush prone from the sky like summer hail.
All, dropping swiftly or settling slow,
Meet, and are still in the depths below;
Flake after flake
Dissolved in the dark and silent lake.

Here delicate snow-stars, out of the cloud,
Come floating downward in airy play,
Like spangles dropped from the glistening crowd
That whiten by night the Milky Way;
There broader and burlier masses fall;
The sullen water buries them all, —
Flake after flake, —
All drowned in the dark and silent lake.

And some, as on tender wings they glide
From their chilly birth-cloud, dim and gray,
Are joined in their fall, and, side by side,
Come clinging along their unsteady way;
As friend with friend, or husband with wife,
Makes hand in hand the passage of life;
Each mated flake
Soon sinks in the dark and silent lake.

Lo! while we are gazing, in swifter haste
Stream down the snows, till the air is white,
As, myriads by myriads madly chased,
They fling themselves from their shadowy height.
The fair, frail creatures of middle sky,
What speed they make, with their grave so nigh;
Flake after flake
To lie in the dark and silent lake!

I see in thy gentle eyes a tear;
They turn to me in sorrowful thought;
Thou thinkest of friends, the good and dear,
Who were for a time, and now are not;
Like these fair children of cloud and frost,
That glisten a moment and then are lost, —
Flake after flake, —
All lost in the dark and silent lake.

Yet look again, for the clouds divide;
A gleam of blue on the water lies;
And far away, on the mountain-side,
A sunbeam falls from the opening skies.
But the hurrying host that flew between
The cloud and the water no more is seen;
Flake after flake
At rest in the dark and silent lake.

WILLIAM CULLEN BRYANT.

SNOW.—A WINTER SKETCH.

THE blessed morn has come again;
The early gray
Taps at the slumberer's window-pane,
And seems to say,
Break, break from the enchanter's chain
Away, away!

WINTER SCENES.

"Through the hushed air the whitening shower descends
At first thin wavering; till at last the flakes
Fall broad and wide and fast, dimming the day
With a continual flow."

'T is winter, yet there is no sound
 Along the air
Of winds along their battle-ground;
 But gently there
The snow is falling, — all around
 How fair, how fair!

RALPH HOYT.

SNOW-FLAKES.

OUT of the bosom of the Air,
 Out of the cloud-folds of her garments shaken,
Over the woodlands brown and bare,
 Over the harvest-fields forsaken,
 Silent and soft and slow
 Descends the snow.

Even as our cloudy fancies take
 Suddenly shape in some divine expression,
Even as the troubled heart doth make
 In the white countenance confession,
 The troubled sky reveals
 The grief it feels.

This is the poem of the air,
 Slowly in silent syllables recorded;
This is the secret of despair,
 Long in its cloudy bosom hoarded,
 Now whispered and revealed
 To wood and field.

HENRY WADSWORTH LONGFELLOW.

THE MOTHER'S SACRIFICE.

THE cold winds swept the mountain's height,
 And pathless was the dreary wild,
And mid the cheerless hours of night
 A mother wandered with her child:
As through the drifting snow she pressed,
The babe was sleeping on her breast.

And colder still the winds did blow,
 And darker hours of night came on,
And deeper grew the drifting snow:
 Her limbs were chilled, her strength was gone.
"O God!" she cried in accents wild,
"If I must perish, save my child!"

She stripped her mantle from her breast,
 And bared her bosom to the storm,
And round the child she wrapped the vest,
 And smiled to think her babe was warm.
With one cold kiss, one tear she shed,
And sunk upon her snowy bed.

At dawn a traveler passed by,
 And saw her 'neath a snowy veil;
The frost of death was in her eye,
 Her cheek was cold, and hard, and pale.
He moved the robe from off the child, —
The babe looked up and sweetly smiled!

SEBA SMITH.

A SNOW-STORM.

SCENE IN A VERMONT WINTER.

'T IS a fearful night in the winter time,
 As cold as it ever can be;
The roar of the blast is heard like the chime
 Of the waves on an angry sea.
The moon is full; but her silver light
The storm dashes out with its wings to-night;
And over the sky from south to north
Not a star is seen, as the wind comes forth
 In the strength of a mighty glee.

All day had the snow come down, — all day
 As it never came down before;
And over the hills, at sunset, lay
 Some two or three feet, or more;
The fence was lost, and the wall of stone;
The windows blocked and the well-curbs gone;
The haystack had grown to a mountain lift,
And the wood-pile looked like a monster drift,
 As it lay by the farmer's door.

The night sets in on a world of snow,
 While the air grows sharp and chill,
And the warning roar of a fearful blow
 Is heard on the distant hill;
And the norther, see! on the mountain peak
In his breath how the old trees writhe and shriek!
He shouts on the plain, ho-ho! ho-ho!
He drives from his nostrils the blinding snow,
 And growls with a savage will.

Such a night as this to be found abroad,
 In the drifts and the freezing air,
Sits a shivering dog, in the field, by the road,
 With the snow in his shaggy hair.
He shuts his eyes to the wind and growls;
He lifts his head, and moans and howls;
Then crouching low, from the cutting sleet,
His nose is pressed on his quivering feet, —
 Pray, what does the dog do there?

A farmer came from the village plain, —
 But he lost the traveled way;
And for hours he trod with might and main
 A path for his horse and sleigh;
But colder still the cold winds blew,
And deeper still the deep drifts grew,

And his mare, a beautiful Morgan brown,
At last in her struggles floundered down,
  Where a log in a hollow lay.

In vain, with a neigh and a frenzied snort,
  She plunged in the drifting snow,
While her master urged, till his breath grew short,
  With a word and a gentle blow;
But the snow was deep, and the tugs were tight;
His hands were numb and had lost their might;
So he wallowed back to his half-filled sleigh,
And strove to shelter himself till day,
  With his coat and the buffalo.

He has given the last faint jerk of the rein,
  To rouse up his dying steed;
And the poor dog howls to the blast in vain
  For help in his master's need.
For a while he strives with a wistful cry
To catch a glance from his drowsy eye,
And wags his tail if the rude winds flap
The skirt of the buffalo over his lap,
  And whines when he takes no heed.

The wind goes down and the storm is o'er, —
  'T is the hour of midnight, past;
The old trees writhe and bend no more
  In the whirl of the rushing blast.
The silent moon with her peaceful light
Looks down on the hills with snow all white,
And the giant shadow of Camel's Hump,
The blasted pine and the ghostly stump,
  Afar on the plain are cast.

But cold and dead by the hidden log
  Are they who came from the town, —
The man in his sleigh, and his faithful dog,
  And his beautiful Morgan brown, —
In the wide snow-desert, far and grand,
With his cap on his head and the reins in his hand, —
The dog with his nose on his master's feet,
And the mare half seen through the crusted sleet,
  Where she lay when she floundered down.

CHARLES GAMAGE EASTMAN.

O WINTER! WILT THOU NEVER GO?

O WINTER! wilt thou never, never go?
O summer! but I weary for thy coming,
Longing once more to hear the Luggie flow,
And frugal bees, laboriously humming.
Now the east-wind diseases the infirm,
And must crouch in corners from rough weather;
Sometimes a winter sunset is a charm, —
When the fired clouds, compacted, blaze together,
And the large sun dips red behind the hills.
I, from my window, can behold this pleasure;
And the eternal moon, what time she fills
Her orb with argent, treading a soft measure,
With queenly motions of a bridal mood,
Through the white spaces of infinitude.

DAVID GRAY.

VIEW FROM THE EUGANEAN HILLS,* NORTH ITALY.

MANY a green isle needs must be
In the deep wide sea of misery,
Or the mariner, worn and wan,
Never thus could voyage on
Day and night, and night and day,
Drifting on his dreary way,
With the solid darkness black
Closing round his vessel's track;
Whilst above, the sunless sky,
Big with clouds, hangs heavily,
And behind, the tempest fleet
Hurries on with lightning feet,
Riving sail and cord and plank
Till the ship has almost drank
Death from the o'erbrimming deep;
And sinks down, down, like that sleep
When the dreamer seems to be
Weltering through eternity;
And the dim low line before
Of a dark and distant shore
Still recedes, as ever still
Longing with divided will,
But no power to seek or shun,
He is ever drifted on
O'er the unreposing wave
To the haven of the grave.

. . . . . .

Ay, many flowering islands lie
In the waters of wide agony:
To such a one this morn was led
My bark, by soft winds piloted.
— Mid the mountains Euganean
I stood listening to the pæan
With which the legioned rooks did hail
The sun's uprise majestical:
Gathering round with wings all hoar,
Through the dewy mist they soar
Like gray shades, till the eastern heaven
Bursts, and then, as clouds of even,
Flecked with fire and azure, lie
In the unfathomable sky,
So their plumes of purple grain,
Starred with drops of golden rain,
Gleam above the sunlight woods,
As in silent multitudes
On the morning's fitful gale
Through the broken mist they sail;

* The lonely mountains which surround what was once the retreat, and is now the sepulcher, of Petrarch.

And the vapors cloven and gleaming
Follow down the dark steep streaming,
Till all is bright and clear and still
Round the solitary hill.

Beneath is spread like a green sea
The waveless plain of Lombardy,
Bounded by the vaporous air,
Islanded by cities fair;
Underneath day's azure eyes,
Ocean's nursling, Venice, lies, —
A peopled labyrinth of walls,
Amphitrite's destined halls,
Which her hoary sire now paves
With his blue and beaming waves.
Lo! the sun upsprings behind,
Broad, red, radiant, half reclined
On the level quivering line
Of the waters crystalline;
And before that chasm of light,
As within a furnace bright,
Column, tower, and dome, and spire
Shine like obelisks of fire,
Pointing with inconstant motion
From the altar of dark ocean
To the sapphire-tinted skies;
As the flames of sacrifice
From the marble shrines did rise,
As to pierce the dome of gold
Where Apollo spoke of old.

Sun-girt city! thou hast been
Ocean's child, and then his queen;
Now is come a darker day,
And thou soon must be his prey,
If the power that raised thee here
Hallow so thy watery bier.
A less drear ruin then than now,
With thy conquest-branded brow
Stooping to the slave of slaves
From thy throne among the waves,
Wilt thou be when the sea-mew
Flies, as once before it flew,
O'er thine isles depopulate,
And all is in its ancient state,
Save where many a palace-gate
With green sea-flowers overgrown
Like a rock of ocean's own,
Topples o'er the abandoned sea
As the tides change sullenly.
The fisher on his watery way
Wandering at the close of day
Will spread his sail and seize his oar
Till he pass the gloomy shore,
Lest thy dead should, from their sleep
Bursting o'er the starlight deep,
Lead a rapid mask of death
O'er the waters of his path.
. . . . . .

Noon descends around me now:
'T is the noon of autumn's glow,
When a soft and purple mist
Like a vaporous amethyst,
Or an air-dissolvèd star
Mingling light and fragrance, far
From the curved horizon's bound
To the point of heaven's profound,
Fills the overflowing sky;
And the plains that silent lie
Underneath; the leaves unsodden
Where the infant frost has trodden
With his morning-wingèd feet,
Whose bright print is gleaming yet;
And the red and golden vines
Piercing with their trellised lines
The rough, dark-skirted wilderness;
The dun and bladed grass no less,
Pointing from this hoary tower
In the windless air; the flower
Glimmering at my feet; the line
Of the olive-sandaled Apennine
In the south dimly islanded;
And the Alps, whose snows are spread
High between the clouds and sun;
And of living things each one;
And my spirit, which so long
Darkened this swift stream of song, —
Interpenetrated lie
By the glory of the sky;
Be it love, light, harmony,
Odor, or the soul of all
Which from heaven like dew doth fall,
Or the mind which feeds this verse
Peopling the lone universe.

Noon descends, and after noon
Autumn's evening meets me soon,
Leading the infantine moon
And that one star, which to her
Almost seems to minister
Half the crimson light she brings
From the sunset's radiant springs:
And the soft dreams of the morn
(Which like wingèd winds had borne
To that silent isle, which lies
Mid remembered agonies,
The frail bark of this lone being)
Pass, to other sufferers fleeing,
And its ancient pilot, Pain,
Sits beside the helm again.

Other flowering isles must be
In the sea of life and agony;
Other spirits float and flee
O'er that gulf; even now, perhaps,
On some rock the wild wave wraps,
With folding winds they waiting sit

For my bark, to pilot it
To some calm and blooming cove,
Where for me, and those I love,
May a windless bower be built,
Far from passion, pain, and guilt,
In a dell mid lawny hills,
Which the wild sea-murmur fills,
And soft sunshine, and the sound
Of old forests echoing round,
And the light and smell divine
Of all flowers that breathe and shine.
— We may live so happy there,
That the spirits of the air,
Envying us, may even entice
To our healing paradise
The polluting multitude;
But their rage would be subdued
By that clime divine and calm,
And the winds whose wings rain balm
On the uplifted soul, and leaves
Under which the bright sea heaves;
While each breathless interval
In their whisperings musical
The inspired soul supplies
With its own deep melodies;
And the love which heals all strife
Circling, like the breath of life,
All things in that sweet abode
With its own mild brotherhood.
They, not it, would change; and soon
Every sprite beneath the moon
Would repent its envy vain,
And the earth grow young again!

PERCY BYSSHE SHELLEY.

GRONGAR HILL.

[The Vale of the Towy embraces, in its winding course of fifteen miles, some of the loveliest scenery of South Wales. If it be less cultivated than the Vale of Usk, its woodland views are more romantic and frequent. The neighborhood is historic and poetic ground. From Grongar Hill the eye discovers traces of a Roman camp; Golden Grove, the home of Jeremy Taylor, is on the opposite side of the river; Merlin's chair recalls Spenser; and a farmhouse near the foot of Llangumnor Hill brings back the memory of its once genial occupant, Richard Steele. Spenser places the cave of Merlin among the dark woods of Dinevawr.]

SILENT nymph, with curious eye,
Who, the purple even, dost lie
On the mountain's lonely van,
Beyond the noise of busy man,
Painting fair the form of things,
While the yellow linnet sings,
Or the tuneful nightingale
Charms the forest with her tale, —
Come, with all thy various hues,
Come, and aid thy sister Muse.
Now, while Phœbus, riding high,
Gives luster to the land and sky,
Grongar Hill invites my song, —
Draw the landscape bright and strong;
Grongar, in whose mossy cells
Sweetly musing Quiet dwells;
Grongar, in whose silent shade,
For the modest Muses made,
So oft I have, the evening still,
At the fountain of a rill,
Sat upon a flowery bed,
With my hand beneath my head,
While strayed my eyes o'er Towy's flood,
Over mead and over wood,
From house to house, from hill to hill,
Till Contemplation had her fill.
  About his checkered sides I wind,
And leave his brooks and meads behind,
And groves and grottoes where I lay,
And vistas shooting beams of day.
Wide and wider spreads the vale,
As circles on a smooth canal.
The mountains round, unhappy fate!
Sooner or later, of all height,
Withdraw their summits from the skies,
And lessen as the others rise.
Still the prospect wider spreads,
Adds a thousand woods and meads;
Still it widens, widens still,
And sinks the newly risen hill.
  Now I gain the mountain's brow;
What a landscape lies below!
No clouds, no vapors intervene;
But the gay, the open scene
Does the face of Nature show
In all the hues of heaven's bow!
And, swelling to embrace the light,
Spreads around beneath the sight.
  Old castles on the cliffs arise,
Proudly towering in the skies;
Rushing from the woods, the spires
Seem from hence ascending fires;
Half his beams Apollo sheds
On the yellow mountain-heads,
Gilds the fleeces of the flocks,
And glitters on the broken rocks.
  Below me trees unnumbered rise,
Beautiful in various dyes:
The gloomy pine, the poplar blue,
The yellow beech, the sable yew,
The slender fir that taper grows,
The sturdy oak with broad-spread boughs;
And beyond, the purple grove,
Haunt of Phyllis, queen of love!
Gaudy as the opening dawn,
Lies a long and level lawn,
On which a dark hill, steep and high,
Holds and charms the wandering eye;
Deep are his feet in Towy's flood;
His sides are clothed with waving wood;
And ancient towers crown his brow,

That cast an awful look below;
Whose ragged walls the ivy creeps,
And with her arms from falling keeps;
So both a safety from the wind
In mutual dependence find.
'T is now the raven's bleak abode;
'T is now the apartment of the toad;
And there the fox securely feeds;
And there the poisonous adder breeds,
Concealed in ruins, moss, and weeds;
While, ever and anon, there fall
Huge heaps of hoary, moldered wall.
Yet Time has seen, — that lifts the low
And level lays the lofty brow, —
Has seen this broken pile complete,
Big with the vanity of state.
But transient is the smile of Fate!
A little rule, a little sway,
A sunbeam in a winter's day,
Is all the proud and mighty have
Between the cradle and the grave.
  And see the rivers, how they run
Through woods and meads, in shade and sun,
Sometimes swift, sometimes slow, —
Wave succeeding wave, they go
A various journey to the deep,
Like human life to endless sleep!
Thus is Nature's vesture wrought
To instruct our wandering thought;
Thus she dresses green and gay
To disperse our cares away.
  Ever charming, ever new,
When will the landscape tire the view!
The fountain's fall, the river's flow;
The woody valleys, warm and low;
The windy summit, wild and high,
Roughly rushing on the sky;
The pleasant seat, the ruined tower,
The naked rock, the shady bower;
The town and village, dome and farm, —
Each gives each a double charm,
As pearls upon an Ethiop's arm.
  See on the mountain's southern side,
Where the prospect opens wide,
Where the evening gilds the tide,
How close and small the hedges lie!
What streaks of meadow cross the eye!
A step, methinks, may pass the stream,
So little distant dangers seem;
So we mistake the Future's face,
Eyed through Hope's deluding glass;
As yon summits, soft and fair,
Clad in colors of the air,
Which, to those who journey near,
Barren, brown, and rough appear;
Still we tread the same coarse way, —
The present 's still a cloudy day.
  O, may I with myself agree,
And never covet what I see;
Content me with a humble shade,
My passions tamed, my wishes laid;
For while our wishes wildly roll,
We banish quiet from the soul.
'T is thus the busy beat the air,
And misers gather wealth and care.
  Now, even now, my joys run high,
As on the mountain-turf I lie;
While the wanton Zephyr sings,
And in the vale perfumes his wings;
While the waters murmur deep;
While the shepherd charms his sheep;
While the birds unbounded fly,
And with music fill the sky, —
Now, even now, my joys run high.
  Be full, ye courts; be great who will;
Search for Peace with all your skill;
Open wide the lofty door,
Seek her on the marble floor:
In vain you search; she is not there!
In vain you search the domes of Care!
Grass and flowers Quiet treads,
On the meads and mountain-heads,
Along with Pleasure, — close allied,
Ever by each other's side, —
And often, by the murmuring rill,
Hears the thrush, while all is still
Within the groves of Grongar Hill.

JOHN DYER.

DOVER CLIFF.

FROM "KING LEAR."

COME on, sir; here 's the place: stand still! How fearful
And dizzy 't is, to cast one's eyes so low!
The crows and choughs that wing the midway air
Show scarce so gross as beetles: half-way down
Hangs one that gathers samphire, — dreadful trade!
Methinks he seems no bigger than his head:
The fishermen, that walk upon the beach,
Appear like mice; and yon tall anchoring bark,
Diminished to her cock; her cock, a buoy
Almost too small for sight: the murmuring surge,
That on the unnumbered idle pebbles chafes,
Cannot be heard so high. — I 'll look no more;
Lest my brain turn, and the deficient sight
Topple down headlong.

SHAKESPEARE.

ALPINE HEIGHTS.

ON Alpine heights the love of God is shed;
    He paints the morning red,
    The flowerets white and blue,
    And feeds them with his dew.
On Alpine heights a loving Father dwells.

On Alpine heights, o'er many a fragrant heath,
The loveliest breezes breathe;
So free and pure the air,
His breath seems floating there.
On Alpine heights a loving Father dwells.

On Alpine heights, beneath his mild blue eye,
Still vales and meadows lie;
The soaring glacier's ice
Gleams like a paradise.
On Alpine heights a loving Father dwells.

Down Alpine heights the silvery streamlets flow;
There the bold chamois go;
On giddy crags they stand,
And drink from his own hand.
On Alpine heights a loving Father dwells.

On Alpine heights, in troops all white as snow,
The sheep and wild goats go;
There, in the solitude,
He fills their hearts with food.
On Alpine heights a loving Father dwells.

On Alpine heights the herdsman tends his herd;
His Shepherd is the Lord;
For he who feeds the sheep
Will sure his offspring keep.
On Alpine heights a loving Father dwells.

From the German of KRUMMACHER,
by CHARLES T. BROOKS.

THE GREAT ST. BERNARD.

NIGHT was again descending, when my mule,
That all day long had climbed among the clouds,
Higher and higher still, as by a stair
Let down from heaven itself, transporting me,
Stopped, to the joy of both, at that low door
So near the summit of the Great St. Bernard;
That door which ever on its hinges moved
To them that knocked, and nightly sends abroad
Ministering spirits. Lying on the watch,
Two dogs of grave demeanor welcomed me,
All meekness, gentleness, though large of limb;
And a lay-brother of the Hospital,
Who, as we toiled below, had heard by fits
The distant echoes gaining on his ear,
Came and held fast my stirrup in his hand,
While I alighted.

On the same rock beside it stood the church,
Reft of its cross, not of its sanctity;
The vesper-bell, for 't was the vesper-hour,
Duly proclaiming through the wilderness,
"All ye who hear, whatever be your work,
Stop for an instant, — move your lips in prayer!"
And just beneath it, in that dreary dale, —
If dale it might be called so near to heaven, —
A little lake, where never fish leaped up,
Lay like a spot of ink amid the snow;
A star, the only one in that small sky,
On its dead surface glimmering. 'T was a scene
Resembling nothing I had left behind,
As though all worldly ties were now dissolved; —
And to incline the mind still more to thought,
To thought and sadness, on the eastern shore
Under a beetling cliff stood half in shadow
A lonely chapel destined for the dead,
For such as, having wandered from their way,
Had perished miserably. Side by side,
Within they lie, a mournful company
All in their shrouds, no earth to cover them;
Their features full of life, yet motionless
In the broad day, nor soon to suffer change,
Though the barred windows, barred against the wolf,
Are always open!

SAMUEL ROGERS.

THE DESCENT.

MY mule refreshed, his bells
Jingled once more, the signal to depart,
And we set out in the gray light of dawn,
Descending rapidly, — by waterfalls
Fast frozen, and among huge blocks of ice
That in their long career had stopt midway;
At length, unchecked, unbidden, he stood still,
And all his bells were muffled. Then my guide,
Lowering his voice, addressed me: — "Through this chasm
On, and say nothing, — for a word, a breath,
Stirring the air, may loosen and bring down
A winter's snow, — enough to overwhelm
The horse and foot that, night and day, defiled
Along this path to conquer at Marengo."

SAMUEL ROGERS.

SONG OF THE BROOK.

I COME from haunts of coot and hern:
I make a sudden sally
And sparkle out among the fern,
To bicker down a valley.

By thirty hills I hurry down,
Or slip between the ridges,
By twenty thorps, a little town,
And half a hundred bridges.

Till last by Philip's farm I flow
To join the brimming river,
For men may come and men may go,
But I go on forever.

I chatter over stony ways,
  In little sharps and trebles,
I bubble into eddying bays,
  I babble on the pebbles.

With many a curve my banks I fret
  By many a field and fallow,
And many a fairy foreland set
  With willow-weed and mallow.

I chatter, chatter, as I flow
  To join the brimming river;
For men may come and men may go,
  But I go on forever.

I wind about, and in and out,
  With here a blossom sailing,
And here and there a lusty trout,
  And here and there a grayling,

And here and there a foamy flake
  Upon me, as I travel
With many a silvery waterbreak
  Above the golden gravel,

And draw them all along, and flow
  To join the brimming river;
For men may come and men may go,
  But I go on forever.

I steal by lawns and grassy plots:
  I slide by hazel covers;
I move the sweet forget-me-nots
  That grow for happy lovers.

I slip, I slide, I gloom, I glance,
  Among my skimming swallows;
I make the netted sunbeam dance
  Against my sandy shallows;

I murmur under moon and stars
  In brambly wildernesses;
I linger by my shingly bars;
  I loiter round my cresses;

And out again I curve and flow
  To join the brimming river;
For men may come and men may go,
  But I go on forever.

ALFRED TENNYSON.

THE RHINE.

FROM "CHILDE HAROLD."

THE castled crag of Drachenfels
  Frowns o'er the wide and winding Rhine,
Whose breast of waters broadly swells
  Between the banks which bear the vine,
And hills all rich with blossomed trees,
  And fields which promise corn and wine,
And scattered cities crowning these,
  Whose far white walls along them shine,
Have strewed a scene, which I should see
With double joy, wert *thou* with me.

And peasant-girls, with deep-blue eyes,
  And hands which offer early flowers,
Walk smiling o'er this paradise;
  Above, the frequent feudal towers
Through green leaves lift their walls of gray,
  And many a rock which steeply lowers,
And noble arch in proud decay,
  Look o'er this vale of vintage-bowers;
But one thing want these banks of Rhine, —
Thy gentle hand to clasp in mine!

I send the lilies given to me,
  Though long before thy hand they touch
I know that they must withered be, —
  But yet reject them not as such;
For I have cherished them as dear,
  Because they yet may meet thine eye,
And guide thy soul to mine even here,
  When thou behold'st them drooping nigh,
And know'st them gathered by the Rhine,
And offered from my heart to thine!

The river nobly foams and flows,
  The charm of this enchanted ground,
And all its thousand turns disclose
  Some fresher beauty varying round:
The haughtiest breast its wish might bound
  Through life to dwell delighted here;
Nor could on earth a spot be found
  To nature and to me so dear,
Could thy dear eyes in following mine
Still sweeten more these banks of Rhine?

LORD BYRON.

ON THE RHINE.

'T WAS morn, and beautiful the mountain's brow —
  Hung with the clusters of the bending vine —
  Shone in the early light, when on the Rhine
We sailed and heard the waters round the prow
In murmurs parting; varying as we go,
  Rocks after rocks come forward and retire,
  As some gray convent wall or sunlit spire
Starts up along the banks, unfolding slow.
Here castles, like the prisons of despair,
  Frown as we pass; — there, on the vineyard's side,
  The bursting sunshine pours its streaming tide;
While Grief, forgetful amid scenes so fair,
Counts not the hours of a long summer's day,
Nor heeds how fast the prospect winds away.

WILLIAM LISLE BOWLES.

THE VALLEY BROOK.

FRESH from the fountains of the wood
 A rivulet of the valley came,
And glided on for many a rood,
 Flushed with the morning's ruddy flame.

The air was fresh and soft and sweet;
 The slopes in spring's new verdure lay,
And wet with dew-drops at my feet
 Bloomed the young violets of May.

No sound of busy life was heard
 Amid those pastures lone and still,
Save the faint chirp of early bird,
 Or bleat of flocks along the hill.

I traced that rivulet's winding way;
 New scenes of beauty opened round,
Where meads of brighter verdure lay,
 And lovelier blossoms tinged the ground.

"Ah, happy valley stream!" I said,
 "Calm glides thy wave amid the flowers,
Whose fragrance round thy path is shed
 Through all the joyous summer hours.

"O, could my years, like thine, be passed
 In some remote and silent glen,
Where I could dwell and sleep at last,
 Far from the bustling haunts of men!"

But what new echoes greet my ear?
 The village school-boy's merry call;
And mid the village hum I hear
 The murmur of the waterfall.

I looked; the widening vale betrayed
 A pool that shone like burnished steel,
Where that bright valley stream was stayed
 To turn the miller's ponderous wheel.

Ah! why should I, I thought with shame,
 Sigh for a life of solitude,
When even this stream without a name
 Is laboring for the common good.

No longer let me shun my part
 Amid the busy scenes of life,
But with a warm and generous heart
 Press onward in the glorious strife.

JOHN HOWARD BRYANT.

AFTON WATER.

FLOW gently, sweet Afton, among thy green braes;
Flow gently, I 'll sing thee a song in thy praise;
My Mary 's asleep by thy murmuring stream,
Flow gently, sweet Afton, disturb not her dream.

Thou stock-dove whose echo resounds through the glen,
Ye wild whistling blackbirds in yon thorny den,
Thou green-crested lapwing, thy screaming forbear;
I charge you disturb not my slumbering fair.

How lofty, sweet Afton, thy neighboring hills,
Far marked with the courses of clear winding rills!
There daily I wander as noon rises high,
My flocks and my Mary's sweet cot in my eye.

How pleasant thy banks and green valleys below,
Where wild in the woodlands the primroses blow!
There oft as mild evening weeps over the lea,
The sweet-scented birk shades my Mary and me.

Thy crystal stream, Afton, how lovely it glides,
And winds by the cot where my Mary resides;
How wanton thy waters her snowy feet lave,
As, gathering sweet flowerets, she stems thy clear wave!

Flow gently, sweet Afton, among thy green braes;
Flow gently, sweet river, the theme of my lays;
My Mary 's asleep by thy murmuring stream,
Flow gently, sweet Afton, disturb not her dream.

ROBERT BURNS.

THE SHADED WATER.

WHEN that my mood is sad, and in the noise
 And bustle of the crowd I feel rebuke,
I turn my footsteps from its hollow joys
 And sit me down beside this little brook;
The waters have a music to mine ear
It glads me much to hear.

It is a quiet glen, as you may see,
 Shut in from all intrusion by the trees,
That spread their giant branches, broad and free,
 The silent growth of many centuries;
And make a hallowed time for hapless moods,
A sabbath of the woods.

Few know its quiet shelter, — none, like me,
 Do seek it out with such a fond desire,
Poring in idlesse mood on flower and tree,
 And listening as the voiceless leaves respire, —
When the far-traveling breeze, done wandering,
Rests here his weary wing.

And all the day, with fancies ever new,
 And sweet companions from their boundless store,
Of merry elves bespangled all with dew,
 Fantastic creatures of the old-time lore,
Watching their wild but unobtrusive play,
I fling the hours away.

THE VALLEY BROOK.

"Fresh from the fountains of the wood
A rivulet of the valley came,
And glided on for many a rood,
Flushed with the morning's ruddy flame."

A gracious couch—the root of an old oak
  Whose branches yield it moss and canopy—
Is mine, and, so it be from woodman's stroke
  Secure, shall never be resigned by me;
It hangs above the stream that idly flies,
Heedless of any eyes.

There, with eye sometimes shut, but upward bent,
  Sweetly I muse through many a quiet hour,
While every sense on earnest mission sent,
  Returns, thought-laden, back with bloom and flower;
Pursuing, though rebuked by those who moil,
A profitable toil.

And still the waters, trickling at my feet,
  Wind on their way with gentlest melody,
Yielding sweet music, which the leaves repeat,
  Above them, to the gay breeze gliding by,—
Yet not so rudely as to send one sound
Through the thick copse around.

Sometimes a brighter cloud than all the rest
  Hangs o'er the archway opening through the trees,
Breaking the spell that, like a slumber, pressed
  On my worn spirit its sweet luxuries,—
And with awakened vision upward bent,
I watch the firmament.

How like its sure and undisturbed retreat—
  Life's sanctuary at last, secure from storm—
To the pure waters trickling at my feet
  The bending trees that overshade my form!
So far as sweetest things of earth may seem
Like those of which we dream.

Such, to my mind, is the philosophy
  The young bird teaches, who, with sudden flight,
Sails far into the blue that spreads on high,
  Until I lose him from my straining sight,—
With a most lofty discontent to fly
Upward, from earth to sky.

WILLIAM GILMORE SIMMS.

TO SENECA LAKE.

ON thy fair bosom, silver lake,
  The wild swan spreads his snowy sail,
And round his breast the ripples break,
  As down he bears before the gale.

On thy fair bosom, waveless stream,
  The dipping paddle echoes far,
And flashes in the moonlight gleam,
  And bright reflects the polar star.

The waves along thy pebbly shore,
  As blows the north-wind, heave their foam,
And curl around the dashing oar,
  As late the boatman hies him home.

How sweet, at set of sun, to view
  Thy golden mirror spreading wide,
And see the mist of mantling blue
  Float round the distant mountain's side.

At midnight hour, as shines the moon,
  A sheet of silver spreads below,
And swift she cuts, at highest noon,
  Light clouds, like wreaths of purest snow.

On thy fair bosom, silver lake,
  O, I could ever sweep the oar,
When early birds at morning wake,
  And evening tells us toil is o'er!

JAMES G. PERCIVAL.

THE BUGLE.

FROM "THE PRINCESS."

THE splendor falls on castle walls
  And snowy summits old in story:
The long light shakes across the lakes,
  And the wild cataract leaps in glory.
Blow, bugle, blow, set the wild echoes flying,
Blow, bugle; answer, echoes, dying, dying, dying.

O hark! O hear! how thin and clear,
  And thinner, clearer, farther going!
O sweet and far, from cliff and scar,
  The horns of Elfland faintly blowing!
Blow, let us hear the purple glens replying:
Blow, bugle; answer, echoes, dying, dying, dying.

O love, they die in yon rich sky,
  They faint on hill or field or river;
Our echoes roll from soul to soul,
  And grow forever and forever.
Blow, bugle, blow, set the wild echoes flying,
And answer, echoes, answer, dying, dying, dying.

ALFRED TENNYSON.

THE FALL OF NIAGARA.

THE thoughts are strange that crowd into my brain,
While I look upward to thee. It would seem
As if God poured thee from his hollow hand,
And hung his bow upon thine awful front,
And spoke in that loud voice which seemed to him
Who dwelt in Patmos for his Saviour's sake
The sound of many waters; and had bade
Thy flood to chronicle the ages back,
And notch his centuries in the eternal rocks.

Deep calleth unto deep. And what are we,
That hear the question of that voice sublime?
O, what are all the notes that ever rung
From war's vain trumpet, by thy thundering side?
Yea, what is all the riot man can make
In his short life, to thy unceasing roar?
And yet, bold babbler, what art thou to Him
Who drowned a world, and heaped the waters far
Above its loftiest mountains? — a light wave,
That breaks, and whispers of its Maker's might.

JOHN G. C. BRAINARD.

THE CATARACT OF LODORE.

DESCRIBED IN RHYMES FOR THE NURSERY.

"How does the water
Come down at Lodore?"
My little boy asked me
Thus, once on a time;
And moreover he tasked me
To tell him in rhyme.
Anon at the word,
There first came one daughter,
And then came another,
To second and third
The request of their brother,
And to hear how the water
Comes down at Lodore,
With its rush and its roar,
As many a time
They had seen it before.
So I told them in rhyme,
For of rhymes I had store;
And 't was in my vocation
For their recreation
That so I should sing;
Because I was Laureate
To them and the King.

From its sources which well
In the tarn on the fell;
From its fountains
In the mountains,
Its rills and its gills;
Through moss and through brake,
It runs and it creeps
For a while, till it sleeps
In its own little lake.
And thence at departing,
Awakening and starting,
It runs through the reeds,
And away it proceeds,
Through meadow and glade,
In sun and in shade,
And through the wood-shelter,
Among crags in its flurry,
Helter-skelter,
Hurry-skurry.
Here it comes sparkling,
And there it lies darkling;
Now smoking and frothing
Its tumult and wrath in,
Till, in this rapid race
On which it is bent,
It reaches the place
Of its steep descent.

The cataract strong
Then plunges along,
Striking and raging
As if a war waging
Its caverns and rocks among;
Rising and leaping,
Sinking and creeping,
Swelling and sweeping,
Showering and springing,
Flying and flinging,
Writhing and ringing,
Eddying and whisking,
Spouting and frisking,
Turning and twisting,
Around and around
With endless rebound:
Smiting and fighting,
A sight to delight in;
Confounding, astounding,
Dizzying and deafening the ear with its sound.

Collecting, projecting,
Receding and speeding,
And shocking and rocking,
And darting and parting,
And threading and spreading,
And whizzing and hissing,
And dripping and skipping,
And hitting and splitting,
And shining and twining,
And rattling and battling,
And shaking and quaking,
And pouring and roaring,
And waving and raving,
And tossing and crossing,
And flowing and going,
And running and stunning,
And foaming and roaming,
And dinning and spinning,
And dropping and hopping,
And working and jerking,
And guggling and struggling,
And heaving and cleaving,
And moaning and groaning;

And glittering and frittering,
And gathering and feathering,
And whitening and brightening,
And quivering and shivering,

And hurrying and skurrying,
And thundering and floundering;

Dividing and gliding and sliding,
And falling and brawling and sprawling,
And driving and riving and striving,
And sprinkling and twinkling and wrinkling,
And sounding and bounding and rounding,
And bubbling and troubling and doubling,
And grumbling and rumbling and tumbling,
And clattering and battering and shattering;

Retreating and beating and meeting and sheeting,
Delaying and straying and playing and spraying,
Advancing and prancing and glancing and dancing,
Recoiling, turmoiling and toiling and boiling,
And gleaming and streaming and steaming and beaming,
And rushing and flushing and brushing and gushing,
And flapping and rapping and clapping and slapping,
And curling and whirling and purling and twirling,
And thumping and plumping and bumping and jumping,
And dashing and flashing and splashing and clashing;
And so never ending, but always descending,
Sounds and motions for ever and ever are blending
All at once and all o'er, with a mighty uproar, —
And this way the water comes down at Lodore.

ROBERT SOUTHEY.

WHAT THE WINDS BRING.

WHICH is the wind that brings the cold?
The north-wind, Freddy, and all the snow;
And the sheep will scamper into the fold
When the north begins to blow.

Which is the wind that brings the heat?
The south-wind, Katy; and corn will grow,
And peaches redden for you to eat,
When the south begins to blow.

Which is the wind that brings the rain?
The east-wind, Arty; and farmers know
That cows come shivering up the lane
When the east begins to blow.

Which is the wind that brings the flowers?
The west-wind, Bessy; and soft and low
The birdies sing in the summer hours
When the west begins to blow.

EDMUND CLARENCE STEDMAN.

THE ORIENT.

FROM "THE BRIDE OF ABYDOS."

KNOW ye the land where the cypress and myrtle
Are emblems of deeds that are done in their clime;
Where the rage of the vulture, the love of the turtle,
Now melt into sorrow, now madden to crime?
Know ye the land of the cedar and vine,
Where the flowers ever blossom, the beams ever shine;
Where the light wings of Zephyr, oppressed with perfume,
Wax faint o'er the gardens of Gúl in her bloom?
Where the citron and olive are fairest of fruit,
And the voice of the nightingale never is mute;
Where the tints of the earth, and the hues of the sky,
In color though varied, in beauty may vie,
And the purple of ocean is deepest in dye;
Where the virgins are soft as the roses they twine,
And all, save the spirit of man, is divine?
'T is the clime of the East; 't is the land of the Sun, —
Can he smile on such deeds as his children have done?
O, wild as the accents of lover's farewell
Are the hearts which they bear and the tales which they tell!

LORD BYRON.

SYRIA.

FROM "PARADISE AND THE PERI."

Now, upon Syria's land of roses
Softly the light of eve reposes,
And, like a glory, the broad sun
Hangs over sainted Lebanon,
Whose head in wintry grandeur towers,
And whitens with eternal sleet,
While summer, in a vale of flowers,
Is sleeping rosy at his feet.

To one who looked from upper air
O'er all the enchanted regions there,
How beauteous must have been the glow,
The life, how sparkling from below!
Fair gardens, shining streams, with ranks
Of golden melons on their banks,
More golden where the sunlight falls;
Gay lizards, glittering on the walls
Of ruined shrines, busy and bright
As they were all alive with light;
And, yet more splendid, numerous flocks
Of pigeons, settling on the rocks,
With their rich restless wings, that gleam
Variously in the crimson beam
Of the warm west, — as if inlaid

With brilliants from the mine, or made
Of tearless rainbows, such as span
The unclouded skies of Peristan!
And then, the mingling sounds that come,
Of shepherd's ancient reed, with hum
Of the wild bees of Palestine,
Banqueting through the flowery vales;—
And, Jordan, those sweet banks of thine,
And woods, so full of nightingales!

THOMAS MOORE.

THE VALE OF CASHMERE.

FROM "THE LIGHT OF THE HAREM."

WHO has not heard of the Vale of Cashmere,
With its roses the brightest that earth ever gave,
Its temples, and grottoes, and fountains as clear
As the love-lighted eyes that hang over their wave?

O, to see it at sunset,—when warm o'er the lake
Its splendor at parting a summer eve throws,
Like a bride, full of blushes, when lingering to take
A last look of her mirror at night ere she goes!—
When the shrines through the foliage are gleaming half shown,
And each hallows the hour by some rites of its own.
Here the music of prayer from a minaret swells,
Here the Magian his urn full of perfume is swinging,
And here, at the altar, a zone of sweet bells
Round the waist of some fair Indian dancer is ringing.
Or to see it by moonlight,—when mellowly shines
The light o'er its palaces, gardens, and shrines;
When the waterfalls gleam like a quick fall of stars,
And the nightingale's hymn from the Isle of Chenars
Is broken by laughs and light echoes of feet
From the cool shining walks where the young people meet.
Or at morn, when the magic of daylight awakes
A new wonder each minute as slowly it breaks,
Hills, cupolas, fountains, called forth every one
Out of darkness, as they were just born of the sun;
When the spirit of fragrance is up with the day,
From his harem of night-flowers stealing away;
And the wind, full of wantonness, woos like a lover
The young aspen-trees till they tremble all over;
When the east is as warm as the light of first hopes,
And day, with its banner of radiance unfurled,
Shines in through the mountainous portal that opes,
Sublime, from that valley of bliss to the world!

THOMAS MOORE.

A FOREST HYMN.

THE groves were God's first temples. Ere man learned
To hew the shaft, and lay the architrave,
And spread the roof above them,—ere he framed
The lofty vault, to gather and roll back
The sound of anthems; in the darkling wood,
Amidst the cool and silence, he knelt down,
And offered to the Mightiest solemn thanks
And supplication. For his simple heart
Might not resist the sacred influences
Which, from the stilly twilight of the place,
And from the gray old trunks that high in heaven
Mingled their mossy boughs, and from the sound
Of the invisible breath that swayed at once
All their green tops, stole over him, and bowed
His spirit with the thought of boundless power
And inaccessible majesty. Ah, why
Should we, in the world's riper years, neglect
God's ancient sanctuaries, and adore
Only among the crowd, and under roofs
That our frail hands have raised? Let me, at least,
Here, in the shadow of this aged wood,
Offer one hymn,—thrice happy if it find
Acceptance in his ear.

Father, thy hand
Hath reared these venerable columns, thou
Didst weave this verdant roof. Thou didst look down
Upon the naked earth, and forthwith rose
All these fair ranks of trees. They in thy sun
Budded, and shook their green leaves in thy breeze,
And shot towards heaven. The century-living crow,
Whose birth was in their tops, grew old and died
Among their branches, till at last they stood,
As now they stand, massy and tall and dark,
Fit shrine for humble worshiper to hold
Communion with his Maker. These dim vaults,
These winding aisles, of human pomp or pride
Report not. No fantastic carvings show
The boast of our vain race to change the form
Of thy fair works. But thou art here,—thou fill'st
The solitude. Thou art in the soft winds
That run along the summit of these trees
In music; thou art in the cooler breath

That from the inmost darkness of the place
Comes, scarcely felt; the barky trunks, the ground,
The fresh moist ground, are all instinct with thee.
Here is continual worship; — nature, here,
In the tranquillity that thou dost love,
Enjoys thy presence. Noiselessly around,
From perch to perch, the solitary bird
Passes; and yon clear spring, that, midst its herbs,
Wells softly forth and wandering steeps the roots
Of half the mighty forest, tells no tale
Of all the good it does. Thou hast not left
Thyself without a witness, in these shades,
Of thy perfections. Grandeur, strength, and grace
Are here to speak of thee. This mighty oak, —
By whose immovable stem I stand and seem
Almost annihilated, — not a prince,
In all that proud old world beyond the deep,
E'er wore his crown as loftily as he
Wears the green coronal of leaves with which
Thy hand has graced him. Nestled at his root
Is beauty, such as blooms not in the glare
Of the broad sun. That delicate forest flower
With scented breath, and look so like a smile,
Seems, as it issues from the shapeless mold,
An emanation of the indwelling Life,
A visible token of the upholding Love,
That are the soul of this wide universe.

My heart is awed within me when I think
Of the great miracle that still goes on,
In silence, round me, — the perpetual work
Of thy creation, finished, yet renewed
Forever. Written on thy works I read
The lesson of thy own eternity.
Lo! all grow old and die; but see again,
How on the faltering footsteps of decay
Youth presses, — ever gay and beautiful youth
In all its beautiful forms. These lofty trees
Wave not less proudly that their ancestors
Molder beneath them. O, there is not lost
One of Earth's charms! upon her bosom yet,
After the flight of untold centuries,
The freshness of her far beginning lies,
And yet shall lie. Life mocks the idle hate
Of his arch-enemy Death, — yea, seats himself
Upon the tyrant's throne, the sepulcher,
And of the triumphs of his ghastly foe
Makes his own nourishment. For he came forth
From thine own bosom, and shall have no end.

There have been holy men who hid themselves
Deep in the woody wilderness, and gave
Their lives to thought and prayer, till they outlived
The generation born with them, nor seemed
Less aged than the hoary trees and rocks
Around them; — and there have been holy men
Who deemed it were not well to pass life thus.
But let me often to these solitudes
Retire, and in thy presence reassure
My feeble virtue. Here its enemies,
The passions, at thy plainer footsteps shrink
And tremble, and are still. O God! when thou
Dost scare the world with tempests, set on fire
The heavens with falling thunderbolts, or fill,
With all the waters of the firmament,
The swift dark whirlwind that uproots the woods
And drowns the villages; when, at thy call,
Uprises the great deep, and throws himself
Upon the continent, and overwhelms
Its cities, — who forgets not, at the sight
Of these tremendous tokens of thy power,
His pride, and lays his strifes and follies by?
O, from these sterner aspects of thy face
Spare me and mine, nor let us need the wrath
Of the mad unchained elements to teach
Who rules them. Be it ours to meditate,
In these calm shades, thy milder majesty,
And to the beautiful order of thy works
Learn to conform the order of our lives.

WILLIAM CULLEN BRYANT.

THE PRIMEVAL FOREST.

FROM THE INTRODUCTION TO "EVANGELINE."

THIS is the forest primeval. The murmuring pines and the hemlocks,
Bearded with moss, and in garments green, indistinct in the twilight,
Stand like Druids of old, with voices sad and prophetic,
Stand like harpers hoar, with beards that rest on their bosoms.
Loud from its rocky caverns, the deep-voiced neighboring ocean
Speaks, and in accents disconsolate answers the wail of the forest.
This is the forest primeval; but where are the hearts that beneath it
Leaped like the roe, when he hears in the woodland the voice of the huntsman?

HENRY W. LONGFELLOW.

SONG OF THE SOUTH.

OF all the garden flowers,
The fairest is the rose;
Of winds that stir the bowers,
O, there is none that blows
Like the south, the gentle south;
For that balmy breeze is ours.

Cold is the frozen North,
In its stern and savage mood;

Mid the gales come drifting forth
Bleak snows and drenching flood;
But the South, the gentle South,
Thaws to love the willing blood.

Bethink thee of the vales,
With their birds and blossoms fair, —
Of the darkling nightingales,
That charm the starry air,
In the South, the gentle South;
Ah! our own dear home is there!

Where doth beauty brightest glow
With each rich and radiant charm,
Eyes of night and brow of snow,
Cheery lips, and bosom warm?
In the South, the gentle South, —
There she waits and works her harm.

Say, shines the star of love
From the clear and cloudless sky,
The shadowy groves above,
Where the nestling ring-doves lie?
From the South, the gentle South,
Gleams its lone and lucid eye.

Then turn ye to the home
Of your brethren and your bride;
Far astray your steps may roam,
And more joys for thee abide
In the South, our gentle South,
Than in all the world beside.

DAVID M. MOIR.

THE GREENWOOD.

O, WHEN 't is summer weather,
And the yellow bee, with fairy sound,
The waters clear is humming round,
And the cuckoo sings unseen,
And the leaves are waving green, —
O, then 't is sweet,
In some retreat,
To hear the murmuring dove,
With those whom on earth alone we love,
And to wind through the greenwood together.

But when 't is winter weather,
And crosses grieve,
And friends deceive,
And rain and sleet
The lattice beat, —
O, then 't is sweet
To sit and sing
Of the friends with whom, in the days of spring,
We roamed through the greenwood together.

WILLIAM LISLE BOWLES.

THE BRAVE OLD OAK.

A SONG to the oak, the brave old oak,
Who hath ruled in the greenwood long;
Here 's health and renown to his broad green crown,
And his fifty arms so strong.
There's fear in his frown when the sun goes down,
And the fire in the west fades out;
And he showeth his might on a wild midnight,
When the storm through his branches shout.

Then here 's to the oak, the brave old oak,
Who stands in his pride alone;
And still flourish he, a hale green tree,
When a hundred years are gone!

In the days of old, when the spring with cold
Had brightened his branches gray,
Through the grass at his feet crept maidens sweet,
To gather the dew of May.
And on that day to the rebeck gay
They frolicked with lovesome swains;
They are gone, they are dead, in the churchyard laid,
But the tree it still remains.
Then here 's, etc.

He saw the rare times when the Christmas chimes
Were a merry sound to hear,
When the squire's wide hall and the cottage small
Were filled with good English cheer.
Now gold hath the sway we all obey,
And a ruthless king is he;
But he never shall send our ancient friend
To be tossed on the stormy sea.
Then here 's, etc.

HENRY F. CHORLEY.

THE ARAB TO THE PALM.

NEXT to thee, O fair gazelle,
O Beddowee girl, beloved so well;

Next to the fearless Nedjidee,
Whose fleetness shall bear me again to thee;

Next to ye both, I love the palm,
With his leaves of beauty, his fruit of balm;

Next to ye both, I love the tree
Whose fluttering shadow wraps us three
With love and silence and mystery!

Our tribe is many, our poets vie
With any under the Arab sky;
Yet none can sing of the palm but I.

The marble minarets that begem
Cairo's citadel-diadem
Are not so light as his slender stem.

He lifts his leaves in the sunbeam's glance,
As the Almehs lift their arms in dance, —

A slumberous motion, a passionate sign,
That works in the cells of the blood like wine.

Full of passion and sorrow is he,
Dreaming where the beloved may be;

And when the warm south-winds arise,
He breathes his longing in fervid sighs,

Quickening odors, kisses of balm,
That drop in the lap of his chosen palm.

The sun may flame, and the sands may stir,
But the breath of his passion reaches her.

O tree of love, by that love of thine,
Teach me how I shall soften mine!

Give me the secret of the sun,
Whereby the wooed is ever won!

If I were a king, O stately tree,
A likeness, glorious as might be,
In the court of my palace I 'd build for thee;

With a shaft of silver, burnished bright,
And leaves of beryl and malachite;

With spikes of golden bloom ablaze,
And fruits of topaz and chrysoprase;

And there the poets, in thy praise,
Should night and morning frame new lays, —

New measures sung to tunes divine;
But none, O palm, should equal mine!

BAYARD TAYLOR.

THE PALM-TREE.

Is it the palm, the cocoa-palm,
On the Indian Sea, by the isles of balm?
Or is it a ship in the breezeless calm?

A ship whose keel is of palm beneath,
Whose ribs of palm have a palm-bark sheath,
And a rudder of palm it steereth with.

Branches of palm are its spars and rails,
Fibers of palm are its woven sails,
And the rope is of palm that idly trails!

What does the good ship bear so well?
The cocoa-nut with its stony shell,
And the milky sap of its inner cell.

What are its jars, so smooth and fine,
But hollowed nuts, filled with oil and wine,
And the cabbage that ripens under the Line?

Who smokes his nargileh, cool and calm?
The master, whose cunning and skill could charm
Cargo and ship from the bounteous palm.

In the cabin he sits on a palm-mat soft,
From a beaker of palm his drink is quaffed,
And a palm thatch shields from the sun aloft!

His dress is woven of palmy strands,
And he holds a palm-leaf scroll in his hands,
Traced with the Prophet's wise commands!

The turban folded about his head
Was daintily wrought of the palm-leaf braid,
And the fan that cools him of palm was made.

Of threads of palm was the carpet spun
Whereon he kneels when the day is done,
And the foreheads of Islam are bowed as one!

To him the palm is a gift divine,
Wherein all uses of man combine, —
House and raiment and food and wine!

And, in the hour of his great release,
His need of the palm shall only cease
With the shroud wherein he lieth in peace.

"Allah il Allah!" he sings his psalm
On the Indian Sea, by the isles of balm;
"Thanks to Allah, who gives the palm!"

JOHN GREENLEAF WHITTIER.

THE HOLLY-TREE.

O READER! hast thou ever stood to see
The holly-tree?
The eye that contemplates it well perceives
Its glossy leaves
Ordered by an intelligence so wise
As might confound the atheist's sophistries.

Below, a circling fence, its leaves are seen
Wrinkled and keen;
No grazing cattle, through their prickly round,
Can reach to wound;
But as they grow where nothing is to fear,
Smooth and unarmed the pointless leaves appear.

I love to view these things with curious eyes,
And moralize;
And in this wisdom of the holly-tree
Can emblems see
Wherewith, perchance, to make a pleasant rhyme,
One which may profit in the after-time.

Thus, though abroad, perchance, I might appear
Harsh and austere ;
To those who on my leisure would intrude,
Reserved and rude ;
Gentle at home amid my friends I 'd be,
Like the high leaves upon the holly-tree.

And should my youth — as youth is apt, I know —
Some harshness show,
All vain asperities I, day by day,
Would wear away,
Till the smooth temper of my age should be
Like the high leaves upon the holly-tree.

And as, when all the summer trees are seen
So bright and green,
The holly-leaves their fadeless hues display
Less bright than they ;
But when the bare and wintry woods we see,
What then so cheerful as the holly-tree ?

So, serious should my youth appear among
The thoughtless throng ;
So would I seem, amid the young and gay,
More grave than they ;
That in my age as cheerful I might be
As the green winter of the holly-tree.

ROBERT SOUTHEY.

THE SPICE-TREE.

The spice-tree lives in the garden green ;
Beside it the fountain flows ;
And a fair bird sits the boughs between,
And sings his melodious woes.

No greener garden e'er was known
Within the bounds of an earthly king ;
No lovelier skies have ever shone
Than those that illumine its constant spring.

That coil-bound stem has branches three ;
On each a thousand blossoms grow ;
And, old as aught of time can be,
The root stands fast in the rocks below.

In the spicy shade ne'er seems to tire
The fount that builds a silvery dome ;
And flakes of purple and ruby fire
Gush out, and sparkle amid the foam.

The fair white bird of flaming crest,
And azure wings bedropt with gold,
Ne'er has he known a pause of rest,
But sings the lament that he framed of old :

"O princess bright ! how long the night
Since thou art sunk in the waters clear !
How sadly they flow from the depth below, —
How long must I sing and thou wilt not hear ?

"The waters play, and the flowers are gay,
And the skies are sunny above ;
I would that all could fade and fall,
And I, too, cease to mourn my love.

"O, many a year, so wakeful and drear,
I have sorrowed and watched, beloved, for thee !
But there comes no breath from the chambers of death,
While the lifeless fount gushes under the tree."

The skies grow dark, and they glare with red ;
The tree shakes off its spicy bloom ;
The waves of the fount in a black pool spread ;
And in thunder sounds the garden's doom.

Down springs the bird with a long shrill cry,
Into the sable and angry flood ;
And the face of the pool, as he falls from high,
Curdles in circling stains of blood.

But sudden again upswells the fount ;
Higher and higher the waters flow, —
In a glittering diamond arch they mount,
And round it the colors of morning glow.

Finer and finer the watery mound
Softens and melts to a thin-spun veil,
And tones of music circle around,
And bear to the stars the fountain's tale.

And swift the eddying rainbow screen
Falls in dew on the grassy floor ;
Under the spice-tree the garden's queen
Sits by her lover, who wails no more.

JOHN STERLING.

THE GRAPE-VINE SWING.

Lithe and long as the serpent train,
Springing and clinging from tree to tree,
Now darting upward, now down again,
With a twist and a twirl that are strange to see ;
Never took serpent a deadlier hold,
Never the cougar a wilder spring,
Strangling the oak with the boa's fold,
Spanning the beech with the condor's wing.

Yet no foe that we fear to seek, —
The boy leaps wild to thy rude embrace ;
Thy bulging arms bear as soft a cheek
As ever on lover's breast found place ;
On thy waving train is a playful hold
Thou shalt never to lighter grasp persuade ;
While a maiden sits in thy drooping fold,
And swings and sings in the noonday shade !

O giant strange of our southern woods!
  I dream of thee still in the well-known spot,
Though our vessel strains o'er the ocean floods,
  And the northern forest beholds thee not;
I think of thee still with a sweet regret,
  As the cordage yields to my playful grasp, —
Dost thou spring and cling in our woodlands yet?
  Does the maiden still swing in thy giant clasp?

WILLIAM GILMORE SIMMS.

TO BLOSSOMS.

FAIR pledges of a fruitful tree,
    Why do ye fall so fast?
    Your date is not so past
But you may stay yet here awhile
    To blush and gently smile,
      And go at last.

What! were ye born to be
    An hour or half's delight,
    And so to bid good night?
'T is pity Nature brought ye forth,
    Merely to show your worth,
      And lose you quite.

But you are lovely leaves, where we
    May read how soon things have
    Their end, though ne'er so brave;
And after they have shown their pride
    Like you awhile, they glide
      Into the grave.

ROBERT HERRICK.

ALMOND BLOSSOM.

BLOSSOM of the almond-trees,
April's gift to April's bees,
Birthday ornament of spring,
Flora's fairest daughterling; —
Coming when no flowerets dare
Trust the cruel outer air,
When the royal king-cup bold
Dares not don his coat of gold,
And the sturdy blackthorn spray
Keeps his silver for the May; —
Coming when no flowerets would,
Save thy lowly sisterhood,
Early violets, blue and white,
Dying for their love of light.
Almond blossom, sent to teach us
That the spring days soon will reach us,
Lest, with longing over-tried,
We die as the violets died, —
Blossom, clouding all the tree
With thy crimson broidery,
Long before a leaf of green
On the bravest bough is seen, —
Ah! when winter winds are swinging
All thy red bells into ringing,
With a bee in every bell,
Almond bloom, we greet thee well!

EDWIN ARNOLD.

THE PLANTING OF THE APPLE-TREE.

COME, let us plant the apple-tree.
Cleave the tough greensward with the spade;
Wide let its hollow bed be made;
There gently lay the roots, and there
Sift the dark mold with kindly care,
  And press it o'er them tenderly,
As round the sleeping infant's feet
We softly fold the cradle-sheet;
  So plant we the apple-tree.

  What plant we in this apple-tree?
Buds, which the breath of summer days
Shall lengthen into leafy sprays;
Boughs where the thrush with crimson breast,
Shall haunt, and sing, and hide her nest;
  We plant, upon the sunny lea,
A shadow for the noontide hour,
A shelter from the summer shower,
  When we plant the apple-tree.

  What plant we in this apple-tree?
Sweets for a hundred flowery springs
To load the May-wind's restless wings,
When, from the orchard row, he pours
Its fragrance through our open doors;
  A world of blossoms for the bee,
Flowers for the sick girl's silent room,
For the glad infant sprigs of bloom,
  We plant with the apple-tree.

  What plant we in this apple-tree!
Fruits that shall swell in sunny June,
And redden in the August noon,
And drop, when gentle airs come by,
That fan the blue September sky,
  While children come, with cries of glee,
And seek them where the fragrant grass
Betrays their bed to those who pass,
  At the foot of the apple-tree.

  And when, above this apple-tree,
The winter stars are quivering bright,
And winds go howling through the night,
Girls, whose young eyes o'erflow with mirth,
Shall peel its fruit by cottage hearth,
  And guests in prouder homes shall see,
Heaped with the grape of Cintra's vine

And golden orange of the Line,
The fruit of the apple-tree.

The fruitage of this apple-tree
Winds and our flag of stripe and star
Shall bear to coasts that lie afar,
Where men shall wonder at the view,
And ask in what fair groves they grew;
And sojourners beyond the sea
Shall think of childhood's careless day
And long, long hours of summer play,
In the shade of the apple-tree.

Each year shall give this apple-tree
A broader flush of roseate bloom,
A deeper maze of verdurous gloom,
And loosen, when the frost-clouds lower,
The crisp brown leaves in thicker shower.
The years shall come and pass, but we
Shall hear no longer, where we lie,
The summer's songs, the autumn's sigh,
In the boughs of the apple-tree.

And time shall waste this apple-tree.
O, when its aged branches throw
Thin shadows on the ground below,
Shall fraud and force and iron will
Oppress the weak and helpless still?
What shall the tasks of mercy be,
Amid the toils, the strifes, the tears
Of those who live when length of years
Is wasting this apple-tree?

"Who planted this old apple-tree?"
The children of that distant day
Thus to some aged man shall say;
And, gazing on its mossy stem,
The gray-haired man shall answer them:
"A poet of the land was he,
Born in the rude but good old times;
'T is said he made some quaint old rhymes
On planting the apple-tree."

WILLIAM CULLEN BRYANT.

THE MAIZE.

"That precious seed into the furrow cast
Earliest in springtime crowns the harvest last."

PHŒBE CARY.

A SONG for the plant of my own native West,
Where nature and freedom reside,
By plenty still crowned, and by peace ever blest,
To the corn! the green corn of her pride!
In climes of the East has the olive been sung,
And the grape been the theme of their lays,
But for thee shall a harp of the backwoods be strung,
Thou bright, ever beautiful maize!

Afar in the forest the rude cabins rise,
And send up their pillars of smoke,
And the tops of their columns are lost in the skies,
O'er the heads of the cloud-kissing oak;
Near the skirt of the grove, where the sturdy arm swings
The ax till the old giant sways,
And echo repeats every blow as it rings,
Shoots the green and the glorious maize!

There buds of the buckeye in spring are the first,
And the willow's gold hair then appears,
And snowy the cups of the dogwood that burst
By the red bud, with pink-tinted tears.
And stripèd the bolls which the poppy holds up
For the dew, and the sun's yellow rays,
And brown is the pawpaw's shade-blossoming cup,
In the wood, near the sun-loving maize!

When through the dark soil the bright steel of the plow
Turns the mold from its unbroken bed
The plowman is cheered by the finch on the bough,
And the blackbird doth follow his tread.
And idle, afar on the landscape descried,
The deep-lowing kine slowly graze,
And nibbling the grass on the sunny hillside
Are the sheep, hedged away from the maize.

With springtime and culture, in martial array
It waves its green broadswords on high,
And fights with the gale, in a fluttering fray,
And the sunbeams, which fall from the sky;
It strikes its green blades at the zephyrs at noon,
And at night at the swift-flying fays,
Who ride through the darkness the beams of the moon,
Through the spears and the flags of the maize!

When the summer is fierce still its banners are green,
Each warrior's long beard groweth red,
His emerald-bright sword is sharp-pointed and keen,
And golden his tassel-plumed head.
As a host of armed knights set a monarch at naught,
That defy the day-god to his gaze,
And, revived every morn from the battle that's fought,
Fresh stand the green ranks of the maize!

But brown comes the autumn, and sear grows the corn,
And the woods like a rainbow are dressed,
And but for the cock and the noontide horn
Old Time would be tempted to rest.

The humming bee fans off a shower of gold
  From the mullein's long rod as it sways,
And dry grow the leaves which protecting infold
  The ears of the well-ripened maize!

At length Indian Summer, the lovely, doth come,
  With its blue frosty nights, and days still,
When distantly clear sounds the waterfall's hum,
  And the sun smokes ablaze on the hill!
A dim veil hangs over the landscape and flood,
  And the hills are all mellowed in haze,
While Fall, creeping on like a monk 'neath his hood,
  Plucks the thick-rustling wealth of the maize.

And the heavy wains creak to the barns large and gray,
  Where the treasure securely we hold,
Housed safe from the tempest, dry-sheltered away,
  Our blessing more precious than gold!
And long for this manna that springs from the sod
  Shall we gratefully give Him the praise,
The source of all bounty, our Father and God,
  Who sent us from heaven the maize!

WILLIAM W. FOSDICK.

THE POTATO.

I'M a careless potato, and care not a pin
  How into existence I came;
If they planted me drill-wise or dibbled me in,
  To me 't is exactly the same.
The bean and the pea may more loftily tower,
  But I care not a button for them;
Defiance I nod with my beautiful flower
  When the earth is hoed up to my stem.

ANONYMOUS.

THE PUMPKIN.

ON the banks of the Xenil, the dark Spanish maiden
Comes up with the fruit of the tangled vine laden;
And the Creole of Cuba laughs out to behold
Through orange-leaves shining the broad spheres of gold;
Yet with dearer delight from his home in the North,
On the fields of his harvest the Yankee looks forth,
Where crook-necks are coiling and yellow fruit shines,
And the sun of September melts down on his vines.

Ah! on Thanksgiving Day, when from East and from West,
From North and from South come the pilgrim and guest,
When the gray-haired New-Englander sees round his board
The old broken links of affection restored,
When the care-wearied man seeks his mother once more,
And the worn matron smiles where the girl smiled before,
What moistens the lip, and what brightens the eye?
What calls back the past like the rich pumpkin-pie?

O, fruit loved of boyhood! the old days recalling,
When wood-grapes were purpling and brown nuts were falling!
When wild, ugly faces we carved in its skin,
Glaring out through the dark with a candle within!
When we laughed round the corn-heap, with hearts all in tune,
Our chair a broad pumpkin, our lantern the moon,
Telling tales of the fairy who traveled like steam
In a pumpkin-shell coach, with two rats for her team!

Then thanks for thy present! — none sweeter or better
E'er smoked from an oven or circled a platter!
Fairer hands never wrought at a pastry more fine,
Brighter eyes never watched o'er its baking, than thine!
And the prayer, which my mouth is too full to express,
Swells my heart that thy shadow may never be less,
That the days of thy lot may be lengthened below,
And the fame of thy worth like a pumpkin-vine grow,
And thy life be as sweet, and its last sunset sky
Golden-tinted and fair as thy own pumpkin-pie!

JOHN GREENLEAF WHITTIER.

HYMN TO THE FLOWERS.

DAY-STARS! that ope your frownless eyes to twinkle
  From rainbow galaxies of earth's creation,
And dew-drops on her lonely altars sprinkle
    As a libation.

Ye matin worshipers! who bending lowly
  Before the uprisen sun, God's lidless eye,
Throw from your chalices a sweet and holy
    Incense on high.

Ye bright mosaics! that with storied beauty,
  The floor of Nature's temple tesselate,
What numerous emblems of instructive duty
    Your forms create!

'Neath cloistered boughs, each floral bell that swingeth
And tolls its perfume on the passing air,
Makes Sabbath in the fields, and ever ringeth
A call to prayer.

Not to the domes where crumbling arch and column
Attest the feebleness of mortal hand,
But to that fane, most catholic and solemn,
Which God hath planned;

To that cathedral, boundless as our wonder,
Whose quenchless lamps the sun and moon supply;
Its choir the winds and waves, its organ thunder,
Its dome the sky.

There, as in solitude and shade I wander
Through the green aisles, or stretched upon the sod,
Awed by the silence, reverently ponder
The ways of God,

Your voiceless lips, O flowers! are living preachers,
Each cup a pulpit, every leaf a book,
Supplying to my fancy numerous teachers
From loneliest nook.

Floral apostles! that in dewy splendor
"Weep without woe, and blush without a crime,"
O, may I deeply learn, and ne'er surrender
Your lore sublime!

"Thou wert not, Solomon, in all thy glory,
Arrayed," the lilies cry, "in robes like ours!
How vain your grandeur! ah, how transitory
Are human flowers!"

In the sweet-scented pictures, heavenly artist,
With which thou paintest Nature's wide-spread hall,
What a delightful lesson thou impartest
Of love to all!

Not useless are ye, flowers! though made for pleasure;
Blooming o'er field and wave, by day and night,
From every source your sanction bids me treasure
Harmless delight.

Ephemeral sages! what instructors hoary
For such a world of thought could furnish scope?
Each fading calyx a *memento mori*,
Yet fount of hope.

Posthumous glories! angel-like collection!
Upraised from seed or bulb interred in earth,
Ye are to me a type of resurrection
And second birth.

Were I in churchless solitudes remaining,
Far from all voice of teachers and divines,
My soul would find, in flowers of God's ordaining,
Priests, sermons, shrines!

HORACE SMITH.

FLOWERS.

I WILL not have the mad Clytie,
Whose head is turned by the sun;
The tulip is a courtly quean,
Whom, therefore, I will shun;
The cowslip is a country wench,
The violet is a nun;—
But I will woo the dainty rose,
The queen of every one.

The pea is but a wanton witch,
In too much haste to wed,
And clasps her rings on every hand;
The wolfsbane I should dread;
Nor will I dreary rosemarye,
That always mourns the dead;—
But I will woo the dainty rose,
With her cheeks of tender red.

The lily is all in white, like a saint,
And so is no mate for me;
And the daisy's cheek is tipped with a blush,
She is of such low degree;
Jasmine is sweet, and has many loves,
And the broom's betrothed to the bee;—
But I will plight with the dainty rose,
For fairest of all is she.

THOMAS HOOD.

THE ROSE.

FROM "HASSAN BEN KHALED."

THEN took the generous host
A basket filled with roses. Every guest
Cried, "Give me roses!" and he thus addressed
His words to all: "He who exalts them most
In song, he only shall the roses wear."
Then sang a guest: "The rose's cheeks are fair;
It crowns the purple bowl, and no one knows
If the rose colors it, or it the rose."
And sang another: "Crimson is its hue,
And on its breast the morning's crystal dew
Is changed to rubies." Then a third replied:
"It blushes in the sun's enamored sight,
As a young virgin on her wedding night,

When from her face the bridegroom lifts the veil."
When all had sung their songs, I, Hassan, tried.
"The rose," I sang, "is either red or pale,
Like maidens whom the flame of passion burns,
And love or jealousy controls, by turns.
Its buds are lips preparing for a kiss;
Its open flowers are like the blush of bliss
On lovers' cheeks; the thorns its armor are,
And in its center shines a golden star,
As on a favorite's cheek a sequin glows; —
And thus the garden's favorite is the rose."
The master from his open basket shook
The roses on my head.

BAYARD TAYLOR.

THE ROSE.

THE rose had been washed, just washed in a shower,
Which Mary to Anna conveyed,
The plentiful moisture encumbered the flower,
And weighed down its beautiful head.

The cup was all filled, and the leaves were all wet,
And it seemed, to a fanciful view,
To weep for the buds it had left with regret,
On the flourishing bush where it grew.

I hastily seized it, unfit as it was
For a nosegay, so dripping and drowned,
And swinging it rudely, too rudely, alas!
I snapped it, it fell to the ground.

And such, I exclaimed, is the pitiless part
Some act by the delicate mind,
Regardless of wringing and breaking a heart
Already to sorrow resigned.

This elegant rose, had I shaken it less,
Might have bloomed with its owner awhile;
And the tear that is wiped with a little address,
May be followed perhaps by a smile.

WILLIAM COWPER.

THE MOSS ROSE.

THE angel of the flowers, one day,
Beneath a rose-tree sleeping lay, —
That spirit to whose charge 't is given
To bathe young buds in dews of heaven.
Awaking from his light repose,
The angel whispered to the rose:
"O fondest object of my care,
Still fairest found, where all are fair;
For the sweet shade thou giv'st to me
Ask what thou wilt, 't is granted thee."
"Then," said the rose, with deepened glow,
"On me another grace bestow."
The spirit paused, in silent thought, —
What grace was there that flower had not?
'T was but a moment, — o'er the rose
A veil of moss the angel throws,
And, robed in nature's simplest weed,
Could there a flower that rose exceed?

From the German of KRUMMACHER.

THE ROSE.

FROM "THE LADY OF THE LAKE."

"THE rose is fairest when 't is budding new,
And hope is brightest when it dawns from fears;
The rose is sweetest washed with morning dew,
And love is loveliest when embalmed in tears.
O wilding rose, whom fancy thus endears,
I bid your blossoms in my bonnet wave,
Emblem of hope and love through future years!"
Thus spoke young Norman, heir of Armandave,
What time the sun arose on Vennachar's broad wave.

SIR WALTER SCOTT.

TO PRIMROSES, FILLED WITH MORNING DEW.

WHY do ye weep, sweet babes? Can tears
Speak grief in you,
Who were but born
Just as the modest morn
Teemed her refreshing dew?
Alas! you have not known that shower
That mars a flower,
Nor felt the unkind
Breath of a blasting wind;
Nor are ye worn with years,
Or warped as we,
Who think it strange to see
Such pretty flowers, like to orphans young,
Speaking by tears before ye have a tongue.

Speak, whimp'ring younglings, and make known
The reason why
Ye droop and weep;
Is it for want of sleep,
Or childish lullaby?
Or that ye have not seen as yet
The violet?
Or brought a kiss
From that sweet heart to this?
No, no; this sorrow shown
By your tears shed,
Would have this lecture read, —
"That things of greatest, so of meanest worth,
Conceived with grief are, and with tears brought forth."

ROBERT HERRICK.

TO THE FRINGED GENTIAN.

THOU blossom, bright with autumn dew,
And colored with the heaven's own blue,
That openest when the quiet light
Succeeds the keen and frosty night;

Thou comest not when violets lean
O'er wandering brooks and springs unseen,
Or columbines, in purple dressed,
Nod o'er the ground-bird's hidden nest.

Thou waitest late, and com'st alone,
When woods are bare and birds are flown,
And frosts and shortening days portend
The aged Year is near his end.

Then doth thy sweet and quiet eye
Look through its fringes to the sky,
Blue — blue — as if that sky let fall
A flower from its cerulean wall.

I would that thus, when I shall see
The hour of death draw near to me,
Hope, blossoming within my heart,
May look to heaven as I depart.

WILLIAM CULLEN BRYANT.

THE PRIMROSE.

ASK me why I send you here
This sweet Infanta of the yeere?
Ask me why I send to you
This Primrose, thus bepearled with dew?
I will whisper to your eares,
The sweets of love are mixt with tears.

Ask me why this flower does show
So yellow-green and sickly too?
Ask me why the stalk is weak
And bending, yet it doth not break?
I will answer, these discover
What fainting hopes are in a lover.

ROBERT HERRICK.

THE EARLY PRIMROSE.

MILD offspring of a dark and sullen sire!
Whose modest form, so delicately fine,
Was nursed in whirling storms
And cradled in the winds.

Thee, when young Spring first questioned Winter's sway,
And dared the sturdy blusterer to the fight,
Thee on this bank he threw
To mark his victory.

In this low vale the promise of the year,
Serene, thou openest to the nipping gale,
Unnoticed and alone,
Thy tender elegance.

So Virtue blooms, brought forth amid the storms
Of chill adversity; in some lone walk
Of life she rears her head,
Obscure and unobserved;

While every bleaching breeze that on her blows
Chastens her spotless purity of breast,
And hardens her to bear
Serene the ills of life.

HENRY KIRKE WHITE.

THE RHODORA.

LINES ON BEING ASKED, WHENCE IS THE FLOWER?

IN May, when sea-winds pierced our solitudes,
I found the fresh rhodora in the woods,
Spreading its leafless blooms in a damp nook,
To please the desert and the sluggish brook:
The purple petals fallen in the pool
Made the black waters with their beauty gay, —
Here might the red-bird come his plumes to cool,
And court the flower that cheapens his array.
Rhodora! if the sages ask thee why
This charm is wasted on the marsh and sky,
Dear, tell them, that if eyes were made for seeing,
Then beauty is its own excuse for being.
Why thou wert there, O rival of the rose!
I never thought to ask; I never knew,
But in my simple ignorance suppose
The selfsame Power that brought me there brought you.

RALPH WALDO EMERSON.

THE BROOM-FLOWER.

O, THE broom, the yellow broom!
The ancient poet sung it,
And dear it is on summer days
To lie at rest among it.

I know the realms where people say
The flowers have not their fellow;
I know where they shine out like suns,
The crimson and the yellow.

I know where ladies live enchained
In luxury's silken fetters,
And flowers as bright as glittering gems
Are used for written letters.

But ne'er was flower so fair as this,
In modern days or olden;

It groweth on its nodding stem
  Like to a garland golden.

And all about my mother's door
  Shine out its glittering bushes,
And down the glen, where clear as light
  The mountain-water gushes.

Take all the rest; but give me this,
  And the bird that nestles in it, —
I love it, for it loves the broom, —
  The green and yellow linnet.

Well, call the rose the queen of flowers,
  And boast of that of Sharon,
Of lilies like to marble cups,
  And the golden rod of Aaron:

I care not how these flowers may be
  Beloved of man and woman;
The broom it is the flower for me,
  That groweth on the common.

O, the broom, the yellow broom!
  The ancient poet sung it,
And dear it is on summer days
  To lie at rest among it.

MARY HOWITT.

VIOLETS.

WELCOME, maids of honor!
    You do bring
    In the Spring,
And wait upon her.

She has virgins many,
    Fresh and fair;
    Yet you are
More sweet than any.

Y' are the maiden Posies,
    And, so graced,
    To be placed
'Fore damask roses.

Yet though thus respected,
    By and by
    Ye do lie,
Poor girls, neglected.

ROBERT HERRICK.

THE VIOLET.

O FAINT, delicious, springtime violet!
    Thine odor, like a key,
Turns noiselessly in memory's wards to let
    A thought of sorrow free.

The breath of distant fields upon my brow
    Blows through that open door
The sound of wind-borne bells, more sweet and low,
    And sadder than of yore.

It comes afar, from that belovèd place,
    And that belovèd hour,
When life hung ripening in love's golden grace,
    Like grapes above a bower.

A spring goes singing through its reedy grass;
    The lark sings o'er my head,
Drowned in the sky — O, pass, ye visions, pass!
    I would that I were dead! —

Why hast thou opened that forbidden door,
    From which I ever flee?
O vanished joy! O love, that art no more,
    Let my vexed spirit be!

O violet! thy odor through my brain
    Hath searched, and stung to grief
This sunny day, as if a curse did stain
    Thy velvet leaf.

WILLIAM W. STORY.

TO A MOUNTAIN DAISY.

ON TURNING ONE DOWN WITH THE PLOW, IN APRIL, 1786.

WEE, modest, crimson-tippèd flower,
Thou 's met me in an evil hour,
For I maun crush amang the stoure
    Thy slender stem;
To spare thee now is past my power,
    Thou bonny gem.

Alas! it 's no thy neibor sweet,
The bonny lark, companion meet,
Bending thee 'mang the dewy weet,
    Wi' speckled breast,
When upward springing, blithe to greet
    The purpling east.

Cauld blew the bitter-biting north
Upon thy early, humble birth;
Yet cheerfully thou glinted forth
    Amid the storm,
Scarce reared above the parent earth
    Thy tender form.

The flaunting flowers our gardens yield,
High sheltering woods and wa's maun shield:
But thou beneath the random bield
    O' clod or stane,
Adorns the histie stibble-field,
    Unseen, alane.

There, in thy scanty mantle clad,
Thy snawie bosom sunward spread,

Thou lifts thy unassuming head
In humble guise ;
But now the share uptears thy bed,
And low thou lies !

Such is the fate of artless maid,
Sweet floweret of the rural shade !
By love's simplicity betrayed,
And guileless trust,
Till she, like thee, all soiled, is laid
Low i' the dust.

Such is the fate of simple bard,
On life's rough ocean luckless starred !
Unskillful he to note the card
Of prudent lore,
Till billows rage, and gales blow hard,
And whelm him o'er !

Such fate to suffering worth is given,
Who long with wants and woes has striven,
By human pride or cunning driven
To misery's brink,
Till wrenched of every stay but Heaven,
He, ruined, sink !

Even thou who mourn'st the daisy's fate,
That fate is thine, — no distant date :
Stern Ruin's plowshare drives, elate,
Full on thy bloom,
Till crushed beneath the furrow's weight
Shall be thy doom !

ROBERT BURNS.

THE DAISY.

STAR of the mead ! sweet daughter of the day,
Whose opening flower invites the morning ray,
From the moist cheek and bosom's chilly fold
To kiss the tears of eve, the dew-drops cold !
Sweet daisy, flower of love ! when birds are paired,
'T is sweet to see thee, with thy bosom bared,
Smiling in virgin innocence serene,
Thy pearly crown above thy vest of green.
The lark with sparkling eye and rustling wing
Rejoins his widowed mate in early spring,
And, as he prunes his plumes of russet hue,
Swears on thy maiden blossom to be true.
Oft have I watched thy closing buds at eve,
Which for the parting sunbeams seemed to grieve ;
And when gay morning gilt the dew-bright plain,
Seen them unclasp their folded leaves again ;
Nor he who sung "The daisy is so sweet !"
More dearly loved thy pearly form to greet,
When on his scarf the knight the daisy bound,
And dames to tourneys shone with daisies crowned,
And fays forsook the purer fields above,
To hail the daisy, flower of faithful love.

JOHN LEYDEN.

THE SUNFLOWER.

AH, sunflower ! weary of time,
Who countest the steps of the sun,
Seeking after that sweet golden clime,
Where the traveler's journey is done ;

Where the youth pined away with desire,
And the pale virgin shrouded in snow,
Arise from their graves, and aspire
Where my sunflower wishes to go.

WILLIAM BLAKE.

THE DAISY.

THERE is a flower, a little flower
With silver crest and golden eye,
That welcomes every changing hour,
And weathers every sky.

The prouder beauties of the field
In gay but quick succession shine ;
Race after race their honors yield,
They flourish and decline.

But this small flower, to Nature dear,
While moons and stars their courses run,
Inwreathes the circle of the year,
Companion of the sun.

It smiles upon the lap of May,
To sultry August spreads its charm,
Lights pale October on his way,
And twines December's arm.

The purple heath and golden broom
On moory mountains catch the gale ;
O'er lawns the lily sheds perfume,
The violet in the vale.

But this bold floweret climbs the hill,
Hides in the forest, haunts the glen,
Plays on the margin of the rill,
Peeps round the fox's den.

Within the garden's cultured round
It shares the sweet carnation's bed ;
And blooms on consecrated ground
In honor of the dead.

The lambkin crops its crimson gem ;
The wild bee murmurs on its breast ;
The blue-fly bends its pensile stem
Light o'er the skylark's nest.

'T is Flora's page, — in every place,
In every season, fresh and fair ;
It opens with perennial grace,
And blossoms everywhere.

On waste and woodland, rock and plain,
  Its humble buds unheeded rise;
The rose has but a summer reign;
  The daisy never dies!

JAMES MONTGOMERY.

DAFFODILS.

I WANDERED lonely as a cloud
  That floats on high o'er vales and hills
When all at once I saw a crowd, —
  A host of golden daffodils
Beside the lake, beneath the trees,
Fluttering and dancing in the breeze.

Continuous as the stars that shine
  And twinkle on the Milky Way,
They stretched in never-ending line
  Along the margin of a bay:
Ten thousand saw I, at a glance,
Tossing their heads in sprightly dance.

The waves beside them danced, but they
  Outdid the sparkling waves in glee;
A poet could not but be gay
  In such a jocund company;
I gazed — and gazed — but little thought
What wealth the show to me had brought.

For oft, when on my couch I lie,
  In vacant or in pensive mood,
They flash upon that inward eye
  Which is the bliss of solitude;
And then my heart with pleasure fills,
And dances with the daffodils.

WILLIAM WORDSWORTH.

DAFFODILS.

FAIR daffodils, we weep to see
  You haste away so soon;
As yet the early-rising sun
  Has not attained its noon.
    Stay, stay,
  Until the hastening day
    Has run
  But to the even-song;
And, having prayed together, we
  Will go with you along.

We have short time to stay as you,
  We have as short a spring;
As quick a growth, to meet decay,
  As you or anything.
    We die,
  As your hours do, and dry
    Away,
  Like to the summer's rain,
Or as the pearls of morning's dew,
  Ne'er to be found again.

ROBERT HERRICK.

THE VOICE OF THE GRASS.

HERE I come creeping, creeping everywhere;
    By the dusty roadside,
    On the sunny hillside,
    Close by the noisy brook,
    In every shady nook,
I come creeping, creeping everywhere.

Here I come creeping, smiling everywhere;
    All round the open door,
    Where sit the aged poor;
    Here where the children play,
    In the bright and merry May,
I come creeping, creeping everywhere.

Here I come creeping, creeping everywhere;
    In the noisy city street
    My pleasant face you 'll meet,
    Cheering the sick at heart
    Toiling his busy part, —
Silently creeping, creeping everywhere.

Here I come creeping, creeping everywhere;
    You cannot see me coming,
    Nor hear my low sweet humming;
    For in the starry night,
    And the glad morning light,
I come quietly creeping everywhere.

Here I come creeping, creeping everywhere;
    More welcome than the flowers
    In summer's pleasant hours;
    The gentle cow is glad,
    And the merry bird not sad,
To see me creeping, creeping everywhere.

Here I come creeping, creeping everywhere;
    When you 're numbered with the dead
    In your still and narrow bed,
    In the happy spring I 'll come
    And deck your silent home, —
Creeping, silently creeping everywhere.

Here I come creeping, creeping everywhere;
    My humble song of praise
    Most joyfully I raise
    To Him at whose command
    I beautify the land,
Creeping, silently creeping everywhere.

SARAH ROBERTS.

THE IVY GREEN.

O, A DAINTY plant is the ivy green,
That creepeth o'er ruins old!
Of right choice food are his meals, I ween,
In his cell so lone and cold.
The walls must be crumbled, the stones decayed,
To pleasure his dainty whim;
And the moldering dust that years have made
Is a merry meal for him.
Creeping where no life is seen,
A rare old plant is the ivy green.

Fast he stealeth on, though he wears no wings,
And a stanch old heart has he!
How closely he twineth, how tight he clings
To his friend, the huge oak-tree!
And slyly he traileth along the ground,
And his leaves he gently waves,
And he joyously twines and hugs around
The rich mold of dead men's graves.
Creeping where no life is seen,
A rare old plant is the ivy green.

Whole ages have fled, and their works decayed,
And nations have scattered been;
But the stout old ivy shall never fade
From its hale and hearty green.
The brave old plant in its lonely days
Shall fatten upon the past;
For the stateliest building man can raise
Is the ivy's food at last.
Creeping where no life is seen,
A rare old plant is the ivy green.

CHARLES DICKENS.

THE DEATH OF THE FLOWERS.

THE melancholy days are come, the saddest of the year,
Of wailing winds, and naked woods, and meadows brown and sear.
Heaped in the hollows of the grove, the autumn leaves lie dead;
They rustle to the eddying gust, and to the rabbit's tread.
The robin and the wren are flown, and from the shrubs the jay,
And from the wood-top calls the crow through all the gloomy day.

Where are the flowers, the fair young flowers, that lately sprang and stood
In brighter light and softer airs, a beauteous sisterhood?
Alas! they all are in their graves; the gentle race of flowers
Are lying in their lowly beds with the fair and good of ours.
The rain is falling where they lie; but the cold November rain
Calls not from out the gloomy earth the lovely ones again.

The wind-flower and the violet, they perished long ago,
And the brier-rose and the orchis died amid the summer glow;
But on the hill the golden-rod, and the aster in the wood,
And the yellow sunflower by the brook in autumn beauty stood,
Till fell the frost from the clear cold heaven, as falls the plague on men,
And the brightness of their smile was gone from upland, glade, and glen.

And now, when comes the calm mild day, as still such days will come,
To call the squirrel and the bee from out their winter home;
When the sound of dropping nuts is heard, though all the trees are still,
And twinkle in the smoky light the waters of the rill;
The south-wind searches for the flowers whose fragrance late he bore,
And sighs to find them in the wood and by the stream no more.

And then I think of one who in her youthful beauty died,
The fair meek blossom that grew up and faded by my side.
In the cold moist earth we laid her, when the forests cast the leaf,
And we wept that one so lovely should have a life so brief;
Yet not unmeet it was that one, like that young friend of ours,
So gentle and so beautiful, should perish with the flowers.

WILLIAM CULLEN BRYANT.

THE USE OF FLOWERS.

GOD might have bade the earth bring forth
Enough for great and small,
The oak-tree and the cedar-tree,
Without a flower at all.
We might have had enough, enough
For every want of ours,
For luxury, medicine, and toil,
And yet have had no flowers.

AUTUMN.

"When the sound of dropping nuts is heard, though all the trees are still,
And twinkle in the smoky light the waters of the rill."

Then wherefore, wherefore were they made,
  All dyed with rainbow light,
All fashioned with supremest grace
  Upspringing day and night: —
Springing in valleys green and low,
  And on the mountains high,
And in the silent wilderness
  Where no man passes by?

Our outward life requires them not, —
  Then wherefore had they birth? —
To minister delight to man,
  To beautify the earth;
To comfort man, — to whisper hope,
  Whene'er his faith is dim,
For who so careth for the flowers
  Will care much more for him!

MARY HOWITT.

BETROTHED ANEW.

THE sunlight fills the trembling air,
  And balmy days their guerdons bring;
The Earth again is young and fair,
  And amorous with musky Spring.

The golden nurslings of the May
  In splendor strew the spangled green,
And hues of tender beauty play,
  Entangled where the willows lean.

Mark how the rippled currents flow;
  What lusters on the meadows lie!
And hark! the songsters come and go,
  And trill between the earth and sky.

Who told us that the years had fled,
  Or borne afar our blissful youth?
Such joys are all about us spread;
  We know the whisper was not truth.

The birds that break from grass and grove
  Sing every carol that they sung
When first our veins were rich with love,
  And May her mantle round us flung.

O fresh-lit dawn! immortal life!
  O Earth's betrothal, sweet and true,
With whose delights our souls are rife,
  And aye their vernal vows renew!

Then, darling, walk with me this morn;
  Let your brown tresses drink its sheen;
These violets, within them worn,
  Of floral fays shall make you queen.

What though there comes a time of pain
  When autumn winds forbode decay?
The days of love are born again;
  That fabled time is far away!

And never seemed the land so fair
  As now, nor birds such notes to sing,
Since first within your shining hair
  I wove the blossoms of the spring.

EDMUND CLARENCE STEDMAN.

THE LION'S RIDE.

THE lion is the desert's king; through his domain so wide
Right swiftly and right royally this night he means to ride.
By the sedgy brink, where the wild herds drink, close couches the grim chief;
The trembling sycamore above whispers with every leaf.

At evening, on the Table Mount, when ye can see no more
The changeful play of signals gay; when the gloom is speckled o'er
With kraal fires; when the Caffre wends home through the lone karroo;
When the boshbok in the thicket sleeps, and by the stream the gnu;

Then bend your gaze across the waste, — what see ye? The giraffe,
Majestic, stalks towards the lagoon, the turbid lymph to quaff;
With outstretched neck and tongue adust, he kneels him down to cool
His hot thirst with a welcome draught from the foul and brackish pool.

A rustling sound, a roar, a bound, — the lion sits astride
Upon his giant courser's back. Did ever king so ride?
Had ever king a steed so rare, caparisons of state
To match the dappled skin whereon that rider sits elate?

In the muscles of the neck his teeth are plunged with ravenous greed;
His tawny mane is tossing round the withers of the steed.
Up leaping with a hollow yell of anguish and surprise,
Away, away, in wild dismay, the camelopard flies.

His feet have wings; see how he springs across the moonlit plain!
As from their sockets they would burst, his glaring eyeballs strain;

In thick black streams of purling blood, full fast his life is fleeting;
The stillness of the desert hears his heart's tumultuous beating.

Like the cloud that, through the wilderness, the path of Israel traced, —
Like an airy phantom, dull and wan, a spirit of the waste, —
From the sandy sea uprising, as the water-spout from ocean,
A whirling cloud of dust keeps pace with the courser's fiery motion.

Croaking companion of their flight, the vulture whirs on high;
Below, the terror of the fold, the panther fierce and sly,
And hyenas foul, round graves that prowl, join in the horrid race;
By the footprints wet with gore and sweat, their monarch's course they trace.

They see him on his living throne, and quake with fear, the while
With claws of steel he tears piecemeal his cushion's painted pile.
On! on! no pause, no rest, giraffe, while life and strength remain!
The steed by such a rider backed may madly plunge in vain.

Reeling upon the desert's verge, he falls, and breathes his last;
The courser, stained with dust and foam, is the rider's fell repast.
O'er Madagascar, eastward far, a faint flush is descried: —
Thus nightly, o'er his broad domain, the king of beasts doth ride.

From the German of FERDINAND FREILIGRATH.

THE BLOOD HORSE.

GAMARRA is a dainty steed,
Strong, black, and of a noble breed,
Full of fire, and full of bone,
With all his line of fathers known;
Fine his nose, his nostrils thin,
But blown abroad by the pride within!
His mane is like a river flowing,
And his eyes like embers glowing
In the darkness of the night,
And his pace as swift as light.

Look, — how round his straining throat
Grace and shifting beauty float;
Sinewy strength is in his reins,
And the red blood gallops through his veins:
Richer, redder, never ran
Through the boasting heart of man.
He can trace his lineage higher
Than the Bourbon dare aspire, —
Douglas, Guzman, or the Guelph,
Or O'Brien's blood itself!

He, who hath no peer, was born
Here, upon a red March morn.
But his famous fathers dead
Were Arabs all, and Arab-bred,
And the last of that great line
Trod like one of a race divine!
And yet, — he was but friend to one
Who fed him at the set of sun
By some lone fountain fringed with green;
With him, a roving Bedouin,
He lived (none else would he obey
Through all the hot Arabian day),
And died untamed upon the sands
Where Balkh amidst the desert stands.

BRYAN W. PROCTER (BARRY CORNWALL).

THE TIGER.

TIGER! Tiger! burning bright,
In the forests of the night;
What immortal hand or eye
Could frame thy fearful symmetry?

In what distant deeps or skies
Burned the fire of thine eyes?
On what wings dare he aspire?
What the hand dare seize the fire?

And what shoulder, and what art,
Could twist the sinews of thine heart?
And when thy heart began to beat,
What dread hand? and what dread feet?

What the hammer, what the chain?
In what furnace was thy brain?
What the anvil? what dread grasp
Dare its deadly terrors clasp?

When the stars threw down their spears,
And watered heaven with their tears,
Did he smile his work to see?
Did He, who made the Lamb, make thee?

Tiger! Tiger! burning bright,
In the forests of the night,
What immortal hand or eye
Dare frame thy fearful symmetry?

WILLIAM BLAKE.

TO A MOUSE,

ON TURNING HER UP IN HER NEST WITH THE PLOW, NOVEMBER, 1785.

Wee, sleekit, cow'rin', tim'rous beastie,
O, what a panic 's in thy breastie!
Thou need na start awa' sae hasty,
Wi' bickering brattle!
I wad be laith to rin an' chase thee,
Wi' murd'ring pattle!

I 'm truly sorry man's dominion
Has broken nature's social union,
An' justifies that ill opinion
Which makes thee startle
At me, thy poor earth-born companion,
An' fellow-mortal!

I doubt na, whyles, but thou may thieve;
What then? poor beastie, thou maun live!
A daimen icker in a thrave
'S a sma' request;
I 'll get a blessin' wi' the laive,
And never miss 't!

Thy wee bit housie, too, in ruin!
Its silly wa's the win's are strewin'!
An' naething now to big a new ane
O' foggage green!
An' bleak December's winds ensuin',
Baith snell and keen!

Thou saw the fields laid bare an' waste,
An' weary winter comin' fast,
An' cozie here, beneath the blast,
Thou thought to dwell,
Till, crash! the cruel coulter past
Out through thy cell.

That wee bit heap o' leaves an' stibble
Has cost thee mony a weary nibble!
Now thou 's turned out, for a' thy trouble,
But house or hald,
To thole the winter's sleety dribble,
An' cranreuch cauld!

But, Mousie, thou art no thy lane,
In proving foresight may be vain:
The best-laid schemes o' mice an' men
Gang aft a-gley,
An' lea'e us naught but grief and pain,
For promised joy.

Still thou art blest, compared wi' me!
The present only toucheth thee:
But, och! I backward cast my e'e
On prospects drear;
An' forward, though I canna see,
I guess an' fear.

ROBERT BURNS.

LAMBS AT PLAY.

Say, ye that know, ye who have felt and seen
Spring's morning smiles, and soul-enlivening green, —
Say, did you give the thrilling transport way,
Did your eye brighten, when young lambs at play
Leaped o'er your path with animated pride,
Or gazed in merry clusters by your side?
Ye who can smile — to wisdom no disgrace —
At the arch meaning of a kitten's face;
If spotless innocence and infant mirth
Excites to praise, or gives reflection birth;
In shades like these pursue your favorite joy,
Midst nature's revels, sports that never cloy.
A few begin a short but vigorous race,
And indolence, abashed, soon flies the place:
Thus challenged forth, see thither, one by one,
From every side, assembling playmates run;
A thousand wily antics mark their stay,
A starting crowd, impatient of delay;
Like the fond dove from fearful prison freed,
Each seems to say, "Come, let us try our speed";
Away they scour, impetuous, ardent, strong,
The green turf trembling as they bound along
Adown the slope, then up the hillock climb,
Where every mole-hill is a bed of thyme,
Then, panting, stop; yet scarcely can refrain, —
A bird, a leaf, will set them off again:
Or, if a gale with strength unusual blow,
Scattering the wild-brier roses into snow,
Their little limbs increasing efforts try;
Like the torn flower, the fair assemblage fly.
Ah, fallen rose! sad emblem of their doom;
Frail as thyself, they perish while they bloom!

ROBERT BLOOMFIELD.

FOLDING THE FLOCKS.

Shepherds all, and maidens fair,
Fold your flocks up; for the air
'Gins to thicken, and the sun
Already his great course hath run.
See the dew-drops, how they kiss
Every little flower that is;
Hanging on their velvet heads,
Like a string of crystal beads.
See the heavy clouds low falling
And bright Hesperus down calling
The dead night from underground;
At whose rising, mists unsound,
Damps and vapors, fly apace,
And hover o'er the smiling face
Of these pastures; where they come,
Striking dead both bud and bloom.
Therefore from such danger lock
Every one his lovèd flock;

And let your dogs lie loose without,
Lest the wolf come as a scout
From the mountain, and ere day,
Bear a lamb or kid away;
Or the crafty, thievish fox,
Break upon your simple flocks.
To secure yourself from these,
Be not too secure in ease;
So shall you good shepherds prove,
And deserve your master's love.
Now, good night! may sweetest slumbers
And soft silence fall in numbers
On your eyelids. So farewell:
Thus I end my evening knell.

BEAUMONT and FLETCHER.

THE SONGSTERS.

FROM "THE SEASONS."

Up springs the lark,
Shrill-voiced and loud, the messenger of morn.
Ere yet the shadows fly, he mounted sings
Amid the dawning clouds, and from their haunts
Calls up the tuneful nations. Every copse
Deep-tangled, tree irregular, and bush
Bending with dewy moisture, o'er the heads
Of the coy quiristers that lodge within,
Are prodigal of harmony. The thrush
And woodlark, o'er the kind-contending throng
Superior heard, run through the sweetest length
Of notes; when listening Philomela deigns
To let them joy, and purposes, in thought
Elate, to make her night excel their day.
The blackbird whistles from the thorny brake;
The mellow bullfinch answers from the grove;
Nor are the linnets, o'er the flowering furze
Poured out profusely, silent: joined to these,
Innumerous songsters, in the freshening shade
Of new-sprung leaves, their modulations mix
Mellifluous. The jay, the rook, the daw,
And each harsh pipe, discordant heard alone,
Aid the full concert; while the stockdove breathes
A melancholy murmur through the whole.
'T is love creates their melody, and all
This waste of music is the voice of love;
That even to birds and beasts the tender arts
Of pleasing teaches.

JAMES THOMSON.

DOMESTIC BIRDS.

FROM "THE SEASONS."

The careful hen
Calls all her chirping family around,
Fed and defended by the fearless cock,
Whose breast with ardor flames, as on he walks,
Graceful, and crows defiance. In the pond
The finely checkered duck before her train
Rows garrulous. The stately-sailing swan
Gives out her snowy plumage to the gale;
And, arching proud his neck, with oary feet
Bears forward fierce, and guards his osier-isle,
Protective of his young. The turkey nigh,
Loud-threatening, reddens; while the peacock spreads
His every-colored glory to the sun,
And swims in radiant majesty along.
O'er the whole homely scene, the cooing dove
Flies thick in amorous chase, and wanton rolls
The glancing eye, and turns the changeful neck.

JAMES THOMSON.

CHORUS OF ENGLISH SONGSTERS.

FROM THE "PARADISE OF BIRDS."

In the springtime, chaffinch gay, —
"Vanished is the winter snow;
Days grow longer" (you shall say);
"Apple-blossoms soon will blow.
Haste, ye wingless lovers, then,
Take your pleasure ere 't is late,
Birds are building, maids and men,
Every one selects his mate.
Now St. Valentine is past,
April will in time be May;
Youth that lingers will not last;
There 's a sunset every day.
Birds and poets both have sung,
'Love comes only to the young.'"

Sing, O nightingale, in June:
"Now it is the shortest night,
And to-morrow's sun by noon
Will have climbed his yearly height.
Rarer sounds the blackbird's pipe;
Redder grows the apricot;
Everything is still and ripe;
From to-morrow all things rot.
Life 's climacteric of power
Is the half-way house of Death;
Man's decline, like bird and flower,
Dates from parting of a breath.
Night must now shift hands with day;
Fullest ripeness brings decay."

Swallow, in September sing:
"Quit we now our northern eaves;
All the gnats are perishing;
Sere and sapless look the leaves.
Where are flown the summer flies?
Like men's riches they have wings.
Vanity of vanities!
Fleeting are all feathered things!
We have read our horoscope,
But in summer we forget;

Every spring awakes new hope,
Every autumn new regret.
'T is the truth (but truth is strange)
Naught 's immutable but change."

Snow-bunting, in winter cry:
"Misery, and cold, and dearth!
Darkness in the shrouded sky!
Silence o'er the snowy earth!
Every tree looks white and wan,
Barbed with icicles, unclad,
Like some featherless old man,
Withered, toothless, poor, and sad.
Yet be trustful, Man and Bird;
Winter shall not kill the soul.
Life on earth is hope deferred,
Since beyond it lies the Pole.
Death, whose bounds are snow and ice,
Is the door of Paradise."

WILLIAM JOHN COURTHOPE.

A BIRD'S NEST.

BUT most of all it wins my admiration
To view the structure of this little work, —
A bird's nest, mark it well within, without:
No tool had he that wrought, no knife to cut,
No nail to fix, no bodkin to insert,
No glue to join: his little beak was all;
And yet how neatly finished! What nice hand,
With every implement and means of art,
And twenty years' apprenticeship to boot,
Could make me such another? Fondly then
We boast of excellence, where noblest skill
Instinctive genius foils.

JAMES HURDIS.

BIRDS.

FROM "THE PELICAN ISLAND."

— BIRDS, the free tenants of land, air, and ocean,
Their forms all symmetry, their motions grace;
In plumage, delicate and beautiful,
Thick without burden, close as fishes' scales,
Or loose as full-blown poppies to the breeze;
With wings that might have had a soul within them,
They bore their owners by such sweet enchantment,
— Birds, small and great, of endless shapes and colors,
Here flew and perched, there swam and dived at pleasure;
Watchful and agile, uttering voices wild
And harsh, yet in accordance with the waves
Upon the beach, the winds in caverns moaning,
Or winds and waves abroad upon the water.
Some sought their food among the finny shoals,
Swift darting from the clouds, emerging soon
With slender captives glittering in their beaks;
These in recesses of steep crags constructed
Their eyries inaccessible, and trained
Their hardy broods to forage in all weathers:
Others, more gorgeously appareled, dwelt
Among the woods, on nature's dainties feeding,
Herbs, seeds, and roots; or, ever on the wing,
Pursuing insects through the boundless air:
In hollow trees or thickets these concealed
Their exquisitely woven nests; where lay
Their callow offspring, quiet as the down
On their own breasts, till from her search the dam
With laden bill returned, and shared the meal
Among her clamorous suppliants, all agape;
Then, cowering o'er them with expanded wings,
She felt how sweet it is to be a mother.
Of these, a few, with melody untaught,
Turned all the air to music within hearing,
Themselves unseen; while bolder quiristers
On loftiest branches strained their clarion-pipes,
And made the forest echo to their screams
Discordant, — yet there was no discord there,
But tempered harmony; all tones combining,
In the rich confluence of ten thousand tongues,
To tell of joy and to inspire it. Who
Could hear such concert, and not join in chorus?

JAMES MONTGOMERY.

PLEA FOR THE BIRDS.

FROM "THE BIRDS OF KILLINGWORTH."

PLATO, anticipating the reviewers,
From his republic banished without pity
The poets: in this little town of yours,
You put to death, by means of a committee,
The ballad-singers and the troubadours,
The street-musicians of the heavenly city,
The birds, who make sweet music for us all
In our dark hours, as David did for Saul.

The thrush, that carols at the dawn of day
From the green steeples of the piny wood;
The oriole in the elm; the noisy jay,
Jargoning like a foreigner at his food;
The bluebird balanced on some topmost spray,
Flooding with melody the neighborhood;
Linnet and meadow-lark, and all the throng
That dwell in nests, and have the gift of song, —

You slay them all! and wherefore? For the gain
Of a scant handful more or less of wheat,
Or rye, or barley, or some other grain,
Scratched up at random by industrious feet
Searching for worm or weevil after rain;
Or a few cherries, that are not so sweet

As are the songs these uninvited guests
Sing at their feast with comfortable breasts.

Do you ne'er think what wondrous beings these?
Do you ne'er think who made them, and who taught
The dialect they speak, where melodies
Alone are the interpreters of thought?
Whose household words are songs in many keys,
Sweeter than instrument of man e'er caught!
Whose habitations in the tree-tops even
Are half-way houses on the road to heaven!

Think, every morning when the sun peeps through
The dim, leaf-latticed windows of the grove,
How jubilant the happy birds renew
Their old melodious madrigals of love!
And when you think of this, remember too
'T is always morning somewhere, and above
The awakening continents, from shore to shore,
Somewhere the birds are singing evermore.

Think of your woods and orchards without birds!
Of empty nests that cling to boughs and beams,
As in an idiot's brain remembered words
Hang empty mid the cobwebs of his dreams!
Will bleat of flocks or bellowing of herds
Make up for the lost music, when your teams
Drag home the stingy harvest, and no more
The feathered gleaners follow to your door?

What! would you rather see the incessant stir
Of insects in the windrows of the hay,
And hear the locust and the grasshopper
Their melancholy hurdy-gurdies play?
Is this more pleasant to you than the whirr
Of meadow-lark, and its sweet roundelay,
Or twitter of little fieldfares, as you take
Your nooning in the shade of bush and brake?

You call them thieves and pillagers; but know
They are the wingèd wardens of your farms,
Who from the cornfields drive the insidious foe,
And from your harvests keep a hundred harms;
Even the blackest of them all, the crow,
Renders good service as your man-at-arms,
Crushing the beetle in his coat of mail,
And crying havoc on the slug and snail.

How can I teach your children gentleness,
And mercy to the weak, and reverence
For Life, which, in its weakness or excess,
Is still a gleam of God's omnipotence,
Or Death, which, seeming darkness, is no less
The selfsame light, although averted hence,
When by your laws, your actions, and your speech,
You contradict the very things I teach?

H. W. LONGFELLOW.

BIRDS BY MY WINDOW.

A JUNE SONG.

SWEET birds that by my window sing,
Or sail around on careless wing,
Beseech ye, lend your caroling,
While I salute my darling.

She 's far from me, away, away,
Across the hills, beyond the bay,
But still my heart goes night and day
To meet and greet my darling.

Brown wren, from out whose swelling throat
Unstinted joys of music float,
Come lend to me thine own June note,
To warble to my darling.

Sweet dove, thy tender, lovelorn coo
Melts pensively the orchard through:
Grant me thy gentle voice to woo,
And I shall win my darling.

Lark, ever leal to dawn of day,
Pause ere thou wingst thy skyward way,—
Pause, and bestow one quivering lay,
One anthem for my darling.

Ah, mocker! rich as leafy June,
Thou 'lt grant, I know, one little boon,
One strain of thy most matchless tune,
To solace my own darling.

Bright choir, your peerless song shall stir
The rapturous chords of love in her;
But who shall be our messenger,
When we salute my darling?

O voiceless swallow, crown of spring,
Lend us awhile thy swift curved wing:
Straight as an arrow thou shalt bring
This greeting to my darling!

EDWARD SPENCER.

THE MOCKING-BIRD.

FROM "OUT OF THE CRADLE ENDLESSLY ROCKING."

ONCE, Paumanok,
When the snows had melted, and the Fifth-month grass was growing,
Up this sea-shore, in some briers,
Two guests from Alabama,—two together,
And their nest, and four light-green eggs, spotted with brown,
And every day the he-bird, to and fro, near at hand,
And every day the she-bird, crouched on her nest, silent, with bright eyes,
And every day I, a curious boy, never too close, never disturbing them,
Cautiously peering, absorbing, translating.

"Shine! shine! shine!
Pour down your warmth, great Sun!
While we bask — we two together.

"Two together!
Winds blow south, or winds blow north,
Day come white, or night come black,
Home, or rivers and mountains from home,
Singing all time, minding no time,
If we two but keep together."

Till, of a sudden,
Maybe killed, unknown to her mate,
One forenoon the she-bird crouched not on the nest,
Nor returned that afternoon, nor the next,
Nor ever appeared again.

And thenceforward, all summer, in the sound of the sea,
And at night, under the full of the moon, in calmer weather,
Over the hoarse surging of the sea,
Or flitting from brier to brier by day,
I saw, I heard at intervals, the remaining one, the he-bird,
The solitary guest from Alabama.

"Blow! blow! blow!
Blow up, sea-winds, along Paumanok's shore!
I wait and I wait, till you blow my mate to me."

Yes, when the stars glistened,
All night long, on the prong of a moss-scalloped stake,
Down, almost amid the slapping waves,
Sat the lone singer, wonderful, causing tears.

He called on his mate;
He poured forth the meanings which I, of all men, know.

. . . . .

"Soothe! soothe! soothe!
Close on its wave soothes the wave behind,
And again another behind, embracing and lapping, every one close,
But my love soothes not me, not me.

"Low hangs the moon — it rose late.
O, it is lagging — O, I think it is heavy with love, with love.

"O, madly the sea pushes, pushes upon the land,
With love — with love.

"O night! do I not see my love fluttering out there among the breakers?
What is that little black thing I see there in the white?

"Loud! loud! loud!
Loud I call to you, my love!
High and clear I shoot my voice over the waves;
Surely you must know who is here, is here;
You must know who I am, my love!

"Low-hanging moon!
What is that dusky spot in your brown yellow?
O, it is the shape, the shape of my mate!
O moon, do not keep her from me any longer.

"Land! land! O land!
Whichever way I turn, O, I think you could give me my mate back again, if you only would;
For I am almost sure I see her dimly whichever way I look.

"O rising stars!
Perhaps the one I want so much will rise, will rise with some of you.

"O throat! O trembling throat!
Sound clearer through the atmosphere!
Pierce the woods, the earth;
Somewhere listening to catch you, must be the one I want.

"Shake out, carols!
Solitary here — the night's carols!
Carols of lonesome love! Death's carols!
Carols under that lagging, yellow, waning moon!
O, under that moon, where she droops almost down into the sea!
O reckless, despairing carols!

"But soft! sink low;
Soft! let me just murmur;
And do you wait a moment, you husky-noised sea;
For somewhere I believe I heard my mate responding to me,
So faint — I must be still, be still to listen;
But not altogether still, for then she might not come immediately to me.

"Hither, my love!
Here I am! Here!
With this just-sustained note I announce myself to you;
This gentle call is for you, my love, for you.

"Do not be decoyed elsewhere!
That is the whistle of the wind — it is not my voice;
That is the fluttering, the fluttering of the spray;
Those are the shadows of leaves.

"O darkness! O in vain!
O, I am very sick and sorrowful."

WALT WHITMAN.

TO THE CUCKOO.

HAIL, beauteous stranger of the grove!
  Thou messenger of spring!
Now Heaven repairs thy rural seat,
  And woods thy welcome sing.

Soon as the daisy decks the green,
  Thy certain voice we hear.
Hast thou a star to guide thy path,
  Or mark the rolling year?

Delightful visitant! with thee
  I hail the time of flowers,
And hear the sound of music sweet
  From birds among the bowers.

The school-boy, wandering through the wood
  To pull the primrose gay,
Starts, thy most curious voice to hear,
  And imitates thy lay.

What time the pea puts on the bloom,
  Thou fliest thy vocal vale,
An annual guest in other lands,
  Another spring to hail.

Sweet bird! thy bower is ever green,
  Thy sky is ever clear;
Thou hast no sorrow in thy song,
  No winter in thy year!

O, could I fly, I 'd fly with thee!
  We 'd make, with joyful wing,
Our annual visit o'er the globe,
  Attendants on the spring.

JOHN LOGAN.

THE BELFRY PIGEON.

ON the cross-beam under the Old South bell
The nest of a pigeon is builded well.
In summer and winter that bird is there,
Out and in with the morning air;
I love to see him track the street,
With his wary eye and active feet;
And I often watch him as he springs,
Circling the steeple with easy wings,
Till across the dial his shade has passed,
And the belfry edge is gained at last;
'T is a bird I love, with its brooding note,
And the trembling throb in its mottled throat;
There 's a human look in its swelling breast,
And the gentle curve of its lowly crest;
And I often stop with the fear I feel, —
He runs so close to the rapid wheel.
  Whatever is rung on that noisy bell, —
Chime of the hour, or funeral knell, —
The dove in the belfry must hear it well.
When the tongue swings out to the midnight moon,
When the sexton cheerly rings for noon,
When the clock strikes clear at morning light,
When the child is waked with "nine at night,"
When the chimes play soft in the Sabbath air,
Filling the spirit with tones of prayer, —
Whatever tale in the bell is heard,
He broods on his folded feet unstirred,
Or, rising half in his rounded nest,
He takes the time to smooth his breast,
Then drops again, with filmèd eyes,
And sleeps as the last vibration dies.
  Sweet bird! I would that I could be
A hermit in the crowd like thee!
With wings to fly to wood and glen,
Thy lot, like mine, is cast with men;
And daily, with unwilling feet,
I tread, like thee, the crowded street,
But, unlike me, when day is o'er,
Thou canst dismiss the world, and soar;
Or, at a half-felt wish for rest,
Canst smooth the feathers on thy breast,
And drop, forgetful, to thy nest.
  I would that in such wings of gold
I could my weary heart upfold;
I would I could look down unmoved
(Unloving as I am unloved),
And while the world throngs on beneath,
Smooth down my cares and calmly breathe;
And never sad with others' sadness,
And never glad with others' gladness,
Listen, unstirred, to knell or chime,
And, lapped in quiet, bide my time.

NATHANIEL PARKER WILLIS.

THE SKYLARK.

    BIRD of the wilderness,
    Blithesome and cumberless,
Sweet be thy matin o'er moorland and lea!
    Emblem of happiness,
    Blest is thy dwelling-place, —
O, to abide in the desert with thee!
    Wild is thy lay and loud
    Far in the downy cloud,
Love gives it energy, love gave it birth.
    Where, on thy dewy wing,
    Where art thou journeying?
Thy lay is in heaven, thy love is on earth.
    O'er fell and fountain sheen,
    O'er moor and mountain green,
O'er the red streamer that heralds the day,
    Over the cloudlet dim,
    Over the rainbow's rim,
Musical cherub, soar, singing, away!
    Then, when the gloaming comes,
    Low in the heather blooms

Percy B. Shelley.

J. B. FORD & Co NEW YORK.

Sweet will thy welcome and bed of love be!
Emblem of happiness,
Blest is thy dwelling-place,
O, to abide in the desert with thee!

JAMES HOGG.

TO THE SKYLARK.

HAIL to thee, blithe spirit!
Bird thou never wert,
That from heaven, or near it,
Pourest thy full heart
In profuse strains of unpremeditated art.

Higher still and higher
From the earth thou springest,
Like a cloud of fire;
The blue deep thou wingest,
And singing still dost soar, and soaring ever singest.

In the golden lightening
Of the setting sun,
O'er which clouds are brightening,
Thou dost float and run;
Like an embodied joy whose race is just begun.

The pale purple even
Melts around thy flight;
Like a star of heaven,
In the broad daylight
Thou art unseen, but yet I hear thy shrill delight.

Keen as are the arrows
Of that silver sphere,
Whose intense lamp narrows
In the white dawn clear,
Until we hardly see, we feel that it is there.

All the earth and air
With thy voice is loud,
As, when night is bare,
From one lonely cloud
The moon rains out her beams, and heaven is overflowed.

What thou art we know not;
What is most like thee?
From rainbow clouds there flow not
Drops so bright to see,
As from thy presence showers a rain of melody.

Like a poet hidden
In the light of thought,
Singing hymns unbidden,
Till the world is wrought
To sympathy with hopes and fears it heeded not;

Like a high-born maiden
In a palace tower,
Soothing her love-laden
Soul in secret hour
With music sweet as love, which overflows her bower;

Like a glow-worm golden,
In a dell of dew,
Scattering unbeholden
Its aerial hue
Among the flowers and grass which screen it from the view;

Like a rose embowered
In its own green leaves,
By warm winds deflowered,
Till the scent it gives
Makes faint with too much sweet these heavy-wingèd thieves.

Sound of vernal showers
On the twinkling grass,
Rain-awakened flowers,
All that ever was
Joyous and fresh and clear thy music doth surpass.

Teach us, sprite or bird,
What sweet thoughts are thine;
I have never heard
Praise of love or wine
That panted forth a flood of rapture so divine.

Chorus hymeneal,
Or triumphant chant,
Matched with thine, would be all
But an empty vaunt, —
A thing wherein we feel there is some hidden want.

What objects are the fountains
Of thy happy strain?
What fields, or waves, or mountains?
What shapes of sky or plain?
What love of thine own kind? What ignorance of pain?

With thy clear, keen joyance
Languor cannot be;
Shadow of annoyance
Never come near thee;
Thou lovest, but ne'er knew love's sad satiety.

Waking or asleep,
Thou of death must deem
Things more true and deep
Than we mortals dream,
Or how could thy notes flow in such a crystal stream?

We look before and after,
And pine for what is not;
Our sincerest laughter
With some pain is fraught;
Our sweetest songs are those that tell of saddest thought.

Yet if we could scorn
Hate and pride and fear,
If we were things born
Not to shed a tear,
I know not how thy joy we ever should come near.

Better than all measures
Of delightful sound,
Better than all treasures
That in books are found,
Thy skill to poet were, thou scorner of the ground!

Teach me half the gladness
That thy brain must know,
Such harmonious madness
From my lips would flow,
The world should listen then, as I am listening now.

PERCY BYSSHE SHELLEY.

HARK, HARK! THE LARK—

HARK, hark! the lark at heaven's gate sings,
And Phœbus 'gins arise,
His steeds to water at those springs
On chaliced flowers that lies;
And winking Mary-buds begin
To ope their golden eyes;
With everything that pretty bin,
My lady sweet, arise;
Arise, arise!

SHAKESPEARE.

TO THE SKYLARK.

ETHEREAL minstrel! pilgrim of the sky!
Dost thou despise the earth where cares abound?
Or, while the wings aspire, are heart and eye
Both with thy nest upon the dewy ground?
Thy nest, which thou canst drop into at will,
Those quivering wings composed, that music still!

To the last point of vision, and beyond,
Mount, daring warbler! — that love-prompted strain,
'Twixt thee and thine a never-failing bond,
Thrills not the less the bosom of the plain;
Yet mightst thou seem, proud privilege! to sing
All independent of the leafy spring.

Leave to the nightingale her shady wood;
A privacy of glorious light is thine,
Whence thou dost pour upon the world a flood
Of harmony, with instinct more divine;
Type of the wise, who soar, but never roam, —
True to the kindred points of Heaven and Home!

WILLIAM WORDSWORTH.

THE THRUSH.

SWEET bird! that sing'st away the early hours
Of winters past or coming, void of care;
Well pleasèd with delights which present are,
Fair seasons, budding sprays, sweet-smelling flowers, —
To rocks, to springs, to rills, from leafy bowers
Thou thy Creator's goodness dost declare,
And what dear gifts on thee he did not spare,
A stain to human sense in sin that lowers.
What soul can be so sick which by thy songs
(Attired in sweetness) sweetly is not driven
Quite to forget earth's turmoils, spites, and wrongs,
And lift a reverent eye and thought to heaven!
Sweet, artless songster! thou my mind dost raise
To airs of spheres, — yes, and to angels' lays.

WILLIAM DRUMMOND.

THE ENGLISH ROBIN.

SEE yon robin on the spray;
Look ye how his tiny form
Swells, as when his merry lay
Gushes forth amid the storm.

Though the snow is falling fast,
Specking o'er his coat with white, —
Though loud roars the chilly blast,
And the evening 's lost in night, —

Yet from out the darkness dreary
Cometh still that cheerful note;
Praiseful aye, and never weary,
Is that little warbling throat.

Thank him for his lesson's sake,
Thank God's gentle minstrel there,
Who, when storms make others quake,
Sings of days that brighter were.

HARRISON WEIR.

THE ROBIN.

MY old Welsh neighbor over the way
Crept slowly out in the sun of spring,
Pushed from her ears the locks of gray,
And listened to hear the robin sing.

Her grandson, playing at marbles, stopped,
And cruel in sport, as boys will be,
Tossed a stone at the bird, who hopped
From bough to bough in the apple-tree.

"Nay!" said the grandmother; "have you not heard,
My poor bad boy! of the fiery pit,
And how, drop by drop, this merciful bird
Carries the water that quenches it?

"He brings cool dew in his little bill,
And lets it fall on the souls of sin;
You can see the mark on his red breast still
Of fires that scorch as he drops it in.

"My poor Bron rhuddyn! my breast-burned bird,
Singing so sweetly from limb to limb,
Very dear to the heart of our Lord
Is he who pities the lost, like him!"

"Amen!" I said to the beautiful myth;
"Sing, bird of God, in my heart as well;
Each good thought is a drop wherewith
To cool and lessen the fires of hell.

"Prayers of love like rain-drops fall,
Tears of pity are cooling dew,
And dear to the heart of our Lord are all
Who suffer like him in the good they do!"

JOHN G. WHITTIER.

THE BOBOLINK.

BOBOLINK! that in the meadow,
Or beneath the orchard's shadow,
Keepest up a constant rattle
Joyous as my children's prattle,
Welcome to the north again!
Welcome to mine ear thy strain,
Welcome to mine eye the sight
Of thy buff, thy black and white!
Brighter plumes may greet the sun
By the banks of Amazon;
Sweeter tones may weave the spell
Of enchanting Philomel;
But the tropic bird would fail,
And the English nightingale,
If we should compare their worth
With thine endless, gushing mirth.

When the ides of May are past,
June and summer nearing fast,
While from depths of blue above
Comes the mighty breath of love,
Calling out each bud and flower
With resistless, secret power,—
Waking hope and fond desire,
Kindling the erotic fire,—
Filling youths' and maidens' dreams
With mysterious, pleasing themes;
Then, amid the sunlight clear
Floating in the fragrant air,
Thou dost fill each heart with pleasure
By thy glad ecstatic measure.

A single note, so sweet and low,
Like a full heart's overflow,
Forms the prelude; but the strain
Gives us no such tone again;
For the wild and saucy song
Leaps and skips the notes among,
With such quick and sportive play,
Ne'er was madder, merrier lay.

Gayest songster of the spring!
Thy melodies before me bring
Visions of some dream-built land,
Where, by constant zephyrs fanned,
I might walk the livelong day,
Embosomed in perpetual May.
Nor care nor fear thy bosom knows;
For thee a tempest never blows;
But when our northern summer's o'er,
By Delaware's or Schuylkill's shore
The wild rice lifts its airy head,
And royal feasts for thee are spread.
And when the winter threatens there,
Thy tireless wings yet own no fear,
But bear thee to more southern coasts,
Far beyond the reach of frosts.

Bobolink! still may thy gladness
Take from me all taints of sadness;
Fill my soul with trust unshaken
In that Being who has taken
Care for every living thing,
In summer, winter, fall, and spring.

THOMAS HILL.

THE O'LINCOLN FAMILY.

A FLOCK of merry singing-birds were sporting in the grove:
Some were warbling cheerily, and some were making love:
There were Bobolincon, Wadolincon, Winterseeble, Conquedle,—
A livelier set was never led by tabor, pipe, or fiddle,—
Crying, "Phew, shew, Wadolincon, see, see, Bobolincon,
Down among the tickletops, hiding in the buttercups!
I know the saucy chap, I see his shining cap
Bobbing in the clover there,—see, see, see!"

Up flies Bobolincon, perching on an apple-tree,
Startled by his rival's song, quickened by his raillery,
Soon he spies the rogue afloat, curveting in the air,
And merrily he turns about, and warns him to beware!
"'T is you that would a-wooing go, down among the rushes O!
But wait a week, till flowers are cheery, — wait a week, and, ere you marry,
Be sure of a house wherein to tarry!
Wadolink, Whiskodink, Tom Denny, wait, wait, wait!"

Every one 's a funny fellow; every one 's a little mellow;
Follow, follow, follow, follow, o'er the hill and in the hollow!
Merrily, merrily, there they hie; now they rise and now they fly;
They cross and turn, and in and out, and down in the middle, and wheel about, —
With a "Phew, shew, Wadolincon! listen to me, Bobolincon! —
Happy 's the wooing that 's speedily doing, that 's speedily doing,
That 's merry and over with the bloom of the clover!
Bobolincon, Wadolincon, Winterseeble, follow, follow me!

WILSON FLAGG.

THE TELLTALE.

ONCE, on a golden afternoon,
With radiant faces and hearts in tune,
Two fond lovers in dreaming mood
Threaded a rural solitude.
Wholly happy, they only knew
That the earth was bright and the sky was blue,
That light and beauty and joy and song
Charmed the way as they passed along:
The air was fragrant with woodland scents;
The squirrel frisked on the roadside fence;
And hovering near them, "Chee, chee, chink?"
Queried the curious bobolink,
Pausing and peering with sidelong head,
As saucily questioning all they said;
While the ox-eye danced on its slender stem,
And all glad nature rejoiced with them.
Over the odorous fields were strown
Wilting windrows of grass new-mown,
And rosy billows of clover bloom
Surged in the sunshine and breathed perfume.

Swinging low on a slender limb,
The sparrow warbled his wedding hymn,
And, balancing on a blackberry-brier,
The bobolink sung with his heart on fire, —
"Chink? If you wish to kiss her, do!
Do it, do it! You coward, you!
Kiss her! Kiss, kiss her! Who will see?
Only we three! we three! we three!"

Under garlands of drooping vines,
Through dim vistas of sweet-breathed pines,
Past wide meadow-fields, lately mowed,
Wandered the indolent country road.
The lovers followed it, listening still,
And, loitering slowly, as lovers will,
Entered a low-roofed bridge that lay,
Dusky and cool, in their pleasant way.
Under its arch a smooth, brown stream
Silently glided, with glint and gleam,
Shaded by graceful elms that spread
Their verdurous canopy overhead, —
The stream so narrow, the boughs so wide,
They met and mingled across the tide.
Alders loved it, and seemed to keep
Patient watch as it lay asleep,
Mirroring clearly the trees and sky
And the flitting form of the dragon-fly,
Save where the swift-winged swallow played
In and out in the sun and shade,
And darting and circling in merry chase,
Dipped, and dimpled its clear dark face.

Fluttering lightly from brink to brink
Followed the garrulous bobolink,
Rallying loudly, with mirthful din,
The pair who lingered unseen within.
And when from the friendly bridge at last
Into the road beyond they passed,
Again beside them the tempter went,
Keeping the thread of his argument —
"Kiss her! kiss her! chink-a-chee-chee!
I 'll not mention it! Don't mind me!
I 'll be sentinel — I can see
All around from this tall birch-tree!"
But ah! they noted — nor deemed it strange —
In his rollicking chorus a trifling change:
"Do it! do it!" with might and main
Warbled the telltale — "Do it *again!*"

ANONYMOUS.

ROBERT OF LINCOLN.

MERRILY swinging on brier and weed,
Near to the nest of his little dame,
Over the mountain-side or mead,
Robert of Lincoln is telling his name:
Bob-o'-link, bob-o'-link,
Spink, spank, spink;

Snug and safe is that nest of ours,
Hidden among the summer flowers.
Chee, chee, chee.

Robert of Lincoln is gayly dressed,
Wearing a bright black wedding coat;
White are his shoulders and white his crest,
Hear him call in his merry note:
Bob-o'-link, bob-o'-link,
Spink, spank, spink;
Look, what a nice new coat is mine,
Sure there was never a bird so fine.
Chee, chee, chee.

Robert of Lincoln's Quaker wife,
Pretty and quiet, with plain brown wings,
Passing at home a patient life,
Broods in the grass while her husband sings:
Bob-o'-link, bob-o'-link,
Spink, spank, spink;
Brood, kind creature; you need not fear
Thieves and robbers while I am here.
Chee, chee, chee.

Modest and shy as a nun is she,
One weak chirp is her only note,
Braggart and prince of braggarts is he,
Pouring boasts from his little throat:
Bob-o'-link, bob-o'-link,
Spink, spank, spink;
Never was I afraid of man;
Catch me, cowardly knaves, if you can.
Chee, chee, chee.

Six white eggs on a bed of hay,
Flecked with purple, a pretty sight!
There as the mother sits all day,
Robert is singing with all his might:
Bob-o'-link, bob-o'-link,
Spink, spank, spink;
Nice good wife, that never goes out,
Keeping house while I frolic about.
Chee, chee, chee.

Soon as the little ones chip the shell
Six wide mouths are open for food;
Robert of Lincoln bestirs him well,
Gathering seed for the hungry brood.
Bob-o'-link, bob-o'-link,
Spink, spank, spink;
This new life is likely to be
Hard for a gay young fellow like me.
Chee, chee, chee.

Robert of Lincoln at length is made
Sober with work, and silent with care;
Off is his holiday garment laid,
Half forgotten that merry air,
Bob-o'-link, bob-o'-link,
Spink, spank, spink;
Nobody knows but my mate and I
Where our nest and our nestlings lie.
Chee, chee, chee.

Summer wanes; the children are grown;
Fun and frolic no more he knows;
Robert of Lincoln 's a humdrum crone;
Off he flies, and we sing as he goes:
Bob-o'-link, bob-o'-link,
Spink, spank, spink;
When you can pipe that merry old strain,
Robert of Lincoln, come back again.
Chee, chee, chee.

WILLIAM CULLEN BRYANT.

THE HEATH-COCK.

Good morrow to thy sable beak
And glossy plumage dark and sleek,
Thy crimson moon and azure eye,
Cock of the heath, so wildly shy:
I see thee slyly cowering through
That wiry web of silvery dew,
That twinkles in the morning air,
Like casements of my lady fair.

A maid there is in yonder tower,
Who, peeping from her early bower,
Half shows, like thee, her simple wile,
Her braided hair and morning smile.
The rarest things, with wayward will,
Beneath the covert hide them still;
The rarest things to break of day
Look shortly forth, and shrink away.

A fleeting moment of delight
I sunned me in her cheering sight;
As short, I ween, the time will be
That I shall parley hold with thee.
Through Snowdon's mist red beams the day,
The climbing herd-boy chants his lay,
The gnat-flies dance their sunny ring, —
Thou art already on the wing.

JOANNA BAILLIE.

PERSEVERANCE.

A swallow in the spring
Came to our granary, and 'neath the eaves
Essayed to make a nest, and there did bring
Wet earth and straw and leaves.

Day after day she toiled
With patient art, but ere her work was crowned,
Some sad mishap the tiny fabric spoiled,
And dashed it to the ground.

She found the ruin wrought,
But, not cast down, forth from the place she flew,
And with her mate fresh earth and grasses brought
And built her nest anew.

But scarcely had she placed
The last soft feather on its ample floor,
When wicked hand, or chance, again laid waste
And wrought the ruin o'er.

But still her heart she kept,
And toiled again, — and last night, hearing calls,
I looked, — and lo! three little swallows slept
Within the earth-made walls.

What truth is here, O man!
Hath hope been smitten in its early dawn?
Have clouds o'ercast thy purpose, trust, or plan?
Have faith, and struggle on!

R. S. S. ANDROS.

THE WINGED WORSHIPERS.

[Addressed to two swallows that flew into the Chauncy Place Church during divine service.]

GAY, guiltless pair,
What seek ye from the fields of heaven?
Ye have no need of prayer;
Ye have no sins to be forgiven.

Why perch ye here,
Where mortals to their Maker bend?
Can your pure spirits fear
The God ye never could offend?

Ye never knew
The crimes for which we come to weep.
Penance is not for you,
Blessed wanderers of the *upper deep*.

To you 't is given
To wake sweet Nature's untaught lays;
Beneath the arch of heaven
To chirp away a life of praise.

Then spread each wing
Far, far above, o'er lakes and lands,
And join the choirs that sing
In yon blue dome not reared with hands.

Or, if ye stay,
To note the consecrated hour,
Teach me the airy way,
And let me try your envied power.

Above the crowd
On upward wings could I but fly,
I 'd bathe in yon bright cloud,
And seek the stars that gem the sky.

'T were heaven indeed
Through fields of trackless light to soar,
On Nature's charms to feed,
And Nature's own great God adore.

CHARLES SPRAGUE.

THE SWALLOW.

THE gorse is yellow on the heath,
The banks with speedwell flowers are gay,
The oaks are budding; and beneath,
The hawthorn soon will bear the wreath,
The silver wreath of May.

The welcome guest of settled spring,
The swallow too is come at last;
Just at sunset, when thrushes sing,
I saw her dash with rapid wing,
And hailed her as she passed.

Come, summer visitant, attach
To my reed-roof thy nest of clay,
And let my ear thy music catch,
Low twittering underneath the thatch,
At the gray dawn of day.

As fables tell, an Indian sage,
The Hindustani woods among,
Could in his desert hermitage,
As if 't were marked in written page,
Translate the wild bird's song.

I wish I did his power possess,
That I might learn, fleet bird, from thee,
What our vain systems only guess,
And know from what wild wilderness
Thou camest o'er the sea.

CHARLOTTE SMITH.

THE DEPARTURE OF THE SWALLOW.

AND is the swallow gone?
Who beheld it?
Which way sailed it?
Farewell bade it none?

No mortal saw it go; —
But who doth hear
Its summer cheer
As it flitteth to and fro?

So the freed spirit flies!
From its surrounding clay
It steals away
Like the swallow from the skies.

Whither? wherefore doth it go?
'T is all unknown;
We feel alone
That a void is left below.

WILLIAM HOWITT.

THE NIGHTINGALE.

THE rose looks out in the valley,
And thither will I go!
To the rosy vale, where the nightingale
Sings his song of woe.

The virgin is on the river-side,
Culling the lemons pale:
Thither, — yes! thither will I go,
To the rosy vale, where the nightingale
Sings his song of woe.

The fairest fruit her hand hath culled,
'T is for her lover all:
Thither, — yes! thither will I go,
To the rosy vale, where the nightingale
Sings his song of woe.

In her hat of straw, for her gentle swain,
She has placed the lemons pale:
Thither, — yes! thither will I go,
To the rosy vale, where the nightingale
Sings his song of woe.

From the Portuguese of GIL VICENTE,
by JOHN BOWRING.

THE NIGHTINGALE.

PRIZE thou the nightingale,
Who soothes thee with his tale,
And wakes the woods around;
A singing feather he, — a winged and wandering sound;

Whose tender caroling
Sets all ears listening
Unto that living lyre,
Whence flow the airy notes his ecstasies inspire;

Whose shrill, capricious song
Breathes like a flute along,
With many a careless tone, —
Music of thousand tongues, formed by one tongue alone.

O charming creature rare!
Can aught with thee compare?
Thou art all song, — thy breast
Thrills for one month o' the year, — is tranquil all the rest.

Thee wondrous we may call, —
Most wondrous this of all,
That such a tiny throat
Should wake so loud a sound, and pour so loud a note.

From the Dutch of MARIA TESSELSCHADE VISSCHER,
by JOHN BOWRING.

THE NIGHTINGALE BEREAVED.

FROM "THE SEASONS"

OFT when, returning with her loaded bill,
Th' astonished mother finds a vacant nest,
By the hard hand of unrelenting clown
Robbed, to the ground the vain provision falls;
Her pinions ruffle, and low-drooping scarce
Can bear the mourner to the poplar shade;
Where, all abandoned to despair, she sings
Her sorrows through the night; and on the bough
Sole-sitting, still at every dying fall
Takes up again her lamentable strain
Of winding woe, till, wide around, the woods
Sigh to her song, and with her wail resound.

JAMES THOMSON.

PHILOMELA.

HARK! ah, the nightingale!
The tawny-throated!
Hark! from that moonlit cedar what a burst!
What triumph! hark, — what pain!
O wanderer from a Grecian shore,
Still, — after many years, in distant lands, —
Still nourishing in thy bewildered brain
That wild, unquenched, deep-sunken, Old-World pain, —
Say, will it never heal?
And can this fragrant lawn,
With its cool trees, and night,
And the sweet, tranquil Thames,
And moonshine, and the dew,
To thy racked heart and brain
Afford no balm?

Dost thou to-night behold,
Here, through the moonlight on this English grass,
The unfriendly palace in the Thracian wild?
Dost thou again peruse,
With hot cheeks and seared eyes,
The too clear web, and thy dumb sister's shame?
Dost thou once more essay
Thy flight; and feel come over thee,
Poor fugitive! the feathery change
Once more; and once more make resound,
With love and hate, triumph and agony,
Lone Daulis, and the high Cephisian vale?

Listen, Eugenia, —
How thick the bursts come crowding through the leaves !
Again — thou hearest !
Eternal passion !
Eternal pain !

MATTHEW ARNOLD.

TO THE NIGHTINGALE.

As it fell upon a day,
In the merry month of May,
Sitting in a pleasant shade
Which a grove of myrtles made,
Beasts did leap, and birds did sing,
Trees did grow, and plants did spring ;
Everything did banish moan,
Save the nightingale alone.
She, poor bird, as all forlorn,
Leaned her breast up-till a thorn ;
And there sung the doleful'st ditty
That to hear it was great pity.
Fie, fie, fie ! now would she cry ;
Teru, teru, by and by ;
That, to hear her so complain,
Scarce I could from tears refrain ;
For her griefs, so lively shown,
Made me think upon mine own.
Ah ! (thought I) thou mourn'st in vain ;
None takes pity on thy pain ;
Senseless trees, they cannot hear thee ;
Ruthless bears, they will not cheer thee ;
King Pandion, he is dead ;
All thy friends are lapped in lead :
All thy fellow-birds do sing,
Careless of thy sorrowing !
Whilst as fickle Fortune smiled,
Thou and I were both beguiled,
Every one that flatters thee
Is no friend in misery.
Words are easy, like the wind ;
Faithful friends are hard to find.

RICHARD BARNFIELD.

THE MOTHER NIGHTINGALE.

I HAVE seen a nightingale
On a sprig of thyme bewail,
Seeing the dear nest, which was
Hers alone, borne off, alas !
By a laborer : I heard,
For this outrage, the poor bird
Say a thousand mournful things
To the wind, which, on its wings,
To the Guardian of the sky
Bore her melancholy cry,
Bore her tender tears. She spake
As if her fond heart would break :
One while in a sad, sweet note,
Gurgled from her straining throat,
She enforced her piteous tale,
Mournful prayer and plaintive wail ;
One while, with the shrill dispute
Quite outwearied, she was mute ;
Then afresh, for her dear brood,
Her harmonious shrieks renewed.
Now she winged it round and round ;
Now she skimmed along the ground ;
Now from bough to bough, in haste,
The delighted robber chased,
And, alighting in his path,
Seemed to say, 'twixt grief and wrath,
"Give me back, fierce rustic rude,
Give me back my pretty brood,"
And I heard the rustic still
Answer, "That I never will."

From the Spanish of ESTEVAN MANUEL DE VILLEGAS,
by THOMAS ROSCOE.

THE PELICAN.

FROM "THE PELICAN ISLAND."

AT early dawn I marked them in the sky,
Catching the morning colors on their plumes ;
Not in voluptuous pastime reveling there,
Among the rosy clouds, while orient heaven
Flamed like the opening gates of Paradise,
Whence issued forth the angel of the sun,
And gladdened nature with returning day :
— Eager for food, their searching eyes they fixed
On ocean's unrolled volume, from a height
That brought immensity within their scope ;
Yet with such power of vision looked they down,
As though they watched the shell-fish slowly gliding
O'er sunken rocks, or climbing trees of coral.
On indefatigable wing upheld,
Breath, pulse, existence, seemed suspended in them :
They were as pictures painted on the sky ;
Till suddenly, aslant, away they shot,
Like meteors changed from stars to gleams of lightning,
And struck upon the deep, where, in wild play,
Their quarry floundered, unsuspecting harm ;
With terrible voracity, they plunged
Their heads among the affrighted shoals, and beat
A tempest on the surges with their wings,
Till flashing clouds of foam and spray concealed them.
Nimbly they seized and secreted their prey,
Alive and wriggling in the elastic net,
Which Nature hung beneath their grasping beaks,
Till, swollen with captures, the unwieldy burden

Clogged their slow flight, as heavily to land
These mighty hunters of the deep returned.
There on the cragged cliffs they perched at ease,
Gorging their hapless victims one by one;
Then, full and weary, side by side they slept,
Till evening roused them to the chase again.

. . . . .

Love found that lonely couple on their isle,
And soon surrounded them with blithe companions.
The noble birds, with skill spontaneous, framed
A nest of reeds among the giant-grass,
That waved in lights and shadows o'er the soil.
There, in sweet thraldom, yet unweening why,
The patient dam, who ne'er till now had known
Parental instinct, brooded o'er her eggs,
Long ere she found the curious secret out,
That life was hatching in their brittle shells.
Then, from a wild rapacious bird of prey,
Tamed by the kindly process, she became
That gentlest of all living things, — a mother;
Gentlest while yearning o'er her naked young,
Fiercest when stirred by anger to defend them.
Her mate himself the softening power confessed,
Forgot his sloth, restrained his appetite,
And ranged the sky and fished the stream for her.
Or, when o'erwearied Nature forced her off
To shake her torpid feathers in the breeze,
And bathe her bosom in the cooling flood,
He took her place, and felt through every nerve,
While the plump nestlings throbbed against his heart,
The tenderness that makes the vulture mild;
Yea, half unwillingly his post resigned,
When, homesick with the absence of an hour,
She hurried back, and drove him from her seat
With pecking bill and cry of fond distress,
Answered by him with murmurs of delight,
Whose gutturals harsh to her were love's own music.
Then, settling down, like foam upon the wave,
White, flickering, effervescent, soon subsiding,
Her ruffled pinions smoothly she composed;
And, while beneath the comfort of her wings,
Her crowded progeny quite filled the nest,
The halcyon sleeps not sounder, when the wind
Is breathless, and the sea without a curl,
— Nor dreams the halcyon of serener days,
Or nights more beautiful with silent stars,
Than in that hour, the mother pelican,
When the warm tumults of affection sunk
Into calm sleep, and dreams of what they were, —
Dreams more delicious than reality.
He sentinel beside her stood, and watched
With jealous eye the raven in the clouds,
And the rank sea-mews wheeling round the cliffs.
Woe to the reptile then that ventured nigh!
The snap of his tremendous bill was like
Death's scythe, down-cutting everything it struck.
The heedless lizard, in his gambols, peeped
Upon the guarded nest, from out the flowers,
But paid the instant forfeit of his life;
Nor could the serpent's subtlety elude
Capture, when gliding by, nor in defense
Might his malignant fangs and venom save him.

Ere long the thriving brood outgrew their cradle,
Ran through the grass, and dabbled in the pools;
No sooner denizens of earth than made
Free both of air and water; day by day,
New lessons, exercises, and amusements
Employed the old to teach, the young to learn.
Now floating on the blue lagoon behold them;
The sire and dam in swan-like beauty steering,
Their cygnets following through the foamy wake,
Picking the leaves of plants, pursuing insects,
Or catching at the bubbles as they broke:
Till on some minor fry, in reedy shallows,
With flapping pinions and unsparing beaks,
The well-taught scholars plied their double art,
To fish in troubled waters, and secure
The petty captives in their maiden pouches;
Then hurried with their banquet to the shore,
With feet, wings, breast, half swimming and half flying.
But when their pens grew strong to fight the storm,
And buffet with the breakers on the reef,
The parents put them to severer proof:
On beetling rocks the little ones were marshaled;
There, by endearments, stripes, example, urged
To try the void convexity of heaven,
And plow the ocean's horizontal field.
Timorous at first they fluttered round the verge,
Balanced and furled their hesitating wings,
Then put them forth again with steadier aim;
Now, gaining courage as they felt the wind
Dilate their feathers, fill their airy frames
With buoyancy that bore them from their feet,
They yielded all their burden to the breeze,
And sailed and soared where'er their guardians led;
Ascending, hovering, wheeling, or alighting,
They searched the deep in quest of nobler game
Than yet their inexperience had encountered;
With these they battled in that element,
Where wings or fins were equally at home,
Till, conquerors in many a desperate strife,
They dragged their spoils to land, and gorged at leisure.

JAMES MONTGOMERY.

TO A WATERFOWL.

WHITHER, midst falling dew,
While glow the heavens with the last steps of day,
Far, through their rosy depths, dost thou pursue
Thy solitary way?

Vainly the fowler's eye
Might mark thy distant flight to do thee wrong,
As, darkly painted on the crimson sky,
Thy figure floats along.

Seek'st thou the plashy brink
Of weedy lake, or marge of river wide,
Or where the rocking billows rise and sink
On the chafed ocean-side?

There is a Power whose care
Teaches thy way along that pathless coast, —
The desert and illimitable air, —
Lone wandering, but not lost.

All day thy wings have fanned,
At that far height, the cold, thin atmosphere,
Yet stoop not, weary, to the welcome land,
Though the dark night is near.

And soon that toil shall end;
Soon shalt thou find a summer home, and rest,
And scream among thy fellows; reeds shall bend,
Soon, o'er thy sheltered nest.

Thou 'rt gone, the abyss of heaven
Hath swallowed up thy form; yet, on my heart
Deeply hath sunk the lesson thou hast given,
And shall not soon depart:

He who, from zone to zone,
Guides through the boundless sky thy certain flight,
In the long way that I must tread alone,
Will lead my steps aright.

WILLIAM CULLEN BRYANT.

TO A BIRD

THAT HAUNTED THE WATERS OF LAAKEN IN THE WINTER.

O MELANCHOLY bird, a winter's day
Thou standest by the margin of the pool,
And, taught by God, dost thy whole being school
To patience, which all evil can allay.
God has appointed thee the fish thy prey,
And given thyself a lesson to the fool
Unthrifty, to submit to moral rule,
And his unthinking course by thee to weigh.
There need not schools nor the professor's chair,
Though these be good, true wisdom to impart:
He who has not enough for these to spare,
Of time or gold, may yet amend his heart,
And teach his soul by brooks and rivers fair, —
Nature is always wise in every part.

EDWARD HOVEL (LORD THURLOW).

THE SANDPIPER.

ACROSS the narrow beach we flit,
One little sandpiper and I;
And fast I gather, bit by bit,
The scattered driftwood bleached and dry.
The wild waves reach their hands for it,
The wild wind raves, the tide runs high,
As up and down the beach we flit, —
One little sandpiper and I.

Above our heads the sullen clouds
Scud black and swift across the sky:
Like silent ghosts in misty shrouds
Stand out the white lighthouses high.
Almost as far as eye can reach
I see the close-reefed vessels fly,
As fast we flit along the beach, —
One little sandpiper and I.

I watch him as he skims along,
Uttering his sweet and mournful cry;
He starts not at my fitful song,
Or flash of fluttering drapery;
He has no thought of any wrong,
He scans me with a fearless eye.
Stanch friends are we, well tried and strong,
The little sandpiper and I.

Comrade, where wilt thou be to-night
When the loosed storm breaks furiously?
My driftwood-fire will burn so bright!
To what warm shelter canst thou fly?
I do not fear for thee, though wroth
The tempest rushes through the sky:
For are we not God's children both,
Thou, little sandpiper, and I?

CELIA THAXTER.

THE LITTLE BEACH BIRD.

THOU little bird, thou dweller by the sea,
Why takest thou its melancholy voice?
Why with that boding cry
O'er the waves dost thou fly?
O, rather, bird, with me
Through the fair land rejoice!

Thy flitting form comes ghostly dim and pale,
As driven by a beating storm at sea;
Thy cry is weak and scared,
As if thy mates had shared
The doom of us. Thy wail —
What does it bring to me?

Thou call'st along the sand, and haunt'st the surge,
Restless and sad; as if, in strange accord

With motion, and with roar
Of waves that drive to shore
One spirit did ye urge —
The Mystery — the Word.

Of thousands thou both sepulcher and pall,
Old ocean, art! A requiem o'er the dead,
From out thy gloomy cells,
A tale of mourning tells, —
Tells of man's woe and fall,
His sinless glory fled.

Then turn thee, little bird, and take thy flight
Where the complaining sea shall sadness bring
Thy spirit nevermore.
Come, quit with me the shore,
For gladness and the light,
Where birds of summer sing.

RICHARD H. DANA.

THE STORMY PETREL.

A THOUSAND miles from land are we,
Tossing about on the stormy sea, —
From billow to bounding billow cast,
Like fleecy snow on the stormy blast.
The sails are scattered abroad like weeds;
The strong masts shake like quivering reeds;
The mighty cables and iron chains,
The hull, which all earthly strength disdains, —
They strain and they crack; and hearts like stone
Their natural, hard, proud strength disown.

Up and down! — up and down!
From the base of the wave to the billow's crown,
And amidst the flashing and feathery foam
The stormy petrel finds a home, —
A home, if such a place may be
For her who lives on the wide, wide sea,
On the craggy ice, in the frozen air,
And only seeketh her rocky lair
To warm her young, and to teach them to spring
At once o'er the waves on their stormy wing!

O'er the deep! — o'er the deep!
Where the whale and the shark and the sword-fish sleep, —
Outflying the blast and the driving rain,
The petrel telleth her tale — in vain;
For the mariner curseth the warning bird
Which bringeth him news of the storm unheard!
Ah! thus does the prophet of good or ill
Meet hate from the creatures he serveth still;
Yet he ne'er falters, — so, petrel, spring
Once more o'er the waves on thy stormy wing!

BRYAN W. PROCTER (BARRY CORNWALL).

LINES TO THE STORMY PETREL.

THE lark sings for joy in her own loved land,
In the furrowed field, by the breezes fanned;
And so revel we
In the furrowed sea,
As joyous and glad as the lark can be.

On the placid breast of the inland lake,
The wild duck delights her pastime to take;
But the petrel braves
The wild ocean waves,
His wing in the foaming billow he laves.

The halcyon loves in the noontide beam
To follow his sport on the tranquil stream:
He fishes at ease
In the summer breeze,
But we go angling in stormiest seas.

No song-note have we but a piping cry,
That blends with the storm when the wind is high.
When the land-birds wail
We sport in the gale,
And merrily over the ocean we sail.

ANONYMOUS.

THE EAGLE.

FRAGMENT.

HE clasps the crag with hookèd hands;
Close to the sun in lonely lands,
Ringed with the azure world, he stands.

The wrinkled sea beneath him crawls;
He watches from his mountain walls,
And like a thunderbolt he falls.

ALFRED TENNYSON.

THE OWL.

IN the hollow tree, in the old gray tower,
The spectral owl doth dwell;
Dull, hated, despised, in the sunshine hour,
But at dusk he 's abroad and well!
Not a bird of the forest e'er mates with him;
All mock him outright by day;
But at night, when the woods grow still and dim,
The boldest will shrink away!
O, when the night falls, and roosts the fowl,
Then, then, is the reign of the hornèd owl!

And the owl hath a bride, who is fond and bold,
And loveth the wood's deep gloom;
And, with eyes like the shine of the moonstone cold,
She awaiteth her ghastly groom;
Not a feather she moves, not a carol she sings,
As she waits in her tree so still;

But when her heart heareth his flapping wings,
She hoots out her welcome shrill!
O, when the moon shines, and dogs do howl,
Then, then, is the joy of the hornèd owl!

Mourn not for the owl, nor his gloomy plight!
The owl hath his share of good:
If a prisoner he be in the broad daylight,
He is lord in the dark greenwood!
Nor lonely the bird, nor his ghastly mate,
They are each unto each a pride;
Thrice fonder, perhaps, since a strange, dark fate
Hath rent them from all beside!
So, when the night falls, and dogs do howl,
Sing, ho! for the reign of the hornèd owl!
We know not alway
Who are kings by day,
But the king of the night is the bold brown owl!

BRYAN W. PROCTER (BARRY CORNWALL).

TO THE HUMBLEBEE.

Burly, dozing humblebee!
Where thou art is clime for me;
Let them sail for Porto Rique,
Far-off heats through seas to seek,
I will follow thee alone,
Thou animated torrid zone!
Zigzag steerer, desert cheerer,
Let me chase thy waving lines;
Keep me nearer, me thy hearer,
Singing over shrubs and vines.

Insect lover of the sun,
Joy of thy dominion!
Sailor of the atmosphere;
Swimmer through the waves of air,
Voyager of light and noon,
Epicurean of June!
Wait, I prithee, till I come
Within earshot of thy hum, —
All without is martyrdom.

When the south-wind, in May days,
With a net of shining haze
Silvers the horizon wall;
And, with softness touching all,
Tints the human countenance
With the color of romance;
And infusing subtle heats
Turns the sod to violets, —
Thou in sunny solitudes,
Rover of the underwoods,
The green silence dost displace
With thy mellow breezy bass.

Hot midsummer's petted crone,
Sweet to me thy drowsy tone
Tells of countless sunny hours,
Long days, and solid banks of flowers;
Of gulfs of sweetness without bound,
In Indian wildernesses found;
Of Syrian peace, immortal leisure,
Firmest cheer, and birdlike pleasure.

Aught unsavory or unclean
Hath my insect never seen;
But violets, and bilberry bells,
Maple sap, and daffodels,
Grass with green flag half-mast high,
Succory to match the sky,
Columbine with horn of honey,
Scented fern, and agrimony,
Clover, catchfly, adder's-tongue,
And brier-roses, dwelt among:
All beside was unknown waste,
All was picture as he passed.
Wiser far than human seer,
Yellow-breeched philosopher,
Seeing only what is fair,
Sipping only what is sweet,
Thou dost mock at fate and care,
Leave the chaff and take the wheat.
When the fierce northwestern blast
Cools sea and land so far and fast, —
Thou already slumberest deep;
Woe and want thou canst outsleep;
Want and woe, which torture us,
Thy sleep makes ridiculous.

RALPH WALDO EMERSON.

A SOLILOQUY;

OCCASIONED BY THE CHIRPING OF A GRASSHOPPER.

Happy insect! ever blest
With a more than mortal rest,
Rosy dews the leaves among,
Humble joys, and gentle song!
Wretched poet! ever curst
With a life of lives the worst,
Sad despondence, restless fears,
Endless jealousies and tears.
In the burning summer thou
Warblest on the verdant bough,
Meditating cheerful play,
Mindless of the piercing ray;
Scorched in Cupid's fervors, I
Ever weep and ever die.
Proud to gratify thy will,
Ready Nature waits thee still;
Balmy wines to thee she pours,
Weeping through the dewy flowers,
Rich as those by Hebe given
To the thirsty sons of heaven.
Yet, alas, we both agree.
Miserable thou like me!

Each, alike, in youth rehearses
Gentle strains and tender verses;
Ever wandering far from home,
Mindless of the days to come
(Such as aged Winter brings
Trembling on his icy wings),
Both alike at last we die;
Thou art starved, and so am I!

WALTER HARTE.

THE GRASSHOPPER.

HAPPY insect! what can be
In happiness compared to thee?
Fed with nourishment divine,
The dewy morning's gentle wine!
Nature waits upon thee still,
And thy verdant cup does fill;
'T is filled wherever thou dost tread,
Nature's self's thy Ganymede.
Thou dost drink and dance and sing,
Happier than the happiest king!
All the fields which thou dost see,
All the plants belong to thee;
All the summer hours produce,
Fertile made with early juice.
Man for thee does sow and plow,
Farmer he, and landlord thou!
Thou dost innocently joy,
Nor does thy luxury destroy.
The shepherd gladly heareth thee,
More harmonious than he.
Thee country hinds with gladness hear,
Prophet of the ripened year!
Thee Phœbus loves, and does inspire;
Phœbus is himself thy sire.
To thee, of all things upon earth,
Life is no longer than thy mirth.
Happy insect! happy thou
Dost neither age nor winter know;
But when thou 'st drunk and danced and sung
Thy fill, the flowery leaves among,
(Voluptuous and wise withal,
Epicurean animal!)
Sated with thy summer feast,
Thou retir'st to endless rest.

From the Greek of ANACREON,
by ABRAHAM COWLEY.

THE GRASSHOPPER AND CRICKET.

THE poetry of earth is never dead;
When all the birds are faint with the hot sun
And hide in cooling trees, a voice will run
From hedge to hedge about the new-mown mead.
That is the grasshopper's, — he takes the lead
In summer luxury, — he has never done
With his delights; for, when tired out with fun,
He rests at ease beneath some pleasant weed.
The poetry of earth is ceasing never.
On a lone winter evening, when the frost
Has wrought a silence, from the stove there shrills
The cricket's song, in warmth increasing ever,
And seems, to one in drowsiness half lost,
The grasshopper's among some grassy hills.

JOHN KEATS.

THE GRASSHOPPER AND CRICKET.

GREEN little vaulter in the sunny grass,
Catching your heart up at the feel of June, —
Sole voice that 's heard amidst the lazy noon
When even the bees lag at the summoning brass;
And you, warm little housekeeper, who class
With those who think the candles come too soon,
Loving the fire, and with your tricksome tune
Nick the glad silent moments as they pass!

O sweet and tiny cousins, that belong,
One to the fields, the other to the hearth,
Both have your sunshine; both, though small, are strong
At your clear hearts; and both seem given to earth
To sing in thoughtful ears this natural song, —
In doors and out, summer and winter, mirth.

LEIGH HUNT.

THE CRICKET.

LITTLE inmate, full of mirth,
Chirping on my kitchen hearth,
Whereso'er be thine abode
Always harbinger of good,
Pay me for thy warm retreat
With a song more soft and sweet;
In return thou shalt receive
Such a strain as I can give.

Thus thy praise shall be expressed,
Inoffensive, welcome guest!
While the rat is on the scout,
And the mouse with curious snout,
With what vermin else infest
Every dish, and spoil the best;
Frisking thus before the fire,
Thou hast all thy heart's desire.

Though in voice and shape they be
Formed as if akin to thee,
Thou surpassest, happier far,
Happiest grasshoppers that are;
Theirs is but a summer's song, —
Thine endures the winter long,
Unimpaired and shrill and clear,
Melody throughout the year.

Neither night nor dawn of day
Puts a period to thy play :
Sing then — and extend thy span
Far beyond the date of man.
Wretched man, whose years are spent
In repining discontent,
Lives not, aged though he be,
Half a span, compared with thee.

WILLIAM COWPER.

KATYDID.

I LOVE to hear thine earnest voice,
Wherever thou art hid,
Thou testy little dogmatist,
Thou pretty Katydid !
Thou mindest me of gentlefolks, —
Old gentlefolks are they, —
Thou say'st an undisputed thing
In such a solemn way.

Thou art a female, Katydid !
I know it by the trill
That quivers through thy piercing notes,
So petulant and shrill.
I think there is a knot of you
Beneath the hollow tree, —
A knot of spinster Katydids, —
Do Katydids drink tea ?

O, tell me where did Katy live,
And what did Katy do ?
And was she very fair and young,
And yet so wicked too ?
Did Katy love a naughty man,
Or kiss more cheeks than one ?
I warrant Katy did no more
Than many a Kate has done.

OLIVER WENDELL HOLMES.

TO A LOUSE,

ON SEEING ONE ON A LADY'S BONNET AT CHURCH.

HA ! whare ye gaun, ye crawlin' ferlie ?
Your impudence protects you sairly :
I canna say but ye strunt rarely
Owre gauze an' lace ;
Though, faith ! I fear ye dine but sparely
On sic a place.

Ye ugly, creepin', blastit wonner,
Detested, shunned by saunt an' sinner,
How dare you set your fit upon her,
Sae fine a lady ?
Gae somewhere else, and seek your dinner
On some poor body.

Swith, in some beggar's haffet squattle ;
There ye may creep and sprawl and sprattle
Wi' ither kindred, jumping cattle,
In shoals and nations :
Whare horn nor bane ne'er daur unsettle
Your thick plantations.

Now haud you there, ye 're out o' sight,
Below the fatt'rels, snug an' tight ;
Na, faith ye yet ! ye 'll no be right
Till ye 've got on it,
The very tapmost tow'ring height
O' Miss's bonnet.

My sooth ; right bauld ye set your nose out,
As plump and gray as ony grozet ;
O for some rank, mercurial rozet,
Or fell, red smeddum !
I 'd gie you sic a hearty dose o't,
Wad dress your droddum !

I wad na been surprised to spy
You on an auld wife's flannen toy ;
Or aiblins some bit duddie boy,
On 's wyliecoat ;
But Miss's fine Lunardi, fie !
How daur ye do 't ?

O Jenny, dinna toss your head,
An' set your beauties a' abread !
Ye little ken what cursèd speed
The blastie 's makin' !
Thae winks and finger-ends, I dread,
Are notice takin' !

O wad some power the giftie gie us
To see oursel's as others see us !
It wad frae monie a blunder free us,
And foolish notion :
What airs in dress an' gait wad lea'e us,
And ev'n devotion !

ROBERT BURNS.

REMONSTRANCE WITH THE SNAILS.

YE little snails,
With slippery tails,
Who noiselessly travel
Along this gravel,
By a silvery path of slime unsightly,
I learn that you visit my pea-rows nightly.
Felonious your visit, I guess !
And I give you this warning,
That, every morning,
I 'll strictly examine the pods ;
And if one I hit on,
With slaver or spit on,
Your next meal will be with the gods.

I own you 're a very ancient race,
And Greece and Babylon were amid;
You have tenanted many a royal dome,
And dwelt in the oldest pyramid;
The source of the Nile! — O, you have been there!
In the ark was your floodless bed;
On the moonless night of Marathon
You crawled o'er the mighty dead;
But still, though I reverence your ancestries,
I don't see why you should nibble my peas.

The meadows are yours, — the hedgerow and brook,
You may bathe in their dews at morn;
By the aged sea you may sound your *shells*,
On the mountains erect your *horn*;
The fruits and the flowers are your rightful dowers,
Then why — in the name of wonder —
Should my six pea-rows be the only cause
To excite your midnight plunder?

I have never disturbed your slender shells;
You have hung round my aged walk;
And each might have sat, till he died in his fat,
Beneath his own cabbage-stalk:
But now you must fly from the soil of your sires;
Then put on your liveliest crawl,
And think of your poor little snails at home,
Now orphans or emigrants all.

Utensils domestic and civil and social
I give you an evening to pack up;
But if the moon of this night does not rise on your flight,
To-morrow I 'll hang each man Jack up.
You 'll think of my peas and your thievish tricks,
With tears of slime, when crossing the *Styx*.

ANONYMOUS.

THE HOUSEKEEPER.

THE frugal snail, with forecast of repose,
Carries his house with him where'er he goes;
Peeps out, — and if there comes a shower of rain,
Retreats to his small domicile again.
Touch but a tip of him, a horn, — 't is well, —
He curls up in his sanctuary shell.
He 's his own landlord, his own tenant; stay
Long as he will, he dreads no Quarter Day.
Himself he boards and lodges; both invites
And feasts himself; sleeps with himself o' nights.
He spares the upholsterer trouble to procure
Chattels; himself is his own furniture,
And his sole riches. Wheresoe'er he roam, —
Knock when you will, — he 's sure to be at home.

CHARLES LAMB.

TO A MOSQUITO.

FAIR insect, that, with thread-like legs spread out,
And blood-extracting bill, and filmy wing,
Dost murmur, as thou slowly sail'st about,
In pitiless ears, full many a plaintive thing,
And tell'st how little our large veins should bleed,
Would we but yield them freely in thy need;

. . . . .

I call thee stranger, for the town, I ween,
Has not the honor of so proud a birth;
Thou com'st from Jersey meadows, broad and green,
The offspring of the gods, though born on earth.

. . . . .

At length thy pinions fluttered in Broadway, —
Ah, there were fairy steps, and white necks kissed
By wanton airs, and eyes whose killing ray
Shone through the snowy veils like stars through mist!
And, fresh as morn, on many a cheek and chin,
Bloomed the bright blood through the transparent skin.

O, these were sights to touch an anchorite! —
What, do I hear thy slender voice complain?
Thou wailest, when I talk of beauty's light,
As if it brought the memory of pain:
Thou art a wayward being, — well, come near,
And pour thy tale of sorrow in my ear.

What say'st thou, slanderer? "Rouge makes thee sick,
And China bloom at best is sorry food;
And Rowland's Kalydor, if laid on thick,
Poisons the thirsty wretch that bores for blood"?
Go, 't was a just reward that met thy crime, —
But shun the sacrilege another time.

That bloom was made to look at, not to touch,
To worship, not approach, that radiant white;
And well might sudden vengeance light on such
As dared, like thee, most impiously to bite.
Thou should'st have gazed at distance, and admired,
Murmured thy adoration, and retired.

Thou 'rt welcome to the town; but why come here
To bleed a brother poet, gaunt like thee?
Alas! the little blood I have is dear,
And thin will be the banquet drawn from me.
Look round, — the pale-eyed sisters, in my cell,
Thy old acquaintance, Song and Famine, dwell.

Try some plump alderman: and suck the blood
Enriched with generous wine, and costly meat;
In well-filled skins, soft as thy native mud,
Fix thy light pump, and raise thy freckled feet.

Go to the men for whom, in ocean's halls,
The oyster breeds, and the green turtle sprawls.

There corks are drawn, and the red vintage flows,
To fill the swelling veins for thee; and now
The ruddy cheek, and now the ruddier nose,
Shall tempt thee as thou flittest round the brow;
And when the hour of sleep its quiet brings,
No angry hand shall rise to brush thy wings.

WILLIAM CULLEN BRYANT.

GOD EVERYWHERE IN NATURE.

How desolate were nature, and how void
Of every charm, how like a naked waste
Of Africa, were not a present God
Beheld employing, in its various scenes,
His active might to animate and adorn!
What life and beauty, when, in all that breathes,
Or moves, or grows, his hand is viewed at work!
When it is viewed unfolding every bud,
Each blossom tingeing, shaping every leaf,
Wafting each cloud that passes o'er the sky,
Rolling each billow, moving every wing
That fans the air, and every warbling throat
Heard in the tuneful woodlands! In the least
As well as in the greatest of his works
Is ever manifest his presence kind;
As well in swarms of glittering insects, seen
Quick to and fro within a foot of air,
Dancing a merry hour, then seen no more,
As in the systems of resplendent worlds,
Through time revolving in unbounded space.
His eye, while comprehending in one view
The whole creation, fixes full on me;
As on me shines the sun with his full blaze,
While o'er the hemisphere he spreads the same,
His hand, while holding oceans in its palm,
And compassing the skies, surrounds my life,
Guards the poor rushlight from the blast of death.

CARLOS WILCOX.

www.ingramcontent.com/pod-product-compliance
Lightning Source LLC
LaVergne TN
LVHW021221110826
845150LV00002B/211
9781425564216